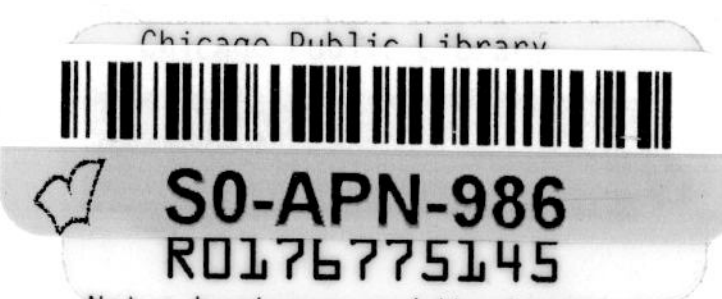

.NET e-Business Architecture

Don Benage, Product Manager

Jody Socha, Program Manager

Robert Amar, Matthew Baute, Mark Benatar, Eric Brown, David Burgett, Remco Jorna, Chris Koenig, Cor Kroon, Richard Lassan, Roger Miller, Brian Mueller, Baya Pavliashvili, Bry Pickett, and John Pickett

201 West 103rd St., Indianapolis, Indiana, 46290 USA

.NET e-Business Architecture

International Standard Book Number: 0-672-32219-6

Library of Congress Catalog Card Number: 2001093570

Printed in the United States of America

First Printing: November 2001

04 03 02 01 4 3 2 1

Trademarks

All terms mentioned in this book that are known to be trademarks or service marks have been appropriately capitalized. Sams Publishing cannot attest to the accuracy of this information. Use of a term in this book should not be regarded as affecting the validity of any trademark or service mark.

Warning and Disclaimer

Every effort has been made to make this book as complete and as accurate as possible, but no warranty or fitness is implied. The information provided is on an "as is" basis. The authors and the publisher shall have neither liability nor responsibility to any person or entity with respect to any loss or damages arising from the information contained in this book or from the use of the programs accompanying it.

Associate Publisher
Linda Engelman

Acquisitions Editor
Karen Wachs

Development Editor
Grant Munroe

Managing Editor
Charlotte Clapp

Project Editor
Heather McNeill

Copy Editor
Ned Snell

Indexer
Ginny Bess

Proofreader
Marcia Deboy
Plan-it Publishing

Technical Editor
Beth Breidenbach
Jawahar Puvvala

Team Coordinator
Lynne Williams

Media Developer
Dan Scherf

Interior Designer
Gary Adair

Cover Designer
Aren Howell

Overview

Introduction **1**

Part I Preliminaries and Planning

1 .NET—The Big Picture **9**

2 gasTIX: A Sample .NET e-Business **47**

3 Enabling Inter-Application Communications **75**

Part II Designing .NET e-Business Solutions

4 Tools of the Trade **91**

5 Implementing .NET Presentation Services **123**

6 Implementing .NET Business Services **155**

7 Implementing .NET Data Services **179**

8 Handling Security **233**

9 COM+ Integration **251**

Part III Building .NET e-Business Sites

10 gasTIX Event Searching **287**

11 Purchasing a Ticket **321**

12 Fulfillment **351**

13 .NET Remoting **395**

Part IV Testing and Deploying .NET Sites

14 Debugging a .NET Application **413**

15 Performance Tuning in .NET **435**

16 Deploying the Application **469**

Appendix

A Design Documents **521**

Index **547**

Table of Contents

Introduction 1

Who Should Use This Book? 1
How This Book Is Organized 1
Part I: Preliminaries and Planning 2
Part II: Designing .NET e-Business Solutions 2
Part III: Building .NET e-Business Sites 3
Part IV: Testing and Deploying .NET Sites 4
Conventions Used In This Book 4

PART I Preliminaries and Planning

1 .NET—The Big Picture 9

The Internet Rules! 10
A Level Playing Field 11
Standards—So Many to Choose From 11
Enterprise-Level Attributes 14
The Evolution of the Programming Model 15
Clients and Servers 16
Applications Become Sites 17
Scale Up Versus Scale Out 20
Balancing the Load 20
A Matter of State 21
Incorporating Services 22
Services 101 23
The Passport Service 24
The Role of SOAP 25
SOAP on a ROPE (The SDK for VS6) 25
DISCO and UDDI 26
Cast of Characters 27
CLR: The Common Language Runtime 28
ASP.NET and Internet Information Services (IIS) 30
.NET Enterprise Services (COM+) 32
The .NET Framework 32
Microsoft Message Queue 33
ADO.NET 34
Windows and the .NET Servers 35
The Microsoft .NET Enterprise Servers 37
BizTalk: The Concept 44
From Here 45

2 gasTIX: A Sample .NET e-Business 47

Introducing gasTIX: The Sample Application 48
Background 48
Problem Statement....49
Vision Statement 49
Solution Concept 49
Business Goals....51
Design Criteria....51
Architecting the System 52
The .NET Architectural Foundation 52
gasTIX Conceptual Architecture 53
gasTIX Use Cases 56
Web Site Flow....65
Home Page....65
Artists/Teams by Name 66
Subcategories by Category 66
Artists by Subcategory 66
State List/US Map 66
Venue Search Page 67
Cities with Venues List 67
Venues by City/State 67
Venues by Name 67
Events by Venue 67
Events by Artist/Team 68
Seating Chart 68
Event Details 68
Event Pricing Details....68
Ticket Purchase 69
Purchase Confirmation 69
Update Profile 69
Shipment Status....69
Project Design and Approach: The Microsoft Solutions Framework 70
Development Process Overview 71
A Note on the Sample Application 73
From Here....73

3 Enabling Inter-Application Communications 75

Challenges of Inter-Application Communications....76
XML—Extensible Markup Language 77
XML and HTML....78
XSD Schema 79
SOAP and Web services 82
WSDL, DISCO, and UDDI....84

Microsoft BizTalk Server 2000 85
Business Document Exchange 85
BizTalk Orchestration 86
BizTalk Messaging 87
From Here 88

Part II Designing .NET e-Business Solutions

4 Tools of the Trade 91

.NET Architectural Tools 92
.NET Framework Classes 93
Common Language Runtime (CLR) 97
Common Type System (CTS) / Common Language Specification (CLS) 99
Metadata 101
Server Integration and Device Independence 104
Security and Authentication 106
Performance and Scalability 107
.NET Architectural Tools Summary 108
.NET Language Tools 108
Visual C# .NET 108
Visual Basic .NET 109
Language Choice 110
Other Languages 111
.NET Language Tools Summary 112
.NET Developer Productivity Tools 112
Visual Studio .NET 112
ILDasm 119
Command Line Compilers 120
.NET Developer Productivity Tools Summary 121
From Here 122

5 Implementing .NET Presentation Services 123

Why Should Developers Switch to ASP.NET? 125
The Page Object 128
What Are Web Controls? 130
Event-Driven Programming 133
Using Web Controls in Visual Studio .NET 134
Advanced Features of Web Controls 145
User Controls 150
Separation of UI and Code 153
From Here 154

6 Implementing .NET Business Services 155

Architectural Goals 156
- Interoperability 157
- Performance 158
- Availability 159
- Scalability 159
- Security 160

gasTIX Business Services—A Closer Look 161
- Business Façade 161
- Business 162
- Data 163
- Data Access 163
- System Framework 164
- Web services 165

What's New for Component Development? 167
- Remoting Versus DCOM 168
- ADO.NET 169

From Here 177

7 Implementing .NET Data Services 179

Data Modeling 181
- Relational Versus Dimensional Models 181
- Physical Modeling 183

Indexing for Performance 189
- Number of Indexes 189
- Clustered Versus Non-Clustered Indexes 189
- Long or Short Index Keys? 193
- Index Tuning Wizard 193

Transact-SQL 194
- Variables in Transact SQL 194
- Parameters in Transact SQL 196
- Transact SQL Cursors 198
- Functions in Transact SQL 200

Views 201
- Advantages of Using Views 202
- Disadvantages of Using Views 203
- Partitioned Views 203
- Indexed Views 204

Stored Procedures 206
- Creating Stored Procedures 206
- Stored Procedure Performance Issues 207

Triggers 210
AFTER Triggers 211
INSTEAD OF Triggers 213
User-Defined Functions 213
Inline Table-Valued Functions....................214
Multistatement Table-Valued Functions 214
XML Support in SQL Server 2000 216
Transact-SQL XML extensions....................216
OPENXML 225
Integration of SQL Server and IIS 227
From Here....................231

8 Handling Security 233
Security Concepts 234
Authentication and Authorization....................234
Authenticating Users 236
Authorization—Working with Role-Based Security....................243
Working with Code-Access Security 246
Signing Assemblies 247
Code Permissions and Associated Tools 248
From Here....................250

9 COM+ Integration 251
A Legacy from the Past 252
The Need for Legacy Components 252
To Migrate or Not to Migrate 252
A Sample Architecture 256
Technology Overview....................257
Managed versus Unmanaged Code....................257
Calling the Operating System 258
Wrapping It All Up 259
Approaches to Partial Ports....................261
Advanced Topics....................266
Typed Transitions and the Stack 266
Controlling the Marshalling Mechanism....................268
Detailed Walkthrough....................269
What We Need....................269
Creating a Simple Visual Basic 6 DLL....................270
Calling the DLL from a Web Service 271
Calling the DLL from a Visual Basic .NET Class Library....................277
Calling the Class Library from a Visual Basic 6 Executable....................279
From Here… 283

PART III Building .NET e-Business Sites

10 gasTIX Event Searching 287

Building Presentation Services with ASP.NET 288
  Presentation Service Goals 288
  ASP.NET Web Controls 290
Building the ASP.NET Project 294
  The gasTIX Search Project 294
  Separation of Code and Design in gasTIX 296
  Using ASP.NET Web Controls 297
  Using Repeater Controls 301
User Controls 310
  A Simple User Control 310
  Building a Nested User Control 314
From Here....320

11 Purchasing a Ticket 321

Setting Up the Examples 322
  Web.Config 322
  Global.asax 323
Middle-Tier Objects Versus XML Web services 324
  Business Objects 324
  Using XML Web services via Soap 325
Building the gasTIX Purchasing User Interface....326
Organization and Flow of the User Interface 327
  Event Details 328
  Payment Information....332
  Confirming the Purchase....337
  Displaying a Receipt 339
  Viewing the Seating Chart....341
The UI for Purchasing a Ticket 342
Tools 345
  Visual Studio .NET 345
  Command-Line Tools 348
From Here....349

12 Fulfillment 351

Communication Overview 353
Notification of New Orders 354
  Message Format and Structure 355
  Message Transport....355
  Message Transport Alternatives 358

Sending the Order 359
BTS Messaging Definitions 360
Creating the Organizations and Applications 360
Creating the Port 361
Creating the Channel 363
Formatting the Order 365
Functoids 367
Alternatives 370
Processing the Order 370
Receiving the Order 371
Activating Orchestration from BTS Messaging 371
TPA Orchestration Overview 372
Creating the Business Process 372
Receiving Messages in the Schedule 373
Creating the Components 375
Creating the Component Ports 376
Mapping the Data 377
Delivery Receipts 378
Transport Acknowledgement and Retry 378
BTS Queues 379
Receipts 379
BTS Framework Reliable Delivery 380
Limitations 381
Order Status Return and Enhanced Receipts 381
Transactions in Orchestration Schedules 383
Correlation 388
Implementation Choices 393
Updating Order Status 393
From Here 394

13 .NET Remoting 395

Application Domains 396
Remotable Versus Non-Remotable Objects 397
Marshal-By-Value 397
Marshal-By-Reference 398
Channels 400
Serializing Messages 401
Remoting Configuration Options 402
Hosting a Remote Object 403
Hosting in a Managed .EXE or Managed Service 404
Internet Information Server (IIS) 405
.NET Component Services Framework 406

Consuming a Remote Object 406
Activation and Lifetime Control....408
Server Activation 409
Client Activation 410
Object Lifetimes 410
From Here....410

PART IV Testing and Deploying .NET Sites

14 Debugging a .NET Application 413
.NET Debugging—The Basics 414
Debugging gasTIX 415
Attaching to gasTIX Web 418
Just-In-Time Debugging 420
Trace and Debug Classes....421
Debugging an ASP.NET Web Application 423
ASP.NET Tracing 424
Debugging and Testing a Web Service 425
Exception Handling 427
The `Exception` Object 427
Fundamentals....430
Best Practices....432
From Here....433

15 Performance Tuning in .NET 435
Performance Tuning Concepts 436
Why Performance Tune?....436
How to Performance Tune....437
When To Performance Tune? 438
.NET Performance Mechanisms....439
ASP.NET Caching Technologies....440
.NET Application Profiling 441
Asynchronous Processing in .NET 446
Install-Time Code Generation 446
Other .NET Performance Considerations 448
.NET Performance Tuning Tools 450
Tuning the .NET Presentation Tier with Application Center Test (ACT)....451
Tuning the .NET Business Tier with Visual Studio Analyzer 457
Tuning the .NET Data Tier 461
From Here....467

16 Deploying the Application 469

Putting the Application Together 470
The Presentation Tier....471
The Business Tier 472
The Data Tier....473
Infrastructure Considerations 473
Technical Requirements for Deployment 473
Application-Imposed Requirements 474
Performance Considerations 474
Scaling Up Versus Scaling Out 475
Deployment Platform for gasTIX Sites....476
Executing Deployments with Visual Studio .NET 477
Visual Studio .NET Deployment Projects....477
Dissecting the Web Setup Project 477
Deploying a .NET Application to the World 484
File System 485
Registry 487
User Interface 488
Custom Actions 490
Creating Web Clusters with Application Center 2000 513
About Application Center 2000....513
Preparing a Web Cluster for Use with .NET and AC2K....515
Deploying .NET Applications on Application Center 2000 Clusters....516
From Here....518

A Design Documents 521

gasTIX Requirements....522
Implemented Functionality 522
Future Functionality 523
gasTIX Use Cases....526
Use Case 1—Select Event by Category 526
Use Case 2—Select Event by Venue....526
Use Case 3—Select Event by State....527
Use Case 4—Select Event by Artist/Team Name....528
Use Case 5—Pricing/Availability Check 528
Use Case 6—View Seating Chart 528
Use Case 7—Purchase Tickets 529
gasTIX Site Map....529
gasTIX Object Models 531
gasTIX Data Model 541

Index 547

Note from Greg Sullivan

G.A. Sullivan sprang from humble beginnings as the IBM PC was being launched—with just one other person (who still works here!) and me writing code, working at the kitchen table. Our organization has experienced dramatic growth in the past 19 years (visit our Web site for details), but our motivations, decisions, and investments are still colored by my beginnings as a software developer, and I still get excited when I see great new technology.

The Microsoft .NET platform and toolset is exciting, comprehensive, and powerful. We have been using Microsoft tools and technologies since the release of Microsoft's first C compiler for the DOS platform. We've grown up with Microsoft, and are proud of the strong partnership we enjoy with Microsoft today. In reviewing the comprehensive scope and power of the .NET platform, I'm reminded of those early days, and feel the same sense of excitement and impending possibility.

The .NET platform represents an incredible opportunity for our industry to create new systems that work well on the Internet and allow unprecedented levels of integration with business partners and customers, all using standard Internet protocols.

Web services, which are described in detail in this book, play a key role in the .NET story. Microsoft is once again "betting the ranch" on a new initiative, and challenging our thinking on what it means to write an application or create a Web site. With their own Web services initiative, they have staked out a true leadership position in this emerging market. I believe the world will follow their lead.

It is important to realize, however, that .NET does *not* represent technology created for its own sake. Leveraging technologies such as XML and SOAP, and products like the collection of .NET Enterprise Servers, Microsoft has provided a platform that delivers real business value. This value is exemplified by improved quality, rapid time to market, and tighter integration between a company, its customers, and its business partners.

So here is our seventh book. We have tried to describe how the .NET platform can be used to create practical, real-world applications. I hope you enjoy it!

Greg Sullivan
CEO

About the Authors

G.A. Sullivan, Inc. is a global .NET application development company focused on delivering Microsoft .NET solutions to middle market and Fortune 1000 companies. G. A. Sullivan was among the first in the world to become a Microsoft Gold Certified Partner for E-Commerce Solutions and currently has five locations that have earned this designation. Since 1982, the company has partnered with clients to streamline business processes and implement leading-edge technologies through complete strategic, technical and creative expertise. G. A. Sullivan is among the fastest growing private companies in America, with nearly 300 software development professionals in six United States and two European locations. The company has ranked on the Deloitte & Touche Technology FAST 500 for four consecutive years, and has appeared for three years on *Inc.* magazine's *Inc.* 500.

G. A. Sullivan is a recognized leader in the technology industry, known for building complex solutions that are flexible, scalable and highly reliable. Vertical industry specialization includes Financial Services (banking, insurance and securities), Healthcare, Manufacturing, Government, and Retail. Technical specialization includes the Microsoft Windows DNA platform, and the new Microsoft .NET platform and toolset. The company has high-level expertise building e-Commerce, Business Intelligence, Knowledge Management, Security and Mobile solutions.

G. A. Sullivan has built a solid team of industry leaders committed to sharing their technical expertise. Members of the G. A. Sullivan team frequently speak at national and international industry conferences. In addition to writing technical books, the company publishes an ongoing white paper series, writes articles for trade publications, and organizes numerous community development seminars and informative roundtable discussions across the United States and Europe.

For additional information about G. A. Sullivan, visit `www.gasullivan.com`.

About the Individual Authors

As a Consultant for G.A. Sullivan, **Robert Amar** has worked with a wide variety of clients and industries to implement Microsoft platform-based solutions. Robert has experience in developing traditional object-oriented and Web-based user interfaces using a diverse set of languages and development tools. Recently Robert has worked on cutting-edge applications for the life insurance industry that implement the ACORD XML transaction standards for the life insurance industry and use BizTalk Server as a means of communicating between underwriters, agents, and insurance companies. Robert is an MCP in Visual Basic.

Robert would like to thank his fiancé Nicha Chowpaknam for all her encouragement and support.

As a Senior Technical Architect in G.A. Sullivan's e-Business Group, **Matthew Baute** helps clients design, implement, and tune leading-edge technology solutions for the Microsoft platform. In addition to extensive Windows DNA experience, Matthew recently completed the early phase of a large, distributed C# and ASP.NET project involving OLAP and Digital Dashboard technology. Matthew is an MCSD in Visual Basic and SQL Server whose authoring credits include a white paper entitled *Multi-Tier Performance Tuning* and a chapter on Visual Basic and ADO in G.A. Sullivan's previous title, *Building Enterprise Solutions with Visual Studio 6.*

Matthew would like to express special thanks to Helena, and to Mom and Dad.

As G.A. Sullivan's Chief Technology Officer (CTO), **Don Benage** leads the daily operations of the company's Technology Center. Specialties include application development, e-business and Internet technologies, and XML-based, loosely coupled, highly scalable systems. Prior to joining G.A. Sullivan in 1995, he spent five years at Microsoft Corporation. Don has also directed several of G.A. Sullivan's authoring teams, serving as the lead author of technical books for Pearson's Que and SAMS labels, including *Building Enterprise Solutions with Visual Studio 6* and *Special Edition Using Microsoft BackOffice* (Editions 1 and 2).

Don would like to thank Diane and Andy.

Eric Brown spends most of his time helping G.A. Sullivan's customers and developers architect, develop, and design large-scale e-Business systems. Eric is an accomplished developer with over eight years of experience building distributed systems using various languages. Eric spends time as a presenter and author educating both customers and developers on .NET technologies. He has contributed to three previous publishing efforts, including G.A. Sullivan's previous title, *Building Enterprise Solutions with Visual Studio 6.*

Eric thanks Rebecca and Emily, as well as Larry, Curley, Moe, Shemp, The Pirates Who Don't Do Anything, and The Yodeling Veterinarian of the Alps.

As a Senior Consultant for G.A. Sullivan, **David Burgett** helps determine the technical direction of clients by identifying business challenges and educating and assisting the client with the implementation of the technology best suited to meet the challenge. David has extensive Web development experience, creating solutions on both the server and client side, with a variety of languages and platforms. David also evangelizes technology within the G.A. Sullivan community, with topics ranging from Dynamic HTML to .NET development. David is an active author and technical presenter; he has contributed to three books and two technical white papers and has recently presented at the TechEd conference and the Office XP launch. David is an MCSD and an MCDBA.

David would like to thank Susan for encouraging him to contribute to this book, for putting up with him while he worked on it, and for sticking by him as he finished it. Also to Sable, Sashka, and Chloe for always making him smile.

As a Managing Consultant in G.A. Sullivan's Line of Business Financial Services, **Remco Jorna** helps financial institutions identify and design technology solutions based on the Microsoft .NET Platform. Remco is an MCSD and has recently completed the logical and technical design of two .NET Framework applications for Employee Benefit and Knowledge Management solutions which use ASP.NET and Visual Basic .NET.

As a Senior Consultant for G.A. Sullivan, **Chris Koenig** works with clients to help them discover and solve their business problems using the latest technologies on the Microsoft platform. Chris has extensive software development experience including large-scale client-server and multi-tier Web applications. Chris is also an active technical evangelist for G.A. Sullivan and helps to educate both clients and consultants about .NET and Web Development. Chris is a Charter Member of the MCSD community and an MCDBA.

Chris would like to thank Laura, David, Christine, Stephen, and Brian for their patience and understanding, and to Shawn for the opportunity.

As a Technical Lead for G.A. Sullivan's Dutch office, **Cor Kroon** helps translate clients' needs into a technical design and implementation that best suits their business goals. Cor has extensive Web development experience, covering all layers of the Windows DNA model. Cor is an MCSD in Visual Basic and Web development, but his experience also includes other platforms and languages, such as UNIX and C. His recent contributions to the G.A. Sullivan community include the design and implementation of an XML-based, multi-lingual version of the company Web site, targeted towards the European market.

Cor would like to thank his wife Jolanda and his sons Niels and Lars for their support and encouragement during his writing efforts.

As a Senior Consultant in G.A. Sullivan's Nashville office, **Richard Lassan** focuses on learning and evangelizing the benefits of the .NET platform. Richard's authoring credits include "ASP+ Validator Controls" for *ASPToday*, and "Working with DataGrids" and "Validating User Input" in a forthcoming book on ASP.NET. Richard is also currently contributing to a book on the C# language.

Richard would like to thank William & Eleanor Lassan, Billy, Ed and Steve, and his wife Karen, for her patience and encouragement while contributing to this book.

As a Senior Consultant for G.A. Sullivan, **Roger Miller** helps architect, implement, and deploy enterprise-wide solutions for clients. Roger manages and mentors large teams of consultants to produce high-quality, on-time solutions. Roger recently presented a Microsoft Solution Series on BizTalk across the Midwest. Roger has worked with a variety of languages and platforms, ranging from handheld devices to Web sites to F-15 fighter jets. Roger holds both a B.S. and an M.S. in Computer Science.

Roger would like to thank his wife Melissa and his children Hayden and Gwendolyn for their support and patience during the development and authoring process, and says, "I promise I won't lock myself in the basement ever again."

Brian Mueller is a senior developer and architect for G.A. Sullivan who specializes in developing Web-based, n-tier business systems utilizing a variety of technologies, and is presently leading the development of a large Visual Basic .NET and ASP.NET portal solution. He also has extensive experience migrating existing applications to new technologies and architectures. Brian is an MCSD, MCDBA, and MCSE.

As a software consultant, **Baya Pavliashvili** has worked on a number of projects specializing in database development and administration. Baya has authored articles about developing in Transact-SQL, configuring replication, and building and maintaining data warehouses with SQL Server. He has assisted with editing and reviewing several technical titles. Baya is the president of the Nashville SQL Server Users Group, and holds the MCSE, MCSD, and MCDBA certifications.

Baya would like to thank Jerry Post and Thomas Baldwin for their tireless efforts, and for developing world-class professionals.

Bry Pickett is a software engineer with G. A. Sullivan and has over six years experience designing and developing distributed applications using Microsoft tools and technologies. He contributes development skills to a wide variety of projects using various languages and platforms including the Microsoft .NET Enterprise Solutions Platform. Bry is an MCSD, MCSE, and MCDBA focusing on middle-tier business logic and data access components as well as user interface components.

Bry would like to thank Layne for being here, and Betty and John for getting him here.

John Pickett has spent most of the last ten years applying new technologies to a wide range of industry solutions. While serving as a Senior Architect in G.A. Sullivan's e-Business group, his primary role is to provide technical leadership to G.A. Sullivan's customers, project teams, and sales staff. John's leadership participation extends to all phases of the software development process, from envisioning and development through stabilization. John has been involved with several previous publishing efforts, and recently presented the gasTIX application at TechEd 2001 Europe in Barcelona, Spain.

John would like to thank his parents, John and Betty, as well as Kathy, Jennaka, and Giovanni.

As a Senior Consultant for G. A. Sullivan, **Jody Socha** helps clients with all facets of software development, from requirements to project management to design and implementation. He has over five years experience in developing applications for the financial services industry, with a focus on enterprise-class applications and business integration strategies. Jody's authoring credits include a white paper entitled *Using Visual Component Manager and the Microsoft Repository*, and chapters in both of the last two books from G.A. Sullivan on Microsoft Visual Studio.

Dedication

For Larry Millett, Shirley Phelps, and Kim Williamson.

Acknowledgments

At G.A. Sullivan

John Alexander
Mark Benatar
Chris Brauss
Gary Dzurny
Bill Edwards
Richard Gower
Shelley Hawkins
Stefanie Hill
Tom Klein
Mike Lichtenberg
Gary Loberg
Tom Luther
Steve Miller
Mark Munie
Dan Norton
Brian Pursley
Greg Sullivan
Debb Wiedner
Kim Williamson
Deana Woldanski

At Microsoft

Bryan Alsup
Craig Jaris
Judy Kolde
Dave Mendlen
Cathy Menees
Piet Obermeyer

Erik Olson
Shannon S. Pahl
Brad Rhodes
Marius Rochon
Merrill Schebaum
Kent Sharkey

At SAMS

Charlotte Clapp
Leah Kirkpatrick
Heather McNeill
Grant Munroe
Karen Wachs

Others

Eddie Gulley
Kenny Hall
John Navratil
Mark Sundt

About the Tech Reviewers

Beth Breidenbach is a Technical Architect for Getronics, a Netherlands-based provider of software and infrastructure solutions throughout the world. Her group develops enterprise-wide software applications targeted to toptier financial institutions. A self-professed "data geek," Beth has an abiding interest in all aspects of data design, storage, transmission, and translation—which was a natural lead-in to exploring the possibilities inherent in the new family of .NET technologies. Her most recent project was the application of XML and database technologies to rule-processing engines. Getronics is a member of Microsoft's .NET Early Adopter Program, and Beth is currently exploring .NET business and data-tier design issues as a member of that development team. Beth is a Charter Member of the MCSD community.

Jawahar (JP) Puvvala is currently working as a senior developer. He has worked extensively with both Microsoft and Java technologies, designing and developing enterprise systems. He has two Masters degrees and currently holds MCSD, MCSE, and MCDBA certifications.

Tell Us What You Think!

As the reader of this book, *you* are our most important critic and commentator. We value your opinion and want to know what we're doing right, what we could do better, what areas you'd like to see us publish in, and any other words of wisdom you're willing to pass our way.

As an Associate Publisher for Sams Publishing, I welcome your comments. You can fax, email, or write me directly to let me know what you did or didn't like about this book—as well as what we can do to make our books stronger.

Please note that I cannot help you with technical problems related to the topic of this book, and that due to the high volume of mail I receive, I might not be able to reply to every message.

When you write, please be sure to include this book's title and author as well as your name and phone or fax number. I will carefully review your comments and share them with the author and editors who worked on the book.

Fax: 317-581-4770

Email: `feedback@samspublishing.com`

Mail: Linda Engelman
Sams Publishing
201 West 103rd Street
Indianapolis, IN 46290 USA

Introduction

Who Should Use This Book?

.NET e-Business Architecture is meant to be read by *technical architects* and *software developers* responsible for designing and building Internet-based applications for the .NET platform. It provides detailed information on implementing a .NET system design, and presents the best practices and lessons learned along the way. Coding techniques using the Visual Studio .NET tool suite are demonstrated throughout the book. The sample code is based on the actual implementation of an enterprise-scale sample application, gasTIX.

.NET e-Business Architecture is also appropriate for *information system managers* faced with planning issues. This book explains the key concepts behind the most important technologies in the .NET platform. Visual C# .NET, Visual Basic .NET, ASP.NET, ADO.NET, SOAP, and XML-based Web services are all covered. More importantly, this book provides practical examples of how to effectively implement these technologies, as well as when and why they should be considered.

How This Book Is Organized

This book is organized to follow an application development cycle, beginning with a look at the basics of the .NET platform. An introduction to the sample gasTIX application is given, along with an overview of the business and technical goals of this fictional company. Subsequent sections cover design and implementation details, and the final section explores .NET testing and deployment issues.

The chapters in Part I, "Preliminaries and Planning," introduce the concepts behind the .NET Framework. They discuss how the Internet and the pervasiveness of XML enable us to begin offering a new generation of software applications. The sample application referenced throughout the book is introduced, along with a chapter covering the communication mechanisms between the multiple layers of a .NET e-Business application.

The chapters in Part II, "Designing .NET e-Business Solutions," cover .NET application design considerations from each of the three logical tiers: presentation, business, and data. Security topics are explored, which are an area of primary concern for architects, managers, and administrators alike. Issues relating to integration with COM+ services are also covered in this section.

The chapters in Part III, "Building .NET e-Business Sites," consider the implementation of the sample gasTIX application from a functional point of view. A chapter is devoted to each of the main site functions (event searching, ticket purchasing, fulfillment/order processing), from the top tier to the bottom tier, demonstrating how data is passed between application layers. An abundance of code samples provides you with ideas and techniques that you can include in your own .NET applications.

The chapters in Part IV, "Testing and Deploying .NET Sites," explore the necessity of debugging and performance tuning a .NET e-Business application prior to release. An entire chapter is dedicated to the issues surrounding deploying a .NET application. This section rounds out a complete discussion of the software development life cycle for a .NET e-Business application.

Part I: Preliminaries and Planning

Chapter 1, ".NET—The Big Picture," provides a high-level overview of the major features of the .NET Framework and the Visual Studio .NET programming tools. An introductory chapter is necessary because of the true evolutionary nature of the .NET release. The central role of the Internet and standard protocols such as XML and SOAP are discussed, along with the importance of designing loosely coupled systems. This chapter prepares the reader to drill down to the more solution-focused chapters that follow.

Chapter 2, "gasTIX: A Sample .NET e-Business," introduces the sample application referenced throughout the remainder of the book. The sample application is an online ticketing Web site that sells tickets to major sporting and concert events across the country. The chapter provides an overview of the requirements and business drivers behind the technical approach chosen. Thoughts on team composition and effective project management for a .NET e-Business implementation are also included.

Chapter 3, "Enabling Inter-Application Communications," discusses how independent applications can work together in a .NET collaborative environment. Concepts such as XML, XML Web services, SOAP, and Orchestration in BizTalk Server 2000 are covered.

Part II: Designing .NET e-Business Solutions

Chapter 4, "Tools of the Trade," discusses the various architectural, language, and productivity tools at the disposal of designers and developers programming for the .NET platform. The .NET Framework is covered in more depth, along with the two major .NET languages, Visual C# .NET and Visual Basic .NET. New productivity features in the Visual Studio .NET integrated development environment (IDE) are explored.

Chapter 5, "Implementing .NET Presentation Services," covers the design considerations for the Web user interface in a .NET application. ASP.NET Web Forms are introduced, along with the new state management options. Approaches for how HTML can be separated from ASP.NET code are given, and server-side versus client-side rendering issues are also covered.

Chapter 6, "Implementing .NET Business Services," discusses approaches to designing the middle tier in a .NET e-Business application. The design of the gasTIX business services is discussed, as well as new issues for component developers, including ADO.NET and .NET Remoting. A discussion of the gasTIX XML Web services is another important topic covered in this chapter.

Chapter 7, "Implementing .NET Data Services," looks at design considerations for the data tier in a .NET application. This chapter explores some of the new features of SQL Server 2000 and how they integrate into the gasTIX Web site. Issues related to the use of stored procedures, XML, and indexes in SQL Server 2000 are explored through evaluating the implementation choices made in the sample application.

Chapter 8, "Handling Security," discusses application security issues and how .NET handles them. Role-based security is explored, including authentication and authorization using cookies and certificates. Code-access security through assembly signing is also covered, along with the different tools used in this regard.

Chapter 9, "COM+ Integration," shows how interaction with COM+ legacy components can be accomplished. This chapter provides a discussion of the issues encountered when porting a COM+ application to .NET managed code. It also presents an overview of how to best leverage your current investment in existing COM+ components.

Part III: Building .NET e-Business Sites

Chapter 10, "gasTIX Event Searching," discusses how a user can browse the gasTIX site to find a specific event. One of the search methods is discussed in detail by focusing on ASP.NET implementation techniques using several of the Web Controls, along with a custom User Control. An advanced User Control is also built for use on the home page of gasTIX.

Chapter 11, "Purchasing a Ticket," presents the area of the site where a user actually purchases a ticket. The focus of the chapter is a walkthrough of purchasing a ticket on gasTIX, and its implementation as a Web service. The gasTIX purchasing XML Web services, consumed by the gasBAGS Web site (a fictional band who wishes to offer its fans event ticket purchasing functionality), are discussed in this chapter.

Chapter 12, "Fulfillment," demonstrates how communication is handled between the main gasTIX site and a site run by a third-party responsible for printing and shipping tickets. BizTalk issues are discussed, including message queuing, routing, and workflow orchestration.

Chapter 13, ".NET Remoting," discusses the important concepts for developing and hosting .NET objects remotely. The use of remoting in the gasTIX application is examined, along with the differences between providing application functionality via remoting and via SOAP XML Web services.

Part IV: Testing and Deploying .NET Sites

Chapter 14, "Debugging a .NET Application," discusses tools and techniques developers can use to efficiently debug a .NET application. The major debugging enhancements in Visual Studio .NET are explored.

Chapter 15, "Performance Tuning in .NET," covers general performance testing concepts, along with the various performance mechanisms in .NET such as ASP.NET output caching. The main .NET tuning tools, Application Center Test (ACT), Visual Studio Analyzer (VSA), and SQL Profiler, are all discussed. These tools help you find and eliminate system bottlenecks.

Chapter 16, "Deploying the Application," walks the reader through the steps required to deploy a .NET application to a production environment. Important issues that should be considered for proper application configuration are addressed. Specific consideration is given to configuring and managing the sample gasTIX application in Application Center 2000.

Conventions Used In This Book

Special design features enhance the text material:

- Notes
- Tips
- Cautions

NOTE

Notes explain interesting or important points that can help you understand the described concepts and techniques.

TIP

Tips are little pieces of information that can help you in real-world situations. Tips often offer shortcuts or alternative approaches to make a task easier and faster, and are written based on the author's personal experiences, to help you increase your productivity.

CAUTION

Cautions alert you to an action that can lead to an unexpected or unpredictable result, including loss of data. The text provides an explanation of how you can avoid such a result. Pay careful attention to Cautions.

Rather than have you wade through all the details relating to a particular function of an application in a single chapter before you progress to the next topic, this book provides special cross-references to help you find the information you need. These cross-references follow the material they pertain to, as in the following sample reference:

See "Another Section or Another Chapter."

This book also uses various typesetting styles to distinguish between explanatory and instructional text and text you enter. Onscreen messages, program code, and commands appear in a special monospaced font. Placeholders, or words that you replace with actual code, are indicated with monospace italic. Text that you are to type appears in monospace boldface.

When a line of code is too long to fit on one line of this book, it is broken at a convenient place and continued to the next line. A code continuation character (➥) precedes the continuation of a line of code. (You should type a line of code that has this character as one long line without breaking it.)

Key combinations that you use to perform Windows operations are indicated by joining the keys with a plus sign: Alt+F4, for example, indicates that you press and hold the Alt key while pressing the F4 function key.

Preliminaries and Planning

PART I

In this section we introduce the concepts behind the .NET Framework. We introduce the ways in which the Internet and the pervasiveness of XML enable enterprises to begin offering a new generation of software applications. The sample application referenced throughout the book is introduced, along with a chapter covering the communication mechanisms between the multiple layers of a .NET e-Business application.

IN THIS PART

- **Chapter 1: .NET—The Big Picture 9**
- **Chapter 2: gasTIX: A Sample .NET e-Business 47**
- **Chapter 3: Enabling Inter-Application Communications 75**

.NET—The Big Picture

by Don Benage and Mark Benatar

CHAPTER

1

IN THIS CHAPTER

- The Internet Rules! 10
- The Evolution of the Programming Model 15
- Incorporating Services 22
- Cast of Characters 27
- From Here 45

Change is constant in our lives. In every area of human endeavor the ongoing flow of progress continues, and computer technology is no exception. Just as we begin to feel comfortable with a particular platform and toolset, another is introduced and the learning process begins anew. Though we may occasionally lament the effort required to keep up with the latest advancements in technology, the constant pace of innovation is also very exciting.

The term ".NET" carries multiple meanings. It is, first and foremost, an umbrella marketing term used to describe the entire Microsoft platform, much as Windows DNA described the previous platform. But the astute observer will notice that .NET is also used to refer to one or more elements of the overall platform in addition to the entire platform as a whole, which can lead to confusion. The exact meaning of the term depends on the context, and what is most important to the speaker. Here is a short list of different elements, all covered in this book, that are described by the term .NET:

- The collection of Microsoft's Enterprise Servers
- The Common Language Runtime (CLR)
- The .NET Framework
- An approach to software development emphasizing the role of XML Web services and the use of standard Internet protocols
- The collection of Microsoft's "core" XML Web services, codenamed Hailstorm

The Microsoft .NET platform is a comprehensive overhaul in the evolution of Microsoft's software development toolset. Some elements of the platform have been under development for four years, and almost every facet has been changed in some way. This book is designed as a thorough introduction to .NET, and how to use it to create e-Business applications and web sites. The authoring team also acted as a software development team, creating a comprehensive sample comprising two Web sites, and then describing the techniques that were used in the following chapters. Welcome to the world of .NET.

The Internet Rules!

As organizations of all sizes and descriptions capture and analyze information, formulate strategies, and ponder their futures, it is clear that the Internet has changed everything. The impact that this multifaceted entity has on our businesses, our schools, our governments, and our lives is profound. This has been stated so often it has already become a cliché, barely worth mentioning.

We are not here to prognosticate on which way the wind is blowing, or the fate of "the dot coms." But to understand the significance and the impetus of .NET you must begin here: the Internet is the thing. It has become a major factor in the way that businesses interact with suppliers, with customers, and with business partners. It has dramatically altered the availability of information, accelerating the pace of information flow, and increasing customer expectations. Its impact is sometimes obvious, but it has also caused pervasive and subtle changes in the way we think about the world which are only beginning to be fully understood.

A Level Playing Field

What makes the Internet so important? One reason is that the Internet offers a reasonably level playing field for a large number of participants. The Internet operates with no single organizing force, no single group or individual holding ultimate power. English is not a standard on the worldwide Web, but Hypertext Transfer Protocol (HTTP) and Hypertext Markup Language (HTML) are, as well as Extensible Markup Language (XML). Large corporate entities from leading industrialized nations certainly exert a great deal of influence, but no conglomerate owns the Internet, and it is not governed by the laws of any single country. Of course there are political maneuverings, and people from all over the world are engaging in debates and machinations aimed at a favorable outcome for their constituencies and themselves. But by and large the Internet is a place with very low barriers to entry, very little regulation, and lots of opportunity.

Standards—So Many to Choose From

A wise man once said, "The nice thing about standards is there are so many to choose from!" This is true even if we limit our investigation to web-based protocols, or even those primarily associated with application development and deployment. There are many standards. We like to think of this in a positive way, looking at these standards as many technologies in our toolkit, waiting for the appropriate situation to be used.

Why are standards so important? With so many people participating in this shared endeavor, we must agree on some rudimentary approaches to conducting our conversations, our transactions, our business. Absolute anarchy serves only the nihilist. If we wish to accomplish something constructive, we need building blocks with which to work. Standard Internet protocols serve as these building blocks.

As a guiding principle, we'd prefer to "be one of the many, not one of the few." In other words, we'd generally like to select mature technologies that are used by many other organizations. And, in general, we'd like standards that are controlled by an independent organization that is not primarily a profit-making entity.

This chapter won't delve deeply into specific protocols, but it will make a few key points about XML and Simple Object Access Protocol (SOAP) because of the central role they play in .NET.

XML

Among its many benefits, XML is a primary enabling technology when we wish to build loosely coupled systems. To appreciate this benefit, some history is in order.

Among the lessons we've learned over the past ten years is the value of building our systems to be resilient in the face of change. Things always change, usually before we can deploy Version 1.0 of a new system!

As we have struggled to deal with this constant need to adapt, we have learned that if the interface between two systems is highly constrained, any changes must be made at the same time to both systems. This is bad enough, but if we have a single system that connects to many other systems, the result is particularly pernicious. Changing all the related systems in synchronization with one another is nearly impossible. Things become so difficult to change we may decide instead to institutionalize the current practice. XML provides a flexibility that can solve this problem.

In the past, it was common practice to define a highly structured data transmission protocol. If one application needed to transmit information to another application, the information was often represented in a compressed, binary format. This was done in an effort to reduce the size of the transmission to maximize the use of relatively scarce bandwidth. An unwelcome offshoot of this approach is a tight coupling between the two applications communicating with one another. If we need to change the content of the transmission, we must change both applications at the same time. Software designed, for example, to interpret the first six characters of a data transmission as an inventory number is, *by its design*, going to yield a tightly coupled system.

But suppose we don't build a preconceived notion of the exact positioning of the invoice number into our software. Suppose, instead, that we look for the invoice number between two tags, `<invno>` and `</invno>`, that must appear somewhere within the data stream. Now that's being a bit more reasonable. We might wish to define a schema that represents, for us, the proper syntax for a valid invoice. We might be willing to consider a subset of the information optional. This would allow us to make changes to one system without the other being affected—loose coupling!

So, we've seen how the design of XML allows us tremendous flexibility and power in the exchange of business documents. The same approach can obviously be used with information of all kinds. This is one of the primary reasons that the use of XML has attracted so much attention. Is there another way to leverage this simple but elegant protocol? Yes, and that way is SOAP.

SOAP

SOAP is an XML-based protocol that allows applications to exchange structured data over the Web. SOAP is the glue that ties together disparate services through industry-standard protocols. SOAP allows developers to build XML Web services, which expose programmatic functionality over the Internet.

NOTE

For more information about SOAP, visit `msdn.microsoft.com/soap`.

Let's assume we have a distributed system made up of two or more computers, each running its own operating system, that are connected by various networking protocols (predominantly TCP/IP). For some years there have been passionate debates about object models, application development models, software architectures, and related technologies. As distributed computing and component-based approaches grew in popularity, the competition grew for the hearts and minds of developers. The major vendors involved in providing tools for building enterprise-class applications are often bitter enemies, and compete vigorously against one another. The playing field is replete with acronyms representing various approaches: CORBA versus COM/DCOM, Enterprise Java Beans (EJB) versus Windows DNA, J2EE versus .NET.

Of course, under the surface there are many similarities in all of these approaches. In particular, all of them offer a way for a process executing on a particular computer to call a remote procedure executing in another process on the same machine, or on an entirely different computer. We need a way to specify the procedure, send one or more arguments, and receive results in the form of return arguments. And every Remote Procedure Call (RPC) should be uniquely resolveable in an unambiguous way, leading us to the correct executable module on the correct computer.

Every platform finds a way to do this, and the differences in implementation are perhaps less interesting than the similarities. And yet they *are* different. Systems built with one platform are incompatible with others. This gave rise to such things as COM/CORBA gateways that provide interoperability between two different platforms. But such gateways, living with one foot in each world, suffer from the problems of both, and are nearly always an undesirable compromise. There are frequent inconsistencies in how either side of the gateway deals with data types and parameters, as well as the inevitable performance hit incurred by the translation process.

Enter the Web, and expectations have changed. The message being sent by the marketplace is this: whatever we build, it must work on the Web. And it must interoperate with other systems. If difficult and capricious requirements exist for interacting with a given system, the time and expense of doing so will become too great. All systems must adhere to a reasonably straightforward way of interoperating with external systems. This is the way organizations wish to conduct business today.

And so we see something happening that was unanticipated by most, professionals and pundits alike. An elegant protocol has been devised for calling a remote procedure that runs over standard Internet protocols, is firewall-friendly, and is not "owned" by any single vendor. Take the contents of a remote procedure call, format them with XML, and send this payload over HTTP protocols. What could be simpler? Forget your COM/CORBA gateways, your façade classes wrapping remote, dissimilar systems and architectures. Let's all speak SOAP!

NOTE

For more information on the implementation and performance of SOAP calls, see Chapter 13, ".NET Remoting."

Enterprise-Level Attributes

Offering a high degree of interoperability through the use of standard web-based protocols is clearly a good thing. It is not enough, however. In this age of e-Business, and the rise of the "dot coms," sites must be prepared to deliver more. What if we decide to invite the whole world to visit our site following the NFL's Super Bowl or the World Cup soccer finals? What if we want to service a worldwide clientele, in multiple time zones?

The characteristics we need are sometimes described as the "ilities," or more eloquently as enterprise class attributes. We've already discussed interoperability. What are the other "ilities"? They include:

- Scalability
- Reliability
- Manageability
- Flexibility

When we say a site should be scalable, we are referring to the ability to handle a large "load"—to perform lots of work. This usually means a large number of concurrent clients, but may also mean relatively fewer clients each engaged in tasks that require the system to perform a lot of work on their behalf. We need reasonable performance for the first user to visit our site, and as the amount of work increases, that performance should not degrade below a well-defined minimum acceptable level.

The site should also be reliable. Depending on the nature of the site we may even wish to approach the elusive "five nines," 99.999% uptime. Since many of the elements we use to build sites do not typically offer this level of reliability, we must usually incorporate redundant elements. By eliminating any single point of failure, an individual element whose failure will bring down the entire site, we can dramatically improve reliability. This goal also impacts our ability to perform scheduled maintenance. No longer can we use late night hours after the close of business for operations that will have a major effect on performance. Our business may not "close!"

Large organizations are subject to many outside influences. There are regulatory and statutory requirements imposed by governments, and competitive pressures exerted by other organizations. The life cycle of a typical automated system has shrunk steadily over the past few decades. Everyone is in a hurry. In order to respond quickly to change, we must design our systems from the very beginning to support change. We must select an architecture that enables change. Earlier in the chapter we discussed loose coupling as a technique to enable change. Building a system out of discrete components that encapsulate their functionality is another approach that supports this goal. If we don't address this need, our system is doomed to a very brief useful lifespan.

Perhaps flexibility isn't enough. In many situations, our systems need to go beyond being flexible—they must be *agile.* As our site operates day-by-day, supporting the needs of our organization and navigating the competitive landscape, we may need agility to be successful. This combines the idea of flexibility with an element of timeliness, and also connotes the ability to be nimble, to be sure-footed. We can make changes with confidence and land on our feet when faced with the need to change.

As system architects and developers have pursued these lofty goals, the tools and techniques they use have undergone a constant evolution. The Microsoft .NET platform is seen in this light as the current incarnation of an evolving process, one that continues to this day and beyond. An understanding of how this process has unfolded and its major milestones can be helpful in developing a complete understanding of our current status. Therefore, a brief summary of this process is provided in the next section.

The Evolution of the Programming Model

Developers must learn many things during the course of their career. The first of these is, obviously, at least one programming language. In addition to this, there are broader issues that must be mastered. What are the characteristics of the target platform? What operating system will be running on the computers making up the system? What are its capabilities, and how should they be leveraged to deliver the desired application specific features? Also of interest is the development platform. What editor or environment will be used? What Application Programming Interface(s) (API) or object model(s) are relevant? In other words, what is the programming model?

The .NET Framework has the benefits of Microsoft's many years of experience building both low-level and rapid application development (RAD) languages and environments. The .NET Framework has been specifically designed to handle the challenges faced by today's developers.

Clients and Servers

Not so long ago, developers who wrote applications for PCs were targeting individual users sitting at disconnected computers. If they were connected to a network, they might load and save files from a shared server or print on a shared printer, but very little was required of the developer to utilize these services. Networking system software intercepted calls directed at the local operating system and redirected them to shared devices.

Microsoft Windows and other similar operating environments offered a Graphical User Interface (GUI) that gave developers a whole new programming model—event-driven programming. The application was essentially a loop that watched for messages sent by the operating system to notify the application of events as they occurred: keyboard activity, mouse movement, mouse clicks, etc.

Over time, networked PCs were increasingly used to deliver applications for groups of users, perhaps a department within an organization. The need for large amounts of structured data grew, and Database Management Systems (DBMS) became popular. This led to the creation of client/server computing, a different way of building applications (see Figure 1.1). For the first time, executable modules making up the application executed on more than one computer—the birth of distributed computing. Client/server computing offered important advantages. Server-based databases were capable of enforcing centrally defined business rules (for example, "Don't allow anyone to delete a customer that still owes us money!"), and allowed more computing power to be applied to a problem.

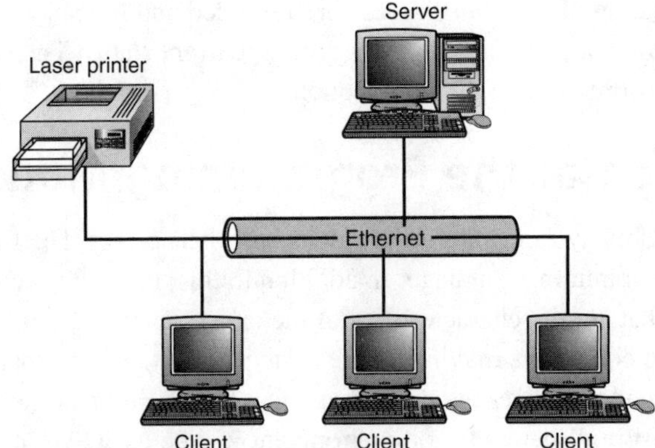

FIGURE 1.1
The client/server programming model was a significant departure from monolithic, single-module applications.

As the use of this programming model increased, new problems arose. Among the most serious was the cost of deploying the client portion of the application. In fact, in some cases, the cost of deployment was greater than the cost of creating or acquiring the application. It was very expensive to install a collection of executable modules and configuration settings on dozens or hundreds of computers. In addition, the protocols that were used for connecting client and server were not designed to work well in a highly distributed environment like the Internet. The growing use of firewalls presented significant challenges.

For these and other reasons, application developers began exploring the use of web browsers such as Netscape Navigator and Microsoft's Internet Explorer. At first, using a browser as a "container" for the client-side application meant serious compromises in the feature set available on the client. Far fewer bells and whistles were possible for clients hosted in a browser. Compatibility differences among rapidly changing browsers from different vendors were also a challenge.

Perhaps more importantly, the limitations of using Structured Query Language (SQL) to implement business rules were increasingly apparent. SQL is a non-procedural, set theory-based language ideal for specifying data-centric operations on a database. It is not designed to provide the services of a general purpose programming language.

As these developments were taking place, another paradigm shift was unfolding—the growth of Object Oriented Programming (OOP). OOP offered a programming model with important advantages such as encapsulation and inheritance. Many problems facing developers were easier to solve when viewed from this perspective. And OOP also offered a greater opportunity to achieve one of the most elusive goals of large-scale software development—reuse.

Applications Become Sites

Combining elements of client/server and OOP, yet another programming model emerged. Component-based development viewed the application as a collection of modules that could be deployed on networked computer systems. But instead of a 2-tier client/server approach, applications were separated into three logical tiers (see Figure 1.2). These were usually referred to as presentation services, mid-tier business logic, and data services. Called 3-tier or, in more complex arrangements, N-tier or multi-tier, this programming model is ideally suited for web-based environments, as well as standard application developments. It is arguably the predominant programming model for non-scientific applications at the time this book is being written.

Presentation services are delivered by the combination of web browsers and web servers working in concert with one another. Microsoft's Active Server Pages (ASP) and similar technologies allow application logic on the web server to execute, ultimately producing HTML for delivery to the browser where it is rendered. Optionally, client-side logic can also be created for execution directly on the client computer. Presentation services are primarily concerned with allowing the user to navigate through the various screens and dialogs that make up the application, accepting input from the user, and presenting results on the client computer's display.

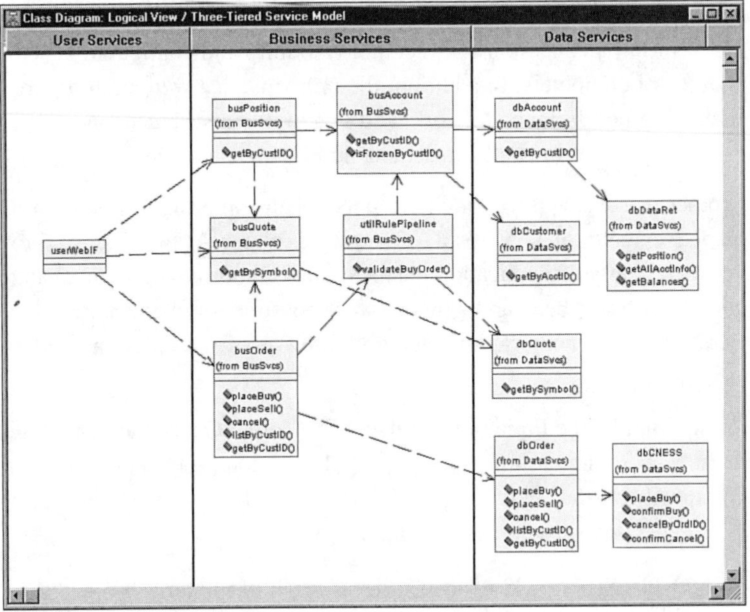

FIGURE 1.2

A logical three-tier architecture provided a separation of the business rules embedded in a system.

In the middle tier, the rules that define how an organization operates are implemented. We might, for example, create components that calculate taxes and apply those taxes only when appropriate. Mid-tier business logic is most often implemented using component-based techniques, which rely on system software to provide services for creating, managing, and destroying components on a server. Microsoft's first offering in this area, Microsoft Transaction Server (MTS), has evolved into a set of services provided by COM+ for managing components and transactional behavior. This allows the use of object oriented approaches and leaves the database to do the things for which it is best suited.

Data services are concerned with the storage and retrieval of information in a persistent store, usually a relational database. Data service components often are designed to encapsulate the exact details of physical data storage and present a "friendly" façade to mid-tier services. This allows the developers of business logic to simply request customer information, for example, and not worry about what tables the information is stored in, the relationships between various tables, and how they are indexed.

It is important to note that there is a distinction between logical tiers and the physical implementation of these elements. It is tempting to think of presentation services occurring on a client computer, mid-tier services executing on a web server and/or application server, and data services on a database server. In reality, it is a bit more subtle and complicated than this simplified picture, as shown in Figure 1.3.

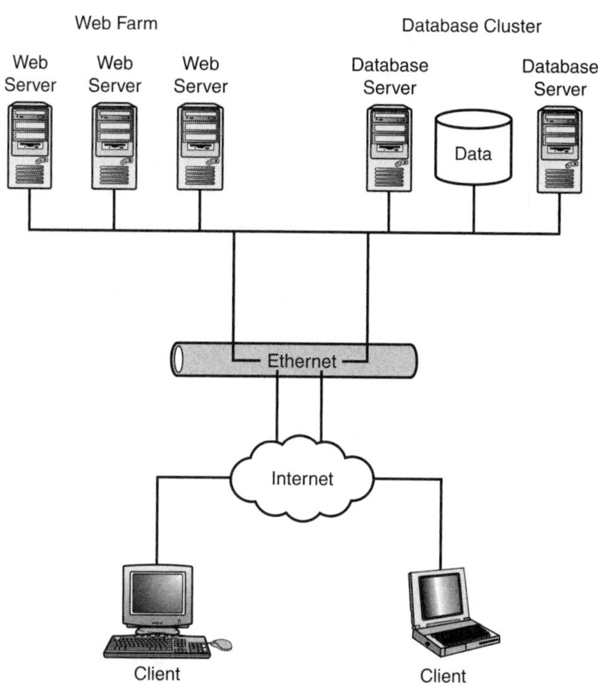

FIGURE 1.3
The physical architecture of a large web site may be made up of many servers working together to function as a single system.

As the use of web-based approaches has grown, the concept of an "application" is now most often physically implemented as a "site"—a distributed collection of elements that deliver the functionality of the application. Large web sites are not implemented on a single computer. The "front door" of the site is often implemented as a web farm, a collection of load-balanced computers that are all configured in essentially the same way. Middle tier components implementing business rules run either co-resident on the web servers, or in a physically separate middle tier, which may also be implemented as a load-balanced collection of servers. Finally, the database is most often run on a cluster of two or more machines sharing a high-performance data storage system. So sites that are experienced by users as a single entity are actually run on a distributed set of specially configured servers, each playing a particular role.

Scale Up Versus Scale Out

A central and ongoing debate focuses on the issue of how to deliver the maximum computing power to a particular application. Is it better to build very large multi-processor systems with massive amounts of memory, or should collections of relatively normal sized, commodity-priced servers be used? Both techniques are now possible, and they are referred to respectively as scaling up and scaling out.

Scaling up is the most common approach to providing maximum power with the database. This is primarily due to the complexity associated with partitioning a large database made up of many tables, indexes, views, triggers, and other elements into a collection of more or less uniform servers. It is possible for any reasonably talented database administrator to do this job manually, but *when* the partitioning scheme needs to be adjusted (and sooner or later it *always will*) you are faced with a difficult and time-consuming job almost certain to require scheduled downtime. SQL Server 2000 offers new support for partitioning a database, and for some applications this makes sense, but as a general rule it is easier to scale the database up, not out. Scale up approaches also match up well with failover clustering for reliability, particularly important for the transactional nature of most databases.

A scale out approach is most often used for web servers, grouping them into a load-balanced web farm. The elements that make up the web server's portion of a distributed, component-based application (for example, scripted web pages, graphics, and configuration files and settings) are deployed in a uniform fashion to each server in the farm. Once this is accomplished, incoming HTTP requests are distributed to one of the servers. Ideally, the amount of work performed by any given server is very close to the amount of work performed by each of the other servers—an equal load.

Balancing the Load

There are a number of approaches to load balancing, some hardware-based and some software-based. One of the first approaches was a simple "round robin" distribution that can be provided by the same Domain Name System (DNS) that directs traffic for the Internet. Instead of configuring only one entry in the DNS table for a particular domain name, a group of IP addresses could all be associated with a site name (for example, `www.gasullivan.com`). This worked, but didn't offer much resilience when one of the servers went down. DNS would continue to send an equal share of incoming requests to the down (and unavailable) server, causing the client to experience a long wait and eventual timeout of the application, or worse.

Networking and router vendors such as Cisco and F5 have offered products for several years that address this problem. In addition to distributing incoming requests, these products will typically sense when a server has gone down and remove it (temporarily) from the web farm. Microsoft acquired and refined similar software-based technology. The Windows Load

Balancing Service (WLBS) was first offered as a free download from Microsoft's web site, then was subsequently renamed and incorporated into Windows 2000 as Network Load Balancing (NLB). A number of industry pundits have predicted that load balancing a web farm is rapidly on its way to becoming a commodity service, and the pricing for this capability continues to drop as additional features are added and performance improves.

Load balancing is not necessarily a trivial task, however. For example, certain applications may perform a great deal of work using mid-tier components. Such an application might warrant a multi-tier approach that implements a physically distinct collection of mid-tier servers (in other words, the mid-tier components are *not* run on the web servers). Now we are faced with a more difficult task than equally distributing incoming requests across the server farm. Ideally, we would equally distribute the actual *work*, not just the component requests.

The algorithms for providing this capability are non-trivial. Among the problems that must be faced is the need to measure and characterize the load being sustained by a given server. What exactly should be measured? Clearly you want to measure the use of one or more of a server's resources such as the Central Processing Unit (CPU), memory, or disk access, but which and in what combination? Also, it is clearly important not to just look at resource utilization at some particular instant, but to measure load over time. But we need to be careful or we will waste precious resources in order to accomplish the measuring.

Finally, there is the question of how to distribute the load. Assuming we know at any given instant which server should receive the next request, what is the actual mechanism that accomplishes this task? Do we send a multi-cast request and depend on the least busy server to answer first? Or do we provide a traffic manager (potentially a single point of failure) to dole out work? Microsoft has grappled with these issues, and offers a Component Load Balancing (CLB) capability in addition to NLB.

A Matter of State

The multi-tier programming model helped solve many problems faced by developers and system architects, but also brought some new challenges. The use of a web farm to handle very large numbers of users is a great benefit, but as these systems were deployed, tested, and tuned it became obvious that state management was an issue. Most web server platforms offer an object model with some type of Session construct for managing interaction with a particular user. It is possible to use session variables to store information about a particular session—choices made by the user, user preferences, and other information collectively referred to as "the current state." Doing so, however, can put a considerable burden on the resources of the server.

An even more difficult problem arises when we allow each request for a new page to be load balanced. If we force a particular client session to "stick" to a particular server, creating what is called server affinity, we must do extra work to provide this session capability over HTTP, which is essentially a session-less protocol. Furthermore, this will almost certainly cause a less even distribution of the load.

It would be easier in some respects to allow each request for a new page to be serviced by any server in the web farm. This would likely provide a more uniform distribution of load, and simplify our session management chores. But, what about state? If there is any current state information that should be maintained, how is it to be managed when the user is redirected to an entirely different server? As we will explore in some detail in Chapter 11, "Purchasing a Ticket," the .NET platform offers several alternatives to address this dilemma:

- Use session variables as in the past. Though this limits scalability, it is the fastest alternative with a single web server.
- Configure a "state server" running as a Windows NT service. A single state server can provide state management for an entire web farm, providing a balance between performance and scalability. This potentially introduces a single point of failure.
- Configure the web farm to store state information in SQL Server. Though this adds the most overhead, and hence compromises performance somewhat, it is the most reliable. The admittedly slower performance will continue to be a problem as the number of users grows very large.

In addition to maintaining state information for a user session, it is also clearly important to be able to identify a particular session. This can be done in a variety of ways, each with its own strengths and weaknesses. The most common method is to use HTTP cookies, strings of specially coded information stored directly on the user's computer and passed to the server with each request. However, cookies can be seen as invasive and are a privacy concern to some users, and most browsers can be configured to disallow the use of cookies. Therefore an alternate method must be provided.

The most widely used alternative to cookies is to imbed the same information directly into the Uniform Resource Locator (URL) that is passed from client to server. Although this circumvents the problem with cookies, it is not as reliable since all session information is lost if a server goes down.

Incorporating Services

The metamorphosis from applications to sites becomes even more interesting when we introduce the concept of XML Web services, as described in the previous section, SOAP. XML Web services blur the definition of the term *site*. We will explore the concept of software as a service in detail in the next section, but for now we will introduce the idea with a simple example. To avoid confusion, it is perhaps best to note immediately that this use of the word "service" is similar to, but distinct from, its normal English definition—the act of helping or doing work for another or for a community. It is also distinct from a Windows NT-style service, which refers to a specific type of process running on a Windows NT or Windows 2000 computer (similar to a Unix daemon).

Suppose we are creating a web site whose purpose is to sell an inventory of items that vary in size and weight. We wish to charge our customers for the items they order and offer a range of shipping alternatives including overnight delivery as well as normal delivery that may take several days. How do we calculate the charge for shipping?

We could, of course, review the process a person would use to manually calculate shipping charges for using a particular carrier. We could create a database table representing the current rates for various sizes, weights, and distances. Then we could create one or more business rule components that calculate shipping charges according to the current rules for that carrier. We could then repeat this process for each carrier we wished to use.

The information in these tables, and the rules expressed in the components, will need to be changed periodically, perhaps frequently. A multi-tier approach facilitates this process, but we don't really wish to become quite so intimate with the calculation of shipping charges. Perhaps the main concern is that this effort does not represent our core competency. Getting this right is not our primary concern. We want to sell our inventory; we are not in the shipping business.

It would be very nice if we could somehow outsource this calculation to those for whom it is a primary concern, namely the carriers themselves. What if we could send an electronic request for the calculation of a shipping charge to send an item of specified size and weight from a particular location to another location, and quickly receive a response containing the cost? This is the central idea behind a web service.

Services 101

Our shipping calculation example leaves many important details of web services undefined. Which shipping companies offer such a web-based service, if any? Exactly what do I send in the request? Do I specify the to and from locations using a street address, Global Positioning System (GPS) coordinates, or latitude and longitude? In what form will the results be returned? Can I ask for optional information or must I make multiple requests? And what protocol do I use to send the request?

We could use a variety of protocols to implement XML Web services, but a standard way of doing the job would make sense in this cooperative endeavor. SOAP seems like a natural fit for much of the job we need to accomplish. Our request for a shipping calculation is essentially a remote procedure call. With the addition of a few extra elements, we have the foundation for a powerful new way to build web-based applications.

NOTE

For more information on alternatives to SOAP when calling web services, see chapter 13, ".NET Remoting."

A directory of XML Web services would be useful, one that we could consult to see which shipping carriers offered such a service, for example. It is beyond the scope of this chapter to provide a comprehensive description of the work in this area, but one effort leading to such a directory is known as Universal Description, Discovery, and Integration (UDDI). UDDI was created through the collaborative efforts of Microsoft, Ariba, and IBM. It encompasses a process for the definition and creation of the UDDI Business Registry (UBR) and related artifacts, the operation of the UBR itself, and the eventual licensing of the intellectual property and control of the UBR and future directions to an independent third party.

The benefits of UDDI include:

- All XML Web services are described in a similar fashion.
- UDDI only describes XML Web services, so it does it well.
- It uses standard HTTP, so it is available anywhere on the Internet, including through firewalls.

NOTE

For more information on locating and using XML Web service, see Chapter 11, "Purchasing a Ticket."

The Passport Service

Back-end "megaservices" are a key component to making web services an attractive way to build applications. Megaservices are simply services designed to handle a huge number of services calls every day. Microsoft has already delivered one such megaservice in the form of Passport. Already, several hundred partners have rid themselves of the problems of building and maintaining their own authentication systems. This enables them to reduce administrative overhead. They can cut their time to market significantly, and in a fast moving age, this is important. They have outsourced the building and debugging of the software. It also means that the users have a single sign-on to any site that uses Passport authentication. They don't have to worry about remembering the sign-on to your web site.

Passport consists of three main services:

- **Passport Single Sign-in (SSI) service.** Site developers can map sign-in names to information in their databases, which will allow them to offer Passport members a personal web experience through targeted ads, promotions, and content. Using Passport in this way can help increase customer loyalty, sales, and advertising revenues.
- **Kids Passport Service.** This service is an optional part of Sign-in service and helps parents protect their children's online privacy by allowing them to determine whether their child can use participating web sites' services that collect personally identifiable information. Kids Passport is the first turnkey solution available to web sites for managing parental consent and helping sites comply with the Children's Online Privacy Protection Act (COPPA), which requires web sites to obtain parental consent before collecting and/or disclosing a child's personal information.
- **Passport Express Purchase Service.** This allows Passport members to store credit card and shipping information in one secured electronic wallet. The purchase process is streamlined because members do not have to retype this information. To make purchases, members click an Express Purchase button or text link next to the products they want to purchase. Then, they simply click to select the credit card and shipping address to use for the purchase, and the information is sent to the supplier's site to complete the transaction.

Businesses can implement the SSI service, the Express Purchase service, or both. On the sample site that accompanies this book, we will eventually be implementing Passport services.

The Role of SOAP

Earlier in this chapter, we talked about what SOAP is. It is also important to understand what SOAP is not.

- It does not perform distributed garbage collection (memory cleanup).
- It has no type safety, versioning, or pipelining of messages.
- It does not use objects-by-reference.
- It has no activation (which requires objects-by-reference).

SOAP builds on HTTP security, both HTTPS and X.509 certificates. We can choose which methods to expose explicitly. There is no application code included in SOAP messages. It is also firewall-friendly.

SOAP on a ROPE (The SDK for VS6)

If you have an existing COM component, the web services SDK makes it easy to turn it into a web service and to consume it in VB. It includes a tool that will extract the type library from an existing COM component and turn it into an XML "contract" that represents that component's capabilities. (You can also generate this contract by hand.) Once you have a contract, an extension for VB will automatically turn the contract into a proxy that you can program against just like a local COM component (complete with VB features such as IntelliSense). The SDK also contains a "listener" that will receive SOAP calls that come in and direct them to the appropriate service.

This Toolkit enables you to:

- **Expose a service**. If the service you want to expose is a COM component, you can just run the Toolkit's "dehydrator," which extracts an XML service description. Otherwise, you can hand-code your service description according to the rules published in the SDL specification.
- **Consume a service**. Once the service description is generated, the Toolkit's automatic Remote Object Proxy Engine (ROPE) pulls it down into Visual Basic and instantiates it as a VB proxy that the programmer can treat as though it were a local COM object.
- **Run against a service**. When you run the client application, the proxy makes calls across the network using SOAP to the Toolkit's Listener application (either the ASP or ISAPI version). The Listener then handles starting up the XML Web service and interacting with the actual application.

TIP

Remember, you can expose XML Web services using any programming language, object model, or operating system. Your XML Web services can also communicate with any other programming language, object model or operating system.

DISCO and UDDI

The discovery of web services (DISCO) protocol and UDDI, discussed earlier, are both concerned with finding what services a Web site can offer. Before we can access a web service, we need to know where it is, what its capabilities are, and how this is formatted. Web service discovery is the process of locating and interrogating web service descriptions.

We can use a program to carry out the discovery when a web service publishes a discovery (.disco) file, which is an XML document that contains links to other resources that describe the web service. The following shows an example of the structure of a discovery document:

```
<?xml version="1.0" ?>
<disco:discovery  smlns:disco="http://schemas.xmlsoap.org/disco
xmlns:scl="http://schemas.xmlsoap.org/disco/scl">
  <scl:contractRef ref="http://MyWebServer/UserName.asmx?SDL"/>
</disco:discovery>
```


NOTE

The discovery document is a container for elements that typically contain links (URLs) to resources that provide discovery information for a web service. If the URLs are relative, they are assumed to be relative to the location of the discovery document. However, a web site that implements a web service need not support discovery. Another site could be responsible for describing the service, or there may not be a public means of finding the service, such as when the service has been created for private use.

As electronic businesses grow and expand, it becomes more important to have standards. Standard descriptions of the business services that a web site offers and how they can be accessed are needed.

A service registry architecture is needed that presents a standard way for businesses to build a registry, query other businesses, and enable those registered businesses to interoperate and share information globally in a distributed manner, just as the Internet was intended to be used. A web services framework and public registry will enable buyers and sellers and marketplaces to share information, to connect web services at low cost, and to support multiple standards.

To address this challenge, a group of technology and business leaders have come together to develop the UDDI specification, an initiative introduced earlier that creates a global, platform-independent, open framework to enable businesses to:

1. Discover each other,
2. Define how they interact over the Internet, and
3. Share information in a global registry that will more rapidly accelerate the global adoption of B2B eCommerce.

Cast of Characters

The .NET platform consists of a comprehensive cast of characters ranging from new ones, like the CLR, to old veterans like Windows and the Microsoft Message Queue (MSMQ). It is important to remember, however, that the .NET platform is not limited to the technologies and products listed here. It will continue to be expanded in the future, adopting new technologies, servers, and programming languages.

CLR: The Common Language Runtime

For software developers, the beating heart at the center of the .NET platform is the CLR. In August of 2001, DevelopMentor hosted their first annual Conference.NET, with over 1000 people in attendance. There, seminal events in the development history of the .NET platform were described for the first time to a large, public audience.

The software that would eventually be called the CLR was first introduced in June of '97 at the Component Object Runtime System Design Review (SDR). Team composition and project startup occurred in November of '97, as work on the SOAP specification was just beginning. Web services had not yet been conceived.

By November of 2000, the key design goals had been refined to a list that includes primary features we see today in the CLR:

- New memory management, featuring the use of garbage collection rather than reference counting and deterministic finalization
- Just in Time (JIT) compilation. Various designs were implemented, explored and refined, including Optimizing JIT and Fast JIT models
- Thread and process management
- Virtual Object System
- Remoting
- Common Type System (CTS)
- Code Access Security (CAS)
- Support for debugging and profiling
- Unmanaged code support
- Simplified, flexible deployment model

The CLR enables a development environment with many desirable features. These include cross-language integration, a strongly-typed shared type system, self-describing components, simplified deployment and versioning, and integrated security services.

Since the CLR is used to load code, create objects, and make method calls, it can perform security checks and enforce policy as managed code is loaded and executed. Code access security allows the developer to specify the permissions that a piece of code needs in order to execute. For example, permission may be needed to read a file or access environment settings. This information is stored at the assembly level, along with information about the identity of the code.

In addition to code access security, the runtime supports role-based security. This builds on the same permissions model as code access security, except permissions are now based on user identity rather than code identity. Roles represent categories of users and can be defined at development time and assigned at deployment time. Policies are defined for each role. At runtime, the identity of the user on whose behalf the code is running is determined. The runtime checks what roles the user is a member of and then grants permissions based on those roles.

The CLR encourages moving away from scripted languages compiled at run time to the concept of managed code. Managed code means a clearly defined level of cooperation between an executing component and the CLR itself. Responsibility for many tasks, like creating objects and making method calls, is delegated to the CLR, which provides additional services to the executing component.

Source code is compiled into Microsoft Intermediate Language (MSIL) that is then consumed by the CLR. In addition to MSIL, .NET compilers also produce metadata. This is information the CLR uses to carry out a variety of actions such as locate and load class types in a file, lay out object instances in memory, and resolve method invocations and field references.

The metadata that the .NET Framework compilers produce includes class definitions and configuration information. It allows an application to totally describe itself. The metadata includes information about dependencies that can be used as part of versioning policies to indicate which version of a particular component should be used when running a particular component. This greatly eases the complexities of application installation and DLL versioning.

The .NET Framework introduces the assembly, a group of resources and types, along with metadata about those resources and types, which is deployed as a unit. The metadata is called an assembly manifest and includes information such as a list of types and resources visible outside the assembly. By using manifests, the developer has support for per-application policies to control the locating and loading of components.

Through the use of MSIL and assembly metadata, code written in many languages can be debugged together, with no loss of information or control as you step through multi-language projects. An exception thrown by a component written in one language can be dealt with using a component written in another language. Cross-language inheritance is supported.

Assemblies can be made private to an application or can be shared by multiple applications. Multiple versions of an assembly can be deployed on a machine at the same time. Application configuration information defines where to look for assemblies, thus the runtime can load different versions of the same assembly for two different applications that are running concurrently. This means that installing an application now becomes as simple as copying the necessary files to a directory tree, provided security permissions are satisfied.

One of the most important benefits of the CLR is that it provides developers with high-level services that are not restricted to a particular hardware platform or Operating System. Code written to the CLR does not need to be re-written to run on different platforms and under different Operating Systems. One immediate benefit is that the same code can run on all of the various flavors of 32-bit Windows and also 64-bit Windows. It extends the familiar ideas of runtime libraries, template libraries and the Java Virtual Machine. It means that developers can reuse more code and develop less in the way of the more basic services. The CLR and .NET simplify the programming model and make it more consistent.

Initially, the CLR will support four languages: Visual Basic .NET, Visual C++ .NET, Visual C# .NET and Visual J# .NET. Many companies are working on other compilers that produce managed code for languages including Cobol, Pascal and Perl.

ASP.NET and Internet Information Server (IIS)

The success of Windows servers has been fueled primarily by their use as application servers and web servers. Although Microsoft and its competitors argue over market share numbers, Internet Information Server (IIS) is certainly one of the most widely used web server platforms on the Internet. Used in conjunction with the family of .NET Enterprise Servers, IIS provides a feature-rich environment for running Internet and intranet applications.

Web servers play a central role in current application development practice. Most often, a client connects to a web server using a web browser. Typically the web server will be running an ASP.NET application hosted on IIS. The application can then connect to, and consume the services of, various .NET Enterprise Servers and megaservices such as .NET My Services, returning the results to the client. The results often are returned in some form of an XML-based document.

NOTE

The .NET Enterprise Server family is described in the next section of this chapter and includes (in alphabetical order):

- Application Center 2000
- BizTalk Server 2000
- Content Management Server 2001
- Commerce Server 2000
- Exchange Server 2000
- Host Integration Server 2000
- Internet Security and Acceleration Server 2000
- Mobile Information Server 2001
- SharePoint Portal Server 2000
- SQL Server 2000

They are listed here to serve as a convenient reference.

ASP.NET is an updated version of Active Server Pages (ASP) which is a web-based application environment that has been available for some time on Windows NT and Windows 2000 servers. This new version allows applications to be written in all CLR-based languages including Visual Basic .NET (VB. NET) and Visual C# .NET (C#). Previous versions of ASP were limited to the use of scripting languages with limited feature sets.

ASP.NET also boasts dramatically improved performance due to support for enhanced caching capabilities, and great improvements in the separation of code and design content, code deployment, configuration, and state management. It has been designed to allow deployment on any Web server platform, but certainly IIS will be used the vast majority of the time, and no plans to release a version for another platform have been announced.

IIS allows an organization to host multiple web sites on a single computer. Process throttling lets administrators limit the amount of CPU time a web application or site can use during a time interval to ensure that processor time is available to other web sites or to non-web applications. Per web site bandwidth throttling lets administrators regulate the amount of server bandwidth each site uses. This lets an ISP, for example, guarantee a predetermined amount of bandwidth to each site.

Web-based authentication can be fully integrated with a Kerberos security infrastructure. The Kerberos Version 5 authentication protocol, which provides fast, single logon, can replace NTLM as the primary security protocol for access to resources within or across Windows 2000 domains. In addition, Windows servers also support the following standard authentication protocols, which are applicable to web-based users and ordinary network users alike:

- Digest Authentication: An authentication standard of the World Wide Web Consortium (W3C)
- Server-Gated Cryptography (SGC): A system used by financial institutions to transmit private documents via the Internet
- Fortezza: A U.S. government security standard

Digest Authentication enables secure authentication of users across proxy servers and firewalls. It offers the same features as basic authentication, but improves on it by "hashing" the password traveling over the Internet, instead of transmitting it as clear text. For those who choose not to use Digest Authentication, Anonymous, HTTP Basic, and integrated Windows authentication (formerly called Windows NT Challenge/Response authentication) and NT LAN Manager (NTLM) authentication are still available.

Secure Sockets Layer (SSL) and Transport Layer Security (TLS) provide a secure way to exchange information between clients and web servers. In addition, SSL and TLS provide a way for the server to verify client identity before logon. Beginning with IIS 5.0, programmers can track users through their sites. Also, IIS 5.0 lets administrators control access to system resources based on X.509 client certificates. It is anticipated that a new release, IIS 6.0, will be included in the new .NET server products planned for release sometime in 2002.

.NET Enterprise Services (COM+)

The collection of services that were called COM+ services are now referred to collectively as .NET Enterprise Services. Originally developed by the COM team, these run-time services are now "baked in", tightly integrated directly into all server versions of Windows operating systems, with some optional features and capabilities only available on the high-end editions. These include support for transactions, object context and call context management, object pooling, and data connection management.

Beginning with Microsoft Transaction Server (MTS), Microsoft has steadily refined their mid-tier component strategy, enhancing object pooling performance and control. Transactional behavior can still be indicated by the developer at design time, through the same mechanisms introduced with Windows DNA, and now with the use of attributes in CLR-based languages. Settings can be overridden by the application administrator in the deployed environment using the appropriate Microsoft Management Console (MMC) based administrative console.

The .NET Framework

Using Microsoft's previous development tools, Visual C++ developers programmed against one set of Windows APIs while Visual Basic developers programmed against another. The ODBC API was an interface programmed against for data access, and the CDO library was the API used for e-mail. Microsoft product groups released dozens of other APIs at different times, each API providing an interface into bits of functionality provided by the underlying Windows operating system. Releasing a multitude of APIs in this fashion meant that there was no clear relation between the many different interfaces, and there was no easy way for an application programmer to locate specific functionality that was needed. Additionally, when a program that used a specific API was deployed, we needed to make sure that a specific DLL was deployed and registered on the target machine.

The .NET Framework base class library is designed to remedy these issues. All functionality is now contained within the same, universal API set and is made available to developers of any .NET programming language. No longer do C++ programmers use one set of APIs while VB programmers use another. Every development language uses the same interfaces, making switching between languages a matter of syntax rather than functionality. Microsoft now categorizes functionality into *namespaces*, making it easier to find the functionality needed for an application.

At the root level of the .NET Framework class library is the `System` namespace. Access to Web Forms, Windows Forms, data access, networking, messaging, and all other functionality is contained in some namespace underneath System. For example, `System.Web.UI` contains functionality to create Web controls on an ASP.NET page. `System.Data` contains functionality that lets us connect to databases and manipulate data using ADO.NET. Although the different namespaces are physically implemented in multiple assemblies (.DLLs), from a programmer's point of view they are now more integrated and easier to navigate.

Because the target machine on which a .NET application will be deployed must have the .NET Framework installed, we no longer have to worry about making sure a specific DLL is delivered and registered. The design of the .NET Framework base class library thus makes life easier for administrators, as well as developers. For more information on the .NET Framework base class library, and for the namespaces particularly relevant to developing .NET e-Business applications, see Chapter 4, "Tools of the Trade."

Microsoft Message Queue

Microsoft Message Queue (MSMQ) is a technology introduced in Windows NT 4.0. The use of queuing as an element in application design is not new. There are a number of scenarios where a queue can play an important role in making systems more reliable and more available. For example, perhaps an application must communicate with another computer system that is frequently offline or unavailable. By introducing a queue, the application can simply store requests or messages destined for the other system until it is once again available. More generally, a queue may be useful in any scenario involving asynchronous or delayed processing.

MSMQ features include:

- COM-based access. MSMQ services are readily accessible through COM interfaces. This makes them usable for both Windows DNA and .NET applications now. It is expected that tighter integration with the .NET platform will be provided in the next release.
- Support for transactions. Both transactional and non-transactional queues may be created. MSMQ operations can be included in transactions with full ACID properties to preserve data integrity and provide simplified error recovery semantics.
- Prioritization. All messages may not be equally important, and MSMQ allows priorities to be assigned to messages and queues. It then manages routing and delivery based on these priorities.
- Notification. MSMQ can notify a sending application that messages were (or were not) received and processed correctly. Rather than polling to find out if a message was properly handled, this capability lets applications know if failures occurred, allowing them to take corrective action as needed.
- Built-in data integrity, data privacy, and digital signature services. Security continues to grow in importance, and MSMQ provides strong security support. It can digitally sign and encrypt messages for transfer across the network, protecting messages from being viewed or changed during transmission, even when sent over public networks such as the Internet.

- Simplified application integration. MSMQ can simplify the design of complex systems by providing an easy-to-use messaging infrastructure that can connect disparate systems with different operational semantics.
- Network protocol independence. MSMQ features do not depend on the use of a particular network protocol (such as TCP/IP). Applications running on systems using different protocols can share the same queues provided the server or servers running MSMQ are configured with multiple (and appropriate) protocols.
- Message journaling. An optional copy of messages sent or received by applications can be kept, providing an audit trail. Journaling can also simplify recovery from certain types of failure.

Flexible, reliable asynchronous communications between component-based applications are critical for building large applications, especially when those applications must communicate with disparate systems running other platforms. MSMQ's services are an important compliment to .NET Enterprise Services, and will remain a key design element as the platform continues to evolve.

ADO.NET

It should come as no surprise that a main function on any e-Business application is to read data from and write data to a database, whether it be SQL Server 2000 or Oracle. Databases capture orders, maintain customer lists, aggregate data for OLAP reporting, and archive historical information. It goes without saying, then, that .NET e-Business developers need a strong programming interface for manipulating and processing such data. This interface is ADO.NET, a significant evolution of Microsoft's ActiveX Data Objects (ADO) technology that has been around for some time.

ADO.NET is based on XML, as is the .NET platform as a whole. The concept of loose coupling and data interchange is key to the .NET concept, and therefore the data access layer should reflect this concept. ADO.NET does in fact reflect this design goal, and the XML support built into the technology is evident. Not only is XML support pervasive, but a whole new way of manipulating data in memory is supported. ADO.NET allows developers to represent multiple tables and their relationships in memory for processing on the client side using a `DataSet`. This is an important evolution of the technology, and provides a great deal of power to the developer that was previously unavailable.

A key design goal of many .NET e-Business applications is high scalability, and ADO.NET supports this with disconnected recordsets. This prevents a middle tier object from having to keep a database connection open, which can be a significant hindrance to scalability. The `System.Data.SqlClient` namespace is also provided as an optimized interface for working with SQL Server. For more information on ADO.NET and its application in the sample application, see Chapter 7, "Implementing .NET Business Services."

Windows and the .NET Servers

The power of a distributed application consists of two major factors: the ability of distributed components to communicate and the power of those components individually. The recent release of Windows XP marks a new chapter in the evolution of operating systems. Windows XP eases the migration path of both professional and home users to a single operating system. This defines a path into the future where users can access distributed components in an identical fashion from both their work and home PCs.

In addition to the benefits of a single code base, Windows XP incorporates the Internet and networking into the operating system better than any previous version. This allows more home users to access the Internet and greatly decreases the effort required to set up and administer even complicated networks. Windows XP inherently understands and utilizes XML. Much of the .NET platform depends on XML, from XML Web services to SQL Server XML result sets. Applications run on Windows XP will benefit from using the operating system's built-in XML parser rather than depending on a plug-in version. This will also greatly ease application deployment in the future. Since Windows XP is currently only available in Home and Professional versions, we must also take a look at the more advanced flavors of Windows 2000 available today.

DataCenter Server 2000

Even the most ardent admirers of the Windows family of operating systems have occasionally questioned its reliability. Software developers who have spent a significant amount of time working with Windows have probably experienced the "blue screen of death", a screen displaying the contents of various memory locations and CPU registers that Windows displays when a fatal crash occurs. One of the fundamental problems in trying to address this serious problem has been the large number of hardware devices and corresponding device drivers supported by Windows. Device drivers, by their nature, must directly access hardware and can cause fatal errors if not properly designed and thoroughly tested.

In order to address this issue, Microsoft has teamed up with hardware vendors to provide the Windows 2000 Datacenter Server, which includes device drivers that have passed the very rigorous Datacenter Server Hardware Compatibility Tests. This version of Windows is only available directly from the hardware vendor. This is further augmented by an integrated approach to support that includes both hardware and software, and application certification specifically for this platform.

In addition to addressing reliability concerns, Datacenter Server includes features that are important for very large installations and applications. It supports up to 32 processors and up to 64 GB of RAM. In addition to providing all the services and features of Windows 2000 Server and Advanced Server, it provides:

- Process Control, a new tool in Datacenter Server that uses job objects to organize, control, and manage the processes on a system, along with the resources they use
- Four-node failover clustering support based on a "Shared Nothing" model
- Enterprise Memory Architecture (EMA). EMA supports two distinct models for enhancing the use of memory:
    - Physical Address Extension (PAE). This allows the operating system kernel to use all available physical memory, including memory above 4 GB (up to 64 GB). Applications need not be rewritten to benefit from the reduced paging provided by this support, however individual applications cannot utilize the full address space without using a new API called Address Windowing Extensions (AWE).
    - Application-Memory Tuning-sometimes referred to as 4-gigabyte tuning (4GT)
- Winsock Direct, a feature that provides substantial performance improvement for Winsock applications without requiring modification. It is essentially an optimized TCP/IP stack capable of very efficient, high-bandwidth, low-latency messaging. This reduces processor utilization, conserving processor time for application use.

Server and Advanced Server

Windows 2000 is based on the earlier Windows NT operating system. All members of the Windows 2000 family share a core feature set, with additional functionality and options added to higher end versions.

At the time of this writing, Windows XP has been released in both Home and Professional editions, however Server and Advanced Server editions are not yet available. It is anticipated that when they are released, they will provide specific enhancements to directly support the .NET platform. The exact naming of these editions has not yet been announced, although industry watchers expect that there will still be Server and Advanced Server editions. Until updated server operating systems are released, the Windows 2000 server family remains the available offering.

Windows 2000 Server is the entry-level version of the family. It supports between one and four processors and a maximum of 4GB of RAM. The base feature set, which is shared by all members of the Server family, includes:

- Enhanced protection of operating system files and registry settings, to prevent inadvertent destruction, removal, or replacement of key elements of Windows 2000.
- Fewer operations requiring a system reboot. Administrators have requested attention to this area for some time. Whether an outage is due to system failure, or a scheduled system upgrade, a reboot still makes the server unavailable and disrupts connected sessions.
- Fast Recovery from System Failure. If your system does fail, Windows 2000 includes an integrated set of features that speed recovery.

Windows 2000 Advanced Server builds on the feature set of the standard version of Windows 2000 Server, and includes additional features to support applications requiring higher levels of scalability and availability. It supports up to 8 processors and up to 8 GB of RAM. Among the additional features are:

- Two-node failover clustering support. In this configuration, two systems share a hard disk subsystem. The machines need not be identically configured or be running the same tasks. When one server fails, the other picks up its load.
- Up to 32-node NLB support. Another form of clustering, this capability is most often exploited to build web farms.
- Rolling Upgrade Support. Using Microsoft Clustering Services (MSCS) and NLB, downtime caused by planned maintenance or upgrades is avoided by using rolling upgrades. Applications are migrated onto one node. The other node is then upgraded and the workload is migrated back without taking the application off line.

The Microsoft .NET Enterprise Servers

ASP.NET and IIS provide the engine for web-based development efforts, but there are many other services that are required to build enterprise applications. These include relational database management, support for mobile communications access, integration with host systems, and advanced management tools. A collection of .NET Enterprise Servers provides a growing set of services to .NET applications. The current collection is described in following sections; additional servers and updated versions of these products will be added over time.

Application Center Server 2000

Application Center Server 2000 is a tool for deploying and managing web applications across clusters of servers. It provides software-scaling services that allow applications to achieve very high scalability (both peak load and sustained load as characterized by number of users or resource utilization) and mission critical levels of availability. It also reduces operational costs and complexity.

Application Center Server allows us to manage our applications using a single high-level definition. This definition includes all of its content, components and configuration settings. All configuration changes are made through a standard MMC snap-in. Performance and event log data from one or all participating machines can be viewed from one place. This keeps application content and configuration settings consistent and synchronized across all servers in a cluster. Synchronization can be automated, with timed or on demand updates. Rudimentary "self-healing" capabilities can be used to improve reliability.

Application Center Server can provide change management for applications. You can deploy versions from a development cluster to testing, then to staging and finally to production automatically, reducing downtime. You can manually rollback a failed deployment, and when necessary, replicate the "last known good" application image. This facilitates rapid recovery from failed deployments.

Windows 2000 Advanced Server contains Network Load Balancing (NLB) services that balance network traffic across multiple servers in a web farm. Application Center Server configures and controls NLB. It also configures and controls COM component execution across multiple servers through its Component Load Balancing (CLB) services.

Application Center Server provides advanced fault tolerance. A properly designed site can withstand software and hardware failures at any single point in the system without disrupting application service. The performance and health of the system can be monitored from a single console. Performance data for any server in the cluster, or for the entire cluster, can be gathered and analyzed.

BizTalk Server 2000

BizTalk Server 2000 is a server platform designed to make it easier to integrate business processes across company boundaries to include partners, vendors, and customers. This is all done using XML-based documents. This document exchange infrastructure allows secure and reliable company relationships to be quickly implemented independent of operating system, programming model or programming language.

The foundation of BizTalk Server 2000 is its rules-based document routing, transformation, and tracking capability. SQL Server provides high-performance storage and easy-to-schedule transformation capabilities for data from BizTalk Server.

BizTalk adheres to a set of guidelines defining the structure of business documents, such as purchase orders and invoices. Each business document defined by a schema. The manner in which one company publishes the information on its purchase order forms may be totally different from what a supplier expects. Using XML, the information contained on a form is easily mapped to a particular schema-defined layout, and then sent to the partner company.

BizTalk Server 2000 contains a host of rich graphical tools for building XML schema, performing schema transformation, establishing trading partner relationships over the Internet, and tracking and analyzing data and documents that are exchanged. It also contains graphical tools that make it easy for business analysts and application developers to model and implement company specific solutions.

BizTalk Server 2000 is built on a foundation of public standards and specifications including XML, HTTP, and EDI. It incorporates security standards such as public key encryption and digital signatures. BizTalk Server 2000 can take an EDI data stream, translate the information it contains into XML, and send it to a trading partner. This makes it a useful tool in EDI integration scenarios.

Commerce Server 2000

Commerce Server 2000 is a tool for managing e-commerce web sites. To support the operation of an effective site, it helps the site operator to attract and engage customers through the use of scheduled online marketing and advertising campaigns and targeted promotions. It also assists with management of the transactions generated on the site. Finally, it analyzes the usage patterns and reactions to the content on the site.

Commerce Server 2000 has tools that allow the site to be personalized for particular customer types in various ways:

- A secure and scalable environment is provided for order capture and management.
- Marketing actions and promotions can be built to reward frequent shoppers. For example, two-for-the-price-of-one promotions can easily be set up. The end user experience can be modified to greet returning customers personally.
- Customer profiles can be built and maintained and knowledge of your customers buying habits can be used to improve the site.
- Product catalogs and price lists can be built and used for business partners. Millions of products can be managed.
- Business process pipelines provide a framework for defining and linking together stages of a business process. Analogous to the process of completing a wizard, pipelines allow tailored processing of orders, advertising, merchandizing, content selection and direct mailing.
- Decision support tools are available to help understand and refine an online business. This incorporates all relevant information, including click-stream data.

In any business, figuring out what sells and what doesn't is very important. Which of the various product lines on offer are visitors interested in? Commerce Server actively manages the web content and analyzes the usage data, providing answers to this sort of question. Pre-configured analysis reports can be used or site managers can build custom reports for mining usage data to uncover important trends about activity on the site.

Content Management Server 2001

Content Management Server 2001 is a relative newcomer to the .NET Enterprise Server family. Large web sites require a constant flow of new content to interest users, and to keep up with necessary changes. Many people who are responsible for creating this content are not members of a technical staff in an IT department. Content Management Server 2001 simplifies the management, scheduling, and flow of content. It lowers management costs, and organizes the process of keeping an application or site refreshed with up to date information. It is designed to support sites with high scalability and availability requirements.

Exchange Server 2000

Exchange Server 2000 is the latest release of the Exchange messaging platform. It is closely integrated with the Windows 2000 operating system and Active Directory. It uses the new Web Storage System to add the accessibility and openness of the web to the reliability and scalability of Exchange Server. Exchange 2000 Conferencing Server provides a platform for complete data, audio, and video conferencing services, establishing a foundation for new avenues of collaboration.

The Web Storage System includes built-in indexing for high-speed searches, enabling users to find content quickly and easily. All content in the Web Storage System is indexed, including messages, standalone documents, contacts, tasks, calendar items, and collaboration data. Indexing is accomplished by an indexing "crawl" of the content in the Web Storage System, using the same technology used in Internet Information Services (IIS) and SQL Server 7.0. Users of Outlook 2000 can search for documents in the Web Storage System as easily as they can search for e-mail messages, increasing user productivity.

Its native support for XML and HTTP is typical of the standards support included in .NET Enterprise Servers. It also includes support for OLE DB 2.5 to integrate with SQL Server, and other OLE DB compliant products.

Exchange 2000 includes two OLE DB providers, a remote provider for server access from client applications, such as Outlook 2000, and a local provider implemented natively in Exchange for high-performance COM access from applications, such as virus scanning programs and workflow engines. Application designers can also use ADO to navigate, query, filter, and sort Exchange Server data. This allows developers familiar with developing SQL applications to easily write applications that use data stored in the Web Storage System using the same tools and expertise.

Host Integration Server 2000

Host Integration Server is the latest release of the product formerly named Microsoft SNA Server. It includes a comprehensive set of integration components for connecting host-based data and transactions with new web-based applications. Host Integration Server provides traditional gateway integration, data access and database replication, as well as integration of both tightly and loosely coupled systems. In most scenarios, it utilizes only Windows-based code with no host footprint, a fact appreciated by most host administrators.

HIS provides a wide variety of integration technologies that enables developers to integrate various host technologies. It offers services that extend a Microsoft interface to traditionally non-Microsoft platforms, including:

- SNA or TCP Protocols. HIS inherits the strengths of predecessor SNA Server for gateway connectivity. While the protocol trend is clearly towards TCP, many host shops still require support for SNA-based applications.

- The OLE DB for DB2 Provider that provides COM+ objects with data access and distributed transactional integration with DB2. These give developers the flexibility to quickly and easily build n-tier applications that integrate COM+ with IBM's DB2, CICS and IMS transactions.
- COMTI (COM Transaction Integrator) allows customers to expose mainframe CICS and IMS transactions as COM objects. It even includes support for distributed two-phase commit. All this is done without requiring any changes to the host application. (This technology has been shipping in Microsoft SNA Server since Version 4.0 in November, 1997.)
- Integrating MSMQ with MQ Series using the MSMQ Bridge, which is responsible for routing application messages between Microsoft's MSMQ and IBM's MQ Series. The bridge allows MSMQ to communicate and exchange messages directly with MQ Series platforms.

HIS 2000 provides these services either via SNA or TCP/IP, without requiring any changes to the host or any host code to be loaded. It supports the native host interfaces and standards and is therefore non-intrusive.

XML integration in HIS is provided via integration with BizTalk. BizTalk has the ability to transform and manipulate documents. Once the incoming information is transformed, BizTalk can utilize HIS 2000 for either of the two following integration methods:

- Synchronous or COM+-based Integration: BTS 2000 supports a COM interface (Ipipeline) that can be used to invoke a COM+ business process. This process in turn executes either a DB2 SQL statement via OLE DB or a CICS/IMS transaction via COMTI.
- Message-Oriented Middleware (MOM)-based Integration: HIS 2000 provides a MSMQ to MQSeries Bridge to allow BizTalk to easily and effectively exchange documents asynchronously via MOM.

As an SNA gateway solution, HIS 2000 runs on Windows NT Server and Windows 2000 Server to connect PC-based local area networks (LANs) to IBM System/390 mainframe and AS/400 midrange systems. HIS 2000 enables users of the leading desktop systems-including Windows 2000 Professional, Windows NT Workstation, Windows 95, Windows 3.x, Macintosh, UNIX, MS-DOS, and IBM OS/2-to share resources on mainframes and AS/400s without installing SNA protocols on the PC or deploying any software on the host.

The HIS 2000 gateway functions handle the translation between the PC LAN transport protocol-whether TCP/IP, IPX/SPX, NetBEUI, or other supported protocols-and the SNA LU protocols running to the host. By allowing each machine to run its native protocols, SNA Server minimizes resource requirements on each PC and on the host system. The configuration also reduces administrative costs by enabling centralized management of the gateways.

Internet Security and Acceleration Server 2000

Internet Security and Acceleration Server 2000 (ISA Server) is Microsoft's new enterprise firewall and web caching server. The main problems that need to be addressed by system administrators and business managers alike include:

- How to prevent hackers and unauthorized persons from accessing the internal network.
- Who has access to the internal network? Who has access to the Internet? How are they using it? Is the internal network exposed?
- How to provide faster Internet access to improve worker productivity as well as serve e-commerce customers quickly.
- How to control bandwidth usage and costs. When thousands of requests go out to the Internet for the same static content it is inefficient and costly.
- How to manage a network as simply as possible. Managing a network and keeping it secure are complex issues. Solving some of the preceding issues can lead to more problems. If you add a cache to improve performance and reduce connection costs, a separate set of resources and expertise are required to manage it.

ISA Server includes the following major capabilities:

- It securely routes requests and responses between the Internet and client computers on a private network. It serves as a firewall, separating a protected private network from the Internet. ISA Server can help defend your network from hackers, unauthorized access and virus attacks by filtering and analyzing traffic prior to routing.
- It provides a high-performance Web Cache Server. This improves web site access performance for network clients by storing frequently requested Internet sites locally. It can be used to speed up performance for internal users accessing the Internet, or external clients accessing your web server.
- It combines the benefits of both a firewall and a web cache with integrated management. ISA Server applies the same access policies to the firewall and the cache. It takes advantage of Windows server features such as QoS, VPN, advanced authentication, NAT and Active Directory.

NOTE

For more information about ISA Server, visit http://www.Microsoft.com/security

Mobile Information Server 2001

Mobile Information Server 2001 is a platform for extending the reach of Microsoft .NET Enterprise applications, enterprise data, and intranet content to the mobile user. This server product will allow mobile users to stay connected to their corporate intranets and applications using devices such as hand held PCs or mobile phones. They will be able to securely access their e-mail, contacts, calendar, tasks, or any intranet line-of-business application. Mobile Information Server integrates with the .NET Enterprise Servers with multiple hardware platforms. It will also integrate with new speech technologies, allowing voice-control of applications.

SharePoint Portal Server 2000

Share Point Portal Server is a new document management portal solution. It allows users to find, share and publish information easily. It provides features such as document management, search, subscriptions, and online discussions. It becomes the single place for information, combining normal office documents with web pages and emails. New documents are saved and checked in and out document stores capturing relevant metadata.

The document management capabilities allow changes in multiple drafts to be tracked as a document is edited, reviewed and approved. SharePoint Portal Server is designed around industry and Internet standards, such as OLE DB, XML, and Microsoft Web Distributed Authoring and Versioning (WebDAV).

SQL Server 2000

Microsoft SQL Server 2000 is the latest release of the SQL Server family. It was designed to provide all the tools needed to build powerful e-business applications. It includes built in support for XML, simplifying back office system integration and data transfer. Data can be retrieved directly as XML and XML can be stored relationally.

This XML functionality allows web developers, for example, to use technologies like XPath, URL queries, and XML updategrams instead of needing in-depth knowledge of relational database programming. Similarly, database developers are not required to learn an object-oriented language or understand all the facets of XML. They can provide XML access to an existing relational database with the FOR XML clause that returns XML data from a SELECT statement and the OPENXML T-SQL keyword.

As well as retrieving data as XML, it is important to be able to store data efficiently as XML, maintaining the relationships and a hierarchy of data while taking full advantage of the speed offered by a relational database. SQL Server 2000 can provide an XML View of relational data as well as map XML data into relational tables.

OpenXML allows XML documents to be addressed with relational SQL syntax. OpenXML is a T-SQL keyword that provides an updateable rowset interface for in-memory XML documents. The records in the rowset can be stored in database tables, just as rowsets provided by tables and views. OpenXML can be used in SELECT and SELECT INTO statements wherever rowset providers, such as table, view, or OPENROWSET, can appear.

The new services engineered into this latest version make SQL Server 2000 more scalable and easier to program. Analysis Services offers built-in data mining tools and storage options that make it possible to build and analyze data warehouses of any size. They have been expanded to allow OLAP cubes to be accessed and analyzed over the web using HTTP, offering remote users, including suppliers and trading partners outside the intranet, the ability to use SQL Server analysis tools. Significant upgrades to the querying tools make it easier for developers to build natural language queries.

SQL Server also includes new features that allow the workload to be partitioned for increased scalability. This is done by "horizontally" partitioning data across multiple servers typically based on some data-driven attribute (such as last name or Account ID). These servers manage the partitioned data together, but operate independently.

The partitioning of data is transparent to applications accessing the database. An application "sees" a full copy of all tables. All servers accept connections and process both queries and updates, distributing scans and updates as needed. The SQL Server 2000 query processor contains a number of enhancements so that partitioned views can be efficiently updated, and to increase distributed query performance.

SQL Server includes the ability to perform differential backups. It also incorporates many important security and availability features. It has been enhanced with security features built on the Windows security model and incorporates flexible role-based security for server, database, and application profiles; integrated tools for security auditing; and support for file and over-the-wire encryption. This augments operating system security and helps to fulfill legal requirements for storing sensitive data.

SQL Server 2000 is tightly integrated with many of the other members of the .Net Enterprise Server family. Microsoft Commerce Server 2000 provides services that include user profiling, product catalogs, and Business Internet Analytics (BIA)-the analysis of customer web click-stream data to make predictions about customer behavior and drive personalization. These services are built on SQL Server 2000.

Microsoft BizTalk Server 2000 also works with SQL Server. BizTalk Server 2000 provides the infrastructure and tools to enable e-commerce business communications. SQL Server 2000 and BizTalk Server 2000 support the same XML data-reduced schema. This allows documents to be transmitted directly from SQL Server to BizTalk Server and vice versa.

BizTalk: The Concept

Many people think of BizTalk as simply another Microsoft product. Actually, BizTalk can also refer to the BizTalk Organization, the BizTalk Initiative, BizTalk orchestration or all four parts as a whole. In order to understand BizTalk completely, it is important to understand the sum of the parts, as well as the individual pieces.

The Organization

The BizTalk organization was formed several years ago. It is an independent organization, but it was founded at Microsoft's initiative. Its goal is to be a resource center for business and software communities for learning about and using XML in document and information sharing over the Internet. It is an online resource rather than a consortium or a standards body.

This site is a library where XML and XSL schema can be located, managed and published. It contains information models and business processes supported by applications that support the BizTalk Framework.

NOTE

For more information, visit http://www.biztalk.org.

When two companies want to communicate electronically over the Internet, documents such as purchase orders, order acknowledgements, shipping documents and so on can be defined in XML. The problem is that the two companies that want to communicate need to agree on how the documents are to be expressed in XML, and this definition is a scheme. Here, people are actively encouraged to publish your own schema.

The Initiative

The *Biztalk Initiative* is made up of the Microsoft BizTalk Framework, various cross-industry investments including the BizTalk.org business document library, as well as Microsoft BizTalk Server 2000. These investments are being made with industry standards groups, technology and service providers, as well as key global organizations. The first set of investments surround the BizTalk Framework, and this is a set of implementation guidelines that any organization can use to define and route business data using XML.

The *BizTalk Framework* itself is not a standard. XML is the standard. The goal of the BizTalk Framework is to accelerate the rapid adoption of XML. The BizTalk Framework implementation guidelines are documented and accessible on `www.biztalk.org`. Since the BizTalk Framework is 100 percent compliant with the World Wide Web Consortium (W3C) XML 1.0 standard, it is operating system-, programming model-, and programming language-independent. BizTalk documents are being used by applications on many different platforms today. The framework provides the implementation guidelines for XML-based document routing.

The BizTalk Steering Committee drives the BizTalk Framework. The steering committee is made up of more than 20 industry standards organizations, large software companies, and multinational corporations that share the interest of promoting the use of XML to provide better interoperability between applications and processes.

BizTalk Orchestration

Every business process is comprised of well-defined steps. Each step starts by the receipt of a message, in a certain pre-defined format and from a particular location. Each step also ends with the sending of a message, again in a certain format, to a particular location. Automating these processes and messages is called orchestration. A design tool hosted in Microsoft Visio allows a business analyst to flowchart a particular business process. That diagram can then be mapped to physically implemented components in the .NET runtime environment. An XLANG messaging infrastructure will typically be used to deliver control information among the distributed elements of the system.

From Here

You are on your way to developing a full understanding of .NET, and learning how to build e-commerce applications using this new technology. The next chapter introduces the sample application that will be used throughout the remainder of the book to illustrate most of the concepts and techniques that are important when building .NET applications.

gasTIX: A Sample .NET e-Business

by Jody Socha

CHAPTER

2

IN THIS CHAPTER

- Introducing gasTIX: The Sample Application 48
- Architecting the System 52
- Web Site Flow 65
- Project Design and Approach: The Microsoft Solutions Framework 70
- From Here 73

This chapter introduces the gasTIX corporation. It includes the high-level vision and business goals of the planned development effort, a discussion of the high-level conceptual architecture of the system using the .NET framework, and a presentation of the approach for designing and developing that system.

Introducing gasTIX: The Sample Application

The sample application being showcased for this book is a Web site handling ticket-selling operations for a fictitious company, *gasTIX*. This section introduces this company and the requirements of the system to be developed.

Background

gasTIX was created as a merger of several other fictitious regional ticket sellers joined together to form a national presence in the ticket-selling market. As part of this newly formed organization, the company decided it needed a new ticket selling system to meet these needs:

- Move each of the disparate companies to a standard platform.
- Aid in streamlining business processes in a standard set of procedures.
- Promote a new single brand and identity for the ticket seller nation-wide.

The company has managed to sign exclusive deals for selling tickets to major venues throughout the country. To maximize profits, this company wants to make the ticket sales available through the largest number of outlets available, including a Web site. Potential sources for selling the tickets are as follows:

- **Internet users**—The new company Web site should enable users to purchase tickets for any of the venues for which the company sells.
- **Phone sales**—Customers should also be able to call a central phone number to purchase tickets.
- **Kiosks**—Customers could purchase tickets from kiosks located in key locations such as nightclubs and airports. These kiosks could also include information about events.
- **Venue box offices**—Many users will want the ability to purchase tickets directly at the venue.
- **Retail box offices**—Various retail stores can provide additional outlets for buying tickets in person.
- **Internet partners**—gasTIX plans to actively look for partners on the Internet so that tickets can be purchased from other sites than just the gasTIX main site.
- **Wireless services**—The company also wants users to be able to buy tickets using devices such as cell phones.

Problem Statement

The problem statement identifies the business issue that the potential solution is trying to solve.

gasTIX currently uses several ticket-selling and administration systems resulting in the following problems for the company:

- Information is distributed across each of the systems, which limits the company's ability to perform centralized progress and financial reporting.
- Different business processes are used throughout the company, which limits the company's ability to streamline operations.
- Because of limitations in each of the current legacy systems, the ability to expand ticket sales to a larger number of alternative outlets is limited.
- Future plans for expanding the company overseas or into merchandise sales are on hold until a more robust system architecture is established.

Vision Statement

The vision statement provides a short description of the solution that this project is promoting. The vision statement for gasTIX is as follows:

- To build a state-of-the-art Web site and ticketing engine to provide gasTIX with a single application for managing ticket sales while opening up sales to the largest number of outlets possible.

Solution Concept

The solution concept presents the general approach planned for implementing the vision statement. The solution concept for gasTIX is as follows.

The gasTIX team has elected to build a new system from scratch to take advantage of all that the Internet has to offer. Not only would it allow potential customers the largest variety of options for purchasing the tickets, but it would also provide the most flexible implementation for combining disparate systems to provide gasTIX with an enterprise-wide solution. In general, the following steps were planned:

- Develop a gasTIX ticketing engine that can support ticket purchases from a variety of sources.
- Develop an interface for each of the various ticket purchasing options to take advantage of the engine.

- Interface with a separate fulfillment system that handles printing and mailing tickets to online customers. Box offices will have their own ticket printing system locally. Also, the ticket needs to be available at the box office rather than through mailing when there is not enough time to mail the ticket to the purchaser.
- Interface with an accounting system in order to track general ledger information.

NOTE

Of course, there are other potential solutions, such as picking one of the legacy systems and modifying it for company-wide use. These alternatives were not seriously considered for this book partly because any existing system probably would not provide the best foundation for future development and partly because the foundation for this book would not exist. Some type of cost-benefit analysis should be performed in order to select the best solution for any organization's needs.

A key to successfully planning this project is trying to understand gasTIX's overall priorities. One useful technique for discussing those priorities lies in the use of a project trade-off matrix (see Table 2.1). The following matrix defines the trade-off expectations for the development project and is used to guide the change management decision process. To properly fill in the matrix, the following rules must be followed:

- One column must be checked in each row indicating how that attribute will be managed.
- No column can be checked more than once in order to avoid conflicting strategies.

TABLE 2.1 Project Trade-Off Matrix

	Constrained	*Optimized*	*Negotiated*
Resources		✓	
Ship date	✓		
Features			✓

Here are definitions of the trade-off terms listed in Table 2.1:

- **Resources**—Cost of the project.
- **Ship date**—The date the system goes online.
- **Features**—The capability of the system.
- **Constrained**—The parameter is tightly specified.

- **Optimized**—The parameter is bound within a range.
- **Negotiated**—The parameter is free for negotiation.

In Table 2.1, the project's ship date is constrained, which means that the gasTIX corporation has decided that rolling out a new system in a timely manner is its highest priority. Its need to get its business units on a common platform is important enough that there is limited room for negotiation on the final ship date. As always, costs are important for the company to control. As a result, the costs of the project need to be as low as possible, but there is room for negotiation if the additional cost is justified to help meet the ship date. In return for these requirements, gasTIX recognizes that there must be room for negotiating the feature set and that not all the desired functionality will likely be on the site.

Inevitably, some features will not be implemented in each of the product increments. The benefits delivered by releasing the product in a timely manner outweigh the opportunity cost lost to a feature's absence. This strategy is sometimes characterized by the phrase "shipping is a feature."

Business Goals

The business goals of a project define how the project will benefit the company. The overall business objectives that this project addresses are as follows:

- To position `gasTIX.com` as the premier ticket provider for venues in the United States.
- To provide customers the greatest flexibility in terms of locations for obtaining tickets for a concert or event of their choice.
- To enable partnering with outside companies to provide additional outlets for ticket sales.
- To reduce administrative costs across the company by providing a common platform for purchasing tickets and administering the ticket system.
- To position the company to easily branch out into new ventures, including overseas operations and selling of event-related merchandise and memorabilia.
- To build the foundation for using historical data to track, analyze, and predict sales trends across the enterprise by regional sales, seasonal patterns, and so on.

Design Criteria

Design criteria identify constraints that limit how a project can be developed. Such constraints can be technical, operational, or organizational in nature. The following lists outlines the overarching design criteria used to guide this project:

- Demonstrate how to use .NET in building a fully functioning application.
- As this is a public-oriented Web site with customer credit card information, ensure that the system is as secure as possible.
- Ensure the capability to scale in order to handle high demand when popular concerts go on sale.
- Ensure code base is effectively managed and versioned to reduce maintenance and administrative costs including all source code, database schemas, and implementation plans as a minimum.
- The application will have to interface with several external systems. Ensure that the interfaces are prepared to reduce the costs associated with maintenance and interoperability.
- Design the system so that the major components are as loosely coupled as possible so that portions of the system can be replaced or upgraded without having to rewrite the whole application.

Architecting the System

Although there are many advances to the .NET environment—including the Common Language Runtime (CLR) and strong typing—the main thrust of .NET is to enable the creation of loosely coupled, service-based applications that will become common as we move forward into the Internet age. This section provides a brief overview of this concept and how the gasTIX architecture functions on top of that foundation.

The .NET Architectural Foundation

With the advent of Microsoft Transaction Server (MTS) and its successor, COM+, Microsoft created an environment in which components can interact when carrying out various transactions on behalf of one client or another. MTS provided the framework for many key application functions such as security and transaction management. This frees the developer to focus on business functionality. An environment was created in which applications can truly be implemented using a set of reusable, business-oriented components—a huge improvement over the previous structured approach for building applications.

Unfortunately, there was a problem with deciding how to take advantage of these components in rolling out enterprise-wide applications. In order to get components on remote MTS servers to work together, developers needed to know where those components were located. Furthermore, to take advantage of those components, developers had to write to a COM-based interface, which introduces several middleware-related issues in communicating with legacy, CORBA, or EJB-based systems.

In the Internet age, the need for data exchange between applications will become more important than ever as the different components of an enterprise's supply chain become more strongly integrated. We cannot assume that these disparate systems will be located in the same country, let alone on the same network backbone. We also can't assume that these applications will be built using the same technologies. Because of this, the applications will require some type of middleware to glue it all together.

So, how does .NET position its applications for the Internet age? There are three basic components:

- Establishment of the .NET platform and its suite of servers to provide a secure, stable, and scalable platform upon which to build sites.
- Introduction of Web services to provide an implementation-independent method for interaction between systems.
- Providing a framework via BizTalk for enabling messaging and workflow between these various sites and services.

A much more thorough discussion of the .NET concept can be found in Chapter 1, ".NET—The Big Picture" of this book.

gasTIX Conceptual Architecture

With the new .NET concepts in mind, gasTIX decided to imagine the site as a set of as many interactive sites and services as possible to provide the greatest flexibility for implementing, and later extending, the site. Each major application is viewed as a site that provides a set of services for the other sites to consume.

Furthermore, this site and service concept ensures the most flexibility in adding new outlets and new functionality. For example, if another Web site expressed interest in linking to gasTIX for ticket information, the presence of the service concept provides an existing and quick means for interfacing with this other site. This concept even spilled over into recasting traditional applications as services to provide greater flexibility in how certain functionality is provided. For example, by breaking the printing and shipping of tickets into a separate fulfillment service, greater flexibility was provided in determining when and where the tickets were developed. Obtaining a third party to provide the service became a possibility.

The rest of this section provides a description of the sites and related service categories required to support gasTIX. Figure 2.1 provides a depiction of these services and how they are related.

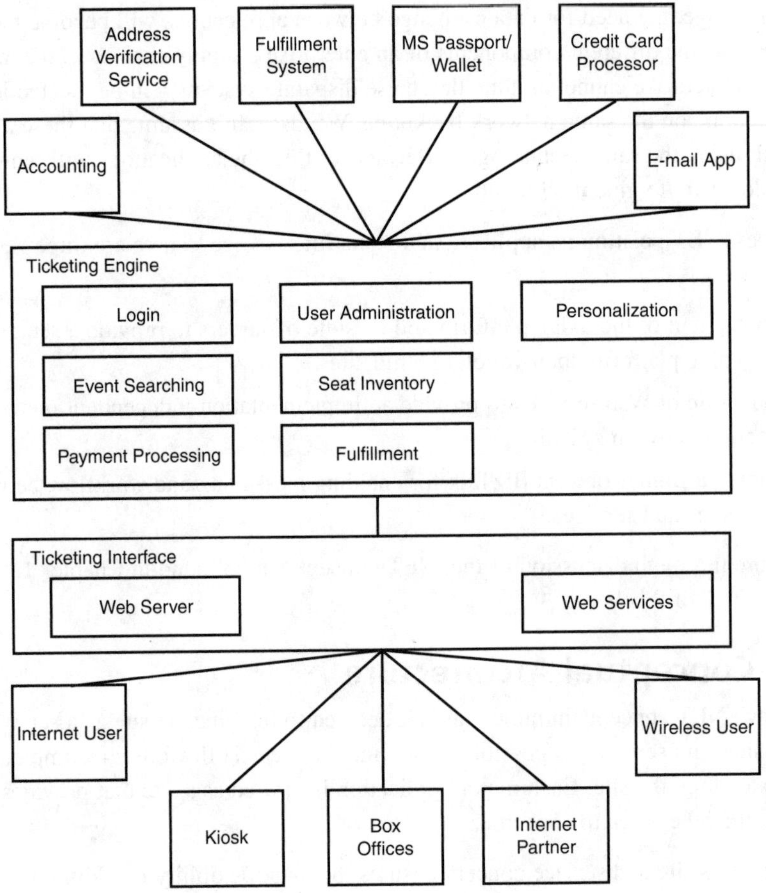

FIGURE 2.1
The gasTIX architectural environment.

Purchasing Mechanisms

To maximize potential ticket sales, gasTIX will allow purchases from a variety of sources. The sources that gasTIX will support are as follows:

- **Internet users**—Represents the set of users attempting to purchase the tickets using their Web browser through the gasTIX Web site.
- **Kiosk**—In some cases, gasTIX will want to place stands in appropriate locations to allow people to purchase tickets on the spot. Examples of potential locales for the kiosks include venue sites, outside of box offices for after-hours purchases, or at various promotional events.

- **Box offices**—These are traditional outlets for purchasing tickets. Examples of locations included in this category include box offices located at the various venues, retail stores that are partnering with the main ticket distribution company, and centers set up to handle telephone purchases.
- **Internet partners**—In some cases, gasTIX might partner with outside Web sites to provide a mechanism for allowing their site users to purchase tickets.
- **Wireless users**—As soon as possible, gasTIX wants to handle users interested in obtaining tickets from a mobile device of some kind.

Ticketing Interface

There are several mechanisms for allowing users to access the site. The service needed depends on the users' location and to what extent they will use the site. The following two mechanisms are available for providing that access:

- **Traditional Web server**—Access to the system is provided through a traditional Web server. This technique provides enhanced performance and additional functionality.
- **Web services interface**—Access to the system is also provided through a new set of services through which other Web sites or similar consumers can access the system. These interfaces will be limited in functionality compared to the internal interfaces.

Ticket Engine

This is the heart of the site and provides the ticket sales and processing on behalf of any service through which a customer can purchase tickets. Through these interfaces, the engine provides a set of base functionality that these consumers can access. This functionality is divided as follows:

- **Login and security**—Provides a means to validate the users and control their access to site features accordingly.
- **Site administration**—Provides the mechanism for managing and configuring the users, sites, events, and performers of the system.
- **Event searching**—Provides the capability to find an event of the user's choice through a variety of criteria.
- **Seat inventory**—Provides the capability to find seats available for the given event and to reserve those seats for potential purchase.
- **Payment processing**—Provides for obtaining and charging the user's credit card to handle actual purchasing of the seats.
- **Personalization**—A certain amount of limited personalization of the site allows the users to specify their favorite categories.
- **Fulfillment**—Provides the mechanism for having the tickets shipped to the purchaser as well as reporting information about the shipment status.

Back Office Support

Not all functionality is directly provided by the ticket engine. Where possible, gasTIX looked for partners to provide functionality for the site. The following services are to be used by or interfaced with the gasTIX system:

- **Accounting**—Financial information is fed to the company's accounting system on a regular basis.
- **Address verification service**—An outside service ensures that address information provided to the site is accurate.
- **Fulfillment system**—An outside service actually prints and ships the tickets to the purchaser. In some cases, the printing portion of the system is located at the various box offices so they can be given to the purchaser directly. The fulfillment system also must be able to tell the ticket engine when the tickets have been printed and shipped.
- **Microsoft Passport/Wallet**—Maintenance of user information is performed by an outside service that can make that information available to gasTIX on an as-needed basis. An example of such a service is the Passport site from Microsoft, which allows Web users to centrally store personal data.
- **Credit card processor**—Authorization and actual charging of credit card transactions are provided by an outside agency. The credit card information is first obtained from the user or from Passport and then run through the processor.
- **Email application**—A service is required for sending emails to customers as necessary.

Future Considerations

There are several other requirements for gasTIX that, although not implemented initially, are important to consider when architecting the site to allow for adding these options. Following is a list of several such enhancements for gasTIX that can be made in the future.

- **Advanced personalization**—Develop a whole suite of services that allow users to customize the functionality of the site as well as obtain specific data of interest on an as needed basis.
- **Extended product line**—Eventually the company might want to sell (or link to someone who sells) related merchandise such as posters and t-shirts.
- **Internationalization**—The company is planning to branch out into selling overseas and will therefore need to handle multiple languages and currencies.

gasTIX Use Cases

The following use case diagram, shown in Figure 2.2, and related descriptions provide an overview of the requirements for the gasTIX Web site. The descriptions provided here are not intended as detailed task lists, but, rather, provide a general overview of the Web site functionality from a user point of view. This section first provides definitions of the various actors and then covers each use case in turn.

The use case descriptions are organized into the following headings:

- **Actor**—Lists the user(s) and system(s) responsible for carrying out the functionality described by the use case.
- **Assumption**—Specifies the conditions that should have occurred before the functions in the use case can be carried out.
- **Purpose**—Defines the basic objective that the use case accomplishes.
- **Outputs**—Presents the expected outcome of the use case function.
- **Description**—Provides the detailed explanation of the tasks involved in the use case.

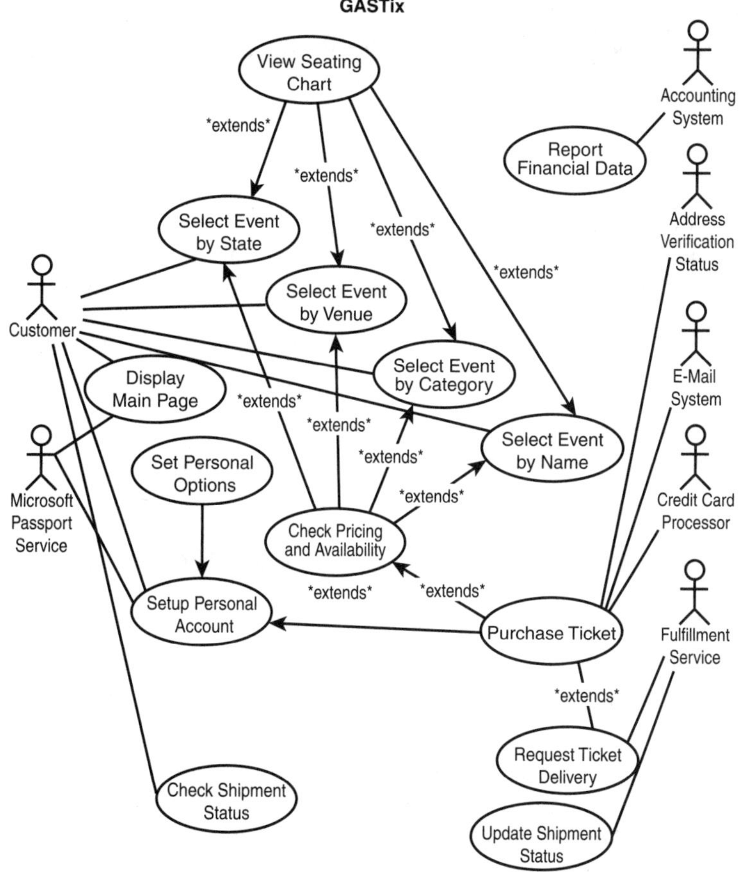

FIGURE 2.2
The gasTIX Web site provides a variety of services.

Actors

The actors involved in the various use cases are described here. Several of the actors represent outside systems with which gasTIX will operate. These are:

- **Customer**—Includes a user attempting to purchase tickets through the site.
- **Microsoft Passport Service**—Includes both the Passport and Wallet sections for providing information about registered customers and their credit information.
- **Accounting system**—Provides general ledger processing on behalf of gasTIX.
- **Address verification service**—Provides a check of user-supplied address data to ensure there are no irregularities.
- **Email system**—Provides forwarding of email messages as required.
- **Credit card processor**—Provides the services for authorizing and charging credit cards for purchases made on the site.
- **Fulfillment service**—Includes the capability to print and deliver tickets to the customers. This can include mailing the tickets as necessary.

NOTE

The first version of gasTIX will not include support for Passport; this functionality will be deferred until a .NET version of Passport is made available. Use cases which require the Passport Actor will indicate manual entry of personal information in the first version of gasTIX.

Display Main Page

Actor: Customer, MS Passport

Assumption: None

Purpose: To show the main page according to the customer's defined preferences.

Outputs: The main page is shown.

Description: Whenever customers visit the main page, the Web site checks to see whether the users have successfully logged into MS Passport. If they have, the site checks to see whether the associated username is stored in the database along with the customer's selected preferences. If the preferences have been set, the list of the user's preferred categories is retrieved from the database. The main page is then displayed with only the customer's preferred categories displayed. If no Passport account is found or no preferences have been set, the main page defaults to showing all categories.

Select Event by State

Actor: Customer

Assumption: The actor can cancel this use case at any time.

Purpose: To select an event based on the state in which the event is located.

Outputs: Detailed information about a specific event.

Description: A list of states along with a graphical US state map is displayed to the customer. The customer selects a state, and a list of artist or team names with events in the state is displayed, ordered by category. The customer selects an artist or team name and the system displays a list of events for the selected name. The customer then selects a specific event and the system displays detailed information about that event.

Select Event by Venue

Actor: Customer

Assumption: The actor can cancel this use case at any time.

Purpose: Select an event based on the venue in which an event is being held.

Outputs: Detailed information about a specific event.

Description: The customer decides whether to search for the venue by name or by state/city and proceeds according to one of the following two paths:

1. Venue search
    - The customer inputs the name of a venue and issues the search for a venue command. The system determines that the number of characters input is greater than or equal to one character in length. If not, the customer is prompted to enter a venue name and must restart the process.
    - Upon successful venue name entry, the system searches for the venue input by the customer. A list of venues is displayed to the customer if matches are found. A "no venues found" message is displayed if no matches are found.
    - The customer picks a venue from the list of matches and a list of events at that venue with summary information is displayed. The actor then selects a specific event and the system displays detailed information about that event.
2. Select venue by state/city
    - A list of states along with a graphical US state map is displayed to the customer, who then picks a state. A list of cities with a covered venue is displayed. If no covered venue cities are found for the selected state, a "no venues found" message is displayed.

- Next, the customer selects a city and a list of venues is displayed. The customer picks a venue and a list of events at that venue with summary information is displayed. The customer then selects a specific event and the system displays detailed information about that event.

Select Event by Category

Actor: Customer

Assumption: The actor can cancel this use case at any time.

Purpose: Select an event based on the category of the artist/team.

Outputs: Detailed information about a specific event.

Description: The customer picks a category and a list of subcategories for that category are displayed. The customer then picks a subcategory and a list of artist or team names with events fitting the category is displayed. The customer then picks a specific artist or team name, and a list of events for that artist or team with summary information is displayed. The customer next selects a specific event and the system displays detailed information about that event.

Select Event by Artist/Team Name

Actor: Customer

Assumption: The actor can cancel this use case at any time.

Purpose: Select an event based on the name of the artist/team.

Outputs: Detailed information about a specific event.

Description: The customer inputs the name of an artist or team name and issues the search for artist/team name command. The system determines that the number of characters input is greater than or equal to one character in length. If not, the customer is prompted to enter an artist or team name and must restart the process.

Upon successful artist/team name entry, the system searches for the name. A list of names is displayed if matches are found. A "no artists/teams found" message is displayed if no matches are found.

The customer picks an artist/team name from the list, and a list of events for that name with summary information is displayed. The customer then selects a specific event and the system displays detailed information about that event.

View Seating Chart

Actor: Customer

Assumption: The actor can cancel this use case at any time. A venue must be selected in order to proceed with this use case.

Purpose: To provide the actor with a graphical view of the seating chart for a specific venue.

Outputs: A graphical display for the selected venue.

Description: The customer picks the view seating chart option for a specific venue. If a seating chart is available for the venue, it is displayed. If no chart is available, a "no seating chart available" message is displayed. The customer can view the different seating configurations for the venue, if available.

Check Pricing and Availability

Actor: Customer

Assumptions: The actor can cancel this use case at any time. A specific event has been selected in order to run this use case.

Purpose: Determine which seats are still available for a specific event and the price for those seats.

Outputs: A list of available seats and prices for a specific event. The Purchase Tickets use case begins immediately.

Description: The customer selects the section in which they want to sit along with the number of seats desired. The system then looks for the best available seats meeting the criteria. If the system does not find seats available, it will return a message indicating no seats found. If the system does find seats, it returns a message showing the seats and section numbers found. At this point the seats are marked as reserved by the system. A button is shown giving the customer the option to purchase the tickets at this time.

Purchase Tickets

Actor: Customer, MS Passport Service, Address Verification Service, Email System

Assumptions: The actor cannot cancel this use case after the final purchase has been submitted. However, the actor can cancel at any time prior to final purchase. A specific event has been selected, and a pricing/availability check has been run for this event.

Purpose: Enable the actor to purchase a specific number of tickets at a specific price for a specific event.

Outputs: A confirmation of purchase for the selected event, pricing, and seating.

Description: The seats are collectively reserved for no more than five minutes to allow the customer the opportunity to provide the necessary purchase information. The reservation is lifted if the five minutes expire, if the customer conducts a new search, or if the customer closes his/her browser.

If the customer presses the purchase button, he or she is taken to the purchase screen. At this point, the customer enters the shipping option, billing address, and credit card information. Optionally, if this customer is logged in through MS Passport, the billing information is read from the personal account profile contained in Wallet and the fields are populated automatically. The customer will have the option to log into Passport at any time during this process. The customer will have the ability to edit the populated data.

NOTE

The seats are reserved in the Check Pricing and Availability use case rather than when the user selects the purchase button so that the seats aren't sold to another customer during the few seconds it takes to send the message to the Web site. This requirement is critical for events with extremely high interest in which tickets sell out in a matter of hours. Naturally, the five-minute time limit is then imposed to prevent the customers from reserving seats indefinitely.

When the customer selects the purchase button, the information is verified. The system verifies that a shipping option is picked, that required billing address fields are completed, and that credit card information is complete. If any of these items fail, the system displays an error message to the customers and provides them with an opportunity to fill in the required fields.

The customer's address data is also validated with the outside address verification service. If a success indicator or no response is received from the service, the address is considered acceptable. If an error is returned, a message is displayed stating that there might be an issue with the address data. The customer will have the opportunity to correct the data or to accept it as is.

The customer is then taken to a confirmation page detailing the purchase information. The customer can now accept or cancel the order at this time.

Once the system determines that all the information is entered correctly, the system calls the purchase ticket function. The credit card information is processed and the appropriate data is sent to the financial system. The system removes the seats purchased from the available list for the event. The system displays a confirmation and generates an email with the same information to the customer. If any errors are encountered during the purchasing process, the purchase is rolled back and aborted. Any error messages are displayed to the customer, who is given the opportunity to resubmit the purchase if appropriate.

Request Ticket Delivery

Actor: Fulfillment Service

Assumption: A ticket purchase has been successfully processed by the system.

Purpose: Generates the request to deliver the tickets to the customer.

Outputs: A message to the fulfillment service.

Description: Upon completion of a successful sale, a request is generated to the fulfillment service to print and deliver them to the customer. The request must be confirmed by the fulfillment service as having been received. Otherwise, the request will need to be resent until it's successfully delivered.

Update Shipment Status

Actor: Fulfillment Service

Assumption: A ticket purchase has been successfully made and the ticket delivery request message has been sent to the fulfillment service.

Purpose: To update the system with the status of a ticket delivery request.

Outputs: An updated status in the system.

Description: The fulfillment service is required to inform gasTIX of the status of a ticket purchase. The status is sent on two occasions:

- A message is sent when the ticket is shipped to the customer.
- Alternatively, if the ticket has not been shipped within a preset number of days, a status is sent providing an expected ship date. This message is resent according to an agreed-upon schedule until the tickets are successfully shipped. The purpose of this message is to ensure that the ticket delivery request has not been lost.

Delivery of this message must be guaranteed. Therefore, gasTIX must acknowledge receipt of the message to the fulfillment system.

Set up Personal Account

Actor: Customer, Microsoft Passport

Assumption: The actor can cancel this use case at any time.

Purpose: Enable the actor to create a personal account for holding billing and contact information.

Outputs: A confirmation of the personal account creation.

Description: The customer picks the Create New Personal Account function. The customer is then taken to the MS Passport area where he or she will be prompted to either log in or modify their account information as appropriate.

Once the customer exits the Passport site and returns to gasTIX, the actor's Passport username is returned. At this point, if the actor's username is not already stored, it is added into the system and a "personal account created" message is displayed.

Set Personal Options

Actor: Customer

Assumption: The customer selects the set personal preferences option. The customer can cancel this use case at any time. The user has successfully logged into the Microsoft Passport site.

Purpose: Allow the customers to set up their personal preferences for how the site behaves.

Outputs: A confirmation of the personal account update.

Description: The customer selects the set preferences option. A screen then shows all the categories available. The customer can then select those categories in which they are primarily interested. Once the selections are made, the customer commits the selection. The system then saves the personal account information and a "personal account updated" message appears.

Check Shipment Status

Actor: Customer

Assumption: None

Purpose: Allow the actor to see the status of a shipment.

Outputs: Shipment status

Description: The actor selects the check shipment status option. A screen prompts the customers for an order number. If the order is found, the status of the shipment is then provided. Otherwise, an error message is returned indicating that the order number is invalid.

Report Financial Transactions

Actor: Accounting System

Assumption: None

Purpose: To provide information about financial transactions for accounting purposes.

Outputs: An export of financial data for general ledger processing.

Description: At regular intervals, gasTIX will compile data about all purchases since the last extract to the accounting system.

Web Site Flow

The final step of the gasTIX requirements phase was to lay out a site map showing expected Web pages and how they interrelate (see Figure 2.3). This section describes each of those pages along with how they relate to the use cases discussed previously.

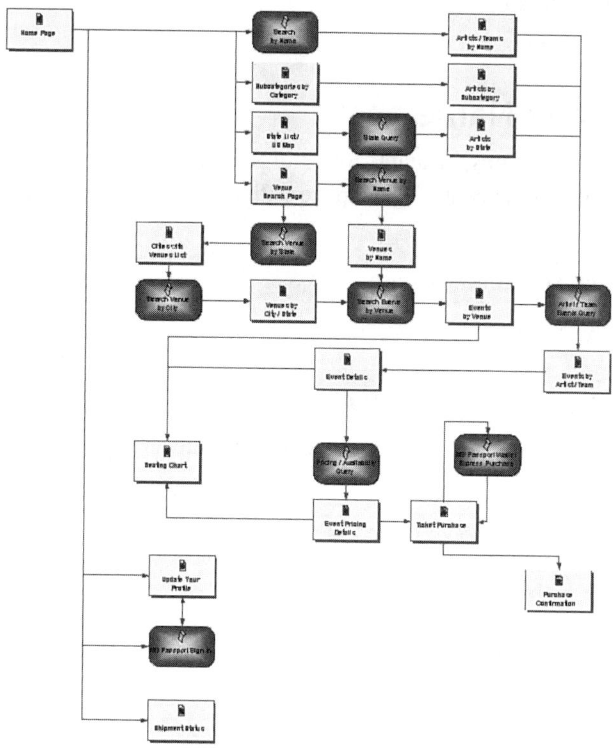

FIGURE 2.3
Map of the pages for the Web site.

Home Page

The main page is the base starting point for the gasTIX site. It presents a variety of options for searching the site for an event of the customer's choice. These options include presenting the set of categories available in the system. Upon visiting the main page, if the user is determined to have been logged into Passport, the list of available categories is modified based on the user's stated preferences. Also from here, the user can sign in to Microsoft Passport and access profile settings.

This Web page supports the following use cases:

- Display Main Page
- Select Event by State
- Select Event by Venue
- Select Event by Category
- Select Event by Name

Artists/Teams by Name

This page lists all artists, groups, or teams found in the system as the result of a name search. The artists are listed down the center of the page with a link to gather more information about the artist.

This Web page supports the following use case:

- Search Event by Name

Subcategories by Category

This page lists all subcategories of a given category. The subcategories are linked to find all events for that subcategory.

This Web page supports the following use case:

- Select Event by Category

Artists by Subcategory

This page lists all artists found in the system for a given subcategory. The events are linked to provide a list of events for that artist.

This Web page supports the following use case:

- Select Event by Category

State List/US Map

This page provides a map of the United States. Each state is linked to show all artists performing in that state.

This Web page supports the following use case:

- Select Event by State

Venue Search Page

This page also provides a map of the United States from which to select. Each state is linked to show all venues available in that state. Optionally, the customer can enter a string to serve as search criteria for a venue name.

This Web page supports the following use case:

- Select Event by Venue

Cities with Venues List

This page lists all cities with known venues for a given state. Each city is linked to provide a list of venues in that city.

This Web page supports the following use case:

- Select Event by Venue

Venues by City/State

This page lists all venues located in a given city and state. Each venue is linked to provide a list of events in that venue.

This Web page supports the following use case:

- Select Event by Venue

Venues by Name

This page lists all venues that match the given criteria for the venue's name. The customer can then issue another search. Alternatively, each venue is linked to provide a list of events in that venue.

This Web page supports the following use case:

- Select Event by Venue

Events by Venue

This page lists all events occurring at a given venue. Each event is linked to provide detailed information about that event.

This Web page supports the following use case:

- Select Event by Venue

Events by Artist/Team

This page lists all events associated with a given artist or team. Each event is linked to provide detailed information about that event.

This Web page supports the following use cases:

- Select Event by State
- Select Event by Category
- Select Event by Name

Seating Chart

This page shows the seating chart of a given venue.

This Web page supports the following use case:

- View Seating Chart

Event Details

This page provides detailed information about a given event, including performer, location, and event times as a minimum. The customers can check for available seating by specifying the section and number of seats desired within the venue.

This Web page supports the following use cases:

- Select Event by State
- Select Event by Venue
- Select Event by Category
- Select Event by Name
- Check Pricing and Availability

Event Pricing Details

This page shows the customer the best seats available for the criteria provided. The customer sees a message indicating that he or she has five minutes (or some other agreed-upon time frame) to purchase the tickets. The user can then elect to begin the purchase process.

This Web page supports the following use cases:

- Check Pricing and Availability
- Purchase Tickets

Ticket Purchase

This page prompts the customer to provide data to complete the purchase including shipping and billing information. The customers have the option to use the Express Purchase option where they will be taken to the MS Passport site to log in and confirm their data. Passport will then provide the customer data back to gasTIX to populate the given form. The user then elects to confirm the purchase.

At this point, the customer receives a confirmation of the purchase by email and the shipping request is made to the fulfillment service.

This Web page supports the following use cases:

- Purchase Tickets
- Request Ticket Delivery

Purchase Confirmation

This page provides the customer with a confirmation that the purchase was processed successfully.

This Web page supports the following use case:

- Purchase Tickets

Update Profile

This page provides the customers with the capability to define their display preferences when visiting the site. Basically, the page lists all categories available and the customers can select which ones to display. Once the profile is updated, the customers see a message indicating the changes are complete.

The customers must have successfully logged into Microsoft Passport before being allowed to visit this page. If they have not, they will be redirected to Passport where they will log in or set up an account, as appropriate.

This Web page supports the following use case:

- Set up Personal Account

Shipment Status

This page provides the customers with the capability to check on the status of any shipment. The customers are prompted to provide an order number, at which point they are provided with the shipping date (or expected shipping date if not already shipped) and shipping destination.

This Web page supports the following use case:

- Check Shipment Status

Project Design and Approach: The Microsoft Solutions Framework

The success of most technology projects depends on proper planning and the adoption of a formal methodology to fulfill the business objectives through effective project management and development. The use of a framework within which to operate is even more important as larger development efforts are undertaken. Therefore, care was taken by the authoring and development team to implement the sample application within a development framework that would ensure the quality of the resulting application.

For that framework, the team used the Microsoft Solution Framework (MSF). MSF presents a collection of industry-wide best practices, concepts, and models that help lay the foundation for planning, constructing, and administering development efforts. This foundation aids an organization in defining required resources and timetables for meeting key project objectives and deliverables.

NOTE

One key point about MSF is that it is a framework, not a methodology. Consider MSF a map that shows key landmarks and possible routes to a destination as opposed to specific driving instructions that lay out the specific route you have to take to reach the destination.

There are actually several models included within MSF:

- **Team model**—Presents the key roles and responsibilities of development team members.
- **Process model**—Presents the main phases and deliverables included within the software development lifecycle.
- **Applications model**—Presents the basic structure for best implementing applications.

For the purpose of this book, only the process model is discussed. The remainder of this section provides a brief overview of that development process and provides a foundation for understanding the overall structure of the book.

NOTE

For more information on the Microsoft Solutions Framework, visit `http://www.microsoft.com/msf`.

Development Process Overview

The MSF process model presents the basic steps involved in a software development project. According to the framework, as presented in Figure 2.4, development is divided into four basic phases. These are:

- Envisioning
- Planning
- Developing
- Stabilizing

Borrowing from the spiral approach to software development, the process model calls for each of the four phases to be repeated in an iterative manner as often as necessary. Each iteration results in a new, fully functional version of the software. This is the reason why Figure 2.4 shows the end of the stabilization phase leading into the envisioning phase of a new version of the product.

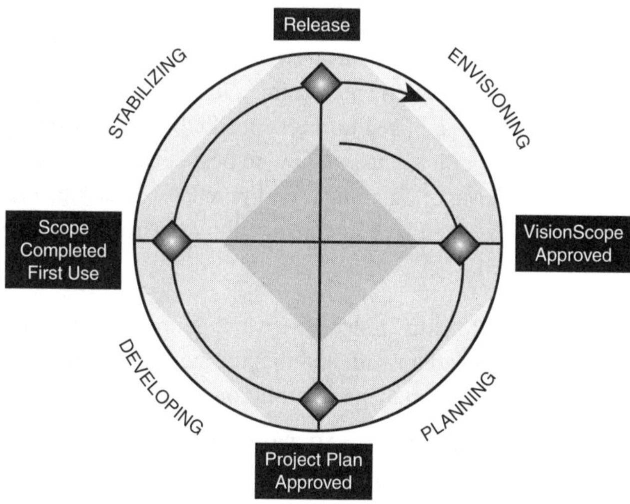

FIGURE 2.4
The MSF process is circular.

Each of those phases consists of a set of intermediate milestones discussed in the subsections that follow.

Envisioning

This phase concludes with the "Vision/Scope Approved" milestone, which represents an agreement on long-range vision motivating the effort, as well as short-range scope of what will be accomplished. At this time, the team members share opportunities, risks, and assumptions.

In relation to this book, Part I, "Preliminaries and Planning," consists of chapters outlining the .NET architecture and presents the high-level requirements of the application.

Planning

This phase concludes with the "Project Plan Approved" milestone, which represents an agreement on project deliverables, features and priorities, and the targeted release date. All team members buy into and commit to the delivery schedule.

Part II of this book, "Designing .NET e-Business Solutions," focuses on the architectural options available in configuring an n-tier application under the .NET architecture. Hence, the chapters are focused on the technical design of the overall system that is part of the planning phase and not on program management issues.

Developing

This phase concludes with the "Scope Complete/First Use" milestone, which represents an agreement that all features have been built to specification, yet accepting that the solution is not completely stable.

Part III of this book, "Building the .NET e-Business," presents code examples of how specific aspects of system functionality are implemented using .NET. The goal is to highlight examples of how different tools within .NET are used to meet specific business or design criteria. This chapter is not concerned with program issues of how to best develop code and it does not discuss use of unit tests, code reviews, or other such best practices. This subject matter is outside of the scope of this book and has been well documented in numerous other books.

Stabilizing

This phase concludes with the "Release" milestone, which represents an agreement that all outstanding stability issues have been addressed, and that the support and operations organization is sufficiently prepared to deploy and manage the solution.

Part IV of this book, "Testing and Deploying .NET Sites," focuses on technical issues associated with testing, debugging, and deploying applications within the .NET Framework. The focus is not on how to best track bugs or reach a "golden release" as, again, such subject matter is outside of the scope of this book and has been well documented in other books.

A Note on the Sample Application

For the purposes of this book, not all aspects of gasTIX were developed by the development team. Only a subset of the entire system has been implemented. Aspects that were necessary to demonstrate the principles of building a .NET application were implemented here.

This does not mean that the sample site is not robust. On the contrary, the site has been rigorously tested to ensure the highest stability and scalability. Rather, not all functionality has necessarily been implemented. The following list shows the overall gasTIX company infrastructure provided in the sample application:

- **gasTIX site**—This is the main site in support of the Internet users. The complete site includes the Web server code, the ticketing engine, and the supporting database.
- **gasBAGS site**—This is a mockup site for a fictitious partner site supporting a bagpipe band called the gasBAGS. The objective of this site is to demonstrate consumption of Web services provided by gasTIX.
- **Fulfillment site**—The fulfillment site is a simple set of services implemented purely to show the use of BizTalk in communications. The site exists primarily to implement the fulfillment side's interface and does not actually print or handle the shipping of the tickets.
- **Address verification**—This is a simplified version of what a full-blown address-verification site provides. This site was created to demonstrate consumption of services needed by gasBAGS and to simulate a large-scale database application running on Microsoft DataCenter Server.
- **Microsoft Passport**—Interfacing with Passport will be implemented to demonstrate the techniques involved in accessing this key service from Microsoft.

The online version of gasTIX will continue to evolve and incorporate this functionality over time. Visit it often at `www.gastix.net` to see the latest implementation.

From Here

Now that you are familiar with the concepts and requirements behind the gasTIX system, the rest of this book takes you inside the design and implementation decisions used to build gasTIX. The study begins in the next section, which focuses on design issues.

Enabling Inter-Application Communications

by Bry Pickett

CHAPTER

3

IN THIS CHAPTER

- Challenges of Inter-Application Communications 76
- XML—Extensible Markup Language 77
- SOAP and Web services 82
- Microsoft BizTalk Server 2000 85
- From Here 88

Problems stemming from independent software applications not communicating well with other applications have an extraordinary cost for companies in both time and money. These self-contained applications cost more to develop and integrate, consume more personnel resources, and hinder built-in features of peer applications by not providing the necessary interfaces to implement a particular application feature set. The result is that many software engineers spend their time thinking of complex ways to link stand-alone systems together, instead of planning and building distributed software applications that integrate well.

This chapter introduces you to the tools and technologies available today that make it possible to produce great distributed software systems using the Microsoft .NET Enterprise Solutions Platform. We will discuss industry-standard technologies such as XML and SOAP, and learn about the tools available to create distributed software systems.

In this chapter, you will:

- Come to understand industry standard technologies used to enable communication between different software applications.
- Learn about the tools provided by the Microsoft .NET Framework to solve inter-application communication challenges.
- Acquire a foundation for building your own solutions for application communication business problems.

We will start by taking a look at the challenges and benefits of inter-application communications, addressing the topics of distributed software systems, incompatible protocols and data formats, and then move on to discussions about industry standard technologies such as XML and SOAP. Next we will cover the tools that Microsoft provides to develop software that targets the Microsoft .NET Enterprise Solutions Platform. The goal of this chapter is to establish a foundation for these concepts which can be extended to meet your own application integration challenges.

Challenges of Inter-Application Communications

The problem of application integration stems from the fact that different applications use dissimilar protocols and data formats. Traditional client/server applications are usually built with the same underlying protocols and data types. As a result, application integration is straightforward because client/server systems are designed from the start to work together.

Unfortunately, as most developers have experienced, applications usually evolve into something that wasn't originally planned for as new products become available, or as the organizational structure of the company changes. Enabling this communication between dissimilar systems is much more difficult than doing so between systems that were designed from the ground up to co-exist. Different communication protocols, operating systems, data types, and many other factors must all work together to produce a cohesive distributed software system.

In many organizations, multiple applications may execute independently of one another. For example, consider a hospital. A hospital may have a system for registering patients, a system for managing radiology services, a system that controls surgery scheduling, and other systems for billing and inventory control. Since these systems were likely developed and deployed at varying times, each one might describe patient demographic information in a different way. Each system may be built in a different programming language, or run on a different operating system. Each application must fluidly communicate with the others in order to achieve any amount of patient satisfaction.

Taking this scenario a bit further, the inventory control department may need to integrate with external suppliers in order to maintain acceptable stock levels of bandages and medicine. This introduces systems beyond the immediate control of the hospital staff. The situation becomes even more complex as different corporate cultures and business philosophies are introduced.

We are now beginning to understand the necessity of enabling application-to-application communication within one organization, as well as across multiple organizations. The following sections discuss the .NET set of tools derived from technologies that help enable inter-application communication.

XML—Extensible Markup Language

XML provides the foundation for enabling inter-application communication between disparate software systems. XML is a general-purpose markup language which allows developers to structurally describe data independent of specific software applications. The ability to independently describe data facilitates information exchange across organizations by making software applications easier to design, build, deploy, and maintain. Since XML is self-describing, the applications that use it to communicate do not need to worry about specific formatting.

It is easy to learn how to create and read XML documents. They are similar in appearance to HTML and typically include standard English terminology instead of code language. Listing 3.1 shows an XML document that describes several pets found in a typical family household.

LISTING 3.1 An XML Description of Household Pets

```
<household>
    <pets>
        <pet type="cat">
            <breed>Domestic Short Hair</breed>
            <name>Daisy</name>
            <color>Brown</color>
            <weight>16 pounds</weight>
        </pet>
        <pet type="cat">
```

LISTING 3.1 Continued

```
            <breed>Domestic Short Hair</breed>
            <name>Hana</name>
            <color>BrownishBlack</color>
            <weight>6 pounds</weight>
        </pet>
        <pet type="dog">
            <breed>Australian Shepard</breed>
            <name>Nellie</name>
            <color>Blue Merle</color>
            <weight>24 pounds</weight>
        </pet>
    </pets>
</household>
```

The listing above shows that XML documents are comprised of elements and attributes to create a structured representation of data. This particular set of data describes three household pets, two cats and a dog, and contains four pieces of information for each pet. The `<household>` element is the root element and contains all other elements and attributes in the household pet document. The `<pets>` tag is a collection of individual `<pet>` tags, each describing an individual pet. The type attribute on the `<pet>` element allows us to further describe a pet using simple name-value pairs. Each XML tag can have zero or more name-value pairs to indicate the specific properties of the tag instance.

When authoring your own XML documents there are a few key guidelines to follow in order to create well-formed XML:

- Each element must have an end tag.
- Elements cannot overlap.
- Attribute values must be enclosed in quotation marks.
- Documents must have a unique root node.

By following these four simple rules you can create highly descriptive and well-formed documents that represent a variety of business data. Many companies have already published XML schemas for use in a specific industry or with specific types of data.

XML and HTML

As shown above, XML is used to describe the content of data. Contrast this to HTML, Hypertext Markup Language, which details how to display data in a web browser. Using HTML, we can tell a browser to display data using a particular font type and size, or act as a hyperlink for site navigation. Using XML together with HTML, we can extend the value of business data by separating content from presentation. This allows a single set of data to be reused in multiple presentations and a single presentation to display multiple sets of data.

One of the benefits of using a standard markup language such as XML to represent our data is that we can easily integrate data from different sources. For example, we can aggregate content from relational databases, spreadsheets, text files, or legacy corporate applications, into a single XML document. This document can then be merged with HTML for robust presentation in a web browser. Instead of displaying in a web browser, we could also deliver the XML to a software application in a different enterprise thus providing a link between the two standalone applications and producing a truly distributed software system.

As we shall see shortly, XML is the technology which provides the infrastructure for distributed software concepts like Simple Object Access Protocol (SOAP) and Web services.

NOTE

A complete discussion of XML is beyond the scope of this chapter, as entire books have been written about XML. Our intention isn't to create XML experts but instead merely to provide a basic introduction to XML. For those interested in learning more please visit the following web links for additional information on XML:

Microsoft XML Developer Center: `www.msdn.microsoft.com/XML`

W3C XML: `www.w3c.org/XML`

XML-Zone: `www.XML-Zone.com/`

XSD Schema

One question we need to address is, "How do we define our own XML document and data structures?" The answer is via an XSD schema. The *XML Schema Definition* (XSD) is a language, based on XML, that allows us to define the structure and data types for XML documents. When we author an XSD schema we actually use a set of elements, attributes, and data types that conform to the World Wide Web Consortium (W3C) XSD Schema Definition language. This specification serves as the blueprint for authoring XSD schemas, and in turn, schemas serve as blueprints for XML document instances.

XSD schemas are a bit more difficult to create than simple XML documents, since XSD schemas serve as blueprints for XML documents. The relationship between XSD schemas and XML documents is similar to that between classes and objects. XML documents are instances of XSD schemas, just as objects are instances of classes in object oriented programming.

Since XSD schemas are defined using XML, all schemas must have a top-level node. The W3C specification states this node must be the `<schema>` element and its definition must include the `www.w3.org/2001/XMLSchema` namespace.

NOTE

According to the W3C standards body, "An XML namespace is a collection of names, identified by a URI reference, which are used in XML documents as `element types` and `attribute names`. XML namespaces differ from the 'namespaces' conventionally used in computing disciplines in that the XML version has internal structure and is not, mathematically speaking, a set." See `www.w3.org/TR/REC-xml-names/` for more information.

Since `<schema>` is the top-level node, all elements and attributes used to author a schema must appear between the begin and end `<schema>` tags. The specification also describes the exact elements and attributes authors may utilize to develop XSD schemas.

Let's work by example. Listing 3.2 shows the XSD schema that defines the household pet XML document that was studied earlier in the chapter.

LISTING 3.2 Household Pets XSD Schema

```
<xsd:schema id="household" targetNamespace="" xmlns=""
xmlns:xsd="http://www.w3.org/2001/XMLSchema" xmlns:msdata="urn:schemas-
microsoft-com:xml-msdata">
 <xsd:element name="household" msdata:IsDataSet="true">
   <xsd:complexType>
    <xsd:choice maxOccurs="unbounded">
     <xsd:element name="pets">
       <xsd:complexType>
        <xsd:sequence>
         <xsd:element name="pet" minOccurs="0" maxOccurs="unbounded">
           <xsd:complexType>
            <xsd:sequence>
             <xsd:element name="breed" type="xsd:string" minOccurs="0"
msdata:Ordinal="0" />
             <xsd:element name="name" type="xsd:string" minOccurs="0"
msdata:Ordinal="1" />
             <xsd:element name="color" type="xsd:string" minOccurs="0"
msdata:Ordinal="2" />
             <xsd:element name="weight" type="xsd:string" minOccurs="0"
msdata:Ordinal="3" />
```

LISTING 3.2 Continued

```
            </xsd:sequence>
            <xsd:attribute name="type" type="xsd:string" />
            <xsd:attribute name="pets_Id" type="xsd:int" use="prohibited" />
           </xsd:complexType>
         </xsd:element>
        </xsd:sequence>
        <xsd:attribute name="pets_Id" msdata:AutoIncrement="true"
type="xsd:int" msdata:AllowDBNull="false" use="prohibited" />
       </xsd:complexType>
      </xsd:element>
     </xsd:choice>
    </xsd:complexType>
    <xsd:unique name="Constraint1" msdata:PrimaryKey="true">
     <xsd:selector xpath=".//pets" />
     <xsd:field xpath="@pets_Id" />
    </xsd:unique>
    <xsd:keyref name="pets_pet" refer="Constraint1" msdata:IsNested="true">
     <xsd:selector xpath=".//pet" />
     <xsd:field xpath="@pets_Id" />
    </xsd:keyref>
  </xsd:element>
</xsd:schema>
```


As we can see, the schema (Listing 3.2) is more complex than its instance (Listing 3.1). Our `household` pet schema, like all schema, begins with the `<schema>` element. Looking through the listing we find `<element>` declarations for our `household`, `pets`, `pet`, `breed`, `name`, `color`, and `weight` elements, as well as an `<attribute>` element that defines the type attribute of the `<pet>` element. Properties such as `MinOccurs` and `MaxOccurs` define the minimum number of times a tag can occur. For instance, the `<pet>` tag has a `MinOccurs` value of `0` and an unbounded `MaxOccurs` value, indicating that for any `household`, there can be 0 or more pets.

NOTE

The XSD schema in Listing 3.2 was generated using the Microsoft .NET Framework XML schemas support utility (xsd.exe). This program allows solution developers to efficiently interoperate between schemas and .NET classes, and is available in the Microsoft .NET Framework SDK.

Up to this point we've discussed XML and studied a simple document instance. We've learned how the separation of content and presentation is important in bringing together data from different sources. We talked briefly about XSD Schema and looked at an example declaration for our household pet example. In the next section, we will discuss technologies that extend XML to create a new set of tools that facilitate inter-application communications.

SOAP and Web services

The Simple Object Access Protocol (SOAP) and Web services play a major role in the Microsoft .NET Enterprise Solutions platform. A Web Service is a piece of application code made available over the Web via standard Internet protocols such as HTTP and TCP/IP. SOAP is a lightweight protocol that travels on top of HTTP. It provides the information transport layer for application communication via Web services. Software engineers developing solutions that target the Microsoft .NET Enterprise Solutions Platform build applications that exchange data between various Web services to produce a single, cohesive distributed software application.

Simplicity is the fundamental principle behind the development of SOAP. SOAP does not introduce new technological innovations, but instead builds upon reliable, well known Internet standards like XML and HTTP. As a result, software engineers can leverage existing knowledge of the Internet to develop SOAP-based Web services targeting the Microsoft .NET Enterprise Solutions Platform.

That said, we can formulate three important points about what SOAP is:

- SOAP is formatted using XML and transported through HTTP requests. A client sends a SOAP message to a server via HTTP and the server performs application logic based on the client request.
- SOAP needs HTTP, nothing else. SOAP is not concerned with operating systems, development languages, or application object models.
- SOAP works with existing firewalls, routers, and proxy servers. A network administrator does not have to go out and buy new hardware to support SOAP-based software systems.

Now that we have covered what SOAP is, we will discuss the two distinct types of SOAP messages:

1. Clients send SOAP messages to a server using a Call message.
2. Servers respond back using a Response message.

Listing 3.3 illustrates a SOAP Call message.

LISTING 3.3 SOAP Call Message

```
POST /RegisterPets HTTP/1.1
Host: www.gasullivan.com
Content-Type: text/xml
```

LISTING 3.3 Continued

```
Content-Length: xxxx
SOAPMethodName: http://www.gasullivan.com/PetService

<SOAP:Envelope xmlns:SOAP="urn:schemas-xmlsoap-org:soap.v1">
    <SOAP:Body>
        <AddPetsToRegistry>
            <XML Payload Goes Here!>
        </AddPetsToRegistry>
    </SOAP:Body>
</SOAP:Envelope>
```

The first four lines in Listing 3.3 are common HTTP syntax. POST is the request type. `Hostname`, `Content-Type`, and `Content-Length` are required for all HTTP messages. Notice the Content-Type of `text/xml`. XML keeps popping up everywhere! The text/xml value indicates that the payload of this HTTP request is XML. In fact, the SOAP message is a well-formed XML document comprised of a required `<SOAP:Envelope>` element, a required `<SOAP:Body>` element, and an optional `<SOAP:Header>` element. The `<SOAP:Header>` is not shown in the listing, but would exist between the `Envelope` and `Body` elements. A server receiving this message sees the `SOAPMethodName` in the HTTP Header and executes an `AddPetsToRegistry` procedure call to add our household pets to a fictitious pet repository at G.A. Sullivan.

Listing 3.4 shows a response to the SOAP Call message above.

LISTING 3.4 SOAP Response Message

```
HTTP/1.1 200 OK
Content-Type: text/xml
Content-Length: xxxx

<SOAP:Envelope xmlns:SOAP=" urn:schemas-xmlsoap-org:soap.v1"
    <SOAP:Body>
        <AddPetsToRegistryResponse>
            <return><XML Payload Goes Here!><return>
        </AddPetsToRegistryResponse>
    </SOAP:Body>
</SOAP:Envelope>
```

Here we see a typical HTTP 1.1 response with an XML document as the response body. The top three lines are similar to the SOAP Call request. The first line is the HTTP response code and the second and third lines describe content type and length. Again we see the XML based SOAP message with the `<AddPetsToRegistryResponse>` element containing a `<return>`

element. The actual payload of the response would be an XML document traveling as a child of the <return> element.

WSDL, DISCO, and UDDI

A Web Service accepts messages from a client, performs work based on information contained in the message, and sends a response back to the client. How does a client, or Web Service consumer, learn about the methods a Web Service exposes? This process is enabled through WSDL, the Web Service Description Language. This section explains WSDL and how it fits into the Web services picture.

WSDL is an XML specification that developers use to detail which methods, parameters, and protocols a Web Service exposes. WSDL can be loosely compared to a text-based COM type library that is not specific to any particular operating system platform. It acts as a contract between a Web Service consumer and the Web Service itself.

Imagine a set of cool web services that exist at a site called gasTIX.com. The gasTIX Web services allow customers to search for tickets to upcoming concerts and sporting events. As developers, all we know about is gasTIX.com, not specific endpoints at the site that expose WSDL documents to develop against. The Discovery Protocol (DISCO) defines an XML-based discovery document format, along with a protocol, giving us the ability to scour gasTIX.com for services of interest. The discovery page lists all Web services and the methods available for those services. It also details the expected parameters for each method and a description of the return value.

Taking this one step further, pretend we do not know the specific URL for the Web services we are interested in. The Universal Description, Discovery, and Integration (UDDI) specification allows Web Service authors to advertise the location of their services and gives Web Service consumers the ability to find these services.

NOTE

For more information on SOAP and Web services, see the following web links:

Microsoft Web services Developer Center: `msdn.microsoft.com/webservices/`

SOAP Specification Version 1.1: `msdn.microsoft.com/xml/general/soapspec.asp`

Web services Description Language 1.1: `msdn.microsoft.com/xml/general/wsdl.asp`

Microsoft BizTalk Server 2000

Microsoft BizTalk Server 2000 is a .NET Enterprise Class server product with powerful development and execution features capable of orchestrating business processes within one organization, as well as among many organizations. BizTalk Server 2000 provides us with the ability to define XML-based business document specifications, and to configure what transformations must take place on these documents as they travel between software applications. BizTalk facilitates application development by allowing both software developers and business analysts to participate in the development of business process software applications.

BizTalk is designed to provide us with a comprehensive interface for managing the types of application interoperability issues that we have been discussing, which can often become quite complex. BizTalk is a technology that helps enable the efficient implementation of business processes and workflow within an organization. It can import XML and XSD schemas after initial configuration customized for a company's e-Business requirements has been completed. As a member of the .NET Enterprise Server family, BizTalk can communicate with SOAP web services.

The sections below are an introduction to the primary application-level features of BizTalk Server and are intended as a foundation for later chapters about gasTIX.com and Microsoft BizTalk Server 2000. For more information on the implementation of BizTalk in the gasTIX application, refer to Chapter 12, "Fulfillment."

Business Document Exchange

Microsoft BizTalk Server 2000 provides a powerful execution engine that enables business document exchange both within and between enterprises. A business document is a text document, or message, that drives a business process. Examples include purchase orders, receivables statements, product specifications, or any other critical pieces of information on which businesses depend for their operations. Different software applications utilize different document formats. BizTalk Server 2000 helps integrate different applications by supporting both XML and common flat-file formats. These message formats are described below:

- XML documents. Any XML document that conforms to the XML 1.0 specification can be exchanged using Microsoft BizTalk Server 2000.
- Delimited flat-files can also be used with BizTalk. The data fields of delimited flat-files are separated by a specified character delimiter. Common delimiters are commas, colons, pipes, and tab characters.
- Fixed-length data fields comprise positional flat-files. A collection of data fields on one row in the flat-file is called a record. Flat-file records can either be fixed or variable length, depending on the structure of the data.

In order for BizTalk to comprehend the content of these different data formats, we must create message specifications. BizTalk message specifications are similar to the XSD Schema we learned about earlier in this chapter. They are blueprints for what type of information a message can contain, and thus enable BizTalk to understand specific rules for business document exchange.

BizTalk Orchestration

The highest layer of abstraction in BizTalk Server 2000 is Orchestration. BizTalk Orchestration is used to design business processes that manage overall application business logic.

In the past, the design and implementation of a business process occurred in two separate pieces. First, a business analyst would gather business requirements and construct some type of diagram, like a flowchart or interaction diagram, describing the business process in a graphical manner. Next, a software developer would review the business process diagram and map requirements to an implementation model and perform the coding and testing to produce the required software solution.

The BizTalk Orchestration Designer gives both the business analyst and software developer a common tool for designing and implementing business processes. Business process creation using BizTalk Orchestration generally follows four distinct steps. These are:

- Business analysts create an XLANG Schedule drawing using a set of well known flowchart-like shapes. Each shape represents a logical step in the business process.
- Software developers provide an implementation for the XLANG Schedule by attaching each shape in the drawing to software which implements that shape.
- Orchestration Designer provides a way to visually define the flow of data between different shapes in the diagram. This work can either be accomplished by a business analyst or software developers.
- The XLANG Schedule drawing is then compiled into an XLANG Schedule. XLANG Schedules are executable business process files used by the BizTalk runtime to complete the business process.

A powerful feature of Orchestration Designer is its ability to create long-running business processes. When designing an XLANG Schedule, we can configure it to stay alive for as long as it takes to complete the business process. For example, a book ordered over the Internet may have to be ordered directly from the publisher, which could take weeks to complete. BizTalk Orchestration treats this as a loosely-coupled process and is able to compensate for the added work required to complete the book order.

BizTalk Messaging

BizTalk Messaging Services provide us with the ability to receive messages and route them into a business process, or to send out messages as a result of a process. Messaging enables business partner integration, as well as integration of existing applications by acting as the low-level transport and support layer for BizTalk Orchestration Services. Messaging and Orchestration are designed to be used closely together, with Messaging providing the receipt and delivery capability that Orchestration relies on.

The major features of BizTalk Messaging include the following:

- Transport services
- Data parsing
- Data validation
- Reliable document delivery
- Security

Transport services represent the different protocols and applications that transmit business documents to their destinations. BizTalk Messaging supports standard Internet protocols like HTTP, SMTP, and HTTPS, as well as file-based document delivery. Custom software, termed *Application Integration Components*, can be also be used by BizTalk Messaging, as well as Message Queuing technology.

All documents that pass through BizTalk Messaging are XML-based. We all know that a business process may consume data that conforms to a variety of industry standard formats like ASNI X12, EDIFACT, or even use flat-file formats. BizTalk Server provides a set of data parsers (converters) that translate these non-XML formats to XML. BizTalk Messaging even allows us to customize its services and develop our own parsers for use with proprietary data formats.

BizTalk enforces data integrity rules by validating each document instance against a specification. If a document instance does not conform to specifications, it is transferred to a temporary holding queue for additional inspection.

Reliable document delivery ensures a document reaches its intended destination in a reasonable amount of time. BizTalk Messaging stores each document in a central repository. In the unlikely event of server failure, BizTalk allows other servers to take control and process orphaned documents from the central repository.

BizTalk Server supports public key encryption for documents transmitted using BizTalk Messaging Services. On the receive side of messaging operations, BizTalk supports decryption as well as signature verification.

From Here

In this chapter we explored XML, SOAP and Web services, and Microsoft BizTalk Server 2000. We discovered how XML is the underlying data format for technologies like SOAP, Web services, and BizTalk Server, and how XSD Schema can be used to create blueprints for XML documents. We studied how SOAP and Web services enable application to application communication using standard Internet protocols like TCP/IP and HTTP. We introduced the basic features of BizTalk Server 2000. We discussed the flow of events for creating business process drawings using BizTalk Orchestration. Also, we talked about the features of Business Document Exchange and BizTalk Messaging Services.

To learn more about building Web services and the gasTIX example, see Chapter 11, "Purchasing a Ticket." For more information on how BizTalk Server is used to integrate the gasTIX website with a third-party fulfillment company, see Chapter 12, "Fulfillment." For a more detailed discussion of the XML, SOAP, or UDDI standards, please visit the websites noted in this chapter.

PART

II

Designing .NET e-Business Solutions

Here we cover .NET application design considerations from each of the three logical tiers: presentation, business, and data. Security topics are explored, which are an area of primary concern for architects, managers, and administrators alike. Issues relating to integration with COM+ services are also covered in this section.

IN THIS PART

- **Chapter 4: Tools of the Trade 91**
- **Chapter 5: Implementing .NET Presentation Services 123**
- **Chapter 6: Implementing .NET Business Services 155**
- **Chapter 7: Implementing .NET Data Services 179**
- **Chapter 8: Handling Security 233**
- **Chapter 9: COM+ Integration 251**

Tools of the Trade

by Matthew Baute

CHAPTER

4

IN THIS CHAPTER

- .NET Architectural Tools 92
- .NET Language Tools 108
- .NET Developer Productivity Tools 112
- From Here 122

Microsoft's release of the .NET platform marks an important step forward in software development. Several years in the making, the framework includes a comprehensive set of class libraries that provides a robust toolset for developers, built from the ground up with the Internet, XML, and distributed processing in mind. Strong language interoperability, easier application deployment and versioning, automatic memory management, and SOAP Web services support were all key design goals for the .NET Framework. .NET delivers on these goals, providing an improved development environment that will make developers much more productive for years to come.

Although JScript and Visual C++ have been updated for .NET, the primary languages targeted for the .NET Framework by Microsoft are Visual C# .NET and Visual Basic .NET. These languages both fully meet the stated design goals of .NET. C# is a new language from Microsoft, marketed as providing the Rapid Application Development (RAD) features of VB, combined with the power of C++. The C# language syntax will feel quite familiar to C++, Java, and even JavaScript developers. C# was designed and built with the .NET Framework in mind, and is de facto the .NET language of choice. This new language is already garnering a great amount of interest in the development community, and is also attracting Java developers who want to target applications for the .NET platform. Visual Basic .NET is a significant overhaul of the popular Visual Basic 6.0 programming language. Many major improvements have been made to the language, greatly enhancing the robustness of the tool.

This chapter explores the most important features of the .NET platform from an architectural perspective. It examines how .NET solves the challenges particular to the distributed Internet-based systems being developed today. It then provides an overview of the two premier .NET languages, Visual C# .NET and Visual Basic .NET, along with thoughts about which language to select for your own development. Visual Studio .NET, the latest and much improved release of Microsoft's Integrated Development Environment (IDE), will be reviewed in depth.

.NET Architectural Tools

With the introduction of XML, SOAP, and Web services, applications can now be easily integrated without regard to geographical location or the underlying operating system. This should bring about a better online experience for end-users because applications that we build can now comprehensively gather and process data that might, in part, live on servers that someone else owns and maintains. Without XML Web services, users are often forced to manually work with data from our site, and then go to several other sites to complete a high-level task. Indeed, this idea of system integration and data sharing via XML is central to Microsoft's .NET vision. Microsoft believes that vast integration will drive application development over the next several years, transforming the common user experience and bringing about the "third generation" of Internet applications.

NOTE

The Internet is entering its third generation of applications. First generation applications were static, read-only HTML pages, with little interactivity. The second generation, of which we are nearing the end, offered more interactivity. Users could make purchases online, submit product information requests, and participate in newsgroup discussions. Second generation Microsoft Internet applications are architected using Windows Distributed Internet Architecture (DNA) solutions, consisting of Active Server Pages (ASP), VB COM components, and SQL Server. Third generation applications will be driven largely by the acceptance of SOAP, XML, and Web services. Microsoft is offering .NET as a premier development environment and platform for these next-generation applications.

Myriad challenges face the application designers architecting and implementing the distributed, Internet-based systems that have exploded onto the scene in the last few years. The same architectural design goals that drove Windows DNA development (scalability, maintainability, reliability, interoperability, extensibility) remain relevant in this new landscape. By design, Microsoft continues to provide more robust tools for architects and implementation teams in order to help meet these goals. .NET represents a major step forward in the evolution of Internet-based application development, and this section explores the enabling foundational architecture of this new platform.

.NET Framework Classes

Although the .NET platform includes a great number of different pieces, a large collection of classes called the .NET Framework is one of its most important features. Developers can take advantage of a tremendous variety of functionality through this framework, ranging from file IO and data access, to threading and Web UI construction. The .NET Framework classes are the single API used to program in .NET. Anything and everything we might want to accomplish programmatically in a .NET application, we will do through some class in this framework.

Because the .NET Framework contains hundreds of classes, it can be overwhelming at first. However, it is vital that we gain a solid understanding of the framework in order to develop applications effectively for .NET. To help organize the framework into logical groupings, the designers of .NET have categorized the classes into namespaces. This makes the scope of the .NET classes more approachable when we are first learning about them.

Table 4.1 shows the namespaces that are the most widely used in constructing e-Business applications with .NET. Many different functions occur in a typical e-Business application:

dynamically constructing and serving Web pages, accessing databases, wrapping a transaction around a set of functions, and calling SOAP methods on external servers. Such functionality is implemented through the following important .NET namespaces:

TABLE 4.1 The main .NET namespaces for e-Business applications

Class Name	*Functional Description*
System.Configuration	Supports a variety of application install and uninstall classes; compatible with Windows Installer.
System.Data	Use this namespace to access relational databases such as SQL Server 2000 through ADO .NET classes. An improved construct called a DataSet provides the equivalent of an in-memory database, allowing operations on hierarchical representations of tables.
System.Diagnostics	When something goes wrong in our application, we usually want to write an exception to the event log. We may also want to examine system performance counters, or create our own. Both types of functionality are found in this namespace.
System.DirectoryServices	Features support for interacting with Active Directory Services (ADSI).
System.EnterpriseServices	This namespace is used when we need to enlist COM+ services such as transactions and object pooling. (In .NET, Microsoft still relies on the COM+ infrastructure built into Windows 2000.)
System.IO	This namespace includes file I/O and StreamReader/StreamWriter classes, used for reading and writing data to disk.
System.Messaging	This namespace is used when our application requires asynchronous processing based on Microsoft Messaging technology (formerly MSMQ).
System.NET	WebRequest and WebResponse classes are included in this networking namespace, along with support for other protocols such as TCP/IP and Sockets. This functionality is used to open networking ports and perform specific tasks over them.
System.Runtime	Serialization methods such as the SoapFormatter and the BinaryFormatter are implemented in this namespace. Interoperability with unmanaged COM components is also facilitated by this namespace.

TABLE 4.1 Continued

Class Name	*Functional Description*
System.Security	This namespace includes Cryptography and Policy classes for helping to lock down a .NET application.
System.Text	Classes in this namespace provide functionality for dealing with text-based data. StringBuilder can be used for efficient manipulation of strings, and RegularExpressions provide powerful string validation functionality.
System.Threading	This namespace includes classes for building multi-threading support into a .NET application.
System.Web	This large namespace includes support for the creation of Web services, Web Forms, and for mechanisms such as output caching to improve the performance of a Web application.
System.XML	XML and XSL functionality, increasingly prevalent in Web applications, is found in this namespace. Support for XPath is also included.

The diagram on the next page presents a high-level view of potential e-Business application functionality mapped to the corresponding .NET Framework base class. We can use Figure 4.1 to locate the top-level namespaces that we need to program against when we have a specific e-Business requirement to meet.

One approach to proficiency with the .NET Framework classes is focusing on fluency with the namespaces listed above. We will probably use functionality provided by these major namespaces in nearly every .NET e-Business Web application that we build. Specialized functionality required by a specific application can then drive further exploration into the less frequently used namespaces. If we concentrate on these few namespaces and learn them inside and out, they should provide us with almost everything we need for building business applications on the Web.

Offering a single API for developers of all .NET languages is a big step forward. Previously, Visual C++ developers programmed directly against the Win32 API, against the ODBC API, and against MFC or ATL. Visual Basic developers had their own language-specific class library (VBRun), RDO and ADO for data access, and only occasionally programmed directly against the Win32 API, with some caveats. In the .NET world, no matter whether we program in the Managed Extensions for C++, Visual Basic .NET, Visual C# .NET, or even a third-party language such as COBOL .NET, we now only need to learn a single API. This is a significant and welcome shift in developing on the Microsoft platform. Programming against a single API will help facilitate better communication between teams working in different languages. Although syntactical implementation may differ across languages, the .NET Framework class library will now serve as a common point of reference.

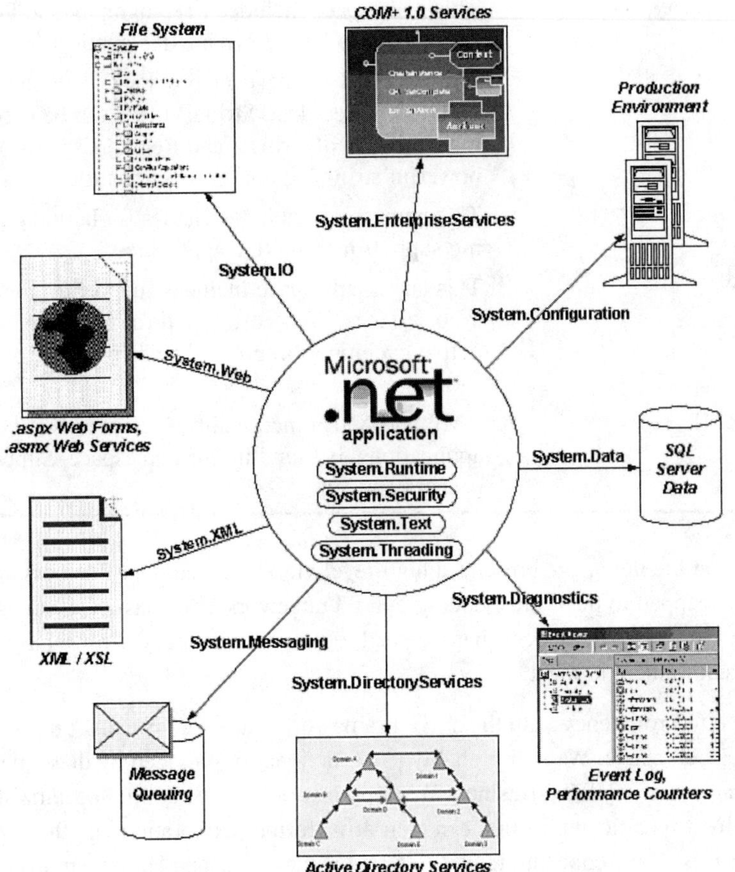

FIGURE 4.1

A graphical view of the main .NET e-Business namespaces.

When developers create the functionality custom to the application they are implementing, they categorize the various components in classes within an application-specific namespace. This allows clients to declare and use the application code in the same manner as the .NET Framework base classes are used. For example, in the gasTIX sample application, all classes providing business functionality specific to our application are implemented in a namespace we have called "gasTIX":

```
namespace gasTIX.Data
{
    using System;
    using System.Data;
    using System.Data.SQL;

public sealed class Category : DataAccess
    {
```

C++ and Visual Basic developers will now have much more in common than ever before, increasing the potential for knowledge sharing and for helping each other and the projects they are working on succeed. The contention between these two camps has often been acrimonious, and has sometimes undermined the success of projects because of language bias. It has long been time for these groups to work productively together, and .NET facilitates this important transition to mutual respect and co-productivity.

Common Language Runtime (CLR)

The CLR is at the heart of the .NET platform. The CLR is a run-time engine that compiles IL code into native machine-language code when a Web page or middle-tier method is invoked. It catches system exceptions, manages memory, and loads and unloads application code.

A major feature of the CLR is its "write once, run anywhere" execution model. Prior to being run by the CLR, the code we write in C# or VB .NET is compiled into Microsoft Intermediate Language, as shown in Figure 4.2. Better known as IL, this low-level language is roughly similar to assembly language.

When IL code is first executed on a target machine, it is compiled into native machine language code for that platform by an important component of the CLR, the .NET Just-In-Time (JIT) compiler. Figure 4.3 shows how code is JIT-compiled to native machine language for each method that is called, and is then cached for quick execution.

Microsoft may choose to release JIT compilers for platforms other than Windows. This will allow .NET code that we write in C# on a Windows 2000 machine to not only run on Windows 2000 Servers, but also on Linux boxes if a JIT compiler becomes available for that platform.

There is no longer a separate runtime for VB, C++, and C#. No matter in which language we choose to code, all source gets compiled to IL. Theoretically, the IL produced by the VB .NET compiler should be the same as what is produced by the C# compiler. (Microsoft comes close, but there still remain differences in the IL generated by the two compilers.) A single runtime is needed to JIT-compile and then execute the managed code, regardless of the language in which the code was initially written. Again, this should help facilitate communication by developers across languages, since they are all targeting the same runtime, the .NET CLR.

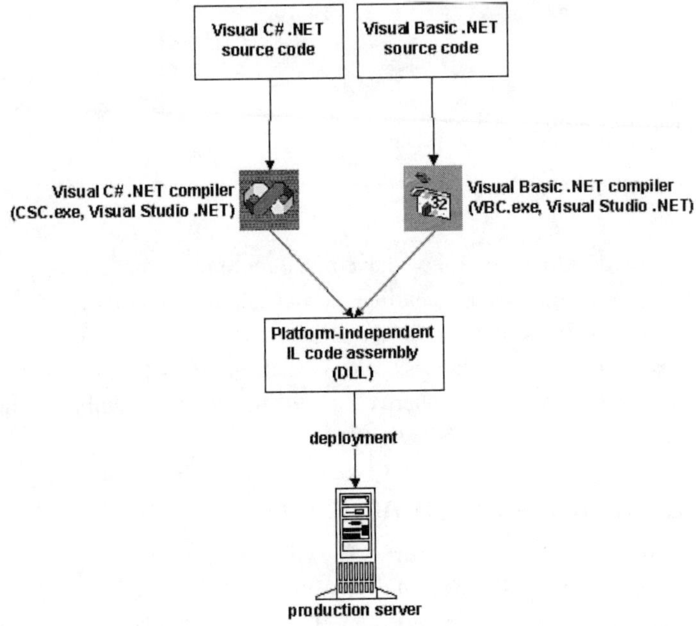

FIGURE 4.2
.NET compilation step 1, converting source code to IL.

> **NOTE**
>
> Unlike Java, there is no .NET virtual machine interpreting byte-code line-by-line. .NET IL code is always JIT-compiled by the CLR to the native machine language of the platform. Although Java JIT compilers exist for some platforms, Java code is normally executed as interpreted code by a virtual machine. Generally speaking, this should make the .NET execution environment faster than Java because .NET code runs in the platform's native machine language. However, the only .NET CLR currently available is for Windows, while a Java Virtual Machine exists for several platforms.

The CLR features automatic memory management, called Garbage Collection. The .NET runtime decides when to release object references based on usage patterns. No longer are developers explicitly required to release object references or free memory. This should mean improved application reliability because fewer memory leaks can occur. Tracking down memory leaks can be a long, arduous task, and having the CLR automatically manage this marks a big improvement in application reliability.

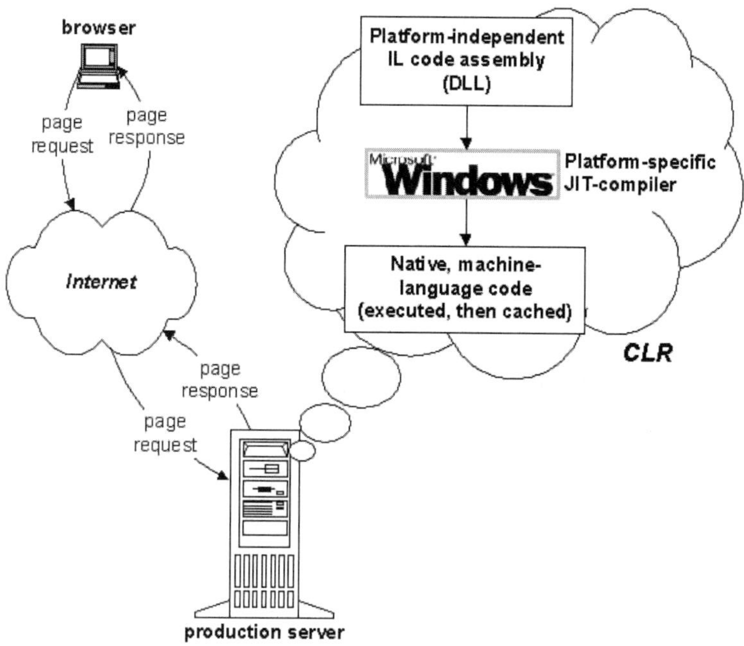

FIGURE 4.3
.NET compilation step 2, converting IL to native code.

> **CAUTION**
>
> Remember that only memory resources are automatically managed by the CLR. We must still explicitly release other resources such as file handles and database connections.

Common Type System (CTS) / Common Language Specification (CLS)

Another powerful architectural feature of the .NET platform is the CTS that all languages share. We are no longer forced to perform a special cast on a VB member when calling a method imported from a C++ class. All languages now share the same types, shown in Table 4.2 (although aliases to these base types may differ per language). The CTS enables the cross-language interoperability that is a major feature in .NET. As long as a language complies with the Common Language Specification (CLS), base types can be passed to and from objects written in that language without incompatibilities.

TABLE 4.2 The .NET base types, with VB .NET and C# aliases

Type Name	*Description*	*Visual Basic .NET Alias*	*Visual C# .NET Alias*
Byte	8-bit unsigned integer	Byte	byte
SByte	8-bit signed integer	*Not supported*	sbyte
Int16	16-bit signed integer	Short	short
Int32	32-bit signed integer	Integer	int
Int64	64-bit signed integer	Long	long
UInt16	16-bit unsigned integer	*Not supported*	ushort
UInt32	32-bit unsigned integer	*Not supported*	uint
UInt64	64-bit unsigned integer	*Not supported*	ulong
Single	single-precision (32-bit) floating-point number	Single	float
Double	double-precision (64-bit) floating-point number	Double	double
Char	Unicode character (a 16-bit character)	Char	char
String	immutable, fixed length string of Unicode characters	String	string
Decimal	12-byte decimal value	Decimal	decimal
Boolean	Boolean value (true or false)	Boolean	bool
DateTime	8-byte date and time value	Date	*no alias* (use DateTime)

Objects can also be inherited across languages because of the CTS and the CLS. This offers developers the powerful ability to implement in C# an inherited abstract base class written in VB .NET. This is because all types, even primitive types such as Boolean and Int32, inherit from the abstract base class System.Object. At a minimum, a certain amount of functionality, including `Equals( )`, `GetHashCode( )`, and `ToString( )`, is guaranteed to be supported by each and every type, whether built-in or custom-implemented.

Additionally, all variables are strongly-typed, meaning we define variables with an explicit type such as Integer, rather than as a Variant. In fact, the concept of Variant does not exist in .NET. Although we can still perform late binding when needed, the majority of time we will declare variables with an explicit type and reap the benefits of a strongly-typed system. This should help catch more errors at compile time, rather than having the user see them at run time. Unsafe type conversions and uninitialized variable assignments will not be allowed to compile. ASP programmers accustomed to declaring variables with only a Dim statement will now enjoy declaring variables specifically as Integer or String, catching any errors at compile time if an inappropriate value is assigned.

.NET languages adhering to the CLS share many additional features dealing with types, properties, and other class members. The CLS has been developed to ensure maximum language interoperability in the .NET Framework, a feature that will provide new options for programmers currently working with Microsoft technologies, and for programmers working in languages that previously could not execute on the Windows platform. COBOL programmers, for example, will now be able to extend their reach into new sectors and take advantage of the Internet when vendors for this language develop .NET CLS-compliant compilers.

CAUTION

Because .NET languages are required to meet only the minimum specifications set forth in the CLS, we should not expect non-CLS language features to be inheritable across language boundaries. A language that might inherit our class may not support the language-specific feature we implement (e.g. unsigned integers and operator overloading are valid in Visual C# .NET, but are not supported in Visual Basic .NET).

Metadata

Metadata, information that describes various characteristics of a piece of code, is widespread throughout the .NET Framework. Metadata is used by the CLR to locate and load classes, to allocate memory for type instances, to check security settings, and to compile IL code to native code. Metadata enables the richness of the .NET design, debugging, and profiling tools. Visual Studio .NET provides IntelliSense support, and the Intermediate Language Disassembler (ILDasm) offers graphical inspection capabilities via metadata, helping developers optimize productivity.

Metadata is compiled directly into an assembly and cannot become separated from the component that it describes. This is a big improvement over the COM metadata model, where type libraries (TLB files), Interface Definition Language (IDL) files, or a variety of other files were separate from the DLL components that they described. If a TLB file was deleted inadvertently from a developer's system, the developer would no longer get IntelliSense support for the component in Visual Studio. This situation cannot occur in .NET.

Metadata also enables a simpler development model called attribute-based programming. .NET classes and methods can be marked with various properties (attributes) which are stored as metadata. These attributes tell the CLR how to handle certain aspects of execution. Examples include SOAP-enabling a method with the `[WebMethod( )]` attribute, and marking the COM+

1.0 transaction requirements of a class with an attribute such as `[Transaction(TransactionOption.Required)]`. The following code listing, from the UpdateOrder class in the Business namespace, shows a few of the attributes used in gasTIX:

```
namespace gasTIX.Business
{
using System;
    using System.Data;
    using System.Runtime.InteropServices;
    using gasTIX;
    using gasTIX.Data;
    using System.EnterpriseServices;

        [
        ComVisible(true),
        Transaction(TransactionOption.RequiresNew),
        Guid("13DF3124-0995-464d-A0AE-1A965A51FF70")
    ]
    public class UpdateOrder : ServicedComponent
    {
      public UpdateOrder()
      {
        }

        [ AutoComplete ]
        public void Add(OrderData order)
        {
```

Attribute-based programming is another big improvement over the COM/DNA model, because attributes are compiled into the code. In DNA, even if a class was marked with "Transaction=Required," this could be overwritten by an administrator within the MTS Explorer. Faulty program execution could then occur because certain conditions might be encountered that the developer did not account for or intend.

Custom attributes can also be implemented in the .NET Framework. These special attributes can be whatever we want them to be, such as method and property documentation. Other developers that use the components into which we compile custom attributes discover them at runtime using the System.Reflection classes.

The .NET platform simplifies component versioning because of metadata. Problems with versioning were a continual source of frustration in the DNA environment, because although we weren't supposed to ever break an interface, it happened all the time.

Versioning is facilitated in .NET through a *major.minor.build.revision* numbering scheme at the assembly level. Built-in to the .NET CLR is a version-checking algorithm that will look to see if a compatible component exists.

```
//
// Version information for an assembly consists of the following four values:
//
//      Major Version
//      Minor Version
//      Revision
//      Build Number
//
// You can specify all the value or you can default the Revision and Build
Numbers
// by using the '*' as shown below:

[assembly: AssemblyVersion("2.1.4.*")]
```

If the major or minor number has changed, the component will be considered incompatible and will not be used. However, if the build or revision number has changed, but the major or minor numbers remain the same, the source is considered to be basically the same, and will be used. Windows DNA had no such version-checking scheme built-in.

When a shared assembly is installed into a machine's Global Assembly Cache (GAC), it will create a subdirectory for it with a unique name. This allows two versions of the same component, identically named, to be installed on a machine. Clients that are dependent on the first version can still use that version, while newer clients can take advantage of the new functionality in the second version.

TIP

Method overloading also helps improve versioning in .NET. Ever had a method that you wanted to add a new parameter to after it had been in use for a time? This occurs often, since requirements change and are further defined during a normal project lifecycle. In Windows DNA this meant breaking the interface, causing potential incompatibilities and errors. In .NET, simply add another method with a different parameter list. The runtime will determine which method to call based on the number and type of parameters. Old clients will not break, even though a new method signature has been added.

Deployment becomes simpler in .NET due to the prevalence of metadata. Since types are self-describing through their compiled-in metadata, there is no longer a need to register types or classes in the Registry. File locations are specified in the assembly manifest, and this metadata cannot become separated from the IL code it describes (whereas with COM, registry entries could be inadvertently deleted). See Chapter 16, "Deploying the Application," for more information on deployment in .NET.

TIP

Deploy assemblies as private whenever possible. Private assemblies live in the application folder and are not registered in the GAC. Assemblies should only be deployed as shared when they contain functionality that several applications will use. The CLR has to go through more work when resolving types within shared assemblies.

Remoting in the .NET Framework is also enabled through metadata. Remoting is the concept of instantiating a method on some object on a remote machine. The CLR uses the metadata of the type and method signature to allocate the proper amount of memory for the method call before it is serialized. For a detailed discussion of remoting concepts, see Chapter 13, ".NET Remoting."

Server Integration and Device Independence

Microsoft believes that XML and Web services, standardized in the SOAP protocol, will transform the way the Internet is used over the next few years. The ability to call functions on a server somewhere on the Internet is a powerful model (see Figure 4.4). Instead of designing, writing, and debugging a thorny tax calculation algorithm, we can now search a site such as `www.uddi.org` for a trusted authority that already provides such a calculation, callable through a SOAP Web Service. This lets us focus on what we do best (implement the business functionality custom to our application's needs), and lets others focus on what they do best (worry about things like thorny, ever-changing tax calculations).

Because Microsoft firmly believes in this evolving model, deep support for SOAP has been incorporated in the .NET platform. XML, XSD, XPath, XSL, and other standard protocols are all built into the platform and framework in various ways. A visual designer for XML and XSD schemas is built into Visual Studio .NET (see the Visual Studio .NET section later in this chapter). Integration with BizTalk Server 2000-generated schemas is simple, as BizTalk exports transformed XML documents. See Chapter 12, "Fulfillment," for detailed information on how BizTalk is integrated into the gasTIX site.

Providing support for the variety of client devices that might access our Web application is just as important as providing back-end integration with other servers. Ever spent long hours trying to get an HTML page to look and behave the same in both Internet Explorer and Netscape Navigator? Cross-browser compatibility has been a major headache ever since DHTML support in the browsers diverged with version 4. The designers of .NET have understood the significant cost to project budgets related to this issue, and have addressed it in the latest release of Active Server Pages (ASP) technology, known as ASP.NET. When constructing a page, a Web Form will read the HTTP_USER_AGENT header and determine what type of device is requesting a page. It will render JavaScript/DHTML to more intelligent browsers, and HTML 3.2 to "down-level" browsers (for more information, see Chapter 5, "Implementing .NET Presentation Services"). Because this type of cross-browser programming is now built into the framework, the life of the everyday Web developer will be made easier.

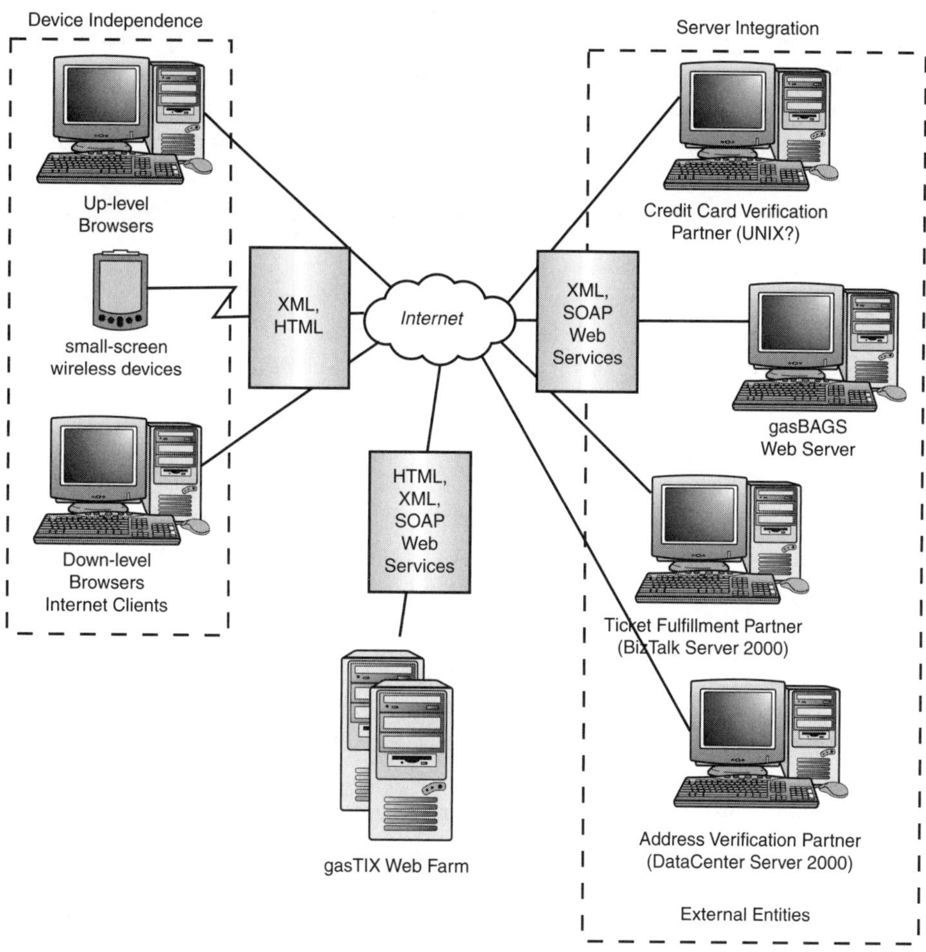

FIGURE 4.4
.NET facilitates server integration and device independence.

Part of the long-term vision for .NET is to provide the information a user might want on any device. Wireless device usage continues to grow rapidly, and Microsoft has released support for these devices and for the Wireless Markup Language (WML) in the .NET Mobile SDK. This technology will detect the type of mobile device requesting the page and render accordingly, similar to the intelligent rendering capability of ASP.NET. This enables our .NET applications to be accessible from "any device, any time," meeting part of the primary .NET vision.

During the design phase for a typical e-Business application, we should think about the functionality we want to offer to our end users in two very different ways. First, consider the normal Web browser client that will be accessing our application, probably at a resolution of 800×600 or higher. This implementation should be very rich and full-featured, offering the most powerful online experience. Next, consider how to present the application to mobile device users. We might port a lot of functionality to the mobile space, or perhaps a scaled-down subset of the application would be more appropriate. Because we need to design for small-screen wireless devices, we will likely end up providing users with a significantly different experience.

More and more people will soon be browsing our sites with Pocket IE or some other mobile browser, so any new application we develop should remember these users. .NET helps us target these users by providing a toolset that makes this aspect of Web development easier.

Security and Authentication

All platforms must incorporate strong security measures to obtain widespread adoption. Microsoft has learned this lesson, sometimes the hard way, over the course of the last few iterations of its Windows operating system and IIS Web server. .NET includes robust security features such as public key signing of .NET components, role-based security support, and run-time managed code verification checking.

Passport, Microsoft's identity technology that enables users to login to a variety of partner sites with a single ID and password, is fully integrated into the .NET Framework. Passport is a key strategy for Microsoft in offering software as a service (the Windows XP operating system even supports Passport as a login option). Because of its central role and importance to forthcoming technologies, we should strongly consider implementing Passport Single Sign-In (SSI) technology into our e-Business applications. This will set the stage for taking advantage of the services collectively known as "HailStorm."

HailStorm services will be hosted by Microsoft and will be accessed via Passport. Basic services such as `MyCalendar`, `MyInbox`, `MyLocations`, `MyNotifications`, and others will be included. Microsoft is committing large resources to stabilizing its data centers and security, hoping to convince a large number of users to allow their data to be hosted, furthering the conceptual shift to a service model from a model in which software is largely hosted locally.

Many computer users move from computer to computer several times during the day. Having data residing in the Internet "cloud," accessible from any machine (or even any wireless device), is a big usability win. No longer will we be forced to manually synchronize or update contacts and inboxes. These services will create new business opportunities for companies, and a more powerful experience for users. Passport is the key to this world, so investigate it further if you plan on integrating with these services in the future.

NOTE

Passport version 3.0 is the official .NET release that brings full integration with the .NET Framework base classes. HailStorm-enabled Web services should begin to emerge after the official HailStorm release sometime in calendar year 2002.

Performance and Scalability

Microsoft has continued to make great strides in improving the scalability and performance of its products. Many new features have been included in the ASP.NET release specifically aimed at improving Web application performance and scalability.

IIS session state provides developers with the ability to maintain information about a Web site user between page requests. It can now be utilized without scalability concerns, as session information for Web farms can be stored in a SQL Server or on a separate machine running an instance of the Session State service.

ASP.NET is now a compiled environment, unlike its predecessor, which was an interpreted scripting environment. Any code parsed line-by-line will implicitly be slower than the same code compiled, all other things being equal.

ASP.NET also includes output caching, a technology that allows frequently viewed pages that are more static in nature to be cached on the Web server for subsequent requests. This way, only the first user who requests a page will experience the full wait for page processing. Subsequent users will receive the page in the time it takes to push it over the wire. This mechanism is configurable, so parameters can be set on a page-by-page basis.

Because all .NET languages can be multi-threaded, any components written in .NET can take advantage of COM+ 1.0 object pooling. This is especially helpful for components that take a long time to initially load. Multi-threading itself greatly improves the performance of components.

Automatic error and overload detection to restart and manage applications and components is supported for ASP.NET applications. This is a powerful feature that will prevent many applications from locking up the server. Every 20 minutes or every 5000 page requests, a "preventive restart" is performed for each ASP.NET worker process. The cache is cleared and memory is released, preventing problems that can arise when applications run unchecked for hours on end.

.NET Architectural Tools Summary

The .NET Framework brings tremendous improvements in the ability to develop robust, enterprise-class solutions. A host of architectural features simplifies common Internet development tasks, ensures cross-language interoperability, and improves overall program execution. As a result, well-designed applications targeted for the .NET platform will be highly scalable, maintainable, reliable, and extensible. They will also interoperate well with other Internet applications, a feature designed into the platform from the beginning.

Now that the most important architectural characteristics of .NET have been examined, let's look at how the two primary .NET languages, Visual C# .NET and Visual Basic .NET, implement these concepts.

.NET Language Tools

Microsoft has introduced a new language called Visual C# .NET that has been designed specifically with the .NET Framework in mind. The popular Visual Basic 6.0 language has also been given a significant overhaul to comply with the .NET CLS. This section explores the major features of these two languages and provides some insights on which language to choose when beginning a project.

Visual C# .NET

Visual C# .NET is a new language that has been in development at Microsoft for several years. It is gaining wide acceptance at Microsoft; in fact, parts of ASP.NET and Visual Studio .NET are written in C#. The Visual C# .NET language was designed specifically to take full advantage of the .NET Framework. It is a component-based language by design, with support for methods, properties, and events. It also features full support for the Object-Oriented Programming (OOP) concepts of inheritance, polymorphism, and encapsulation.

C#, as its name implies, maintains many basic features of the C and C++ family of languages, but with a new beginning. It was indeed time to design a new language from the ground-up with OOP, the Internet, and components in mind. C# is the product of this new start. Internet features are available in C++, but largely as add-on features. Java is designed for the Internet, but XML and SOAP support is lacking. C# is now the most modern development language available, fully supporting the latest types of Internet applications.

The overwhelming number of C++ constructs and macros proved too high a barrier of entry for most new programmers. To remedy this, C# does away with the many anachronisms of the C++ language. It provides newer programmers with a much more concise, integrated toolset which still enables building robust, interoperating applications. The power of C# is provided by the .NET Framework base classes, rather than through a variety of different APIs as in C++. Novice developers will now be able to dive more quickly into a full-featured, modern language than ever before.

Java programmers will also be attracted to the C# programming language. Because Java is a C-style language, the syntax of C# will feel very familiar to Java developers. Interestingly enough, many Web developers who have programmed JavaScript for client-side validation in HTML pages will also feel at home in C# because JavaScript syntax is similar to C# syntax.

Visual Basic .NET

The latest incarnation of the popular Visual Basic programming language is called Visual Basic .NET. This is the most significant overhaul of VB to date. Support for OOP concepts such as inheritance, polymorphism, and encapsulation are included. This marks a very different way to think for VB programmers, and may present one of the biggest challenges for current VB developers in moving to this new version.

Multi-threading support is also included in VB .NET. In previous versions of Visual Basic, programmers could only write single-threaded programs, greatly limiting application performance. With multi-threading support, Visual Basic applications can now perform on a par with lower-level languages such as C++. This is another new way to think for VB developers—new concepts such as threading synchronization must be mastered.

Structured exception handling is another new feature of Visual Basic .NET. Clumsy VB `On Error Goto` syntax is replaced with the more logical `try...catch...finally` syntax. Method overloading now enables developers to call different implementations of the same method name by passing different parameters.

Type safety is a welcome feature of Visual Basic .NET. In VB 6.0, undesired type conversions would sometimes occur when the programmer did not intend it. With the introduction of the Option Strict directive in VB .NET, these types of errors cannot occur, and will be caught at compile time.

With all these new features, Visual Basic .NET offers more power and flexibility than ever before to its loyal legion of followers.

Language Choice

A great debate is currently raging over which .NET language to use on future development projects: Visual C# .NET or Visual Basic .NET. This is an important question, but it does not have easy answers.

The decision of which language to use should be the result of carefully weighing development staff strengths and weaknesses, along with current market trends. It is still too early in the life cycle of these languages, and the .NET platform in general, to reach a substantive conclusion about which of these two languages will dominate in the marketplace. However, the following thoughts provide insights which may help with this decision.

Although the languages are named after C/C++ and Visual Basic, neither Visual C# .NET nor Visual Basic .NET bears much resemblance to its predecessors. C# bears more resemblance to Java than it does to C or C++. VB .NET has changed so much (primarily in order to support OOP concepts) that it requires a significant shift in mindset for current Visual Basic programmers to make the transition. If VB programmers make the assumption that VB .NET programs should be implemented similar to Visual Basic 6.0 programs, they will make serious programming errors.

Part of the popularity of Visual Basic 6.0 is its simplicity. Business managers have been able to put together simple applications to meet their needs with little or no help from IT departments. Taking advantage of the significant strides made with the release of VB .NET will require a fairly significant learning curve. It is not certain that the business managers who used VB 6.0 so successfully will be able to use VB .NET in a similar fashion.

There is a substantial base of VB programmers that need an upgrade path into the .NET world. Conservative estimates state that there are over three million Visual Basic programmers today. If a significant part of the VB world moves to VB .NET, there will be a large base of support for VB .NET programming, regardless of its stature as a language.

Microsoft has used Visual C# .NET as their programming language of choice for constructing parts of the .NET infrastructure. The C# compiler is likely better optimized because of the heavy focus on this new language at Microsoft. However, consider that C and C++ were used to write most of the existing Windows infrastructure and programs, yet VB became the language of choice for business applications, not C or C++. Widespread acceptance at Redmond, however, makes the future of the C# language more certain.

There are a few advanced functions in C# that are not available in VB .NET. Operator overloading, unsigned integers, and XML documentation support are a few of the more notable. Although these features may be released in a future version of VB .NET, they are three examples of functionality that C# provides today that VB .NET does not.

TIP

Regardless of the language in which we decide to implement our .NET applications, becoming a *.NET developer* should be our goal. A ".NET developer" will focus heavily on mastering the .NET Framework base classes, and will thus be able to jump from Visual Basic .NET to Visual C# .NET and back with little difficulty. Much of the challenge in coming up to speed on .NET is learning how to effectively apply the wide variety of functionality found in the base classes. Proficiency with the .NET platform as a whole is often times more valuable to companies and projects than focusing deeply on a single .NET language.

Other Languages

Although this chapter has dealt only with Visual Basic .NET and Visual C# .NET, Microsoft has also released an update to its Visual C++ and JScript languages.

The Managed Extensions for C++ enables C++ developers to target applications for the .NET Framework, and to call into unmanaged, "unsafe" C++ code when pointers and other constructs not allowed by the CLS are needed. JScript is now a compiled language, with support for OOP. Although these two languages are not garnering a great amount of interest from the development community at large, they will continue to have their loyal devotees, and Microsoft is committed to them in the near future.

Compilers for other languages adhering to the CLS will soon be released, enabling a large variety of languages to run on the .NET platform. Developers skilled in Ada, APL, COBOL, Fortran, Pascal, Perl, Python, SmallTalk, and several other languages will now be able to market solutions for the .NET platform. They will get a new lease on life by having the power of the .NET Framework at their fingertips, as far as their respective compilers include support for .NET platform constructs.

Microsoft's upgrade path to .NET for current Visual J++ and Java developers is called the Java Upgrade Migration Plan (JUMP). The J++ language will not be upgraded to .NET largely because of the litigation over the past few years between Microsoft and Sun, and because the combination of C# and .NET offers a viable alternative. Microsoft will continue to support J++ 6.0, so any solutions based on this language will have Microsoft's support for now. However, the future of this language is uncertain, and it is quite likely that Microsoft will not release additional upgrades. Any J++ applications should probably be ported to C# and .NET if business requirements warrant new functionality, or if the application must live for several more years. (See `msdn.microsoft.com/visualj/jump/default.asp` for more details on the JUMP initiative.)

.NET Language Tools Summary

Both Visual C# .NET and Visual Basic .NET provide developers with the most modern programming constructs, including support for component and object-oriented programming. These languages enable developers to take advantage of the vast amount of functionality found in the .NET Framework base classes.

Choosing a .NET language in which to work can be difficult, and depends on many factors. Mastering the .NET Framework base classes should be the primary goal of any computer professional desiring to participate in the burgeoning .NET world. The language chosen to implement the underlying constructs does not hold the same importance as it once did because all languages now sit on top of the same API and CLR.

.NET Developer Productivity Tools

The Visual Studio .NET development suite and other important utilities such as the .NET disassembler ILDasm bring great productivity gains for developers. This section will explore the new features of Visual Studio, along with several other important .NET tools.

Visual Studio .NET

Microsoft has significantly reworked the Visual Studio development environment. It features a single IDE for all languages, support for debugging across language boundaries, Web services support, XML/XSD visual design tools, and a host of other usability enhancements.

Single IDE

The .NET release of the Visual Studio product suite finally realizes the vision of an all-encompassing IDE. Microsoft's single IDE is enabled by the cross-language features of the .NET Framework such as the CLR and the CLS. Whether we program in Visual C# .NET, Visual Basic .NET, or Managed Extensions for C++, we will use Visual Studio .NET as our main development environment.

Having just one IDE to work with is a great productivity gain for developers. In past incarnations of Visual Studio, each language came with its own IDE, with different function keys, menu bars, and various quirks. Switching back and forth between Visual Basic 6.0, Visual C++ 6.0, and Visual InterDev was challenging, especially for programmers new to the Microsoft world. It was hard enough trying to master a language without having another IDE to learn—this just added another layer of unneeded complexity.

In order to maximize existing knowledge and skills, we can still choose to use the keyboard scheme or window layout based on prior language experience. If you're a Visual Basic developer, the IDE can be configured to respond to familiar VB function keys and to arrange windows similar to VB 6.0. As shown in Figure 4.5, these options are configured the first time Visual Studio .NET is started, on the My Profile section of the VS Home Page:

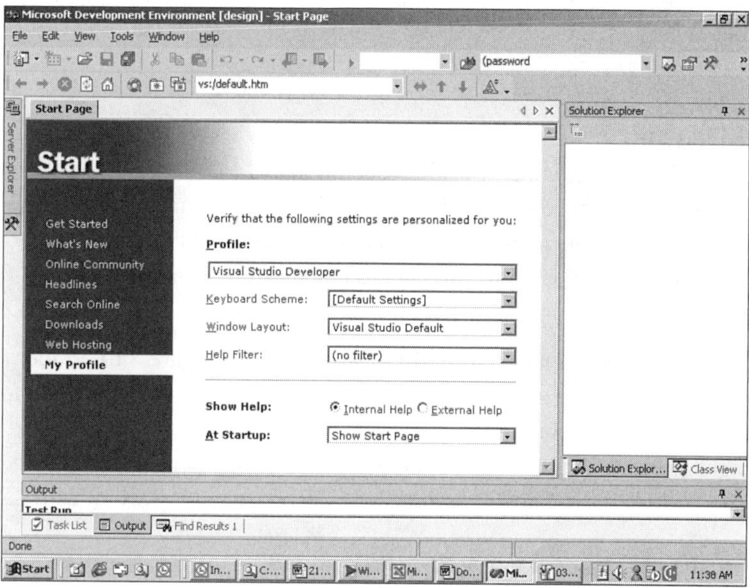

FIGURE 4.5

The Visual Studio .NET Start page enables customization of the IDE.

The Visual Studio Start page contains many other helpful sections, including a link to Microsoft's online developer support area, MSDN. Headlines are retrieved across the Internet from MSDN, enabling the developer to keep current with the latest patches, techniques, and tips. This integration is an effective way to encourage developers to access the thousands of technical documents on MSDN, helping them grow their skills and add value to projects.

Cross-Language Debugging

Having all languages in a single IDE enables another important feature of Visual Studio .NET: cross-language debugging. It is now possible to step from Visual C# .NET code into Visual Basic .NET code, or into any other CLS-compliant language. This powerful debugging capability should help programmers find and correct bugs in less time than ever before.

We also now have the capability to step into SQL Server stored procedures from within the Visual Studio .NET IDE. This enhancement makes tracking down tricky stored procedures bugs quicker. A breakpoint must be set within the stored procedure that you want to debug in order to stop application execution.

NOTE

According to the .NET documentation, the integrated stored procedure debugging feature only works with the ODBC adapter.

Improved Usability

The Visual Studio .NET environment, while based on Visual InterDev 6.0, has been revamped and enhanced with respect to general usability. Fly-in windows (such as the Toolbox and Server Explorer) help keep the majority of screen real estate available for the code window. Once we drag and drop a tool from the Toolbox onto our Web form, the Toolbox "flies" back to the left-hand side.

Another user interface enhancement is multi-tab windows (see Figure 4.6). Rather than seeing just the open window, as in Visual Basic 6.0, multiple tabs now appear across the top of the Visual Studio .NET window, similar to worksheets in Microsoft Excel. This is a convenient method to quickly be reminded of what windows are currently open. It also provides an easy way to navigate back and forth among several code or form windows we're working with.

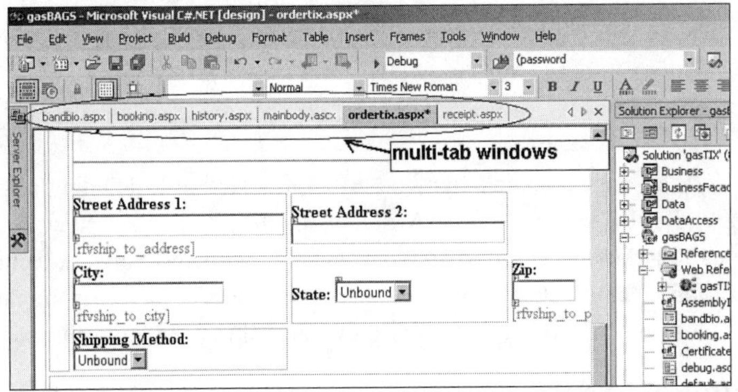

FIGURE 4.6

The Visual Studio .NET environment features multi-tab windows.

A feature that will especially benefit newer developers is Dynamic Help. Although this feature causes some slow-down in performance, it is worth the penalty, especially when learning the Visual Studio .NET IDE or the .NET Framework. Note how in Figure 4.7, the keyword `Protected` has been highlighted. Dynamic Help searches its database for entries related to this keyword and displays matches in the Dynamic Help window at the right.

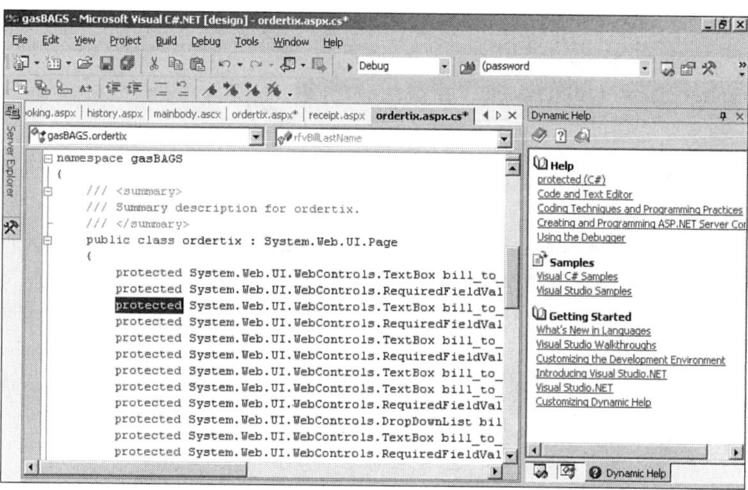

FIGURE 4.7
Dynamic Help in Visual Studio .NET especially helps programmers new to the .NET Framework.

The Visual Studio .NET Server Explorer, shown in Figure 4.8, contains any and all parts of a server against which code can be written. Message queues, performance counters, event logs, and many other components all live within the Server Explorer.

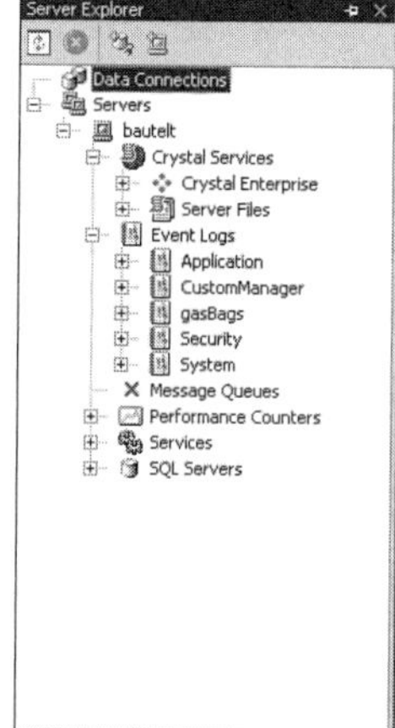

FIGURE 4.8
VS .NET Server Explorer enables "Rapid Application Development (RAD) for the Server."

A component in the Server Explorer can be dragged and dropped onto a Web form, double-clicked, and programmed against. This is a feature that Microsoft calls "RAD for the Server." It provides programmers with a quick, visual method for incorporating non-visual components into applications.

The Task List is another helpful window that makes the overall development process in Visual Studio .NET more robust. Not only does this window display all compile-time errors, but it will also display any TO DO items that we mark in our code. This provides us with a quick way to mark sections of code that we want to revisit later.

With the prevalence of XML in the .NET platform, Microsoft has introduced new visual design tools to support XML. The XML and XSD visual designers, shown in Figure 4.9, allow programmers who are not experts in XML syntax to generate robust schemas and files by using familiar visual tools, similar to database design tools.

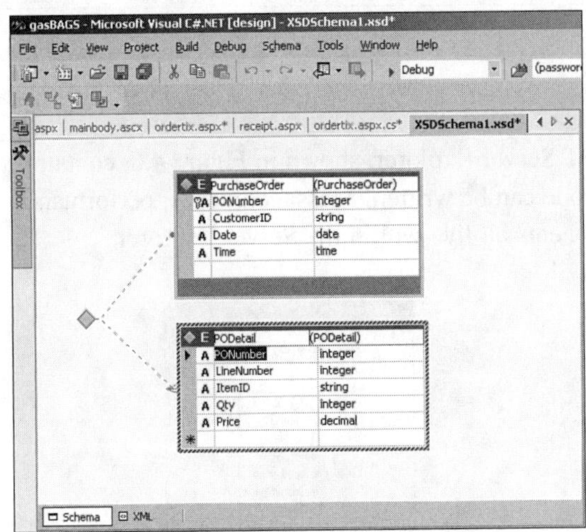

FIGURE 4.9
The VS .NET XSD schema designer offers a way to visually create schemas.

IntelliSense, the statement auto-completion feature that we often wonder how we ever programmed without, is improved in Visual Studio .NET. VS .NET gives auto-complete functionality when writing XML files, generated by reading the accompanying XSD schema. IntelliSense is also supported for HTML statement completion.

Web services Support

The SOAP protocol is strongly supported in the Visual Studio .NET environment. Visual Studio .NET includes productivity features that keep developers from having to know the intimate details of the underlying infrastructure of any SOAP calls. This is achieved by adding a Web reference to the Solution Explorer, similar to how a reference to a library or namespace located on the local machine is added. The difference is that the SOAP call will likely be going over the Internet, but the enabling infrastructure is abstracted from the developer.

After right-clicking on the Solution and selecting Add Web Reference…, a dialog box such as the one in Figure 4.10 is displayed. This screen allows the developer to browse to the Web Service on the Internet, or to search for a type of service through UDDI.

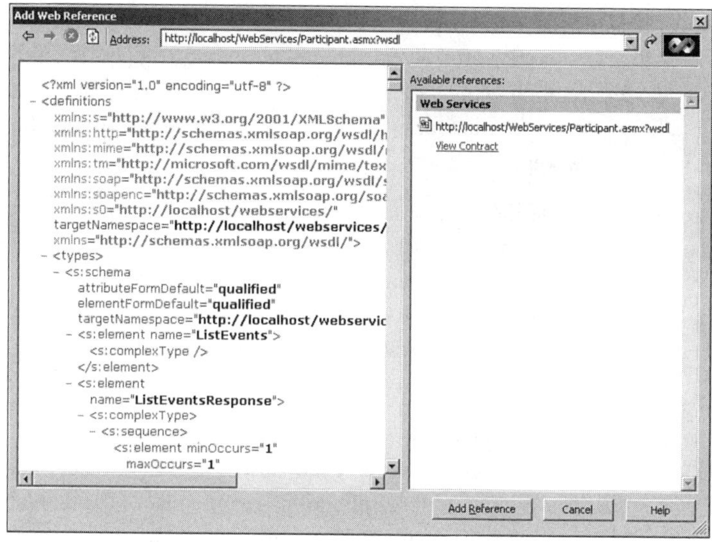

FIGURE 4.10
Adding a Web Reference in Visual Studio .NET is easy.

The developer can view a Web Service's SDL contract to get more detailed information about the service. When the correct Web Service has been located, the developer picks it, and the Web Service is included within the Visual Studio .NET solution. The SOAP contract is downloaded to the local machine for IntelliSense support. This allows the developer to use IntelliSense help even for methods called over the Internet.

The new Web services programming model is a significant shift in mindset for many developers, but it holds great promise for driving the creation of an entirely new generation of applications. Visual Studio .NET abstracts enough of the SOAP protocol plumbing to make it easy for developers to begin writing and consuming Web services. Microsoft believes that tools like those found in VS .NET will begin driving widespread acceptance of Web services in the industry.

Application Lifecycle Tools

Modeling, design, testing, and source-code control tools are all tightly integrated into the Enterprise edition of Visual Studio .NET. Having a toolset at our disposal within the VS .NET environment that covers the entire software development lifecycle from start to finish is a big win for our project teams. No longer is the Visual Studio development environment simply a set of programming languages. It has evolved to become a toolset that supports the analysis, design, development, testing, and deployment phases of the software development lifecycle.

Visual Studio .NET includes tools for the industry-standard Unified Modeling Language (UML) for application modeling. Support is included for use cases, sequence diagrams, activity diagrams, class diagrams, and more. The VS .NET modeling tool builds on the previous version of Visual Modeler, which was itself a subset of the popular Rational Rose product. UML modeling is helpful for communicating application requirements and architecture across project teams through visual representations of various system components.

In addition to support for modeling application code, database modeling tools are also included in VS .NET. The Database Designer provides the developer with the ability to add new tables, columns, relationships, and more, all within the VS .NET IDE. Query Designer provides an Access-like way of visually generating SQL queries with drag and drop. The Script Editor provides keyword color-coding when working with triggers and stored procedures.

When an application has reached the appropriate development stage, it can be tested within the VS .NET IDE with Application Center Test (ACT, formerly known as Web Application Stress Tool, or Homer). This tool places a heavy load on the various XML Web services and HTML/ASPX Web pages that comprise the application. Test pages for XML Web services are generated automatically by the Visual Studio .NET environment, and these pages can be included in automated ACT stress-tests. This tool helps testers track down potential bottlenecks before the application is ever deployed. Developers can then attack each bottleneck until test performance metrics meet the specified business requirements.

Applications can be tested at a lower level using Visual Studio Analyzer. This tool tracks interactions between objects, threads, and the various application tiers. Results are presented in an easy-to-use graphical format.

Throughout the life of a project, application documents and code must be protected from inadvertent changes, and from multiple programmers unknowingly working on the same piece of code at the same time. Visual SourceSafe (VSS) is Microsoft's tool for solving these problems. The .NET release of VSS brings a tighter integration with the Visual Studio .NET environment for ease of use.

The Visual Studio .NET environment also includes support for deploying a .NET application after it has been developed and tested. See Chapter 16, "Deploying the Application," for an in-depth look at the deployment features of VS .NET.

Enterprise Features

Microsoft continues to strive to meet the needs of enterprise-class development projects. Companies with sizable development projects and staff often wish to standardize application architecture across many different projects. With Visual Studio .NET, senior developers and technical architects can now develop baseline application architectures. Templates established by these more experienced team members can then be used as starting points by team members. This is much more effective than each developer starting with a blank slate and coming up with his own design.

Senior developers and technical leads can also define Visual Studio .NET policies that dictate whether certain menu items or components appear in a developer's VS .NET IDE. These policies are defined through an XML meta-language called the Template Description Language (TDL). For example, seeing only the relevant components on a toolbar, rather than having to choose from every component available out-of-the-box, helps developers implement forms that are consistent with the policy laid out by those responsible for delivery.

Support for Architectural Templates and Policy Definition within Visual Studio .NET helps senior architects share their knowledge more effectively with team members. This will enable better application integrity and will help ensure consistency across the work of all the developers on a project or across an enterprise.

ILDasm

The IL Disassembler, or ILDasm, is a utility used for looking at the inner workings of assemblies. It is located in the `C:\Program Files\Microsoft.NET\FrameworkSDK\Bin` folder. Such a detailed view of an assembly is possible because of the prevalence of metadata compiled into every assembly. The metadata describes everything about an assembly: its types, its version number, its cultural locale, etc.

We might want to view the inner workings of an assembly to determine why a program is behaving like it is, or to help us find out about all the functionality that is implemented. As shown in Figure 4.11, the parts of an assembly that ILDasm will display include namespaces, classes, interfaces, methods, events, properties, and more.

By double-clicking on a member of a type, we can view the IL code that defines the inner workings of the member. A sample detail view of a DataSet member function is shown in Figure 4.12.

ILDasm is useful for figuring out how the underlying .NET Framework behaves, and provides a means of going "deep" into the detailed implementation when needed.

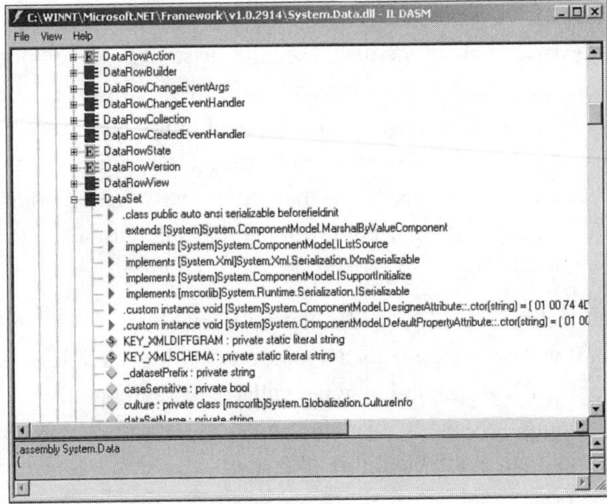

FIGURE 4.11
The ILDasm utility offers an inside look into assemblies.

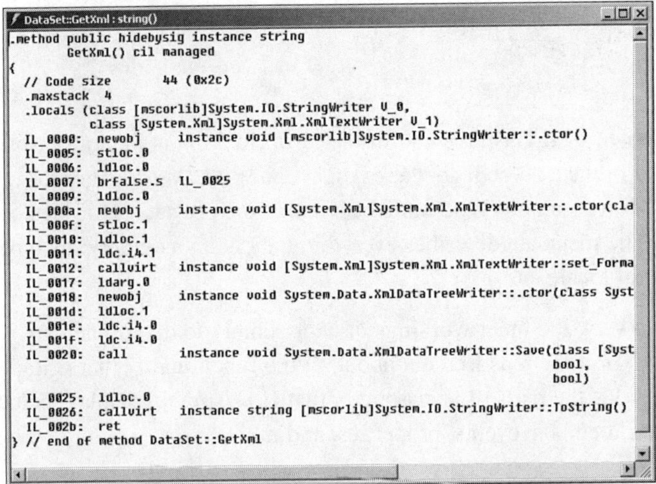

FIGURE 4.12
Double-clicking a type member displays the supporting IL code.

Command Line Compilers

Included with both Visual C# .NET and Visual Basic .NET is a command-line compiler. This allows us to write code outside of the Visual Studio .NET environment with the editor of our choice. This is also helpful for administrators who use build scripts to pull the latest code from VSS and compile it on a regular basis.

CAUTION

Work outside of the Visual Studio .NET IDE at your own peril. The productivity gains that VS.NET provides for us are exceptional. Creating typed datasets, programming against Web references, and calling other functions that require plumbing work "behind the scenes" is made simple in the graphical IDE of VS .NET.

The Visual Basic .NET compiler is VBC.exe and the Visual C# .NET compiler is CSC.exe. Both compilers provide a variety of switches that control compilation options, as shown in Figure 4.13.

```
C:\WINNT\System32\cmd.exe
C:\WINNT\Microsoft.NET\Framework\v1.0.2914>csc /?
Microsoft (R) Visual C# Compiler Version 7.00.9254 [CLR version v1.0.2914]
Copyright (C) Microsoft Corp 2000-2001. All rights reserved.

                      Visual C# Compiler Options

                        - OUTPUT FILES -
/out:<file>             Output file name (derived from first source file if not
                        specified)
/target:exe             Build a console executable (default) (Short form:
                        /t:exe)
/target:winexe          Build a windows executable (Short form: /t:winexe)
/target:library         Build a library (Short form: /t:library)
/target:module          Build a module that can be added to another assembly
                        (Short form: /t:module)
/define:<symbol list>   Define conditional compilation symbol(s) (Short form:
                        /d)
/doc:<file>             XML Documentation file to generate

                        - INPUT FILES -
/recurse:<wildcard>     Include all files in the current directory and
                        subdirectories according to the wildcard specifications
/reference:<file list>  Reference metadata from the specified assembly files
                        (Short form: /r)
/addmodule:<file list>  Link the specified modules into this assembly

                        - RESOURCES -
/win32res:<file>        Specifies Win32 resource file (.res)
/win32icon:<file>       Use this icon for the output
/resource:<resinfo>     Embeds the specified resource (Short form: /res)
/linkresource:<resinfo> Links the specified resource to this assembly (Short
                        form: /linkres)

                        - CODE GENERATION -
/debug[+|-]             Emit debugging information
/debug:{full|pdbonly}   Specify debugging type ('full' is default, and enables
                        attaching a debugger to a running program)
/optimize[+|-]          Enable optimizations (Short form: /o)
/incremental[+|-]       Enable incremental compilation (Short form: /incr)

                        - ERRORS AND WARNINGS -
/warnaserror[+|-]       Treat warnings as errors
```

FIGURE 4.13
The language compilers offer a variety of compilation options.

.NET Developer Productivity Tools Summary

Visual Studio .NET finally realizes the long-awaited vision of a single IDE for all Microsoft development languages. This will bring more synergy to programming teams and will allow developers to move more easily between languages. Visual Studio .NET brings a host of other productivity features that make it the premier development environment for building distributed e-Business applications on the market today. In addition to using Visual Studio .NET, developers should also become familiar with the ILDasm tool. This utility can help drive a deeper understanding of the way the .NET Framework is designed and implemented.

From Here

The new .NET platform is the end result of a tremendous effort by Microsoft. The company believes that the Internet is poised to evolve into a new generation of applications and services, interconnecting data on levels previously not possible. .NET is designed from the ground up with this model of large-scale data integration and sharing in mind.

Because of its powerful architectural foundation, robust language implementations, and developer productivity tools, the .NET platform and toolset is poised to deliver the enterprise-class performance and extensibility that will enable Microsoft e-Business solutions to play in the space once reserved for larger-scale Unix and AS/400 systems. This chapter has introduced the .NET architecture and tools. Read on to learn more about designing each of the three logical tiers in .NET, presentation, business, and data.

Implementing .NET Presentation Services

by David Burgett

CHAPTER

5

IN THIS CHAPTER

- Why Should Developers Switch to ASP.NET? 125
- The Page Object 128
- What Are Web Controls? 130
- Advanced Features of Web Controls 145
- From Here 154

The presentation layer of the gasTIX Web site is implemented using ASP.NET pages written with Visual Basic .NET. The use of ASP.NET offers the following benefits over classic ASP during development: much shorter development time, separation of design and code, better encapsulation and reusability, and much easier maintenance. This chapter examines the major features of ASP.NET with particular focus on how those features were leveraged in the gasTIX Web site.

When Microsoft first introduced Active Server Pages (ASP) in 1997, developers were suddenly able to dynamically publish information to the Web and customize Web pages very easily while using their existing Visual Basic skills. Visual Basic had already gained a large following, so this advancement made dynamic Web development instantly available to a very large group of developers. ASP boasted very easy development, an interpreted script language, and the ability to interact cleanly with standard HTML files. All of those features were great in 1997 since only a small percentage of companies had dynamic Web sites and fewer ones trusted the Internet to handle their core business functionality. With the success of ASP, this philosophy began to change.

ASP quickly became the de facto standard for adding personalization to Web sites, publishing data, and displaying continuously updated information across Intranets. However, even as Microsoft was enjoying a great response to the first version of ASP, their developers had already recognized that the vision of the Internet was changing and they were already hard at work on the next evolution of the technology, ASP.NET.

In the last few years, we have seen the Internet explode from a public novelty to a fundamental business component. As bandwidth and security have increased, more and more companies are placing their business processes on the Web while hundreds of new companies have emerged whose entire business depends on the Web for its existence. Transactions written in XML and transferred through the Internet are rapidly becoming the core of business-to-business communication. As companies place more of their business on the Web, they need increasingly more robust, more streamline solutions that can handle the increased volume. ASP.NET meets these requirements while offering many other new features.

ASP.NET is a radical change from previous versions of ASP. It is much more than simply an upgrade. In fact, some previously developed ASP applications and pages will not be easily upgraded to ASP.NET. This marks a significant departure from past ASP upgrades and will no doubt anger some ASP developers. Microsoft did not, however, make this decision lightly. In designing ASP.NET, Microsoft realized that the benefits easily outweigh the problems associated with limited backwards compatibility. It was a small price to pay, but one which will be praised in the long run. The rest of this chapter is devoted to demonstrating the overwhelming benefits of ASP.NET and demonstrating why developers will want to make the switch.

Why Should Developers Switch to ASP.NET?

Classic ASP code suffers from all the symptoms of non-object-oriented programming. They are: poor reusability, increased difficulty when using a distributed development team, and increased maintenance challenges. These problems are actually worse in ASP than other non-object-oriented languages, since ASP inherently mixes two different development languages into a single code base. By mixing HTML design code with ASP scripting code (whether it be VBScript, JScript, or another language), the resulting page is much more difficult to read and maintain. Additionally, classic ASP code becomes tied to the design making it easier to break and more difficult to reuse in other pages. This problem is often referred to as "spaghetti code," in that the lines of code are intertwined amongst one another like a mound of spaghetti, with no discernible beginning or end to any strand.

While there are techniques for overcoming many of the non-object-oriented problems associated with classic ASP, none of them are part of the technology itself. It is possible to use COM controls, for instance, to improve encapsulation and reusability. However, the COM control cannot be written in the same VBScript that the page is written in. It is written against a different object model, and requires different development skills to produce. ASP.NET improves upon this by integrating all of the solutions into a single development package.

Classic ASP also suffers from many of the problems inherent in immature languages, such as limited functionality and poor performance. Since the default language for classic ASP is VBScript, which is a subset of the Visual Basic language, developers have often complained about the limited functionality available to ASP pages. Developers familiar with the full Visual Basic language or other application-level languages, such as C or C++, have found it difficult to work within the limits of VBScript. The power of VBScript was enhanced with the ability to run COM controls, but this power came at the expense of having to code and maintain multiple languages.

In addition to the limited functionality, VBScript incurs serious performance penalties due to its interpreted nature. Every line of code must be parsed and interpreted each time a page is requested. This has severely limited the ability of classic ASP pages to scale to the level of an enterprise application.

ASP.NET addresses each of these issues through a variety of evolutions of the object model, underlying languages, and deployment infrastructure. First, the ASP object model has been completely rewritten in order to gain the benefits of object orientation. This results in a complete change in the way that ASP pages are written. ASP.NET pages now separate the scripting code from the design code, allowing developers to write code and designers to design the pages. This minimizes the amount of design work that developers need to do and the amount of ASP knowledge that designers must have, allowing each group to focus on what they do best.

gasTIX is an excellent example of this separation of code and design. A team of designers created the HTML code using server-side ASP controls (explained later in this chapter) using a pre-determined naming scheme. The developers then wrote the code for their respective pages in a separate file, referencing the named controls. This allowed the designers and developers to be located in geographically different locations without impacting either's work. This separation resulted in the developer never having to see where the controls were on the page, while the designers never had to see the developer's code. They were able to working completely independent of each other.

To improve on the performance of classic ASP pages, ASP.NET is now fully compiled. All of the code in an ASP.NET Web page is compiled into a single .DLL that, by default, resides in the "bin" sub-directory in the root Web directory. By compiling code into a .DLL and storing it in memory, ASP.NET executes pages very quickly and eliminates much of the overhead associated with the executing multiple pages. This offers significant performance gains over classic ASP, which simply interprets each page upon demand, which includes interpreting the same page many times.

One of the benefits of interpreted languages over compiled languages is the ability to just drop new code into place and run it immediately. ASP.NET features this benefit despite being a compiled language. ASP.NET allows the developer to define where the project .DLL is to be placed and update that .DLL by simply dropping a new version on top of the old one. It is no longer necessary to manually register a .DLL using regsvr32; the system automatically registers .DLL's upon demand. The first time an ASP.NET page uses the new .DLL, the system will register the .DLL for future use. This incurs a significant performance penalty the first time a page is run, but allows future calls to the .DLL to be run with the best possible performance.

TIP

Always test your ASP.NET application after each compilation. Not only is this good development practice, but it will also ensure that you experience the time-consuming .DLL registration period, saving your users the frustration of waiting for the page to run the first time.

The limited functionality problem in classic ASP has been alleviated in ASP.NET through two new features. These are new features in the general .NET platform and new features in how the ASP.NET uses .NET compiled code. The .NET platform now allows all .NET languages to be compiled for the Common Language Runtime (CLR). This means that whether you write your code in VB .NET, C#, or any one of the other thirty third-party .NET languages, your code will be compiled for the same CLR. This feature, coupled with ASP.NET's ability to use any CLR compiled code, means that developers are now free to write their ASP.NET pages in any .NET language they're comfortable with. Additionally, different pages within a single ASP.NET pages can be written in different .NET languages, allowing easier team development.

Since ASP.NET pages now fully support the developer's favorite language, whatever it might be, ASP applications are now only limited by the functionality of the chosen language. ASP applications can now make Windows API calls, control multiple system threads, and do many other language features that, in the past, have been reserved for application development.

Since the gasTIX presentation layer was developed in Visual Basic .NET, all code examples in this chapter will use Visual Basic .NET. Since ASP.NET supports the CLR, these examples can be easily ported to C# or any other .NET language.

There are many other features of ASP.NET that should motivate serious developers into considering making the switch. For instance, ASP.NET supports classic ASP pages as well, allowing class ASP pages to be executed side by side with ASP.NET pages. ASP.NET pages use the file extension ".aspx" instead of the classic ".asp". This allows the IIS Web server to differentiate between ASP and ASP.NET pages and execute the appropriate code. These pages can call one another and pass data through query strings, though they cannot share information in state management objects due to ASP.NET's vastly improved state management features.

NOTE

It might be unclear at this point how ASP.NET manages .aspx pages and compiled ASP.NET code. Each ASP.NET Web form has one .aspx page and one code-behind class. All of the code-behind classes in a project are compiled into a single .DLL, which is used when any of the .aspx pages are requested. This allows ASP.NET to keep all of the application code compiled and waiting in cache, while maintaining separate .aspx pages.

Another feature of ASP.NET is the ability to expose and consume Web services. A *Web service* is basically an object method call that is exposed through the Inter/intranet for consumption by other applications or services. This service is exposed through a group of standard technologies such as XML and UDDI. This allows users to locate the service and learn about its definition. The service is likewise used, or consumed, using the same standards. This greatly increases the encapsulation and reusability of components and allows a distributed team of developers to create a single system. See Chapter 11, "Puchasing a Ticket," for more information on publishing and consuming Web Services.

All of the .NET languages offer enhanced support for XML. XML is a maturing language and has been accepted by many major companies as an information exchange standard. gasTIX makes use of this native XML support by passing all event, venue, and participant data between tiers in XML format. Using a single, standard way of representing data makes it very easy for the presentation service layer to understand the format of the data offered by all of the business objects. There is no need for the presentation tier to understand a separate data object model since it already understands XML natively. This greatly simplifies the presentation layer and makes it easier to expose the same data through other interfaces, such as Web services. See Chapter 11 "Purchasing A Ticket" for an example of how the presentation layer uses XML provided by the business layer.

The Page Object

All ASP.NET Web pages are full-fledged derivatives of the page class. This ensures that all ASP.NET pages have the have the same basic properties, methods, and events. Complete integration of ASP.NET development with a clearly-defined object model is an integral part of the development platform and offers short design cycles, improved reusability, and easier maintenance.

When a developer creates a new ASP.NET Web page, the .aspx page is compiled into an object derived from the Web form class. This ensures that all ASP.NET pages adhere to the object model while allowing the flexibility for developers to derive their own classes from the page class. This makes it easy for developers to create their own custom page classes for easy re-use. Custom page classes may define standard colors, include default controls, etc.

Since the .aspx file is a simple text file and not an actual class, the Page directive supplies the necessary information to the compiler so that it can be treated as a module.

Each .aspx file requires a page directive with an *Inherits* parameter specifying a class from which the Web form is inherited. The class specified in the Inherits property must be derived from the *Page* class or some sub-class of the Page class. The following page directive for the gasTIX home page specifies that Visual Basic is used (`Page Language="vb"`), that events must be connected to handlers explicitly (`AutoEventWireup="false"`), the code-behind file (`Codebehind="Home.vb"`), and the class from which the page is inherited (`Inherits="Search.Home"`).

```
<%@ Page Language="vb" AutoEventWireup="false" Codebehind="Home.vb"
Inherits="Search.Home"%>
```

Page directives in gasTIX also use the following attributes:

- `AspCompat`—True or False. Specifies whether an ASP.NET page is compatible with ActiveX .DLL's written for class ASP pages.
- `ContentType`—Specifies the HTTP content type. Any standard MIME type is acceptable.

- `Description`—Specifies a textual description of the page.
- `EnableSessionState`—True or False. Enables or disables session state for the page. A third option, ReadOnly, is also available if session state can be read but not changed.
- `ErrorPage`—Specifies the URL to load if an unhandled page error is encountered.
- `MaintainState`—True or False. Specifies that ViewState should be maintained across page requests. (See "Round Tripping and ViewState" later in this chapter.)
- `Trace`—True or False. Tells the Web server to output trace information for this page.

In addition to the page directive, ASP.NET pages can also contain one or more of each of the following five types of directives:

- `@ Control`—Used to define that a page is a user control instead of a standard ASP.NET Web form.

  This directive is mutually exclusive with the @ Page directive.
- `@ Import`—Defines a namespace to be imported into the page. This is used to make available classes and interfaces not automatically included in the page. Each @ Import directive can have only a single namespace, but each page or user control can have multiple @ Import directives.
- `@ Register`—Defines aliases for user controls on a .aspx page. When we build a user control, the @ Register directive is used to tell our Web form where it can find the user control.
- `@ Assembly`—Defines an assembly (a compiled .DLL) to be linked to this page. This makes the assembly's classes and interfaces available to the page.
- `@ OutputCache`—Defines how long the Web server should retain the page in the output cache.

Page directives are just one of ten syntactical elements that can appear on an ASP.NET page. The most common used are *HTML control* and *custom control* elements. An HTML control element is simply an HTML element on the page which you can manipulate at design-time or run-time. This allows the developer to work with standard HTML objects in server-side code. A custom control element is a specialized version of one or more HTML controls. This includes the standard ASP.NET Web controls such as TextBox, Label, and DataGrid. In order to clearly define the control desired, all server-side Web control must include an alias; the alias for included Web controls is "asp:" while the alias for user controls is defined in the @ Register directive.

In order to add functionality to the objects defined in the control syntax sections, the *code declaration* and *code render* blocks allow developers to write code against the controls. The code declaration block includes all member variables, properties, and methods that will be compiled into the .NET class. The code render section defines expressions that will be executed in order to render the page. These expressions can be included inline, within the .aspx file itself, or in a code-behind file. The third code section is reserved for data binding expressions to allow the developer to programmatically bind controls to exposed data sources.

Finally, an ASP.NET page can include three server-side elements: *object tags*, *include directives*, and *comments*. Code in the object tags section declares and instantiates both COM and .NET Framework objects for use within the page. The include directives insert the contents of a specified file directly into the ASP.NET page. The contents of this file are not parsed or executed; they are simply dumped into the file "as-is." Comments, of course, are simply server-side definitions that prevent code from executing during the page render and are available to the developer to aid maintainability.

Additional content found in an ASP.NET page that does conform to one of these categories is defined as literal text. This often includes such things as standard text and standard HTML. It is important to note that even this text is fully object oriented; for each section of literal text found, a LiteralControl object is built and placed into the page's object model. These LiteralControl objects can be manipulated programmatically like any other ASP.NET object.

What Are Web Controls?

For die-hard ASP developers, the best new feature of ASP.NET is undoubtedly Web forms and Web controls. That's a bold statement to make, given the diversity of over one million ASP developers in the world today. However, most Web developers agree that the most vexing problem facing them today is browser compatibility: the never-ending quest to make a single set of code work in every available browser on every available operating system. Web Forms and Web Controls promise to solve this problem.

A Web Form is a server side construct designed to contain Web Controls. When the ASP.NET page is parsed, the Web Form is translated into a standard HTML form while the Web Controls are translated into their respective HTML counterparts. There are several benefits to using Web Forms and Controls, most important being browser independence and event-driven programming.

Web Controls offer true cross-platform development and achieve true browser independence by parsing server-side controls into browser-compliant HTML. The Web server recognizes the specific type and version of the browser making the page request and creates the most advanced version of HTML allowed by the browser. This means that the HTML created by a single ASP.NET control definition may look differently in Internet Explorer than it does in Netscape, as shown in Figure 5.1. Because of this, generated pages may not be identical within the same browser if their versions differ. Give credit to Microsoft for developing a solution to this problem and recognizing the reality of user and browser diversity.

The definition of the HTML that is created when the Web server parses the Web control is also dependent on the operating system on which the browser resides; the HTML created for Internet Explorer running on Windows may look different than HTML created for Internet Explorer running on a Macintosh. When you consider other browsers like the Opera Web browser and UNIX/Linux platforms as well, it is easy to understand how a single Web control can have literally dozens of HTML definitions.

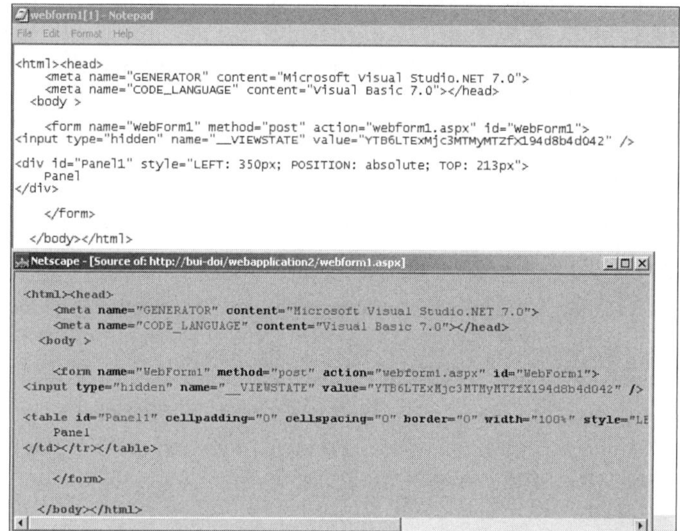

FIGURE 5.1

A single Web Control can create multiple versions of HTML, depending on the browser requesting the page.

Web controls are similar to Microsoft's Design-Time Control (DTC) definition used with classic ASP pages. The difference is that DTC's had to be authored in a COM-compliant language such as Visual Basic or MS Visual C++ instead of VBScript with the rest of the ASP pages. The DTC was then compiled and included as a server-side definition on the ASP page where it was forced to work within the ASP page. The improvement of Web controls over DTC's is that they are fully integrated with the ASP.NET object model and are programmed using the same language and object model as the Web forms. Thus, they do not incur the overhead or learning curve of an additional language.

Obviously, the benefit of allowing server-side controls to write HTML is the ability to create a single page of code that is automatically translated for any browser request. Most current Web development is built on the premise that a specific browser/version/operating system combination is chosen and the pages are built to support that version. By definition, this automatically involves more work than is necessary: browsers and versions have to be evaluated, functionality must be "dumbed down" to the level of that browser, and additional testing is required to ensure compatibility. ASP.NET moves that effort from the developer to the Web server, where it belongs.

It is important to understand that ASP.NET Web controls are not just "dumbed down" to the lowest supported browser/version. In fact, Web controls are pushed to expose the highest functionality allowable within the browser making the request. That means that a single Label Web control with a Cascading Style Sheet (CSS) transition defined on it will automatically be displayed with the transition in Internet Explorer version 5 and will simply be displayed without the transition in Netscape version 4.

Since Web controls are parsed into pure HTML before the client ever sees them, the end-user will not be able to tell the difference between Web controls and standard HTML controls. The two are fully compatible and can be freely interspersed on a single page. For examples of using Web Controls, see Chapter 10, "gasTIX Event Searching."

Of course, Web controls are not a silver bullet for every possible browser incompatibility. The solution is dependent on the rules embedded on the Web server, which dictate how the HTML is defined. These rules are, of course, subject to discrepancies within the browsers and the ravages of time and new browser versions. The Web server needs to be updated or patched for every new browser version that becomes available in order to ensure the highest level of compatibility and functionality. Microsoft is still evaluating the best method for keeping these rules up to date.

Another concern for Web developers is the increasing number of handheld devices now accessing the Web. These devices have severely limited functionality, compared to their desktop counterparts. Furthermore, the functionality limitations vary drastically from device to device, from the inability to display images all the way to being limited to 100 characters or fewer on the screen. These devices create an entirely new set of cross-browser development problems, one that even ASP.NET Web controls cannot easily fix. The first release version of ASP.NET does not include built into compatibility with handheld devices, although support is available from Microsoft in a separate Software Development Kit. Future versions of ASP.NET promise to include full support for handheld devices.

TIP

You can download the .NET Mobile Web SDK at `www.microsoft.com/mobile/downloads/default.asp`

Despite these concerns, Web controls go a long way towards solving the problems of cross-browser development. The initial version of ASP.NET clearly demonstrates this progress by including controls which do not have a standard HTML counterpart. ASP.NET ships with support for numerous additional controls such as the Calendar and Ad Rotator controls. While there is no HTML equivalent of these controls, ASP.NET automatically creates a set of standard HTML controls and arranges them as necessary on the page to create the effect of a single control. ASP.NET automatically supports down-level browsers as well, applying its standard rules for creating HTML controls for each browser.

Third-party controls will also be available for ASP.NET which should allow developers to easily use advanced controls in their Web development without having to worry about downgrading their applications for older browsers. ASP.NET even makes it easy for developers to make their own user controls to maximize code-reuse and portability (see the "User Controls" section later in this chapter).

Event-Driven Programming

Web Controls also allow Web developers to code more like application developers by offering event-driven programming. In a typical application built in Visual Basic or C++, application functionality is only executed in response to some event. This may be the user clicking a button, pressing a key on the keyboard, or even the arrival of new email. This allows developers to break the functionality of their code into small manageable chunks that are only executed when the event they represent occurs. This improves application performance by only executing the necessary pieces of code and makes code much easier to maintain.

Event-driven programming has become the standard in application development, but it has never been available in server-side Web development. The problem is that the events and the event handlers exist in different realms: the event has to occur on the client end of the Web, while the event handler for server-side pages has to be run on the server. There are methods for passing information from the client-side to the server-side, and vice-versa, however there is no intrinsic ability built into an HTML textbox, or any other HTML control, that allows the developer to hook client-side events to server-side handlers. Web controls offer this ability.

When the original HTML specification was written, it was created to display information, not serve as an application development platform. There was no defined way to dynamically change object properties or respond to an object's events. In fact, no events were even defined in the HTML specification. Event handling did not become possible until Web browsers started supporting another construct: scripting. Most commonly using JavaScript, browsers slowly began supporting client-side event handling and dynamic property assignment. Though this marriage of two specifications is not perfect, it has evolved to work fairly well for basic event handling and dynamic property assignment.

There are two major drawbacks with the existing relationship of HTML and client-side script. The first is the requirement to include specific code on every Web page that allows for basic event handling and property manipulation. All mature application development languages hide these basic details from the developer. While this problem leads to bloated code and additional development risks, the second drawback is much more problematic for true application development.

The second drawback is the requirement that event-handlers must be defined on the client-side. The event-handler is constrained by the limited environment of the Web browser. Most Web browsers impose strict restrictions on the actions client-side code can execute, restricting access to the file system, other applications, and system settings. These restrictions severely limit the functionality that can be achieved in client-side code in order to protect the end machine and operating system from deviant acts by rogue programmers. Different browsers also implement variations of the client-side script engine, requiring multiple code versions.

Moreover, placing additional code on the client-side not only increases the file size of the pages being downloaded, but it also imposes the burden of executing the code on the client machine. The end result is large code blocks that are downloaded and executed on a slow client machine instead of being executed on a high performance Web server.

Another holdback to event-driven Web programming is the Web's inherent statelessness. Internet pages are stateless, that is, they do not maintain any information about their own state between calls. Thus, when a call to a page is made, the page has no idea what happened during the previous call. In fact, the page has no way of knowing how the page making the request came into being at all. The only information available to the server is the current state of the page: textbox values, list selections, etc. Thus, if the user has changed a value in a textbox, the server-side code responding to the changed text only knows the current value of the textbox; it has no inherent way to know the previous value. Each page is recreated from scratch each time it is loaded, degrading performance. This is a common scenario in application programming and one that cannot be easily duplicated in Web development…until now.

Using Web Controls in Visual Studio .NET

One of the goals of ASP.NET is to bring Web development closer to the more mature world of application development. Web controls and Visual Studio .NET make great strides in this direction by allowing developers to design Web pages with What You See Is What You Get (WYSIWYG) control and property dialogs as shown in Figure 5.2.

When ASP developers begin working with Visual Studio .NET, the first thing they will likely notice is that Visual InterDev is missing. Since Visual Basic .NET and C# are fully supported for ASP.NET development, ASP.NET projects do not need a separate Integrated Development Environment (IDE). To create a new ASP.NET project in Visual Basic .NET, simply choose

File|New|Project from the Visual Studio .NET menu. Select Visual Basic Projects from the Project Types list on the left-hand side of the New Project dialog and highlight Web Application from the Templates list on the right. Change the application name and location if desired and click OK (See Figure 5.3).

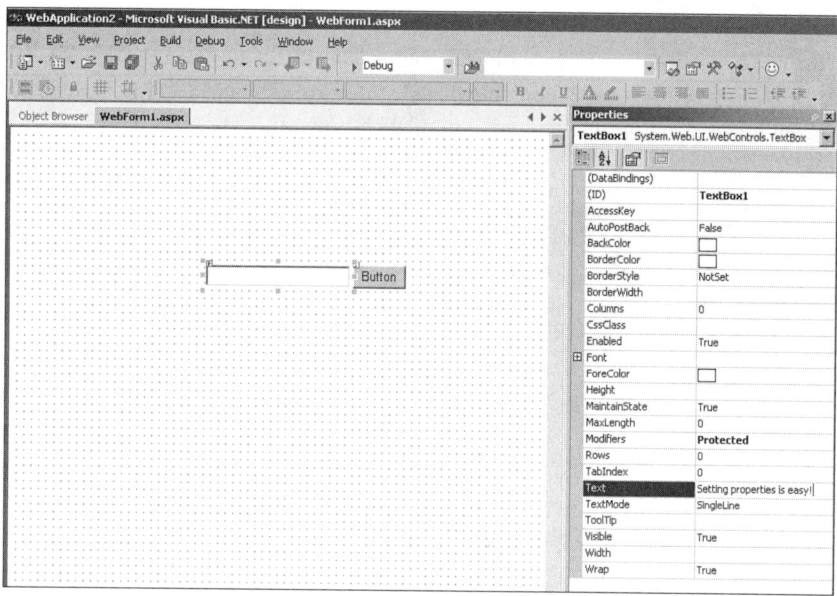

FIGURE 5.2

You set properties for your Web controls just like application controls.

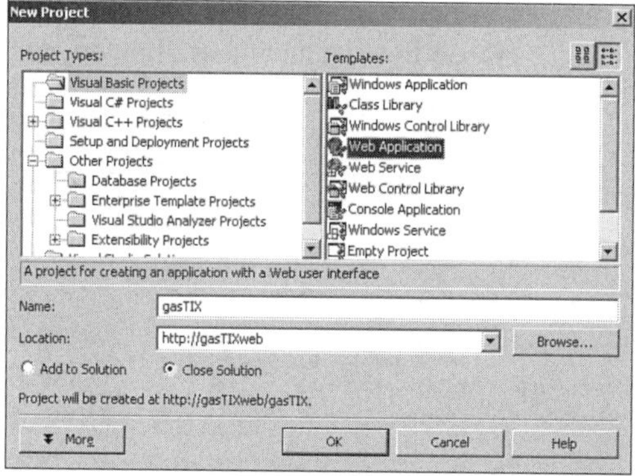

FIGURE 5.3

The New Project dialog offers a variety of templates for Visual Basic, C#, and C++.

By default, the WebForm1.aspx is displayed in linearLayout mode, meaning that controls dropped on to the Web form will line up top to bottom, left to right. If you drag a control from the Toolbox onto the form, it will automatically reposition itself in the next available position to the right and below the most recent control added. Click on the form and change the pageLayout property on the properties dialog to gridLayout. Notice that a grid appears on the Web form. Now, drag another control onto the form. Notice how it remains where you dropped it on the form. The gridLayout feature of Web pages automatically generates HTML table or CSS definitions to position your Web controls as you desire. The positioning is designed to be compatible with every major type and version of Web browser.

NOTE

> You may have to hover over the Toolbox menu item along the left side of your IDE to display the toolbox. You should also ensure that you've selected the "Web Forms" tab before selecting controls to add to a Web form.

You will find a variety of controls in the toolbox, some familiar, some new. The TextBox and Button controls are familiar to Web developers and are named consistently with their HTML counterparts, while the common HTML Anchor tag (<A>) is called "HyperLink" in the Visual Studio .NET toolbox. New controls include the DataGrid, the Repeater, and the Validator controls. For more information about these controls, see Chapter 11, "Purchasing a Ticket."

The Visual Studio .NET IDE offers you two views of each Web form: Design and HTML. This is similar to the design feature of Visual InterDev 6 ASP pages, though it has been greatly enhanced to accommodate the many new features of Web controls. Click on the HTML tag at the bottom of the Web form to view the server-side code generated by the design page, as shown in Figure 5.4. Here you can examine the table definition created to accommodate the absolute positioning of your controls.

```
<%@ Page Language="vb" AutoEventWireup="false" Codebehind="WebForm1.vb" Inherits="WebApplication2.WebForm1"%>
<html><head>
    <meta name="GENERATOR" content="Microsoft Visual Studio.NET 7.0">
    <meta name="CODE_LANGUAGE" content="Visual Basic 7.0"></head>
  <body ms_positioning="GridLayout">

    <form id="WebForm1" method="post" runat="server">
<asp:TextBox id=TextBox1 style="LEFT: 210px; POSITION: absolute; TOP: 141px"
                runat="server">Setting properties is easy!</asp:TextBox>
<asp:Button id=Button1 style="LEFT: 368px; POSITION: absolute; TOP: 141px"
                runat="server" Text="Button"></asp:Button>


    </form>

  </body></html>
```

FIGURE 5.4

The IDE automatically generates the necessary code to create the Web controls.

Scroll through the HTML code to find one of the controls you placed on the form. Notice how the definition is similar to a standard HTML control definition prefaced with the designation, `ASP:`. This is the namespace alias for the control and indicates to the Web server where to look to find the HTML definition for the control. Also common to all of the controls you created is the `runat="server"` property. This indicates to the Web server that processing should be completed before the HTML is sent to the client.

Each Web control is defined with the same name it is given in the tool box, i.e. a HyperLink control is defined as `<ASP:HyperLink>`, not `<A>` as you might expect. The translation into common HTML controls, such as HyperLinks into anchor tags, will take place only when a browser requests the page.

Handling Events

Web controls in ASP.NET have the ability to respond to client-side events with server-side handlers as shown in Figure 5.5. This new functionality allows developers to create controls that can define event handlers on both the client and server side of the page. The event handler is simply a piece of code that is executed in response to a defined event, such as a button click. It is important to note that controls cannot have both client- and server-side handlers defined for a single event.

Perhaps the most important new feature in the IDE is the support for server-side event handlers. This gives developers the ability to simply double-click on a Web control to be taken to the code for that control. Visual Basic .NET responds to double-clicks by displaying the default event for the specified control. This allows the developer to quickly and easily place controls on a form and specify event handlers for those controls. Return to the Design view of your Web form and double-click on one of the controls.

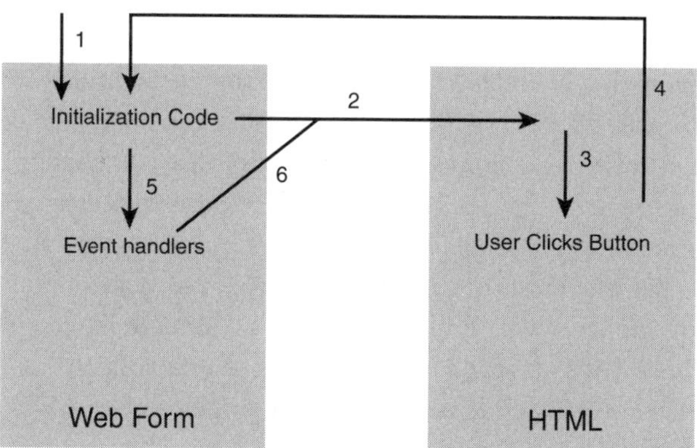

FIGURE 5.5

ASP.NET pages have self-submitting forms that allow server-side event handlers to be executed.

1. A request for a Web form is made.
2. The Web form returns standard HTML to the client.
3. The user raises an event, such as clicking a button.
4. Execution is passed back to the Web form on the server.
5. Code in the appropriate event handler is executed.
6. A new version of the HTML is returned to the client.

Standard ASP programming restricts communication between the client and server to form submissions and page requests. Web controls enhance this communication by enabling event handlers for all controls. Thus, a list box can execute code in response to the user selecting a different option and a radio button can respond when the user selects a new value. This enhanced functionality eliminates the need for the developer to manually create extraneous HTML forms whose only purpose is to send control of the page to the Web server.

TIP

Remember that the event handler code is executed on the server side, not the client-side!

The code for the event handler will be immediately familiar to any Visual Basic programmer. The event handler name is simply the name of the control appended with an underscore (_) and the name of the event. In the case of a new list box value selection, the event handler is `ListBox1_SelectedIndexChanged`. Passed as arguments to the event handler is a reference to the object that raised the event and an object of type `System.EventArgs`, which specifies details about the event itself.

In addition to the event handler created by double-clicking the control, you will notice two other event handlers created for every Web form: `WebForm_Load` and `WebForm_Init`. The `Load` event of the WebForm is fired just before the Web controls are parsed into HTML by the Web server. This allows the page the opportunity to make any necessary changes to the controls before the processing occurs. For instance, it is common practice to populate a label control with the name of the person currently signed into the Web site. You've probably seen this on Web sites such as Amazon.com where the site indicates, "You are logged in as David Burgett. If you are not David…" If the current user name is stored in a Session variable, the `WebForm_Load` event would be used to change the text property of an ASP.NET Label Web control to indicate the actual name of the user. This is an excellent example of event-driven programming in ASP.NET since the label caption is being populated in response to an event (the Web form's load event), not just as code on the page itself. The second standard event handler, WebForm_Init, defines the code necessary to create the Web form and controls and is generally hidden within the IDE.

NOTE

Use caution when editing the WebForm_Init method. Changing this code may cause your form to load incorrectly and not display in design mode.

To create a simple demonstration of Web controls event handling, add a Label Web control and a ListBox Web control to your Web form. Select the ListBox and set the AutoPostBack property to True. Open the Items property and add several items to the ListBox. Double-click the ListBox to view the ListBox1_SelectedIndexChanged event handler. Enter the following code:

```
Label1.Text=ListBox1.SelectedItem.Text
```

This code simply changes the text property of the Label to the value selected in the ListBox. Pressing F5 runs the code and selects an item in the ListBox; the Label control automatically updates to reflect the item selected in the ListBox. You might have to wait several seconds the first time you load the page and the first time you click an item in the ListBox. The reason for this wait is that ASP.NET is automatically checking for new versions of a compiled .DLL and new Web pages for this application. Click a different item in the ListBox and you will notice that the response is immediate.

TIP

Be prudent when setting AutoPostBack=True in order to avoid pages which make frequent, repeated trips to the server.

NOTE

By default, only the button click events are automatically posted back to the server. This closely resembles the standard HTML form submission model.

Some developers will undoubtedly complain that Web controls do not offer anything that was not available previously. Indeed, it is possible with classic ASP, or any other server-side Web development language, to create server-side handlers for client-side events. It is true that

ASP.NET simply uses common tools, such as HTML form submission and JavaScript, which are readily available today. It is important to note, however, that ASP.NET offers all of this functionality in a WYSIWYG, rapid application development environment, drastically reducing development time, all without compromising browser independence. This represents a significant advancement for Web development.

Round-Tripping and ViewState

Now that you have seen Web control event handling in action, you are no doubt wondering, "How does it do it?"

In order to bind client-side events to server-side event handlers, ASP.NET uses a toolbox consisting of client-side scripts, HTML forms submissions, and state management. Each time a handled event occurs on the client-side, the page uses a combination of JavaScript and form submissions to pass processing back to the server-side code. Each ASP.NET page submits back to itself, allowing controls and their event handlers to be defined on a single page. In ASP, forms usually post to a second page, breaking the controls and their events into separate sets of code. When an ASP.NET event is raised, the server-side handler is executed and a new page is delivered to the client. This is called "round-tripping." During this round-trip, state management is employed to ensure that each of the controls not affected by the event retain their current properties.

NOTE

Due to the overhead of each round trip to the server, some events which occur frequently on a page, such as OnMouseOver, do not call server-side event handlers.

Client-side JavaScript is required to force a browser to make a call to the server in circumstances where it normally would not. An example of this is shown in Listing 5.1. In our previous example, this consisted of a user making a selection in a list box. Since HTML has no support for making a page request in response to a list box selection, ASP.NET examines the browser making the request to determine if it supports JavaScript. If it does, then ASP.NET automatically creates simple JavaScript to force the browser to make a request to the server to handle the event. If the browser does not support JavaScript, then the event cannot be automatically handled and will instead be cached and handled on the next form submission.

LISTING 5.1 ASP.NET Automatically Creates the Necessary JavaScript to Force the Browser to Respond to the OnChange Event of This Textbox

```
<script language="javascript">
<!--
    function __doPostBack(eventTarget, eventArgument) {
        var theform = document.WebForm1
        theform.__EVENTTARGET.value = eventTarget
        theform.__EVENTARGUMENT.value = eventArgument
        theform.submit()
    }
// -->
</script>

<input name="TextBox1"
    type="text"
    value="Setting properties is easy!"
    id="TextBox1"
    onchange="javascript:__doPostBack('TextBox1','')"
    style="LEFT: 210px; POSITION: absolute; TOP: 141px" />
<input type="submit" name="Button1" value="Button" id="Button1" style="LEFT:
368px; POSITION: absolute; TOP: 141px" />

    </form>
```

In order to translate requests to run an event handler in a syntax that HTML can understand, all Web forms are required to have an HTML form. The HTML form acts as a conduit for events, passing page execution from the client back to the server for event handling. Client-side events are processed by setting form properties and then executing a programmatic submission of the form. Since forms are a very basic HTML requirement, this model ensures that the widest possible range of browser types and versions can support the ASP.NET programming model.

In addition to describing a means of communication between the client-side events and the server-side handlers, ASP.NET also defines a method for storing an object's state. This allows the Web controls to act as independent objects, maintaining their own properties despite changes in other page objects. When a classic ASP page makes a form submission, all of the HTML controls on the page are destroyed and recreated. The developer then must programmatically repopulate the controls with the appropriate values.

ASP.NET handles this automatically, using a hidden form field named `__VIEWSTATE`. The ViewState form field holds an encrypted string which describes all of the Web controls on the page and their state when the page was loaded (see Listing 5.2). On the server-side, the `__VIEWSTATE` property directly translates to the `State` property of the page class. This allows the developer to access the state information programmatically within event handlers.

LISTING 5.2 The Hidden VIEWSTATE Field Stores Encrypted Web Control State Information

```
<html><head>
    <meta name="GENERATOR" content="Microsoft Visual Studio.NET 7.0">
    <meta name="CODE_LANGUAGE" content="Visual Basic 7.0"></head>
  <body ms_positioning="GridLayout">
    <form name="WebForm1" method="post" action="webform1.aspx" id="WebForm1">
<input type="hidden" name="__EVENTTARGET" value="" />
<input type="hidden" name="__EVENTARGUMENT" value="" />
<input type="hidden" name="__VIEWSTATE"
value="YTB6MTk4ODc0NjcyX19feA==f2f03fae" />
```

There are two important elements to note about the `ViewState` field. The first important note is that the `ViewState`, as mentioned above, is encrypted. The information is encrypted and decrypted on the server, which is important because it ensures that the user never has the opportunity to alter the existing state information. This is critical in e-Commerce applications where the text property of a Web label on a shopping cart page would display the total amount of the purchase. Without the `ViewState`'s encryption, a savvy user could fairly easily alter this information, setting any price they like for the purchase, all without the application's knowledge. The encryption of the `ViewState` information prevents tampering and makes using Web controls much more secure.

The second important note about the `ViewState` field is a warning to Web developers: be careful how much information you store in the `ViewState`. Each Web control has a maintainState property which allows the developer to determine whether or not the state information for the control should be stored in the `ViewState`. This is a critical decision when you consider the amount of information any given Web control might contain. In the case of gasTIX, a simple label Web control may contain only a few dozen characters, like the name of a band. A multi-line text box on the same page may contain several hundred words in a description of that band's albums. Consider, however, the amount of data contained within a DataGrid displaying a list of upcoming concerts. There could easily be thousands of lines of text describing venue names, locations, show times, and opening bands. It is important to take into consideration the fact that you may be increasing the size of the page downloaded to the client by 50-100k or more when setting `maintainState` to `true` for dataGrids full of data.

While the potential size and increased download time of the `ViewState` field is imposing, the upside of using `ViewState` is easier development and improved page performance. Consider the common scenario of a user updating his personal information. When the page loads, a database query must be run to retrieve all pertinent information about the user. This information is stored in the appropriate Web controls on the Web page. Suppose that the user then updates some of his information and submits the form. In addition to executing the appropriate update statements, classic ASP pages must request the entire dataset again in order to populate the HTML controls. An ASP.NET page, however, has automatically populated the textboxes with the appropriate values before the event is handled.

The `State` property of the Page class offers another benefit which experienced Web developers will appreciate. Many Web developers use the trick of using hidden form fields to pass important information from one page to another. The problem with using these hidden form fields is that they really aren't hidden very well; a user needs only to view the HTML source of the page to view the "hidden" information. ASP.NET can now save this information in the page state property instead of hidden form fields. The data still gets passed to the client and back like hidden form fields, but it is now encrypted in the `__VIEWSTATE` form field and hidden from prying eyes.

The Life Cycle of a Page Object

As you have already seen, the Web is a stateless programming model. Each page that is requested must be created from scratch since no information about the page is stored on the server. This is what allows the use of Web farms, where two different servers may be used to fulfill subsequent requests for a single page.

In order to understand how the state information described in the previous section is used, it is necessary to understand how each page is created. Each page object undergoes a predefined set of steps necessary to load the object, bind data objects, handle events, and perform cleanup (see Figure 5.6).

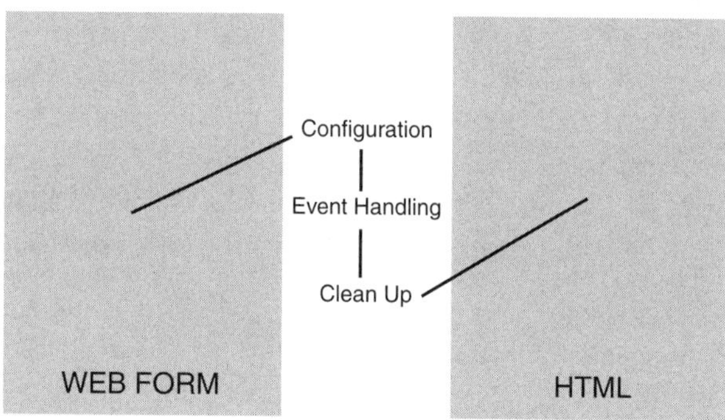

FIGURE 5.6
Each page goes through three stages during processing: configuration, event handling, and clean up.

The first stage of the page life cycle is configuration. This stage allows the page to restore the state information for the page object and each of its constituent controls. During this stage, the `Page_Load` event fires, thus checking the status of the `IsPostBack` property of the Page object.

The IsPostBack property is a simple Boolean value which specifies whether the page is being created from scratch or in reference to a post back. When an event is encountered on the client-side of the page, the page automatically (if the `AutoPostBack` property is set) posts back to itself to handle the event.

Since the ASP.NET page automatically stores the state of Web controls on the page, the IsPostBack property is checked to determine whether controls need to be initialized or not. If the IsPostBack property is set to true, meaning that the page has been loaded previously and is currently responding to an event, then controls on the page do not need to be reinitialized. This drastically improves processing speed by eliminating database calls to set control properties.

At the time the `Page_Load` event fires, all controls on the page are created and initialized with either their default or ViewState properties. This event is typically used to set control properties, as well as perform initial data binding and to reevaluate data binding expressions on subsequent round trips. Data binding is a very powerful way to quickly load data from a database into list boxes, datagrids, and other controls.

The second stage in the page object life cycle is event handling. This stage is skipped if `IsPostBack` is set to `false`, indicating that this page is not being requested in response to an event. ASP.NET automatically fires the handler associated with the specified event, as well as handlers for any cached events. For more information about cached events, see the next section, "Advanced Features of Web Controls."

The event handling stage typically includes actions such as database updates, state management updates, and control property updates. If the user has updated the information stored in the database, the event handler for the change (i.e. `TextBox_TextChanged`) would be used to execute a SQL update statement. If the page is maintaining specific state management information, such as the number of users logged on the system, this information could be updated in the event handler. Likewise, event handlers are frequently used to update control properties, such as the text property of a status label control. If the page contains validation controls, the IsValid property of each validation control is checked during the event handling stage and the appropriate action is taken.

The final stage of the life cycle is cleanup. This stage fires the `Page_Unload` event which should be used to close files and database connections and explicitly discard any objects created by the page.

NOTE

Even though the .NET CLR includes automatic garbage collection, it is recommended that the page explicitly close database connections and other expensive resources to ensure that they do not continue to consume resources after the page is unloaded.

Advanced Features of Web Controls

Web controls include many advanced features which significantly ease the development and add impressive functionality to ASP.NET Web applications. From a development standpoint, the consistent object model is probably the most important step towards bringing Web application development into line with standard application development.

The current HTML specification has been pieced together by different groups and affected by a variety of browsers, which has led to fragmenting of the HTML object model. The type and version differences of available scripting languages accepted by different browsers has futher exacerbated the problem. To ease Web development, the ASP.NET development team worked diligently to ensure that all ASP.NET Web controls share a common object model and consistent naming convention. Each of the Web controls packaged with ASP.NET derive from a common ancestor, System.Web.UI, as shown in Figure 5.7. Since all Web controls derive from a single control, they share similarly named properties. For instance, both TextBox and a Label Web controls have "text" properties, despite the fact that they map into HTML quite differently. This consistency makes ASP.NET much easier for novices to learn and removes some of the burdens for experienced programmers.

Another improvement in ASP.NET is the enhanced WYSIWYG page designer. Previous versions of Visual Studio .NET created a WYSIWYG interface for Web page design by trying to cobble together client-side HTML elements with different interfaces and properties. The new Visual Studio .NET makes use of the server-side processing and the unified object model to create an interface which allows developers to easily drag and drop Web controls into place and modify their properties within a single properties dialog.

Visual Studio .NET also provides support for absolute positioning of controls on the page using CSS absolute positioning. The developer simply drags the controls to the desired location, just as he would in Visual Basic, and the Web server automatically defines style attributes with the absolute positioning definition. For maximum backwards compatibility, Visual Studio .NET also supports the use of tables to position elements on the page. Switching between these two positioning models, CSS and tables, is achieved by simply specifying the targetSchema property of the page object to either HTML 4.0 or HTML 4.2.

Web controls also improve the event handling model by adding support for nested and cached events. Nested, or bubbled, events occur in Web controls that act as containers for other controls. For instance, the Repeater control, explained in Chapter 10, creates a variety of Web controls for each row that exists in the database. Each of the Web controls contained within the Repeater is a full-fledged Web control with its own properties, methods, and the ability to raise events. In order to avoid requiring developers to write event handlers for every control contained within the Repeater, events of the child controls will automatically bubble up to the container to be handled by a single set of code. The `OnItemCommand` event of the Repeater control (as well as the DataGrid and DataList controls) passes along a parameter which specifies which child code created the actual event.

System.Web.UI.Design.WebControls Hierarchy

```
System.Object
  -System.ComponentModel.BaseComponentEditor
    -System.WinForms.Design.WinFormsComponentEditor
      -BaseDataListComponentEditor
        -DataGridComponentEditor
        -DataListComponentEditor
  -System.ComponentModel.Design.ComponentEditor
    -System.Web.UI.Design.ControlDesigner
      -System.Web.UI.Design.HtmlControlDesigner
        -System.Web.UI.Design.UserControlDesigner
        -System.Web.UI.Design.WebControlDesigner
          -AdRotatorDesigner
          -BaseValidatorDesigner
          -ButtonDesigner
          -CalendarDesigner
          -CheckBoxDesigner
          -HyperLinkDesigner
          -LabelDesigner
          -LinkButtonDesigner
          -ListControlDesigner
          -PageletDesigner
          -System.Web.UI.Design.ReadWriteControlDesigner
            -PanelDesigner
          -System.Web.UI.Design.TemplatedControlDesigner
            -BaseDataListDesigner
              -DataGridDesigner
              -DataListDesigner
        -RepeaterDesigner
  -System.Drawing.Design.UITypeEditor
    -RegexTypeEditor
    -System.ComponentModel.Design.CollectionEditor
      -ListItemsCollectionEditor
      -TablecellsCollectionEditor
      -TableRowsCollectionEditor
  -System.MarshalByRefObject
    -System.ComponentModel.MarshalByRefComponent
      -System.WinFormsControl
```

FIGURE 5.7
All Web controls, including pages, derive from a single ancestor in this portion of the ASP.NET object model.

Events can also be cached on the client-side. As explained previously, Web controls have an `AutoPostBack` property which, when set to True, specifies that the control should automatically post back to the server when an event is triggered. There are situations, however, where the developer will not want every control to trigger a post back, so ASP.NET allows events to be cached for later processing. When an event is triggered on a Web control with AutoPostBack set to false, the client automatically adds that event to a list of events that need to be handled when processing is sent back to the server. When another event is encountered for which `AutoPostBack` is set to `True`, processing is transferred to the server, where all cached events are handled and then the posting event is handled as well.

CAUTION

There is no specified order in which cached events will be handled. Do not write code that is dependent on the execution of a specific order of event handlers.

Data binding is the process of automatically attaching a user interface control to a data source. The control then displays information retrieved from the database. Data binding has been available in Windows application development for many years and has seen some limited functionality in Web development in the more recent past. Data binding in ASP.NET, however, is revolutionary in that it no longer limits the types of objects that can be bound to or how the bound data is displayed.

Many Web controls can be data bound in ASP.NET to either simple or complex data sources. Furthermore, most of the basic properties of each Web control can be bound, not just the text property as in the past. A simple data source is any property or variable that is of the correct type for the property being bound to. Thus, the text property of a text box can be bound to a string variable while the height property can be bound to a numeric variable. Likewise, either property can be bound to a similar property on another text box or any other type of control.

Data binding offers great flexibility in defining properties for a wide range of controls and applications while making it easy to bind a string of controls together so that they always share the same property values. It is trivial, for instance, to create multiple image controls on a page, binding each one's height and width to the height and width of a specified image. This would ensure that every image on the page would always have the same height and width.

In addition, for simple data binding, that is, binding to a single value, ASP.NET fully supports binding to complex data sources. A complex data source is a collection of data, such as a database query result set. In fact, Web controls can be bound to any structure that implements the `IEnumerable` interface, as show in Figure 5.8. This includes not only information retrieved from a database, but also Arrays, Dictionaries, Queues, and Stacks. It also includes any collection of data exposed by a control's property, such as the list box's `ObjectCollection` property. Since `XMLNodeList` implements the `IEnumerable` interface as well, Web controls can even bind directly to XML documents, as demonstrated in gasTIX. The flexibility to bind to other controls, XML documents, and simple, programmatic constructs enables a whole new world of Web application development. See Chapters 10 and 11 for more examples of data binding.

System.Collections Hierarchy

```
System.Object
  -ArrayList
  -BitArray
  -CaseInsensitiveComparer
  -CaseInsensitiveHashCodeProvider
  -Comparer
  -Dictionary
  -HashTable
    -CaseInsensitiveHashtable
  -NameObjectCollectiontable
    -NameValueCollection
  -ObjectList
  -Queue
  -SortedList
    -CaseInsensitiveSortedList
  -Stack
  -StringCollection
  -StringTable
  -System.ValueType
    -DictionaryEntry

Interfaces

ICollection
IComparer
IDictionary
IDictionaryEnumerator
IEnumerable
IEnumerator
IHashCodeProvider
IList
```

FIGURE 5.8
Web controls can be bound to any derivative of the IEnumerable interface.

The second improvement in data binding involves displaying the data that has been bound to the control. The most obvious improvement for displaying this data is the ability to create data binding expressions. A data binding expression is simply a reference to the particular column or field of data being bound with a function applied to it. The function can be simple or complex and can change anything about the data, including the type. Thus, a string property could be bound to a numeric data source by appending a `toString()` method to the data reference.

Displaying bound data has also been greatly improved through the introduction of templates. Templates offer much more control over the user interface of both packaged and custom controls. Templates allow developers to pass in more than just a few simple properties to controls. Instead, multiple templates are defined within the beginning and ending tags of the control definition. The Repeater, DataGrid, and DataList controls all use templates to display data retrieved from a database. See Chapter 10 for more information on these controls.

Each of the three data controls accepts templates for normal items, for alternating items, and for the header and footer. The basic template common to all repeating data controls is "ItemTemplate." This template specifies not only cosmetic items such as font and color, but also functional items such as hyperlinks and buttons for every item retrieved from the database. Separating the logic and design of each item from the code needed to apply a dataset to it creates cleaner code and easier maintenance.

In Listing 5.3, the `ItemTemplate` defines hyperlinks to information about performers displayed in gasTIX. Likewise, the `AlternatingItemTemplate` creates the same information on a grey background for every other row, improving readability.

LISTING 5.3 The `ItemTemplate` and `AlternatingItemTemplate` Tags Allow Data To Be Easily Formatted

```
<asp:Repeater id=rptParticipants runat="server">
<template name="HeaderTemplate">
  <table>
</template>
<template name="ItemTemplate">
    <tr><td>
        <a href='EventsByParticipant.aspx?Participant_ID=
<%#Container.DataItem("Participant_ID")%>'>
                                        <%#Container.DataItem("Participant_Name") %>
</a>
    </td></tr>
</template>
<template name="AlternatingItemTemplate">
    <tr><td bgcolor="C0C0C0">
        <a href='EventsByParticipant.aspx?Participant_ID=
<%#Container.DataItem("Participant_ID")%>'>
  <%#Container.DataItem("Participant_Name") %>
</a>
    </td></tr>
</template>
<template name="FooterTemplate">
  </table>
</template>

</asp:Repeater>
```

The `AlternatingItemTemplate`, if present, overrides the `ItemTemplate` for every even numbered item. This makes it trivial to create tables of data where every other row has a different color background in order to facilitate easier reading. The `Header` and `Footer` templates allow the developer to specify text and controls, such as record count or sort buttons, which belong at the top or bottom of the data.

Validation controls are a specific type of Web controls which perform a simple function: validating user input. Validation controls can validate that the data input by the user falls within a specified range or matches a specified pattern or parameter. Custom validation controls can even be written to allow developers to create their own validation rules.

Validation happens automatically on a page level. If any control on the page fails validation, the entire page is marked as invalid. ASP.NET will not submit a form until the page passes the validation stage successfully. The developer can also programmatically validate controls on an individual basis. When validation fails, a customized error message is displayed to the user that includes information about all failed controls. This message is configurable and can be placed anywhere on the Web page. For more information about validation controls, see Chapter 11.

User Controls

Two of the main goals of object-oriented programming are encapsulation and improved reusability. Encapsulation is the process of hiding the implementation details of some piece of code in a convenient package. This improves team development and eases maintenance by grouping related functionality into small, manageable objects. If these objects are programmed carefully, they can be widely reused in a variety of applications, none of which need to know the internal workings of the objects. ASP.NET finally brings the benefits of object-oriented programming into the Web development world with the advent of User Controls.

User controls are typically small, reusable chunks of Web UI and logic that form a functional unit. This unit can be reused in a variety of situations on multiple pages, reducing development time and improving maintainability. A user control is similar to a Web form, in that it contains Web controls and HTML controls, as well as the code behind these controls. User controls cannot, however, stand alone; they require a container document.

User controls follow standard ASP.NET page conventions, with the exception that they cannot have page-level tags, such as `<HTML>`, `<BODY>`, or `<FORM>` tags. Since user controls can only be displayed within a parent ASP.NET page object, the user control will make use of the existing page-level tags within the parent page. Including additional page-level tags in a user control will create multiple tags in the HTML sent to the client, which will cause the page to be displayed incorrectly.

A typical user control will encapsulate common functionality that is needed on multiple pages, even across multiple Web applications. Common uses for user controls include:

- login controls, which provide textboxes for the user to enter a name and password and a button to submit the information
- search criteria, which include a text box for entering text to search for and list or check boxes for setting the search options
- search results, which would define the formatting of the search results

Each of these examples defines a small, concrete set of functionality that is required on multiple pages and multiple applications. Any well-defined piece of work can be encapsulated in a user control to be included across multiple pages.

TIP

If you find yourself writing the same code on more than one page, you could save time and improve maintainability by making a user control to encapsulate the desired functionality.

The gasTIX Web site makes use of several user controls for including the navigation bar, creating personalized content, and displaying performer information. Each page within the Search portion of the gasTIX Web site makes use of two user controls to define the navigation bar along the left side of the page and to create the information panel along the top of the page, as shown in Figure 5.9.

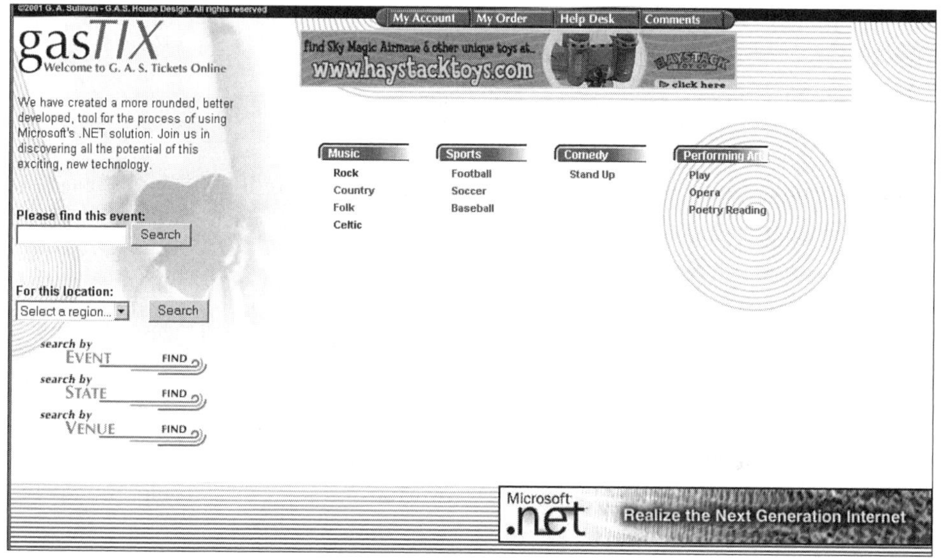

FIGURE 5.9

Each page in the gasTIX search application uses two user controls to create a consistent look and feel across the entire Web site.

Instantiating the template user controls for each search page is very similar to performing a server-side include. The difference is that user controls are fully object oriented and can accept properties and perform methods that include files cannot. User control properties are well defined, allowing the developer to perform bounds checking on their values and make programmatic modifications if necessary. User controls have full access to the ASP.NET object model and act as standard Web controls in terms of allowing and gaining access to other controls.

User controls can also define events. Events raised within a user control can be handled internally in the user control itself, or raised as an event to the page containing the control. This allows developers great flexibility in creating user controls that handle all intrinsic functionality while offering some control to the containing page. For instance, a user control that allows users to enter search criteria may need to internally handle events when options are set to validate the selected options, while allowing the parent page to handle the search button click event. This would allow developers using the search user control to write their own database queries while not forcing them to validate the user-selected options on every page that uses the control.

User controls are stored like standard Web forms, except they must have the file extension .ascx. User controls are included in a Web page by creating a page directive that tells the page how the control will be called and where the file is that should be used. The following code registers the gasTIX TemplateTop user control with the page:

```
<%@ Register TagPrefix="gasTIXSearch" TagName="TemplateTop"
src="TemplateTop.ascx" %>
```

Once a register directive has been placed on a page, the user control is added to the page like any other control. Instead of the typical `ASP:` prefix used for Web controls, the prefix defined in the register directive must be used. The definition of a gasTIX TemplateTop user control would be:

```
<gasTIXSearch:TemplateTop runat="server">
```

Just like standard Web controls, user controls can be added to a Web page programmatically using the `LoadControl` method of the Page object. The `LoadControl` method takes a string path to the .aspx file of the user control and types the newly loaded control by replacing the dot with an underscore. Thus, `LoadControl(TemplateTop.ascx)` creates a control of type `TemplateTop_aspx`.

The gasTIX Web site also uses user controls to display categories and subcategories of performers for whom tickets are available. Each performer is categorized into a generic category and then further specified by a subcategory. For instance, the gasBAGS bag pipe band is categorized under the “Celtic” subcategory of the generic “Music” category.

The relationship between categories and their subcategories is something that needs to be displayed in several places across the gasTIX Web site, thus a category user control was created to encapsulate this functionality. The category user control displays information about categories defined in the SQL Server 2000 database and uses a nested subcategory control that displays information about the subcategories under each category. This allows developers to quickly create an organized list showing parent-child relationships by simply dropping a control and setting a couple of properties, and ensures display consistency across the Web site.

Separation of UI and Code

Another benefit of ASP.NET is an improved separation of the code from the user interface (UI). One of the largest problems facing developers building large, traditional ASP applications is the combination of design and code in a single page. The UI defined by the HTML in a traditional ASP is often inextricably tied to the code used to modify the UI. This not only makes maintenance of both the UI and the code much more difficult, it makes the initial creation of the page more complicated as well.

Several challenges arise from the fact that both the UI designer and the code developer have to modify a single set of code. The most obvious is that the designer and the developer cannot work on the page at the same time. The second challenge is the potential for one to inadvertently alter the other's work, breaking either the form or the functionality. Web forms largely eliminate this problem by enabling "code-behind" classes, where the event handlers for a Web page are stored in a separate file. This allows the designer to create the .aspx page while the developer works on a .vb page which contains code for the .aspx page. The two pages are tied together through the CodeBehind attribute of the Page directive.

While it is still possible to use traditional inline scripting instead of code behind, it is strongly recommended that code behind be used whenever possible. The added maintainability of the code easily justifies the small learning curve needed to adjust to the new style of ASP programming. The samples in this book and the gasTIX Web site use code behind exclusively, as demonstrated in Listing 5.4.

LISTING 5.4 The Code Behind Page for gasTIX Search Pages Sets the Text Property of the lblHeader Control

```
<body>
<form id=RegionList method=post runat="server">
<gastix:templatetop id=TemplateTop runat="Server"></gastix:templatetop>

<asp:label runat="Server" id="lblHeader" cssclass="Header"></asp:label>

Code Sample: Each gasTIX search page has a Label web control defined by the
designer; all the developer needs to know is the name.
          Dim SC As New gasTIX.BusinessFacade.Subcategory()
          Dim dvXML As DataView
```

LISTING 5.4 Continued

```
            Dim dsTemp As New DataSet()
            dsTemp.ReadXml(New StringReader
(SC.ListParticipants(Request.QueryString("SubCategory_ID").ToInt32())))
            If Request.QueryString("debug") <> "" Then
                response.Write(Request.QueryString("Name"))
               Response.Write(server.htmlencode
(SC.ListParticipants(Request.QueryString("SubCategory_ID").ToInt32())))
            End If
            If dsTemp.Tables.Count > 0 Then
                dvXML = dsTemp.Tables("Participant").DefaultView
                With rptParticipants
                     .DataSource = dvXML
                     .DataBind()
                End With
            Else
                lblNoRecords.Text = "There are no participants in this
subcategory."
            End If
            lblHeader.Text = "Participants in the <span style=""color:#FF0000"">
Category..SubCategory Name</span>
 (" & rptParticipants.Items.Count & " records found)"
```

Each results page in the gasTIX Search application has a Label Web control defined on the page to indicate to the user the search for which the results are presented and the number of results found. For example, if the user clicks the “Celtic” subcategory on the home page, the results page displays a label indicating that one record was found in the “Music..Celtic” category. Since the developer knows that a Web control named “lblHeader” will be present somewhere on the page, he simply instructs the code behind page to specify the text property of the label. He never needs to know the style or location of the label, just its name.

From Here

ASP.NET finally brings the benefits of object-oriented programming into the world of Web development. ASP.NET features much better encapsulation and reusability then ever before, allows developers and designers to work separately on a single project, and allows developers to write code in the language of their choice. In addition, performance improvements, enhanced security, and interoperability with the .NET servers make ASP.NET an excellent choice for larger scale, enterprise critical applications.

Implementing .NET Business Services

CHAPTER

6

by Eric Brown

IN THIS CHAPTER

- Architectural Goals 156
- gasTIX Business Services—A Closer Look 161
- What's New for Component Development 167
- From Here 177

The business services layer of the gasTIX application is the tier that is responsible for enforcing business rules, processing information, and managing transactions. It is in the business services layer that a developer builds reusable components. Business services components are not tied to any specific client, and can service multiple applications, as well as reside in separate locations from the clients. The business services layer is critical to applications, even though it does not create the look and feel of the application.

With the introduction of .NET, Microsoft has made one of the most significant platform changes since the introduction of Windows to the DOS world. These changes are far more comprehensive than just simple language changes, or the creation of a new language. Many of the changes in .NET affect the implementation of .NET business services, including the framework classes, remoting, and web services, just to name a few. If developers are not prepared for the changes ahead, they may find themselves left behind on the learning curve.

Due to this platform shift, many developers and architects alike are asking how the implementation of enterprise applications and business services will change from Windows DNA to .NET. Perhaps they should also be asking how all these changes affect the design of enterprise applications and business services, as well as what should be the items to think about when architecting .NET applications. The architectural goals for gasTIX would have remained the same, regardless of the implementation platform. However, the actual design of gasTIX does vary in response to the implementation platform. The introduction of the .NET platform has therefore affected both the gasTIX application design and implementation. This chapter begins by discussing the architectural goals of gasTIX. The chapter then covers the design of the gasTIX Business Services and also covers the reasons behind some of the design choices. Lastly the focus is on what is new in component development with .NET.

Architectural Goals

The team that was formed to design gasTIX consisted of several experienced Windows DNA architects and designers. Each team member had previously participated in the design and construction of enterprise-class applications. When the design team met to begin the design process for gasTIX, many of the decisions appeared to already have been made, due to the team's experience. Each member was familiar with both the theoretical best practices for building Windows DNA applications, as well as having formulated their own "real" world best practices from their experiences. Some design changes were appropriate with the introduction of the new features incorporated in the .NET platform that were not present in the Windows DNA platform, but the design and architectural goals remained the same. Most of what has changed with the introduction of .NET is the actual implementation for enterprise systems.

When discussing enterprise applications we often use key words to describe their functionality. These are often used by companies when marketing their new applications to show how "great" and well designed they are. As a result, the following terms have become commonplace within all technology fields:

- Interoperability
- Performance
- Availability
- Scalability
- Maintainability
- Extensibility
- Security

It is an impressive list, but looking past the marketing-speech, what do all these things really mean to designers in the real world? Designing an enterprise system requires carefully weighing each of the items in this list against the requirements and goals of the system. Several of the items on this list are interrelated, and are opposed to each other in certain cases. This means that design decisions that are made can affect multiple items on the list in both positive and negative ways.

For example, designing a system for scalability can often negatively affect the performance of a system. The design team for gasTIX took these interrelationships into account when designing the architecture for gasTIX. The primary design goals set forth included: interoperability, performance, availability, scalability, and security. Maintainability and extensibility were also primary concerns; their implementation is discussed in length in Chapter 4, "Tools of the Trade" and Chapter 10, "gasTIX Event Searching."

Interoperability

Interoperability deals with the system's ability to interact with other disparate systems, potentially on different platforms. In order to have interoperability, it is not required that we choose to use a standard protocol, like SOAP over HTTP. Instead, we can implement a proprietary protocol or interface to communicate between two different systems. Both file-based and API interfaces are commonly used as communication mechanisms between heterogeneous systems. A file-based interoperability system has a few obvious problems. Some of these problems are:

- Transport across networks will not occur if the network doesn't support file-based protocols.
- There is no synchronous communication.
- There is no efficient callback mechanism.

If we implement a file-based protocol (FTP), even if it were to transport through a firewall (which may require firewall configuration) there is no really good way to get a feedback response from the destination. Building a service to poll for feedback would require extra development effort, and is not necessarily the most timely response mechanism that exists. Using an API, which would solve the response mechanism problem, may not transport well through a firewall. Of course, one could open ports on the firewall in order to enable this option to work, but this would introduce a security issue. The best choice is a standard Internet protocol that talks on a port that the firewall will most likely already have open.

The designers chose to use SOAP as the protocol for method invocation for gasTIX. SOAP calls are transported over HTTP, which is a standard Internet protocol, and will pass through most firewalls without the need to reconfigure the firewall. SOAP is not a Microsoft-only supported protocol, so there is little to no custom development involved in building an application on top of a standard messaging protocol.

NOTE

SOAP is a W3C standard protocol that is supported by many web servers including but not limited to IIS, Websphere, and Apache.

The designers had no interest in building a custom protocol over HTTP that would require development on both sides of the pipe to interpret the message. Good tools exist on multiple hardware platforms already to support the plumbing of sending and receiving SOAP messages. Although SOAP is not the most efficient protocol, the developers of gasTIX decided that it was worth the tradeoff for the ease of development, cost of development, and flexibility that it offered.

Performance

Performance refers to the responsiveness of a system to a user's request. It is typically measured by using a set of metrics like the number of pages/sec or the number of transactions/sec. Due to the definition alone, one can see that performance can (and probably should) be talked about using discreet and concrete terms rather than nebulously. Instead of discussing that the system must have good performance, the discussion should focus on finite measures such as the system supporting 50 pages/sec or 200 transactions/sec. Also it is imperative that detailed performance requirements be stated up front in order to take them into account during design. If these requirements are not stated up front, significant amounts of work may be required to modify a constructed system.

There are two main things that can adversely affect performance. The first of these items is building a system for interoperability. Building a system that can interoperate with other systems using standard protocols, like SOAP over HTTP, will cause a decrease in speed over using a binary protocol (TCP is nearly four times the speed of HTTP). HTTP, although portable, is not necessarily the most efficient protocol. The second item that can affect performance is scalability. When building a system for only 10 users, one can optimize knowing that fact. In this scenario, we are able to hold resources for longer periods of time and gain responsiveness in the system. When designing for scalability, one tries to reduce the length that resources are held. This includes even expensive resources like a database connection. Although connection pooling and object pooling can help, performance may suffer due to waiting on acquiring resources.

Availability

Availability refers to the ability of an application to always be able to respond. One view of availability would involve having a web server farm where if one server becomes unavailable, another server would be "available" to handle that server's requests. But availability can go one step further to include building a disaster recovery plan.

A disaster recovery plan addresses the ability to access the system even if, for example, the entire building where the primary equipment is located were to be damaged or destroyed. The latter would require separate installations of software at geographically separate locations. The remote in the alternate location would come on-line and handle user requests at the press of a button, so to speak. Handling the latter of the cases often involves significant expense since duplicate systems are required in different locations. Most companies balance availability by performing fail-over clustering or web farms in case a single machine fails to function. In doing so they accept the level of risk that a single disaster can wipe out their entire system.

Scalability

Scalability refers to the system's capability to handle considerably larger numbers of users while maintaining both performance and availability requirements. As can be seen in the provided definition, scalability is closely related to both availability and performance. Designing a scalable enterprise system requires addressing both the software design and the hardware implementation. When designing Windows DNA applications in the past, the design had to include some mechanism for storing state information (if the client was web-based). .NET provides designers with this feature built-in, so the implementation is simpler than in the DNA world.

The designers of gasTIX know that consumption of server resources is one of the items that affect scalability the most. Object-oriented systems typically require significant numbers of objects in memory, and that consumes precious server resources. Holding a database connection open for each user also consumes significant amounts of resources. If access to resources is a bottleneck, then the scalability of a system will be greatly affected.

We did specific things to address the scalability needs of the application. First, designers decided to use session state management features of ASP.NET that would allow for multiple web servers in the web farm. Second, database connection would not be dedicated to a single user, but would be pooled (as in COM+). Third, "state-aware" components would be designed and built.

When MTS first came into existence, the term "stateless" was used to describe the way components should be built to build scalable systems. Many people built all the components in the business services layer to be "stateless." Stateless components hold no state information at all between method calls. The misunderstood "requirement" of statelessness in all business services components caused and still causes much confusion for developers.

The gasTIX designers do not believe that all classes built in the business services layer are required to be stateless to have a scalable solution. From the view of the presentation services, the business services are "stateless." The business façade (which will be discussed later in more detail) holds no state between calls from the presentation services. Other components in the business services layer behind the business façade may in fact hold state between calls from other objects in the business services layer. The lifetime of these business services components will end when the call from the business façade is completed.

The design of gasTIX also needed to take into account the addition of hardware to support a large increase in users. Scaling the presentation services is traditionally simple, by just building a web farm. The main issue that arises is the issue of sharing session state across web servers, which .NET now takes care of for us. There are two main approaches for scaling the business services layer: deploy the business services components on the same physical machines as the web servers, or build a farm of servers for the business services. The design of gasTIX does not dictate which option will be used.

Security

Security, at least in the case of gasTIX, refers to how protected the site is from those attempting to break into it (crackers). Security also refers to the general principle behind how users will be set up and authenticated, and what encryption mechanism is used to send data security so that it is difficult to read if intercepted.

.NET provides significant security enhancements to the Windows DNA model. The CLR provides an extensive security mechanism (code access security) to determine which users are allowed to run and execute managed and unmanaged code alike. When looking at security, the designers of gasTIX were primarily focused on how to ensure that a consumer of the web service would be authenticated. The designers of gasTIX settled upon using a certificate-based authentication mechanism over secure HTTP (HTTPS). For this, IIS would map the certificate to an Active Directory user, from which the application would query to get the partner's ID (participant, venue, or sponsor). There would also be a security check to ensure that a partner attempting to consume the participant web service was in the participant group in the NT domain.

The main problem with just passing a user name and password on the call to the web service is that it is possible for a partner to impersonate another partner. There is no way to actually tell what partner is using the username and password. Although the username and password is reasonably secure, the use of a certificate would guarantee that the partner was who the gasTIX web service thought the partner was. Any special processing that needed to occur for a specific partner (like a service charge) would be simple to do since the web service façade would be able to identify the partner making the request. For more information on .NET security, see Chapter 8, "Handling Security."

gasTIX Business Services—A Closer Look

Since we have looked at what things the designers of gasTIX took into account when designing gasTIX, it is now time to take a more detailed look at the elements of the gasTIX business services.

The high-level design that was developed can be seen in Figure 6.1. The gasTIX business services were divided into six areas: business façade, business objects, data, data access, system framework, and web services. During implementation, these business services areas were assigned their own namespaces.

Business Façade

NOTE

A façade, according to the dictionary, is the principal face of a building or an artificial or deceptive front. Applying this definition, a business façade is the principal interface to the business services layer.

The business façade has two separate and distinct purposes. First, it is used to abstract the complexity of the business services by providing a simple interface to the gasTIX presentation services client. The presentation services client is not required to understand how the business services layer works; from the view of this client, the business façade *is* the business services layer. Secondly, the business façade makes up the workflow of the business services. The components in the business façade glue the other layers of the business services together. If the order of processing must be changed, the business façade will more than likely be the place to change it. The business facade controls the logic that occurs in the business services layer.

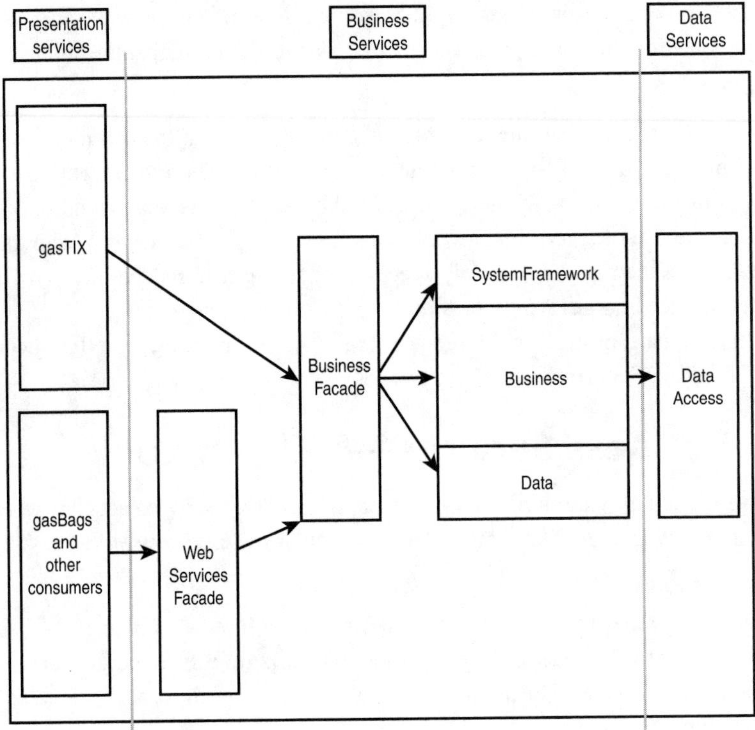

FIGURE 6.1
The gasTIX high-level design.

One item that arose was whether gasTIX should have a `ListEvents` class that had methods named `ListEventsByParticipant` and `ListEventsByVenue`, or have a `Participant` class with a `ListEvents` method and a `Venue` class with a `ListEvents` method. We chose to design `Participant` and `Venue` classes.

First, from a purely object-oriented point of view, a `Participant` and `Venue` intuitively fit the definition of a class. Second, it made sense that since we had `Participant` and `Venue` classes, that each one would know how to list events. The classes require a participant and `venue ID` respectively because objects in the business façade do not hold state between calls from the presentation services.

Business

The classes in the `gasTIX.Business` area of the gasTIX business services layer are responsible for processing and enforcing business rules in the gasTIX application. The presentation services may enforce some business rules, but it is the responsibility of the middle tier to validate the data. Remember that although the existing presentation layer may validate data, it may not be able to validate all business rules. It is also possible that another presentation layer, which has no validation, could be built to call into the business services layer.

One rule that is enforced is that an order may only contain up to eight tickets. Both the gasTIX consumer site and gasBAGS may or may not enforce this rule. The OrderRules class in the Business namespace does enforce this rule. The web services façade calls into the business façade. This is the same business façade that the gasTIX consumer site uses. The business façade in turn calls into the objects in the business namespace. This rule is automatically enforced on both the gasTIX and gasBAGS sites because both consumers end up using the same business logic components. Further, no significant communication is required between gasTIX and the business partner with regards to what business rules that they must enforce in order to consume our service.

The objects in the business namespace also control the transactions that are enlisted. All data access components are set to "supports transactions." This allows the actual data access work to be agnostic of the transactional state of the context it is operating in. When processing the business rules, and preparing to save an object, the business elements determine under which circumstances transactions are enlisted.

Data

It is the `Data` area of the gasTIX business services that contains the actual information retrieved from the database. The classes that reside in this area are in the `gasTIX.Data` namespace. The data objects within are the containers of the actual data retrieved from the database and sent across the wire to the presentation services.

Typed datasets are themselves derived from Dataset. When datasets are sent from the business services layer to the presentation services layer, a copy of the dataset is sent. We decided to use typed datasets to implement our `gasTIX.Data` classes for several reasons, but the primary reason was that we felt it was better to program against a `gasTIX Order` object, rather than a generic dataset. Using a typed dataset prevents the presentation layer from constructing a generic dataset on the fly and attempting to pass it into a function as a parameter where a specific type of dataset is required. Thus we can more tightly control the interface to and from the business services layer. For more information on typed datasets, see the section, "Typed Datasets," later in this chapter.

Data Access

The gasTIX data access objects are used to communicate to the database. They contain the information necessary to send and receive information from the data store. The data access objects themselves do NOT start or complete transactions, but "support" running in or out of a transactional context. The new .NET Framework provides automatic enlistment of transactions through COM+ services. Due to this requirement, these components are hosted in COM+.

ADO.NET contains objects that are used to connect to the database. In gasTIX we built a `Data Access` object that wraps up some ADO.NET functionality and abstracts the logic required to connect to the database and execute queries.

NOTE

Many people have attempted to abstract database connectivity in past versions of Visual Basic. One problem that occurred was that since VB did not support inheritance, developers either had to put all this code in a module or implemented an interface and did what is affectionately known as "cut-and-paste inheritance." Neither solution was a pretty one. Full inheritance in the .NET platform finally makes an elegant solution possible.

The gasTIX `Data Access` objects derive from the base class `gasTIX.DataAccess`. The `gasTIX.DataAccess` baseclass is abstract, so it must be inherited from. It contains the logic to retrieve the connection string for the database from the COM+ `ConstructString`. The base class also contains all the logic to set up a call to execute a stored procedure to retrieve data, but it is up to the derived class to put in the specific information like the stored procedure name and parameters. All other data access objects derive from `gasTIX.DataAccess` and inherit its functionality. This is better than implementing an `IDataAccess` interface, because there is common code in all data access components that can be abstracted out and written only one time.

One other aspect of the design of data access components is noteworthy. Past experience has shown that making multiple calls to a data source is expensive, from a performance point of view. For this reason, one should retrieve large blocks of data in a single call rather that in multiple calls to a data source. For example, say that the business services needs to retrieve three datasets from a data source; it is more efficient to retrieve all three datasets by executing one database call, rather than in three separate calls. In order to update data it is sometimes necessary to execute multiple, separate update statements; just keep in mind that reducing the number of calls across the wire, or across processes, will improve performance.

System Framework

The system framework provides for utility functionality that is used throughout the system. Two of the objects in the `gasTIX.System Framework` namespace are specifically designed to deal with exception handling. These objects are a custom exception, `GASException`, and an error list object, `GASErrors`. The .NET Framework handles exceptions via structured exception handling, even across languages. If an exception is thrown across a SOAP call, the exception is transported back to the caller as a SOAP fault. The purpose behind implementing a custom exception and error list objects was not due to a problem with the .NET exception handling mechanism. But say, for example, that the presentation services team wants to get a list of business rules that failed while the business services were processing data. The exception mechanism built into .NET does not work this way.

.Web services

As you can see from the press coming out of Microsoft, .Web services technology is a cornerstone of .NET. A Web service is a collection of code that provides services and data to other applications using standard Internet and Web protocols like XML and SOAP. The implementation of each Web service is irrelevant, since Web services communicate using these standard web protocols.

Microsoft proposed taking our existing business components and making them Web services simply by adding the `[WebService]` attribute to them. If we are not careful, we could easily get caught up in the marketing hype and make an uninformed, if not ill-advised, decision.

The idea of simply taking business components and making them available as a Web service instigated the most interesting discussions that arose during our entire design process. The design team thought that if our business façade components would be exposed as Web services, why not have the gasTIX consumer sites use the same Web services interface as gasBAGS or any other third-party consumer of the gasTIX Web service? The primary benefit to having all consumers access business services through the Web service was that all consumers would have used a single interface into the business services layer. This single interface would have demanded a simpler conceptual design, as shown in Figure 6.2. Also, there was some thought that there would be less maintenance of code in the future. This concept was abandoned for several reasons.

First, the use of Web services arbitrarily is not a good approach. Web services communicate using the SOAP formatter over HTTP, which is not the most efficient choice for all communication. This communication mechanism is best for interoperability, but if interoperability is not your goal, why use SOAP over HTTP? In general, we should only expose services as a Web service if it is necessary to consume that service by using a standard Internet protocol. If we are only building components that will be consumed within our firewall domain, why not use .NET remoting?

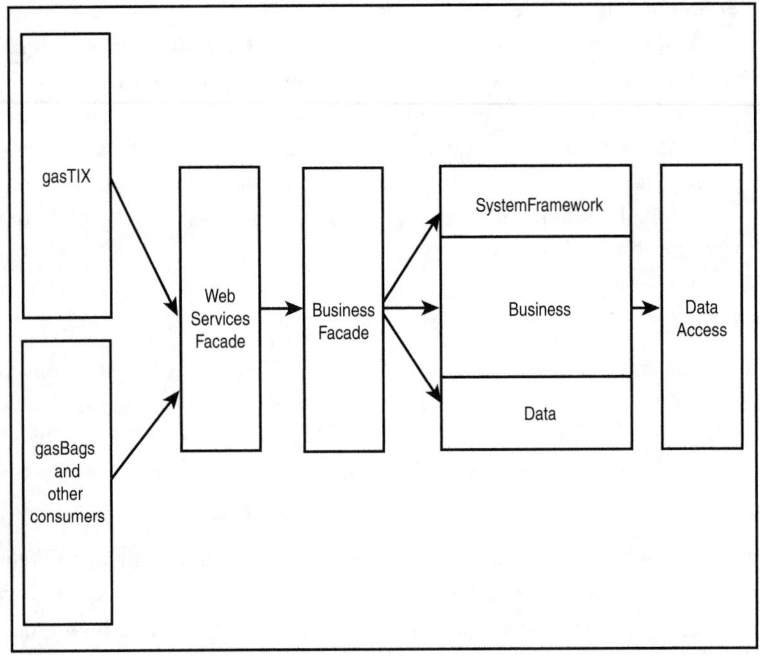

FIGURE 6.2
The gasTIX Proposed design.

Second, the Web service façade does not perform the same functions as the business façade. The Web service façade exposes only those services that the web service is providing for a business partner of gasTIX. A business partner could be a participant, like gasBAGS, a venue, or a sponsor. The Web service façade also executes specific business rules, for example, charging a fee for usage, or waiving shipping charges, depending upon the consumer of the Web service. Third, the web service façade controls access to the particular services themselves.

Consumers of the gasTIX Web services would fall into one of three categories: participant, venues, and sponsors. Only participant-type consumers will be able to call the participant Web service methods. This is also true with both venues- and sponsors-type consumers. This being the case, the obvious question is how do we know which consumers are participants, venues or sponsor types? The answer is with digital certificates.

The gasTIX Web services design requires that a client certificate be passed in on the Web service request. IIS maps the client certificate to a particular domain user in Active Directory (AD). IIS forwards the call to the Web service façade along with the authenticated user. The Web service façade verifies that the authenticated user (implemented in the .NET Framework as `WindowsPrincipal`) of the call is in the appropriate NT group. If the `WindowsPrincipal` identified from the certificate is not in the group, an exception is thrown. If the `WindowsPrincipal` is in the appropriate group, the web service façade queries for the ID of the user in the AD tree and uses that ID on the call to the business façade. This is demonstrated in Figure 6.3.

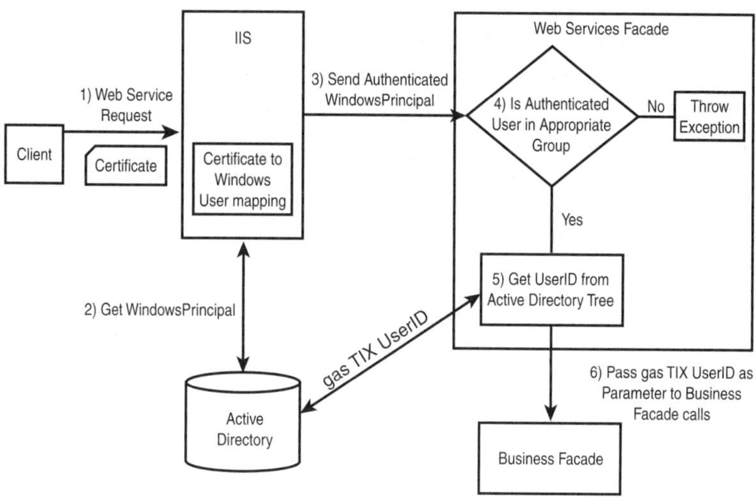

FIGURE 6.3
The gasTIX site uses Client Certificates to authenticate web service requests.

What's New for Component Development?

Enterprise application development has changed since the introduction of .NET. Microsoft's significant technology shift has provided developers with some new choices for implementation that were not previously available in the Windows DNA world. Remember that the .NET platform includes the .NET servers as well as the .NET Framework. The combination of the two provides for some simplification in development, where significant amounts of work were sometimes required before. Implementation changes are usually more significant for the VB developer than for the Visual C++ developer.

The business services layer of gasTIX was implemented using C# and Visual Basic .NET. As you may (or at least should) know, there is no significant difference between the various Microsoft-provided .NET languages. Since all .NET languages adhere to the Common Language Specification (CLS), gasTIX business services could have been written in any .NET language. We chose C# and Visual Basic .NET solely based upon the skill sets of the developers involved in the implementation.

In regards to the custom development effort, .NET has changed the implementation of enterprise systems and components in several ways, and the two that we will discuss are remoting and ADO.NET.

Remoting Versus DCOM

The concept of creating objects that run in a different process or machines is itself not a new concept. In Windows DNA, developers used DCOM (Distributed COM) to do remote calls to objects. DCOM was designed to allow components to be invoked between machines on a LAN. The .NET platform extends the features that DCOM provided. In a way, .NET remoting could be considered DCOM+. As useful as DCOM was, it suffered from a few problems that can be addressed using .NET remoting.

The first problem for DCOM was that the registration allowed for deploying applications in configurations that were not conceived of during the design phase. By altering a few registry entries, it is possible to convert a normal locally registered COM component into a remotely created DCOM component. The developer does not need to do anything to make this happen in the Windows DNA world. This sounds very flexible, but the inherent danger is that modifications at runtime by someone who does not understand the design of the application would affect the performance of the application. In the .NET platform, code must be added into both the server that hosts the object and the consumer of the object in order to enable remoting. Remoting, unlike DCOM, no longer "auto-magically" happens.

A second problem that faced developers using DCOM is that the protocol that DCOM speaks (RPC) is not portable through a firewall with a standard setup. This prevents a person from calling components over DCOM outside of their firewall. DCOM solves this by opening ports on the firewall, which is a security risk and is therefore not a desirable solution. The use of SOAP bypasses this problem. Remoting allows the developer to choose the protocol (HTTP, TCP or other) and the formatter (SOAP, BINARY) to transport information. It is possible, then, to use remoting to invoke methods located behind firewalls using either a SOAP or Binary formatter over HTTP.

This leads to an interesting discussion about when one should use SOAP for remoting (as when using Web services) and when one should use remoting. If you need to access remote services within your LAN, using .NET remoting makes a lot of sense (just as using DCOM in Windows DNA would have made a lot of sense). If you must communicate to the outside world using a standard Internet protocol, SOAP is a good choice. Remoting is a more flexible remoting engine because it allows developers to choose either a binary, SOAP, or other protocol, but Web services only use SOAP. It is conceivable that your remoted component should be able to support multiple protocols. In this case, build your component as a Web service, and at the same time build it to support remoting.

For more information on remoting, see Chapter 13, ".NET Remoting."

ADO.NET

With the development of a new platform comes a new data access library named ADO.NET. Make no mistake, this is not just an update to ADO 2.x ("classic ADO"). One of the most significant differences between ADO.NET and classic ADO is in the object model. ADO.NET clearly separates those objects that retrieve and update data from those objects that represent the data. ADO 2.x combines both of these functions in the ADO recordset.

ADO.NET comes with two data providers: the SqlClient and the OLEDB. The SqlClient provider can be found in the `System.Data.SqlClient` namespace and is designed to talk only with SQL Server. The OLEDB provider can be found in `System.Data.OleDb` and is designed to connect to any OLEDB datasource.

NOTE

At the time of this writing, Microsoft has release an ODBC provider for connecting to any ODBC data source. It can be found in the assembly `System.Data.Odbc.dll` and is in the `System.Data.Odbc` namespace.

In ADO 2.x, we can create a recordset, pass it a stored procedure name, execute the stored proc, and the results are stored in the recordset. The recordset could be either connected or disconnected and then sent across the wire as necessary. In .NET the connected and disconnected objects are separated as well.

ADO.NET contains several new important classes and concepts with which a developer must be familiar. The important classes and concepts that we will focus on are as follows:

- DataReader
- Dataset
- XML view of Data
- Typed Datasets

DataReader

A `DataReader` (`SQLDataReader` or `OleDbDataReader`) is a forward-only, read-only "firehose" cursor with an open connection to the data source. This object is similar to a Recordset in "classic" ADO with a cursor type of forward-only and a lock type of read-only. This object should always be closed when finished so the datasource connection that it holds open can be returned to the connection pool.

An example of using a DataReader to retrieve data out of a datasource can be found in Listing 6.1. The code in the listing is very straightforward. We open a connection and command. We create a reader and set it equal to the ExecuteReader method on the SqlCommand object. We can now retrieve the data out of the reader.

LISTING 6.1 Retrieving Data with the SqlDataReader

```
string connectionString = "server=gasTIXSQL;database=gastix;uid=sa;pwd=";
string queryString = "select * from credit_card_type";
SqlConnection conn = new SqlConnection(connectionString);
SqlCommand cmd = new SqlCommand(queryString, conn);
SqlDataReader reader;

conn.Open();
if(conn.State == ConnectionState.Open)
{
    reader = cmd.ExecuteReader();
    while (reader.Read())
    {
        string outputString = "";
        for (int i=0;i < reader.FieldCount; i++)
            outputString += "reader[" + i + "] = " +
reader[i].ToString() + "  ";
        Console.WriteLine(outputString);
    }
    reader.Close();
    conn.Close();
}
```

A DataReader can be useful for retrieving read-only data, but since it must be connected to the data source in order to access data, a DataReader is very limited. Since the connection is being held open all the time, a server will have issues with scaling as significantly more users come online. If we wanted to do a query and send this data to the presentation services, sending back a DataReader would not be the way to best send the information. We really need a disconnected container for the data. ADO.NET provides this functionality in a Dataset.

Dataset

There is no object in "classic" ADO that can be mapped directly to an ADO.NET Dataset. Similar to a disconnected recordset in "classic" ADO, a Dataset represents data disconnected from the data source. But unlike a recordset, a Dataset consists of DataTables and the relationships between those tables (DataRelation). A DataTable represents a single Select statement. This is similar in some ways to a "shaped" recordset, but ADO uses one single tabular object to do this. A DataAdapter in ADO.NET represents a set of commands and a data source connection and is used to fill a Dataset. Code for retrieving data in a Dataset can be found in Listing 6.2.

LISTING 6.2 Retrieving Data into a Dataset

```
string connectionString = "server=gasTIXSQL;database=gastix;uid=sa;pwd=";
//create a new connection object
SqlConnection conn = new SqlConnection(connectionString);
//create a new command object
SqlCommand cmd = new SqlCommand();
// create a data adapter that will use the command object to get data
SqlDataAdapter da = new SqlDataAdapter(cmd);
//create a dataset
DataSet ds;
cmd.Connection = conn;
conn.Open();
if(conn.State == ConnectionState.Open)
{
    ds = new DataSet("categories");
    //create a SqlParameter to pass a value into a stored procedure
    SqlParameter sqlParam;

    sqlParam = new SqlParameter("@customer_id", SqlDbType.Int, 4);
    sqlParam.Value = customerID;
    sqlParam.Direction = ParameterDirection.Input;
    cmd.Parameters.Add(sqlParam);
    // the command type is a stored proc
    cmd.CommandType = CommandType.StoredProcedure;
    // this is the stored procedure name
    cmd.CommandText = "usp_get_categories_by_customer";
    // map DataTable "Table" to DataTable "category" in the dataSet
    da.TableMappings.Add("Table", "category");
    // load results into the dataset
    da.Fill(ds);

    conn.Close();
}
```

The previous code listing shows retrieving data from a SQL Server database via a stored procedure into a Dataset. We know that the datasource is a SQL Server database because we are using the `SqlClient` namespace objects. A `SqlCommand` and `SqlConnection` are created. The `SqlCommand.Connection` is set to point to the `SqlConnection`. A `SqlDataAdapter` is created, and connected to the `SqlCommand`. The stored procedure parameters are created using the `SqlParameter` object. By default when the results are retrieved, they are put in a DataTable called "Table." If there are multiple tables, then the scheme is "Table," "Table1," ..."Table*n*." We want the DataTable inside the dataset to have the name "category," not "Table," so we use a TableMapping to make this happen. The `SqlDataAdapter.Fill` method loads the DataSet. After this the connection to the database is closed, but the data still exists in the DataSet.

XML View of Data

Another new item in ADO.NET is the way in which XML has been incorporated. ADO.NET datasets allow data to be treated as XML. A Dataset can be loaded from an XML file or XML buffer, and can write its contents out to W3C compliant XML. A Dataset can write its data to XML regardless of the source of the data. This means that we can load a Dataset from a database and write its contents out to XML.

A Dataset can also write its schema as XML Schema Definition Language (XSD). Datasets are serialized as XML, which allows business services to return a Dataset from a method. The presentation services can then apply a style sheet directly on the XML representation of the data in the Dataset. The Dataset provides the following methods: `WriteXMLSchema`, `WriteXML`, and `ReadXML` to work with the data as XML.

It was possible starting with ADO 2.5 to save RecordSets into XML or load them from XML into a RecordSet. It is important to understand the significant advantages that ADO.NET provides over previous incarnations. First, the XML format that was saved was predefined. Using the `DataRelation` and `DataTables`, we can control the format of the XML by changing the node structure. Using `TableMappings`, we control how source tables are mapped into `DataTables`. By using `ColumnMappings`, we can control how the `DataColumn` is mapped when the Dataset is saved as XML. In effect, we could take data in from a data source, load it into a Dataset, and save it as *any* XML document that we want.

Typed Datasets

ADO.NET supports both typed and untyped Datasets. In a typed Dataset, all the DataTables and DataColumns become first class objects in the model. Typed Datasets are supported by Intellisense in the Visual Studio code editor, and are easier to read and understand. Typed Datasets are built from a schema. Because the object model of the Dataset is known, the compiler can do type checking at runtime to ensure that invalid values are not assigned. The code generated for a typed Dataset includes code for events when rows change.

As discussed earlier, the gasTIX application uses typed Datasets. All Datasets returned from the data access layer are returned as typed Datasets. One disadvantage of using a Dataset is that the schema of the Dataset is not type checked during compile time. This means that an invalid table name could be referred to in code and the error would not be discovered until runtime. However when we use typed datasets, the compiler can check column and table names because the schema has been specified.

If we are using a typed Dataset, the code to access the category_name column in the first row can be written simply as:

```
ds.usp_get_participant_detail[0].last_name = "MyLastName";
```

Rather than:

```
ds.Tables["participant_detail"].Rows[0]["last_name"] = "MyLastName";
```

Building a typed Dataset in Visual Studio .NET is very simple. The following list details the steps required:

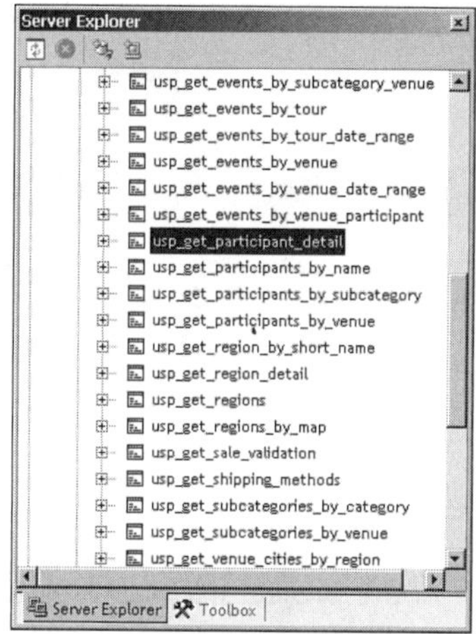

FIGURE 6.4
The Server Explorer.

1. Add a Data Set Component to the project and name it `ParticipantData.xsd`.
2. Open the Server Explorer and create a Data Connection to the database. See Figure 6.4.
3. From the Server Explorer, drag the stored procedure “usp_get_participant_detail” into the designer window.
4. This will create a schema that matches the results of the stored procedure. See Figure 6.5.
5. Save changes.

Now code can be written that uses this new typed Dataset. This schema allows the compiler to check values at compile time rather than at runtime. We could also have dragged multiple objects (tables, stored procedures, or views) into the designer and set up a relationship between them. If the compiler has this information, it can enforce validation checks as well.

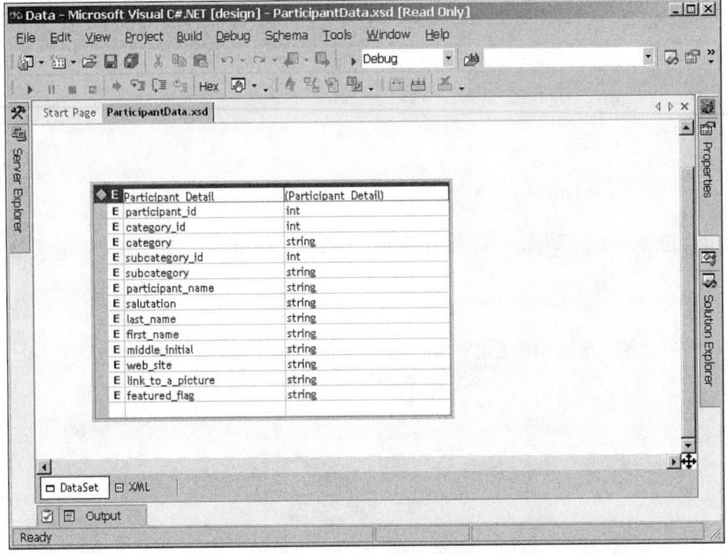

FIGURE 6.5

The XSD Designer supports quick creation of a schema from the results of a stored procedure.

> **NOTE**
>
> By showing the hidden items in the project explorer window, we can see the class that was generated by the designer for the typed Dataset.

The table names and column names that are generated by Visual Studio .NET can be ugly. In our case, the table name in the typed dataset is the same as the source of the data; in other words, the view, stored proc, or table that was the source. The columns are the same name as the source columns. We can change the name of the code generated columns and tables by modifying the underlying XML schema that is generated. In order to do this we must use what are called annotations.

To use an annotated schema, we must make the following change in the XML schema itself. We must insert

```
xmlns:codegen="urn:schemas-microsoft-com:xml-msprop"
```

into the schema line that looks like this

```
<xsd:schema id="ParticipantData"
targetNamespace="http://tempuri.org/ParticipantData.xsd"
```

```
elementFormDefault="qualified" xmlns="http://tempuri.org/ParticipantData.xsd"
xmlns:xsd="http://www.w3.org/2001/XMLSchema" xmlns:msdata="urn:schemas-
microsoft-com:xml-msdata">
```

to produce a line that looks like this:

```
<xsd:schema id="ParticipantData"
targetNamespace="http://tempuri.org/ParticipantData.xsd"
elementFormDefault="qualified" xmlns="http://tempuri.org/ParticipantData.xsd"
xmlns:codegen="urn:schemas-microsoft-com:xml-msprop"
xmlns:xsd="http://www.w3.org/2001/XMLSchema" xmlns:msdata="urn:schemas-
microsoft-com:xml-msdata">
```

Once we have added the `codegen` namespace definition to the XML schema, we can use the `codegen` attributes as shown in Listing 6.3. The `typedName` element is the name that will be generated.

LISTING 6.3 Creating an Annotated schema

```
<?xml version="1.0" encoding="utf-8" ?>
<xsd:schema id="ParticipantData"
targetNamespace="http://tempuri.org/ParticipantData.xsd"
elementFormDefault="qualified" xmlns="http://tempuri.org/ParticipantData.xsd"
xmlns:codegen="urn:schemas-microsoft-com:xml-msprop"
xmlns:xsd="http://www.w3.org/2001/XMLSchema"
xmlns:msdata="urn:schemas-microsoft-com:xml-msdata">
<xsd:element name="ParticipantData" msdata:IsDataSet="true">
<xsd:complexType>
<xsd:choice maxOccurs="1">
<xsd:element name="Participant_Detail"
codegen:typedName="ParticipantDetail"
codegen:typedPlural="ParticipantDetails">
<xsd:complexType>
<xsd:sequence>
<xsd:element name="participant_id"
codegen:typedName="ParticipantID"
codegen:nullValue="-1" msdata:ReadOnly="true"
msdata:AutoIncrement="true" type="xsd:int" />
<xsd:element name="category_id" codegen:typedName="CategoryID"
codegen:nullValue="-1" type="xsd:int" />
<xsd:element name="category" codegen:typedName="Category"
codegen:nullValue="_empty" type="xsd:string" />
<xsd:element name="subcategory_id"
codegen:typedName="SubcategoryID"
codegen:nullValue="-1"
type="xsd:int" minOccurs="0" />
```

LISTING 6.3 Continued

```
<xsd:element name="subcategory" codegen:typedName="Subcategory"
codegen:nullValue="_empty"
type="xsd:string" minOccurs="0" />
<xsd:element name="participant_name"
codegen:typedName="ParticipantName"
codegen:nullValue="_empty"
type="xsd:string" minOccurs="0" />
<xsd:element name="salutation" codegen:typedName="Salutation"
codegen:nullValue="_empty" type="xsd:string"
minOccurs="0" />
<xsd:element name="last_name" codegen:typedName="LastName"
codegen:nullValue="_empty" type="xsd:string"
minOccurs="0" />
<xsd:element name="first_name" codegen:typedName="FirstName"
codegen:nullValue="_empty" type="xsd:string"
minOccurs="0" />
<xsd:element name="middle_initial"
codegen:typedName="MiddleInitial"
codegen:nullValue="_empty" type="xsd:string"
minOccurs="0" />
<xsd:element name="web_site" codegen:typedName="WebSite"
codegen:nullValue="_empty" type="xsd:string"
minOccurs="0" />
<xsd:element name="link_to_a_picture"
codegen:typedName="LinkToAPicture"
codegen:nullValue="_empty" type="xsd:string"
minOccurs="0" />
<xsd:element name="featured_flag"
codegen:typedName="FeaturedFlag"
codegen:nullValue="_empty" type="xsd:string" />
</xsd:sequence>
</xsd:complexType>
</xsd:element>
</xsd:choice>
</xsd:complexType>
</xsd:element>
</xsd:schema>
```

Also notice that on the Participant_Detail table, there are both `typedName` and `typedPlural` attributes. This signifies that the compiler will generate a type for both a single row and the table. This allows us to iterate through all the rows in the table as a collection by using the following code:

```
foreach (ParticipantData.ParticipantDetail x in p.ParticipantDetails)
```

Typed Datasets provide type-safe access to the data that they hold, while simultaneously allowing us to have a logical object hierarchy with which to access the data. Since they are type checked at compile time, some errors can be eliminated before runtime.

From Here

In some ways, Microsoft's changes in the .NET platform affect the *design* of .NET Business Services. There should be no question that these same changes affect the *implementation* of .NET Business Services. Understanding changes to marshaling, remoting, web services, and ADO.NET will prove fundamental to a developer's ability to build reliable and robust business service components in the future.

Implementing .NET Data Services

by Baya Pavliashvili

CHAPTER

7

IN THIS CHAPTER

- Data Modeling 181
- Indexing for Performance 189
- Transact-SQL 194
- Views 201
- Stored Procedures 206
- Triggers 210
- User-Defined Functions 213
- XML Support in SQL Server 2000 216
- From Here 231

Data services are a large part of any business application. The fact that data is one of the most valuable assets for any organization should come as no surprise. With that fact comes the need to select the database platform that most appropriately serves the needs of the organization.

Microsoft completely rewrote its SQL Server database engine with version 7.0 in order to meet the needs of the largest business applications. Some of the major improvements were optimized storage, ease of maintenance, and software reliability.

SQL Server 2000 builds on the foundation of SQL Server 7.0 and adds more long-awaited features such as user-defined functions, array support, partitioned data views, and many others. SQL Server 2000 is also one of the first Database Management Systems (DBMS) to provide native XML support. Furthermore, database management and maintenance tasks are easier than ever before. According to the latest benchmarks, Microsoft SQL Server wins hands-down over any other DBMS on the market as far as reliability and scalability are concerned.

NOTE

For details on DBMS benchmarking, and to view the latest results created by the Transaction Processing Performance Council, an independent consortium of database industry representatives, visit `www.tpc.org`.

As might be expected, SQL Server is more expensive than in the past. However, total cost of ownership is still quite less than comparable DBMSs on the market.

In addition to transactional systems, today's market has a strong demand for business intelligence software, often referred to as data warehousing. SQL Server 2000 provides excellent tools for data warehousing at no additional cost. Moreover, the SQL Server engine is optimized for star schemas, which are at the heart of any data warehouse.

NOTE

Data Transformation Services (DTS), Analysis Services (AS), and Multi-Dimensional eXpressions (MDX) provide sophisticated ways of building and deploying data warehousing applications in SQL Server 2000. DTS allows us to move and "scrub" data from our relational database to a dimensional database. AS and MDX combine to provide dimensional cube generation, drill-down, and drill-through query functionality. The SQL Server 2000 OLAP tools are industry-leading, and offer powerful functionality that previously necessitated purchasing expensive third-party tools.

SQL Server 2000 offers reusable code modules such as views, stored procedures, triggers, and user-defined functions. There are many advantages to using these server-side constructs, as opposed to executing embedded SQL statements from middle-tier and front-end programs. (The advantages of each type of code module will be discussed in the individual sections that follow).

The bottom line is that Microsoft SQL Server 2000 is the best choice for building a transactional application, a decision support system, or a fully-fledged data warehouse.

In this chapter we will present an overview of how data services tie into the big picture of the gasTIX sample .NET e-Business application. Although the basics of SQL Server are beyond the scope of this chapter, we will introduce some of the new SQL 2000 features that gasTIX utilizes. We will also cover examples from the gasTIX data services, and will explore how we can utilize SQL Server 2000 to build our own applications.

Data Modeling

Prior to building the physical database where the data will actually be stored, a logical data model should be constructed. A logical data model consists of related business entities, and maps entity attributes to the data elements that will be stored in the database.

There are many reasons for building a logical data model. First, it helps developers understand the business needs and requirements. Modeling the application data logically is the first step in moving from abstract business requirements listed in a requirements document to a representation of all the items to be tracked, and how they interrelate. Second, it provides an opportunity to think about how to store the data in the format most appropriate for the type of application we are building. These formats vary widely, and picking the best format for the job is crucial to building a successful application. The next section explores the different formats in which data can be stored.

Relational Versus Dimensional Models

All database-related applications fit into one of three general models: on-line transaction processing (OLTP), decision support systems (DSS), or online analytical processing (OLAP). OLAP is often referred to as data warehousing.

OLTP applications are specifically designed to collect data: the gasTIX sample application this book describes selling tickets over the web. It is a perfect example of a high-volume OLTP system. The main purpose of the system is to provide information about available events and to track tickets purchased for those events. The logical model for an OLTP database will usually be highly normalized, as is the gasTIX logical model.

NOTE

When designing OLTP systems it is important to store data in the most efficient manner possible by following the standard rules of normalization. First Normal Form states that repeating groups in tables should be eliminated, and that a primary key should be identified for each table. Second Normal Form states that separate tables should be created for sets of values that apply to multiple records, and that these tables should be related with a foreign key. Third Normal Form states that fields that do not depend on the key should be eliminated. Other rules exist, but are rarely used.

OLTP systems perform well for data-entry purposes, but usually fail to perform well when used for extensive reporting. The reason is that reports typically need to gather data from a large number of tables, and joining many tables usually slows down the report generation process. DSS applications, on the other hand, are specifically optimized for reporting. When we build DSS applications, we add a level of redundancy to our data by de-normalizing the appropriate tables. For example, we may decide to copy the customer name column into a purchase history table so that we don't have to join to the customer table for a purchase history report. Conversely, DSS applications do not perform as well as OLTP applications for data gathering purposes. In an OLTP system, we would not want to duplicate the customer name column in the purchase history table, because every time a customer makes a purchase, we would need to write extra data (customer name) into that table.

TIP

Database modeling has often been called more of an art than a science. Only through extensive experience do we gain the ability to know when to de-normalize appropriately, or to know to what level of normalization we should implement a design. More often than not, we find ourselves making trade-offs during the modeling process. Success comes through staying focused on the business requirements, and through soliciting feedback from others whose opinions we value.

OLAP applications load data from multiple transactional systems into a single storage area. The data may be cleaned up in this staging area, and custom calculations can be performed. When the data transformation process has been completed, it is loaded into the OLAP warehouse, and from this database users can build easily customizable reports.

OLAP applications let the business decision-makers "slice and dice" the data along various dimensions. Such systems represent a *dimensional model*, as opposed to the *relational model* used for OLTP and DSS applications.

The dimensional model consists of a large fact table (or multiple fact tables) and many small dimension tables. The fact table contains foreign keys to each of the dimension tables, and holds the measures that users would like to see on their reports. For instance, gasTIX management might like to see the cities and states with the highest volume of purchases for Backstreet Boys concerts. The dimensions chosen would include the music group (performer) and the customer. The measures would be the number of tickets sold, or the revenue generated.

One of the common mistakes made when modeling data is mixing the relational and the dimensional approaches, or using the same application for both data entry and reporting. Since the gasTIX business will require dimensional OLAP reporting at a later date, we will eventually build DSS or OLAP functionality into the gasTIX data services (although this is not included in this version). Keeping this in mind, we have purposefully designed an OLTP (relational) application for phase one of gasTIX, remembering the need for a future version of the database optimized for reporting. At some later time we may decide to design a dimensional model that will interface with the existing relational model. By no means, however, will we attempt to implement DSS/OLAP functionality solely within the relational model.

Physical Modeling

Perhaps one of the most frequently asked (and debated) questions is the difference between physical and logical data modeling. Logical modeling is done without any consideration of the DBMS that will be used to physically implement the model. Whether we build our database in Microsoft Access, Oracle, Informix, Sybase, or Microsoft SQL Server, the logical data model should be the same.

The physical model, on the other hand, is specific to the DBMS being used. It is in the physical model that we define data types and referential integrity constraints such as primary keys, foreign keys, and triggers. Any other database objects that will participate in the model are also defined, including indexes and views. Data types and database objects can vary widely from one DBMS to the next. Therefore, the physical model built for SQL Server might be quite different from the model built for Informix, although they are based on the same logical model.

In the following sections, we will examine each component of physical data modeling.

Choosing Appropriate Data Types

Physical database design involves choosing the proper data type for each element to be stored in the database. Data type selection should be primarily driven by the stated business requirements. However, we must select from the many data types provided with SQL Server. For instance, numeric data can be stored in the following data types: `BIT`, `TINYINT`, `SMALLINT`, `INT`, `BIGINT`, `REAL`, `DOUBLE`, `NUMERIC`, `FLOAT`, `MONEY`, `SMALLMONEY`, or even `CHAR` and `VARCHAR`.

We should select the data type that provides the necessary range of values, which at the same time uses the smallest number of bytes of storage. For instance, if we are storing a person's age, we can use the BIGINT data type, but we will be better off using TINYINT (unless we expect people in our database to exceed the age of 255)! The difference in storage space between these two types is seven bytes for every row, which will add up quickly if we gather millions of rows. "Narrow" data types create narrow tables and narrow indexes, which are easier to scan for queries.

Varying length data types such as VARCHAR and VARBINARY can also add overhead to a table and can therefore slow down transactions. If we are storing a social security number or a phone number in a column which always has the same length, it makes sense to use the CHAR data type instead of VARCHAR. On the other hand, if the average length of the column is much shorter than the maximum allowed length, variable length data types will actually perform better than fixed length data types.

Another important decision is whether each column in a table should allow nulls. Nullable columns add a slight overhead to a table, and are somewhat slower than the columns that do not allow nulls. However, nullable columns save a lot of space for the tables where only a few rows contain values.

TIP

In general, it is not a good idea to allow nulls in columns "just in case." This can hide exceptions that would otherwise be raised when data that should be provided for a business requirement is missing in an INSERT statement.

When adding a column to a table with existing data, we have to either allow nulls or specify a default value. After we populate all existing rows with non-null values, however, we can change the table definition to disallow nulls for that column. Earlier versions of SQL Server required us to export the data, drop the table, re-create the table, and import the data. With SQL Server 2000, we can simply change the table definition, which is a welcome productivity enhancement.

New Data Types in SQL Server 2000

Among the many welcome additions to the SQL Server programmer's arsenal of tools are several new data types, shown in Table 7.1.

TABLE 7.1 The New Data Types in SQL Server 2000

New Data Type	*Description*
BIGINT	Exact numeric data type that can handle values larger than INT.
CURSOR	Contains a reference to an existing cursor. Can only be used for parameters and variables.

TABLE 7.1 Continued

New Data Type	*Description*
`SQL_VARIANT`	Provides a way to store values without knowing the data type. Similar to the `VARIANT` data type found in other languages such as Visual Basic 6.0.
`TABLE`	Contains up to 1024 columns. Similar to temporary tables, except `TABLE` variables are cleaned up automatically. Can only be used for variables and parameters. Provides an array-like structure.

The first new data type we will discuss is `BIGINT`. This data type allows for very large numeric values between `+9,223,372,036,854,775,807` and `-9,223,372,036,854,775,807`. It consumes eight bytes of storage. Obviously, the majority of our applications can get by just fine with the `INT` data type and will never need to use `BIGINT`. However, for those folks that have stretched SQL Server's limits in the past due to the need to store huge data values, `BIGINT` is the answer.

SQL Server 2000 also adds support for `CURSOR` data types. Variables with the `CURSOR` data type can store a reference to a SQL cursor, which is a Transact SQL programmatic construct that allows us to loop through a recordset row by row. The difference between the `CURSOR` and `TABLE` data types is that a `CURSOR` allows scrolling through the data set one record at a time, while a `TABLE` does not. The `CURSOR` data type can be used to pass an array from one stored procedure to another, but cannot be used for creating table columns. The example shown in Listing 7.1 uses an output parameter with a `CURSOR` data type.

LISTING 7.1 A SQL Server 2000 Stored Procedure Output Parameter Can be Defined and Called with the New `CURSOR` Data Type

```
CREATE PROC return_customers
(@letter CHAR(1),
@cust_cursor CURSOR VARYING OUTPUT)
AS
SET @cust_cursor = CURSOR FOR
SELECT email_address FROM customer
WHERE email_address LIKE @letter + '%'
OPEN @cust_cursor

-- execute the procedure with a CURSOR OUTPUT parameter:
DECLARE @my_cursor CURSOR

EXEC return_customers a, @my_cursor OUTPUT
FETCH NEXT FROM @my_cursor
WHILE @@FETCH_STATUS = 0
BEGIN
```

LISTING 7.1 Continued

```
FETCH @my_cursor
END
CLOSE @my_cursor
DEALLOCATE @my_cursor
```

Another new data type in SQL Server 2000 is `SQL_VARIANT`. This data type is similar to the `VARIANT` data type found in other programming languages. It can be used for storing data of any type, except `TIMESTAMP`, `SQL_VARIANT`, `IMAGE`, `TEXT`, and `NTEXT`. It takes eight bytes of storage, and can be used for table columns, variables, parameters, or return values of user-defined functions. The advantage of `SQL_VARIANT` is that it can be used when we are unsure about the nature of the data to be stored in a parameter or column.

Also available in SQL Server 2000 is the new `TABLE` data type. This data type offers the long-awaited feature of array support. We can declare a variable with a `TABLE` data type and store multi-dimensional arrays in it. As the name states, a `TABLE` variable behaves much like a temporary table. The advantage of using a `TABLE` data type is that it is cleaned up automatically when it goes out of scope; there is no need to issue a `DROP TABLE` statement. For example, the code in Listing 7.2 populates a variable with multiple columns of data.

LISTING 7.2 Multiple Columns of Data Can be Stored in a `TABLE` Variable in SQL Server 2000

```
DECLARE @customer_names TABLE
(last_name VARCHAR(30), first_name VARCHAR(30), email_address VARCHAR(50))

-- populate the table variable
INSERT @customer_names
SELECT last_name, first_name, email_address FROM customer

-- read the values from the table variable
SELECT * FROM @customer_names
```

Keep in mind that the `TABLE` data type cannot be used when specifying column data types; it can be used only with variables.

Adding Referential Integrity Constraints

Referential Integrity (RI) constraints help keep the database in a consistent state. RI lets the database administrator or developer enforce business rules at the database level. It is true that the majority of business rules should be enforced in middle-tier components. However, an additional level of integrity usually does not hurt. Certain business rules are also easier to create and can be more efficiently enforced in the database. For example, we could enforce a rule that a customer record must exist in the customer table before she can place orders. Similarly, we can only delete a customer if all orders for that customer have been canceled. These rules are quite easy to enforce at the database level, while in a middle-tier component they are more complex to implement.

SQL Server 2000 provides a way to cascade referential integrity constraints when UPDATE and DELETE statements are executed. What this means is that if a foreign key column is updated in the primary table, the column in the related table can also be updated. We also have the option to supress such UPDATES and report an error. In previous versions of SQL Server, we had to write a trigger to create this functionality. Let's look at a quick example of a cascading UPDATE statement. In the gasTIX database we have a Participant table, as well as an Event_Participant table (see the Appendix for a full depiction of the gasTIX database schema). Listing 7.3 shows the first few rows of the Event_Participant table.

LISTING 7.3 The First Few Rows of the Event_Participant Table Selected

```
SELECT * FROM Event_Participant

Results:
Event_id    participant_id
1       10
1       11
2       15
...
```

Suppose we add the following foreign key constraint to the Event_Participant table, as shown in Listing 7.4.

LISTING 7.4 A Foreign Key Constraint is Added to the Event_Participant Table

```
ALTER TABLE [dbo].[Event_Participant]
ADD  CONSTRAINT [FK_event_participant_participant]
FOREIGN KEY  ([participant_id])
REFERENCES [dbo].[participant] ([participant_id])
ON UPDATE CASCADE
```

Now, if we change the participant_id column in the Participant table, the participant_id column in the Event_Participant table will also be updated accordingly. This is shown in Listing 7.5.

LISTING 7.5 The Participant_id Column is Changed in the Participant Table

```
UPDATE Participant SET participant_id = 151
WHERE participant_id = 15
GO
SELECT * FROM Event_Participant

Results:
Event_id    participant_id
1       10
1       11
2       151
...
```

Alternatively, we could choose to report an error if anyone attempts to change participant_id, as shown in Listing 7.6.

LISTING 7.6 A Foreign Key Constraint is Added, Specifying that an Error is to be Raised if Violated

```
ALTER TABLE [dbo].[Event_Participant]
DROP CONSTRAINT FK_event_participant_participant
GO
ALTER TABLE [dbo].[Event_Participant]
 ADD CONSTRAINT [FK_event_participant_participant]
FOREIGN KEY
    ([participant_id])
REFERENCES [dbo].[participant] ([participant_id])
ON UPDATE NO ACTION
```

Now, in Listing 7.7, when we try to change the participant_id column back to the way it was originally, we receive an error. The error result we receive lets us know that this change is not acceptable.

LISTING 7.7 An Error is Returned When We Try to Change the Participant_id Column Back to Its Original State

```
UPDATE Participant SET participant_id = 15 WHERE participant_id = 151
Server: Msg 547, Level 16, State 1, Line 1
UPDATE statement conflicted with COLUMN REFERENCE
constraint 'FK_event_participant_participant'.
The conflict occurred in database 'gastix',
table 'Event_Participant', column 'participant_id'.
The statement has been terminated.
```

We could configure similar actions for the DELETE statement. The general syntax is as follows:

```
ON DELETE { CASCADE | NO ACTION }
```

Indexing for Performance

Building and maintaining appropriate indexes on database tables is a necessity for making sure that an application is optimized well. If our indexes are not effective, or if index statistics are out of date, chances are that our queries will not perform to the best of their ability. That is why adding good indexes can make a world of difference in an application's execution speed.

The more indexes we have and the bigger they are, the faster our queries, right? Wrong! Choosing the proper indexes is not that simple, otherwise we could build indexes on every column of every table and rewards would be quickly forthcoming. Actually, our choice of the columns on which to place an index depends on many factors. Some of these factors are examined below.

Number of Indexes

Each index we define will likely improve performance of a SELECT query. However, we need to keep in mind that the same index will slightly degrade the performance of any related INSERT, UPDATE, and DELETE statement. The reason for this is that SQL Server automatically maintains the index keys. Therefore, each time we issue a Data Modification Language (DML) statement such as INSERT, UPDATE, or DELETE, not only does SQL Server have to make changes to the data, but it also has to change each index defined on the affected table. Performance degradation is especially noticeable with large tables containing many indexes, or even a few indexes with long keys.

SQL Server 2000 has come a long way from previous releases when considering index maintenance. However, in some cases, it still makes sense to drop the indexes, issue the data modification statement, and then re-create the indexes. This is especially true when working with large sets of data. For instance, suppose we have a data warehouse with a fact table containing several million rows. Approximately one million rows are added each time we load data. To speed up the queries, we have defined several indexes on the fact table, including the clustered index (covered in the next section) which spans all of the dimension keys. The population of the fact table will be much faster if we drop the indexes, load the data, and rebuild the indexes.

Clustered Versus Non-Clustered Indexes

Another decision to make is whether we need a clustered or a non-clustered index on a particular column or set of columns. This is where it helps to have an understanding of the underlying SQL Server index architecture. SQL Server indexes have a B-tree structure with a root node, intermediate levels, and leaf nodes. For non-clustered indexes the leaf nodes are the keys of the clustered index. For clustered indexes the leaf nodes represent *the data itself*. This brings up two important points:

1. Table data is sorted according to the order of the clustered index.
2. We can only have one clustered index on each table. This makes sense if we refer to the previous point; we cannot expect SQL Server to store the data sorted in two different ways.

To illustrate these points, let us look at the Event table in the gasTIX database. By default this table has the clustered index *event_ind* defined on the event_id column. This means that data in this table will be ordered according to the event_id. Creating a clustered index on a sequentially increasing column is a bad idea, as discussed shortly, so we will drop the current clustered index and replace it, as shown in Listing 7.8.

LISTING 7.8 Creating a Better Clustered Index on the Event Table in gasTIX

```
DROP INDEX event.event_ind
GO
CREATE CLUSTERED INDEX event_date_and_name ON event(event_date, event_name)
```

Now we can examine how the data is physically stored in the table by running a simple `SELECT` statement on the Event table (shown in Listing 7.9). We will force SQL Server to use the clustered index with a query hint since we do not wish to bring the entire table back, just the date and the name of the event.

LISTING 7.9 Examining How Data in the Event Table is Returned Using the Newly Created Clustered Index

```
SELECT event_date, event_name FROM event (INDEX = 1)
event_date     event_name
5/6/01 12:00 AM     Decatur Houseflies vs. Bentonville Polar Bears
5/6/01 12:00 AM     Hayward Rats vs. Decatur Houseflies
5/7/01 12:00 AM     Warwick Houseflies vs. Savannah Houseflies
5/11/01 12:00 AM     Reno Tigers vs. New London Rats
```

We have created a clustered index on the combination of the event date and the event name. This will provide the gasTIX database with the best performance for the majority of its queries, since these are the two columns most frequently searched. It is important to note that we have agreed to the trade-off of decreased performance on `INSERT` and `DELETE` statements on the Event table for improved SELECT performance. This decision fits our business requirement which states that searches will be performed much more frequently than data inserts or deletions.

TIP

Trade-offs between better SELECT statement performance versus better INSERT, UPDATE, and DELETE performance must often be made when implementing a database design. As shown in the previous gasTIX example, the decision should be made based on the relevant business requirements.

A common misperception is that SQL Server stores data according to the order that records are entered into a table. Contrary to this belief, SQL Server actually stores data according to the way we create the clustered index.

A clustered index will be much faster for data retrieval operations than a non-clustered index because the data is ordered according to the clustered index definition. What this means to us as developers is that the clustered index should be placed only on the most important column (or columns) in each table. SQL Server allows up to 249 non-clustered indexes per table. Therefore, if we do need an index on other columns, we can always create a non-clustered index.

NOTE

Keep in mind that SQL Server enforces PRIMARY KEY constraints by placing a unique index on a table. Unless told otherwise, and if there is no clustered index on the table, SQL Server will make the PRIMARY KEY index clustered. When creating indexes other than PRIMARY KEY or UNIQUE KEY indexes, by default SQL Server will create them as non-clustered.

If we have a column marked as an identity column, we should avoid putting a clustered index on that column. Identity columns use an automatically-incremented value generated by SQL Server. For instance, the gasTIX database has the identity property set on the event_id column in the Event table. The first event inserted in this table will have an `event_id = 1`, the second will have `event_id = 2`, etc. It is not likely that our users will ever run queries affecting the identity column since it has no business meaning, and normally users will never see this value.

TIP

It is very important to have a clustered index on every table. If a table does not have a clustered index, all new records will be added to the last data page occupied by the table. This can cause inefficiencies because queries are rarely executed based on the order in which data was originally inserted. If there is a clustered index on a table, new rows can be added to the last page, or to the middle of the table, whichever position is suitable for the new row according to the way data is sorted in the table (according to the way clustered index is defined).

In general, clustered indexes are good for queries that:

- contain a large number of distinct values.
- have a `WHERE` clause that returns values based on `BETWEEN`, or > or < conditions.
- read columns accessed sequentially. That is, if 'lastname' and 'firstname' columns are accessed often in queries, we should create an index on columns *in that order*.
- have a `GROUP BY` and/or `ORDER BY` clause that accesses the first few or all columns comprising the clustered index.

In general, we should avoid placing a clustered index on a frequently changing column. Since SQL Server has to sort the data according to the clustered index definition, frequently changing clustered key values will result in extra work for the database engine, and will degrade the performance of `UPDATE` and `INSERT` operations.

We should also avoid having long keys for clustered indexes, unless our queries refer to the entire combination of all columns in the clustered index frequently. The reason to avoid long keys is that non-clustered indexes on the same table will use the clustered keys for lookups, and will therefore grow very large.

Non-clustered indexes are good for retrieving smaller numbers of rows, and for queries that have exact match (=) conditions in the `WHERE` clause. Generally speaking, we can use non-clustered indexes any time we need to speed up the query on a particular column if the clustered index is already being used by another column.

CAUTION

Keep in mind that each time we rebuild a clustered index (whether we move it to a different column or not) all non-clustered indexes for the table are rebuilt as well. This is because non-clustered indexes use the clustered index values as their lookup keys. When we move the clustered index to a different column, the whole table is copied to temporary storage, ordered according to the clustered index definition, and recreated. Therefore, dropping and re-creating clustered indexes is a resource-intensive and time-consuming operation which should be performed during periods of limited user activity.

Long or Short Index Keys?

When implementing indexes for a database, we must decide how many columns, and which specific columns, to include in our indexes. Most of the time our queries themselves determine whether or not we need to include a particular column in an index. However, we have the option to create more indexes with fewer columns (or index keys). The shorter an index is, the more index keys fit on a single page, and the less space taken up by the index. This means that scanning index pages takes less time, and overall the index is more efficient.

On the other hand, some queries that contain search criteria defined on several columns could benefit from a long index that includes all columns mentioned in the `WHERE` clause. Such an index is referred to as a "covering index." Note that if the index key is too long, SQL Server might actually store more data than index keys on a single page. The covering index keys should fit on a single page in order to be beneficial. If the index is narrower than the actual table, more index keys can be placed on a single page, and therefore the entire index will be easier to scan. For example, suppose we have a report that retrieves event date, event name, tour id associated with the event, and date that tickets go on sale. We could create a covering non-clustered index on the Event table to optimize the query for this report as follows:

```
CREATE NONCLUSTERED INDEX report_index ON

Event(event_date, event_name, tour_id, ticket_sell_start_date)
```

Index Tuning Wizard

SQL Server 2000 includes a useful tool called the Index Tuning Wizard. This tool analyzes the current indexes on a database, based on a workload file generated with SQL Profiler, a selection of queries run within Query Analyzer, or from a trace table (which can also be generated with SQL Profiler). If the Index Tuning Wizard finds that queries can be optimized with new indexes, it provides the option to create the new indexes at the click of a button.

The Index Tuning Wizard is invoked by selecting Tools|Index Tuning Wizard from the menu bar within SQL Profiler, or by selecting the Query|Index Tuning Wizard menu option within SQL Query Analyzer. For detailed information on using this helpful tool, refer to Chapter 15, "Performance Tuning in .NET."

Transact-SQL

Transact SQL is a SQL Server-specific flavor of the Structured Query Language (SQL), the programming language supported by all major database engines. Transact SQL (T-SQL) supports most standard SQL features which are updated every few years by the American National Standards Institute (ANSI).

NOTE

To learn more about the ANSI standards body, visit their web site at `www.ansi.org`. In addition to helping define the ANSI SQL standard, this standards body is involved with defining consistent standards for a wide variety of industries. The National Resource for Global Standards (NSSN) offers a web site at `www.nssn.org` where you can search for a variety of these standards, and view the details behind them.

Transact SQL has powerful extensions that let us program conditional statements, execute server-side cursors, manipulate batches, and work with reusable code modules such as user-defined functions and stored procedures. In this section we will offer a brief overview of the differences between ANSI SQL and Transact SQL with an emphasis on the new features supported in SQL Server 2000. Since this is not a book dedicated to Transact-SQL, we will only focus on the major features and enhancements. The key point to remember is that implementing .NET data services requires smart use of Transact SQL in various places in SQL Server 2000.

Variables in Transact SQL

Variables are user-defined or system-defined objects that hold certain values within a Transact SQL program for a period of time. There are two types of variables in T-SQL: local and global. We will explore both variable types in the following sections.

Local Variables

Local variables are created by developers using the `DECLARE` statement. It is a good idea to create all local variables at the beginning of the T-SQL program (or stored procedure) to make maintenance easier. Variable names must conform to the SQL rules for identifier names, and in addition, they must start with the "@" symbol. They cannot be `TEXT`, `NTEXT`, or `IMAGE` data types.

As mentioned earlier, SQL Server 2000 supports the new `TABLE` data type, which can contain up to 1024 columns. Due to this fact, the variables with data types other than `TABLE` are often referred to as *scalar* variables. The syntax for creating local scalar variables includes simply stating the variable name and the data type, as follows:

```
DECLARE @local_variable data_type
```

Multiple local variables can be created with a single DECLARE statement. For example, the following code creates three local variables:

```
DECLARE @number_of_rows INT, @event_name VARCHAR(20), @event_date SMALLDATETIME
```

There are multiple ways of assigning values to local variables. One way is to use a SELECT statement to assign a specified value to the variable, as shown in the following line (note that all of the following examples assume that the @number_of_rows variable has been declared as INT):


```
SELECT @number_of_rows = 10
```

Another way is to assign a value retrieved by a SELECT statement to the variable, as follows:

```
SELECT @number_of_rows = (SELECT COUNT(row_id)

FROM venue_section_row WHERE section_id = 2)
```

A third way is to use the SET statement to assign a specified value (or value returned from a sub-query) to the variable:

```
SET @number_of_rows = (SELECT COUNT(row_id)

FROM venue_section_row WHERE section_id = 2)
```

A fourth way is to use a variable as a column alias inside a SELECT statement:

```
SELECT @number_of_rows = row_id

FROM venue_section_row WHERE section_id = 2
```

CAUTION

If a SELECT statement, such as the statement shown in the last example, returns multiple values, then the local variable will be assigned the *last* value returned. While not causing a run-time error, this can produce unexpected results if not accounted for.

Scalar local variables can be used for constant values, but cannot be directly referenced as database objects, such as tables or views. For instance, the code in Listing 7.10 generates an error.

LISTING 7.10 Referencing a Scalar Local Variable as a Database Object Causes an Error

```
DECLARE @table VARCHAR(32)
SELECT @table = 'region'
SELECT * FROM @table
Results:
Server: Msg 137, Level 15, State 2, Line 4
Must declare the variable '@table'.
```

The reason this error is raised is that variable values are resolved at compile time. A workaround is to use the `EXECUTE` statement (or the `sp_executesql` system stored procedure), which is resolved at run time rather than at compile time. The statement in Listing 7.11 will execute because the `EXEC` statement is included. It returns all records from the Region table, which is what we were trying to accomplish in the first example.

LISTING 7.11 Using the `EXEC` Statement Allows Us to Reference a Scalar Local Variable as a Database Object

```
DECLARE @table VARCHAR(32), @string VARCHAR(100)
SELECT @table = 'region'
SELECT @string = 'SELECT * FROM ' + @table
EXEC(@string)
```

Global Variables

Global variables are pre-defined system values. Their values cannot be changed by the programmer. Global variables used by any session have the same value at any particular point in time. For instance, the global variable `@@error` always contains the number of the last error that was encountered during program execution. Global variables are helpful when programming in Transact SQL because they provide system-wide information that we often need to inspect to determine an outcome.

Parameters in Transact SQL

Parameters in T-SQL are special kinds of variables used within stored procedures, triggers, and user-defined functions. Just like other local variables, parameters must start with the "@" symbol, and need to be of a particular data type. Unlike local variables, parameters exist only for the duration of a procedure or function, and they can have a default value. General syntax for declaring parameters is as follows:

```
CREATE OR ALTER PROCEDURE proc_name

    [ { @parameter data_type }
        [ VARYING ] [ = default ] [ OUTPUT ]
    ] [ ,...n ]
```

The list of parameters can optionally be enclosed in parentheses. The VARYING keyword applies to output cursor parameters and simply informs SQL Server that the result set is constructed dynamically.

Parameters for both stored procedures and functions can have defaults assigned to them. If the variable does not have a default, and no value is provided, the stored procedure (or function) will fail. Stored procedures can take parameters of any data type, including the TEXT, NTEXT and IMAGE data types. The CURSOR data type can only be used as an output parameter, and we must also specify the VARYING keyword. User-defined functions can only accept scalar data types.

The following procedure from the gasTIX database, shown in Listing 7.12, returns all participants (music artists or sports teams) that appear at a specified venue. Notice that in addition to using a parameter, the procedure also uses a local variable, @today. Also note that the @venue_id parameter is assigned a default value.

LISTING 7.12 A Sample gasTIX Stored Procedure Accepts a Single Input Parameter and Uses a Local Variable

```
CREATE PROCEDURE dbo.usp_get_participants_by_venue
(@venue_id    INT = -1) -- default value of -1
AS
DECLARE @today SMALLDATETIME
select @today = CAST(CONVERT(VARCHAR(10), GETDATE(), 101) AS SMALLDATETIME)
SELECT DISTINCT
    p.participant_id,
    p.participant_name
FROM    venue v
INNER JOIN configuration c ON c.venue_id = v.venue_id
INNER JOIN event e ON
    e.configuration_id = c.configuration_id
    AND e.event_date BETWEEN @today AND DATEADD(m, 3, @today)
    AND e.inactive_flag = 'N'
INNER JOIN event_participant ep ON ep.event_id = e.event_id
INNER JOIN participant p ON p.participant_id = ep.participant_id
WHERE    v.venue_id = @venue_id
```

Output parameters can be specified within a stored procedure if we would like the procedure to return a single value, rather than a recordset. Alternatively, we can return a populated cursor from a stored procedure with a CURSOR data type as the output parameter.

To use output parameters, we simply include the keyword OUTPUT (or just OUT) within the parameter declaration. The example shown in Listing 7.13 retrieves the total amount of revenue generated by ticket sales for a particular venue as an output parameter.

LISTING 7.13 A Sample gasTIX Stored Procedure Uses a Simple Output Parameter

```
CREATE PROC output_param_example @region_id VARCHAR(11),
@total_sales SMALLMONEY OUTPUT
AS
SELECT @total_sales = SUM(total_charged) FROM sale a, region b,
event c, configuration d, venue e
WHERE  a.event_id = c.event_id
AND    b.region_id = e.region_id
AND    d.venue_id = e.venue_id
AND    c.configuration_id = d.configuration_id
AND    e.region_id = @region_id
```

Now, in Listing 7.14, we use the `@total_sales` output parameter in the following batch (which could easily be a stored procedure).

LISTING 7.14 Using the Output Parameter Returned from a gasTIX Stored Procedure

```
DECLARE @total_sales SMALLMONEY
EXECUTE output_param_example
31, @total_sales = @total_sales OUTPUT
SELECT 'the folks from New Jersey have purchased $ '
+ CAST(@total_sales AS VARCHAR(10)) + ' worth of tickets'

Results:
----------------------------------------------------------------
the folks from New Jersey have purchased $ 9627.45 worth of tickets
```

Transact SQL Cursors

Transact SQL is a set-based language. This means we usually don't need to process one row at a time. However, there are times when we need to exercise programming logic when reading the result set row by row. This is when we need to create and use a cursor. A cursor is an in-memory representation of a table or query result that we can manipulate one row at a time.

CAUTION

As expected, reading a table with a million rows one row at a time can be painfully slow. Cursors will usually perform poorer than comparable set-based operations, and should be avoided when another solution is available (such as a `SELECT` statement using a `GROUP BY` clause). However, for certain tasks cursors are the only option.

Perhaps one of the best examples of when to use cursors is when we apply a batch job to a large table. In this case, performance is not as important as reducing the locking contention on the table, or perhaps even as important as filling up the transaction log.

TIP

Cursors in SQL Server generally do not lock multiple pages at a time since they are reading the data set row by row. This reduces the overall amount of locking contention.

Working with cursors in Transact SQL consists of implementing several steps:

1. Create the cursor with the `DECLARE` statement. This command defines a `SELECT` clause, possibly joining multiple tables and views to create the recordset to be referenced by the cursor.
2. Open the cursor with the `OPEN` command. SQL Server will populate the recordset by executing the `SELECT` statement that defined the cursor, but will not return any records.
3. Fetch one row at a time and take the desired programmatic action on each row. Depending on the type of cursor, we might change values in the underlying table or view. We might also move forward and back (scroll) inside the cursor.
4. Once all processing is complete (all rows have been traversed), `CLOSE` the cursor (we can reopen it later if necessary).
5. Once the program has completed its task(s) and it is clear that we will not need the cursor again, remove it from memory with the `DEALLOCATE` command.

Cursors cannot be shared among connections, but they can be declared as local or global, and can thus be shared across the same connection. Declaring a global cursor simply means the cursor is made available for any stored procedure or batch for the duration of the connection. A cursor declared as local has a much more limited scope. It can only be used by the stored procedure or batch in which it is declared. If neither option is specified, the default is determined by the database option `DEFAULT TO LOCAL CURSOR`, which can be modified with the `ALTER DATABASE` command or the `sp_dboption` system stored procedure.

The `SELECT` statement used to declare a cursor cannot contain the `FOR BROWSE` or `FOR XML` clauses, and also cannot use `COMPUTE`, `COMPUTE BY`, or `INTO`. Base tables or views cannot be updated through a cursor if the `SELECT` statement in the cursor declaration contains:

- an aggregate function (such as `SUM`, `COUNT`, etc.)
- a `JOIN` of any kind

- a subquery
- the `UNION` keyword
- the `DISTINCT` keyword
- a `GROUP BY` clause

Functions in Transact SQL

Transact SQL functions are built-in or user-defined code modules that let us manipulate data, perform computations and comparisons, and retrieve other system information. With SQL Server 2000 user-defined functions are also supported.

Functions can be *deterministic* and *non-deterministic*. Deterministic functions return the same result with the same set of input values, regardless of when they are executed. Built-in functions that are always deterministic include `ISNULL`, `CEILING`, `FLOOR`, and others. Non-deterministic functions return a different result depending on when they are executed. For instance, `getdate()` is a non-deterministic function since it returns a different result each time.

CAUTION

If a SQL Server table has a column populated with the result of a non-deterministic function, we cannot build an index on that column. We also cannot create a clustered index on a view that references a non-deterministic function.

The following example uses several built-in functions. `ISNULL` returns a specific value if a `NULL` is encountered. `SUBSTRING` lets us extract a portion of a string. `LEN` lets us determine the number of characters in a string. `CAST` allows us to change the data type of a variable or constant.

LISTING 7.15 A SELECT Statement Can be Made Powerful with the Use of Transact SQL Functions

```
SELECT TOP 3
SUBSTRING(event_name, 1, LEN(event_name)) AS event,
CAST(SUBSTRING(ISNULL(special_instruction, 'not available'), 1,
LEN(ISNULL(CAST(special_instruction AS VARCHAR(100)), 'not available')))
AS VARCHAR(40))
 AS special_instr
FROM event

Results:
event                                                special_instr
---------------------------------------------------- -------------
```

LISTING 7.15 Continued

```
Hayward Polar Bears versus Fort Dodge Polar Bears        not available
Knoxville Rats versus Jackson Polar Bears                not available
Witchita Polar Bears versus Washington Rats              not available
```

Views

Views are stored queries that look and act like virtual tables. A view can be based on one or more tables, or on other views. A view's content is not stored as a table. Rather, the query that defined the view is executed against the base tables each time a view is queried. A view cannot accept parameters and cannot contain multiple `SELECT` statements (with the exception of subqueries, which are allowed).

We can define a view using the `CREATE VIEW` statement (refer to the SQL Server documentation for syntax). Listing 7.16 provides an example of creating a view in the gasTIX database.

LISTING 7.16 Creating a View in the gasTIX Database

```
CREATE VIEW event_participant_names
AS
SELECT participant_name, event_name
FROM event a INNER JOIN event_participant b
ON a.event_id = b.event_id
INNER JOIN participant c
ON c.participant_id = b.participant_id
```

If we wish to rename a view (or any other reusable code module), we can use the `sp_rename` system stored procedure. With SQL Server 2000, we can also modify the `SELECT` statement that created the view without dropping and recreating a view. This can be accomplished by using an `ALTER VIEW` statement, as shown in Listing 7.17.

LISTING 7.17 Altering a View in the gasTIX Database

```
ALTER VIEW event_participant_names
AS
SELECT participant_name, event_name
FROM event a INNER JOIN event_participant b
ON a.event_id = b.event_id
INNER JOIN participant c
ON c.participant_id = b.participant_id
INNER JOIN category d
ON c.category_id = d.category_id
WHERE
category_name = 'music'
```

If we are no longer using a view, we can drop it by executing the `DROP VIEW` statement as follows:

```
DROP VIEW event_participant_names
```

The `SELECT` statement that creates a view cannot contain any of the following:

- `COMPUTE` or `COMPUTE BY`
- `INTO`
- `ORDER BY` clause (unless we also use `TOP` keyword)
- `FOR XML` or `FOR BROWSE`

Note that the `CREATE VIEW` statement cannot be combined with other statements in a batch.

We are allowed to execute Data Modification Language (DML) statements against views with some limitations:

- DML statements must affect only one underlying table. For example, an `INSERT` statement can only add values to one table through a view and it must have the column list specified.
- We cannot insert or update a computed or aggregate column through a view.
- We cannot use `WRITETEXT` to modify `TEXT` data type column inside a view.
- We cannot run an `INSERT` statement against a view without specifying columns for all non-nullable columns of the underlying table, unless those columns have default constraints associated with them.
- If we use the `WITH CHECK` option when defining a view, all data modifications will have to conform to the `SELECT` statement that created the view.

The addition of `INSTEAD OF` triggers to SQL Server 2000 allows developers to build updateable views on multiple base tables. This type of trigger is discussed later in this chapter in the section titled "`INSTEAD OF` Triggers."

Advantages of Using Views

Views are used for several different reasons. The first is to hide data complexity. Instead of forcing our users to learn the T-SQL `JOIN` syntax, we might wish to provide a view that runs a commonly requested SQL statement.

If we have a table containing sensitive data in certain columns, we might wish to hide those columns from certain groups of users. For instance, customer names, addresses, and social security numbers might be stored in the same table. For a group of employees such as shipping clerks, we can create a view that only displays customer name and address. This is referred to as *vertical partitioning* and is accomplished by specifying only the appropriate columns in the `CREATE VIEW` statement.

Another way to secure table data is to create a view that allows reading only certain rows from a table. For instance, we might have a separate view for each department's manager. This way, each manager can provide raises only to the employees of his or her department. This is referred to as *horizontal partitioning* and is accomplished by providing a where clause in the `SELECT` statement creating a view.

We can also use views to enforce simple business rules. For instance, if we wish to generate a list of customers that need to receive a winter catalog of upcoming gasTIX events, we can create a view of customers that have previously bought tickets for artists/teams scheduled to perform during the winter.

Views can also help us export data using the Bulk Copy Program (BCP). BCP is a command-line utility that provides lower-level import and export capabilities for SQL Server. If we are using BCP to export SQL Server data to text files, we can format the data through views, since the formatting ability of the BCP utility is quite limited.

Customizing data is also made easy using views. If we wish to display customized computed values or column names formatted differently than the base table columns, we can do so by creating views.

Disadvantages of Using Views

Even though views can be a great tool for securing and customizing data, they can at times perform slowly. Indeed, they are no faster than the query that defines them. With SQL Server 2000, indexed views (also referred to as *materialized* views) are supported to overcome this limitation. This feature enables us to create a unique clustered index on a view, which causes the view results to be stored similar to how a table with a clustered index is stored. This feature is covered in more detail later in this chapter.

CAUTION

Views based on other views can especially degrade performance. Therefore, it is recommended that views should NOT be created based on other views. All views should be created against base tables.

Partitioned Views

One of the many exciting new features of SQL Server 2000 is the ability to build a group of databases residing on different servers that can act as a single database as far as client applications are concerned. This can be useful if our tables grow so large that we cannot effectively store data on a single server. This concept is referred to as a group of *federated databases*.

Partitioned views are implemented through remote (distributed) queries. A partitioned view is simply a view built on a set of tables residing on local or remote servers. All tables participating in the partitioned view have the same or similar structure. The column names, data types, precision, and scale must be similar for a read-only view, and must be the same to allow updates through a view.

Each server participating in building a partitioned view must be set up as a *linked server* on the local server where the view is defined. DML statements, as well as the `CREATE VIEW` statement, are implemented through `OPENQUERY` or `OPENROWSET` keywords. A table on each server contains a portion of the entire data set. The partitioned views, in effect, are really a way to split a table horizontally for optimizing performance. The column used to split the table into several smaller tables is referred to as the *partitioning column*.

Due to the relatively large size and low price of hard disks, it is likely that most of our applications will not make use of distributed partitioned views. However, if we do encounter the need to use them, it is helpful to know that they are supported.

There are some issues to keep in mind when building and using distributed partitioned views:

- Only the Enterprise and Developer editions of SQL Server support partitioned views.
- Each linked server participating in the partitioned view has to have `lazy schema validation` option set on. This is accomplished through the `sp_serveroption` system stored procedure and advises SQL Server not to request metadata from any linked servers until it is actually needed. Indeed, if our query can be satisfied from the data on the local server, there is no need to run distributed queries.
- The partitioned view must be set up on each of the servers participating in building the view. This means we must set up all participating servers as linked servers for each other.
- A distributed transaction will be initiated if the partitioned view is distributed and updateable, and a DML statement is executed against the view. This also means that the Distributed Transaction Coordinator (DTC) must be running on all participating servers.
- Each server must have `SET XACT_ABORT` option set to on, which ensures that if there are any type of runtime errors when executing a DML statement, the entire transaction will be rolled back.

For a complete discussion of the advantages and limitations of distributed partitioned views, refer to the SQL Server 2000 documentation.

Indexed Views

Another exciting new feature of SQL Server 2000 is the ability to build indexes on views. Just like using a partitioned view, using an indexed view requires some extra work. However, the performance gains that can be achieved make the extra steps worthwhile.

In order to be indexed, a view must be bound to the database schema. It then behaves in a similar fashion to a regular table. As mentioned earlier, unless we bind the view to the schema, it is just a stored query, rather then a physical object. The view created in Listing 7.18 can be indexed because it uses the `WITH SCHEMABINDING` keyword. (Note that in the example we must specify the two-part format for database objects, e.g. `dbo.Venue`, when using the `WITH SCHEMABINDING` option).

LISTING 7.18 Creating a View in the gasTIX Database Using the `WITH SCHEMABINDING` Keyword

```
CREATE VIEW ca_venues WITH SCHEMABINDING
AS
       SELECT venue_id, venue_name
FROM dbo.Venue V, dbo.Region R
WHERE V.region_id = R.region_id
AND R.short_name = 'ca'
```


Now we can define an index on the venue_id column in the view to speed up the query performance:

```
CREATE UNIQUE CLUSTERED INDEX ix_ca_venues ON ca_venues(venue_id)
```

SQL Server can now use the `ix_ca_venues` index not only when reading rows from the view, but also when querying the underlying Venue table (depending on the cost of using the index versus the cost of scanning the entire table or using another index).

In order for SQL Server to use an index defined on a view, the following session settings must be set on:

- `ANSI_NULLS`
- `ANSI_PADDING`
- `ANSI_WARNINGS`
- `ARITHABORT`
- `CONCAT_NULL_YIELDS_NULL`
- `QUOTED_IDENTIFIERS`

In addition, `NUMERIC_ROUNDABORT` must be turned off.

NOTE

According to the SQL Server documentation, requiring that the clustered index for a view be unique improves efficiency. This is because it can more easily locate rows in the index affected by future data modifications.

Stored Procedures

Stored procedures are groups of T-SQL statements executed together. Using stored procedures allows programmers to enclose much of the business logic of a .NET e-Business application inside T-SQL code.

There are multiple advantages to using stored procedures:

- Stored procedures generally perform better than the same group of statements executed individually. When a stored procedure is first invoked, it is compiled, and the execution algorithm is cached. The SQL Server engine reads from this cache on subsequent invocations and does not have to decide how to best run a stored procedure each time it is executed.
- Stored procedures provide a high level of security for SQL Server data. When we write a stored procedure for all DML statements and grant database users access only to these stored procedures, we can tightly control what users can and cannot do with the data.
- Stored procedures can accept and return parameters. With SQL Server 2000, each stored procedure can have up to 2100 parameters.
- Stored procedures allow us to encapsulate business rules within manageable components of code. When the business rule changes, we only have to modify our code in one place.
- Stored procedures can be executed automatically when SQL Server starts up, or they can be invoked explicitly.

Creating Stored Procedures

Stored procedures can be created with the `CREATE PROCEDURE` SQL statement, or through the SQL Enterprise Manager user interface. There are certain rules to keep in mind when using the `CREATE PROCEDURE` statement. First, stored procedure names must follow the general rules for identifier names. Second, the objects that a stored procedure references must exist when it is run. We no longer have to pre-create objects before referencing them, as we did in previous versions of SQL Server. We can now create, populate, and retrieve data from a table or view within a single stored procedure. We just have to make sure that the object is created before it is referenced.

This feature is called *deferred name resolution* because the SQL Server engine does not check for the existence of an object until run-time. Despite the fact that we can create and reference objects within the same procedure, we cannot drop and re-create the object with the same name within a single procedure. So if we drop the gasTIX table named Venue in a stored procedure, we cannot create another table named Venue within the same procedure.

Certain statements are not allowed within stored procedures. These include:

- `CREATE DEFAULT`
- `CREATE PROCEDURE`
- `CREATE RULE`
- `CREATE TRIGGER`
- `CREATE VIEW`
- `SET SHOWPLAN_TEXT`
- `SET SHOWPLAN_ALL`

Stored procedures can be nested up to 32 levels deep. The maximum size of a stored procedure is 128 MB (although a stored procedure of this size would be hard to maintain)! Local temporary tables created within a stored procedure go out of scope as soon as procedure execution has completed.

Certain Data Definition Language (DDL) statements (`ALTER TABLE`, `CREATE INDEX`, etc.) as well as the `UPDATE STATISTICS` and `DBCC` commands need to specify the two-part format when referencing database objects (object owner along with object name). This rule holds true only if users other than the object owner will execute the stored procedure.

We can use the `sp_helptext` stored procedure to read the text of any existing stored procedure within a database. This saves a fair amount of time if we use stored procedures as templates for other procedures. The text of stored procedures is available in the `SYSCOMMENTS` table, unless we use the `ENCRYPTION` option.

CAUTION

Although we can query the `SYSCOMMENTS` system table directly to retrieve the text of our stored procedures, Microsoft recommends against querying system tables. It is better to use the `sp_helptext` stored procedure to retrieve this text.

Stored Procedure Performance Issues

One of the main benefits of stored procedures is their ability to execute faster than the same set of T-SQL statements executed individually. This performance gain is due to the fact that stored procedure execution plans are cached and reused after the first execution. At times, however, we need to force SQL Server to choose a different execution plan each time the stored procedure is executed. A good example of this would be when we do not know how much data is going to be created in the temporary tables used by the stored procedure. In such cases, it is advisable to use the `RECOMPILE` option.

There are several different ways to force SQL Server to choose an alternative execution plan:

- Create the stored procedure using the `WITH RECOMPILE` option. This will cause SQL Server to recompile the procedure each time it is called.
- Execute the stored procedure using the `WITH RECOMPILE` option in the `EXEC` command.
- Execute `UPDATE STATISTICS` on any table affected by the stored procedure. SQL Server will flag the affected procedure and will recompile it the next time it is called.
- Drop and recreate the procedure. Alternatively, use the `ALTER PROC` statement.
- Stop and restart SQL Server. All execution plans are recreated when the stored procedures are first executed after a server restart.
- Execute the `sp_recompile` system stored procedure for a particular stored procedure to refresh the query plan.

It is a good idea to recompile stored procedures when indexes have been modified, as well as when the data volume affected by a stored procedures changes.

Another reason that stored procedures are very efficient is that they reduce network traffic. Instead of sending numerous SQL Statements over the wire, users only have to write a single `EXEC procedure_name` command.

Since there are very few limitations on what we can do with stored procedures, their level of complexity can vary widely. The simplest stored procedures retrieve values from a single table according to a parameter passed in. The example shown in Listing 7.19 retrieves all participants whose name starts with a specified letter.

LISTING 7.19 Creating a Stored Procedure that Takes an Input Parameter and Returns a Resultset

```
CREATE PROCEDURE dbo.usp_get_participants_by_name
( @participant_name VARCHAR(50) )
AS
SET CONCAT_NULL_YIELDS_NULL OFF
SELECT participant_id,
participant_name = CASE
    WHEN salutation IS NULL THEN
        participant_name
    ELSE
        salutation + ' ' + participant_name
    END
FROM participant
WHERE participant_name LIKE '%'+ @participant_name + '%'
UNION
SELECT participant_id,
```

LISTING 7.19 Continued

```
participant_name = CASE
    WHEN middle_initial IS NULL THEN
        salutation + ' ' + first_name + ' ' + last_name
    ELSE
        salutation + ' ' + first_name + ' ' + middle_initial + '. ' + last_name
    END
FROM Participant
WHERE last_name LIKE '%' + @participant_name + '%'
OR first_name LIKE '%'+ @participant_name + '%'
```


The following execution of the stored procedure will bring back all records from the Participant table where the participant's first or last name contains the string "ga":

```
EXEC usp_get_participants_by_name ga
```

More complicated stored procedures may contain looping structures, cursors, large numbers of parameters, conditional processing, and more. The stored procedure shown in Listing 7.20 retrieves the next available row for a specified section at a specified event.

LISTING 7.20 Creating a Stored Procedure in gasTIX that Takes Multiple Input Parameters, Enlists a Transaction, Calculates Functions, and Returns a Value

```
CREATE PROC usp_get_available_row
(@event_id INT, @section_id INT)
AS
DECLARE @row_id INT
BEGIN TRAN
SELECT @row_id = MIN(row_id) FROM event_section_row WITH (XLOCK)
WHERE section_id = @section_id
AND event_id = @event_id
AND purchased_flag = 'n'
AND (DATEDIFF(mi, locked_time, GETDATE()) > 5 OR locked_time IS NULL)
UPDATE event_section_row SET locked_time = GETDATE()
WHERE row_id = @row_id
AND section_id = @section_id
AND event_id = @event_id
IF @@ERROR <> 0
    BEGIN
    RAISERROR ('error occured while retrieving the best available row', 16, 1)
    ROLLBACK TRAN
    RETURN 1 -- failure
END
COMMIT TRAN
SELECT row_id FROM event_section_row
```

LISTING 7.20 Continued

```
WHERE row_id = @row_id
AND section_id = @section_id
and event_id = @event_id
RETURN 0 --success
```

Triggers

A trigger in SQL Server is a piece of code run whenever a DML (INSERT, UPDATE, or DELETE) statement is executed against the database, but before the data transaction is completed. This provides us with the opportunity to validate or check data prior to letting the SQL Server engine complete the transaction. If a certain condition is encountered, we can choose to disallow the DML operation and roll the data change back.

Triggers can perform just about any operation supported in a stored procedure. In addition, triggers have access to the pseudo-tables named INSERTED and DELETED that store the rows affected by INSERT, UPDATE and DELETE statements. Within triggers, we can define local variables, use conditional and looping structures, and call powerful functions.

Triggers can call each other, a concept referred to as *nested triggers*. This occurs if table_a has a trigger that includes an INSERT, UPDATE, or DELETE statement against table_b. Table_b, on the other hand, might have a trigger that includes an INSERT, UPDATE, or DELETE statement against table_a. The nested triggers setting must be enabled on the server for triggers to be able to call each other; this setting can be modified by executing the sp_configure system stored procedure, or through SQL Enterprise Manager.

CAUTION

Triggers can be nested up to 32 levels deep. This is a rather dangerous setting, however, which can easily lead to an infinite loop. Nested triggers should therefore be implemented with caution. In SQL Server 2000, if we do happen to initiate an infinite loop with nested triggers, the loop will automatically be terminated as soon as the nesting level exceeds the allowed limit.

Another powerful yet potentially dangerous setting is RECURSIVE_TRIGGERS. This option can be set by using the sp_dboption system stored procedure, and lets a trigger include a DML statement that will cause it to execute itself again. For example, an UPDATE trigger might itself include an UPDATE statement, and will therefore initiate another execution of the trigger.

Statements not permitted inside triggers include the following:

- ALTER DATABASE
- DISK INIT
- DISK RESIZE
- CREATE DATABASE
- DROP DATABASE
- RECONFIGURE
- RESTORE DATABASE
- RESTORE LOG
- LOAD DATABASE
- LOAD LOG

TIP

We cannot call a trigger explicitly. Therefore, the only way to test a trigger is to execute a DML statement against the table on which a trigger is defined.

AFTER Triggers

AFTER triggers are the triggers executed after a record has been inserted, updated, or deleted. AFTER triggers have been around since the early versions of SQL Server. They are used to maintain referential integrity and to enforce business rules. In fact, before SQL Server added support for Declarative Referential Integrity (DRI), triggers were the only way to maintain RI.

With SQL Server 2000, we can have multiple INSERT, UPDATE, and DELETE triggers defined on a table. We can also define a trigger for any combination of INSERT, UPDATE, and DELETE.

Listing 7.21 restricts the deletion of a venue associated with an event through a trigger.

LISTING 7.21 Creating a Trigger in gasTIX that Restricts Deletion of a Venue with an Associated Event, Enforcing Referential Integrity

```
CREATE TRIGGER del_venue ON venue
FOR DELETE
AS
IF EXISTS (SELECT E.* FROM Event E, Configuration C, Deleted D
WHERE E.configuration_id = C.configuration_id
AND D.venue_id = C.venue_id)
BEGIN
```

LISTING 7.21 Continued

```
    RAISERROR('You cannot delete a Venue associated with an Event', 16, 1)
    ROLLBACK
END
```

The example shown in Listing 7.22 ensures that a Participant category matches the category of the Event prior to adding or modifying an Event_Participant record. This ensures, for example, that we do not assign a musician to a football game accidentally.

LISTING 7.22 Creating a Trigger in gasTIX that Ensures the Participant and Event Categories Match

```
CREATE TRIGGER ins_upd_event_participant ON event_participant
FOR INSERT, UPDATE
AS
DECLARE @category_id INT, @participant_id INT
SELECT @category_id = (SELECT E.category_id FROM Inserted I, Event E
            WHERE I.event_id = E.event_id)
SELECT @participant_id = (SELECT participant_id FROM inserted)

IF
    (SELECT category_id FROM participant
    WHERE participant_id = @participant_id) <> @category_id
    BEGIN
        RAISERROR ('The Participant''s category does not match the Event
category', 16, 1)
        ROLLBACK
    END
```

In previous versions of SQL Server, programmers often used cascading triggers to maintain referential integrity. Cascading triggers deleted all corresponding rows from related child tables when a particular record was deleted from the parent table. For example, a cascading trigger could delete all records for customer number "2" when that customer record was deleted from the Customer table.

With SQL Server 2000, we can specify cascading updates and deletes without writing triggers. This is accomplished through SQL Enterprise Manager by viewing the table in design view, clicking the relationships button, and selecting the appropriate options. Refer to the "Adding Referential Integrity Constraints" section earlier in this chapter for additional information about cascading updates and deletes.

AFTER triggers are somewhat tricky when enclosed inside transactions due to the fact that there are three transaction states within an AFTER trigger. These are:

- Before changes are made. This is when the transaction begins.
- During data modifications. This is when the INSERTED and DELETED tables are created, and contain both the old and new images of the modified record(s).
- After the changes are completed. This is when the transaction is committed (or rolled back), and the underlying table contains the new version of the record(s). The INSERTED and DELETED tables are dropped.

NOTE

AFTER triggers cannot be created on views. They can only be specified on tables.

INSTEAD OF Triggers

INSTEAD OF triggers are new to SQL Server 2000. They take an action instead of executing a particular DML statement. For instance, instead of deleting a row in a Sales table, a trigger might copy it first to the Sales_History table and then delete it. Keep in mind that the original command that invoked the INSTEAD OF trigger is never executed. Therefore, if we just want to copy the Sales record that was attempted to be deleted, we can do so without actually deleting the record. Notice that INSTEAD OF triggers can still take advantage of the INSERTED and DELETED pseudo-tables, even though the original command does not get executed.

TIP

INSTEAD OF triggers can be defined for views, and can make a view updateable even if it refers to multiple base tables. Since the INSTEAD OF trigger effectively disables the original DML statement, it can substitute multiple DML statements for the single statement executed against a view. This way, we can actually allow updates through a view based on multiple tables.

User-Defined Functions

User-defined functions are a welcome addition to the programmer's arsenal in SQL Server 2000. User-defined functions are useful any time we need to perform a task repeatedly, and any time we need to return a single value or a result set. Sometimes built-in functions are not sufficient for meeting business requirements specific to a .NET e-Business application.

There are three types of user-defined functions: scalar, inline table-valued, and multistatement table-valued functions. These types progress in complexity. Scalar functions return a single value, while the table-valued functions return an entire table. For an inline function the table returned is the resultset of a single `SELECT` statement. The table returned by a multistatement function is built using `INSERT` statements within a `BEGIN` and `END` block.

All user-defined function types can be called directly from `SELECT` statements. Therefore, when granting permissions to a user-defined function, the syntax is to grant `SELECT` (not `EXECUTE`), as follows:

```
GRANT SELECT ON fn_participant_category TO PUBLIC
```

Inline Table-Valued Functions

Inline table-valued functions can be thought of as views that can accept parameters. Such functions can contain only a single `SELECT` statement. No DML statements are allowed within the function. Unlike views, inline table-valued functions can accept parameters and return data accordingly. Additionally, the function's body is *not* enclosed within `BEGIN` and `END` delimiters.

Both inline and multistatement table-valued functions are called with a syntax different from that used with scalar functions. Since table-valued functions return resultsets similar to tables, we can execute them with the `SELECT * FROM dbo.my_table_valued_function_name` syntax.

The example shown in Listing 7.23 creates a simple inline function that returns a list of Sales where the total amount charged is greater than the specified input parameter.

LISTING 7.23 Creating an Inline Table-Valued User-Defined Function

```
CREATE FUNCTION sales_by_total
    (@total SMALLMONEY)
RETURNS TABLE
AS
    RETURN SELECT * FROM Sale
    WHERE Total_Charged > @total
```

Notice that with inline table-valued functions, we do not have to specify the table structure, even though we are returning a rowset (table). To call the function we just created, we simply invoke it by name, passing in the single parameter:

```
SELECT * FROM sales_by_total (255)
```

Multistatement Table-Valued Functions

Multistatement table-valued functions are similar to stored procedures in that we can use control-of-flow statements, assignments, cursors, and other statements. A multistatement function must have a function body enclosed within the BEGIN and END delimiters. The statement within the function body can accomplish any of the following:

- Assign values to local variables inside the function.
- Create, open, and fetch rows from a cursor. The fetch statements returning data to the client are not supported, but we can still assign values to variables with the INTO keyword.
- INSERT, UPDATE, and DELETE rows in table variables local to the function.
- Perform any kind of conditional or loop processing.
- Execute extended stored procedures.

NOTE

We are not allowed to use SQL Server non-deterministic functions within the body of a multistatement function because they might return different values. Hence, we cannot rewrite a stored procedure as a user-defined function if the stored procedure uses non-deterministic built-in functions or executes DML statements outside the scope of the procedure.

The multistatement function shown in Listing 7.24 returns the revenue generated by tickets shipped to various states. The function also assigns a ranking to the amount of revenue generated by each state.

LISTING 7.24 Creating a Multistatement Table-Valued User-Defined Function

```
CREATE FUNCTION fn_revenue_by_state
(@start_date SMALLDATETIME, @end_date SMALLDATETIME)
RETURNS @revenue_by_state
TABLE (state_name VARCHAR(55) NOT NULL,
number_of_events INT,
revenue MONEY NULL,
ranking VARCHAR(20) NULL)
AS
BEGIN

INSERT @revenue_by_state (state_name, number_of_events, revenue)
SELECT long_name, COUNT(*) AS number_of_events, SUM(total_charged) AS revenue
FROM region r, sale s, event e
WHERE  r.region_id = s.ship_to_region_id
AND e.event_id = s.event_id
```

Listing 7.24 Continued

```
AND event_date BETWEEN @start_date AND @end_date
GROUP BY long_name

UPDATE @revenue_by_state SET ranking = CASE
WHEN revenue < 1000 THEN 'poor'
WHEN revenue BETWEEN 1000 AND 5000 THEN 'average'
ELSE 'great' END

RETURN
END
```

We can execute the function we just created as follows:

```
SELECT * FROM dbo.fn_revenue_by_state ('1/1/01', '12/31/01')
```

XML Support in SQL Server 2000

Over the past few years, software developers have used a variety of technologies to retrieve recordsets from relational databases. DAO, RDO, and most recently ADO each had its advantages and drawbacks. Now with the .NET Framework, we can take advantage of the power of ADO.NET. With SQL Server 2000, we are provided with even more options because of the XML functionality built in to the SQL Server architecture.

We can use the SQL Server XML extensions to retrieve a dataset from the database as an XML tree, as opposed to retrieving a recordset. Middle-tier components or front-end code can parse such an XML tree and format it appropriately. The main advantage of using XML is that it is passed as a text string, and is therefore supported by all platforms.

SQL Server 2000 is one of the first DBMSs to fully support XML. T-SQL extensions allow us to read and write data in XML format, while the integration of IIS and SQL Server allows us to access our relational data from the Internet in XML format without writing any code. The following sections discuss both options, and comment on their pros and cons.

Transact-SQL XML extensions

The main XML extension of Transact-SQL is the `FOR XML` clause of the `SELECT` statement. The `FOR XML` clause has many different options, and can be somewhat tricky to master. However, if we spend enough time figuring out the details, we will be pleased to discover what this clause has to offer. The syntax of the `FOR XML` clause is as follows:

```
FOR XML mode [, XMLDATA] [, ELEMENTS][, BINARY BASE64]
```

There are three different modes of the `FOR XML` clause: `AUTO`, `RAW`, and `EXPLICIT`. `AUTO` and `RAW` are extremely easy to use. `AUTO` simply treats the table name as the element and column names as attributes. `RAW` appends a `<row>` tag to the same output and suppresses the table name. For example, Listing 7.25 shows queries that return the top row of the gasTIX Configuration table:

LISTING 7.25 Returning XML from SQL Server 2000 with the `AUTO` and `RAW` Modes

```
SELECT TOP 1 * FROM Configuration FOR XML AUTO
Result (formatted for readability):
XML_F52E2B61-18A1-11d1-B105-00805F49916B
-------------------------------------------------------------
<configuration configuration_id="1"
configuration_name="Morristown Theatre_1"
venue_id="1"
link_to_image="images\seatingcharts\art_seating_bw.gif"/>

SELECT TOP 1 * FROM Configuration FOR XML RAW

Result (formatted for readability):
XML_F52E2B61-18A1-11d1-B105-00805F49916B
-------------------------------------------------------------
<row configuration_id="1"
configuration_name="Morristown Theatre_1"
venue_id="1"
link_to_image="images\seatingcharts\art_seating_bw.gif"/>
```

Neither `AUTO` nor `RAW` offer much flexibility. If we want to return a single-node XML tree for a multitable join using `AUTO`, we must first create a temporary table to hold the results of a non-XML query and then use another `SELECT FOR XML` statement to build and return the XML tree. For example, the query shown in Listing 7.26 returns a hierarchy of two XML nodes, not one.

LISTING 7.26 The `AUTO` Mode Cannot Return a Single-Node XML Tree for a Multitable Join

```
SELECT TOP 1 participant.*, category_name
FROM Participant, Category
WHERE Participant.category_id = Category.category_id
AND Category.category_name = 'comedy'
FOR XML AUTO

Result:
XML_F52E2B61-18A1-11d1-B105-00805F49916B
----------------------------------------
<Participant participant_id="51" category_id="3" subcategory_id="10"
```

LISTING 7.26 Continued

```
participant_name="Isaiah Gardner" salutation="Mr" last_name="Gardner"
first_name="Isaiah" middle_initial="A" web_site="www.isaiahgardner.com"
featured_flag="n" participant_key="D9690100-C78D-48B2-9CFB-35C1E3A47D3C">
<Category category_name="Comedy"/>
</Participant>
```

If we choose to use RAW mode instead of AUTO, a single node will be returned. However, the table name will not be returned as the XML node, as is often desired.

The AUTO option of the FOR XML clause allows us to return column names as separate elements, rather than attributes, by simply adding the ELEMENTS option, as shown in Listing 7.27.

LISTING 7.27 Returning Column Names as Separate Elements Using the ELEMENTS Option

```
SELECT TOP 1 participant.*, category_name
FROM Participant, Category
WHERE Participant.category_id = Category.category_id
AND Category.category_name = 'comedy'
FOR XML AUTO, ELEMENTS

Result:
XML_F52E2B61-18A1-11d1-B105-00805F49916B
-------------------------------------------------------
<Participant>
    <participant_id>51</participant_id>
    <category_id>3</category_id>
    <subcategory_id>10</subcategory_id>
    <participant_name>Isaiah Gardner</participant_name>
    <salutation>Mr</salutation>
    <last_name>Gardner</last_name>
    <first_name>Isaiah</first_name>
    <middle_initial>A</middle_initial>
    <web_site>www.isaiahgardner.com</web_site>
    <featured_flag>n</featured_flag>
    <participant_key>D9690100-C78D-48B2-9CFB-35C1E3A47D3C</participant_key>
    <Category>
        <category_name>Comedy</category_name>
    </Category>
</Participant>
```

The EXPLICIT clause, while offering greater flexibility, is somewhat more cumbersome to use than the AUTO clause. When using EXPLICIT mode, we can define a hierarchy of XML nodes that we wish to see in our output by specifying the TAG and PARENT of each node. The information about the XML hierarchy we define is stored in a "universal table" and is used for formatting our output.

As the top tag in the XML hierarchy has no parent, each SELECT statement using the EXPLICIT mode of the FOR XML statement starts with the following:

```
SELECT 1          AS TAG,
        NULL     AS PARENT
```

Each node in the hierarchy must be defined by a separate SELECT statement, which must contain the column definitions, as well as any aliases we might like to use in our output. For instance, the SELECT statement shown in Listing 7.28, which is a portion of a larger example of EXPLICIT mode, returns columns from the gasTIX Event table.

LISTING 7.28 Querying the Database in EXPLICIT Mode, Part 1

```
SELECT      1                AS TAG,
NULL                AS PARENT,
Event.event_id            AS [Event!1!event_id],
Event.category_id      AS [Event!1!category_id],
Event.subcategory_id     AS [Event!1!subcategory_id],
Event.event_name      AS [Event!1!event_name],
Event.event_time      AS [Event!1!event_time],
NULL                AS [Category!2!category_id],
NULL                AS [Category!2!category_name],
NULL                AS [Subcategory!3!subcategory_id],
NULL                AS [Subcategory!3!subcategory_name]
FROM Event
```

Notice that in addition to specifying the column names from the Event table, the query in the previous example also defines the skeleton for the rest of the statement by providing column names from two other tables, Category and Subcategory. This is necessary because EXPLICIT mode combines outputs from multiple queries with a UNION ALL clause.

CAUTION

Each query participating in a SELECT...FOR XML EXPLICIT statement must be valid, and must contain the same number of columns.

For all SELECT statements that follow in a SELECT statement that uses the EXPLICIT keyword, we can also include the TAG and PARENT columns. However, these keywords are optional, as long as we specify the hierarchy. For example, we could have a second SELECT statement as shown in Listing 7.29.

LISTING 7.29 Querying the Database in EXPLICIT Mode, Part 2

```
SELECT 2, 1,
Event.event_id         AS [Event!1!event_id!hide],
Event.category_id     AS [Event!1!category_id!hide],
Event.subcategory_id    AS [Event!1!subcategory_id!hide],
Event.event_name     AS [Event!1!event_name],
Event.event_time      AS [Event!1!event_time],
Category.category_id    AS [Category!2!category_id!hide],
Category.category_name    AS [Category!2!category_name],
NULL              AS [Subcategory!3!subcategory_id!hide],
NULL              AS [Subcategory!3!subcategory_name]
FROM Event, Category
WHERE Event.category_id = Category.category_id
```

SELECT 2, 1 simply means that 2 will be the tag of the output, and 1 will be the parent. Since the first query contained [event!1!event_id] and [category!2!category_id], the <event> tag will be the parent, and the results of the second query will be enclosed in the <category> tag. Alternatively we could have specified the full syntax simliar to SELECT 2 AS TAG, 1 AS PARENT, etc.

The last query of SELECT...FOR XML EXPLICIT must contain the ORDER BY clause if we want our output to be properly organized. If we fail to provide the ORDER BY clause, our query will still work, but the output will not be exactly what we expect. For instance, Listing 7.30 demonstrates what happens when ORDER BY is omitted.

LISTING 7.30 Not Including the ORDER BY Clause Produces Undesired Results

```
SELECT      1                  AS TAG,
NULL              AS PARENT,
Event.event_id         AS [Event!1!event_id!hide],
Event.category_id     AS [Event!1!category_id!hide],
Event.subcategory_id    AS [Event!1!subcategory_id!hide],
Event.event_name     AS [Event!1!event_name],
Event.event_time     AS [Event!1!event_time],
NULL              AS [Category!2!category_id!hide],
NULL              AS [Category!2!category_name],
NULL              AS [Subcategory!3!subcategory_id!hide],
```

LISTING 7.30 Continued

```
NULL            AS [Subcategory!3!subcategory_name]
FROM Event

UNION ALL

SELECT 2, 1,
Event.event_id         AS [Event!1!event_id!hide],
Event.category_id    AS [Event!1!category_id!hide],
Event.subcategory_id    AS [Event!1!subcategory_id!hide],
Event.event_name    AS [Event!1!event_name],
Event.event_time     AS [Event!1!event_time],
Category.category_id    AS [Category!2!category_id!hide],
Category.category_name    AS [Category!2!category_name],
NULL            AS [Subcategory!3!subcategory_id!hide],
NULL            AS [Subcategory!3!subcategory_name]
FROM Event, Category
WHERE Event.category_id = Category.category_id

UNION ALL

SELECT 3, 1,
Event.event_id              AS [Event!1!event_id!hide],
Event.category_id          AS [Event!1!category_id!hide],
Event.subcategory_id         AS [Event!1!subcategory_id!hide],
NULL                AS [Event!1!event_name],
NULL                AS [Event!1!event_time],
Category.category_id         AS [Category!2!category_id!hide],
Category.category_name         AS [Category!2!category_name],
Subcategory.subcategory_id    AS [Subcategory!3!subcategory_id!hide],
Subcategory.subcategory_name    AS [Subcategory!3!subcategory_name]
FROM Event, Category, Subcategory
WHERE Event.subcategory_id = Subcategory.subcategory_id
AND Event.category_id = Category.category_id
FOR XML EXPLICIT

X
----------------------------------------
<Event event_name="Bentonville Polar Bears vs. Alpena Sloths" event_time="9:00
➥PM"/>
<Event event_name="Bentonville Polar Bears vs. Alpena Sloths" event_time="9:00
➥PM"/>
<Event event_name="Bentonville Polar Bears vs. Alpena Sloths" event_time="9:00
➥PM"/>
<Event event_name="Bentonville Polar Bears vs. Alpena Sloths" event_time="9:00
➥PM"/>
```

LISTING 7.30 Continued

```
<Event event_name="Bentonville Polar Bears vs. Alpena Sloths" event_time="9:00
➥PM"/>

...

<Category category_name="Music"/>
<Category category_name="Music"/>
<Category category_name="Music"/>
<Category category_name="Music"/>
<Category category_name="Music"/>

...

<Subcategory subcategory_name="Celtic"/>
<Subcategory subcategory_name="Celtic"/>
<Subcategory subcategory_name="Celtic"/>
<Subcategory subcategory_name="Celtic"/>
<Subcategory subcategory_name="Celtic"/>
```

Obviously this is not what we intended our output to look like. Instead, we want to see a relational tree where `<event>` is the parent, and `<category>` and `<subcategory>` are children. Listing 7.31 demonstrates the complete statement with proper syntax.

LISTING 7.31 Including the `ORDER BY` Clause in Our XML `SELECT` Statement Produces Desired Results

```
SELECT     1                  AS TAG,
NULL               AS PARENT,
Event.event_id         AS [Event!1!event_id!hide],
Event.category_id    AS [Event!1!category_id!hide],
Event.subcategory_id    AS [Event!1!subcategory_id!hide],
Event.event_name    AS [Event!1!event_name],
Event.event_time    AS [Event!1!event_time],
NULL               AS [Category!2!category_id!hide],
NULL               AS [Category!2!category_name],
NULL               AS [Subcategory!3!subcategory_id!hide],
NULL               AS [Subcategory!3!subcategory_name]
FROM Event

UNION ALL

SELECT 2, 1,
Event.event_id         AS [Event!1!event_id!hide],
```

LISTING 7.31 Continued

```
Event.category_id    AS [Event!1!category_id!hide],
Event.subcategory_id    AS [Event!1!subcategory_id!hide],
Event.event_name    AS [Event!1!event_name],
Event.event_time     AS [Event!1!event_time],
Category.category_id    AS [Category!2!category_id!hide],
Category.category_name    AS [Category!2!category_name],
NULL             AS [Subcategory!3!subcategory_id!hide],
NULL             AS [Subcategory!3!subcategory_name]
FROM Event, Category
WHERE Event.category_id = Category.category_id

UNION ALL

SELECT 3, 1,
Event.event_id              AS [Event!1!event_id!hide],
Event.category_id          AS [Event!1!category_id!hide],
Event.subcategory_id          AS [Event!1!subcategory_id!hide],
NULL                 AS [Event!1!event_name],
NULL                 AS [Event!1!event_time],
Category.category_id          AS [Category!2!category_id!hide],
Category.category_name          AS [Category!2!category_name],
Subcategory.subcategory_id     AS [Subcategory!3!subcategory_id!hide],
Subcategory.subcategory_name     AS [Subcategory!3!subcategory_name]
FROM Event, Category, Subcategory
WHERE Event.subcategory_id = Subcategory.subcategory_id
AND Event.category_id = Category.category_id
ORDER BY [Event!1!event_id!hide],
[Category!2!category_id!hide],
[Subcategory!3!subcategory_id!hide]
FOR XML EXPLICIT

X
----------------------------------------
<Event event_name="Hayward Polar Bears vs. Fort Dodge Polar Bears"
event_time="5:00 PM">
<Category category_name="Sports"/>
<Subcategory subcategory_name="Baseball"/>
</Event>
<Event event_name="Knoxville Rats vs. Jackson Polar Bears" event_time="9:00
➥PM">
<Category category_name="Sports"/>
<Subcategory subcategory_name="Poetry Reading"/>
</Event>
<Event event_name="Witchita Polar Bears vs. Washington Rats" event_time="7:00
➥PM">
```

LISTING 7.31 Continued

```
<Category category_name="Sports"/>
<Subcategory subcategory_name="Play"/>
</Event>
...
```

TIP

Note that in the previous example we used the `hide` directive to exclude the event_id, category_id, and subcategory_id columns from the output. As these columns are used for joining the tables and do not provide any helpful information to the user, there is no need to include them in the output. However, we need these columns to order the result set, so we must include them in the query. The `hide` directive simply gives us a way to use the columns but not display them.

Another point worth noting in this query is that we are using the two child entities `<category>` and `<subcategory>` under the same parent `<event>`. To do so, our hierarchy is organized as follows:

```
SELECT 1            AS TAG,
        NULL        AS PARENT
...
SELECT 2           AS TAG,
AS PARENT
...
SELECT   3           AS TAG,
AS PARENT
```

Other queries might need several levels of nested tags to define the XML hierarchy. For instance, we can retrieve all Subcategories for a particular Category. In this case, we can alter the hierachy slightly by specifying:

```
SELECT 1            AS TAG,
        NULL        AS PARENT
...
SELECT 2            AS TAG,
AS PARENT
...
SELECT 3             AS TAG,
AS PARENT
```

Remember that the key to successfully using the `FOR XML EXPLICIT` clause is to define the "universal table" appropriately, specifying an equal number of columns in each participating `SELECT` statement, and providing a correct `ORDER BY` clause.

OPENXML

The OPENXML function allows us to read an XML string, parse it as a rowset, and take the appropriate action depending on the values contained in the rowset. OPENXML provides an additional benefit to the T-SQL programmer: it also lets us read XML and pass an unlimited number of parameters to our queries (or stored procedures). It is hard to imagine a procedure that will ever exceed the limit of parameters (2100). However, if we just need to pass a huge amount of data, we can put it in an XML string and use OPENXML to parse it. So OPENXML is much like a utility that parses a multidimensional array (enclosed in XML tags) and converts it into a table.

The syntax of OPENXML may seem somewhat convoluted at first. However, system stored procedures do the majority of the hard work; after using OPENXML a few times it will seem much easier. The first system procedure, sp_xml_preparedocument, reads the XML document and creates an internal representation of it in memory. Next, we specify the root node of the XML document that we wish to use for parsing. Finally, the second system procedure, sp_xml_removedocument, removes the XML document from memory. Listing 7.32 demonstrates a simple example.

LISTING 7.32 Using the OPENXML Function

```
DECLARE @idoc INT    -- for sp_xml_preparedocument
DECLARE @doc varchar(1000)
SET @doc ='
<ROOT>
<event event_name="Hayward Polar Bears versus Fort Dodge Polar Bears"
event_time="5:00 PM">
    <category category_name="Sports"/>
</event>
<event event_name="Knoxville Rats versus Jackson Polar Bears" event_time="9:00
➥PM">
    <category category_name="Sports"/>
</event>
<event event_name="Witchita Polar Bears versus Washington Rats"
event_time="7:00 PM">
    <category category_name="Sports"/>
</event>
</ROOT>'

--Create an internal representation of the XML document.
EXEC sp_xml_preparedocument @idoc OUTPUT, @doc

-- Execute a SELECT statement that uses the OPENXML rowset provider.
SELECT    *
```

LISTING 7.32 Continued

```
FROM
OPENXML (@idoc, '/ROOT/event',2)
WITH
(event_name  VARCHAR(55) '@event_name',
event_time VARCHAR(12) '@event_time')
EXEC sp_xml_removedocument @idoc
```

Notice that the `WITH` clause of `OPENXML` lets us specify the column headings and data types for our rowset. It also lets us define the data source for our columns. In the query shown in Listing 7.32, the source of `event_name` was `@event_name under ROOT/event`, and the source of `event_time` was `@event_time under ROOT/event`. We can easily extend this example by adding the category name to the output. To do so, we will have to navigate one level down the XML tree and base our `OPENXML` clause from `ROOT/event/category node`. This will force us to specify which XML node is the data source for each column in the resultset, as shown in Listing 7.33.

LISTING 7.33 Using the `OPENXML` Function to Further Specify which XML Node is the Data Source for Each Column

```
DECLARE @idoc INT    -- for sp_xml_preparedocument
DECLARE @doc varchar(1000)
SET @doc ='
<ROOT>
<event event_name="Hayward Polar Bears versus Fort Dodge Polar Bears"
event_time="5:00 PM">
    <category category_name="Sports"/>
</event>
<event event_name="Knoxville Rats versus Jackson Polar Bears" event_time="9:00
➥PM">
    <category category_name="Sports"/>
</event>
<event event_name="Witchita Polar Bears versus Washington Rats"
event_time="7:00 PM">
    <category category_name="Sports"/>
</event>
</ROOT>'

--Create an internal representation of the XML document.
EXEC sp_xml_preparedocument @idoc OUTPUT, @doc

-- Execute a SELECT statement that uses the OPENXML rowset provider.
SELECT    *
```

LISTING 7.33 Continued

```
FROM
OPENXML (@idoc, '/ROOT/event/category',2)
WITH
(event_name  VARCHAR(55) '../@event_name',
event_time VARCHAR(12) '../@event_time',
category VARCHAR(20) '@category_name')
EXEC sp_xml_removedocument @idoc
```


NOTE

Once the OPENXML keyword converts the XML into a rowset, we can do any type of data manipulation allowed in SQL Server. OPENXML is thus not necessarily just for dressing up output. It can also easily be used to provide parameters to an UPDATE or INSERT statement.

Integration of SQL Server and IIS

SQL Server 2000 offers a way to query a database directly from the Web once the web server is appropriately configured. Configuring XML support in IIS is fairly straightforward. From the Start menu, select Programs|Microsoft SQL Server|Configure SQL XML Support in IIS. This opens the Microsoft Management Console for IIS. Note that the web server must be running at this point.

From the Action menu, select New|Virtual Directory. This will bring up a dialog box that lets us configure all the necessary options. The General tab is quite intuitive; it asks for the virtual directory name and the physical path where the files need to be stored. Unless we are intending to expose template files (discussed shortly), the physical path specified on this tab is irrelevant.

The Security tab, shown in Figure 7.1, lets us define the logon credentials of the users that will access our database through the Web.

CAUTION

If we provide the 'sa' password on the Security screen (as shown in Figure 7.1), every user querying our database will have system administrator privileges. Needless to say, this can easily lead to serious security issues, and should not be allowed.

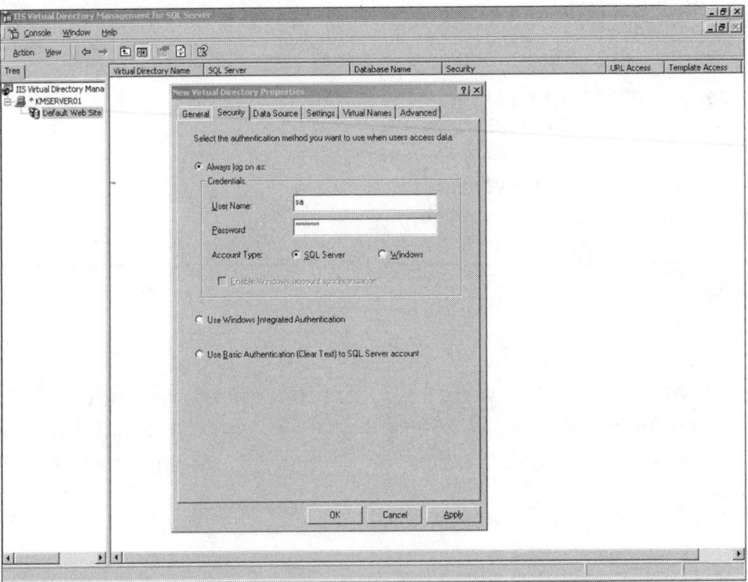

FIGURE 7.1

The Security tab of the New Virtual Directory dialog allows us to restrict access to the directory.

Choosing Windows authentication on this tab lets our users log into SQL Server based on their Windows 2000 permissions. Keep in mind that Windows user accounts still need to be assigned to SQL Server roles. If we choose the 'basic authentication to SQL Server account' option, users must provide their own security credentials. Although the last option is the most secure, it is still limited to clear text authentication, which is fairly simple to intercept.

The Data source tab lets us specify the server and the database we wish to make available through the web. Before we can specify a data source, the security account we specified on the Security tab must have the appropriate permissions to the server and the database to which we are trying to connect. If we chose the basic authentication option on the Security tab, we must specify the valid SQL Server account and password prior to selecting a data source.

The Settings tab shown in Figure 7.2 lets us configure the types of queries allowed through the web.

URL queries allow users to type in a SQL query directly in the location bar of a browser. This option is useful if all of our users can write appropriate queries and we can trust them not to destroy our data. On the other hand, if the types of queries users need to execute become complex, we should opt for template queries.

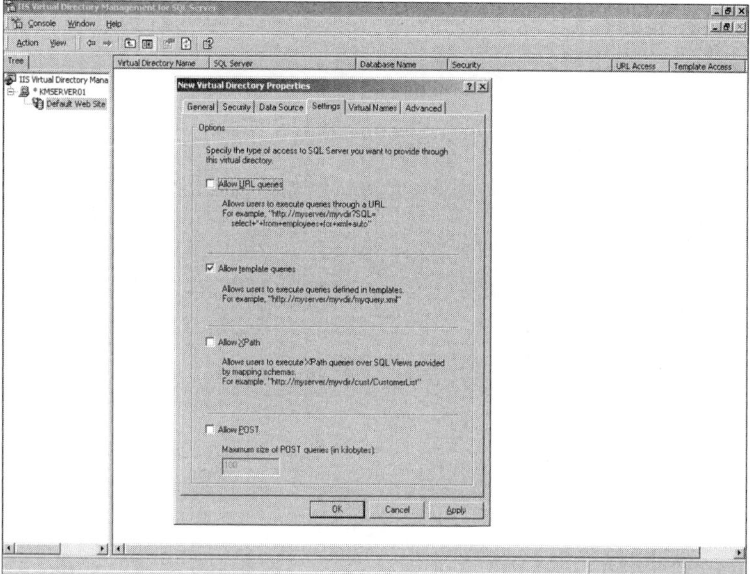

FIGURE 7.2
The Settings tab allows us to set several options for our New Virtual Dialog.

Template queries let the administrator save certain pre-defined queries in the directory specified on the General tab. Users can execute these queries by file name. In a way, template queries resemble navigating to a specific web site, since we are calling a query saved in a directory as a file. Xpath queries are executed against an annotated XML-Data Reduced schema. (Defining this schema requires a fairly good understanding of the Xpath language, and is beyond the scope of this chapter). The 'Allow POST' option allows the users to post data to the database along with retrieving data from the database.

The Virtual Names tab lets us define a shortcut to certain template files we wish to expose through IIS. This can be useful if our directory structure is complicated, and we do not want database users to know the intricacies of our file system.

Finally, the Advanced tab lets us modify the location of the SQLISAPI.DLL, which is the ISAPI filter through which XML support is implemented in IIS. If we have accepted the default options when installing SQL Server, we will not need to make modifications to this tab.

Figure 7.3 demonstrates a URL query executed on the test server. The query simply brings back a few rows from the gasTIX Participant table.

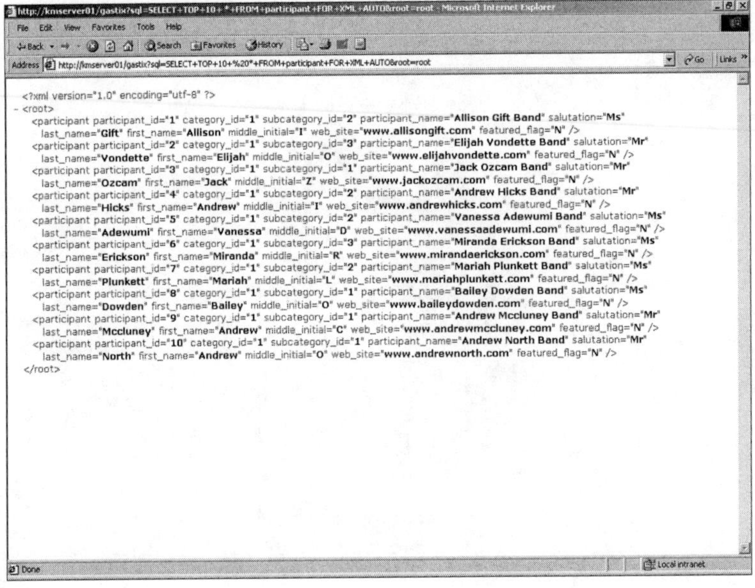

FIGURE 7.3
The URL query returns standard XML in Internet Explorer.

The XML returned from the database is in a very basic format, but it can be easily given a nice shape by applying an XSL stylesheet template.

Although useful for remote SQL Server management and certain intranet applications, the ability to query SQL Server through the Web has security ramifications. For instance, if we allow users to excute queries through their browsers, they could easily delete tables or even the entire database if they have appropriate permissions. The solution to these problems is to secure the data by only allowing users to execute XPath queries or a limited set of stored procedures that do not permit the modification of data structures.

TIP

In order to determine what specific queries are being executed over the Web on a database, we can turn on auditing through SQL Profiler. This tool allows us to track at a detailed level any and all database activity. If desired, we can set a filter for just the activity occurring over the Web.

From Here

SQL Server 2000 is one of the major components of the .NET platform. With a number of improvements to the query engine and many other new exciting features, SQL Server 2000 is emerging as the best overall database platform on which to develop e-Business applications.

This chapter explored samples from the gasTIX application and also offered pointers for developing robust SQL Server 2000 applications. We discussed all of the major improvements to the SQL Server Transact-SQL programming language, and shared tips for designing optimized applications.

Chapter 10, "gasTIX Event Searching," and Chapter 11, "Purchasing a Ticket," discuss building the ASP.NET website which consumes the data services built in this chapter. Chapter 15 explores the details of tuning both .NET data services and other parts of a .NET e-Business application. Finally, Chapter 16, "Deploying the Application," discusses deploying all parts of the gasTIX sample application, including the SQL Server 2000 data services.

Handling Security

by Remco Jorna

CHAPTER

8

IN THIS CHAPTER

- **Security Concepts 234**
- **Authentication and Authorization 234**
- **Working with Code-Access Security 246**
- **From Here 250**

A cracker breaks into a corporate Internet site and downloads thousands of credit cards which he will later sell to any takers. A disgruntled employee discovers that with some subtle manipulations she can access the company payroll information, and gives herself a small raise that no one will notice. An end-user prints a report and is inadvertantly shown prprietary data from a competitor. Each of these scenarios describes unacceptable breaches in security that can wreak havoc for a corporation.

Security Concepts

Security is a growing concern for developers in a world where applications are increasingly composed of multiple, distinct components each providing a specific functionality. The need to verify the security rights of these components is vital to ensuring safe execution of the entire application. This chapter discusses how the .NET Framework implements a security architecture which allows developers to easily incorporate evidence- or role-based security using authentication and authorization.

In order to understand the security mechanisms present within the .NET Framework it is important to first understand some security basics. There are two types of security mechanisms built directly into the .NET Common Language Runtime (CLR) infrastructure:

- Role-based security
- Code-access, or Evidence-based security

An application that uses role-based security grants a user access to resources or data based on the identity and role membership of an user. The identity is determined using the credentials a user provides. A more detailed discussion on role based security is supplied later in this chapter in the section titled "Authorization—Working with Role-Based Security."

Evidence-based security is new in the .NET Framework and is aimed at securing the execution of code that originates from outside resources. It is also referred to as code-access security, since it restricts applications' ability to access individual chunks of code. Examples of such code are third-party controls. Within .NET, you can use this code and assign it execution permissions. This means you can restrict behavior and deny or grant access to certain resources, such as your hard disk. A more detailed discussion on evidence-based or code access security is supplied later in this chapter, in the section "Working with Code-Access Security."

Authentication and Authorization

Security is a two step process that involves both authentication and authorization. These two terms are commonly used interchangeably, but in reality they each have a specific meaning. Authentication is the process of discovering the identity of the connected user and verifying the user's identity with a trusted authority. Authorization, on the other hand, is the process of selecting resources that are accessible by the authenticated user.

The authenticated user is identified using a concept called *principal*. A principal is a given user's identity and any roles that user is a member of. A role is a set of security clearances allowed to a group of users. Common roles are Administrator and Typical User. Breaking security into roles allows developers to easily assign the same security clearances to a dynamically defined set of users.

When we use Windows as our authentication mode, the .NET Framework automatically creates a `WindowsPrincipal` object. This object is part of the `System.Security.Principal` namespace and assumes the rights assigned to the specified Windows user. A generic `Principal` object can also be manually created based on our own custom roles. This allows us to maintain our own database of user/roles and create the appropriate principal object.

Thus, a principal is defined by the security rights an individual user has, combined with the rights offered by roles the user is a member of. The principal therefore has rights to act on the user's behalf. Security rights are cumulative; that is, if a user belongs to two roles, he has the sum of all permissions included in either role. So if the first role allows access to an application but the second role does not, the user can still access the application using the permissions of the first role.

Within the .NET Framework we distinguish between three types of principals:

- A generic principal that represents users and roles independent of the underlying Windows NT or Windows 2000 users and roles. This is the type of principal used by the gasTIX Web site, allowing us to use Digital Certificates, as described later in this chapter.
- A windows principal that represents users and roles based upon the underlying Windows NT or Windows 2000 users and roles that can impersonate another user. Through impersonation a user can get access to resources on behalf of the impersonated user.
- A custom principal that can be defined by an application and can extend the notion of a principal's identity and roles.

As mentioned previously, the process of authenticating users is done by checking the provided credentials with a trusted authority. In general, a variety of mechanisms can be used. Examples of those mechanisms are basic authentication, Microsoft Passport, and digest authentication.

Basic authentication and Microsoft Passport are used throughout this chapter to describe the authentication methods used by gasTIX. Digest authentication is a new feature of IIS 5.0 which encrypts the user's password information instead of using clear text as basic authentication does. This process is designed to thwart the interception of password information being transmitted to the Web site. While this makes the entire process more secure, it comes at an additional cost. In order to encrypt the password information, the client must be running Internet Explorer 5.x or have the .NET Framework installed. This limits the reach of applications using digest authentication; thus gasTIX uses basic authentication in order to maximize our potential audience.

Once the user is authenticated, all information about this user is available and usable within the code. With this information we decide what access should be granted to our code or resources. This is called authorization and is only possible when the authentication process is finished.

Authenticating Users

As stated previously, the authentication process is the process of discovering and verifying the identity of the connected user. There are several methods that can be used to verify this identity. On the Internet, it is not always possible to use built-in authentication, so other methods should be used. Commonly used methods are:

- Using built-in operating system authentication mechanisms such as Windows NT Challenge/Response
- Using username/password type of validations in combination with cookies
- Using Digital Certificates

Using Built-in Authentication Mechanisms

In a built-in or integrated authentication scenario, the user is authenticated using either NTLM Challenge/Response or Kerberos. Built-in security is very secure, since no encrypted passwords are ever sent over the network.

A benefit of integrated security is that you can provide the user with a single-logon policy. This should be considered only when the users have Windows NT Domain or Active Directory accounts behind a corporate firewall (intranet) and use Internet Explorer 3.01 or higher.

Note that Kerberos is only used when the browser is compatible with the Kerberos V5 protocol and Active Directory Services are installed on the server. In this case the authentication process uses both challenge/response and Kerberos.

When you want to use integrated security, the configuration file for the Web site needs to be told to use integrated security. The rest of the process is very straightforward. If the user is not authenticated he will not be given access to the pages on the Web site. Listing 8.1 shows a portion of the Web.config file for gasTIX.com.

LISTING 8.1 A Portion of the Web.config File for gasTIX.com Using Integrated Security

```
<configuration>
  <system.Web>
    <authentication mode="Windows"/>
  </system.Web>
</configuration>
```

Using Username/Password Validation with Cookies

In a username/password scenario, the user will be prompted by the system to enter a valid combination which is checked on the Web site against some store containing the valid combinations. Once this is done, the connection state can be controlled by either using a cookie or storing the credentials in a session variable. For this sample we use cookie-based authentication.

The example contains three pages; the first is the configuration file for the Web Site. In this file we tell the site to use cookie-based authentication, or forms authentication. The second page is the default.aspx page that will be hit by the user when accessing the Web Site. And finally, the third page is a login page where the user will be prompted to enter a valid username/password combination.

The first page tells the Web Site to use cookies. In line three of Listing 8.2, the page tells the compiler to use forms based authentication. Line four defines that when the cookie is not found the user should be redirected to the login page which we have named login.aspx. The name of the cookie is the second parameter, in this case, `.ASPXgasTIXCookie`.

LISTING 8.2 A Portion of the Web.config File for gasTIX.com Using Forms-Based Security

```
<configuration>
  <system.Web>
    <authentication mode="Forms">
      <forms loginUrl="login.aspx" name=".ASPXgasTIXCookie" />
    </authentication>
    <authorization>
      <deny users="?" />
    </authorization>
  </system.Web>
</configuration>
```

Now the Web Site knows to redirect unauthenticated users to the login page when the authorization cookie is not present. The default starting point for a user is the default.aspx file. For this example, the gasTIX page has been reduced to display only the name of the authenticated user. It also contains a button to sign out and clear the cookie. Pushing this button will also redirect us to the login page. In the gasTIX Web Site, the login can be achieved manually, like on this page, or through the use of Microsoft Passport. This is shown in Listing 8.3.

LISTING 8.3 This Simple .aspx page Identifies the Authenticated User and Offers the Option to Sign Out, Clearing the Authentication Cookie

```
<%@ Import Namespace="System.Web.Security " %>

<html>
<head>
<title>Demo - Using username/password validation with cookies</title>
<script language="VB" runat=server>

  Sub Page_Load(Src As Object, E As EventArgs)
      Welcome.Text = "User: " & User.Identity.Name
      Response.Cache.SetCacheability(HttpCacheability.NoCache)
  End Sub

  Sub Signout_Click(Src As Object, E As EventArgs)
      FormsAuthentication.SignOut()
      Response.Redirect("login.aspx")
  End Sub

</script>
</head>
<body>

  <h3>User authenticated page</h3>
  <form runat=server>
    <h3><asp:label id="Welcome" runat=server/></h3>
    <asp:button text="Signout" OnClick="Signout_Click" runat=server/>
  </form>

</body>
</html>
```

The third page in this sample is the login.aspx page. On this page, the user is asked to provide his credentials which will be checked against some custom code. In this simple example, we are simply checking to see if the predetermined values have been entered. This code could also be written to validate the user against Active Directory Services or Hailstorm services.

For our demo we will only accept a username/password combination of gasbags/gastix and depending on the choice of the user we can persist the cookie. When the user is authenticated he is redirected to the URL he typed in to get access to the site, in this case, default.aspx. This is shown in Listing 8.4.

LISTING 8.4 This Code Allows the User to Enter his Credentials for Authentication

```
<%@ Import Namespace="System.Web.Security " %>

<html>

<head>
  <title>Demo - Using username/password validation with cookies (Login
page)</title>

  <script language="VB" runat="server">

      Sub Login_Click(Src As Object, E As EventArgs)
          ' authenticate user: only the combination
          ' "gasbags" and a password of "gastix"
          If UserName.Value = "gasbags" And UserPass.Value = "gastix" Then
              FormsAuthentication.RedirectFromLoginPage(UserName.Value,
PersistCookie.Checked)
          Else
              ErrorMsg.Text = "User could not be verified. Please try again."
          End If
      End Sub

  </script>

</head>
  <body>
  <form runat="server">

    <h3>Login</h3>

    <table>
      <tr>
        <td>Username:</td>
        <td>
          <input id="UserName" type="text" runat=server/>
        </td>
        <td><ASP:RequiredFieldValidator ControlToValidate="UserName"
Display="Static" ErrorMessage="*" runat=server/></td>
      </tr>
      <tr>
        <td>Password:</td>
        <td>
          <input id="UserPass" type="password" runat=server/>
        </td>
        <td><ASP:RequiredFieldValidator ControlToValidate="UserPass"
Display="Static" ErrorMessage="*" runat=server/></td>
```

LISTING 8.4 Continued

```
      </tr>
      <tr>
        <td>Remember Login:</td>
        <td><ASP:CheckBox id="PersistCookie" runat="server" /></td>
        <td></td>
      </tr>
    </table>

    <asp:button text="Login" OnClick="Login_Click" runat=server/>
    <p>
    <asp:Label id="ErrorMsg" ForeColor="red" Font-Name="Verdana" Font-Size="10"
runat="server" />
  </form>

  </body>
</html>
```

Using Certificates

Using Digital Certificates is an excellent security solution for certain scenarios. A Digital Certificate is a piece of software that has been authenticated by a designated third-party, such as Verisign. Information about the certificate is passed along with the Web request, making it easy to verify. This actually provides a simple solution for the client code, as the developer does not need to worry about passing usernames and passwords to be authenticated.

Digital Certificates are not suited for every situation, however. Since the Digital Certificate is a piece of software that must be installed on the machine making the request, it is not an ideal solution for public Web Sites. The average Web user is not willing to install new software on his machine just to browse a Web site. Therefore, the use of Digital Certificates is commonly relegated to business-to-business transactions such as inventory inquiries, order purchasing, and work outsourcing. Digital Certificates are also appropriate for internal applications such as a secure intranet.

The gasTIX XML Web services are designed to check for the presence of an authorized Digital Certificate before allowing certain method calls to be made. Some method calls, such as those for listing events and retrieving venue information do not require secure access. The method calls dealing with credit card transactions, however, do require the additional security provided by the Digital Certificates.

Since the business model for gasTIX calls for a small number of clients consuming the gasTIX XML Web services, this is an appropriate security solution. In our fictional business model, we would require new clients wishing to consume our services to obtain and install a Digital

Certificate on their Web server. This allows the gasTIX Web services to work with full confidence that only registered gasTIX consumers will be able to access the secure credit card processing Web services.

In order for the Web site to use certificates, we need to first update the Web.config file. We will use information from the Digital Certificate to impersonate a user. Impersonating a user means assuming the identity of a known account that has certain permissions. Access to data and resources is controlled by this account.

To make this happen we set up the Web.config file to use Windows authentication by adding the following section (Listing 8.5) into the Web.config file:

LISTING 8.5 This Listing Shows a Portion of the Web.config File for gasTIX.com Using Certificates

```
<configuration>
  <system.Web>
    <authentication mode="Windows" />
    <identity impersonate="true" />
  </system.Web>
</configuration>
```


Next, we need to update the global.asax file so that it will handle the impersonation. This is done with the following code:

```
<%@ Import Namespace="System.Security.Principal" %>

<script language="vb" runat="server">

  Sub Application_OnAuthenticateRequest(src As Object, e As EventArgs)
    Dim ctx As HttpContext = HttpContext.Current
    Dim id As GenericIdentity = new
GenericIdentity(ctx.Request.ClientCertificate("SUBJECTEMAIL"))
    Dim prin As GenericPrincipal = new GenericPrincipal(id, Nothing)
    ctx.User = prin
  End Sub
</script>
```

The impersonation is done by taking the `SUBJECTEMAIL` property from the client certificate and using that to impersonate a Windows user. A `GenericPrincipal` object is created and stored in the `User` property of the current `HttpContext` object. We still have not made sure that the user is allowed to use the Web site, but we have created a Principal, so we are able to use that for the authorization process, for example, by using role-based security mechanisms.

Now we have set up the application Web to allow a Digital Certificate to impersonate a Windows user. All we need to do now is build a Web page that displays some information on the user and information from the client certificate being passed in. In this scenario we will display the name of the impersonated user, the Windows identity and the issuer of the certificate in a simple .aspx page. The code for this page is shown in Listing 8.6. (Note: For the sake of simplicity, the Visual Basic .NET code has been included in the .aspx file.)

LISTING 8.6 This Simple .aspx Page Displays the Name of the Impersonated User, the Windows Identity, and the Issuer of the Digital Certificate

```
<%@ Page Transaction="Disabled" %>
<%@ Import Namespace="System.Security.Principal" %>
<html>
    <head>
        <script runat="server" language="vb">

            sub Page_Load(Src As Object, e As EventArgs)
               UserName.Text = User.Identity.Name
               ThreadUser.Text = WindowsIdentity.GetCurrent().Name
               CertIssuer.Text   = Request.ClientCertificate.Issuer
            end sub

        </script>
    </head>
    <body>
        <H3>Certificates</H3>
        <table>
            <tr>
                <td valign="top" align="right">
                    User:
                </td>
                <td valign="top">
                    <asp:label id="UserName" runat="server" />
                </td>
            </tr>
            <tr>
                <td valign="top" align="right" width="100px">
                    Thread ID:
                </td>
                <td valign="top">
                    <asp:label id="ThreadUser" runat="server" />
                </td>
            </tr>
            <tr>
                <td valign="top" align="right">
                    Issuer:
                </td>
```

LISTING 8.6 Continued

```
                <td valign="top">
                    <asp:label id="CertIssuer" runat="server" />
                </td>
            </tr>
        </table>
    </body>
</html>
```

Authorization—Working with Role-Based Security

Role-based security is a mechanism that enables us to administratively construct an authorization policy for an application. Using role-based security, we can define which users can access which resources, even down to assigning access to individual methods. As we have seen in the gasTIX application, it is common to apply different security restrictions at the method level.

When we want to allow people to access our application we have to assure two things:

- That the user is authenticated, i.e. the user is who he claims to be.
- That the user is authorized; in other words, the user has sufficient permissions based upon his identity.

Take for example the common scenario of expense reimbursement. When an employee spends his own money for company purposes, he is entitled to be reimbursed for those expenses. To do so, the employee must complete an expense report indicating the amount spent and the purpose for the expenditure. An employee is able to submit his expense reports through an application. A clerk in the accounting department receives the expense report and is only allowed to approve expenses up to a certain amount. When the amount on an expense report exceeds that limit, the manager of the accounting department has to approve the report personally. Finally, the CFO has to forward the approved report to the financial department that makes the payment.

Looking at the responsibilities and roles in this scenario, we end up with Table 8.1.

TABLE 8.1 Role-Based Security Restricts Access to Different Areas Based on the Defined Role

Role	*Employees*	*Accounting*	*Accounting Management*	*Executive*
Employee	X			
Clerk	X	X		
Manager	X	X	X	
CFO	X	X	X	X

The table shows that all employees are allowed to submit expense reports. However, there are multiple roles that may be necessary to process the report. For any specific task, only a person in a role with permissions for that task can complete it.

Microsoft provided a role-based security infrastructure with MTS and COM+ services. In .NET the role-based security infrastructure is enhanced with added flexibility and extensibility to meet the requirements of more diverse, integrated applications. The .NET Framework allows the option of using role-based security on both server and client platforms.

Since the role-based security in the .NET Framework extends upon COM+ role-based security, it is useful to compare the two security models. Remember that a *principal* is a user or an agent that acts on a user's behalf. With that in mind, we can take a look at the differences between role-based security in COM+ and in the .NET Framework. Table 8.2 shows the comparison between COM+ and .NET.

TABLE 8.2 .NET and Com+ Security Comparison

Topic	*COM+*	*.NET Framework*
Principals	Based on Windows NT Accounts and tokens	Not necessarily associated with Windows NT Accounts and tokens
Windows NT trust relationships	Required	Optional; applications can require trust relationships, but there is no underlying assumption of trust in the framework
Management of roles	Per-application basis	Application specific roles can be defined. Possibility for runtime mapping between roles and user accounts
Application registration	Application code must be registered with the registration database	No registration required, except for some interoperability scenarios where COM and .NET work together
Mapping between user accounts and roles	Tracked by COM+	The runtime attaches a principal object to the call context, which is always available to the current thread. The principal object contains a reference to an identity object as well as the roles to which the identity belongs

The table shows that the .NET role-based security mechanisms provide far more flexibility than COM+ does. For example, the option to do runtime mapping of roles and responsibilities allows for less administrative overhead.

The .NET Framework provides a mechanism for checking role membership, WindowsPrincipal. The WindowsPrincipal reveals information about the current user, the authorization mechanism used for authentication and the domain.

Example of using WindowsPrincipal:

```
AppDomain.CurrentDomain.SetPrincipalPolicy(PrincipalPolicy.WindowsPrincipal);
WindowsPrincipal user =
     (WindowsPrincipal)System.Threading.Thread.CurrentPrincipal;
Console.WriteLine("User name: {0}", user.Identity.Name);
Console.WriteLine("Authentication type: {0}",
     user.Identity.AuthenticationType);
Console.WriteLine("Is in Administrators group: {0}",
     user.IsInRole(WindowsBuiltInRole.Administrator));
Console.WriteLine("Is in Guests group: {0}",
     user.IsInRole(WindowsBuiltInRole.Guest));
```


The example above shows how to access the WindowsPrincipal information and get some information from it using the `WindowsBuiltInRole` enumeration. We can alternatively replace the fifth line above with the following line of code to accomplish the same effect:

```
Console.WriteLine("Is in Administrators group: {0}",
    user.IsInRole("BUILTIN\\Administrators"));
```

Mind the correct spelling of the groups; case-sensitivity is also very important. It is also possible to check on other domain roles by replacing the `BUILTIN` keyword with the name of the domain to check. For instance, the administrative functions of the gasTIX site validate against the gasTIX\\Administrators' role.

The second option is to use declarative security. Declarative security works by adding metadata about the security restrictions directly to the assembly. From a development standpoint, this is accomplished by adding an attribute to a method, as shown here:

```
[PrincipalPermission(SecurityAction.Demand, Role=@"BUILTIN\Administrators")]
private static string DoSomething() {
 return "Passed ...";
}
```

In this example, the `DoSomething()` method has a security restriction placed on it which states that the principal must be assigned to the BUILTIN\Administrators role in order to execute the method. Thus, the method is only accessible if the user can impersonate the requested role.

TIP

Remember that when using declarative security, `try...catch...finally` constructions have to be used to catch security exceptions.

Working with Code-Access Security

Code-access security is a new mechanism provided by the .NET Framework and designed to combat common security attacks and abuses. The security is placed on the code itself, restricting both access to the code as well as the functions the code can perform. This helps ensure that the code is secure whether it is run directly by a user or indirectly from another set of code.

Security becomes more important and more apparent when systems are being integrated instead of being built from scratch. When an application uses code elements that reside on different machines and are downloaded upon request, we need to be absolutely sure that we are working with trusted code.

Since code can reside anywhere, we need some mechanism that confirms the identity of the developer. We are able to identify the developer based on several elements like a digital signature and the IP address of the Web Site where the code originated.

Using the identity of the developer we are able to gain additional confidence that the code is secure. But even when we can trust the code, since we know the organization or person that wrote it, we might still want to limit execution and access permissions. We also need to be able to verify that every caller in the call stack has every security right demanded by the code.

Code-access security relies on security policies that describe the rules which contain the permissions granted to the code. Those rules are read and followed by the Common Language Runtime (CLR). The beauty of code-access security is that administrators can set policies independent from developers. The developers, on the other hand, can specify which permissions are required for the code to run, which permissions are desirable and which permissions can be denied.

Using code-access security reduces the likelihood of executing malicious code. An application can be given or denied certain permissions. For example, permissions for accessing the file system can be denied. Since permissions are granted or denied on individual components, we must remember that there will likely be multiple sets of permissions being applied to any given application.

When the application calls code that needs additional permissions, the call stack is checked to see if, at every higher calling level, this operation is allowed. This ensures that the component requesting access to the secured resource is always checked to see whether it has the appropriate rights. This eliminates the possibility that code without the appropriate permissions can gain access to secured code modules by using an intermediary code module. If the original caller is found to have sufficient permissions, then the next caller in the stack is authorized, and so on. If any component lacks the necessary permissions, access to the component will be denied.

All code that is executed within the CLR benefits from this code access security, even when it is not explicitly stated. This means that developers do not need to write anything to check the security access of components calling their code; they simply need to check for exceptions raised by the security runtime and handle them appropriately.

Signing Assemblies

Code-access security allows assemblies to be signed by the developer. This allows developers and other assemblies to verify the developer of the original code. Signing an assembly is done using the signcode utility included with the .NET Framework. To make this work you need to have certificates already established that you can use for signing. You can create a test certificate using the makecert utility, run it by the cert2spc utility and then use it with the signcode utility.

We can demonstrate this process using an application included with the SDK samples. In this case we will use the WordCount example. The WordCount sample application demonstrates how to open files and count the number of words contained within. We will digitally sign the application to prove its authenticity. Use the following steps to create a test certificate:

1. Create the sample—Open a command prompt and go to the directory where the sample is located. When the .NET Framework SDK is installed at the default path it should be c:\program files\microsoft.net\ frameworksdk\samples\applications\wordcount.
2. Build the sample using NMAKE ALL.
3. Create a test certificate—Microsoft has a command-line tool that enables the creation of a test certificate. This certificate is for development purposes only, no deployed application should be signed using the certificate.
4. Create the certificate using MAKECERT -sk developer -n CN=developer developer.cer.
5. Create a valid Software Publishers Certificate—The newly created test certificate is a X.509 certificate. When signing an assembly we need a valid Software Publishers Certificate (SPC). This certificate is created by using the CERT2SPC command-line tool.
6. Create the certificate using CERT2SPC developer.cer developer.spc.

7. Check current trust—When an assembly has not been signed there is no way of determining where the code originated from. The origin can be verified using the CHKTRUST command-line tool.
8. Verify the trust using CHKTRUST wordcount.exe. A security warning will pop up stating that the authenticode signature is not found.
9. Sign the assembly—Assembly signing is done using the SIGNCODE command-line tool.
10. Sign the assembly using SIGNCODE -spc developer.spc -k developer wordcount.exe. We can ignore the message that the file has not been timestamped.
11. Re-check trust—Now that the assembly has been signed we should get a message containing information about the publisher and the assigned certificate.
12. Re-check trust using CHKTRUST wordcount.exe.

The above steps have demonstrated how to create a test certificate, convert it into a Software Publisher's Certificate, and sign an assembly with it. We can follow these same steps for any assembly we build for testing. For deployment, we will need to obtain an authentic certificate and use it to sign our assembly.

Code Permissions and Associated Tools

Code-access security controls the type of access a program has to certain resources and operations. Code-access security has been introduced to accommodate the new connected world where we can download pieces of code that will execute on our own machines. It helps protect systems from malicious code and allows for a safe execution environment of this mobile code. We can gain trust about the author by checking the Digital Certificate, but that might not be enough. Even when we know the identity of the developer we might want to prevent access to certain resources, like the file system.

The .NET Framework allows us to set code permissions for all managed code assemblies. However, we cannot set permissions for unmanaged code. Unmanaged code can be called from managed code given the right permissions. Examples of those are invoking methods on COM+ applications. This of course means that allowing access to unmanaged code is a potential security risk which has to be assessed very carefully.

Within .NET, the code permissions are controlled at runtime. Code-access security performs several functions. These are:

- Define permissions and named permission sets that control the right to access system resources.
- Enable system administrators to configure a security policy that associates the permission sets with groups of code.
- Allow code to make a request for required permissions, useful permissions and off-limit permissions.

- Grant permissions to loaded assemblies based on permissions requested by the code and the permissions granted by the security policy.
- Enable code to demand that callers have certain permissions.
- Enforce runtime restrictions on code by comparing the granted permissions of every caller with the required permissions of the code.

Runtime checking of permissions is carried out based on a pre-defined pattern. When code wants to access a resource, the runtime's security system walks the call stack to see if the demanded permissions are in compliance with the granted permissions of each caller. If one of the callers does not have sufficient permission, a security exception is thrown. This mechanism is in place to prevent less trusted code from accessing resources through highly trusted code. This approach incurs additional overhead and a slight performance hit, but the downside is even less attractive.

The .NET Framework provides some command-line utilities to work with permissions and security. Administrators and users can use the caspol utility to modify a security policy for the user policy level and the machine policy level. This tool gives access to the granted permissions of an assembly and those code groups which the assembly belongs to.

NOTE

The command-line utilities described in this section are installed by default with the .NET Framework. If, for some reason, they are not installed on your machine, simply re-run the .NET Framework installation and make sure you have selected the samples for installation.

The permview utility allows us to look at the permissions the assembly requires. Note that required permissions are different than the granted permissions.

The .NET Framework has a good sample related to code permissions. The sample is called PermRequest.cs and demonstrates how an assembly defines which permissions are requested, which permissions are optional and which permissions are refused. The sample uses declarative security:

```
[assembly:EnvironmentPermission(SecurityAction.RequestMinimum,
    Read="PROCESSOR_IDENTIFIER;PROCESSOR_REVISION;NUMBER_OF_PROCESSORS;OS")]
[assembly:EnvironmentPermission(SecurityAction.RequestOptional,
Unrestricted=true)]
[assembly:EnvironmentPermission(SecurityAction.RequestRefuse,
    Read="USERNAME;USERDOMAIN;USERDNSDOMAIN;COMPUTERNAME;LOGONSERVER",
    Write="USERNAME;USERDOMAIN;USERDNSDOMAIN;COMPUTERNAME;LOGONSERVER")]
```

From Here

The .NET Framework is designed to utilize either role- or evidence-based security inherently. This allows developers to write more secure code with less work. The framework also ships with several utilities and examples which make building and enforcing security policies easy to understand and implement. For more information on calling legacy COM+ components from .NET managed code, read on to Chapter 9, "COM+ Integration."

COM+ Integration

by Cor Kroon

CHAPTER

9

IN THIS CHAPTER

- A Legacy from the Past 252
- A Sample Architecture 256
- Technology Overview 257
- Advanced Topics 266
- Detailed Walkthrough 269
- From Here 283

In the previous chapters we have seen how .NET is about to reshape the process of software development. However, companies have made extensive investments in previous technologies, including Microsoft's COM+ technology. In many cases, it will not make sense to move previously developed COM+ components to .NET, at least not initially. As a result, there will be a need to integrate newly developed .NET components with COM+ components. This chapter focuses on tips and techniques for making that happen.

A Legacy from the Past

Those of us who have been around long enough to witness other "major" changes in software development can relate to so-called *legacy* systems. "Legacy" normally refers to any system or product not considered to be state of the art. This does not necessarily mean such systems are not being used anymore. It does not even have to mean everybody *agrees* that these systems are no longer state of the art.

The Need for Legacy Components

There are several reasons why legacy systems survive. In the next three paragraphs we will look at the three major reasons.

- **Momentum, also known as Installed Base**—Replacing a legacy system by a new system takes both time and energy. Often, the energy that was put into building the system keeps it moving forward in its current state for some time to come. The more momentum the system has, the more time or energy it will take to make it change course.
- **The Black Box**—One of the advantages of component-based development is *abstraction*. Developers can hide implementation details from other developers using their components and only expose certain properties, methods and/or events to them. Developers using the component can treat it like a *black box*. If the black box was designed correctly, then there may not be a major reason for updating the software. It is necessary in these cases that newly developed applications be able to adequately interface with those boxes.
- **The Cost of Change**—Rewriting existing software can be expensive in terms of both time and money. Of course, *not* rewriting software may be expensive as well. In the end, it comes down to cost versus benefits, and that analysis may determine it is best to leave the application "as is."

To Migrate or Not to Migrate

There are many things to consider when we look at the possibility of migrating an existing application to the .NET platform. Let's have a look at a typical, but hypothetical, situation, built around the COM+ interface. COM+ has been the standard interface for building n-tier applications based on various incarnations of the Windows operating system. The COM+ interface and n-tier architecture are beyond the focus of this book. We will assume the reader is familiar with both concepts. Figure 9.1 shows a Win32 application called `myApp.exe`. The application calls into one of the COM+ interfaces exposed by `myServer.dll`. A second COM+ component (`myClient.dll`) calls another interface of `myServer.dll`.

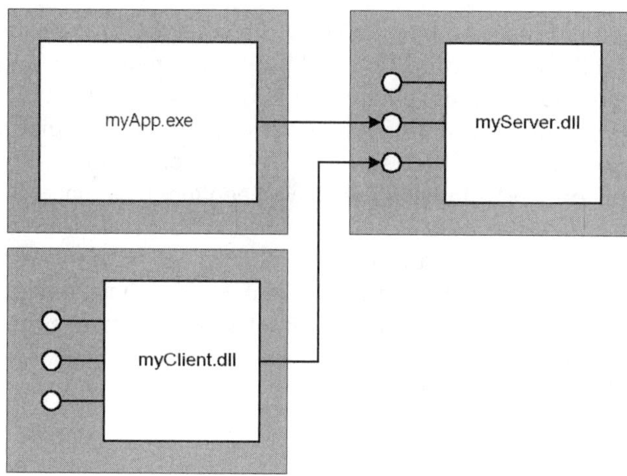

FIGURE 9.1
A sample pre-.NET situation, based on the COM+ interface.

If we look at the interfaces between these components, there are always two parties involved: the *client process* that is making the call (either `myApp.exe` or `myClient.dll`) and the *server process* that is receiving the call (`myServer.dll`). This does not mean that a component's role is fixed. On the contrary—as can be seen in Figure 9.1, `myClient.dll` exposes a number of interfaces itself. It is not unthinkable that another EXE or DLL will call `myClient.dll` and treat it as a server component, while it acts like a client component to `myServer.dll`.

In Figure 9.1, both sides of the COM+ interface contain so-called *native* code. This is code that is compiled to run directly on the target system's processor. In many cases, this will be code that is meant to run on a 32-bit Windows platform using an x86 type of processor. If we look at this situation from a .NET perspective, the situation that would benefit most from the advantages of the .NET platform would be to migrate both sides of the interface to run inside the *Common Language Runtime* (CLR), since this would introduce as little overhead as possible while still making use of the .NET platform. This would require `myApp.exe`, `myClient.dll` and `myServer.dll` to be ported to the .NET platform. We refer to this situation as a "full port."

Obviously, converting every single part of an application can be a lot of work, especially if the source language for the original application cannot be recompiled as part of the .NET platform without making changes to its syntax or to its use of library functions.

NOTE

Visual Basic 6 is one of the most commonly used languages for the creation of COM+ components. With the introduction of Visual Basic .NET, many new features have been added to the Visual Basic language that was not part of Visual Basic 6. Visual Basic .NET is a fully featured programming language for the .NET platform that can compete with other languages such as Visual C++ .NET and Visual C# .NET. One consequence of the changes and additions that have been made to the Visual Basic language and syntax will cause some Visual Basic 6 sources to produce syntax errors when compiled with the Visual Basic .NET compiler. When making the transition, at least some Visual Basic 6 sources will have to be rewritten. Documentation regarding the differences between Visual Basic 6 and Visual Basic .NET can be found on Microsoft's MSDN Web site. Find a list of articles related to moving from VB6 to VB .NET at `msdn.microsoft.com/vbasic/technical/upgrade/guide.asp`.

If the decision to port an application to the .NET platform were an "all-or-nothing" type of choice, we would be facing a tough challenge for the next couple of years. In the previous paragraphs we have already seen that many factors must be considered when making this choice.

To make the transition to .NET go as smoothly as possible, Microsoft has added support for calling COM+ components from within the CLR. This is not just a nice feature for developers; it's an actual must-have for the platform. Because the initial release of the .NET Framework will be based on Microsoft's 32-bit Windows platforms, the operating system itself will still consist of 32-bit "native" code. This means that .NET assemblies will frequently have to call code that resides outside of the CLR. It won't be until Microsoft releases Windows.NET further down the road that we will see the first example of a completely .NET-based platform. Until then, most solutions will be hybrid systems that use both .NET assemblies and COM+ DLLs.

Because support for COM+ interfaces is built into the .NET platform, applications can be a mixture of Win32 code modules and .NET assemblies. Not only can assemblies call COM+ components, but native code can call .NET assemblies as well. This means that we have much more freedom when deciding which parts of our original application will be ported to the .NET platform. When we migrate only part of an application, we refer to this situation as a *partial port*. Table 9.1 shows the possible choices when planning the migration of a client-server interface to the .NET platform.

TABLE 9.1. Possible choices when migrating a COM+ solution

		Server	
		COM+	CLR
Client	COM+	Original situation	Partial port
	CLR	Partial port	Full port

This leaves us with three possible choices to consider:

- No port (original situation)

  Of course choosing not to migrate an existing application to the .NET platform is as much a choice as any other. As we have seen in the previous paragraphs, sometimes migrating is *not* the best choice we can make. There may be technical or financial reasons that dictate us to follow another course of action. We will, however, explore the creation of enterprise solutions using .NET in the remaining chapters of this book.

- Full port to CLR

  The other chapters of this book describe how to build an e-Business solution from scratch by leveraging the many features of the .NET platform. Using the techniques described in these chapters, we can also take an existing application and give it the full .NET treatment. This may or may not involve using the existing source code of our original application. In some cases starting from scratch based on the original case study (or an updated revision) yields certain advantages over line-by-line conversion of the existing code. If this is the case, then COM+ integration is not what we're looking for and we may as well proceed directly to Chapter 10, "gasTIX Event Searching."

- Partial port

  In situations where we want to maintain a COM+ client or server component as part of our solution while still integrating with a .NET assembly, a number of techniques are important. Most are existing techniques that have been re-tooled to work with .NET. There are also some new techniques that are only available within the .NET Framework. The remainder of this chapter will focus on what it takes to make .NET integrate with COM+ interfaces. We will explore the integration of COM+ legacy components with .NET assemblies such as Web services and Class Libraries. We will also look at how .NET Class Libraries can be called from a Win32 application.

A highly detailed discussion of integrating .NET with COM+ is beyond the scope of this chapter. However, we will discuss how to efficiently leverage our existing code base in order to minimize the amount of effort needed to reap the benefits of integrating with .NET.

A Sample Architecture

Since gasTIX is an all-new business case, it doesn't contain any legacy components. This is an advantage in that the resulting application will run more efficiently and can use all of the exciting new features of the .NET Framework. The downside is that we will have to sidestep the gasTIX business case to demonstrate integration with COM+. For this purpose we will look at a simple hypothetical situation. The architecture for this example is shown in Figure 9.2.

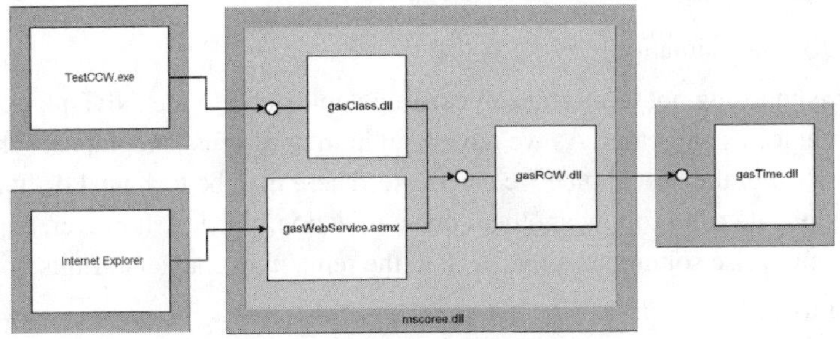

FIGURE 9.2
The COM+ integration example discussed in this chapter makes use of a COM+ DLL, two .NET assemblies, and a .NET Web Service.

The legacy code is an uncomplicated COM+ DLL called `gasTime.dll`. It can be used to determine the current time on the server platform and will be implemented using Visual Basic 6. We will make this DLL available to two assemblies: `gasWebService.asmx` and `gasClass.dll`. These represent a .NET Web Service and a .NET Class Library respectively and both run inside the Common Language Runtime. Let's just ignore the `gasRCW.dll` for the moment. Its purpose will be explained later in this chapter.

We will test the Web Service by querying it using Microsoft Internet Explorer. After testing the Web Service we will write a Visual Basic 6 desktop application to test the Class Library. Since the Class Library is actually just a wrapper DLL, it will call our original VB6 DLL to return the time. The result will be two pieces of native code and two pieces of managed code (`gasRCW.dll` comes into play as well) co-existing within a single application and being able to call one another across the CLR boundary.

NOTE

Since Web services utilize industry standard communication protocols, the Web Service can be tested in any HTTP-compliant browser.

We will have a closer look at this example in the detailed walkthrough later in this chapter. However, before we are ready to start working on the sample application, we should familiarize ourselves with the technologies involved in COM+ integration.

Technology Overview

In this section, we look at the technologies involved in COM+ integration. First we quickly brush up on assemblies and the Common Language Runtime. Then we look at various ways in which managed and unmanaged code can coexist within a single application.

Managed versus Unmanaged Code

All code created using Visual Studio .NET is compiled into one or more *assemblies*. An assembly is a collection of one or more files (.EXE, .DLL, resource files, and so on) that implement a logical application or component. Assemblies are not targeted towards a particular processor or operating system. They consist of MSIL (Microsoft Intermediate Language) instructions instead of native code (a.k.a. machine language). Assemblies also contain metadata that describes the contents of the assembly. We might say that assemblies are the .NET counterpart to Win32 executables.

As a result, assemblies require the .NET Framework in order to run. The .NET Framework performs tasks such as compilation to the native code format, garbage collection, loading and unloading of classes and performing security checks. That's why we say MSIL programs don't just run: They are *managed*. The module that performs all these tasks is called the CLR. We call the programs that run "inside" the CLR *managed code*.

COM+ components, on the other hand, are unmanaged code because they run directly on the platform's CPU, without the intervention of the CLR. Unmanaged code is typically targeted towards a fixed range of processors and operating systems. If we compile our unmanaged application for the standard Windows environment, it will run on x86 CPUs and, most likely, any 32-bit version of Windows. Users with another combination of processor and operating system, say a 68000 processor running Palm OS, are out of luck.

As we have seen before, it is essential that applications be able to contain a mixture of managed and unmanaged modules. Some of these unmanaged modules may be system DLLs like `user32.dll` or `kernel32.dll`. Other unmanaged modules could be COM+ components. But how can we bridge the gap between managed and unmanaged code? Managed code can't run directly on the platform's CPU because it is not in native format, and unmanaged code can't run inside the CLR because it does not contain the metadata required by the CLR.

The answer to this question is .NET *Interoperability Services*. The .NET Framework ships with a namespace called `System.Runtime.InteropServices`. This namespace contains all the services required for running applications across the CLR boundary. A detailed description of InteropServices is beyond the scope of this chapter, but we will explore some of the basic techniques here.

Calling the Operating System

Since calling native Win32 DLLs from within the CLR is likely to happen frequently, InteropServices provides a special mechanism for this purpose. This mechanism is called *Platform Invoke,* or P/Invoke for short. P/Invoke allows us to define a CLR wrapper around an existing DLL's methods. Let's say for example that we would like to invoke the MessageBox method of the user32 system DLL from a Visual Basic .NET program. First we would need to tell Visual Basic .NET that we want to use InteropServices. We do this by including the following line of code:

```
Imports System.Runtime.InteropServices
```

This tells Visual Basic .NET to import the System.Runtime.InteropServices namespace so that we may easily refer to its classes in our code. Next we define a class called Win32 (or any other name that we see fit) and add the following code:

```
Public Class Win32
    Declare Auto Function MessageBox Lib "user32.dll" (Byval hWnd As Integer, _
    Byval txt As String, Byval caption As String, Byval Type As Integer) _
    As Integer
End Class
```

Once this class has been added to our project, we can simply invoke the MessageBox function of the class. A MessageBox will now appear when we execute the following code:

```
Win32.MessageBox(0, "Hello World", "gasTIX Platform Invoke Sample", 0)
```

It will have "gasTIX Platform Invoke Sample" as its title, will display the text "Hello World" and will only have an "OK" button. Of course, since displaying message boxes is an inherent part of the Visual Basic .NET language as well, we could have replaced all of the preceding code with the following simplified code:

```
MsgBox "Hello World", 0, "gasTIX Platform Invoke Sample"
```

Our development experience tells us it would probably have been a lot more efficient as well. But why? Our MessageBox function tells the Visual Basic .NET compiler which parameters to expect. That information is important, because the compiler needs the information to create metadata for the CLR. However, our declaration doesn't tell the CLR what code should be executed. There is no body for the MessageBox function. So what happens when we call it from our managed code?

Our declaration does not tell the CLR what the function is supposed to do, but it does indicate where the function can be found. First, `InteropServices` locates the DLL containing the function as defined by our `Declare` statement and loads it into memory. When the DLL has been loaded, `InteropServices` places our arguments onto the Call Stack and transfers control to the unmanaged function inside the native DLL. The unmanaged function then executes, possibly changing the contents of the Call Stack while it does, and transfers control back to `InteropServices`. Here, any results are collected from the Call Stack and passed back to our managed code.

Those familiar with COM+ will note that this mechanism is similar to the way in which COM+ handles remote procedure calls. The mechanism of placing arguments on a Call Stack is called marshalling and is not unique to the .NET platform. What P/Invoke does is create a proxy class to handle the marshalling for us. We will look into this mechanism in more detail later in this section.

NOTE

Each time we pass arguments and function results in or out of the CLR, data needs to be marshaled across the Call Stack. In addition, a piece of managed code will be created to handle the marshalling and to pass control to native code. The overhead required to perform this marshalling will incur a performance penalty based on the type and amount of data being marshaled. Using a managed code equivalent in place of native DLL's wherever possible will typically offer better application performance.

Wrapping It All Up

Now that we have seen that the .NET platform can wrap a proxy class around a native DLL, how does it work? Whenever a native COM+ object needs to be called, the CLR creates a *Runtime-Callable Wrapper* (RCW) for that object. Only one RCW needs to be created for any COM+ object. The CLR keeps track of the number of references made to the RCW. The RCW acts just like any managed piece of code to the CLR, but exposes a copy of the COM+ object's interfaces to other classes. The wrapper class (including its interfaces) is created based on the type library associated with the COM+ object. The main purpose of the RCW is to invoke the COM+ object and marshal data between managed and unmanaged code based on the object's interface definition. Since the .NET types associated with the interface may differ from those used in the COM+ component, some conversion may be required. We will address this mechanism in more detail in the "Advanced Topics" section later in this chapter. If the COM+ object changes any by-reference arguments or returns a result, these values will have to be marshaled back to the CLR in the same way. Once all references to the RCW have been released, the RCW releases its reference to the COM+ object. The CLR can then perform a garbage collection on the RCW. Figure 9.3 shows a diagram depicting the RCW.

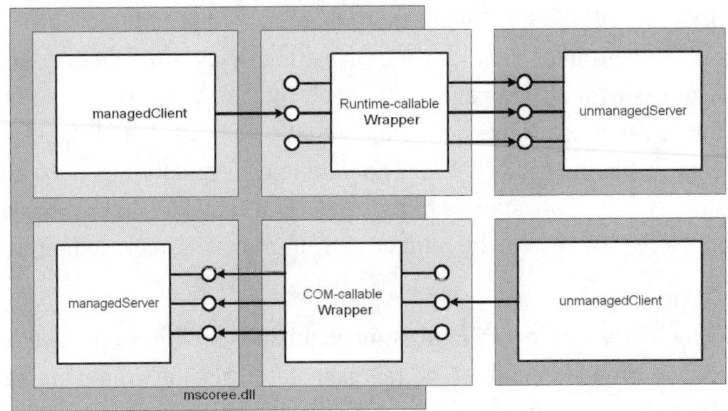

FIGURE 9.3
The RCW and CCW act as proxies across the CLR boundary.

The reverse process (calling managed code from native code) works in much the same way. In this case a *COM-Callable Wrapper* (CCW) is created. Only one CCW is created for any .NET object. The CCW is reference-counted like any other COM+ object so it can be discarded once all references have been released. The CCW holds just one reference to its corresponding .NET object. The CCW exposes COM+ copies of the .NET object's interfaces to native code and marshals arguments and results in the same way the RCW does, only in the opposite direction. The CCW is also shown in Figure 9.3.

Being able to call objects at run-time regardless of which side of the CLR boundary they are located is great, but it's not much use at development time. At development time, we'd like to use early binding to reduce the possibility of run-time compatibility errors. Developers would also like to use Microsoft's IntelliSense features to show property and method names and offer code completion. This should be available not just for COM+ components in Visual Studio 6 and .NET assemblies in Visual Studio .NET, but for any combination of development environment and component type.

When we look at the type of information that both versions of Visual Studio use to describe interfaces, we are faced with a problem. Visual Studio 6 uses type libraries, while Visual Studio .NET inspects the metadata in an assembly. What we would need is some way of translating between the two. Fortunately, Microsoft comes to our aid by shipping a number of very useful tools with Visual Studio .NET. These tools include the Type Library Importer Utility (TlbImp) and the Type Library Exporter Utility (TlbExp). TlbImp takes a type library or COM+ module as argument and produces a .NET DLL containing CLR equivalents of the module's interfaces, including the required metadata. TlbExp does exactly the opposite: it takes a .NET assembly and exports a COM+ compliant type library based on the metadata in the assembly. We will use both tools in building this chapter's sample application.

TIP

TlbImp will not expose standard interfaces like `IUnknown` and `IDispatch`, but will map a COM+ component's interfaces onto a .NET wrapper DLL. The resulting DLL contains all the required metadata we need for setting references in Visual Studio .NET. In the detailed walkthrough later in this chapter, we will look at converting a COM+ DLL using TlbImp and using it in Visual Studio .NET to reference our original COM+ object.

NOTE

Although TlbImp and TlbExp can save us a lot of work by automatically converting between metadata and type libraries or vice versa, there are some situations in which we need more control over the marshalling process. In these cases we need to translate the interfaces by hand. In the "Advanced Topics" section later in this chapter, we will look at the mechanisms involved in marshalling data across the CLR boundary. We will also discuss methods to control the data types used in marshalling.

There is one more tool that needs to be mentioned when using wrapper functions to straddle the CLR boundary. In order to call .NET assemblies through the COM+ interface, COM+ must be able to locate the assembly and its interfaces. Traditionally we make COM+ components available by registering them using the `regsvr32.exe` utility that ships with Windows. Since this utility expects a component with a COM+ compliant interface, it is not much use when trying to register .NET assemblies. Fortunately, Microsoft has included the *.NET Assembly Registration Utility* (or REGASM) with Visual Studio .NET. REGASM takes an assembly and registers it as if it were a COM+ component. This will allow the assembly to be called through a CCW like any "real" COM+ component. We will look at REGASM in more detail at the end of this chapter.

Approaches to Partial Ports

We have now examined the mechanisms involved in calling objects across the CLR boundary. Now we can examine the various ways of employing these mechanisms in order to achieve a partial port of a legacy application.

Partial Port—RCW Approach

In this approach, we have chosen to convert only the client portion of the application. As shown in Figure 9.4, `myClient.dll` has been converted to `myNewClient.dll`. Since myNewClient.dll consists of managed code, it needs an RCW to communicate with myServer.dll, which still consists of native code. We can use TlbImp to automatically generate myServerRCW.dll based on myServer.dll or translate the interface by hand. The advantage of this approach would be that other native components (for example, myApp.exe) could still call myServer.dll without any changes.

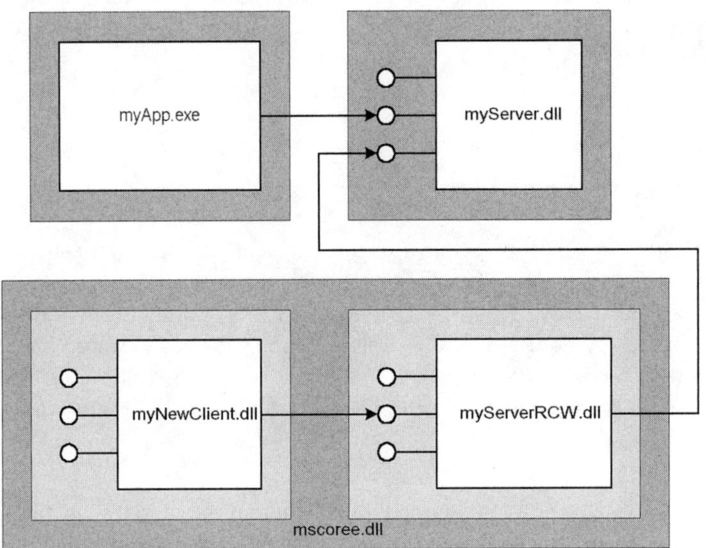

FIGURE 9.4
When only myClient.dll *is converted to managed code, we need a RCW to allow access to* myServer.dll.

Partial Port—Quick Approach

Instead of converting myClient.dll to managed code by hand, there is a much simpler approach. We can use TlbImp to generate an RCW for myClient.dll (called myClientRCW.dll in Figure 9.5) and leave all other code unchanged. Other pieces of managed code can then call upon the interfaces of myClientRCW.dll just as if it was myClient.dll itself. However, this approach only works with native code for which a type library exists. This means that standard EXEs (like myApp.exe in the example) cannot be converted this way.

Partial Port—CCW Approach

The third option to explore in this example is converting myServer.dll to managed code and leaving the client components unchanged. Here we take myServer.dll and rewrite it to managed code that can run inside the CLR. Since our client software still consists of native code, we need a CCW to marshal data back and forth to our new server component. This solution is shown in Figure 9.6.

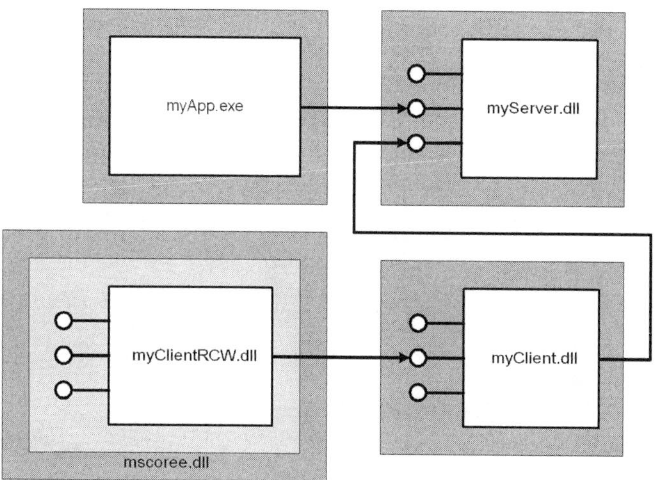

FIGURE 9.5
In the "quick" approach, no source code needs to be converted and the RCW for `myClient.dll` *can be generated automatically by TlbImp.*

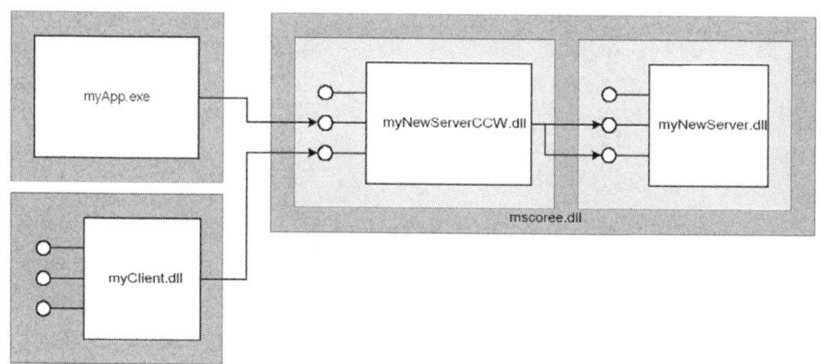

FIGURE 9.6
When only `myServer.dll` *is converted to the CLR, we need a CCW to be able to call it from native code.*

Performance of Partial Ports

An important factor when considering the various approaches is their performance when compared to the original COM+ solution and to a full port. For this purpose, let's consider the situation were `myServer.dll` would contain a class called `Server` and were we would add the following two functions to this class:

```
Public Function DoubleLoop(ByVal value As Double) As Double
    Dim result As Double
    Dim counter As Long

    result = value

    For counter = 0 To 2000000
        result = result + value
        result = result - value
    Next counter

    DoubleLoop = result
End Function

Public Function IntLoop(ByVal value As Integer) As Integer
    Dim result As Integer
    Dim counter As Long

    result = value

    For counter = 0 To 2000000
        result = result + value
        result = result - value
    Next counter

    IntLoop = result
End Function
```

We could call these functions from `myClient.dll` using code like this:

```
Public Sub runTest(ByVal iterations As Integer)
    Dim myObject As myServer.Server
    Dim counter As Long
    Dim doubleResult As Double
    Dim intResult As Integer

    For counter = 1 To iterations
        Set myObject = New myServer.Server
        doubleResult = myObject.DoubleLoop(CDbl(counter))
        Set myObject = Nothing
    Next counter

    For counter = 1 To iterations
        Set myObject = New myServer.Server
        intResult = myObject.IntLoop(CInt(counter))
        Set myObject = Nothing
    Next counter
End Function
```

We could then call `myClient.dll` from a test program that would measure the time required to run `runTest` with a certain number of iterations.

Using the techniques described in the detailed walkthrough later in this chapter, we can produce an "original" Visual Basic 6 version and a full port, as well as a RCW, "Quick" and CCW version of this setup. Although the actual performance of any given solution will depend much on the code involved, it will give us some rules of thumb regarding the performance of the different approaches.

Since any .NET assembly needs to be converted to native code prior to being executed, we might argue that this will inflict a loss on performance compared to the original Win32 application. Even though the CLR's Just-In-Time (JIT) compiler may be able to use optimizations based on the actual processor and platform, while a native code compiler has to settle for the least common denominator, we see a 10 to 15% overall drop in performance for a first run of the test code described above. Exact numbers differ for the type of parameters being used. Because Microsoft's JIT compiler uses a clever caching mechanism, code only needs to be translated on its first execution. This results in subsequent calls of our test code being executed 5 to 20% faster than on the first call. As a result, we have verified that certain functions like `DoubleLoop` may indeed out-perform their native code versions once the JIT compiler has done its job.

When looking at the differences in performance between the partial port approaches and the full port approach, we expect a drop in performance because additional wrapper classes have to be added and executed. Our benchmarks seem to verify this. CCW, RCW and "Quick" approaches decrease performance for our test code by approximately 28%, 36% and 39% respectively when compared to a full port. It is interesting to note that the performance of the "Quick" version is only slightly lower than that of the RCW approach. The CCW typically outperformed both in our tests, probably because it is based on metadata that contains more detailed information than a type library and can use more efficient marshalling code as a result.

TIP

As far as performance is concerned, whenever we need to convert at least part of our application to the .NET platform, the full port approach is preferable. If performance is not a major issue, we might settle for a simple and convenient "Quick" approach and save ourselves a lot of work. Of course these are only rules of thumb, since different scenarios may outperform others in different situations. Because the "Quick" approach is very simple to implement, we should consider using it as a performance test case whenever performance is an issue.

Advanced Topics

Now that we have seen in which situations marshalling is required, we will look at what goes on inside the RCW and CCW. We will also look at ways to control the data types used in marshalling.

Typed Transitions and the Stack

With the introduction of Visual Basic .NET, several changes have been made to the Visual Basic programming language. Since the Visual Basic .NET compiler generates managed code that is targeted towards the .NET platform, all data types must map onto one of the CLR data types. Table 9.2 shows the data types available in Visual Basic .NET, along with their value ranges, storage size (in bytes) and the CLR data type they map unto. Table 9.3 lists the data types available in Visual Basic 6 along with their value ranges and storage sizes.

TABLE 9.2 Overview of Visual Basic .NET Data Types

Visual Basic .NET Data Type	*Value Range*	*Storage Size*	*CLR Type*	*Isomorphic / Nonisomorphic*
Boolean	True / False	2	System.Boolean	NI
Byte	0 to 255	1	System.Byte	I
Char	0 to 65535	2	System.Char	NI
Date	January 1, 0001 to December 31, 9999	8	System.DateTime	NI
Decimal	+/-79,228,162,514,264,337,593,543,950,335 with no decimal point; +/-7.9228162514264337593543950335 with 28 places to the right of the decimal; smallest non-zero number is +/-0.0000000000000000000000000001	16	System.Decimal	NI
Double	-1.79769313486231E308 to -4.94065645841247E-324 for negative values; 4.94065645841247E-324 to 1.79769313486232E308 for positive values	8	System.Double	I
Integer	-2,147,483,648 to 2,147,483,647	4	System.Int32	I
Long	-9,223,372,036,854,775,808 to 9,223,372,036,854,775,807	8	System.Int64	I
Object	Various	4	System.Object	NI
Short	-32,768 to 32,767	2	System.Int16	I

TABLE 9.2 Continued

Visual Basic .NET Data Type	Value Range	Storage Size	CLR Type	Isomorphic / Nonisomorphic
Single	-3.402823E38 to -1.401298E-45 for negative values; 1.401298E-45 to 3.402823E38 for positive values	4	System.Single	I
String	0 to approximately 2 billion Unicode characters	Various	System.String	NI
User- Defined Type	Various	Various	Inherits from System.ValueType	NI
Single dimensional array of isomorphic types	Various	Various	System.Array	I
All other arrays	Various	Various	System.Array	NI

If we compare the two tables we may notice a number of things. Some data types in one version of Visual Basic have no corresponding type in the other. Also, the storage size for a number of data types is different. For example, a Visual Basic .NET `Integer` is equivalent to a Visual Basic 6 `Long`, not to a Visual Basic 6 `Integer`. This is not just a Visual Basic problem, because it affects other .NET languages as well. Not all data types used on the .NET platform have equivalent data types in the world of COM+. However, when we look closely at the table, we can see that some .NET data types can be mapped directly onto COM+ data types and vice versa. We call these types *isomorphic* or *blittable* data types. They can be marshaled from one side of the interface to another without actual data conversion. The types that need conversion are called *nonisomorphic* or *non-blittable.* Table 9.2 shows which Visual Basic .NET data types are isomorphic and which data types are not.

TABLE 9.3 Overview of Visual Basic 6 Data Types

Visual Basic 6 Data Type	Value Range	Storage Size
`Boolean`	`True` / `False`	2
`Byte`	`0` to `255`	1
`Currency`	`-922,337,203,685,477.5808` to `922,337,203,685,477.5807`	8

TABLE 9.3 Continued

Visual Basic 6 Data Type	*Value Range*	*Storage Size*
`Date`	`January 1, 100` to December `31, 9999`	8
`Decimal`	`+/-79,228,162,514,264,337,593,543,950,335` with no decimal point; `+/-7.9228162514264337593543950335` with 28 places to the right of the decimal; smallest non-zero number is `+/-0.0000000000000000000000000001`	14
`Double`	`-1.79769313486231E308` to `-4.94065645841247E-324` for negative values; `4.94065645841247E-324` to `1.79769313486232E308` for positive values	8
`Integer`	`-32,768` to `32,767`	2
`Long`	`-2,147,483,648` to `2,147,483,647`	4
`Single`	`-3.402823E38` to `-1.401298E-45` for negative values; `1.401298E-45` to `3.402823E38` for positive values	4
`String`	`0` to approximately `65,400` characters	Various
`UDT`	Various	Various
`Variant`	Various	Various
`Object`	Various	4

Each instance of a RCW or CCW maintains two copies of the Call Stack: one for the managed side and one for the unmanaged side. To marshal data from one side to the other, data is copied from one Call Stack to the other. If the data type is isomorphic, it can simply be copied byte-by-byte (hence the name *blittable*). If the data type is nonisomorphic, it will have to be converted in the process.

TIP

It shouldn't come as a surprise that the overhead involved in marshalling is proportional to the amount of work required to convert arguments and results from one data type to another. Therefore, if we choose isomorphic types wherever we can, we can significantly increase the performance of our application.

Controlling the Marshalling Mechanism

Based on the data available from metadata or a type library, the CLR will choose a default data type for marshalling. While this will work in most situations, sometimes we want to pick the data type by hand. In this case we can't use TlbImp and TlbExp to create the wrapper class for us. On the other hand we have complete control over the way data is being marshaled across the Call Stack.

Let's look at the wrapper function of the listing shown earlier in this chapter under "Calling the Operating System" again. The `txt` argument is defined as `String` in our function definition. If we want to make sure this argument is marshaled as a particular unmanaged type to `user32.dll`, we can define this type using the `MarshalAs` attribute. Visual Basic .NET references unmanaged data types through the `UnmanagedType` enumerated type. If we change the definition of the `txt` argument to

```
<MarshalAs (UnmanagedType.LPStr)> Byval txt As String
```

the argument will be marshaled as a `LPStr` type. The revised definition of our Win32 class can be found in the following listing. See the Visual Studio .NET documentation for more information on unmanaged data types and the `MarshalAs` attribute.

```
Public Class Win32
    Declare Auto Function MessageBox Lib "user32.dll" (Byval hWnd As Integer, _
    <MarshalAs (UnmanagedType.LPStr)> Byval txt As String, Byval caption As
String, _
Byval Type As Integer) As Integer
End Class
```

CAUTION

Take extreme care when defining `MarshalAs` attributes! If we define types that are not compatible with the types defined in the type library for a given COM+ interface, unexpected things may happen.

Detailed Walkthrough

The remainder of this chapter will demonstrate how to use the techniques discussed in the previous sections. To do so, we will build a sample application consisting of a Visual Basic 6 DLL. We will call this DLL from a Web Service and also from a Visual Basic .NET Class Library. Then we will call the Class Library from a Visual Basic 6 executable. The different components of our example were shown previously in Figure 9.2.

What We Need

If we want to demonstrate the integration of Visual Studio .NET assemblies and Visual Studio 6 COM+ components, we must at least be able to run both versions of Visual Studio. The best way to do this is to have two separate development environments: one running Visual Studio .NET, the other running Visual Studio 6. These environments can either be on separate computers or on separate bootable partitions of the same computer. If we use separate computers, they don't need to be connected through a network. We will only be exchanging small files (that will easily fit on a floppy disk) from one environment to the other.

Please refer to the Microsoft Visual Studio .NET and Visual Studio 6 documentation for information on the system requirements for both development environments and for instructions on how these environments should be installed.

Creating a Simple Visual Basic 6 DLL

First we will create the Visual Basic 6 DLL. Since this book is not primarily about Visual Studio 6, we will keep the DLL very simple. It will only be used to demonstrate COM+ integration.

Telling the Time from Visual Basic 6

The DLL we create will expose one function: `TellTime`. The function will accept one input parameter that will instruct it how to format the current date and/or time. It will use the Visual Basic `Now` function to return the current date and/or time.

First we will switch to the Visual Studio 6 development environment and start Visual Basic 6. From the *New Project* dialog, choose the *New* tab and select *ActiveX DLL*, then click on *Open*. Select `Project1` from the Project Explorer and change its name to `gasTellTime` in the Properties toolbox. Select `Class1` and change its name to `gasTime`. Now go to the code window and add the code below to the class.

```
Public Function TellTime(ByVal strFormat As String) As String
    TellTime = Format(Now, strFormat)
End Function
```

The code for the COM+ sample DLL is very simple.

That is all the code we need for our COM+ DLL. We simply tell the DLL what we want it to report and it will return a formatted string with the requested information. For information on the codes used in the formatting string, please refer to the Visual Basic documentation.

Before we compile our DLL, we first select gasTellTime Properties… from the Project menu and define the DLL as running in Unattended Execution mode by checking the corresponding checkbox. Figure 9.7 shows what the development environment should look like by now. After we have clicked OK on the Project Properties dialog, we save our work and choose Make gasTime.dll… from the File menu to compile our DLL and write it to disk.

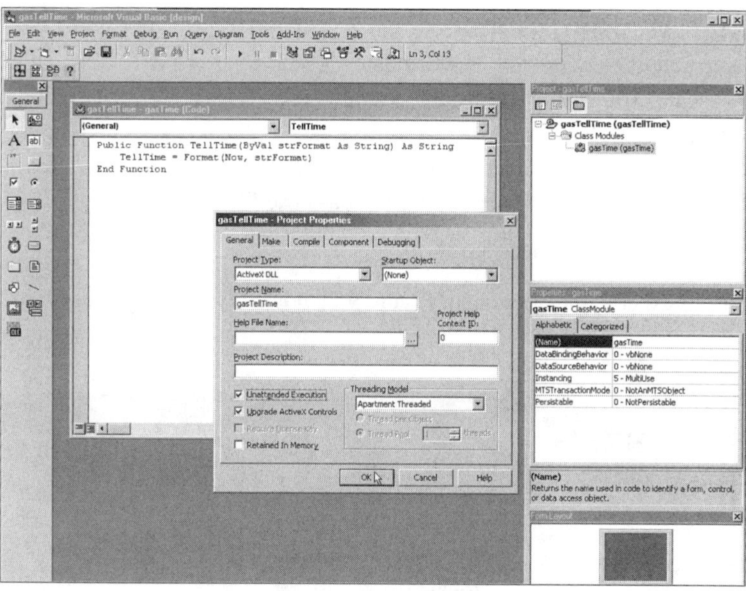

FIGURE 9.7

The COM+ DLL is almost finished.

Registering the DLL on the .NET Machine

Before we can use the COM+ DLL in the .NET environment, we must first copy it to our Visual Studio .NET development environment. Although the actual file location is unimportant, in this example we will assume the DLL was copied to the '`D:\gasTIX\gasTime\`' directory. As with any COM+ DLL, the DLL will have to be registered before it can be used. To do so open, a DOS Command Prompt or select Run… from the START menu, and type

```
regsvr32 d:\gasTIX\gasTime\gasTime.dll
```

and press Enter to register the DLL. A pop-up with the text "DllRegisterServer in d:\gasTIX\gasTime\gasTime.dll succeeded." will appear if the DLL was registered successfully. If this is not the case, check that the DLL has been copied to the correct location and that we reference it correctly.

Calling the DLL from a Web Service

So far everything has been rather straightforward. For most developers creating COM+ DLLs and registering them on a server is just a repetition of old tricks. But don't worry. We are just about to build a .NET Web Service around the `gasTime` DLL.

Creating a RCW using TlbImp

Before we can create the actual Web Service using Visual Studio .NET, we must make sure the .NET Framework has something to call into. For this purpose we will first create a Runtime-Callable Wrapper (RCW) by hand. We will do so by using the Type Library Importer Utility (TlbImp) that ships with Visual Studio .NET. From the "Visual Studio .NET Command Prompt," navigate to the directory containing the `gasTime` DLL, type

```
TlbImp gasTime.dll /out:gasRCW.dll
```

and press Enter to execute the command. Figure 9.8 shows how we can access the Visual Studio .NET Command Prompt.

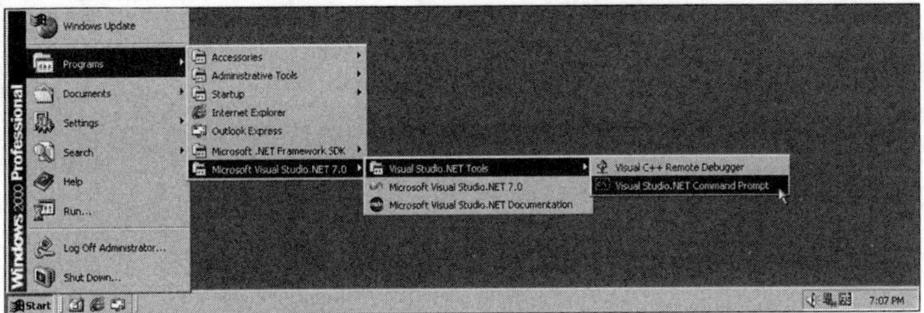

FIGURE 9.8

The Visual Studio .NET Command Prompt can be found as part of the Visual Studio .NET Tools

The TlbImp utility will respond with a message that should look like:

```
TlbImp--Type Library to .NET Assembly Converter Version 1.0.2914.16
Copyright (C) Microsoft Corp. 2001. All rights reserved.

Type library imported to D:\gasTIX\gasTime\gasRCW.dll
```

CAUTION

Use the Visual Studio .NET Command Prompt instead of the "standard" Command Prompt. The standard Command Prompt does not have the correct environment settings for calling the Visual Studio .NET tools from the command line. If you use the standard Command Prompt, utilities like TlbImp will not be recognized unless they reside in your working directory or you type the full path to these utilities.

Executing the above command has created a second DLL that serves as a runtime-callable wrapper to our original COM+ DLL. We can use the `/out:` parameter of TlbImp to define the name of the resulting DLL. To learn more about the optional parameters of TlbImp, type:

```
TlbImp /?
```

or look in the Visual Studio .NET documentation. Some of the most useful options for our purposes are shown in Table 9.4.

TABLE 9.4 Some of TlbImp's Command Line Parameters

Parameter	*Description*
`/out:FileName`	File name of the assembly to be produced
`/namespace:Namespace`	Namespace of the assembly to be produced
`/asmversion:Version`	Version number of the assembly to be produced. The version number must be specified as: Major.Minor.Build.Revision.
`/silent`	Suppresses all output except for errors

Now that we have created the RCW, what does it contain? Let's have a look inside using the Intermediate Language Disassembler Utility (ILDASM). Start the utility and open `gasRCW.dll` from the *File* menu. The result should look like Figure 9.9. When we open the `gasTime` object, we notice that `gasRCW.dll` exposes a method called `TellTime`. `TellTime` takes a string argument and produces a string result, just like our original DLL. This is because it is nothing more than a wrapper function to our original DLL's `TellTime` method.

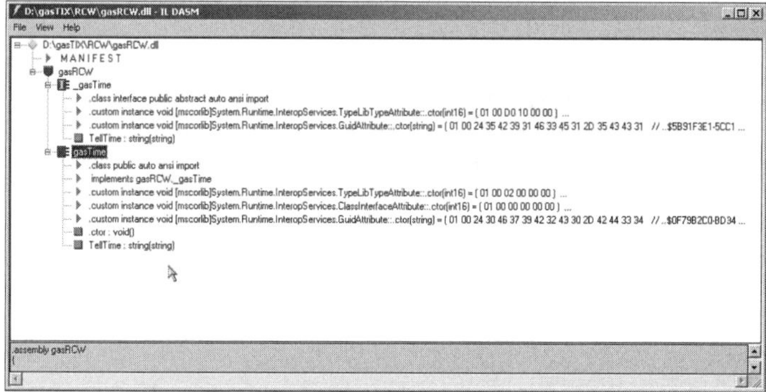

FIGURE 9.9
Our RCW exposes the `TellTime` *method just like our original DLL.*

Making a Simple Web Service

We are now ready to call the RCW from a .NET assembly. For demonstration purposes, we will create a simple Web Service around the RCW DLL. We will test the Web Service using Internet Explorer. First start Visual Studio .NET and choose *New Project* from the Start Page. The New Project dialog is shown in Figure 9.10. Select Visual Basic Projects as Project Type and choose the ASP.NET Web Service template. Name our Web Service `gasWebService` and use `http://localhost` as its location. Then click on OK.

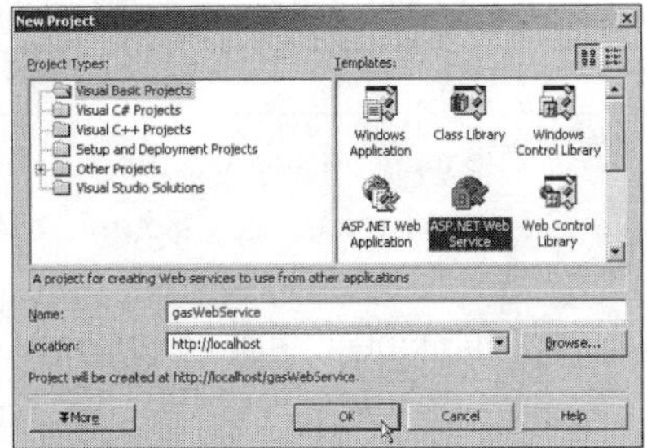

FIGURE 9.10
The New Project dialog in Visual Studio .NET makes it easy to create a new Web Service.

Go to the Solution Explorer and select `Service1.asmx`. In the properties toolbox, change its name to `tellTime.asmx`. Then click on the View Code icon in the Solution Explorer to see the code associated with `tellTime.asmx`. Visual Studio .NET has already added a public class named `Class1` to our project. Change its name to `gasTellTime`. In order to use the RCW DLL from within our Web Service, we must add a reference to the RCW to our project. To do so, go to the Project menu and click on Add Reference. This will display the Add Reference dialog as shown in Figure 9.11.

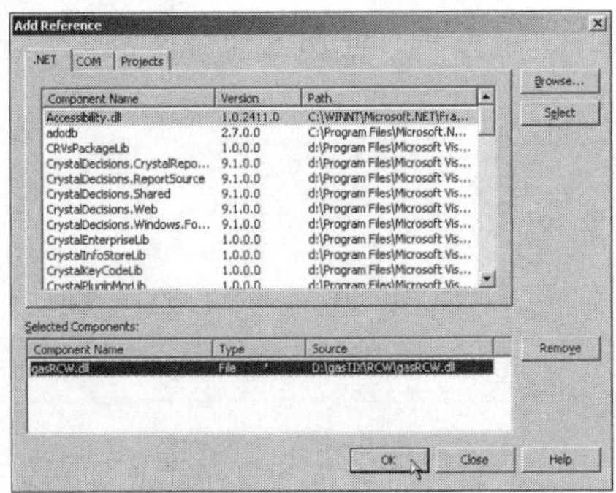

FIGURE 9.11
We can use the Add Reference dialog to set a reference to our RCW DLL in the Web Service project.

Because our RCW DLL is a .NET assembly, we select the .NET tab in the dialog. Since the .DLL is not listed in the list of components, go to Browse, locate `gasRCW.dll` and click OK. The file "`gasRCW.dll`" should now be added to Selected Components as shown in Figure 9.11. To finalize adding a reference to the component, simply click *OK*.

TIP

Since we have already created our RCW by using TlbImp, we can reference it from our project. However, Visual Studio .NET can set references to COM+ components directly by selecting them from the COM tab of the Add Reference dialog. Visual Studio .NET will then give us the option of having the wrapper class generated automatically. Please refer to the Visual Studio .NET documentation for more details.

We will now make the Web Service expose the `TellTime` method of the RCW so that other applications can use it. Go back to the code window of `tellTime.asmx.vb` and add the code below to the `gasTellTime` class.

```
<WebMethod()> Public Function TellTime(ByVal strFormat As String) As String
    Dim myRcwDll As gasRCW.gasTime
    myRcwDll = New gasRCW.gasTime()

    TellTime = myRcwDll.TellTime(strFormat)
End Function
```

Because we have added a reference to `gasRCW.dll` to our Web Service project, the Visual Studio .NET development environment is able to use features like Code Completion and Auto Quick Info (IntelliSense) while we type our code. An example is shown in Figure 9.12. After saving our project, we can select Build from the Build menu. Visual Studio .NET then deploys our Web Service to our development computer (localhost) or any other server that we have specified as location for our Web Service. As has been said before, the Web Service in our example is just a simple wrapper used to expose the RCW to the web. The RCW itself is a wrapper around our original DLL.

It's time to test our Web Service. Let's start Internet Explorer and navigate to `localhost/gasWebService/TellTime.asmx`. We will be presented with a list of possible operations. The only operation available from our Web Service is "TellTime". When we click on the "TellTime" hyperlink, we will jump to a page that can be used to test the `TellTime` Web Method. The page also describes how to call the Web Method using SOAP or HTTP calls. We could have navigated to this page directly by using `localhost/gasWebService/TellTime.asmx?op=TellTime` as the page address.

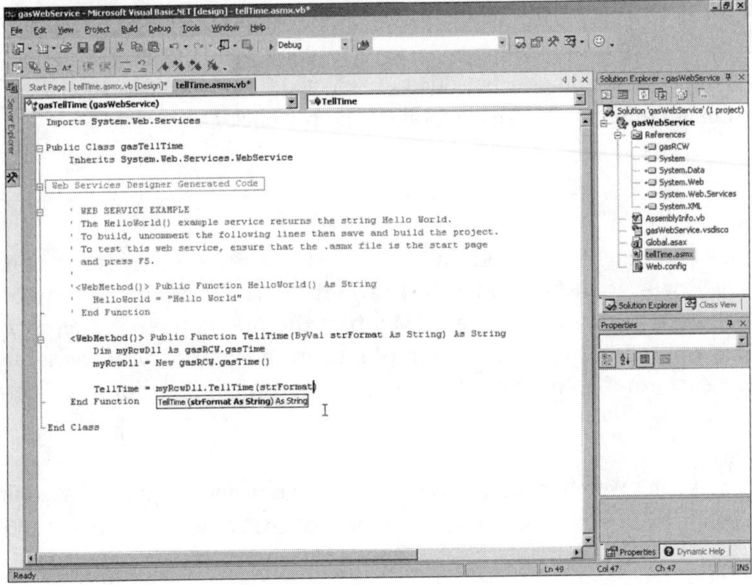

FIGURE 9.12
Visual Studio .NET offers IntelliSense for our RCW's objects and methods.

> **NOTE**
>
> We don't need to add *any* code to produce these pages. They are generated automatically when we invoke a Web Service without specifying its method or the method's parameters. For more information on building and consuming Web services, see Chapters 3 "Enabling Inter-Application Communications" and 6 "Implementing .NET Business Services."

Enter "MMM d yyyy" in the text box for `strFormat`'s value and press the *Invoke* button. A new browser window will appear as shown in Figure 9.13. When we look at the new window's URL, we can clearly see how the `TellTime` Web Method may be called. We simply take the URL for the Web Service and add an extra forward slash, the name of the Web Method, a question mark and the name/value pairs of any parameters we wish to specify. In our example this results in `http://localhost/gasWebService/TellTime.asmx/TellTime?strFormat=MMM+d+yyyy`. Note that the spaces in the parameter string are encoded using plus signs (as is standard behavior when passing parameters using the HTTP GET method).

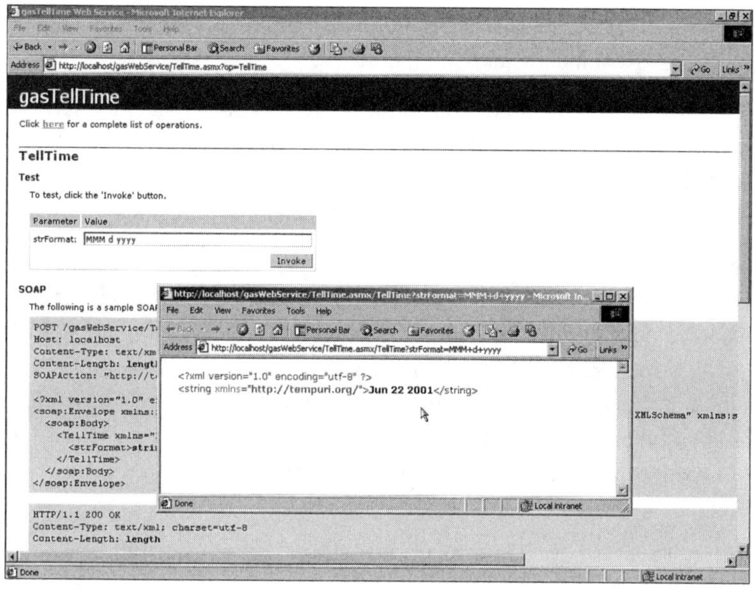

FIGURE 9.13
The .NET platform makes testing a Web Service easy.

Our web Service returns a short XML file that includes the requested information:

```
<?xml version="1.0" encoding="utf-8" ?>
<string xmlns="http://tempuri.org/">Oct 22 2001</string>
```

More information about inter-application communications using XML can be found in Chapter 3.

Calling the DLL from a Visual Basic .NET Class Library

We have already seen that our RCW DLL integrates seamlessly with an ASP.NET Web Service. But what does it take to make the `TellTime` method available through a Visual Basic .NET Class Library? Class Libraries are the .NET equivalent of ActiveX DLLs. In this section, we will create such a Class Library using Visual Basic .NET. Later in this chapter we will call the Class Library from a Visual Basic 6 executable just like a COM+ component.

Setting up the Class Library

To start creating the Class Library, start Visual Studio .NET and choose New Project from the Start Page. Select Visual Basic Projects and choose the Class Library template. Enter `gasClass` as the name for the project and define a location (the default location given by Visual Studio .NET will do). Once the project is created, select `Class1.vb` in the Solution Explorer and change its name to `gasClass.vb`. Visual Studio .NET has already added a public class called `Class1` to our project. Rename this class to `gasTime`.

To be able to use the RCW's method in our project, we will have to add a reference, just like we did for the Web Service project. Go to the Project menu and click on Add Reference. Once again the Add Reference dialog will appear. Select the .NET tab, click on Browse… and locate `gasRCW.dll`. Then click OK to select the DLL and click OK again to add the reference to our project.

Go to the code window for `gasClass.vb` and add the code below to the `gasTime` class. Figure 9.14 shows what the development environment should look like. Adding the `TellTime` function will call the RCW's `TellTime` method and make its result available through the Class Library's `TellTime` method. If this code looks familiar, that is probably because it *is* familiar! It is an almost exact copy of the code that was used to create our Web Service. The only part that is missing is the `<WebMethod()>` attribute. Compare the snippet below to the previous snippet to spot the difference.

```
Public Function TellTime(ByVal strFormat As String) As String
    Dim myRcwDll As gasRCW.gasTime
    myRcwDll = New gasRCW.gasTime()

    TellTime = myRcwDll.TellTime(strFormat)
End Function
```

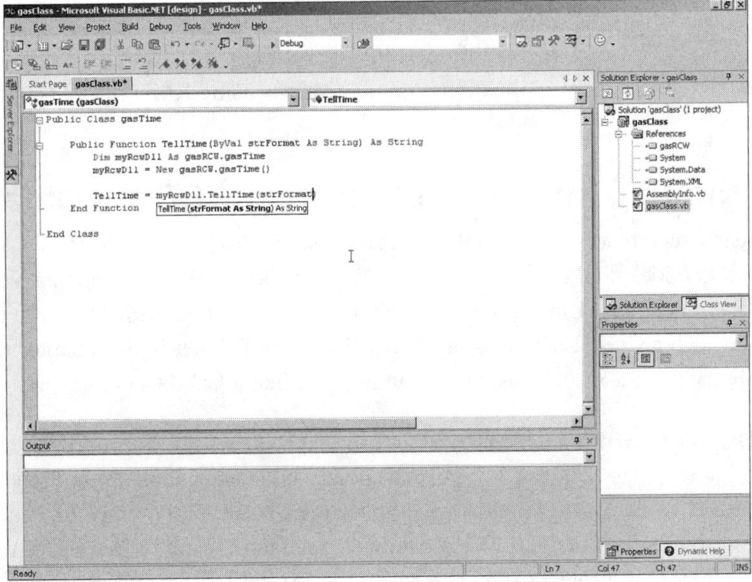

FIGURE 9.14

Our sample class library uses functionality found in our COM+ DLL.

Once again, creating the project is rather straightforward. After saving our work we can select Build from the Build menu to create the `gasClass` assembly.

Calling the Class Library from a Visual Basic 6 Executable

Now that we have created the Class Library, we are almost ready to call it from a Visual Basic 6 executable using the COM+ interface. But since Visual Basic 6 cannot add references to assemblies, we will have to export a type library first.

Exporting the Type Library using TlbExp

Visual Studio .NET ships with a utility called the Type Library Exporter Utility, or TlbExp for short. TlbExp does just the opposite of TlbImp: it takes an assembly and exports a type library based on the assembly's contents. To use it, we open the Visual Studio .NET Command Prompt and navigate to the directory containing the `gasClass` assembly. Then we type

```
TlbExp gasClass.dll /out:gasCCW.tlb
```

and press Enter to execute the command. The TlbExp utility will respond with a message that should look like similar to the following:

```
TlbExp—.NET Assembly to Type Library Converter Version 1.0.2914.16
Copyright (C) Microsoft Corp. 2001. All rights reserved.

Assembly exported to D:\gasTIX\gasClass\gasCCW.tlb
```

Executing the above command has created a type library that we can use to set references to the assembly from Visual Studio 6. We can use the `/out:` parameter of TlbExp to define the name of the resulting type library. To learn more about the optional parameters of TlbExp, type:

```
TlbExp /?
```

or look in the Visual Studio .NET documentation. Another parameter that is worth mentioning is the `/silent` parameter that prevents TlbExp from displaying messages.

Creating a Visual Basic 6 Executable

It is time to switch back to our Visual Studio 6 development environment again. Copy the type library that we produced in the previous paragraph and placc it somewhere within the Visual Studio 6 environment. Next, start Visual Basic 6 so that we can create a simple test application to call the Class Library through a COM+ interface. Select Standard EXE from the New Project dialog. Once the project has been created, select `Project1` from the Project Explorer and change its name to `TestCCW` in the Properties toolbox. Select `Form1` and rename it to `MainForm`. Change its caption to "TestCCW." We will now add some controls to the form. Figure 9.15 shows what the form should look like.

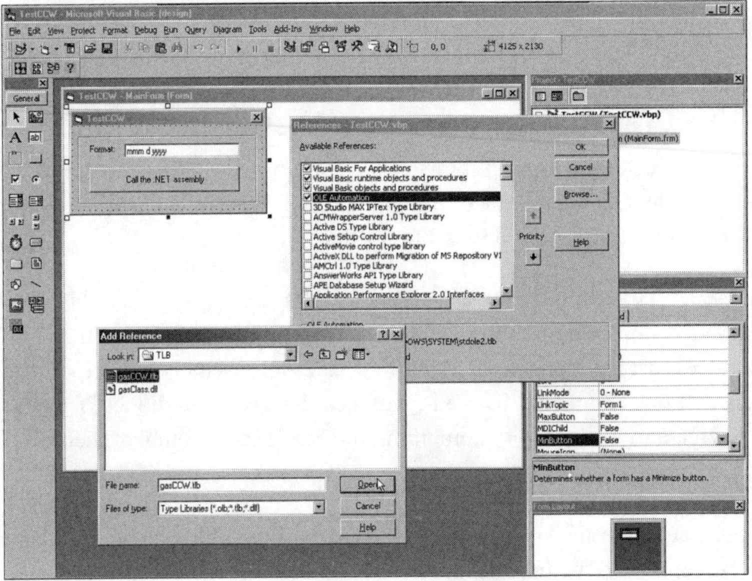

FIGURE 9.15

Setting a reference to the type library exported with TlbExp

We will add a `Label` control and change its caption to `Format:`. Then we will add a `TextBox` control and change its default `Text` property to `mmm d yyyy`. The last control to be added is a `CommandButton`. Change its caption to `Call the .NET assembly`, then change to the code window for `MainForm`. Before we can call the assembly, we will first have to add a reference to its type library. To do so, we select References…from the Project menu. Click on Browse... and locate the type library that we have copied from the Visual Studio .NET development environment. This is shown in Figure 9.15. Click on Open and OK to add the reference to our project. Now add the code of the listing below to the code window. This will create an instance of the assembly when the user clicks the `CommandButton` and show its results in a `MessageBox`.

```
Private Sub Command1_Click()
    Dim myAssembly As gasClass.gasTime
    Set myAssembly = New gasClass.gasTime

    MsgBox myAssembly.TellTime(Text1.Text)

    Set myAssembly = Nothing
End Function
```

NOTE

For more details on defining date/time formats, please refer to the Microsoft Visual Basic documentation. Some of the most useful options for our example are shown in Table 9.5.

TABLE 9.5 Some of the Characters that Can be Used to Define the Date Format

Character	*Description*
`d`	Display the day as a number without a leading zero (`1 - 31`).
`dd`	Display the day as a number with a leading zero (`01 - 31`).
`m`	Display the month as a number without a leading zero (`1 - 12`).
`mm`	Display the month as a number with a leading zero (`01 - 12`).
`mmm`	Display the month as an abbreviation (`Jan` - Dec`)`.
`mmmm`	Display the month as a full month name (`January - December`).
`yy`	Display the year as a 2-digit number (`00 - 99`)
`yyyy`	Display the year as a 4-digit number (`0001 - 9999`)

The only things left to do in the Visual Studio 6 environment are saving our work and building the executable. Copy the executable so we can transfer it to the Visual Studio .NET environment.

Testing the Assembly from Visual Basic 6

After making a final switch to our Visual Studio .NET development environment, we are just about ready to start our test application. Copy `TestCCW.exe` to any directory and copy both `gasClass.dll` and `gasRCW.dll` to the same directory. In our example we will assume that the files have been copied to `D:\gasTIX\TestCCW\`. There is just one thing left to do. If we want to call a COM+ component, it needs to be registered first. Otherwise, COM+ won't be able to locate the component. If we want to call an assembly just like it was a COM+ component, it needs to be registered as well. But since it is not a COM+ component, we can't use `regsvr32.exe` to do the registering for us. We will have to rely on another utility that ships with Visual Studio .NET, RegAsm. RegAsm is to assemblies what `regsvr32` is to Win32 .DLLs. It registers the assembly and allows it to be called through a COM+ interface. To register `gasClass.dll`, start the Visual Studio.NET Command Prompt, navigate to the directory containing `TestCCW.exe` and the two assemblies, and type

```
RegAsm gasClass.dll
```

and press Enter to execute the command. This will register the assembly and should respond with a message like:

```
RegAsm--.NET Assembly Registration Utility Version 1.0.2914.16
CopyRight (C) Microsoft Corp. 2001. All rights reserved.

Types Registered successfully
```

To learn more about the optional parameters of RegAsm, type:

```
RegAsm /?
```

or look in the Visual Studio .NET documentation. Some of the most useful options for our purposes are shown in Table 9.6.

TABLE 9.6 Some of RegAsm's command line parameters

Parameter	*Description*
`/unregister`	Unregister types
`/tlb[:Filename]`	Export the assembly to the specified type library and register it
`/silent`	Prevents displaying of success messages

TIP

Both TlbExp and RegAsm (with `/tlb` parameter) are capable of exporting type libraries. The difference is that RegAsm will also register the assembly, while TlbExp will not. If we want to register an assembly and export its type library at the same time, we can use `RegAsm filename1 /tlb:filename2` as a shorthand form for `RegAsm filename1` followed by `TlbExp filename1 /out:filename2`.

We are now ready to start our test application. We can enter any format string in the text box. When we press the button, a `MessageBox` will show the result. Figure 9.16 shows an example using the default string `mmm d yyyy`. Please note that as was originally shown in Figure 9.2 at the beginning of this chapter, it is our original Visual Basic 6 DLL that produces the actual result. The call from `TestCCW.exe` is transferred into the CLR through `gasClass.dll` and `gasRCW.dll`, and then out of the CLR again to `gasTime.dll`. This clearly is not the most efficient solution, but it demonstrates all the mechanisms involved in COM+ integration.

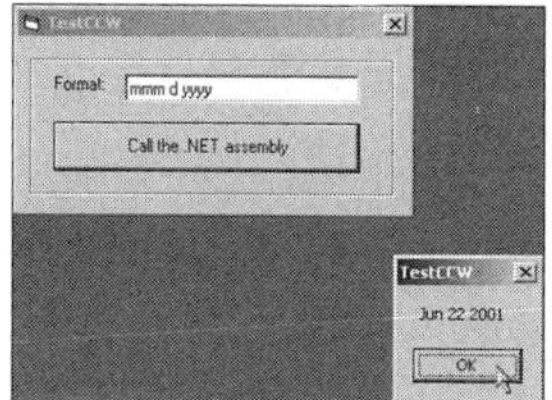

FIGURE 9.16
Our test application is finally running!

From Here

In this chapter we explored the various ways in which managed and unmanaged code can coexist within an application. We looked at Runtime-Callable Wrappers, COM-Callable Wrappers and various utilities that can be used to integrate COM+ components with .NET code.

- To learn more about Web services and inter-application communications, see Chapter 3.
- For more information on performance testing, see Chapter 15, "Performance Tuning in .NET."
- For further information on the integration of .NET and COM+, see the Microsoft Visual Studio .NET documentation.
- For more information on using Visual Studio 6, see *Building Enterprise Solutions with Visual Studio 6—The Authorative Solution*, by Don Benage, Azam Mirza et al, ISBN 0-672-31489-4, Sams Publishing.

Building .NET e-Business Sites

This section considers the implementation of the sample gasTIX application from a functional point of view. We devote a chapter to each of the main site functions (event searching, ticket purchasing, fulfillment/order processing), from the top tier to the bottom tier, demonstrating how data is passed between application layers. An abundance of code samples provides you with ideas and techniques that you can include in your own .NET applications.

IN THIS PART

- **Chapter 10: gasTIX Event Searching 287**
- **Chapter 11: Purchasing a Ticket 321**
- **Chapter 12: Fulfillment 351**
- **Chapter 13: .NET Remoting 395**

gasTIX Event Searching

by David Burgett

CHAPTER

10

IN THIS CHAPTER

- Building Presentation Services with ASP.NET 288
- Building the ASP.NET Project 294
- User Controls 310
- From Here 320

The bulk of the user experience on gasTIX is the process of users searching for particular events for which they wish to buy tickets. We have strived to make it simple for users to easily find events for a specific Participant or Venue, as well as viewing based on categories and sub-categories. The Event Searching portion of gasTIX is built as an ASP.NET project written in Visual Basic .NET. This chapter examines the process of building these pages and building reusable user controls that are instantiated on many of the ASP.NET pages.

The overall goal of the event searching services in the gasTIX presentation layer is to allow users to quickly and easily find information about events and tickets, and to encourage casual site browsers to become buyers.

Building Presentation Services with ASP.NET

In order to build the gasTIX presentation services, we first need to identify the goals of the presentation layer. We need to identify how users will use the website, what information they will search for, and how to make the whole process easy.

The presentation layer holds a special distinction: It is the only code which produces output directly viewed by the user. As anyone who has built an e-commerce site will tell you, it doesn't matter how well a website can handle orders if the website itself does not convince visitors to become buyers.

In order to actually build the gasTIX presentation services, we will use ASP.NET web forms and web controls. In order to effectively use these, it is important to understand the ASP .NET object model and the base classes from which all other web controls are inherited from.

This chapter examines the ASP.NET code that consumes the gasTIX business objects and offers event-searching capabilities to the user.

Presentation Service Goals

There are numerous ways to determine and document the goals of a website; gasTIX uses standard UML use cases to help in this process. These are described in Chapter 2, "gasTIX: A Sample .NET e-Business."

There are four primary goals that gasTIX users have when accessing the site:

- Finding information or tickets for a specific event, such as a concert or football game
- Finding events for a specific performer or venue
- Finding personalized events in which they may be interested
- Making users feel comfortable enough to purchase tickets

Given the goals of gasTIX users, the event-searching capability must allow quick access to ticket information through a variety of search techniques. Users may know the name of the event they would like to purchase tickets for, or simply the name of the performer or venue. Searching on any of these pieces of information should allow gasTIX users to locate events for which they may purchase tickets.

Take the example of our fictional bagpipe band, the gasBAGS. If our user knows that the gasBAGS will be playing at the gasAuditorium sometime in the next two months, he will likely want to search for all upcoming gasBAGS events to find the particular event he is interested in. Or, since they know the particular venue in question, they may search specifically for gasAuditorium. Or, perhaps they know that this particular event is just one event in the "gasBAGS World Tour" and would like to know about the other events scheduled for this tour. In order to minimize the amount of effort required by the user to locate the appropriate information, the gasTIX website must make it possible to easily locate an event based on any of the possible pieces of information.

To that end, the gasTIX website employs a "combined search" feature, which allows users to enter a single piece of information and review multiple types of information that meet the search criteria. For instance, if a user types `gas` into the combined search entry box, a display similar to Figure 10.1 will display events, tour, venues, and performers matching `gas`. Under the Performers category, we find the *gasBAGS* bagpipe band and under the Venues category, we find the gasAuditorium venue. Likewise, under the Tour category, we find a single entry, the "gasBAGS World Tour 2002", and under the Events category, we find multiple events that comprise the world tour.

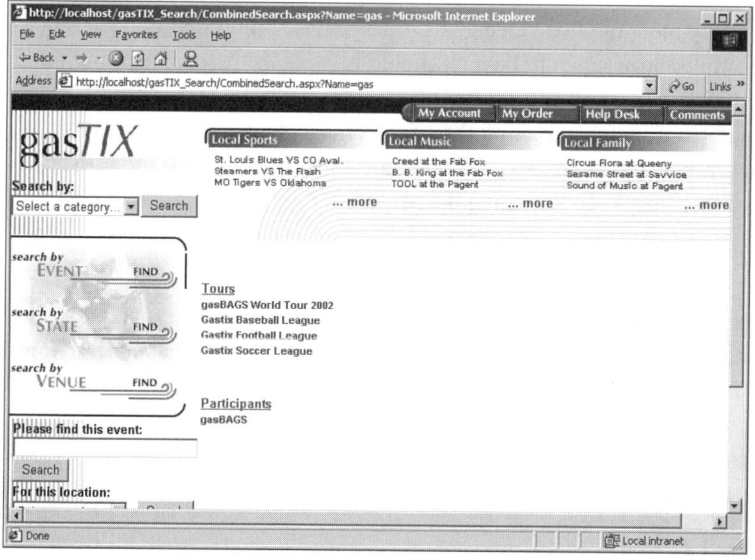

FIGURE 10.1

The combined search feature of gasTIX displays several types of information for a single search entry.

NOTE

The code for the combined search feature of gasTIX is discussed later in this chapter.

Since the entry point for the combined search functionality is found on the gasTIX home page (and duplicated on each subsequent page), users can quickly find information about all aspects of gasTIX data. However, we also need to consider the possibility that the user does not know the specific name they are looking for when searching for information. Perhaps a user is visiting a city and would like to see what events are taking place in that city during the next month. gasTIX needs to allow the user to view a list of venues in the specified city as well as a list of events for each venue.

Or perhaps the user cannot remember the name of our bagpipe band, and instead remembers only that the band they are looking for plays the best Celtic music around. To assist these users, and to allow users to find events or performers similar to those the user already knows of, gasTIX has organized all events and performers into a structured set of categories and subcategories. gasTIX categories are high-level constructs like Music and Sports, while subcategories are further defined into rock, country, or Celtic music. Thus, since our user knows that he likes Celtic music and finds that the gasBAGS band is classified in the Celtic subcategory of the Music category, he can find a band of interest to him. In addition, the user can find other bands that play Celtic music.

If we successfully meet the first three goals of the gasTIX presentation layer, then meeting the fourth goal, turning browsers into buyers, should be easy. If the user can find the tickets he is looking for quickly and easily, he will be much more likely to actually make a purchase than if he has to spend ten minutes searching the site. Web users have a notoriously short patience level; if they can not find what they are looking for quickly, they are more likely to look on another site, rather than keep searching deeper into the original site.

ASP.NET Web Controls

One of the exciting new features of ASP.NET is the consistent object model shared by all web controls, custom controls, and pages. The object model is consistent and independent of language, allowing all ASP.NET developers to program against the same objects, properties, and methods. This allows the developer to focus more energy on the business problem and less on how a particular syntax works. To understand the new object model, we must first discuss the basic objects that all ASP.NET applications will use.

The Control Class

As discussed in Chapter 3, “Enabling Inter-Application Communications,” web forms are the basis of most ASP.NET applications and serve as the starting point for building the gasTIX

Event Searching services. Server-side web controls are added to each web form and manipulated either programmatically or through the use of HTML tag parameters.

For ASP.NET developers, the most pertinent branch of the .NET Framework object model is the `System.Web.UI` namespace. This namespace contains all of the user interface (UI) controls built for use on the web. The first class in this namespace that we will discuss is the Control class. The Control class is the base definition for all ASP.NET server controls and user controls. Standard controls include the TextBox control and Label, while user controls can be created and distributed by any third-party. See the "User Controls" section later in this chapter for more information.

The System.Web.UI.Control class offers the base properties that all visual web controls require, such as an ID, a reference to a parent control, and the visibility of the control. All controls inherit these basic properties from the Control class, as well as basic methods like `GetType`, `FindControl`, and `ToString`. These methods provide the basic functionality all controls need to determine their type, to find child controls, and to return a string representation of themselves.

A method defined on the Control class is the `DataBind()` method. `DataBind` connects the control to a `DataSource` and resolves all data-binding expressions defined within the control. This is typically used to display multiple sets of information returned from a database query, such as a list of states or regions in a drop-down box or a list of events in a DataGrid. However, data binding can also be used to create single-value, data-bound formulas. This method can be used to tie two controls together, so that the value of the second is always based on the value of the first. For more information on data binding, see the section entitled "Using the DataList Control" later in this chapter.

The Control class also defines several events which all controls inherit. These events allow us to execute code when the control is first initialized, when it is actually loaded into a web page, when it is unloaded from memory, and when it is data bound.

The `System.Web.UI` branch of the .NET Framework object model provides the basic structure for all controls we will use in every ASP.NET project and provides a uniform structure for our pages.

The TemplateControl Class

The TemplateControl class inherits directly from the Control class and provides functionality to two other classes ASP.NET developers should become very familiar with, Page and UserControl. The TemplateControl class subclasses the Control class and adds several methods. The primary functionality added is the ability for TemplateControl class objects to contain other controls. This allows page objects to contain controls and user controls to be nested within other user controls.

The TemplateControl class also adds an `Error` event, which occurs when an unhandled exception is thrown. This makes it easy to catch errors at either the page level, or for any individual control.

The TemplateControl class gets its name from the fact that it can obtain instances of an ITemplate interface and apply that template to the controls contained by the TemplateControl. This allows developers to easily define grouping styles for repeatable information in a single location. For more information about using Templates, see "Using the DataList Control" section later in this chapter.

The first class derived from the TemplateControl class is the Page class. Page is the class from which all web pages are instantiated. In classic ASP, a page was simply a text file parsed by the web server. In ASP.NET, the page is now a fully qualified object, derived from TemplateControl, with its own properties and methods. Each time the web server receives a request for a web page, the `Page` object is instantiated and populated with the information stored in the .aspx and code-behind files.

The Page class exposes as properties the standard objects that ASP developers are accustomed to: `Application`, `Request`, `Response`, `Server`, and `Session`. The Page class also offers new properties: `Validators`, which will be discussed in Chapter 11, "Purchasing a Ticket"; Trace, which will be discussed in Chapter 14, "Debugging a .NET Application"; and IsPostBack, which will be used on almost every gasTIX page. Commonly used properties of the page class are shown in table 10.1.

TABLE 10.1 Page Class Properties

Properties	
`Application, Request, Response, Server, Session`	Returns a reference to the current object of the same name
`Cache`	Allows developers to store this page for later use
`Controls`	A collection of controls on the page
`ErrorPage`	The page to display if an unhandled exception occurs
`IsPostBack`	True if the page is being instantiated in response to an event on the page, false otherwise
`Trace`	Returns a reference to the `TraceContext` object
`User`	Returns information about the user who requested the page
`Validators`	Returns a collection of all validation controls on the page

TABLE 10.1 Continued

Methods	
`DataBind`	Connects all databound controls on the page to their appropriate datasource.
`LoadControl`	Instantiates a UserControl from a user control (.ascx) file.
`Validate`	Executes all validation controls on the page.

The second class derived from the TemplateControl is the UserControl class. The UserControl class is the class instantiated when a developer creates a user-defined class stored in an .ascx file. User controls are similar to Page objects in how they are instantiated, however, UserControls require a parent Page object in order to be instantiated. UserControls cannot be created, except within the context of a page object. For more information on UserControls, see the ".NET User Controls" section in this chapter.

Other Key Classes

There are several classes in the System.Web.UI.Control namespace that you should know, as shown in Figure 10.2. These include:

- The WebControl class. This class provides a foundation for all server-side ASP.NET web controls, such as TextBox and Label. The WebControl class provides basic properties such as color and border, as well as events such as `ApplyStyle`. This ensures that all Web Controls share similar property names, a welcome improvement over classic ASP development.
- The HTMLControl class. This class is inherited by all standard HTML element classes, such as `<input>` and `<img>`. This is an important point for developers learning ASP.NET. Using ASP.NET server controls does not exclude you from using standard HTML controls, and using standard HTML controls does not prevent you from having a well-defined object model. An ASP.NET page can instantiate a `System.Web.UI.HTMLControl.HtmlImage` object and programmatically set its normal HTML parameters, such as the `src` and `height` parameters.
- The Repeater and RepeaterItem classes. These two classes work in concert to provide base functionality for template items. The styles defined within the template will be repeated once for each row of bound data. Each `Repeater` object can have one or more RepeaterItems attached to it. The sections "Using our Repeater Control" and "Using the DataList Control" in this chapter offer examples of using objects derived from the Repeater class.

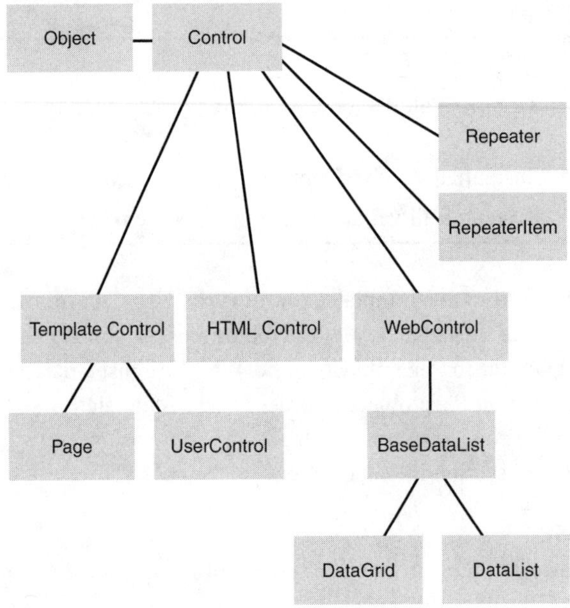

FIGURE 10.2
All ASP.NET controls derive from the Control class.

Building the ASP.NET Project

Now that we have defined the goal for the search portion of the gasTIX website and learned more about the ASP.NET object model, we will jump right into building the project itself. The gasTIX solution was initially developed as multiple Visual Studio .NET projects by developers in geographically distinct places. Much improved project interoperability is an important benefit of ASP.NET, allowing developers to work separately towards a common goal. In this chapter, we will create the gasTIX_Search project allowing users access to the `gasTIX` event searching features. The next chapter, "Purchasing a Ticket" will build the second project in the presentation services layer. These two projects will then be combined with the business layer projects to form the gasTIX solution.

The gasTIX Search Project

To create the gasTIX_Search project, do the following:

1. Open Visual Studio .NET
2. Select New|Project

3. Under Project Types, select "Visual Basic Project" and highlight "ASP.NET Web Application" in the Templates window
4. Change the project name to "gasTIX_Search" and ensure that the location specified points to your local machine.

NOTE

The presentation services require the use of the business objects created for gasTIX. Both the assemblies and source code are available for download at `www.gasTIX.com`. Alternately, the assemblies are available for web service consumption at `www.gasTIX.com/WebServices`. You can reference them locally or through a web service. See Chapter 11, for more information on web services.

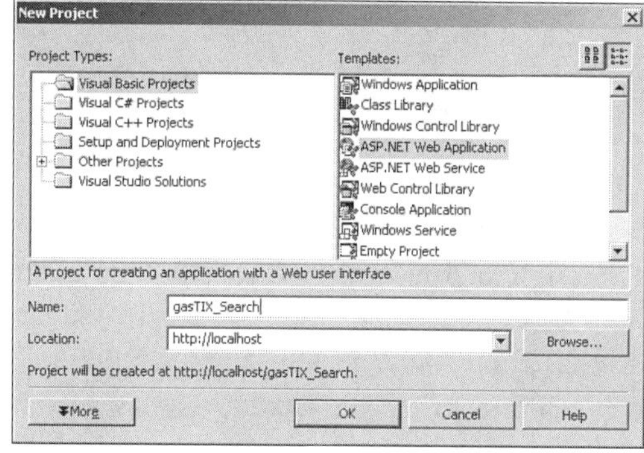

FIGURE 10.3
The New Project dialog offers several languages and project types.

After the new website is created, Visual Studio .NET presents us with a standard ASP.NET application with a default web form called WebForm1.aspx. For this example, rename the web form "CombinedSearch.aspx." The project also creates several other files, as detailed here:

- **Styles.css**—This is a Cascading Style Sheets (CSS) document that describes styles used in the newly created application.
- **Global.asax**—This file handles application-level events such as `Application_BeginRequest` and `Application_Error`.
- **web.config**—This file holds configuration information about the application, such as default language and session state information.
- **AssemblyInfo.vb**—This file contains information to be built into the assembly (.dll) such as version and trademark information.

In order to make use of the gasTIX middle-tier business objects, we first need to add a reference to them. Right-click on References in the Solution Explorer dialog and select Add Reference. Click Browse and locate gasTIX.BusinessFacade.dll. The BusinessFacade assembly provides the basic business objects of gasTIX: `events`, `participants`, `venues`, and so on. Each business object has appropriate methods and properties that will allow our gasTIX_Search pages to retrieve and display the necessary data.

Our ASP.NET project is now initialized and ready for us to add some pages.

TIP

If you have downloaded the entire code for the business objects, instead of just the compiled assemblies, you will find it much easier to work with project references versus assembly references. Simply create a solution that contains all business layer projects and your gasTIX_Search project. When you add references to the business layer projects to your gasTIX_Search project, simply select the references from the Projects tab of the Add References dialog.

Separation of Code and Design in gasTIX

One of the most beneficial design improvements of ASP.NET for building gasTIX is the ability to separate code and design. As mentioned previously, a distributed team of designers and developers working all over the United States and in Europe built gasTIX. The ability to create the design of the website at a different time and location from those creating the code was critical to the development cycle's success.

gasTIX uses code-behind pages extensively for this reason. (For more information on code-behind pages, see Chapter 5, "Implementing .NET Presentation Services.") The developers were able to drop the controls they needed on the web form and write the code in the code-behind page to access those controls. They would then tell the designers what controls were necessary on any given page. The designers would take that information and design an aesthetically pleasing web form using the controls dictated by the developers. When the designers were finished, the developers simply replaced the local web forms (but not the code-behind) with the ones supplied by the designers. Since all of the application logic is stored in the code-behind files, this did not break any of the developers' code. After designers and developers identified which pages were necessary, and which controls each of those pages would contain, each could work at their own pace and in an order that suited their needs.

TIP

The default code-behind file name changed between Beta 1 and Beta 2 of the .NET Framework to include the .aspx before the .vb. However, you can specify any name you like for the file, as long as the `CodeBehind` attribute of the Page or Control directive matches up.

This system, while much better than classic ASP development, is not perfect yet. There are situations in which the code and design still bleed together. One such situation is using DataList controls. Many designers are not comfortable with creating the necessary server-side code to call the `DataBinder.Eval` method. Without this application code, the DataList has no functionality. While the ability to use templates and styles does help separate code and design, some of the design of items in the DataList still needs to go in the ItemTemplate.

Technically, the ItemTemplate can be filled from the code-behind page, but this gets into the issues that have plagued ASP developers for years. When you have server-side code writing client-side HTML, it is both inefficient and ugly. It is much easier to design the HTML code on the HTML page, rather than trying to design it piece by piece in VB .NET code.

Overall, however, the ability to separate code from design allows much more productivity and efficiency.

Using ASP.NET Web Controls

To start building the gasTIX_Search project we will first create a simple Web Form that allows users to perform the "combined search" discussed previously. We will build a single page that will have two simple components: a TextBoxes web control and a Button web control. This section describes how to use simple Web Controls how to add add the controls to a page.

TextBox and Button Controls

The first thing we need to do to build our page is add a TextBox control to our Web Form. This textbox will allow our user to enter the text they would like to search for. Follow these steps:

1. Double-click CombinedSearch.aspx in the Solution Explorer to open it in design mode. Notice the two tabs just below the design area in Figure 10.4. The "Design" and "HTML" views work interchangeably; when one is modified, the other is automatically updated to reflect the change.

TIP

If you are creating your web forms in the HTML view, a quick way to validate your code is to click the Design tab, or press Control-Page Up on your keyboard. Before Visual Studio.NET switches to design mode, it will validate your code and notify you of any errors.

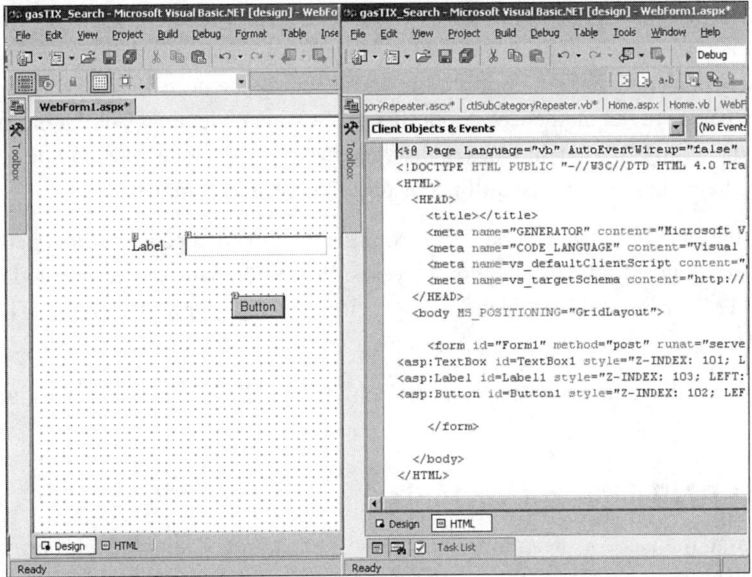

FIGURE 10.4
Visual Studio .NET offers both a design view and an HTML view of every Web Form.

2. To add a textbox web control to our form, we first need to locate the Toolbox menu. This is usually docked on the left-hand side of the screen and is identified by an icon of a hammer and a wrench. If the Toolbox is not visible, simply click the tab and it will unfurl on top of our web form. Locate the textbox control in the toolbox and double-click it to add one to the web form.

TIP

The controls in the toolbox are arranged according to the order in which Microsoft believes they will be most commonly used. The items can also be arranged alphabetically by right-clicking the toolbox and choosing Sort Items Alphabetically.

When you double-click the textbox control, a small text box appears in the upper, left-hand corner of the web form. You can move this control to any location on the web form by simply dragging and dropping it. The control will stay wherever you put it because web forms, by default, are created with their pageLayout property set to GridLayout. The GridLayout option allows you to graphically design the layout of the page and develops HTML to automatically support our design. Visual Studio .NET will create the necessary HTML tables or CSS absolute positioning tags to arrange the web controls on the page. For more information on positioning web controls, see Chapter 5.

3. Change the name of the textbox control to txtCombinedSearch. We also need a button control on our form, so double click the button control in the toolbox and then move the button to an aesthetically pleasing location on the form. We will call the button butSearch. In order to make the form a little more attractive, you can add a label next to the textbox. Change the caption to explain to the user the purpose of the textbox. The form now looks similar to the one shown Figure 10.5.

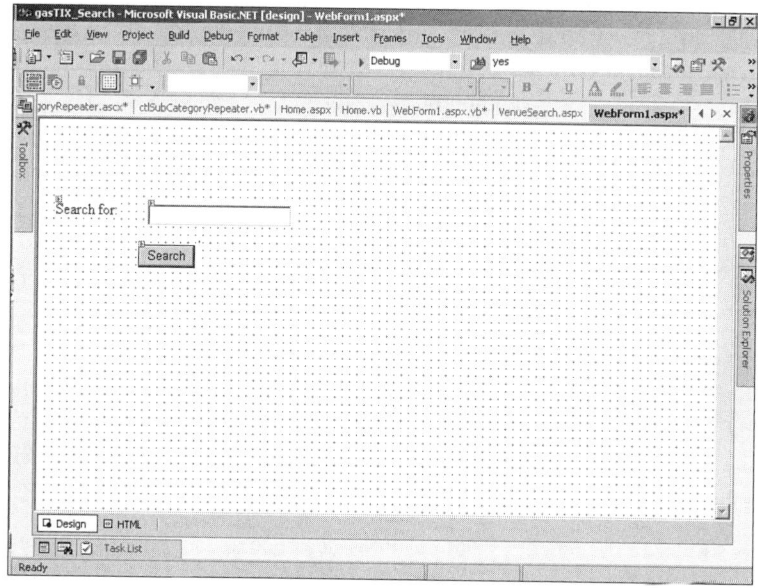

FIGURE 10.5
This simple web form now has the controls we need to perform a search on all events, tours, participants, and venues.

Now that we have added the two basic controls to the web form, take a moment to look at the HTML created by the design view. Click the HTML tab in the bottom left corner of the screen. Find the textbox control we added; the HTML for it should look similar to this:

```
<ASP:TextBox Runat="Server" ID="txtCombinedSearch">
```

There are two important things to note about this HTML tag. The first is the `RunAt` attribute which is set to the value of `Server`. This tells the ASP.NET engine to handle this control on the server, before the page is sent to the client. This is what gives ASP.NET the opportunity to examine the browser making the request and then create customized output based on the browser level.

The other interesting note about this HTML definition is the prefix attached to the TextBox definition. The ASP: prefix tells ASP.NET that this textbox control is part of the standard ASP.NET control collection. All web controls shipped with ASP.NET are part of the ASP package. When we develop our own custom controls later in this chapter, we will change this prefix to tell ASP.NET that we are using controls from our own package.

You now have everything you need on the web form to allow a user to perform a combined search. Next, you need some way to display the data returned from the middle tier objects. For that, you will add a Repeater to the web form.

Repeating Data Controls

The `Repeater` control is one of several web controls shipped with Visual Studio .NET that allows developers to easily display rows of data. Displaying data from a database (or XML file or any other data store) is a very common purpose for web pages, so ASP.NET is designed to make these tasks easy. ASP.NET offers three controls designed to make formatting data easy and reusable. These are:

- `Repeater`
- `DataList`
- `DataGrid`

The `Repeater` control is the simplest of the repeating data controls, because it has no inherent user interface. Thus, repeater controls offer the most output flexibility. However, the trade-off for this flexibility is more effort required on the developer's part. The repeater control is very useful for any type of listed data including spreadsheet-style tables, bulleted point lists, series of images, or even simple comma-delimited lists.

The datalist is similar to the repeater control, but is designed specifically to handle table-style data. The datalist organizes each data record into a single row of a standard data table format. Developers have control over both the display of the table as a whole, and each row of data. If you are looking for a way to display a spreadsheet style table of data, the datalist is a better choice than the repeater because it has the table structure built into it. If you use a repeater control, you need to define the table structure using HTML tables or simple `<BR>` tags. On the other hand, the datalist automatically creates the necessary `<TABLE>`, `<TR>`, and `<TD>` tags to display the data correctly. Datalist controls have full WYSIWYG editing in Visual Studio .NET, using the design mode tools. For example code, see the "Using the Datalist Control" section later in this chapter.

The Datagrid control takes the concept of the datalist one step further. Like the Datalist control, Datagrid controls automatically display data in a grid format. Datagrid controls add additional functionality: automatic paging, data sorting, data editing and deleting. Like Datalist control, Datagrid controls support full WYSIWYG editing in design mode and the design of the grid is highly customizable. If you are looking for a standard table layout with the ability for the user to sort or edit the data, then Datagrid is the best choice. The automatic paging functionality of the datagrid also makes it an excellent choice when you have more data to display than will conveniently fit on a single screen. If, however, you want simple, read-only display of your data, the Datalist or Repeater controls will be a better choice as they incur less overhead.

For the gasTIX combined search page, we will use four Repeater controls to display the data returned by the middle tier. Each Repeater control will display a group of data relating to one of our search categories: Events, Tours, Participants, and Venues. The repeater web control sits in the toolbox like all standard controls and can be easily double-clicked and added to the page. Create four Repeater controls and name them: rptEvents, rptTours, rptVenues, and rptParticipants. Arrange them in a single column below the textbox and button already on the page.

NOTE

It is important that there be a valid datasource with at least one row of data bound to any Repeater, Datalist, or Datagrid. If a repeating data control has no bound data, it will not be rendered on the page.

Using Repeater Controls

Now that we have added a Repeater control to our web page, we need to create some templates for identifying how to lay out the data. Every Repeater control requires an <ItemTemplate> tag to display data. Additionally, each one can have several optional templates as well, such as <AlternatingItemTemplate> and <HeaderTemplate>.

Repeating Data Control Templates

There are five templates available to the Repeater control:

- ItemTemplate
- AlternatingItemTemplate
- HeaderTemplate
- FooterTemplate
- SeparatorTemplate

The ItemTemplate of a Repeater web control identifies the HTML code that will be displayed for each row of data bound to the control. This HTML can be as simple as a comma to build a comma-delimited list, or it can be part of a complex table structure used to position each row of data on the page. The <ItemTemplate> tag of one of our combined search repeater controls looks like this:

```
<ItemTemplate>
 <tr>
  <td>
   Data Goes Here!
  </td>
 </tr>
</ItemTemplate>
```

This is simple enough; for each row of data that is bound to our repeater control, a new HTML table row with a single column will be created. HTML rows cannot be displayed without a <table>..</table> definition. We could place these tags on either side of our repeater control, but there is a better place, as we will discuss later in this section.

There is one problem, however; for every row of data bound to our Repeater control, the phrase "Data Goes Here!" will appear! Since this is clearly not what we want, we need to replace that phrase with the actual data. We do that by using the Eval method of the DataBinder object. Replace "Data Goes Here!" with the following:

```
<%# DataBinder.Eval(Container, "Event_Name") %>
```

This code takes the container object and looks for a piece of data named Event_Name. If the data is found, then it replaces the server-side code with the data that will be displayed within the table cell defined in our ItemTemplate.

TIP

Although Microsoft recommends developers use the previously mentioned method, you can also use the following shortcut to access a container object's data:

```
Container.DataItem("Event_Name")
```

In addition to ItemTemplates, Repeater controls also support HeaderTemplates and FooterTemplates. These templates are only executed once per repeater control instead of once per row, like the ItemTemplate. The HeaderTemplate executes just before the first ItemTemplate and the FooterTemplate executes just after the last row of data is displayed in the ItemTemplate. Thus, we will place the <table> tag in the HeaderTemplate and the </table> tag in the FooterTemplate.

It may seem that these two options are redundant since both achieve the same effect on the resulting web page. However, one of the key concepts in the .NET Framework is modular objects. By including the `<table>` tags in the repeater control, we make the control completely modular and easily moved elsewhere on the page or to another page. The `Repeater` control is designed to be completely self-contained and to require no support from its parent page.

We will add one more feature to the HeaderTemplates of each repeater control for aesthetics. Just after the `<table>` tag, we will add a title row using the following code:

```
<tr><th>Tours</th></tr>
```

We will replace "Tours" with the appropriate title (Events, Participants, Venues) for each of our `Repeater` controls.

There are two more templates supported by the `repeater` control. The first is the SeparatorTemplate, which is inserted between each pair of ItemTemplates. This is useful for creating simple list structures such as delimiters between data items. It is important to note that the SeparatorTemplate is only used between two ItemTemplates; if there is only a single row of data, the SeparatorTemplate will never be used. Two examples of using the `Repeater` templates are showing in Figure 10.6

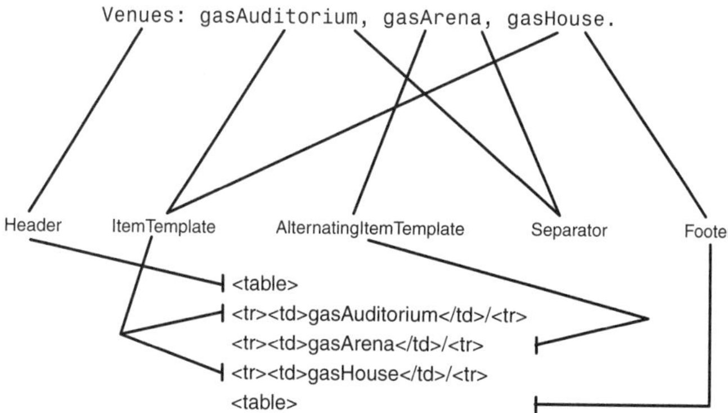

FIGURE 10.6
The `Repeater` control can be used to make comma-delimited lists or organize data into tables.

The final template available to the `Repeater` control is the AlternatingItemTemplate. This innovation is a huge timesaver and productivity enhancer. The AlternatingItemTemplate is used for the second row of data and every even numbered row thereafter. This makes it trivial to create the standard table structure where every other row is shaded differently to enhance readability. In order to enhance our combined search page with alternately shaded output rows, we would add the following template immediately below our ItemTemplate:

```
<AlternatingItemTemplate>
 <tr>
  <td bgcolor="C0C0C0">
   <%# DataBinder.Eval(Container, "Event_Name") %>
  </td>
 </tr>
</ItemTemplate>
```

This creates a table in which every even-numbered row has a light-grey colored background, while the odd-numbered rows have the standard white background, enhancing readability.

NOTE

If an AlternatingItemTemplate is not present, the ItemTemplate is used for every row of data.

Converting a Classic ASP Page to Use a Repeater Control

As discussed in Chapter 5, there are many reasons to convert existing ASP pages to ASP.NET pages. To convert an existing data-driven ASP page into a new ASP.NET page, simply copy the ASP code into the HTML view of the ASP.NET page. Then, insert a `<Repeater>` control on the page, wrapping the ASP code for displaying data. Then, insert Header- and FooterTemplates for any code that is just outside the loop that displays data. Finally, insert an ItemTemplate where you see the following code:

```
do while not rs.eof
```

You can determine the need for an AlternatingItemTemplate by checking to see if there is any code inside the new ItemTemplate that looks likes this:

```
counter=counter+1
if counter mod 2 = 0 then
<td bgcolor="C0C0C0">
 else
<td>
end if
```

The `counter mod 2 = 0` check is a common technique used to qualify every other line. If we increment counter each time through the loop, then `counter mod 2` will evaluate to true every other time.

To use the Repeater control, get rid of the `if...then` construct and move the first `<td>` definition to the AlternatingItemTemplate. Then, copy all of the remaining display code in the ItemTemplate to the AlternatingItemTemplate.

There are two remaining steps necessary to hook the new repeater control up to real data. The first is to replace any existing references to the recordset named `rs` in the old ASP page to the `DataBinder.Eval` method listed in the previous code. So we would convert:

```
<%= rs("event_name") %>
```

into

```
<%# DataBinder.Eval(container,"event_name") %>
```

The last step is to eliminate the code in the ASP page that retrieves data into the recordset. Now you need to create new code that binds the entire `Repeater` construct to a set of data pulled from the database.

Web Control Event Handling

You now have a web form with a text box, a button, and a repeater control that will serve as the basis for the combined search functionality. However, you do not yet have any code to accept input from the user, or to use that input to retrieve events, tours, participants, and venues from the database.

In order to run code to bind the repeater control to a data set, you need a place to run it from. That is, you need an event handler for the button control so that you can write code that will execute only after the user presses the button. This calls for event-driven programming. The concept of event-driven programming is new to ASP, but is very familiar to application programmers. An event-driven program is simply broken into chunks of code that are only executed when certain events occur, or are "fired." When an event fires, the associated code is executed and the application goes back to waiting for the next event. In the world of ASP.NET, events are fired when users press a button, select an item from a list box, or click a link. The event handler code can then respond to the event by changing data on the web form and redisplaying it, or by passing control to a new web form.

The easiest way to create an event handler for the click event of the button control is to simply double-click on the button in design mode. Visual Studio .NET automatically creates the necessary code for the handler and switches the view to the code so that you can immediately start writing the code for the handler. The event handler definition looks like this:

```
Public Sub butSearch_Click(ByVal sender as Object, ByVal e as System.EventArgs)
```

As we examine the code page, we see two other events handlers already defined and filled with code. The `CombinedSearch_Init` and `CombinedSearch_Load` events were automatically created by Visual Studio.NET when we created the CombinedSearch.aspx. These two events handle creating the controls on the web form and allow the developer to execute code before the page is processed and sent to the client. The web form load (`CombinedSearch_Load`) event is very useful for filling default values into textboxes and binding controls to data. It also plays a large role in the separation of design and code, as we will see later in this chapter.

If you switch back to the CombinedSearch.aspx file by clicking the tab just above the code area, and then switch to HTML view, you can see the code inserted into the `ASP:Button` control to tie it to the click event handler. A new parameter has been added to the control:

```
onClick="butSearch_Click"
```

This tells .NET that when the user clicks this button, the control should be passed back to the server to run the "butSearch_Click" event handler. Any code found in the event handler will be executed and the page will be reloaded.

We talked about the two events created automatically for every ASP.NET page. It is important to note that, by default, these events are "wired up" to the page, that is they will be executed every time the page is loaded. It is possible to turn these events off, however, so that they do not execute. Do this by adjusting the `AutoEventWireup` attribute of the Page directive. The first line of the CombinedSearch.aspx HTML is:

```
<%@ Page Language="vb" AutoEventWireUp="true"
Codebehind="CombinedSearch.aspx.vb" Inherits=Project1.CombinedSearch" %>
```

The Page directive gives basic information about the page like the language and location of the code-behind files. The `AutoEventWireUp` attribute tells the ASP.NET page to automatically handle the basic page level events like `Load` and `Init`. This is convenient since most ASP.NET you create will need this basic functionality. There may, however, be instances where the developer does not want events tied to their respective controls automatically. In this case, the developer would set `AutoEventWireUp` to `False` and would fire the events manually. This can be useful in cases where the developer wants to wait and handle multiple events with a single round-trip.

Binding the Repeater Control Data

We now have our controls in place and we have an event handler in which we can place code to retrieve data based on the input of the user. After we retrieve the data, we need to display it on our page by binding our repeater control to it.

First, to retrieve the data, we need to instantiate a `CombinedSearch` business object. The `CombinedSearch` object has a method called ListMultiple which accepts a string parameter specifying the search criteria. It then performs a search of the appropriate database tables and aggregates the results. It converts these results into an XML string and returns it to the caller.

All of the gasTIX middle tier objects return XML data as their basic form of communication. .NET's ability to read these files natively makes them a perfect choice for communication between tiers; if we decide to make the information public at any point in the future, we can simply expose the XML we already have to the world through a web service. Additionally, since SQL Server 2000 can return data as automatically formatted XML, all tiers of the gasTIX application can speak the same language natively.

To instantiate a `CombinedSearch` object from the BusinessFacade assembly, you first need to add a reference to the assembly. Do this by right-clicking the references tree under the project name in the Solution Explorer. Then, click the Browse button on the .NET tab of the Add Reference dialog (see Figure 10.7) and locate the BusinessFacade.dll file. The BusinessFacade assembly is listed in the Selected Components section of the dialog. Click OK to close the dialog.

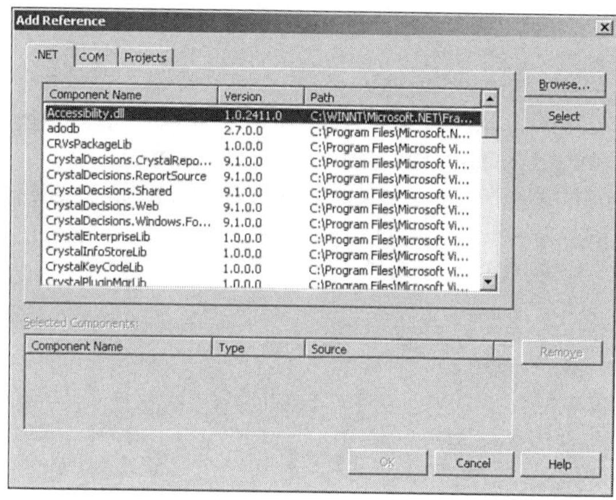

FIGURE 10.7
The Add Reference dialog allows us to add references to .NET assemblies, COM/COM+ objects, and even whole .NET projects.

The `CombinedSearch` object in the BusinessFacade library is located in the `gasTIX` namespace, so the code to instantiate this is:

```
Dim cs as gasTIX.BusinessFacade.CombinedSearch()
```

Add this line to the `butSearch_Click` event handler created previously. You now have an object of type `CombinedSearch`, with which you can retrieve results based on the user's input. You now need to call the `ListMultiple` method, passing in the value that the user has typed in the textbox. Since the method will return a string, you need to define a string variable, `sResult`, and assign it the value of the method call, as show here:

```
Dim sResult as String
sResult = cs.ListMultiple(txtCombinedSearch.Text)
```

Notice that since the `txtCombinedSearch` is a full object, we can simply refer to its text property, passing it as the parameter in to the `ListMultiple` method call. In classic ASP/HTML pages, textboxes are not objects in their own right; they only exist in the context of an HTML form. To access the content of an ASP textbox, you have to refer to an individual value in the form collection, instead of referring to the textbox itself. Since ASP.NET pages are designed to handle their own events, all of the controls are within scope and fully accessible within event handler code.

The `ListMultiple` method has now gone out to the database, retrieved several datasets and returned to us an aggregated XML file. For the purposes of actually getting to see something that we are creating, we will add a line of code to display the results of the `ListMultiple`, as shown here:

```
Response.write (Server.HTMLEncode(sResult))
```

This line takes the XML and runs it through the Server object's `HTMLEncode` method, which fixes any characters which will not display correctly on our HTML page. We can now run our web application by pressing F5. The web form is displayed with a blank textbox and a button. Enter the value "gas" in the textbox and click the button. The page will be reloaded, this time displaying the XML returned by the `CombinedSearch` business object as shown in Figure 10.8.

NOTE

For this page to work, the business objects and SQL Server database must be correctly installed and referenced. See Chapter 16, "Deploying the Application," for more information on deployment of the gasTIX application.

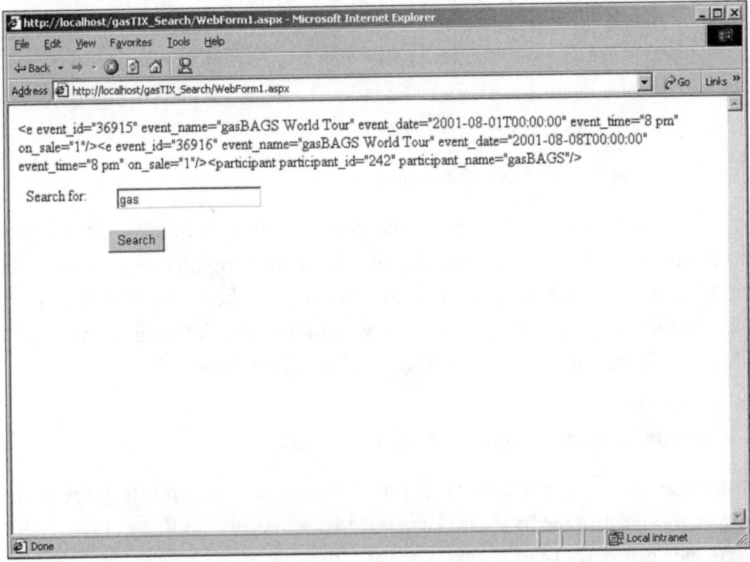

FIGURE 10.8
The CombinedSearch.aspx page now displays the XML returned from our combined search.

We have now successfully made a call to the middle tier object and returned data to the presentation tier. All that is left to do now is to bind the `Repeater` control to the data. `Data-bound` controls cannot bind directly to a string, since a string does not inherently have any enumeration. They can, however, bind to any object that supports the IEnumerable interface. This includes not only the expected DataSet and DataView classes, but also basic structures such as arrays, collections, and dictionaries.

Since our data is currently in an XML string, we need to find a way to get it into a class that supports IEnumberable. There are several ways to do this in the .NET Framework, but we have chosen to make use of the `ReadXML` method of the DataSet class. This method takes a single `StringReader` parameter and reads the XML contained within the string, parsing it into a `Dataset`. The code for this is:

```
Dim dsTemp as New DataSet()
dsTemp.ReadXML (New StringReader(sResult))
```

These two lines define a `DataSet` variable and fill it with the XML data contained in the `sResult` variable. The `StringReader` object created in the parameter call takes our sResult and makes it accessible to the `ReadXML` method.

Since our combined search returns information about several different types of data (events, participants, etc), our dataset will contain multiple tables. We therefore need to loop through all of the `DataSet`'s tables, binding the appropriate table to each of our `Repeater` controls. To do this, we will create a `DataTable` variable, dtTemp, to use in a `For...Each` statement. Within the `For...Each` statement, we will use a `Select` statement to determine which table we are working with so that we can select the correct `Repeater` control to bind to. The code then looks like this:

```
Dim dtTable as DataTable
For Each dtTable in dsTemp.Tables()
Select Case dtTemp.TableName
Case "tour"
With rptTours
     .DataSource = dtTemp.DefaultView
     .DataBind()
End With
Case "event"
With rptEvents
     .DataSource = dtTemp.DefaultView
     .DataBind()
End With
Case "venue"
With rptVenues
     .DataSource = dtTemp.DefaultView
```

```
    .DataBind()
End With
Case "participant"
With rptParticipants
    .DataSource = dtTemp.DefaultView
    .DataBind()
End With
End Select
Next
```

If we run our web application again, and enter `gas` once again in our textbox, when we click the Search button we will see that we now have data visible in two of our four repeater controls, similar to the completed web form shown earlier in Figure 10.1. Since there are tours and participants containing the phrase "gas," those two `Repeater` controls are now visible and filled with data, while the other two repeaters remain un-rendered because they have no data.

User Controls

`User` controls are a new implementation of an old idea: encapsulating commonly used functionality into a reusable package. In classic web development, we have several options for building reusable user interface components for the web. We can use ActiveX controls, Java applets, Macromedia Flash applets or include files. Each of these options has its pros and cons, but the biggest negative shared by all is limited interaction with server-side ASP code.

Since the ActiveX controls, Java and Flash applets were all designed for client-side applications, their interaction with server-side code is mostly implemented secondarily to their true function. Also, each of these three options has limited viability across a variety of platforms and browsers. Server-side include files, on the other hand, are specifically server side constructs. Unfortunately, they offer no user interaction and none of the object-oriented benefits of truly encapsulated components.

User controls are a hybrid of these previous options built specifically for the .NET Framework. They encapsulate both user interface and interaction in an object-oriented design. Best of all, they make use of ASP.NET's ability to render for down-level browsers, so their output is automatically configured to work on a variety of browsers and platforms.

A Simple User Control

To examine how to build and use `User` Controls, we are going to encapsulate the combined search functionality built previously. Once the functionality is encapsulated into a user control, any ASP.NET developer can utilize it by simply instantiating the control on their page. The developer does not need to understand the internal workings of the combined search functionality. This allows the combined search functionality to be used much easier by a much wider audience.

NOTE

Note an important distinction here: `User` Controls are not "included" on a web form, they are "instantiated." `User` controls are full objects, not just flat files.

Building a `User` control is a two step process: first we have to build the `User` control itself in an .ascx file. Then we have to instantiate the `User` control on each web form where its functionality is needed. The combined search functionality will be part of a larger `user` control called `NavBar.ascx` which will be instantiated on every web form presented to the user. This ensures that no matter where the user is in the search or purchase process on gasTIX, he can always easily navigate to the site's main areas or perform a search for desired events.

One of the concerns of new ASP.NET developers is the overhead associated with instantiating multiple server-side controls on a single web form. While this is a valid concern, the performance hit of using server-side controls is actually quite small due to the .NET Framework's use of compiled assemblies and caching techniques. In complex web applications, this performance hit is easily outweighed by the benefits gained from true object-oriented programming techniques. As an additional incentive to use server-side controls, it is important to remember that since everything in the .NET Framework shares the same object model, the performance of controls should be similar no matter what .NET language the control is written in. This eliminates the need to evaluate language options/constraints when trying to increase performance.

Building the gasTIX Navigation User Control

To build a `User` Control, we choose File|New Item and then select Web User Control. We will call the new `User` Control "NavBar.ascx" as shown in Figure 10.9. Since the combined search functionality is only a small part of the functionality included in the `gasTIX NavBar.ascx`, the control built in this chapter will differ significantly from the control downloaded from `www.gasTIX.com`.

The design mode of the `User` Control is very similar to a web form. When we switch to HTML view, however, we notice several important changes. First, the @Page directive at the top of our file has been changed to an @Control directive. This is an important difference because user controls are not instances of the Page class, like web forms are. Instead, they are instances of the user control class, which is a sibling to the page class in the .NET object model. This means that the properties and methods are slightly different for user controls.

Also, we note that user controls do not have `<HTML>` or `<HEAD>` or `<BODY>` tags. The main difference between the Page and User Control classes is that `Page` objects are able to exist on their own, while `User Control` objects require a parent to exist within.

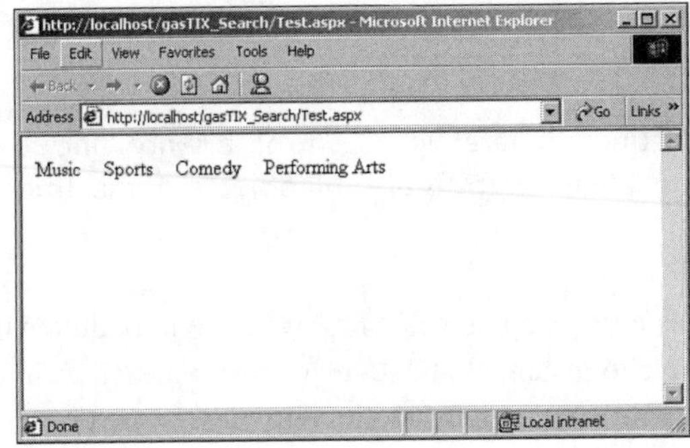

FIGURE 10.9
Encapsulating functionality in a user control is easy with Visual Studio .NET.

For simplicity, we are going to cut and paste code from the `CombinedSearch.aspx` to create a user control. Since the `NavBar` control will only allow users to enter their search criteria, but will not display the results, we want to first copy the HTML code for the textBox and button controls from CombinedSearch.aspx. Paste this code into the HTML view of our user control. Our user control now looks like this:

```
<%@ Control Language="vb" AutoEventWireup="true"
CodeBehind="NavBar.ascx.vb" Inherits="NavBar" %>
<ASP:TextBox Runat="Server" ID="txtCombinedSearch">
<ASP:Button Runat="Server" ID="butSearch">
```

TIP

When you want to add web controls to a web form or user control in HTML, you can ensure that the code-behind has been updated by switching to Design mode. Doing this ensures that the necessary code has been created to instantiate the objects in HTML.

You can now add a new event handler for the click event of the button web control. Do this in the same manner as we did on the web form: simply double-click the control in design mode. Since the display of the combined search results is being left to the CombinedSearch web form, all we need to do in our click event handler is pass execution of the application to that page, passing the search text as a URL parameter.

The code to do this looks like this:

```
Response.Redirect("CombinedSearch.aspx?criteria=" & Textbox1.text)
```

Now that our NavBar control will redirect to the CombinedSearch web form, we need to update the web form code to read its search criteria from the URL instead of a textbox. Change the following line of code in CombinedSearch.aspx.vb:

```
sResult = cs.ListMultiple(txtCombinedSearch.Text)
```

to:

```
sResult = cs.ListMultiple(Request.QueryString("criteria"))
```

This passes the criteria parameter passed in the query string to the ListMultiple method call instead of the contents of the textbox. Since we no longer need the textbox or search button, we can delete them from the web form.

TIP

When deleting controls from a web form or user control, make sure to delete any associated event handlers in the code-behind file. Having extraneous event handlers will not break the application, but it will create excessive overhead for the compiler.

Using the Control

Now that we have a User Control, we need a web form to instantiate it on. Add a new web form to the web application and call it Home.aspx. Switch to HTML view.

In order for the ASP.NET compiler to find a definition for our user control, we need to add an @Register directive to the top of our Home web form. Add the following line of code just below the @Page directive:

```
<%@ Register TagPrefix="gasTIX" TagName="NavBar" src="NavBar.ascx" %>
```

The @Register directive tells the ASP.NET compiler that there will be NavBar controls in the gasTIX project include somewhere on this page. When the compiler finds an instance of the gasTIX:NavBar control, it will instantiate the object found in the defined source (src) file.

Now that the compiler knows where to look for the NavBar control, add one to the page using this code:

```
<gasTIX:NavBar></gasTIX:NavBar>
```

If necessary, you can add attributes inside the opening <gasTIX:NavBar> tag like you would for any other web control. The NavBar user control does not take any additional attributes, so leave it blank for now.

Run the project. You should see a form very similar to the old CombinedSearch web form. It contains a single textbox and button control. When we enter a search criteria and click the button, the button's click event handler fires and passes control to the CombinedSearch.aspx page, which checks the URL for a criteria parameter and displays the search results.

We now have an encapsulated `NavBar` control which can easily be dropped onto any web form in our application, guaranteeing a consistent, easy-to-use combined search interface.

Building a Nested User Control

In the last section, we discussed the power of encapsulating functionality into user controls. The `NavBar` sample we built, however, is a very simple example of a user control. User controls can be much more complex, handling the bulk of a web application's functionality, if appropriate.

One particularly useful enhancement we will discuss is the ability to nest user controls. Since user controls are truly encapsulated objects, we can contain them within any suitable container, such as a web form or even other user controls. This technique is useful for breaking the functionality of a web site down to its most basic components.

For example, take the purchase section of the gasTIX web site. The main goal of these pages is to accept information input from the user. This is accomplished through a series of web forms, each containing several textboxes for input. Each textbox needs a label control next to it to identify the data that should be entered into the textbox. This is a perfect situation for the creation of a user control.

You could create a simple user control that is comprised of a text box and a `label` control. The control would allow the developer to pass in a caption for the label and a name for the textbox. You could then include multiple instances of this control in the web forms to save development time. Since this would, in effect, reduce the number of controls on the web form by one half, it would also significantly improve code maintainability.

Now imagine that there is a particular set of questions that we ask on several web forms. For instance, the first information we need to know about a customer purchasing tickets through gasTIX is their personal information: name, address, email, etc. This is the same information we need to know about new participants when they register with gasTIX. The logical conclusion is to encapsulate this entire personal information form into a user control of its own. Thus we have a new user control comprised of a submit button and multiple children user controls.

To demonstrate the concept of nested user controls, we will build a `Category` user control in the next section of this chapter. The `Category` user control will then be instantiated on the home page of gasTIX.

Using the DataList Control

The purpose of the `Categories` user control is to display a list of gasTIX categories such as Music, Sports, etc. Under each category heading there will be a list of subcategories, such as Rock, Country, and Celtic under the Music category.

In order to display this data, we will use a `DataList` control, since it allows us to easily create a table layout without having to worry about the details. We will instantiate the `Category` business object in order to retrieve a list of categories from the database, which we will then bind our `DataList` to.

To begin creating the `Categories` user control:

1. Select File|New Item.
2. Select Web User Control.
3. Name the new control Categories.ascx.
4. Double-click the DataList icon in the Toolbox to add it to the user control.
5. Rename the data list dlCategories. Your control should now look similar to the one in Figure 10.10.

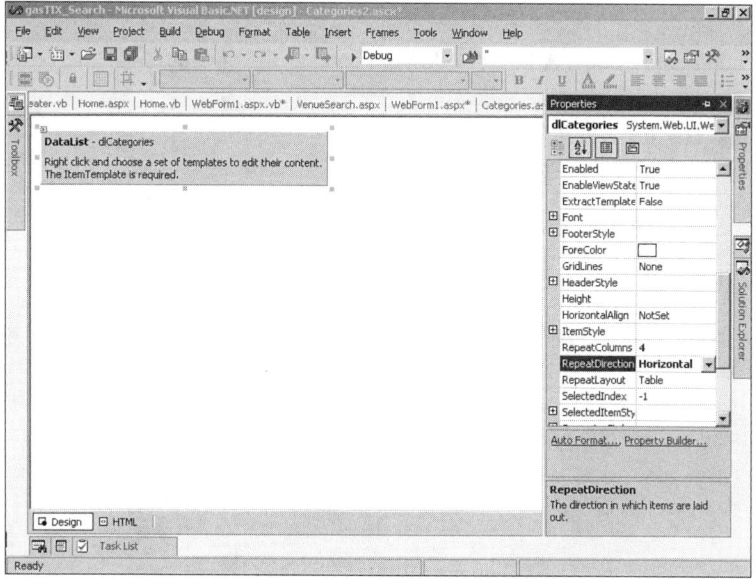

FIGURE 10.10
The Categories user control has a single `DataList` *web control which will display all gasTIX event categories.*

We will add templates to our `DataList` like we did with our repeater controls in the CombinedSearch example. In HTML view, add the following code inside our `<ASP:DataList>` tag:

```
<ItemTemplate>
<%# DataBinder.Eval(container,"category")   
</ItemTemplate>
```

Note that for the moment, we are keeping this simple; we will add any necessary formatting when we polish the web form later. We are also not going to add an `AlternatingItemTemplate` to this `Datalist` control because we want every item to be designed identically. We do want to change one thing about the dlCategories default design however; we want it to display up to four columns of data per row. As we mentioned previously, the `DataList` handles all of the details of arranging the data on the page. All we need to do to force the DataList to create four columns per row is add two attributes to the `<ASP:DataList>` tag, `RepeatDirection` and `RepeatColumns`. Alter the dlCategories definition so that it looks like this:

```
<ASP:DataList id="dlCategories" runat="SERVER"
 RepeaterDirection="Horizontal" RepeatColumns="4">
```

Our `DataList` will now automatically create four columns of data horizontally across the page before continuing in a new row of up to four items below the original row.

Now we need to bind our `DataList` to some data. Double-click the user control in design mode to view the code-behind page. Add the following code to the `Categories_Load` event:

```
dim c as new gasTIX.Category()
dim dsTemp as new DataSet()
dsTemp.ReadXML(New StringReader(c.ListCategories())
With dlCategories
.DataSource = dsTemp.Tables("category").DefaultView
.DataBind()
End With
```

This code instantiates a `Category` business object and uses its `ListCategories()` method to retrieve an XML string representing all current gasTIX categories. This string is passed to the `ReadXML` method of the `dsTemp DataSet` object, which our `DataList` is then bound to. Our user control is now databound and will display a list of categories as shown in Figure 10.11.

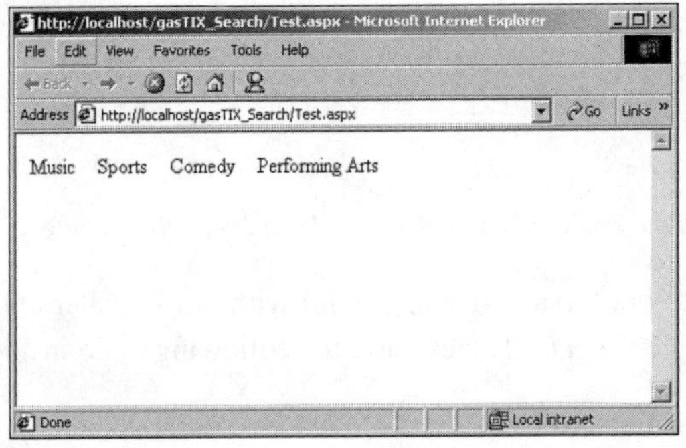

FIGURE 10.11
The `Categories` user control displays a neatly organized list of gasTIX categories.

Other DataList Features

DataLists support several features not found in repeater controls, due to the inherent table structure supported by `DataLists`. In addition to the templates available for `Repeater` controls, `Datalist` controls also support SelectedItem and EditItem templates. These templates let us implement features in our page that allow users to select and edit a particular row of data in our `DataList`. We can use textboxes in place of labels to allow editing of our data and we can place additional text or graphics next to a selected item in our datalist.

There is another type of child tag available for `DataList` and `DataGrids` that is not available for `Repeater` controls: Styles. Style tags allow us to indicate the design elements for the templates in our datalist. We can specify the color, font, alignment, etc. of the data displayed by our templates by using the same prefix for our style. To set the vertical alignment of all of data displayed in our ItemTemplate, for instance, we simply add an `<ItemStyle>` tag to our `Datalist` control, specifying the attribute, `VerticalAlign=top`.

Styles allow us to easily define the design attributes of all data bound to our datalist, without mingling the design attributes with the programming logic. Since the code for displaying the data is stored in separate template tags, the Template and Styles can easily be defined by a developer and designer, working separately. For more information on the separation of design and code, see the “Additional ASP.NET Features” section later in this chapter.

Nesting a Second User Control

Now that we have built the categories user control, we can test it by adding it to our Home.aspx page. This is accomplished using the following code:

```
<%@ Register TagPrefix="gasTIX" TagName="Categories" src="Categories.ascx" %>
<gasTIX:Categories></gasTIX:Categories>
```

Set the Home web form to be the start up form by right-clicking it in the Solution Explorer and choosing Set As Start Page. If you now run the application, you will see the four gasTIX event categories listed horizontally across the page.

As previously mentioned, there are subcategories for each top-level category now listed on the page. The music category, for instance, has Rock, Country, and Celtic subcategories. In order to round out our Categories control, we would like to list all subcategories under the appropriate category heading in a vertical listing.

Our first reaction might be to just include the code to display subcategories in the categories user control. However, there may be times when we want to display just the subcategories, without the category listed at the top. Consider what happens when a user clicks on a category in the categories user control. They should probably be taken to a Category.aspx web form which displays the name of the category, some general information about the type of events users will find in that category, and a list of subcategories they can choose to further refine their search. In this case, we would want to show the subcategory list without the category header information, and we would only want to show subcategories for a single, specified category.

The best way to implement this functionality is to build a separate SubCategories user control that accepts a `CategoryID` parameter specifying which category to display subcategories for. This control can be placed on the Category.aspx web form, and can be nested inside the Categories user control. Inside the `Categories` user control, we would then instantiate a `Subcategories` user control for each category listed.

This is usually easier to understand in practice than theory, so we will get started building it. Add a new user control to the project and call it Subcategories.ascx. We are going to borrow the HTML code from our Categories control to build this control, with a couple of modifications:

```
<%@ Control Language="vb" AuteoEventWireup="false"
CodeBehind="SubCategories.vb" Inherits="gasTIX.SubCategories" %>
<ASP:DataList id="dlSubCategories" runat="server">
<ItemStyle VerticalAlign="top"></ItemStyle>
<ItemTemplate>
   
<%# DataBinder.Eval(container,"SubCategory_Name") %>
</ItemTemplate>
</ASP:DataList>
```

We have made a couple of changes in this code. First, we renamed everything to appropriate names for our new user control. Second, we added three HTML spaces ( ) just before the subcategory name. This will offer the appearance of a tree structure. And finally, we have removed the `RepeatDirection` and `RepeatColumns` attributes of dlSubCategories. The DataList will now use its default attribute of a single column, repeating vertically down the page. This will create the effect we desire, with categories listed horizontally across the page and subcategories listed vertically downward below each category heading.

The code-behind for this user control will look very similar to the Categories user control as well, except for two things: first, instead of the `ListCategories` method, we will use the `ListSubCategories(CategoryID)` method, and second, we will define a custom property to allow us to set the category id. The following code is borrowed from the categories user control:

```
dim c as new gasTIX.Category()
dim dsTemp as new DataSet()
dsTemp.ReadXML(New StringReader(c.ListSubCategories())
With dlCategories
```

```
    .DataSource = dsTemp.Tables("category").DefaultView
    .DataBind()
End With
```

Since user controls are full-fledged objects, they can have property definitions like any other object. When we instantiate a user control on our web form (or in another user control), we will simply specify the property name and assign it a value. In the code for the user control, we can run validation code to ensure that the value entered is acceptable. Here is the code to add a `CategoryID` property to our user control:

```
Private _CategoryID as Integer
Public Property CategoryID() as Integer
Get
    Return _CategoryID
End Get
Set
    _CategoryID = Value
End Set
End Property
```

The code for our property is very simple, but we can easily enhance it to verify, for instance, that the integer value passed in is the ID of an actual category in the database. For the time being, our simple property definition will work fine.

Our `SubCategories` user control is now ready to use. Since we want to add it to our existing Categories control, we need to open the HTML view of that control and add the following code:

```
<%@ Register TagPrefix="gasTIX" TagName="SubCat"
src="SubCategories.ascx" %>
```

Inside the ItemTemplate for dlCategories, add the following code just after the category name:

```
<br><gasTIX:SubCat runat="server" CategoryID="<%#
DataBinder.Eval(container,"category_id") %>" >
```

This code instantiates a `SubCategories` user control, passing in the current value of category_id within the `Categories` user control as an attribute.

When we run our application now, our `Categories` user control looks like Figure 10.12.

We have created a single `Categories` user control, complete with the appropriate subcategories, which can easily be instantiated on any web form in our application. We can easily enhance this user control to make the category and subcategory listings into hyperlinks which will take the user to the appropriate web form for more information.

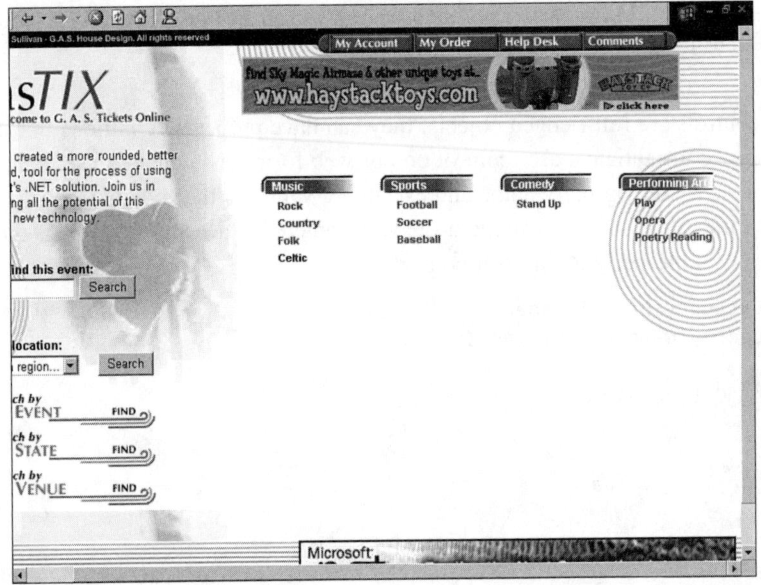

FIGURE 10.12

The `Categories` *user control now displays subcategories under each category header.*

From Here

In this chapter you learned how to build a simple web form which serves as a basis for all web forms in the gasTIX application. You also learned how to build several user controls that are used on multiple pages in the gasTIX website.

If you would like to learn more about the ASP.NET development of the website, read Chapter 11 which discusses the process of purchasing tickets through both the gasTIX and a third-party site using Web services. Chapter 14, “Debugging a .NET Application,” discusses debugging .NET applications, while Chapter 15, evaluates performance-tuning options. Finally, Chapter 16, “Deploying the Application,” helps you deploy the application.

Purchasing a Ticket

by Rick Lassan & Chris Koenig

CHAPTER

11

IN THIS CHAPTER

- Setting Up the Examples 322
- Middle-Tier Objects Versus XML Web services 324
- Building the gasTIX Purchasing User Interface 326
- Organization and Flow of the User Interface 327
- The UI for Purchasing a Ticket 342
- Tools 345
- From Here 349

In the previous chapter, we discussed how to search for any event on the gasTIX Web server via the gasTIX Web site. Now we are going to turn our attention to purchasing tickets for those events. This chapter will demonstrate how to use the gasTIX purchasing services from internal business objects and remotely through Web services. We will discuss specifically how to find the Web service and transfer our application code to use that Web service. We will walk through calling the appropriate Web service methods via the UI, business and data access layers to purchase a ticket.

The main goal for developing the gasBAGS Web site is to demonstrate how to use or "consume" data via Web services using the SOAP protocol from the gasTIX Web site. For an introduction to .NET presentation services, please refer back to Chapter 5, "Implementing .NET Presentation Services." Chapter 10, "gasTIX Event Searching," offers examples of ASP.NET pages which will set the foundation for the examples in this chapter.

Setting Up the Examples

In this section, we discuss how to configure the Web.config and Global.asax file. The two files play an important role in defining actions that occur globally within the Website and control other functions such as security, HTTP handlers, tracing, and error handling.

Web.Config

Since our site is built with ASP.NET, a couple of new features need to be introduced. First, the Web.config file contains all configuration information for ASP.NET. Take a look at the following Web.config file for the gasBAGS site:

```
<configuration>
    <customerrors mode="on" defaultredirect="error.aspx"/>
    <trace enabled="false" requestlimit="40" pageoutput="true"/>
</configuration>
```

All configuration information in the Web.config must be included between the configuration tag elements. In our file, we are using only two tags, the `<customerrors>` and `<trace>` tags. The `<customerrors>` tag has the following attributes defined:

- **`Mode=On|Off`**—When set to OFF, the default, error handling is handled by the .NET runtime. When set to ON, we are indicating to the .NET runtime that we have implemented our own custom error handling. When an error occurs the user is redirected to the error page indicated by the `customerrors` attribute defaultredirect.
- **`Trace Enabled = True|False`**—Indicates whether debug info is displayed inline on the aspx page. Set this to True when debugging is required.

For another example of using the Global.asax file, please refer to Chapter 16, "Deploying the Application," for more on deploying the gasTIX Web site.

Global.asax

Since we are going to use a global error handler in our ASP.NET application, this section serves as an introduction on how to implement the error handler in the Global.asax file.

This file serves the same purpose as the Global.asa in ASP in the pre .NET days; it defines application scope settings. The global.asa file can have any number of purposes, from setting up a global datasource to initializing common variables. The gasBAGS Website uses its global.asax to define an application-wide exception handler. Whenever an exception occurs in one of our Web forms, the following exception handler is executed and an event is logged in the NT event log:

```
<%@ Import Namespace="System.Diagnostics" %>

<script language="C#" runat=server>
void Application_Error(Object sender, EventArgs e) {

   // grab the exception that occured
   Exception ex = Context.Error.GetBaseException();
   String ExceptionMsg = "Message: " + ex.Message
    + "\nSource: " + ex.Source
    + "\nForm: " + Request.Form.ToString()
    + "\nQueryString: " + Request.QueryString.ToString()
    + "\nTargetSite: " + ex.TargetSite
    + "\nStackTrace: " + ex.StackTrace;

   // create a new log for this Website
   String LogName  = "gasBags";
   if (!EventLog.SourceExists(LogName))
      EventLog.CreateEventSource(LogName, LogName);

   // write the entry to the event log
   EventLog Log = new EventLog();
   Log.Source = LogName;
   Log.WriteEntry(ExceptionMsg, EventLogEntryType.Error);
}
</script>
```

TIP

Visual Studio .NET automatically creates the Global.asax file for you. If you are writing ASP.NET pages by hand, you will have to create this file manually.

In the example just shown, we have defined a handler for the `Application_Error` event, which is triggered when any exception occurs in our application. Next, we define a new event log source so that the exception is written to our event log. In our example, we have defined the gasBAGS source log for logging all exceptions that occur in our application.

Middle-Tier Objects Versus XML Web services

In the prior section, we briefly touched on exception handling for Web services. We now turn our attention to using the data that returns from web services and how to handle those exceptions. When we built the gasTIX purchase business objects, we realized that the same functionality could easily be exposed to other Web sites as XML Web services. This would allow bands or sports teams' sites to offer event searching and credit card processing with very little effort. All of the data, e-commerce functionality, and security exist on the gasTIX servers, so the third-party site using our services does not have to worry about anything but building their own Web site. Since offering functionality as an XML Web service is built into the .NET framework, there is very little extra work on our part to expose our internal business objects to the world.

Business Objects

The gasTIX application has been architected to heavily depend on a three-tier architecture. The database, business object, and presentation tiers have been developed separately by different developers in remote geographical locations. This is important because each tier has been abstracted to know very little about the other tiers. The presentation tier (gasTIX and gasBAGS Web Forms) does not know how the business tier objects are written, or in fact, even what language they are written in. This is an important design concept for anyone developing business objects that will be exposed as XML Web services. We cannot depend on consumers of our XML Web services to write a lot of custom code to integrate with our business objects. They need to be able to simply instantiate our objects, set properties and call methods without having an intimate understanding of the internal workings of our objects.

That being said, the gasTIX business objects have been designed to model real world objects like `Events` and `Participants`. This makes it easy for any developer to use the business objects; they simply instantiate the type of real-world objects they are interested in and call a method. For instance, to update an Order status, we can simply instantiate an Order object and execute the UpdateSaleStatus method. For more information on the gasTIX business objects, please see Chapter 6, "Implementing .NET Business Services."

Using the middle-tier objects in gasTIX is simple. We simply add a reference to the BusinessFacade assembly in our Web project. Since all gasTIX development eventually found its way to a single server, despite being developed in many locations, all gasTIX assembly references were made as Project References. That is, all of the gasTIX middle tier objects and the presentation services were incorporated into a single solution. This makes it easy for the presentation tier to reference the entire business object project and makes compiling the project as a whole possible. For an example of setting a project reference to the middle tier business objects, see Chapter 10, "gasTIX Event Searching."

Using XML Web services via Soap

After we built the business objects to be used internally for the gasTIX application, we found that the functionality exposed by those business objects was broadly applicable to other applications as well. Searching for events and purchasing tickets to those events are examples of the functionality that can be used by a variety of web applications beyond gasTIX. Fortunately, the .NET Framework makes it easy to turn business objects into XML Web services.

An XML Web service exposes functionality to the Internet using the standard HTTP protocol. This gives every application that understands HTTP and has an Internet connection access to the functionality. Now web sites for rock bands or sports teams can allow their users to search for events and purchase tickets to those events with very little programming on their part. The magic glue that makes this happen is SOAP.

Simple Object Access Protocol (SOAP) is based on Extensible Markup Language (XML) and allows more robust communication between remote systems. The protocol itself is designed to be very simple and contain very little functionality of its own. Instead, it provides the means for transporting data and object between systems.

Since SOAP uses HTTP, it is broadly applicable to all Internet-enabled systems in use today. Since it is an XML based, non-proprietary protocol, it can be utilized by any operating system on any platform. No longer are systems tied to their business objects by a proprietary operating system or communication protocol. In the XML Web services world, it is not uncommon for either side of the communication to not know where the other end is located or what platform it is using.

The SOAP specification is broken into four main parts. They are:

- The only mandatory part of the SOAP specification is the "extensible envelope," which is used for encapsulating data. This is the most basic unit of exchange between two SOAP enabled systems.
- Optional data encoding rules can be created to represent user- or application-defined data types. These rules can also be used to create a uniform serialization model for non-syntactic data models.
- The third part of the SOAP specification defines the message exchange pattern. This exchange pattern is based on the classic Remote Procedure Call (RPC) request/response

system allowing a SOAP enabled system to send a request message and accept a response message. However, SOAP is designed as a one-way transmission and is not limited to only the request/response style of message handling. Thus, this message exchange pattern is also optional.

- Finally, the SOAP specification includes a binding between SOAP and HTTP. This binding defines how SOAP messages can travel to its destination using the HTTP protocol. However, in order to maximize flexibility, this binding is also optional. SOAP messages can be transported using any valid transport protocol, including SMTP, FTP, or even something as simple as a floppy disk.

SOAP is normally transported over HTTP, thus it will work through firewalls and network security applications. Also, SOAP can be sent and received by any browser on any type of platform that understands XML. The inherent platform- and language-independence of SOAP has advanced its acceptance as a development standard.

The .NET framework makes using objects accessed through SOAP as seamless as using object assemblies on the same development machines. After the developer has referenced the assembly, the code needed to instantiate and use the object is identical, whether it is a local assembly or referenced through the Internet. In order to highlight the differences between similar code in different languages, we have written the gasTIX site in Visual Basic .NET and the gasBAGS site in Visual C# .NET. The examples in this chapter pull from both sets of code, first from gasTIX and later from gasBAGS.

Building the gasTIX Purchasing User Interface

The gasTIX Website is an example site designed to show development using Microsoft's new .NET framework, specifically utilizing Visual Studio .NET, Visual Basic .NET and ASP.NET in an e-commerce setting. Our goals for the purchasing user interface were to:

- Showcase some of the new tools available to the developer in the .NET Framework
- Show how the new tools can be applied to an e-Commerce application using Visual Basic .NET and ASP.NET setting
- Demonstrate how the new development languages of the .NET Framework could interoperate easily together

Since most ASP developers are using VBScript to build their pages today, we selected Visual Basic .NET as the development language for the presentation tier of gasTIX. Visual Basic and VBScript command such a large audience today, that we thought it was the best choice for developing our user interfaces. In a similar fashion, Visual C# .NET was chosen for the business and data tiers based on the number of Visual C++ developers writing that same type of code today. By using multiple languages, we had hoped to show how easy it now is to integrate any of the .NET languages together into one coherent application.

In fact, this worked better than we had expected, as we re-wrote parts of the middle-tier in Visual Basic .NET and parts of the presentation tier in Visual C# .NET. Depending on the particular part of the application we are using, there may be three of four language changes, from Visual Basic .NET to Visual C# .NET and back again. Best of all, it all works seamlessly, just as Microsoft has promised.

The purchase interface of the gasBAGS Web site is very similar to the gasTIX interface, since they use the same business objects. It is important to note, however, that each Web application applies its own design and presentation logic to the data returned by the business objects. This extensible model makes it easy for us to add new third-party Web sites using our XML Web services, while allowing the users of those Websites to remain unaware of the fact that they are actually using gasTIX services.

Organization and Flow of the User Interface

The purchasing user interface is presented as a series of Web pages that each collect a portion of the total amount information required to purchase a ticket in gasTIX. The end result of the purchasing process is a successful purchase of tickets to an event stored in our system. The process for purchasing tickets in gasTIX is depicted in Figure 11.1 below.

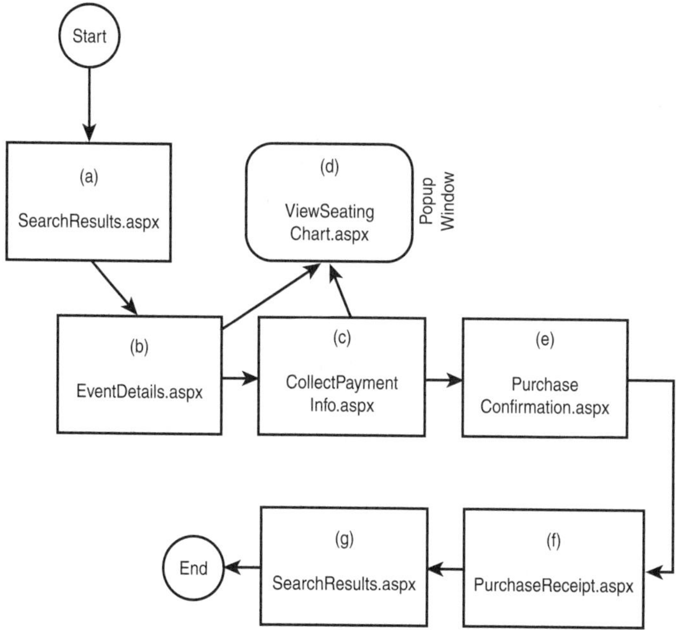

FIGURE 11.1
The purchasing process.

The customer enters the purchasing process from the Search Results page (a) by clicking on an event listing. The Event Details page (b) shows information about the event, and allows the customer to select a section in which to sit and the number of seats to purchase. The system will determine if the customer's selection is valid and if the seats are available before temporarily reserving their seats and sending the customer to the Payment page (c). The Payment page collects the billing, shipping and payment information required for purchase. This page allows the user to enter information manually by typing it in, or by using Microsoft Passport's Express Purchase feature. If the user chooses to view a seating chart for an event (d), a links from the Event Details and the Payment Collection pages are supplied. If the customer does not have a Microsoft Passport account, one can be opened from the Passport site (e).

Once the customer has chosen seats, and entered payment and shipping information, the customer is shown a final confirmation page (f) that displays a summary of all the information collected during this process. From here the customer can either completely cancel out of the current purchase or continue to submit the order for processing. If the order is successfully posted, the customer is shown a receipt page (g) that includes the total dollar amount of the purchase and a tracking number that identifies the order in the system.

Each page in this process will be detailed in the sections that follow, beginning with the Event Details page.

Event Details

The first part of the purchase process involves the selection of seats and is handled by the EventDetails.aspx page. The customer reaches this page by clicking on an event link from the SearchResults.aspx page. On the Event Details page, the customer can view the details for the Event selected, including the name of the venue and the date and time of the event. The EventDetails.aspx page is showing in Figure 11.2.

Event Summary

The top of the page contains the summary of the customer's selected Event. The data displayed includes the name of the event, the place the event is held (also called the event's *venue*) and the date and time the event takes place. This information is gathered from the business layer and data layer objects and displayed using the Label server controls.

The Event Summary section is repeated on the Payment collection page described later in this chapter.

Choosing A Section and Seats

The lower half of the screen contains the data entry area for the page. From here the customer selects which section of the venue he would like. The sections are presented to the customer using the new `DropDownList` server control. This control is used in place of a traditional

HTML <SELECT> control in favor of the data binding capabilities and control enhancements the new server controls supply. For the display of the sections, we can easily bind a DataSetView that is returned from the Business tier objects to this control and successfully display the list of sections, shown in Listing 11.2.

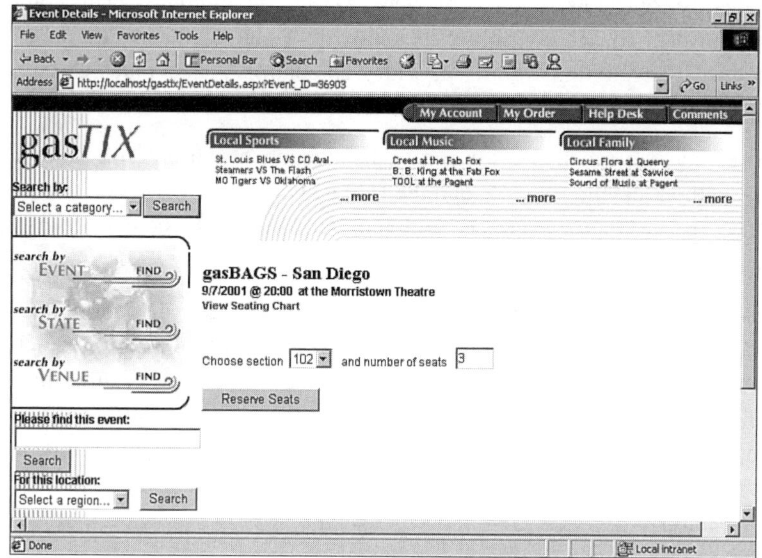

FIGURE 11.2
The EventDetails.aspx page.

LISTING 11.2 `Data Binding` and the `DropDownList` Server Control

```
Dim dvSec As DataView = ed.Tables(VENUE_SECTION_TABLE).DefaultView
With selSection
    .DataSource = dvSec
    .DataTextField = "section_name"
    .DataValueField = "section_id"
    .DataBind()
    .SelectedIndex = 0
End With
```

As you saw in Chapter 7, "Implementing .NET Data Services," the `EventData` object is a subclass of the ADO.NET SerializeableDataSet class. The `DataTable` object identified by the key `VENUE_SECTION_TABLE` contains the names and database codes for the sections that are available inside the current event's configuration. Since each event takes place at a particular venue, and within a particular configuration for that venue, this list must represent only the available sections for the current configuration. This `DataTable` object is also used to display the Purchase Price per Ticket and the Section Name in the header area of this page.

In addition to selecting the section, the customer can choose between one and eight tickets to purchase. The entry control used here is the new `TextBox` server control. This control was chosen over the equivalent HTML control for its ability to be validated using the new ASP.NET Validation controls. Developing Web forms with web controls is also much easier and faster due to their drag-and-drop capabilities and property dialogs.

From the server side, we can also easily access the contents of the text box using the object's Text property, without having to go though the HTML Form object. This not only makes access to the control easier, the access is more familiar to Visual Basic developers than having to address it via the `Request.Form` object.

The two validation controls used on this page are the `RangeValidator` control and the `RequiredField` control. Both validation controls are connected to the Number of Tickets field via their `ControlToValidate` property. The `Range Validator` control ensures that the user has entered a value for the control within a given range for the specified data type. Here, the validation is done on an integer value falling between 1 and 8. If the validation fails, a message is displayed to the user. An instance of the Required Field validator is used to ensure that the field cannot be empty.

TIP

> The `Range Validator` control does not perform validation on its associated control if the control's value is empty. To ensure that a field is not empty, you must use the Required Field validator, or a different type of control like a `DropDownList` or `ListBox` control.

Creating an Order

Once the user has entered the required data, the business tier is asked to create a new order to represent the customer's selections (see Listing 11.3). The selected section id and number of seats information is sent to the `Order` object's `ReserveSeats` method. If the call is successful, and the seats are indeed reserved, an `OrderData` object will be returned. To trap the possibility of this error, we use the Try-Catch error handling syntax new to Visual Basic .NET.

LISTING 11.3 Reserving Seats and Creating an Order

```
Dim od As gasTIX.Data.OrderData
Dim ord As New gasTIX.BusinessFacade.Order()
Try
```

LISTING 11.3 Continued

```
    od = ord.ReserveSeats( _
        hidEventID.Text.ToInt32(), _
        selSection.SelectedItem.Value.ToInt32(), _
        txtNumberOfSeats.Text.ToInt32() _
    )
    Session.Item("OrderData") = od
    Response.Redirect("CollectPaymentInfo.aspx")
Catch
    lblMessage.Text = _
        "I'm sorry, but those seats are not available. " & _
        "Please refine your search and try again.<br/>"
End Try
```

The `OrderData` object that is returned from the `ReserveSeats` method serves as our digital "ticket order form," containing entry fields for all of the information we will need to collect to successfully process the customer's ticket order. Each step in the purchase process will access this order form and update it according to the information it is collecting. Once all the information is collected, we can save the order to the database and display a final invoice to the customer.

We chose the DataSet-based model for representing our order because it provides a single, familiar interface for accessing all of the data that comprises a ticket order. Since there were multiple steps in the ordering process, we knew that we must somehow persist this information we captured so that it would be available on subsequent pages. Basing the `OrderData` object on a `SerializableDataSet` not only gives us an easy way to access and update our data, it also gives us a convenient way to persist data from page to page. As we will see in the next section, the `OrderData` object is persisted from page to page in ASP.NET's new and improved `Session` object.

Saving the Order and Moving On

Now that our seats are reserved, and we have a real `OrderData` object to work with, we must persist the `OrderData` object for use in the rest of the purchasing process. The storage mechanism used by gasTIX to persist this object from one page to the next is via the new ASP.NET `Session` object. With the `Session` object now supporting Web-farm compatible session state, the `Session` object can now be safely used to store data without fear of data loss. For more information, see Chapter 16, "Deploying the Application."

We can store the `OrderData` object we just created into the `Session` object with one simple line of code:

```
Session.Item("OrderData") = od
```

TIP

During development, we noticed that storing and retrieving data out of the `Session` object could be problematic. If an unhandled error is thrown, subsequent access to the object stored in the Session will erroneously raise an `InvalidCastException` error. To solve the problem, you must restart IIS.

Now that the `OrderData` has been saved in the `Session` object, we can access it from our other pages using the syntax

```
Dim od as OrderData = CType(Session.Item("OrderData"), OrderData)
```

The new `CType` function in Visual Basic .NET performs a type casting operation, allowing us to convert objects from one class to another. You might recognize this type of conversion function as something similar to the more familiar `CStr` and `CLng` functions from Visual Basic 6.

You will probably be relieved to know that most of these conversion functions are still around, with the notable exception of `CVar`. That function accompanied the Variant data type on their way out of the Visual Basic programming language. Type conversions are also available as members of the Object class. Refer to the object browser and MSDN library for more information on the new type casting functions in Visual Basic .NET.

If the object can not be converted to the specified class, an `InvalidCastException` error is thrown. The type casting is necessary here as the `Session.Item` method returns an instance of type Object, and we need an instance of type OrderData. Alternatively, we could bypass the error and still eliminate the type cast if we change the Strict option setting to Off at the top of our code for this page:

```
Option Strict Off
```

This option is available to us, but it removes some of the protections strict typing can offer us at compile time and at run time.

Payment Information

After the customer has found a section and some seats, the next step in the purchase process is the collection of billing, shipping, and payment information. This information is collected on a single form, divided into three sections, not counting the Event Summary section at the top. This page is called the CollectPaymentInfo.aspx page, and a screen shot is shown in Figure 11.3.

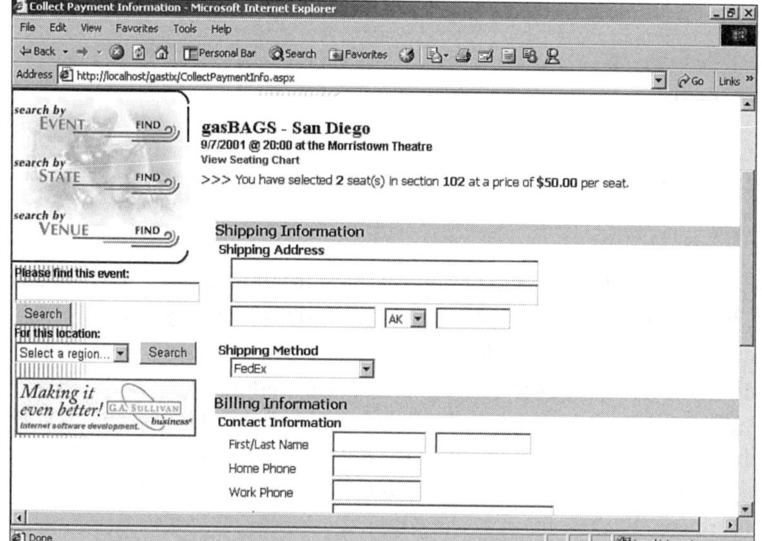

FIGURE 11.3
The CollectPaymentInfo.aspx page.

Although the data entry on this page is extensive, it is not very complicated. Most entry fields are simple `TextBox` server controls. The only other controls on this page, besides the Button server controls at the bottom, are the Shipping State, the Billing State, and the Credit Card Type fields which are the `DropDownList` server controls we covered in the previous section.

Collecting the Information

The Shipping Details section is comprised of the shipping address and the shipping type. The required fields are validated using the Required Field validator. The `Shipping Method` `DropDownList` control is loaded from a DataSet that is populated from an XML string returned from the gasTIX.Data objects. Listing 11.4 shows how this was accomplished. The `DropDownList` server control for the Shipping and Billing State fields are filled in a similar way.

LISTING 11.4 Loading a `DropDownList` Server Control from an XML String

```
Dim objSM As New ShippingMethod()
Dim dsSM As New DataSet()
Dim dvSM As DataView
dsSM.ReadXml(New StringReader(objSM.ListShippingMethods))
dvSM = dsSM.tables("shipping_method").DefaultView
With selShippingMethod
```

LISTING 11.4 Continued

```
    .DataSource = dvSM
    .DataTextField = "provider_name"
    .DataValueField = "shipping_method_id"
    .DataBind()
    .SelectedIndex = 0
End With
```

This method of loading a `DropDownList` control is slightly different than the version we saw in Listing 11.1. In that listing, we were able to bind the control directly to a `DataView` that was returned from our `Business` object. Here, we have to somehow create that `DataView` from a string of XML. The data-tier objects in the gasTIX application use an XML string for all static data that is independent of any order, and a `DataSet` for all data that is returned from a query into the database. This was done to allow us to explore the interoperability between XML and the new Data classes within the .NET Framework. As we will see, working with these new technologies is relatively easy and very versatile.

Before we can bind our `DropDownList` control to a `DataView`, we must create one from the XML string the `Business` object returns to us. Since `DataViews` are a child object of the `DataSet` class we will need a `DataSet` to work with first. We can create an empty `DataSet` simply by using the New keyword. Once we have the `DataSet` created, we have to get data into it. To load our XML into the `DataSet`, we will need to use the StringReader class to help us out. The `DataSet`'s `ReadXml` method takes either a `TextReader`, an `XmlReader` or a `Stream` object as its parameter. The StringReader class allows us to create a type of TextReader that works over an existing String. We create a new instance of this StringReader and pass it into the `ReadXml` method to load the `DataSet` from our XML. Once we have the `DataSet`, we can return the `DataView` that will serve as the `DataSource` for our `DropDownList`.

The Billing Details section is comprised primarily of a Name and Address identifying the person who should receive the bill. These fields are all represented in the same way the Shipping information is collected. Required fields for this section are validated using the Required Field Validator, and the Billing State is managed using a `DropDownList` server control.

The Payment Details section is comprised of the name of the person on the credit card, the type of the credit card, and the card's expiration date. We use the Required Field validator on all required fields, and the Range Validator to ensure that the expiration month and expiration year are of the correct data type and that thy fall within acceptable ranges. The Credit Card Type field is collected via a `DropDownList` server control, similar to the way the Shipping and Billing State fields were collected.

Once all this information is entered, and validated by the Validator controls, the Customer is taken to a summary page (PurchaseConfirmation.aspx) where they may review their order before submitting it for processing.

Microsoft Passport Express Purchase

An alternative to the manual data entry involves integrating our site with Microsoft Passport services, specifically Passport Express Purchase. The Express Purchase service allows us to collect all the information we will need about a Customer using the information they have stored in their Microsoft Wallet account. During processing, we actually leave the gasTIX site and navigate over to Passport where the user can log in, select the information we need to collect and return to our site with all the data. The data is returned in an HTML Form Post, so we can easily access everything from the `Request.Form object.Website`.

Updating the OrderData Object

Once the Customer enters all the information and the page has validated the entries, it is time to once again update the OrderData object with the newly collected values. This time, we have a bunch of information to store in the `SALES_TABLE` DataTable. Listing 11.5 has some examples of updating this section.

LISTING 11.5 Updating the `OrderData` Object

```
Private Function UpdatePurchaseData() As String
    Dim od As gasTIX.Data.OrderData
    Dim dr As DataRow

    ' Retrieve order data from the session
    od = CType(Session.Item("OrderData"), gasTIX.Data.OrderData)
    dr = od.Tables(SALE_TABLE).Rows(0)

    ' *** billing informaiton
    dr.item(BILL_TO_FIRST_NAME) = txtBillingFirstName.Text
    dr.item(BILL_TO_LAST_NAME) = txtBillingLastName.Text
    dr.item(BILL_TO_PHONE_1) = txtBillingHomePhone.Text
    dr.item(BILL_TO_PHONE_2) = txtBillingWorkPhone.Text
    dr.item(BILL_TO_ADDRESS) = txtBillingAddress1.Text
    dr.item(BILL_TO_ADDRESS_2) = txtBillingAddress2.Text
    dr.item(BILL_TO_CITY) = txtBillingCity.Text
    dr.item(BILL_TO_POSTAL_CODE) = txtBillingZipCode.Text
    dr.item(BILL_TO_REGION_ID) = selBillingState.SelectedItem.Value

    ' *** shipping informaiton
    dr.item(SHIP_TO_ADDRESS) = txtshippingAddress1.Text
    dr.item(SHIP_TO_ADDRESS_2) = txtshippingAddress2.Text
```

LISTING 11.5 Continued

```
    dr.item(SHIP_TO_CITY) = txtShippingCity.Text
    dr.item(SHIP_TO_POSTAL_CODE) = txtShippingZipCode.Text
    dr.item(SHIP_TO_REGION_ID) = selShippingState.SelectedItem.Value
    dr.item(SHIPPING_METHOD_ID) = selShippingMethod.SelectedItem.Value

    ' *** credit card data
    dr.item(CREDIT_CARD_TYPE_ID) = selCreditCardType.SelectedItem.Value
    dr.item(CREDIT_CARD_NAME) = txtCreditCardName.text
    dr.item(CREDIT_CARD_NUMBER) = txtCreditCardNumber.Text
    dr.item(CREDIT_CARD_EXPIRATION_DATE) = txtExpireMonth.text & _
        "/" & txtExpireYear.text

    ' cleanup
    o = Nothing
    od = Nothing
    od_r = Nothing
End Function
```

The information for Billing and Shipping data is collected in a similar way using the same technique of accessing the `Text` property of the `TextBox` server control. The State fields, like the Credit Card Type field in the above listing, requires some data conversion from Text to Code in order to save the value into the object.

If the Customer chose to use Passport Express Purchase instead of entering their information into the form, they will actually leave the gasTIX Website and be redirected to the Microsoft Passport site. The Passport site will collect all of the same Shipping, Billing and Credit Card information that we would have otherwise collected in our site, returning the Customer to our site when complete. The HTML anchor tag used to link the customer to the Passport site is shown in Listing 11.6.

LISTING 11.6 Link to the Passport Express Purchase Site

```
<a href="https://current-
wallet.passporttest.com/ppsecure/get.asp?lc=1033&ru=http://www.gastix.com/Walle
tPostAcceptor.aspx&mid=1&ca=visa,mast,amer&pc=visa"><img alt="Check out using
Microsoft Passport." src="images/exp128x26.gif" align=absMiddle border=0></a>
```

The link to the Passport Website contains several items, including:

- **LC**—the locale of the calling site (for internationalization purposes)
- **MID**—the unique SiteID of the calling site

- **CA**—a list of the credit card types we want to support
- **PC**—the "preferred" credit card
- **RU**—a return link to the calling site

The locale parameter is used to allow Passport to show the Express Purchase site in the proper language and format. For us in the USA, that value is `1033`. The `SiteID` parameter is established by the gasTIX developers when we tell Passport what information we wanted to collect from them and return to us. The credit cards we select for display are based on the credit card types the Microsoft Wallet accepts. The `RU` parameter, perhaps the most important parameter, tells Passport where to post the payment information it collects. This page serves as a re-entry point into our site that should contain all the purchasing, billing and shipping information we will need to complete our purchase. The page in gasTIX that serves this purpose for the Express Purchase process is called WalletPostAcceptor.aspx.

NOTE

For more information on Microsoft Passport, Express Purchase, and Microsoft Wallet, please refer to the Microsoft Passport Website at `www.passport.com`.

The WalletPostAcceptor.aspx page contains the same type of server-side processing found in the code we saw in Listing 11.5, but uses the posted Form data from the Passport site instead of the data entered by the Customer on the gasTIX site. We access this information using the `Request.Form` object and use it to update our `OrderData` object.

To make the coding easier to follow, we decided to use a separate page to re-enter the site from Passport instead of using one of the existing pages like the PurchaseConfirmation.aspx or the CollectPaymentInfo.aspx pages. This extra step not only helps the site become more readable by spreading out the code into more discrete steps, it also makes the site a little easier to extend. If we choose to add a new provider for this same type of eWallet service in the future, we can extend the site to them by adding an additional Web page that caters to the new service instead of adding additional complexity to an existing page. Part of the challenge of building effective Websites is making them easy for people to understand and easy to maintain.

Confirming the Purchase

Once the tickets have been selected and payment is arranged, we offer the customer one final chance to back out of their selected purchase. The purchase confirmation page, shown in Figure 11.4, is an example of one such page.

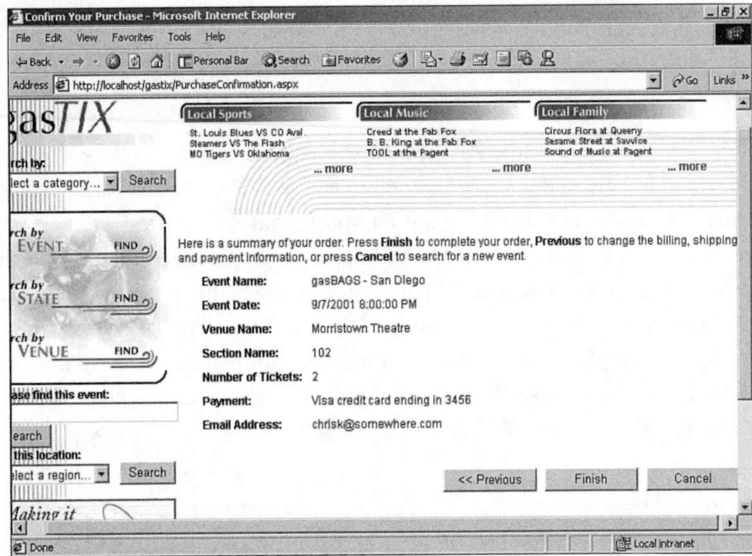

FIGURE 11.4
The PurchaseConfirmation.aspx page.

This page shows a complete summary of the purchase, including event, venue, billing, shipping and purchase information along with their seat and section selections. This page is almost the same as the final invoice page (PurchaseReceipt.aspx) except that it gives the Customer an option to quit before completing their purchase. When the Purchaser chooses the Checkout button, processing is passed to the server side of this page, and the order is updated.

Since we have been using the `OrderData` object throughout the purchase cycle, all of the information we need to post an order is easily available. The business tier provides an `Order` object that we can use to help us complete our order with the help of the `OrderData` object. Listing 11.7 shows a function that the Website uses to save the completed order to the database.

LISTING 11.7 Completing the Purchase

```
Private Function SaveOrder() As String
    Dim o As New gasTIX.BusinessFacade.Order()
    Dim od_r As gasTIX.Data.OrderData
    Dim od as gasTIX.Data.OrderData
    ' save / finalize order and return
    Try
        od_r = o.FinalizeSale(od)
        Session.Item("OrderData") = od_r
        Return ""
    Catch
```

LISTING 11.7 Continued

```
        Return Err.Description
        Session.Item("OrderData") = od
    End Try
End Function
```

Once the `OrderData` is completely filled out, it is only a matter of calling the `FinalizeSale` method on an `Order` object, passing in the `OrderData` object we have been working with during the purchase process. If the purchase is successful, our `OrderData` object will be returned to us after having been updated the total amount of sale, and the purchase tracking number by the purchasing logic. If the purchase is successful, we save the `OrderData` object back to the Session and redirect the user to the PurchaseReceipt.aspx page which serves as their on-line invoice. If the purchase is not successful, we save the original `OrderData` object back to the Session and redisplay the page with the associated error message.

Displaying a Receipt

When the order processing is complete the Customer is shown an electronic receipt that confirms their successful purchase. Much like the traditional paper receipt, this page includes a summary of the Event, details about the tickets that are purchased, and a confirmation tracking number that the Customer can use to track their order.

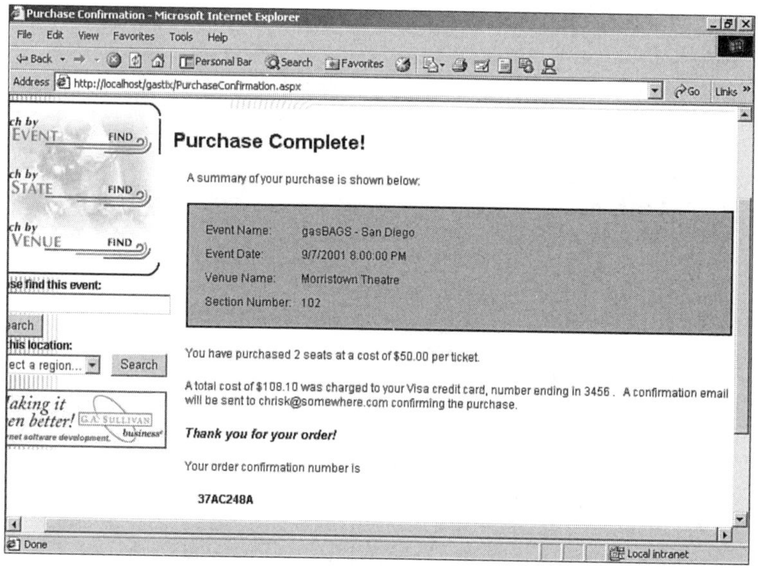

FIGURE 11.5
The PurchaseReceipt.aspx page.

The data on this page is, by now, a familiar sight. The Order, Event and Venue information is all accessed via accustomed means, and displayed to the Customer in a summary form. Listing 11.8 shows the `Load` event for the PurchaseReceipt.aspx page, showing how we retrieve and display this information.

LISTING 11.8 Displaying a Receipt

```
Protected Sub PurchaseReceipt_Load( _
    ByVal Sender As System.Object, ByVal e As System.EventArgs)
    Dim od As gasTIX.Data.OrderData
    Dim dt As System.Data.DataTable
    Dim dr As System.Data.DataRow
    Dim evt As New gasTIX.BusinessFacade.[Event]()
    If Not IsPostback Then    ' Evals true first time browser hits the page
        od = Session.Item("OrderData")
        If od Is Nothing Then
            Response.Redirect("home.aspx")
        Else
            ' load the data row
            dr = od.tables(od.SALE_TABLE).rows(0)

            ' retrieve event information
            Dim iEventID As Integer
            iEventID = dr.Item(od.EVENT_ID).ToString.ToInt32

            Dim ed As EventData = evt.GetEvent(iEventID)
            Dim ed_dt As DataTable = ed.Tables(ed.EVENT_TABLE)
            Dim ed_dr As DataRow = ed_dt.Rows(0)
            lblEventName.Text = ed_dr.Item(ed.EVENT_NAME)
            lblEventDate.Text = ed_dr.Item(ed.EVENT_DATE)
            ed_dr = Nothing
            ed = Nothing
            evt = Nothing

            ' retrieve section information
                lblSectionName.Text = dr.Item(od.SECTION_NAME)
                lblConfirmationNumber.Text = _
                dr.Item(od.CONFIRMATION_NUMBER)
                lblCreditCardNumber.Text = _
                right(dr.Item(od.CREDIT_CARD_NUMBER), 4)
            lblCreditCardType.Text = iif( _
                dr.Item(od.CREDIT_CARD_TYPE_ID) = "VI", _
                "Visa", "MasterCard")
            lblTotalCost.Text = dr.Item(od.TOTAL_CHARGED)
            lblNumberOfSeats.Text = od.tables(od.SEAT_TABLE).Rows.Count
```

LISTING 11.8 Continued

```
            od = Nothing

            ' clean out the order data
            Session.Item("OrderData") = Nothing
        End If
    End If
End Sub
```

Viewing the Seating Chart

To assist the consumer with the purchase, the Event Details and Purchase pages each include a link to view the Seating Chart for the selected event. When purchasing a seat to an event, it is often helpful to see a graphical layout of the venue identifying where all of the sections are located. The seating chart we display will show the arrangement of the section appropriate to the event. This arrangement is sometimes referred to as a seating configuration. If the event is a football game, for example, the seating chart should reflect the venue's seating configuration for a football game, and will not show the seating configuration of a baseball or hockey game. See Figure 11.6 for the ViewSeatingChart.aspx file.

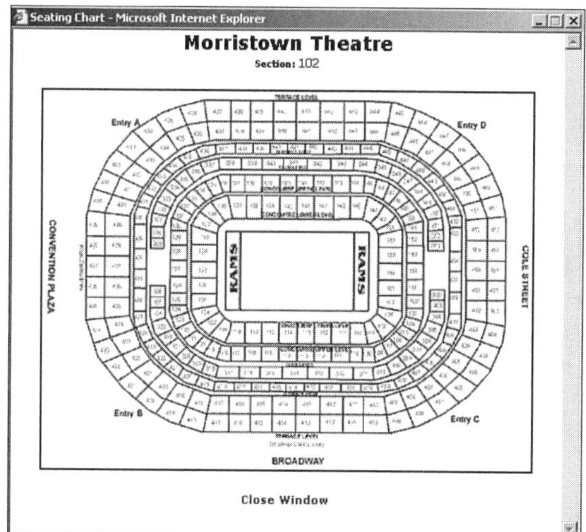

FIGURE 11.6
The ViewSeatingChart.aspx page.

To implement this page, we provide a hyperlink from the event summary on our pages to the ViewSeatingChart.aspx page. This page contains all the code necessary to display the Seating

Chart for the `EventID` it is passed in. The code to render the hyperlink is handled by the new Hyperlink server control. The control's NavigateURL property is dynamically built at runtime based on the `EventID` that was passed in. In ASP, we would have inserted something similar to the following to create this effect.

```
<a href="Page.asp?Parm=<%=myParm%>">Link</a>
```

The downside of this is that the context-switching that is required to make this link dynamic is known to have a negative performance impact to your site. With the `Hyperlink` server control, this context switching is no longer necessary. All of the processing is handled for you by the ASP.NET framework.

To get its data, the ViewSeatingChart.aspx page can use the `EventID` to access the `EventData` object it needs to retrieve the name of the image file to show and the name of the venue it is displaying.

This page is not critical to the operation of the Website, but was provided as a usability benefit to a customer who was unfamiliar with the particular venue. The Seating Chart allows them to get a better view of their seats so they can have a better view of the event. We designed our site so that the Seating Chart is available from the Event Details and the Billing, Shipping, and Payment Collection pages.

The UI for Purchasing a Ticket

At this point in the chapter, we are going to move to purchasing a ticket from the gasBAGS point of view. Recall that gasBAGS is a Website for the fictional gasBAGS band, which consumes the gasTIX purchase XML Web services and uses the data provided.

As mentioned previously, the code for accessing business objects is very similar, whether the reference to those objects is local or made through the Internet. The only difference will come in how each site chooses to design and display its data. In order to highlight both the differences between the Websites and offer proof of the seamless interoperability of the languages, gasBAGS has been written in Visual C# .NET. Figure 11.7 shows the gasBAGS order page.

> **NOTE**
>
> The Web services used in this chapter are built in Chapter 6, Please see that chapter for an understanding of how Web services are created.

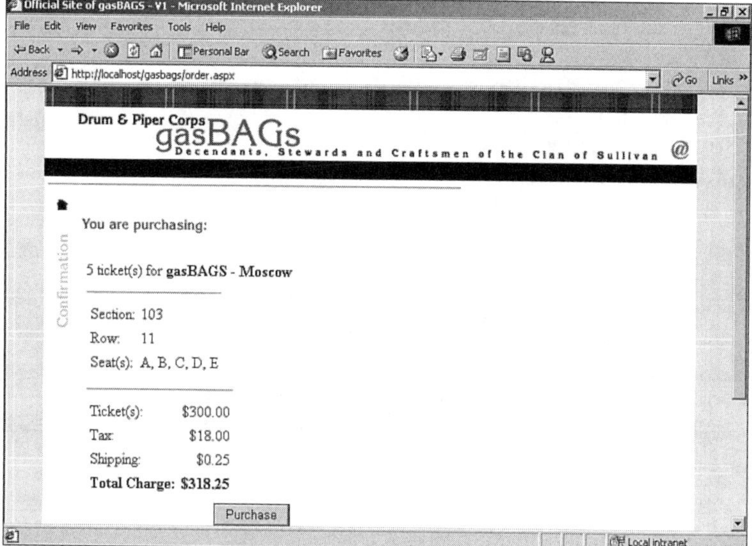

FIGURE 11.7
Order page for the gasBAGS Website as seen from Internet Explorer.

Listing 11.9 demonstrates how to bind the data returned from the Web service to our server controls.

LISTING 11.9 Binding a `DropDownList` to an XML Web Service

```
namespace gasBags {

    using System;
    using System.Web.UI;
    using System.Data;
    using System.IO;
    using gasTix.ParticipantProxy;

    //-- define the Order class
    public class Order : Page {

        protected System.Web.UI.WebControls.DropDownList bill_to_region_id;
...
        //-- this function initializes the pages controls with default values
        protected void LoadPageControls() {
            try {
                //-- get reference to the gasTixWeb Participant assembly
                Participant ParticipantProxy = new Participant();
```

LISTING 11.9 Continued

```
                //-- get regions
                DataSet dsRegions = new DataSet("Regions");
                StringReader srRegions = new
StringReader(ParticipantProxy.ListRegions());
                dsRegions.ReadXml(srRegions);

                //-- load regions for bill to
                bill_to_region_id.DataSource = dsRegions.Tables[0].DefaultView;
                bill_to_region_id.DataTextField = "short_name";
                bill_to_region_id.DataValueField = "region_id";
```

Notice that the Participant class can be instantiated like any other class. Once we have a `Participant` object, we can call the `ListRegions()` method, which returns an XML string of data representing all regions where gasTIX currently sells tickets. We can then bind our `bill_to_region_id TextBox` Web control directly to that XML string. Let's walk through how this is accomplished.

```
Participant ParticipantProxy = new Participant();
```

Here we create our reference to the Participant.DLL, which is our proxy for Web service data. Instead of using Server.CreateObject as in ASP, we just need to create a reference to the DLL located in the bin directory of our Website.

```
//-- get regions
DataSet dsRegions = new DataSet("Regions");
StringReader srRegions = new StringReader(ParticipantProxy.ListRegions());
dsRegions.ReadXml(srRegions);
```

In the above code snippet we make the call to our Web service (implemented via the SOAP protocol) to get a listing of regions to load in our data set. Since our data is being transmitted as String data over the SOAP protocol we use the StringReader call to serialize the data. We then call the `ReadXML` method on the dataset to load our string data.

```
//-- load regions for bill to
bill_to_region_id.DataSource = dsRegions.Tables[0].DefaultView;
bill_to_region_id.DataTextField = "short_name";
bill_to_region_id.DataValueField = "region_id";
bill_to_region_id.DataBind();
```

From here, we just need to assign the dataset as the data source to our `DropDownList` control and specify which fields in the dataset to use. Finally, we call the `BindData` method to bind the data source to the server controls.

All of the preceding code is found in the code-behind page for Order.aspx. Listing 11.10 shows how we wire up the server controls using page directives and server side control definitions.

LISTING 11.10 The HTML Version of the Order.aspx Page.

```
<%@ Register TagPrefix="gasBAGS" TagName="Footer" src="Footer.ascx" %>
<%@ Register TagPrefix="gasBAGS" TagName="Header" src="Header.ascx" %>
<%@ Page Language="c#" Src="Order.cs" Inherits="gasBags.Order"%>
<html><head>
<gasBAGS:Header id="Header" runat="server" />
<form runat="server" ID="Purchase">
...
<b>State:</b>
<asp:dropdownlist id="bill_to_region_id" runat="Server">
</asp:dropdownlist>
...
```

The `@Page` directive in Listing 11.10 informs the ASP.NET parser to include our code behind page specified by the SRC attribute. In this example, the `src` attribute points to the ORDER.CS page discussed earlier. Notice that the form and server controls have the `runat` attribute set to Server.

We specify the `ASP:dropdownlist` control to display a list of the regions supported by gasTIX. Notice that we do not have any inline code for filling the `drop down` control. In "old style" ASP, we would have embedded script logic to fill the control or instantiated a COM object and then looped through building all of the options for the control.

Now, all of the logic is in the order.cs page. This makes for a clean division between the presentation and logic layers of the Web application.

Tools

When using Web services we can use the features in Visual Studio or the command line tools that are also included. However, using the environment in Visual Studio offers a richer development experience when building Web services since Visual Studio offers all of the IntelliSense and syntax checking features.

Visual Studio .NET

This will probably be the preferred method for most developers when consuming XML Web services. We can add references to XML Web services not only from local machines, but also from the following remote locations where:

- The developer is explicitly aware of the XML Web service being exposed and knows the URL for accessing that XML Web service. This is derived from a file with the .disco file extension or the SDL contract from a file with the asmx extension. For more information, see Discovery of Web services (DISCO) at `msdn.microsoft.com/xml/general/disco.asp`.
- The XML Web service is exposed via UDDI (Universal Discovery, Description and Integration). UDDI is a distributed directory of published XML Web services. For more information, see Universal Discovery, Description and Integration at `www.uddi.org`.

The ability to consume both local and remote XML Web services is a huge boon to developers. Now we can create our own XML Web services as building blocks and combine them with other services without regard to physical geography. This greatly broadens the reach and applicability of all development efforts.

Since Visual Studio .NET is tightly integrated with the .NET Framework, this is our tool of choice when building the XML Web services for the gasBAGS Web site. When a Web service is built using Visual Studio .NET, a file with the .vsdisco extension is added to the project. In Managed Visual C++ .NET, this file extension is .disco. When we built our examples for consuming XML Web services from the gasBAGS Website earlier in this chapter, we added Web references from Visual Studio .NET that discovered the methods available by interrogating the .vsdisco files.

Let's get started with Visual Studio .NET and implement the logic to consume an XML Web service from gasTIX. In this example we are going to connect to the gasTIX server and discover the Web services available for use in the gasBAGS Website. To begin, right-click on the project name in the Solution Explorer and select Add a Web Reference. The dialog is shown in Figure 11.8.

From this dialog, we can enter the URL of the Web server where an XML Web service is located, or we can select one of the UDDI directories provided by Microsoft. For the gasBAGS example, enter the name of the gasTIX Web server, `www.gasTIX.com/`. After just a moment, we should see a list of XML Web services that are available for consumption. Select the gasTIX Discovery service. This will display a list of gas XML Web service methods available to us. We will click Add Web Reference to add a reference to this XML Web service and make a copy of the .DLL on our local machine.

In your project you should now see a Web References node, and under that a node referencing the gasTIX Web server. When the gasTIX server node is expanded you will see a WSDL file and a DISCO file. The WSDL file is the XML file describing the methods available in the XML Web service. The DISCO file is the discovery file used by Visual Studio .NET when searching for XML Web services.

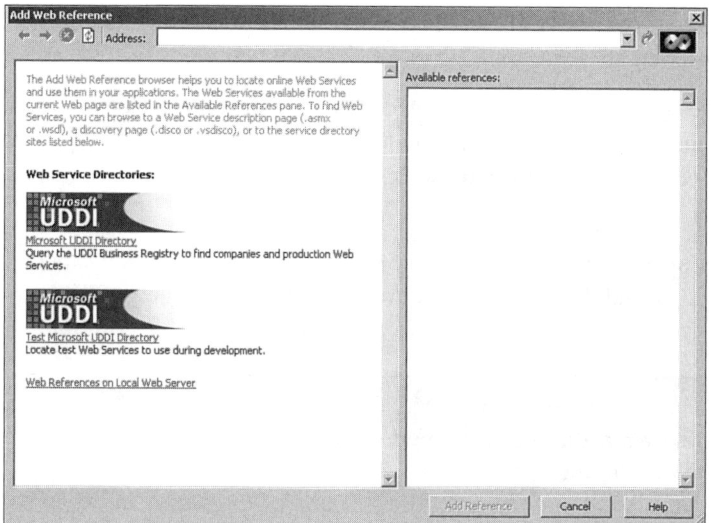

FIGURE 11.8
The Visual Studio .NET Add a Web Reference page.

TIP

It is important to remember that a copy of the XML Web service assembly is copied to our local machine. If the Web service is updated, we need to refresh our Web reference to update our local copy with the new definition.

Now that we have a reference to our XML Web service, we can use it in our code. In our example, double-click on the WebForm1.ASPX file. Right-click on the WebForm1.ASPX file and click View Code. We need to add a reference to the XML Web service that we referenced from the gasTIX XML Web server. Insert the following statement:

```
Using gasBAGS_Demo.gasTix;
```

Now, insert the following code into the `Page_Load` event:

```
DataSet ds = new DataSet("Events");
Participant Events = new Participant();
StringReader sr = new StringReader(Events.ListEvents());
ds.ReadXml(sr);
DataGrid1.DataSource = ds.Tables[0].DefaultView;
DataGrid1.DataBind();
```

As you can see, we only need to create a reference to the object and then we can call the methods of this Web service.

Select View Designer on the WebForm1.ASPX page. If the page is not in Design mode, select that option at the bottom of the page. Drag the `DataGrid` control onto the page layout. Since the default name of the control is `DataGrid1`, we have already referenced this in the `Page Load` event.

Hit the F5 key to build and run the example solution. Once the solution is built, a browser window should pop up and display the list of events available from the gasTIX Web server.

NOTE

If you do have a start up page defined, Visual Studio .NET will ask you to define one before running the application.

As you have seen, finding and using XML Web services through Visual Studio .NET is simple. Once you have a Web reference made, development is completed as though the component was local.

Command-Line Tools

The .NET Framework also supplies command line tools for building ASP.NET pages that consume XML Web services. Each language has its own command-line compiler (csc.exe is the compiler for Visual C# .NET), and the WSDL.exe utility allows developers to build XML Web service proxy DLL's.

TIP

Please refer to the .NET SDK documentation for complete details on all of the command-line options available with the above tools.

After the XML Web service .DLL is generated and copied to our bin directory using the WSDL utility, we can instantiate and call any of the public methods included in the class. So, before we can implement the logic in our ASPX pages, we need to create our module. Open a command prompt and type the following:

```
wsdl /n:gasTix.ParticipantProxy /protocol:SOAP
    http://www.gasTix.com/Participant.asmx?SDL
```

The above command line locates the gasTIX Participant XML Web service and creates a C# proxy class on our machine. We could have specified a different output filename with the `/out:` parameter. Before we compile our source to create our module, let's discuss the command line parameters used. They are:

- **`/n`**—Gives a namespace to our module
- **`/protocol:SOAP`**—Specifies to use the SOAP protocol
- **`www.gasTix.com/Participant.asmx?SDL`**—Specifies the URL where we can find the WSDL contract for this XML Web service.

Also, we did not specify the language on the command line, since C# is the default.

Now that we have generated the source code file, we need to compile it and move it in to our BIN directory. To compile the source file, execute the following line at the command prompt:

```
csc /t:library /r:system.Web.services.dll /r:system.xml.serialization.dll
PARTICIPANT.CS
```

After execution, our assembly is produced and ready to be copied into the BIN directory. As with the WSDL command-line tool, we will examine the command line arguments used to generate the module.

```
/t:library
```

```
This option specifies that we are generating a LIB
file./r:system.Web.services.dll and
/r:system.xml.serialization.dll
```

For each .NET Framework class that we reference, we need to include the `/r` argument followed by the name of the class.

Finally, we specify the name of the source file to be compiled.

While it is not as easy or convenient as using Visual Studio .NET, there are cases where it may be important to be able to reference XML Web services and build C# projects from the command line. The .NET Framework gives you the tools to do so.

From Here

Purchasing a ticket on the gasTIX Website involved a series of steps that each captured a different segment of the order. Some of the things that we accomplished in this section were to:

- use the new Server Controls to efficiently display and collect information from our customer
- use the `DataSet` object to easily retrieve and record our customer's information

- use the `Session` object to persist our DataSet order form from page to page
- successfully interface with a business layer of code that was entirely written in a different programming language: Visual C# .NET

Visual Studio .NET and Visual Basic .NET provide a strong foundation for building the next generation of Web applications. Visual Basic .NET is now a world-class, object-oriented development language with many new and improved features. Visual Studio .NET provides a rich, stable environment for developing applications with the new .NET framework technologies. Also, the improvements to the ASP Session object, and the opportunity to use code-behind pages to simplify our coding, makes ASP.NET the premier Web development technology. All wrapped up together, the .NET framework provides the best suite of tools and technologies to build premier enterprise applications.

In this chapter we took a detailed look at the purchasing process from the gasTix server. We covered the UI, how the data is remoted through the middle tier, and finally committed the transaction to the database. With the advent of .NET and the native XML format, consuming data via XML Web services from any platform is much easier, with a minimal amount of code.

Fulfillment

CHAPTER

12

By Roger Miller and Brian Mueller

IN THIS CHAPTER

- Communication Overview 353
- Notification of New Orders 354
- Sending the Order 359
- Formatting the Order 365
- Processing the Order 370
- Delivery Receipts 378
- Order Status Return and Enhanced Receipts 381
- From Here 394

NOTE

This chapter assumes that the reader has some familiarity with BizTalk Server (BTS). A full discussion of installing and implementing BTS is beyond the scope of this chapter.

This chapter demonstrates how we implemented the gasTIX fulfillment process. In our sample application, this involves printing and shipping tickets to a customer. In many real-world organizations, and in particular e-Business start-ups, there are not sufficient resources to handle fulfillment needs in-house. For this reason, tasks such as warehousing, packaging, shipping, and printing are routinely outsourced to vendors called *third-party administrators* (TPA). A TPA who focuses exclusively on these tasks can be far more effective and efficient in delivering services.

While outsourcing solves one problem, it introduces another. The system which was previously self-contained now must interact with another system over which it has no control. The challenges here can be numerous. State of communications with the vendor's system must be tracked. The status of your data in the vendor's system must be tracked. The transactions with the vendor may be spread out over a significant time. The communication channels may not be reliable (both between computer systems and the among the systems integrators themselves). In spite of these potential challenges, it is a path that is chosen every day. And rather than buy all of the printers and postage machines, gasTIX also chose to outsource our fulfillment operations.

The business requirements for fulfillment are very simple. Once an order for tickets has been placed, the appropriate tickets need to be printed, stuffed in an envelope and shipped to the customer in a timely manner via their shipper of choice. gasTIX also needs to be able to provide the customer with the status of their tickets at any given time. The ticket printing service we chose (which we'll simply refer to as TPA) can provide us all of these functions. Since we also created the TPA for our sample app, we made sure the technologies fit our needs as well. Communication with the TPA is via http over the internet and the messages are encoded in XML. Note that for the purposes of our sample application, tickets are emailed rather then actually printed and mailed.

There are dozens of technologies we could have chosen from to implement fulfillment in the .NET world given the loose requirements above. The possibilities ranged from hard coding everything using old ISAPI calls to using brand new web services. We thought that fulfillment gave us a perfect opportunity to use Microsoft's latest weapon in the battle of systems integration, BizTalk Server 2000 (BTS), a part of the .NET family of servers. BTS has two processing engines, messaging and orchestration. BizTalk messaging provides data transformation and data transport services. BizTalk orchestration provides workflow processing and application integration. We've used both engines to handle communication with the TPA.

Communication Overview

Let's look at the communications involved between the gasTIX site and our TPA and then get into the specifics of each portion. There are processes running on three physical layers that must communicate. First there is the business layer containing all of our .NET components, which resides on our gasTIX web servers. This layer is responsible for kicking off a chain of events when a new order is placed. It must also provide an interface that allows the status of orders to be updated. The second layer is the TPA, which will be running on its own set of servers; it will provide a web interface for submitting orders to be printed. It will also fulfill those orders (via email) and notify the requestor (via an HTTP post) as the status of the order changes during the fulfillment process. The final layer is BTS, which is installed on its own server and will serve as the coordinator between the other two layers.

In a more serial fashion, illustrated in Figure 12.1, here are the steps of order fulfillment:

1. gasTIX middle tier completes an order and notifies BTS.
2. BTS transforms the order to the TPA format.
3. BTS sends the order to the TPA.
4. TPA acknowledges an order was received.
5. TPA processes the order.
6. TPA ships the order, if possible.
7. TPA sends the print order status back to gasTIX.
8. BTS receives the status and notifies the middle tier.

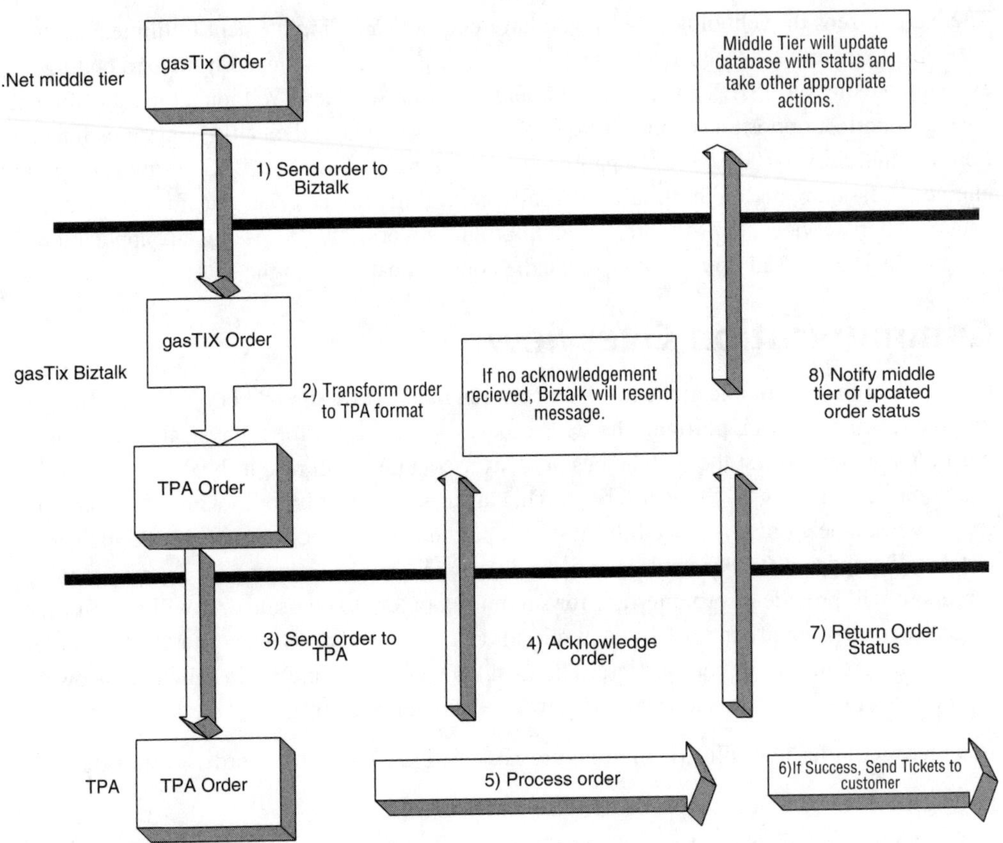

FIGURE 12.1
Overview of communications involved in fulfillment.

Notification of New Orders

Once the customer has finished purchasing their tickets, the middle tier gathers and processes all of the information. Now the fulfillment process begins by passing a message containing an order to BTS. There are three decision points surrounding the passing of a message from the middle tier to BTS. These are:

- The format of the message
- The precise structure of the message
- The technique for transporting the message

With gasTIX, the first two decisions are easy as we will see.

Message Format and Structure

BTS can handle messages in several formats, including XML, comma-separated files, and various EDI formats. XML is the native format for information in BTS; if a message is received in any other format, BTS immediately converts it to XML for internal processing. Since the middle tier is already holding an XML version of the completed order in a data set, this is the most natural format to use. This answers the second question as well. The simplest solution is to use the structure of the XML data set that the middle tier is already using.

One of the marquee features of BTS is data transformation. BTS can take any inbound message it receives and convert it to our trading partner's structure and format. And conversely it can take our trading partner's style and format and convert it to a format our systems can understand. So using the data or message structure that we're already working with is the generally the best solution. The caveat is that all necessary information for our trading partner must be included or derivable from the set of information we're sending. Also, future changes that are likely to be incorporated by our trading partner (or perhaps a future trading partner) should be considered. Some extra information in the message is not a bad thing and may actually save effort in the future. If there is an extra field in the message that our partner may need in six months, we've reduced our future middle tier work and limited changes to the BTS layer, at very little cost to us now.

NOTE

Trading partner is a term used in BizTalk documentation to generically describe an entity that you're doing business with electronically. In our sample application, the TPA is a trading partner.

Message Transport

The final decision to make is what method is used to send the message to BTS. Two choices are available: *receive functions* and *direct COM+ calls*. Receive functions allow BTS to monitor Microsoft Message Queue (MSMQ) and file system locations for messages. A BTS service runs, waiting for an appropriate message to be detected. When this happens, it is picked up and routed to the appropriate BizTalk channel for processing. For MSMQ receive functions, a queue name must be specified. For file receive functions, a file name, with wildcards allowed, and a directory must be specified as shown in Figure 12.2. Either type allows routing directives to be provided to BTS as shown in Figure 12.3. Receive functions are set up and maintained from the BTS administration console.

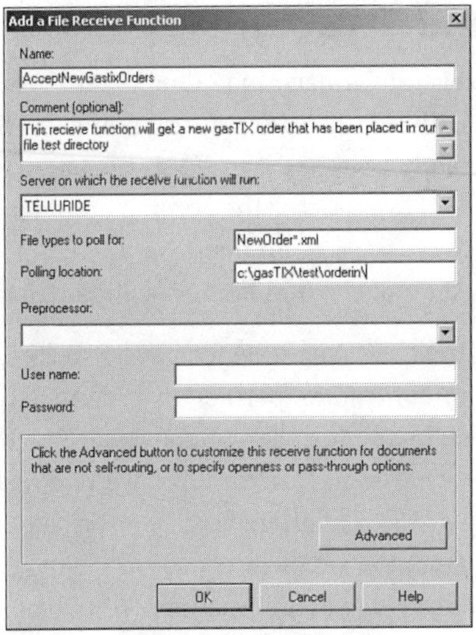

FIGURE 12.2
Dialog for adding a receive function.

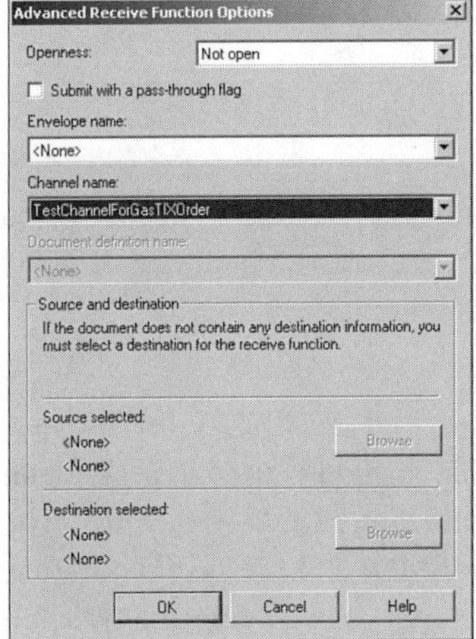

FIGURE 12.3
Dialog for specifying routing directives for a receive function.

The other option for sending messages to BTS is a COM+ call. This interface is provided via the IInterchange class. The `Submit` method of this class allows an asynchronous transmission of the message. Once the message has been submitted to the BTS messaging engine, execution can continue. There is also a `SubmitSynch` method that allows you to wait for the BTS engine to successfully process and transport the message. The format of the `Submit` method is:

```
Submit( OpennessFlag, Document, DocName, SourceQualifier, SourceID,
DestQualifier, DestID, ChannelName, FilePath, EnvelopeName, PassThrough)
```

NOTE

It is worth noting the similarities between the parameters in the Submit call and the routing options available on the properties of a receive function. There is really no loss of functionality by choosing one method over the other since both can take on values like channel, document type, and destination ID. These parameters control how a message is processed in BTS messaging. Every message will take one path through BTS called a channel. When submitting a message to BTS, these parameters can aid BTS in its channel selection process. Very specific information can be provided such as the exact channel to use. More general information can be provided, such as a destination organization or a document name, to aid BTS in selecting a channel. If no information is provided, BTS will look for similar information embedded inside of the message, making this a self-routing document. Finally, lacking any other information, BTS will attempt to determine the format of the message and select a channel accordingly. There is a great deal of flexibility on how messages can be routed through BTS.

TIP

If no routing information is provided to BTS, be careful to ensure your BTS setup is not ambiguous (in other words, only one channel is valid for any anticipated inbound message).

NOTE

BTS claims to accept messages from a myriad of sources such as HTTP, FTP, SMTP, and MSMQ, but there is actually some sleight of hand going on to accomplish this. Currently, the only three methods of getting a message into BTS are via a direct function call via IInterchange, an MSMQ receive function, or a file receive function. The other transports are "implemented" by using the three mentioned. For example, FTP is supported by having a file receive function monitor the FTP target directory. An HTTP post is supported by using an ASP page that passes the message along through either MSMQ or IInterchange. SMTP is supported by using events or event sinks on specific folders that pass their message to BTS via IInterchange. The bare minimum was included in the first release of BTS, with plans for other protocols being directly supported in future releases.

For gasTIX, we chose to make a direct asynchronous call from the middle tier. The reason for this choice was that we wanted to make direct use of a COM+ component from .NET code. The call we made is shown in Listing 12.1.

LISTING 12.1 Function to Submit Message to BizTalk

```
Private Function SubmitOrderToBTM(ByVal orderXML As String) As String
     Dim objSubmit As BTSInterchangeLib.IInterchange = New
BTSInterchangeLib.Interchange()
     Dim strHandle As String
     Dim strChannel As String
     strChannel = "GastixOrderToOrchestration"
     Try
       strHandle = objSubmit.Submit(
BTSInterchangeLib.BIZTALK_OPENNESS_TYPE.BIZTALK_OPENNESS_TYPE_NOTOPEN,
orderXML, "", "", "", "", "", strChannel, "", "", 0)
     Catch e As Exception
       Throw e
     End Try
     Return strHandle
  End Function
```

A reference to the `IInterchange` object was made available to the web/middle tier box by installing an application proxy reference to the BizTalk Server Interchange Application that resides in COM+ on the BTS box. When the reference was set, the Visual Studio .NET IDE actually generated a .NET wrapper library for the COM+ object. The topic of COM+ interoperability is discussed in detail in Chapter 9, "COM+ Integration." A more detailed look at the `Submit` method and its parameters is provided later this chapter, in the section on Correlation.

A call is made using the `Submit` function, which will allow the message to be processed asynchronously. The only parameters passed to the `Submit` function are the openness type, the XML message containing the order itself, and the channel name. In our example, we knew exactly which channel we wanted to go to and specified it. More specific information is always better when it's available. After the call to submit is made, the middle tier can exit its processing for this order. BTS can take over the fulfillment processing.

Message Transport Alternatives

Of the three decision points that were mentioned previously, only the last one is questionable. Using XML was an easy choice since the information was readily available in that format from our site and it is the native format for BTS. The structure of the message was also easy to select, since the message already existed and contained all of the information we needed. The decision to pass the message as a direct call, however, could be argued.

One good alternative would have been to submit the order message to MSMQ instead of directly to BTS. This would solve some reliability problems, since connectivity to the BTS machine would never be an issue. In the case of server or network problems, the message sits in the queue, waiting until system conditions allow it to be delivered. This makes the interface with BTS truly asynchronous. Using a message queue also prevents the web/middle tier servers from being tied directly to particular BTS servers. Being tied to a particular machine introduces reliability and scalability problems. Finally, using MSMQ also eliminates the need to install the application proxies to BTS on the web/mid tier machines.

One variation of the direct call would be to use Application Center's component load balancing. By load balancing BTS across multiple machines, several problems are eliminated. Scalability is no longer an issue. In fact, using Application Center makes scalability as good as, and possibly better than, MSMQ. Since MSMQ receive functions are tied to a single machine, only one machine will read messages from a message queue (although any server in the group could actually process the message once it was read). Multiple machines could each have a MSMQ receive function reading from a queue, although load balancing by having multiple readers of a queue is generally discouraged. We didn't attempt to load balancing receive functions on Application Center to see how they behave.

Application Center load balancing also provides some reliability benefits, in that single server failures aren't a problem. In the case of general network errors, however, MSMQ may have an advantage over Application Center. Ultimately, reliability may be a moot point as well, as most real systems will have a mechanism in place to detect unfulfilled orders (or in our case—unshipped tickets). So if a call fails, it will be handled eventually. This will be discussed more in a following section.

There are several factors to consider in selecting message-passing solutions for any given situation. Regardless of the solution we select, the message will end up in work queue for BTS and be prepared for delivery to the TPA.

Sending the Order

After BTS has received a message, the next step from the point of Figure 12.1 is to transform our message into the TPA's format. For the moment, we will skip ahead to Step 3 and look at how BTS sends the message to the TPA for processing. Just as we did with the receive functions mentioned above, we have several transport options for sending the order to the TPA. Regardless of which transport option we use, though, there are many things common about the way BTS processes messages. BTS has introduced a lot of new terminology that is important for the explanation so let's quickly review some important definitions. Objects represented by these definitions can all be created by the BizTalk Messaging Manager.

BTS Messaging Definitions

Document—This is a specification for a message that will be processed by BizTalk.

Organization—To BizTalk, an organization represents a specific trading partner. Typically, an organization is specified as the source and/or destination for each message.

Home Organization—A default organization that represents our BizTalk server. However, home organization may not be specified as the source or destination for messages. Instead subdivisions called applications are used.

Application—An application is a virtual entity that may or may not correspond to a real software application. It is essentially a point of attachment that allows us to connect to the home organization.

There are a couple of important notes on applications and organizations. Applications are assumed to be internal to our network and, as such, are allowed to directly interface with BTS Orchestration XLANG schedules. Otherwise, the selection of specific applications or organization is mostly important for organization and tracking of messages. And as noted previously, specifying this information can also be used by BTS for routing messages.

Port—This is the destination for our message. This could be an actual organization in which case you're required to provide the specific transport. Transports available include HTTP, SMTP, FTP, COM+ components, and XLANG schedules among others. Or this could be a virtual organization for which the specifics are determined at runtime, in which case the port is considered to have an open destination.

Channel—As previously defined, this is the particular path that a message takes through BTS. A source organization or application may be designated for a channel. Otherwise it is considered to have an open source. The channel specifies the inbound and outbound document definitions. The channel also handles any data transformations that need to occur; these transformations use map files, which we will cover in the next section.

Envelope—A wrapper for inbound and outbound documents. Aids in formatting the message to and from XML. Some formats include X12, EDIFACT and Reliable. Reliable will be used later in the the section on BTS Framework Reliable Delivery.

Creating the Organizations and Applications

We need to create an organization to represent the TPA so we have some place to hook in our port. To do this, simply open the BizTalk Messaging Manager and select create a new organization from the file menu. This will display the dialog shown in Figure 12.4. All we need to do is give a name, so we will just call it TPA. If we had needed to programmatically identify the TPA by some other method than organization name, we could have specified additional information on the Identifiers tab. You can define your own identifiers or use standard one such as ISO 6523 Organization Identification, American Bankers Association number, or DUNS (Dun & Bradstreet) number.

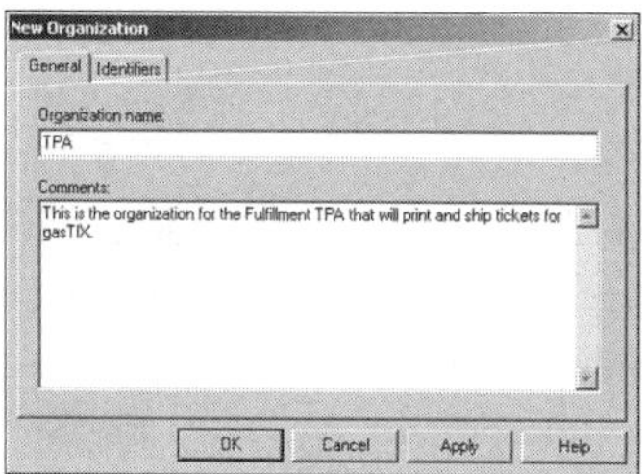

FIGURE 12.4
Dialog for adding the TPA organization.

As stated before, the home organization is a bit different from other organizations because it represents our BizTalk Server. Though we could just attach channels directly to other organizations that represent us, this is not recommended. Instead, to keep things organized, we want to create an application off of our home organization to represent our middle tier. Creating an application is easily done by editing the home organization as shown in Figure 12.5. Notice that the home organization has a third tab that other organizations don't. This is where we can add our application that we will call WebOrder.

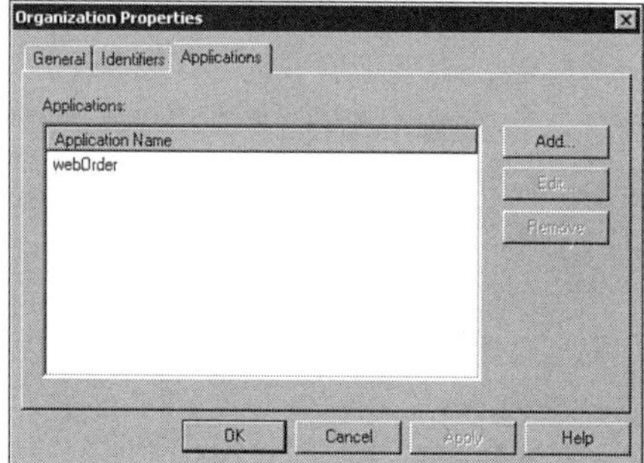

FIGURE 12.5
Applications tab for the Home Organization property sheet.

Creating the Port

Ports are the endpoint of message so we need to create a port for the TPA, which we will name PrintOrderToTPA. To do this, open the BizTalk Messaging Manager and select New

Messaging Port to an Organization from the File menu. Name the port PrintOrderToTPA, and configure the destination organization as shown in the Figure 12.6. Note that we've selected the TPA organization that we just created and specified a primary transport as an HTTP URL where our TPA server is located.

There are a number of port options only some of which are shown in Figure 12.6. Listed here are some of the important ones:

- **Transport**—We selected HTTP for this option. Other transport options available are: Application Integration Component (AIC), which is a COM+ object with a that implements a specific BizTalk interface; file; HTTP; HTTPS; loopback, which returns to the calling XLANG schedule or component; MSMQ; and SMTP. For ports that are attached to an application, XLANG schedules are also an option as discussed in the section on Activating Orchestration from BTS Messaging. We can also select a backup transport that will be used if the primary transport fails.
- **Service Window**—You can restrict the availability of the port to certain hours. Messages received outside of those hours will be queued until the service window is open. This option was not used in our example.
- **Envelopes**—We can associate a number of different envelopes (EDIFACT, X12, flat file, etc.). These can be used to format our messages so they can be read by existing non-XML systems. This option was not used in our example.
- **Encoding, Encryption, and Signature**—These options allow you to MIME encode the document if it contains non-text data and to use Secure MIME if you need public-key encryption. This option was not used in our example.

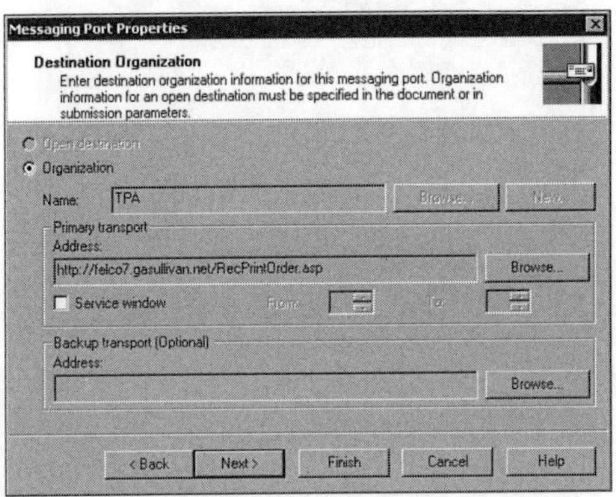

FIGURE 12.6
Dialog for configuring the destination organization.

Once you click Finish, the new messaging port will show up in the list of configured ports. Note that the channel count for the port is zero, so now we need to create a channel to allow the port to receive our message.

TIP

A port can have any number of channels connecting to it. Conversely, we can send a message to multiple ports using a single channel by grouping those ports into distribution lists.

Creating the Channel

A channel runs *from* an application or organization *to* a port. Since our message is coming from an internal source, we will create a channel from an application. Recall from our previous discussion that this is done to help us keep our connections organized. To do this, simply right-click the port (PrintOrderToTPA in this case) and select New Channel From an Application from the context menu. This brings up the new channel/channel properties wizard, which is where we'll name the channel GastixOrderToOrchestration.

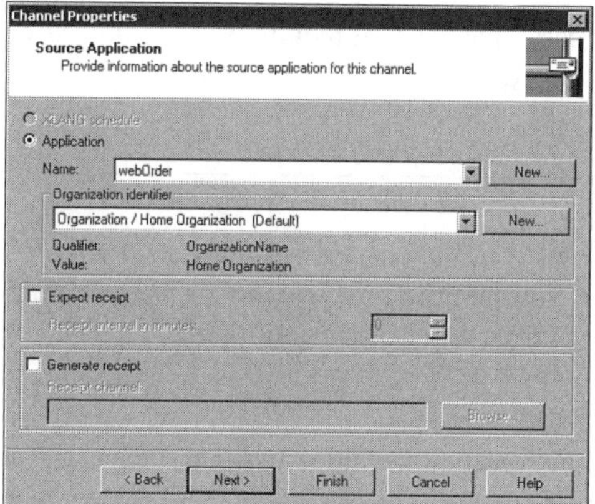

FIGURE 12.7
Dialog for configuring the source application.

Now we need to tell the channel where it will be getting its data from; we do this in the second page of the channel wizard. Because we have only one application—webOrder—assigned to our home organization, we will select webOrder as our source as shown in Figure 12.7. Even though we selected a specific application as our source, data can come from anyone who correctly submits a document to this channel.

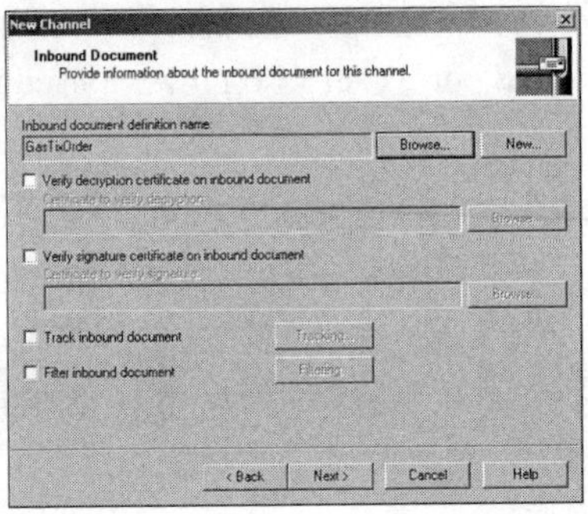

FIGURE 12.8
Dialog for configuring the inbound document.

After telling the channel where to get its data from, we now need to select the inbound and outbound document specifications. For the inbound document, simply select the GasTixOrder specification on the third page of the channel wizard as shown in Figure 12.8. We'll assume that the TPA has its own specification for print orders. For the outbound specification, we will select the TPAPrintOrder specification. Since we are using different inbound and outbound specifications we now must also select a map file. We will discuss the details of mapping later; for now, simply browse to the map file gastixToTpaR1.xml. Figure 12.9 shows the completed dialog. Since we have no particular logging requirements in this case, accept the defaults on the remaining dialogs.

NOTE

For the purposes of this example, we are assuming that we already have the TPA document specification in hand. In practice, we would likely obtain this specification through the BizTalk.org repository or through UDDI.

Channels provide several options that we did not utilize such as the ability to log particular fields or entire documents. Channels also provide the ability to sign and recognize digital signatures and filter what inbound documents are processed based on the contents of particular fields. (Channels also provide the specification of retry options, but this will be covered in more detail in the section entitled, "Receipts.") The path from our schedule to the TPA is now complete. Figure 12.10 summarizes the route our message takes.

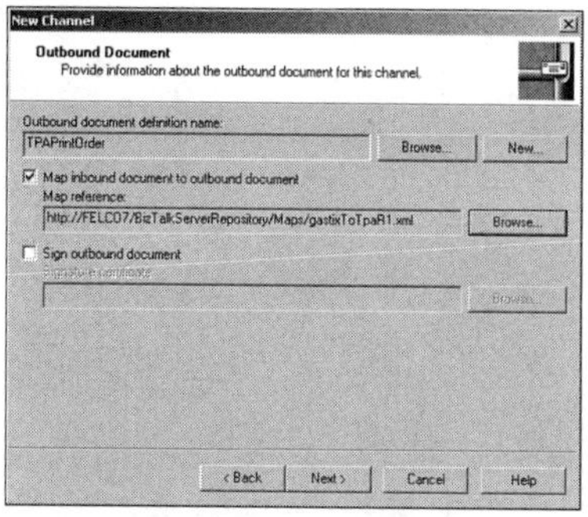

FIGURE 12.9
Dialog for configuring the outbound document.

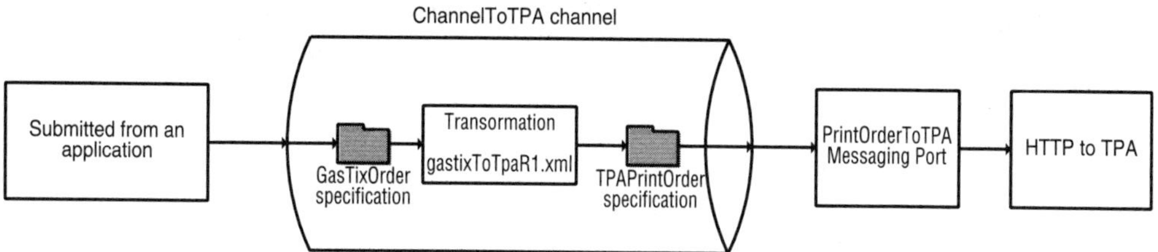

FIGURE 12.10
This diagram demonstrates the message flow to TPA.

Formatting the Order

As we discussed before, the TPA has its own document specification for formatting a ticket order, so we need to transform our order document to match their specification. To do this we will use BizTalk Mapper. This creates a map file will that then be attached to our channel as previously demonstrated and will automatically be applied whenever we send a document through that channel.

BizTalk Mapper is a tool that lets us visually create a transformation between the data elements of two document specifications. This allows us to see the properties of individual data, and also shows the relationship between the two specifications. Figure 12.11 illustrates our map from the gasTIX order format to the TPA format.

Table 12.1 lists the mappings between our order document and the TPA document. Most of these are simple one-to-one mappings, so all we need to do is drag the field from our document to the corresponding field in the TPA document and the connection is done. Some of these mappings, however, are far more complex and that's where functoids—described in the next section—come into play.

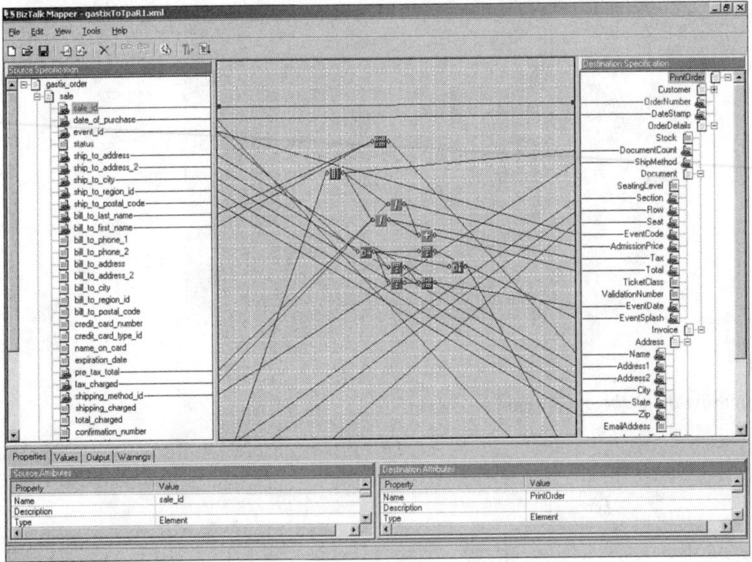

FIGURE 12.11

BixTalk Mapper creates a visual map for transforming a gasTIX order to a TPA order.

TABLE 12.1 GasTIX Fields Map Directly to TPA Fields

Destination	*Source*
/PrintOrder/Customer/OrderNumber	/gastix_order/sale/sale_id
/PrintOrder/Customer/DateStamp	/gastix_order/sale/date_of_purchase
/PrintOrder/Customer/OrderDetails/DocumentCount	Count of /gastix_order/seat
/PrintOrder/Customer/OrderDetails/ShipMethod	/gastix_order/sale/shipping_ method_id
/PrintOrder/Customer/OrderDetails/Document/Section	/gastix_order/sale/section_name
/PrintOrder/Customer/OrderDetails/Document/Row	/gastix_order/sale/row_name
/PrintOrder/Customer/OrderDetails/Document/Seat	/gastix_order/seat/seat_name
/PrintOrder/Customer/OrderDetails/Document/ EventCode	/gastix_order/sale/event_id
/PrintOrder/Customer/OrderDetails/Document/ AdmissionPrice	/gastix_order/sale/pre_tax_total divided by count of gastix_order/seat
/PrintOrder/Customer/OrderDetails/Document/Tax	/gastix_order/sale/tax_charged divided by count of gastix_order/seat

TABLE 12.1 Continued

Destination	*Source*
/PrintOrder/Customer/OrderDetails/Document/Total	/gastix_order/sale/pre_tax_total divided by count of gastix_order/seat
PLUS	
/gastix_order/sale/tax_charged divided by count of gastix_order/seat	
/PrintOrder/Customer/OrderDetails/Document/EventDate	String concatenation of event_date and event_time fields from the database, retrieved by /gastix_order/sale/event_id
/PrintOrder/Customer/OrderDetails/Document/EventSplash	Value of event_name field from the database, retrieved by /gastix_order/sale/event_id
/PrintOrder/Customer/OrderDetails/Invoice/Address/Name	String concatenation of /gastix_order/sale/bill_to_first_name and /gastix_order/sale/bill_to_last_name
/PrintOrder/Customer/OrderDetails/Invoice/Address/Address1	/gastix_order/sale/ship_to_address
/PrintOrder/Customer/OrderDetails/Invoice/Address/Address2	/gastix_order/sale/ship_to_address2
/PrintOrder/Customer/OrderDetails/Invoice/Address/City	/gastix_order/sale/ship_to_city
/PrintOrder/Customer/OrderDetails/Invoice/Address/State	/gastix_order/sale/ship_to_region_id
/PrintOrder/Customer/OrderDetails/Invoice/Address/Zip	/gastix_order/sale/ship_to_postal_code
/PrintOrder/Customer/OrderDetails/Invoice/InvoiceText/Line/Text	Error text returned from database query
/PrintOrder/Correction/DateTimeStamp	/gastix_order/sale/date_of_purchase

Functoids

Functoids are essentially function objects that perform many of the functions we would typically associate with a programming language. There are functoids that concatenate strings, multiply and divide numbers, and apply specific formatting. We can also use functoids to extract data from a database. If none of the standard functoids fit our requirements, we can even create custom functoids written in VBScript. If we need still *more* flexibility, we can go so far as to write a completely custom functoid object, using the IFunctoid interface, that is then added to our functoid palette. Given the effort involved in that task, however, we generally try to make use of the existing functoids when we can.

NOTE

Keep in mind that the end result of compiling the map file is an XSLT style sheet. While many of the functoids compile to standard XSLT elements, some of them (including custom script functoids) add script elements to the style sheet. Since script elements are notorious for slowing down style sheet processing, we need to be careful to ensure that our functoid usage does not create performance issues. For the same reasons, we need to think carefully before writing large blocks of script or invoking COM+ components from script. Just because we *can* do everything in the map does not necessarily mean we should.

TIP

It is possible to manually edit the compiled-map, XLST style sheet to add things that the IDE does not allow. However this can be tedious as the mapper will replace these elements every time you recompile.

Now we will take a closer look at the specific functoids used in our map. Functiods are visually represented in the mapper by boxes in the center of the mapper form as shown in Figure 12.11. The first functoid we use is the `String Concatenation` functoid, which takes strings as inputs and concatenates them together for the output. Any number of inputs can be used with the functoid—to add an input, simply drag the field to the functoid. In this case we are using this functoid to concatenate the customer's first and last names.

The next functoid is the `Record Count` functoid, which simply counts the number of occurrences of one item (and only one) in the document. For example, if we connect the event_id field to a `Record Count` functoid, the output will be the number of seats contained in the document. We use this functoid to count the number of seats (and therefore the number of tickets) ordered. In addition to being stored in the output document directly, this count will be used later to calculate tax and price per ticket.

That brings us to the various mathematical functoids, which provide everything from minimum and maximum value calculations to addition, subtraction, and square roots. For the gasTIXtoTPAr1 mapping, we are simply using the division and addition functoids to convert the total ticket price and total tax listed in the ticket order to the per-ticket values that the TPA wants to see. These calculations work off of the ticket count that we discussed earlier.

All of these functoids so far have operated solely on data that is already present in the source document. Now let's address the need to pull some additional data from the database that isn't present. There are three database functoids that are built for this task. In a typical database mapping all three of them will be used. The first step is always to make a connection to the database using the `Database Lookup` functoid, which takes the following four parameters:

- the database to use (`dsn=gastix;uid=sa;pwd"=`)
- the table we are querying (`event`)
- the column we are querying against `event_id`
- the value we are using to query the database (mapped from the gasTIX `event_id.`)

Note that we have used constants for all of our values except event_id. Figure 12.12 shows the parameters we used for our mapping.

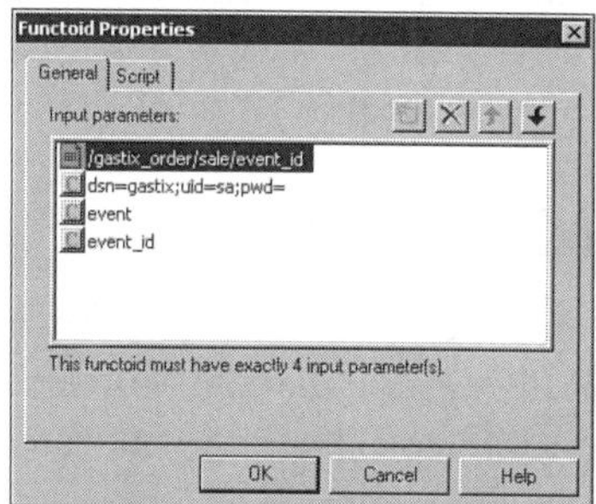

FIGURE 12.12
Dialog for the Database Lookup functoid.

Once we have established a database connection, we need to extract the data. We do this using the `Value Extractor` functoid, which allows us to specify one database field to retrieve. We will use three of these to retrieve the `event_name`, `event_time`, and `event_date` field, which then map to the `EventDate` and `EventSplash` fields in the output document (note that another `String Concatenation` functoid is used to combine the time and date).

If we have trouble setting up our database queries, we can use the `Error Return` functoid. It hands out a string that contains any error messages created during data access.

NOTE

We need to emphasize that a trade-off exists between extracting data from a database and requiring that it instead be supplied in the inbound document. In most cases we would prefer to have the data already present in the document. By doing so, we do not have concerns about the database server being inaccessible, performance problems from an overloaded database server, or other problems that can occur any time an additional system is added to the mix. On the other hand, retrieving data from the database reduces the burden on the supplier of the document, and in some cases, the trading partner or legacy application we are integrating with simply might not have access to the data we need.

Alternatives

Most people note when first considering BizTalk messaging and mapping that there is nothing special about BizTalk that couldn't be developed with more traditional methods. And generally speaking that is true. We could have coded the middle tier to directly generate into the TPA's format. But what happens when the TPA changes their format? Or we change to a different TPA? Or if we decide to use different TPA's for each shipping method? That is when using BizTalk really starts to pay dividends. Perhaps we will not always see the benefits for the first trading or second trading partner but by the third or thirtieth trading partner, we will.

Processing the Order

Now that the order has been formatted and sent to the TPA for processing, we need to take a look at the implementation of the TPA itself. The TPA will receive our order through an ASP page and a BizTalk channel. For our sample, the TPA will then issue ticket(s) to the customer via standard email. A success or failure status will also be sent back to the trading partner that sent the order, which is gasTIX in this case. We have used a BTS orchestration schedule to help process the orders. We are assuming that the TPA mostly uses legacy systems but is starting to modernize and is using BTS orchestration for simple application integration.

NOTE

The term "schedule" has been used rather loosely in this chapter. But in all cases, it refers to the output of the BizTalk Application designer tool. This is the tool that is used to design workflow orchestration and application integration within BizTalk. To be precise XLANG (pronounced "slang") schedules are the compiled output of the tool that can be executed by the XLANG (or orchestration) engine/service. But the terms XLANG schedule, orchestration schedule, and schedule have been used interchangeably.

Receiving the Order

We know that the TPA received the order as an HTTP post to an ASP page. We are using a slightly modified version of an ASP page, provided with the BTS SDK, to process the message. This page extracts the message from the posted data. We could have chosen to activate the XLANG schedule directly and hand it the message. But instead we send the message through BTS messaging, which allows us to demonstrate additional features. The ASP code uses the same submit method to invoke messaging, just like the middle tier code on gasTIX. The name of the channel we will use is IncomingPrintOrder.

Activating Orchestration from BTS Messaging

Most of the setup for BTS messaging is similar to what was done for the gasTIX side, in terms of creating organizations, channels and ports. Only two things differ. First, the document is not mapped, meaning that the channel's inbound document is identical to the outbound document. Second, we let BTS messaging instantiate the orchestration schedule and hand it the message. The messaging port we have created is a port to an application and is called PortToPrinthouseSchedule. The second step of the wizard (shown in Figure 12.13) shows that we are activating a new XLANG schedule (as opposed to using some other transport). This gives the physical location of the compiled XLANG schedule and specifies the port name, IncomingPrintOrder. The rest of the parameters are the typical ones for messaging port specification. After the channel executes, control is handed over to the BTS orchestration engine.

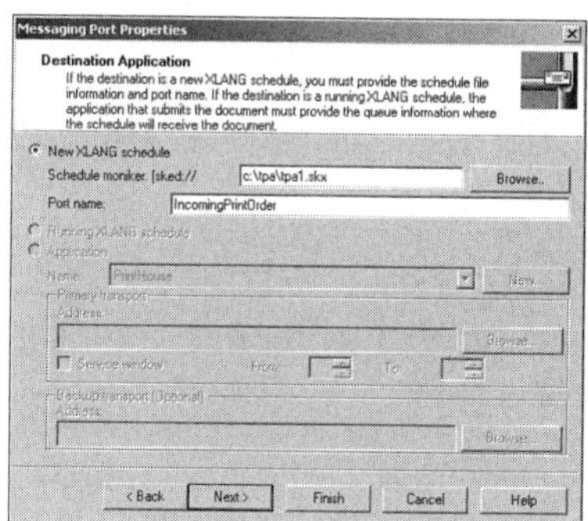

FIGURE 12.13

The Messaging Port Properties dialog allows us to specify a new XLANG schedule.

NOTE

The port, IncomingPrintOrder, referred in the dialog in Figure 12.14 is an orchestration port, not a BTS messaging port. An orchestration port is essentially a logical entry point to the XLANG schedule as we will see shortly. Unfortunately, Microsoft chose to overload the term port when developing BTS.

TPA Orchestration Overview

The TPA is a separate organization with its own servers and business processes. We will create an XLANG schedule to coordinate its part of the fulfillment process. Using the BizTalk Orchestration Designer, we have created a schedule named Tpa1.skv. Figure 12.14 shows the complete orchestration schedule that we use in this section.

The left portion of the diagram is the abstract business process. The right hand side represents physical implementation of message sources or destinations. Currently four types of implementations are allowed to interact with BTS orchestration: BTS messaging, MSMQ, COM+ components and scripting components. The middle represents ports and messages. Ports are logical entry points to the schedule. Messages are shown inside of ports and are the data elements which move in and out of the schedule.

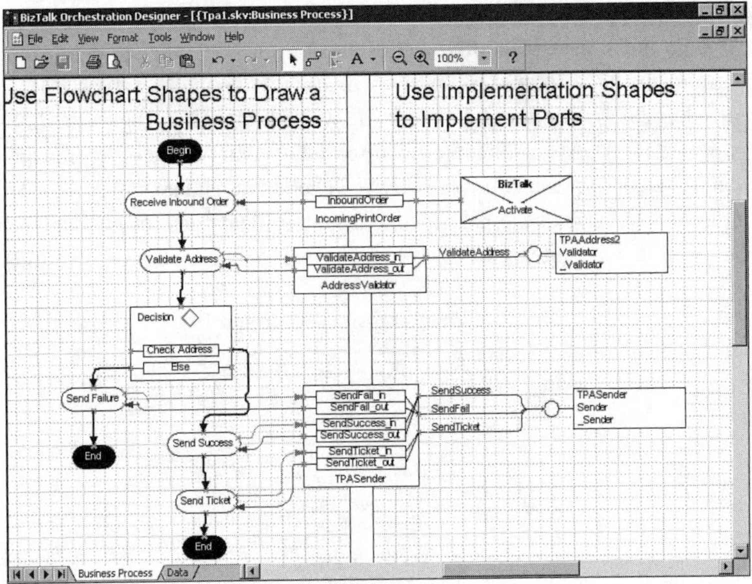

FIGURE 12.14

Creating the Business Process

The business process, shown in Figure 12.15, theoretically is created by a business analyst to summarize the work flow through the system. For our TPA, the business process blocks represent moving messages between different systems. We need to attach these to specific implementations on the right side of the diagram to designate where the data goes. We also need to implement a bit of logic by adding a decision block. This decision block (represented by a rectangle) has one rule named Check Address. The script for this logic can be entered or edited by using the properties of the decision block (see Figure 12.16 for the complete dialog) and is as follows:

```
ValidateAddress_Out.ValidateAddress=TRUE
```

This rule is very simple; it checks the Boolean return value of a function to see if the address validation succeeds. Rules can be, however, very complex. We will cover the address validation port later in this chapter.

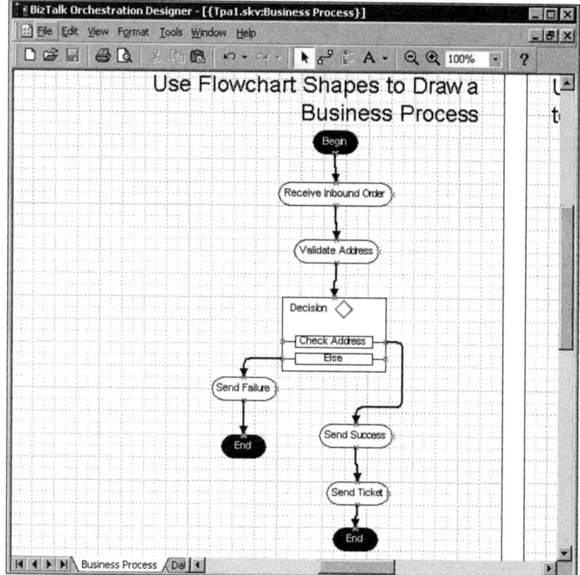

FIGURE 12.15
TPA Business process.

Receiving Messages in the Schedule

Everything else we do will be based on the document coming into the schedule. First, we create a new BizTalk implementation shape. The wizard/properties then prompt you to create a new port or attach to an existing one. We create a new port, named IncomingPrintOrder, which matches the name we specified in the BTS messaging port. On the subsequent tabs, we set it to Receive (Figure 12.17), and specify that the channel activates a new XLANG schedule (Figure 12.18). Then we connect Receive Inbound Order block of the business process to the

IncomingPrintOrder port. This brings up the XML communication wizard which lets us specify the message. The wizard is straightforward and allows us to specify message name, type and associate it with a specification. We associate it with the same specification that we used in BTS messaging channel, TPAPrintOrder.xml.

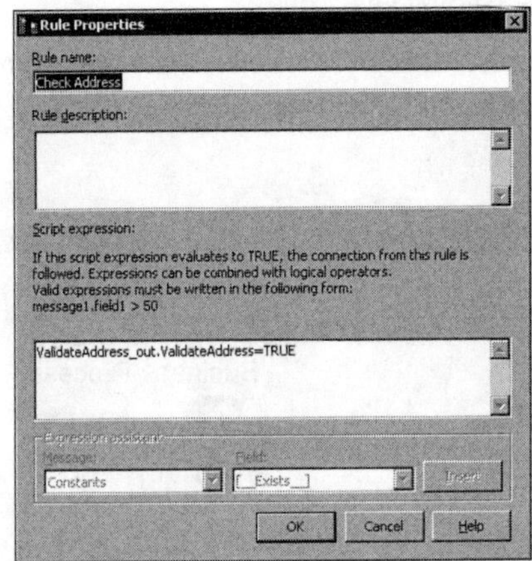

FIGURE 12.16

Dialog for the address validation rule.

> **NOTE**
>
> It's important to be careful when specifying the message type. It must match the name of the root node name when the message is coming from BTS or the label when the message is from MSMQ. If not a mildly informative error will be raised.

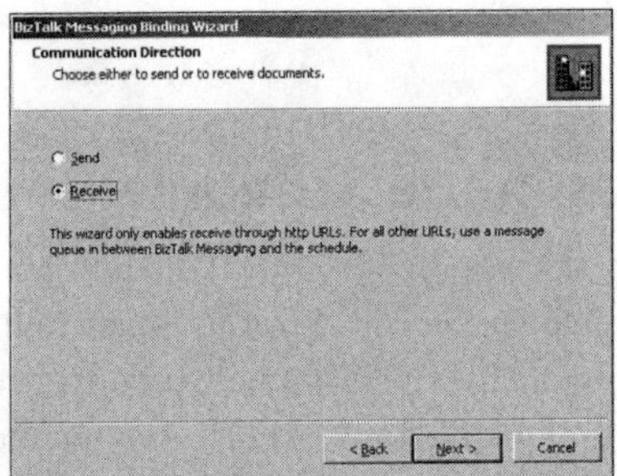

FIGURE 12.17

BizTalk Messaging Binding Wizard—Communication Direction.

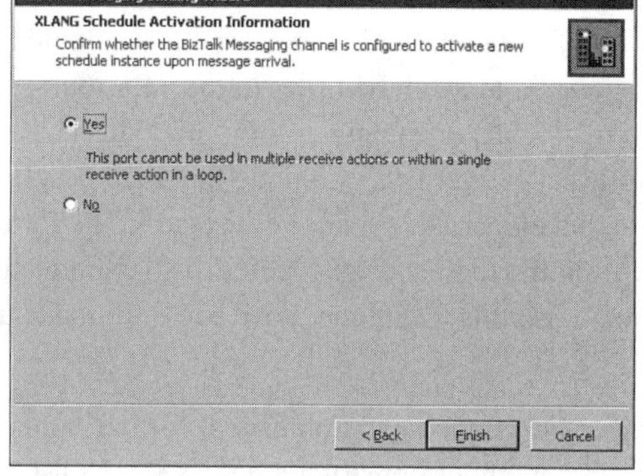

FIGURE 12.18
BizTalk Messaging Binding Wizard—XLANG Schedule Activation Information.

Creating the Components

Now that we have shown how to get a message into our orchestration schedule, we'll show how to integrate some existing components to process that message. We have two existing COM+ applications to integrate with: the address validator and the TPA sender. The address validator component (TPAAddressValidator2) provides a wrapper for services to verify a customer's address data. The implementation for the sample site doesn't actually do anything except return true, but it would be easy to expand it to perform validation. It could even call a web service to do the job, supplied by the postal service or another company. For our purposes, the implementation of the address validator is not important; all that concerns us is the resulting Status, as shown in Listing 12.2. Note that the interface *must* return a Boolean, since the rule in the Decision block expects this return value (the `ValidateAddress` value specified in our Decision block above).

LISTING 12.2 Visual Basic 6.0 declaration for the `ValidateAddress` Function

```
Public Function ValidateAddress( ByVal Document as String, Status as Long) as
Boolean
```

The next component is the TPASender, which has several functions, the most important of which (at least to the customer) is sending the ticket. The `SendTicket` method (see Listing 12.3) is used to interface with an existing system for printing and mailing paper tickets as well as delivering electronic tickets. For demonstration purposes, however, our implementation just formats a simple email message based on information in the order document and sends it to the customer via SMTP.

Next, the `SendSuccess` and `SendFail` methods (Listing 12.3) return the appropriate status to the calling client in the form of a standard XML document. We could have accomplished this with BizTalk messaging as we did to send the order to the TPA, but we elected to take another approach and generate the new XML document entirely in code. This is a somewhat arbitrary choice, but it serves to illustrate an alternate technique that may be very useful in many circumstances. For example, a developer who is not yet versed in the intricacies of BizTalk Mapper and who is under a short deadline might prefer this technique because of its familiarity. One of the best reasons to use this technique, however, is to make use of an existing code base.

Both methods are identical in our implementation except for the status that is returned. The functions underlying these two methods construct a new XML DOM document after extracting some key information from the inbound order (such as the URL to send the status to). The status document is then posted to the destination URL using the server-side XMLHTTP object. Note that the status could also be sent through a BizTalk channel using the IInterchange interface, but a direct HTML Post is adequate for our needs since we do not need receipts and are not implementing any transactions for the transmission of the status.

NOTE

The interfaces shown in the listings are clearly interfaces to COM components and not to .NET assemblies. This is simply because BizTalk Server has not yet been updated to fully understand .NET assemblies. As a result, COM/.NET interoperability (see Chapter 9, "COM+ Integration") becomes a factor for the short term.

LISTING 12.3 Visual Basic 6.0 declaration for the SendSuccess, SendFail, and SendTicket Functions

```
Public Sub SendSuccess( Document as String)
Public Sub SendFail( Document as String)
Public Sub SendTicket( Document as String)
```

Creating the Component Ports

Now that the components have been created, we need to create the ports to attach them to our schedule. Since we have two components we will need two component ports to validate the customer address, send the tickets, and send appropriate status messages back to the trading partner (gasTIX in this case). Since the process for creating each port is identical, we'll briefly discuss the Component Binding Wizard in general. The following steps outline the process:

1. Name the port
2. Select the type of component instantiation. We'll select Static, which means that the XLANG schedule is responsible for creating component instances.
3. Next select the component to use. We'll be using registered components, so simply select the appropriate class for the list.
4. Select the interface that you want to use. (Note: This is only necessary if you have multiple interfaces, which is required to operate within MTS.)
5. The final dialog consists of several advanced options relating to security, state management, and transaction support. We won't be using any of these for the TPA, so we can just accept the defaults.

Once we have created both component ports we need to attach each method to the appropriate objects in the business process. We simply drag a connection from the business process object to the method we want on the component port and select a synchronous call. If the component has multiple methods we also select the method to use and we are done. Next, we will handle the mapping of the data.

Mapping the Data

Now associate the various pieces of data that are attached to the ports as shown in Figure 12.19. The mappings of the TPA are relatively simple; the XML document representing the ticket order is simply passed from port to port, so it is mapped to a string parameter in each component method. The only other piece of data—the Boolean that is returned from the address validator—is used by the decision block and discarded, so we don't need to do anything else with it. The data tab of the BizTalk Orchestration designer will be covered in more detail in the next section.

Looking at the TPA's logic has given us a quick overview of orchestration and given us a taste of integrating orchestration and messaging, but we did the bulk of the work in pre-existing COM+ components. This is one of the sweet spots for orchestration: workflow and integration of existing applications. We'll see more advanced features in upcoming sections, but it is clear how easy it is to move simple pieces of data between different applications or systems. Using BTS messaging to transform or augment data as it moves between systems can further enhance this ability. Now, we will get back to the gasTIX side and start tying up some loose ends.

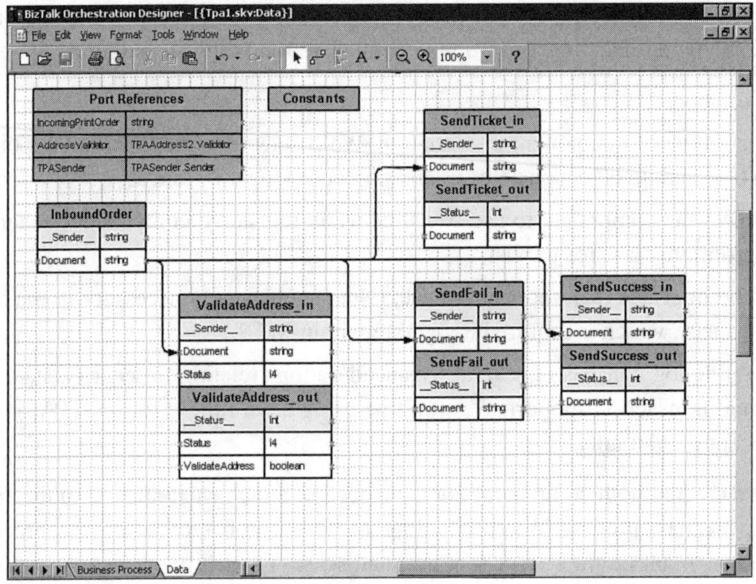

FIGURE 12.19
Data mapping diagram for the TPA schedule.

Delivery Receipts

Even though an advantage of BTS is that it allows us to be loosely coupled with our trading partner, we still need to know that they successfully received our message and if they were able to process it. There are several different levels of acknowledgement, some of which come with no expense when BTS is used. BTS also has built in retry functionality for messages lost in the mail.

Transport Acknowledgement and Retry

The first level of acknowledgement is that the message was successfully transported. Obviously, the mechanics of this vary by the transport used. For example, when using an Application Integration Component (AIC) transport, an error raised by the component will be caught by BTS and indicates failure to BTS. Our example uses an HTTP transport to send the message to the TPA. BTS expects a "200 OK" response from the TPA's web server. Any other response will be interpreted by BTS as a failure and the message will end up in the retry queue. Based on the port settings, future redelivery attempts will be made. If all attempts fail, the message will be placed in the suspended queue.

BTS Queues

At this point, we need to discuss the queues that BTS messaging uses. There are four queues implemented by BTS in SQL server. Each one is a separate table in the shared queue database. The queues are:

- The *work queue* contains documents that are currently being processed by BTS. Unless very large and/or complicated documents are being processed, they will never be seen in the queue because of the speed of processing.
- The *scheduled queue* contains items that have been processed and are awaiting transmission due to a service window constraint.
- The *retry queue* contains items that have failed transmission and are waiting for their retry window to open up. Also, documents awaiting reliable delivery responses are in this queue. The retry parameters are set in the channel that this message was submitted from. Both the retry count and interval can be set.
- The *suspended queue* contains items that have failed at some stage of processing. Items that failed during the transmission phase may be resubmitted.

All of these queues may be viewed and manually managed from the BizTalk Administration console.

TIP

It is a good idea to set up monitoring on the suspended queue. This is fairly straightforward since all of BTS's queues are implemented in SQL Server. The `IInterchange` object also provides a method for monitoring BTS queues. Since it is an automated monitoring, it allows failures to be dealt with in a timely manner—rather than waiting for the customer to inform us that there is a problem.

Receipts

Just because a message was successfully transported does not mean that it was seen by BTS. As previously discussed, this implementation of BTS does not directly receive any message (from a FTP or HTTP server). BTS has two methods to ensure that the remote server has seen our message.

For X12, EDIFACT and other messages with custom parsers, you can use receipts. A receipt in this context is the act of automatically requesting and delivering an acknowledgement message that can be associated (the BTS term is correlated) with the original request. Both the source and destination servers must be set up appropriately, but BTS does provide most of the tools needed to implement receipts. An oversimplified description of the logical steps is as follows:

- Specify the document definition for the receipt
- Set up the source channel. Specify that the channel expects receipts and set a timeout value.
- Set up the destination channel. Specify that it should generate a receipt and specify another channel that it will use to generate the receipt.
- The receipt channel on the destination generates a receipt and returns it to the source.
- Set up a receive mechanism to deliver the receipt to the BTS processing engine on the source.
- If a receipt is not returned to the source within the time limit, the previously described retry mechanism kicks in.

BTS Framework Reliable Delivery

Oddly enough, the receipt mechanism implemented in BTS does not work for XML messages. For this, BTS turns to the BizTalk Framework 2.0 messaging standard. The BizTalk Framework does not concern itself with the details of any particular business like the Rosettanet PIP's and other standards do. Rather the BizTalk Organization (largely driven by Microsoft) developed a framework that is concerned with reliable and standardized delivery of any type of business message (with the assumption that the business message is XML). This is largely accomplished by using SOAP based envelopes to wrap the messages.

TIP

You can find out more about the BizTalk Framework 2.0 and the BizTalk Organization at `www.biztalk.org`.

The element of the framework that we are concerned with is reliable delivery; BTS uses reliable delivery for XML messages in a manner similar to receipts for other formats of messages. However, setting up reliable delivery of XML messages is much easier. This will work with any BizTalk Framework 2.0 compatible server, but if BTS is used, there is minimal setup on the source and no setup required on the destination. This was one of the reasons we chose for the TPA ASP page to pass its message through BTS messaging.

The first step on the server is to set up a global property on the BizTalk group, via the BTS administration tool. On the general tab of the group's properties, there is an entry named Reliable Messaging Reply-to-URL. This is used to specify the address to which reliable delivery acknowledgements will be sent. Typically this is an ASP page that will forward the message to the BTS messaging engine, but other transports can be used as well.

Second, we will create an envelope in BTS messaging manager that has a type of Reliable. Finally for each message that we want a reliable delivery receipt for, we simply select the reliable envelope that we just created for our outbound port. BTS will wrap your message in the reliable delivery envelope and populate the receipt destination with the address that was specified in the group properties. That's it. When the destination BizTalk server gets the envelope, it will know to create a receipt and return it to the reply address.

This is the technique that was initially implemented for gasTIX. For our reply destination, we used a simple ASP page named StandardReceipt.ASP that ships with BTS in the SDK samples section. This ASP page simply reads the XML message sent and dumps it to the BTS messaging engine to be processed. The envelope type allows the BTS messaging engine to decide which channel to route it to. BTS has implicit channels defined to process reliable delivery messages. And finally, if the receipt is not returned, the retry cycle is initiated.

Limitations

Both receipts and reliable delivery are an improvement over simply knowing the message was delivered. But under certain circumstances these techniques still fall short. With reliable delivery, we know the BTS engine received the message but we don't know if processing was completed. This still requires a definitive acknowledgement from our trading partner's processing engine. In many business scenarios, confirmation information is expected as a return value, like an invoice number. We can use this "receipt" as part of an enhanced notification/retry strategy that we will explore in the next section.

Order Status Return and Enhanced Receipts

We previously explained how BTS provided several mechanisms for guaranteeing that the messages it sends are actually delivered. In real business scenarios, it is not sufficient to know that your trading partner's computer or message-processing engine received the message. That is a good start, but we need to confirm that they actually understood and processed the message. This will require some coordination (much like the development of the interface to send the message) and some development on both sides, but it is an essential part of business. In some scenarios (such as the Microsoft's purchase order example for BizTalk), several messages will go back and forth with a trading partner.

In our case, one simple receipt is enough. We will only get a notification after the TPA prints and ships the tickets. The TPA will send a message if it encounters an error processing an order. So the information we need is very simple: order number, order status, shipping date, and possibly a tracking number if the shipper provides one. We can use this information to update our database.

Traditional methods will handle this scenario just fine. We could set up an ASP page to process the acknowledgement; or we could invoke a COM+ or .NET component to do so. We could allow a web service to handle the acknowledgement directly, but we are assuming a standard solution from the TPA. We chose to use BTS orchestration to correlate and process the acknowledgments. This was probably overkill for our simple scenario, but it allowed us to demonstrate some features that will be extremely useful in more elaborate business situations.

So instead of our original processing diagram on the gasTIX side, we have something that looks like Figure 12.20. We are now including orchestration on the gasTIX side. BTS messaging hands the order to our orchestration schedule. Orchestration uses BTS messaging to send the order to the TPA. Finally, on the return trip, messaging hands the order back to the orchestration schedule, which will update the middle tier. This may seem like extra work, but we are using the complementary abilities of the messaging and orchestration engines to achieve the desired effect, as we'll discuss in this section.

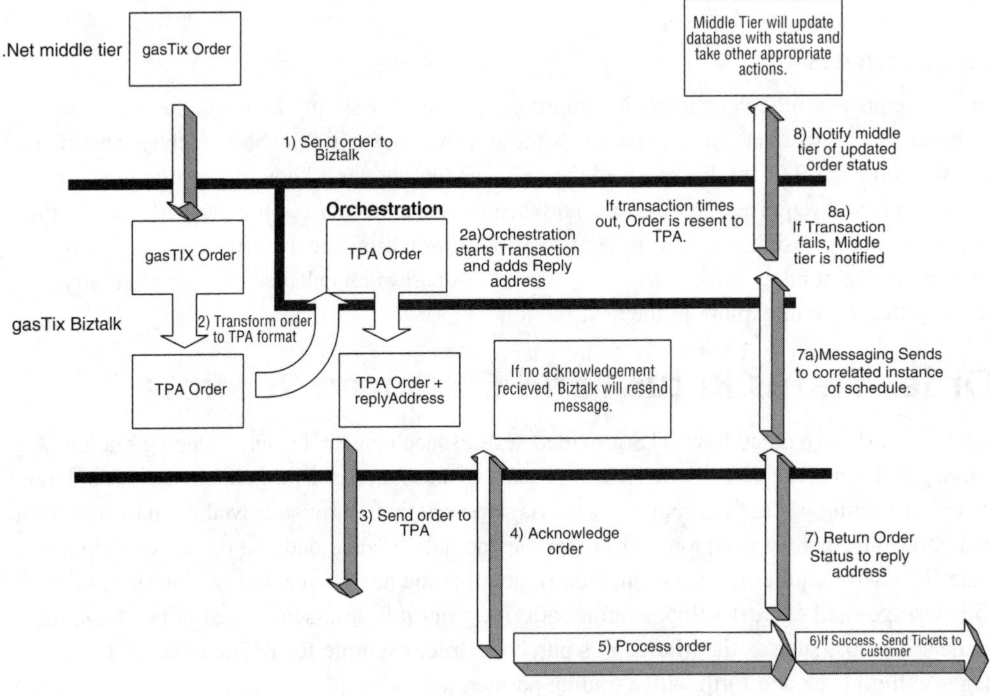

FIGURE 12.20

Updated diagram using orchestration to process enhanced receipts.

The BTS messaging engine does the original transformation of the gasTIX message into the TPA message. Then it hands this message into a BTS schedule that it kicks off. This is identical to how the TPA orchestration schedule was initiated. Now things get more complicated as we use two of the less obvious features of BTS orchestration: transactions and correlation. Transactions inside of an orchestration schedule are used to relate a set of actions. Correlation means that responses to messages sent from a schedule will be returned to the exact same schedule. We will discuss schedule transactions first and then see how we use them.

Transactions in Orchestration Schedules

Given the typical computing definition of transaction, it is fairly obvious that the purpose of grouping actions in a schedule is for the purpose of determining success or failure of that group as a whole. There are three types of transactions in schedules: short lived (DTC style), timed, and long-running. Short-lived transactions will be familiar to COM+ and database programmers. They have the four ACID attributes and upon failure, the DTC will rollback all actions that were initiated in the schedule.

CAUTION

Activities that are inherently non-transactional such as using BTS messaging to do an HTTP post are not affected by transactions that roll back.

Timed and long-running transactions lack the ability to use the DTC to roll back their activities. Timed transactions and short-lived transactions have the additional ability to set a time limit for success. Other than time limit failures, all three types fail for the same reasons: explicit failures (because the "Abort" shape is executed) or because of failure in transactional resources or other objects. Transactions provide the ability for retry counts and back off times, similar to the BTS messaging manager and ports. All three types also share the ability to take alternative action upon failure, which we will use in our application.

TIP

Orchestration schedules also have the ability to nest transactions. Only one level of transaction may be nested and the outer layer may not be short lived. Also if a nested transaction fails, an alternate action may be performed. This is called compensation and is mechanized similar to the action upon failure.

We chose to use a timed transaction to ensure that the TPA has processed our order. We've assumed that contractually the TPA will send out the tickets within a certain period of time. Timed transactions will work well for gasTIX because of this limit. If the TPA hasn't sent us a receipt within the acceptable time frame, we will resend the order message. If we do not receive a response within the expanded retry time, we will update the database (via the middle tier component which we will cover in the next section) and set the status of our print request to failed.

Here is a look at the orchestration schedule that we produced to fulfill this acknowledgement need. Figure 12.21 shows the business process view of our orchestration schedule. As explained earlier in the chapter, this view gives a logical flow of the message(s) through the system. The left side shows the decisions and actions that occur. These are commonly referred to as actions or shapes. The right side shows the entry and exit points from the schedule that the implementation methods chose. In the middle are the connections between the actions and the implementations called ports (not to be confused with BTS messaging ports). Inside of each port are one or more messages which represent the actual data traveling in and out of the system. The same messages are also represented in Figure 12.22; it details all of the messages that travel in and out of the schedule and how their data is related. However this view does not give any clues as to when the data is moved between messages. To get a complete view of the system, both views must be used. This data view will be more fully explained shortly.

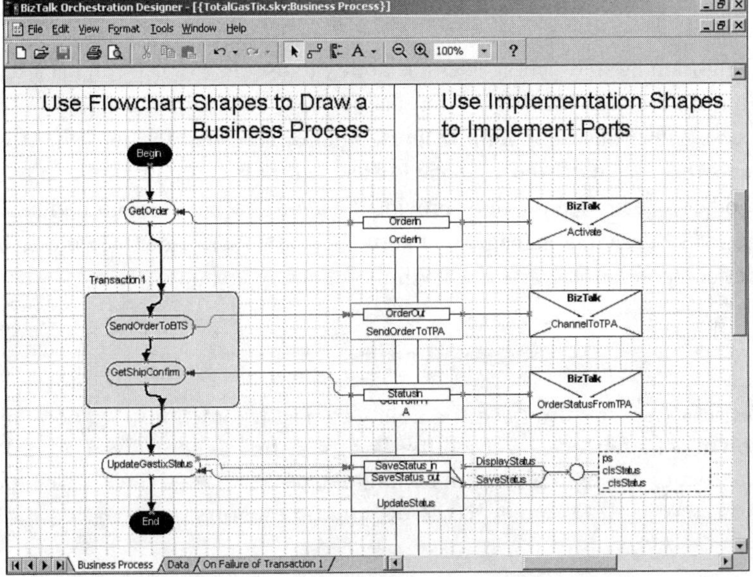

FIGURE 12.21

GasTIX Orchestration Business Process view.

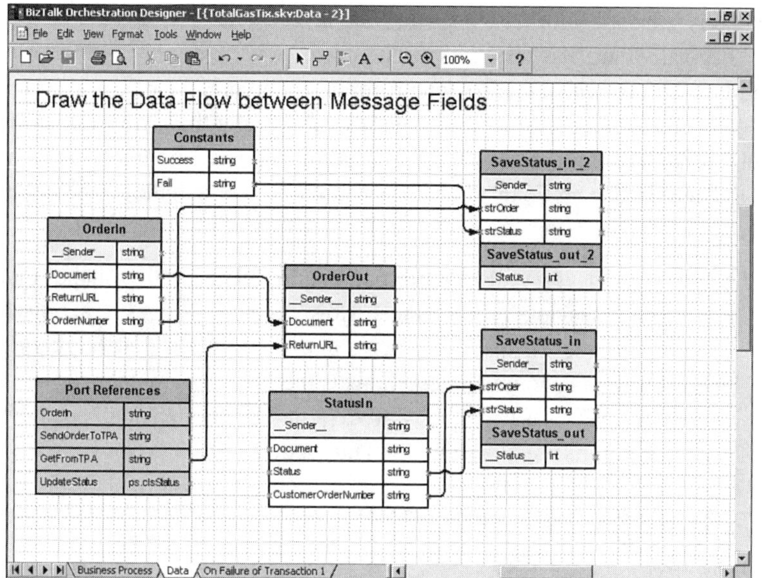

FIGURE 12.22

GasTIX Orchestration data view.

The overall flow of the orchestration schedule is very simple. The first step is to get the order into the schedule. Then it immediately enters the transaction shape named transaction 1. Inside of the transaction, the two actions are to send the order to the TPA and to receive the acknowledgement from the TPA. Both the outbound and inbound messages are routed through BTS messaging. Receiving the acknowledgement completes the transaction. The final action is to update the database with the information received from the TPA using a COM+ object. The success path is very easy, but what happens in the case where no acknowledgement is received? We will start by looking at the property page for Transaction 1 which is shown in Figure 12.23.

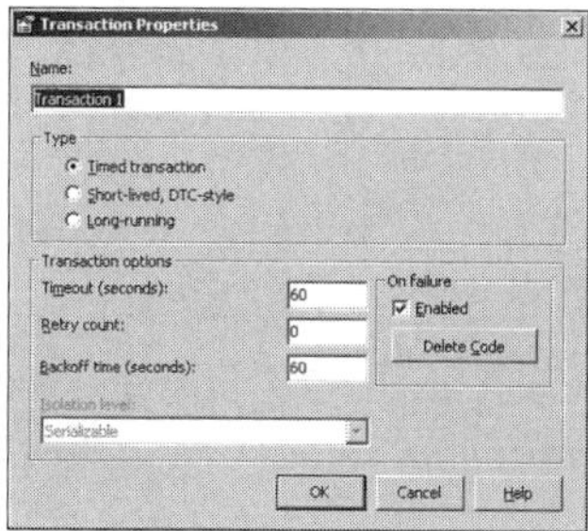

FIGURE 12.23

Property page for Transaction 1.

The page contains standard information such as the name of the transaction and the type. The timeout and retry values are also specified on this form. What we are most interested in is the creation of failure actions which is also done from this page in the On Failure frame. Initially the button is labeled Add Code. After selecting this and closing the form by clicking OK, another sheet will be created in the BizTalk Orchestration Designer named On Failure of Transaction 1. There is also an Enabled checkbox in the frame that allows the failure activities to be disabled.

Selecting the new failure sheet reveals a set of ports and implementation shapes that is identical to that on our original business process sheet. However no messages or actions are displayed. That is the left side of the business process diagram will be blank but the right side will be identical. This list of ports and implementations is the same for every sheet. We can either add new destinations for our messages if they are required or use existing ones. The same is true for messages. Our completed On failure of Transaction 1 sheet is shown in Figure 12.24.

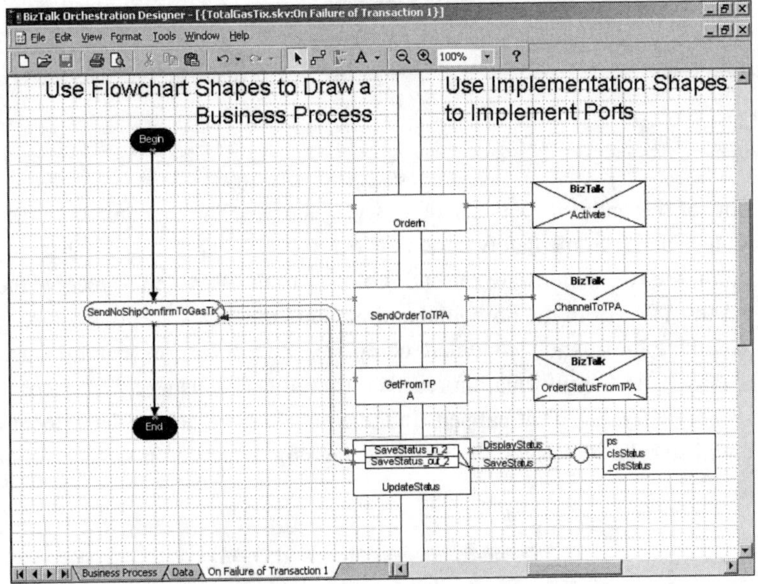

FIGURE 12.24
Orchestration Business process failure page.

Since we want to notify the middle tier of a failure, we will reference the same port to the middle tier object that the success path used. Only a single action that notifies the middle tier of the failure is required. When we connect the action to the port, a new message is created automatically because with COM+ components(and scripts), existing messages may not be reused. Each entry to the port is unique. We named this message "Save_Status_in_2". Now that we have integrated with the COM+ component, only one thing is missing; where do we set the parameters that we will pass to the middle tier? The answer is in the data view represented in Figure 12.22.

As stated earlier, each message on the data view corresponds to a message displayed inside of a port on the business process view. The messages in our schedule are as follows:

- SaveStatus is the message to the COM+ middle tier for the success path.
- SaveStatus2 is the message to the COM+ middle tier for the failure path.
- OrderIn is the message originally passed to the schedule by BTS messaging.
- OrderOut has the same structure as OrderIn but is updated by the schedule (more on this later) and sent to the TPA.
- StatusIn is the acknowledgement message that is received from the TPA.
- Constants is a self-explanatory, system message present on every data view.
- PortReferences is also a system message which will be explained in a later section.

Looking at the data view, we can see that the document for the OrderIn message is linked to the document of the OrderOut message. This means that the entire document is being copied. Looking at the business process view, we can see that this will happen every time the schedule is executed. When an acknowledgement is received from the TPA (our success case), we want to simply send what the TPA gives us. To do this, we created links from the StatusIn status field to the corresponding parameter in the SaveStatus message. Previously, we did the same thing with the order number.

In the case of transaction failure, we do not have any message from the TPA. So in our failure path, we link the order number from the OrderIn message to the order number of the SaveStatus_2 message. A constant, string value is linked to the status. We know the status is always Fail for this path. So when the schedule executes and hits the failure path, it will grab the constant string of Fail and the order number from the OrderIn message and call the COM+ component.

An arbitrary decision on our part (and an incorrect one upon further review) raises an interesting point. For the failure path, we grabbed the order number from the original message because we had no choice. For the success path, we grabbed the order number from the acknowledgement message instead. It appears to not matter since they will be the same; that assumption holds unless the TPA has a problem and sends an erroneous message. There should have been a check to see that the returned order number matched the sent order number.

This discussion brings out something that was implied before that should now be explicitly stated: in our sample application, the acknowledgement message returns to the exact same orchestration schedule that sent the order (i.e the message and the acknowledgement are correlated). If this did not happen, we could not use orchestration transactions to wait for the corresponding acknowledgements. Given the simplicity of gasTIX fulfillment requirements, there are easier methods we could have used to determine if the TPA processed an order and update the status. Use of correlation is not critical for this simplified example. However there are many cases, especially when integrating third party and legacy applications, where correlating to the correct schedule will be invaluable, so we will demonstrate this technique next.

Correlation

Once again, correlation is associating an inbound message as a response to a previously transmitted message. BTS Orchestration facilitates correlation by generating a unique address for messages to return to. The address is implemented by using a private queue that has a GUID in the name. In our example, we are using HTTP as our transport protocol to communicate with our trading partner. As the schedule is executing, it creates a return address and inserts it in the outbound message. The return address is an URL to send the acknowledgement. The URL has two parameters in the query string: the unique queue name and the BTS channel that will return the acknowledgement back to the schedule. Since the queue name is unique for each instance of the schedule, it must be set by the schedule rather than hard coded. This is why the return address is set by the schedule. An example of a generated return address is:

```
HTTP://gastixsql.gasullivan.net/receiveresponse.asp
?channel=orderstatusfromtpa&;
qpath=gastixsql.gasullivan.net\private$\orderstatusfromtpa{2ef8c2ed-8a67-4670-
9837-c80c7f401873}
```

All three elements of the return address (two query string parameters and the URL) can be found by looking at the properties of the BTS messaging implementation shape named OrderStatusfromTPA; this is where the schedule receives the TPA's acknowledgement message. The property page of this shape is actually the BizTalk messaging binding wizard. The name is displayed on the first page, while the second page displays the communication direction as shown in Figure 12.25. Since we are setting properties for acknowledgement, the schedule will receive a message. There is, however, a cryptic message on this tab which clouds things a little. The message states that "This wizard only enables receive through HTTP URLs. For all other URLs use a message queue in between BizTalk messaging and the schedule." The confusion arises from the reference to HTTP URLs when we are setting up the schedule to get a message from BTS. The reason for this will become clear later in this section.

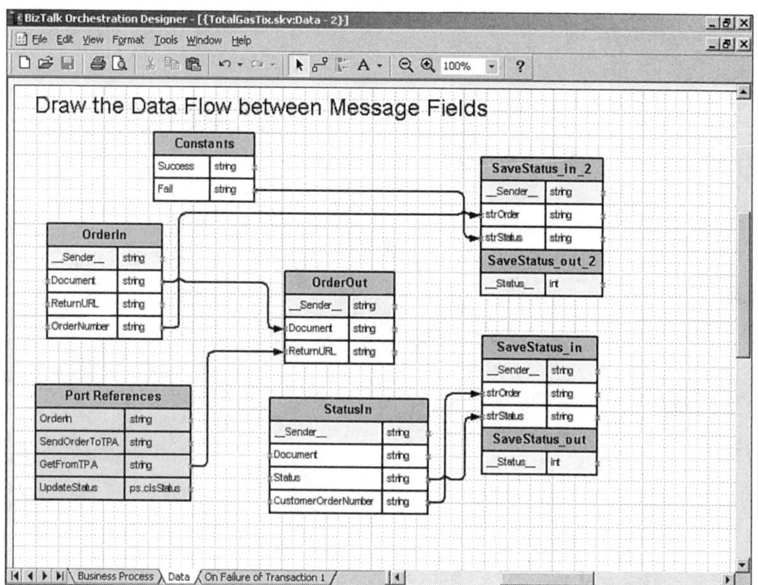

FIGURE 12.25

BizTalk Messaging Binding Wizard pg2—Communication Direction.

The third page has the XLANG schedule activation information as shown in Figure 12.26. The question asked is: "Should BTS messaging create a new schedule?" We have selected "yes" previously in launching both the gasTIX and TPA schedules. But this time since we want to re-enter the same schedule, we'll select no instead. The final page is channel information that is shown in Figure 12.27. Here we specify the BTS messaging Channel Name that is "OrderStatusFromTPA". This tab also provides a text box to enter an HTTP URL address where the BizTalk messaging service receives documents. For our example we have used `gastixsql.gasullivan.net/ReceiveResponse.asp`. We can now see where the URL and the channel in the reply address come from. The final element of the reply address is not shown, but it is implicitly generated because of our selections of receive and activation of new schedule set to "no". This forces a uniquely named queue to be created for each instance of the schedule. So we know where all of the elements of the return address come from, but the question remains: how do they get into the outbound order message OrderOut?

The answer is again on the data view. Notice in Figure 12.22 that the GetFromTPA section of the "Port References" message is linked to the ReturnURL of the "OrderOut" message. When the schedule is executed, the return address is dynamically generated and copied to the ReturnURL. Previously we skipped over the Port References message but we can now see that, in this instance, it can be used to provide a reference to a port allowing it to be accessed externally.

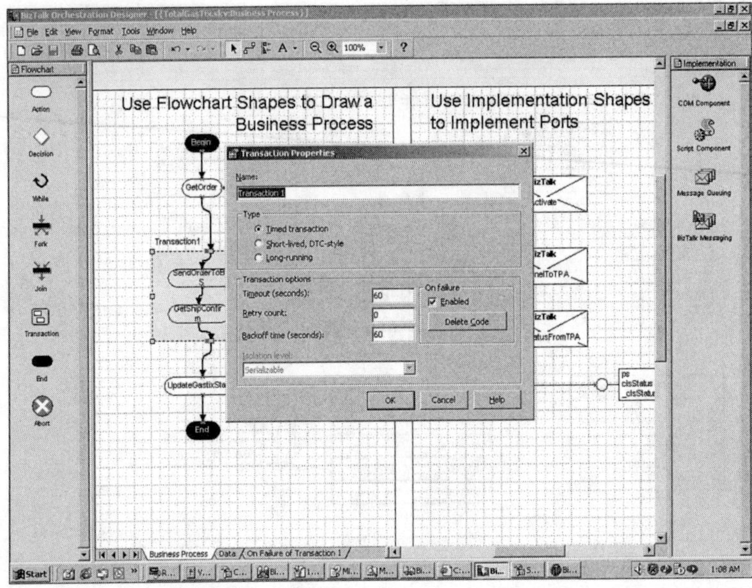

FIGURE 12.26

BizTalk Messaging Binding Wizard page 3—XLANG Schedule Activation Information.

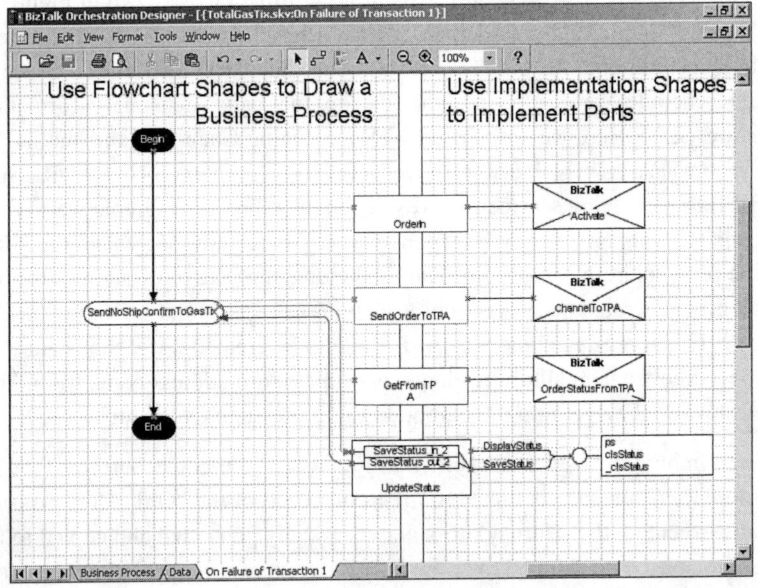

FIGURE 12.27

BizTalk Messaging Binding Wizard page 4—Channel Information.

NOTE

Port references can also receive data, which would make them dynamic. For example a queue name or a pointer to an instantiated COM+ object could be passed in.

The other pieces of the puzzle that make correlation work are found outside of the orchestration schedule. The first is the actual ASP page that is the target of the reply to URL. Remember that this was specified on the properties dialog of the `OrderStatusFromTPA` object in the schedule. This ASP page ships with the BTS SDK and can be found under the SDK at SDK\messaging samples\receive scripts\receiveresponse.asp. The ASP page uses the query string parameters to determine both the channel name and the queue name to use as shown below:

```
queuepath = Request.QueryString("qpath")
queuepath = "queue://Direct=OS:" & queuepath
channelname = Request.QueryString("channel")
```

Notice that the transport type and queue routing type are appended to the queue name. Next it extracts the message body from the body of the `response` object. Then using the IInterchange object, it submits the message to BTS messaging using the following line

```
call interchange.submit (4,PostedDocument,,,,,queuepath,channelname).
```

Only four parameters are filled in. The first parameter is the openness type, which indicates the openness type of the BTS messaging port. Openness is a concept that indicates if a message can be sent or received from any location or only from a specified location. The value of `4` corresponds to a constant BIZTALK_OPENNESS_TYPE_DESTINATION. This simply means that the associated messaging port has no specific destination.

The second parameter is the `posted document`. It contains the actual message body that we've received, in this case the acknowledgement message from the TPA. The third parameter is the `destination ID`. Since the openness type was specified as destination open, this parameter is filled in to indicate the actual address where BTS messaging should send the message. Here we've filled in the queue path that was created earlier. This value was originally derived from the properties of the schedule's receive port.

NOTE

The `destination ID` field has alternate uses depending on the value of the openness type. In can be used in conjunction with the preceding parameter, destination qualifier, to select a destination organization.

The final parameter is the `channel name`. This specifies the channel that the message is submitted to. Again in our case, this is again a value that is originally derived from the properties of the schedule's receive port.

So as the ASP page submits the document to BTS messaging, we have almost made the round trip. For our example, the channel does no mapping; we chose to use the TPA's acknowledgement format directly. Therefore the message goes to the port that will submit the message back to the originating schedule.

The port is tied to a BTS application, which we have seen allows us to interact with schedules. Looking at the properties of the messaging port, the second tab displays the destination application. In previous examples we have selected a new XLANG schedule. This time we will select a running XLANG schedule. It may be unclear how BTS will invoke a schedule because no information is provided here, not even the schedule name. We will assume for the moment that this does send the message back to the appropriate schedule and more precisely to the exact instance of the schedule that sent the request. Finally, the acknowledgement ends up back in the schedule that can inform the middle tier of the order status. But how does this work when only scattered pieces of seemingly unrelated information are provided?

We will start with what appears to go on under the covers and tie this back to the original overview. For all the talk of HTTP transports in the schedule setup, the bottom line is the BTS messaging communicates with a running schedule via a message queue. In orchestration schedules, message queue implementation shapes can be explicitly created or can be dynamic—that is, they always generate a new queue for each instance of the schedule. They do this by appending a GUID to the queue name. When you specify a BizTalk implementation shape to receive a message into an existing schedule, the same thing is done implicitly. This is why a queue name is handed out as part of the return address from the port description.

On the return trip the ASP page does not do anything special either. It simply uses the IInterchange submit method to invoke BTS messaging with an open dynamic destination. When we look at the property page of the messaging port that targets a running XLANG schedule, it gives us no clues as to how BTS messaging will communicate with the schedule, but again implicit work is being done. Behind the scenes, the transport used is MSMQ, and the destination was defined to BTS messaging by the Destination ID parameter. And this was initially supplied by our original schedule's port definition.

So all the mystery can be summed up like this: when you want to return to an existing correlated schedule, a uniquely named message queue is created and the name is handed out by the schedule. Then the returning BTS messaging port (in conjunction with the ASP page) is set up to write back into an open destination—that same message queue that was handed out. The fact that unique user interfaces are provided for this case and the available documentation is subtle at best makes this topic rather confusing—when it is actually rather straightforward.

TIP

Hints were dropped in the preceding explanation that BTS messaging is not the only way to correlate to a running instance of a schedule. The only critical element is that a message queue implementation shape with dynamic queue names be used. Then this queue path name can be handed out. After execution flow leaves the schedule, the only important thing is that the return message ends up back in the queue (properly formatted and with the correct message name, of course).

Implementation Choices

After a rather roundabout trip, we are able to verify that acknowledgements come back in time or that we have updated our order status in the database to the contrary. Was this the best way to achieve this objective? Probably not. All of this effort could have been accomplished with a simple set of logic that scanned our database periodically looking for orders without acknowledgements. It could have resubmitted an overdue message to BizTalk again and mark those that have passed some maximum time limit to failed. Both this process and our schedule could have taken other actions besides simply updating status. The orchestration implementation may have been better suited to handle additional workflow tasks that could involve customer service or IT departments in trying to trouble-shoot the failed messages. This orchestration solution, however, also comes at a higher resource cost.

All of these instances of the schedules hang around until they have completed a path. BTS does have a solution for this called hydration. Essentially, schedules that meet certain criteria and have been idle for a while will be dehydrated—their state saved and stored to a SQL server database. When the appropriate request comes in, they are rehydrated—pulled from the database, restored to their prior state and executed where they left off. This eases the resource load as all of the schedules do not have to be active at the same time. However there are still potentially a large number of schedules active at one time. We have not performed resource testing to gauge the impact—but it will definitely be more than a simple database routine run periodically. Again, more complicated scenarios will clearly show benefits of using this scheme over simpler implementations.

Updating Order Status

The last section of this chapter deals with actually updating the status of the order in the database. We could invoke a Visual Studio 6 component to update the database, but that is not the topic of this book. We cannot directly invoke a .NET component because, as we have previously noted, the messaging and orchestration engines only recognize COM+ components at this point in time. So the choices that are left are to make a .NET component look like a

COM+ component or to directly invoke the web service with a SOAP message. We selected the easiest path and placed a COM+ wrapper around a .NET component. A better reason for this approach is that we are on the same network as the middle tier, so there is no need to actually incur the overhead of using a web service. Traditionally DCOM would be used to fit this need but .NET introduces a new technique called remoting. Similar to DCOM, this allows execution of an assembly to take place on a remote server. For more information on remoting, see Chapter 13 ".NET Remoting."

NOTE

BizTalk Server 2000 is still a maturing product but there are still several good resources available:

- The included help system is actually very good.
- The Official Microsoft site at `www.microsoft.com/biztalk` has a number of white papers and technical articles
- The Microsoft public news groups at `msnews.Microsoft.com` have several good discussions on BizTalk. Paths include `Microsoft.public.biztalk.general`, `Microsoft.public.biztalk.orchestration`, and `Microsoft.public.biztalk.setup`
- There are a number of BizTalk articles and tutorials on the TopXML.com network. This is located at `www.vbxml.com/b2b/`.

From Here

In reviewing the implementation of our fulfillment process, we have seen many different techniques. We have made heavy use both of BizTalk's messaging and scheduling engines. The features and their setup are not always so clear, but their power and flexibility are. For a first generation product, BizTalk is really quite good. It will undoubtedly become an invaluable tool for integrating with trading partners—both internal and external. It will also prove its worth in orchestrating work flow and tying legacy and forward leaning applications together into smoothly flowing process. Again, it may seem easier to lean on existing methods for performing all of these tasks that BTS is performing, but once a minimal level of comfort is reached with the product, it will be faster and easier to use BTS. It will become an essential tool in every development shop's bag of tricks.

To read a more detailed discussion of Remoting in .NET, see Chapter 13.

Chapter 3, "Enabling Inter-Application Communication," discusses the various ways in which distributed .NET systems pass data.

.NET Remoting

By Eric Brown and John Pickett

CHAPTER

13

IN THIS CHAPTER

- Application Domains 396
- Remotable Versus Non-Remotable Objects 397
- Channels 400
- Serializing Messages 401
- Remoting Configuration Options 402
- Hosting a Remote Object 403
- Consuming a Remote Object 406
- Activation and Lifetime Control 408
- From Here 410

One area of .NET that has introduced significant changes from the Windows DNA world is the concept of *remoting*. You can use .NET Remoting to enable different applications to communicate with one another, whether those applications reside on the same computer, on different computers in the same local area network, or across the world in very different networks. The remoting infrastructure abstracts the complexities of interprocess communication.

Remoting is similar to Web services in some ways, but remoting is much more extensible. While XML Web services allow for high-level access to objects via SOAP, remoting allows for low-level control over the actual communication. The remoting infrastructure is more extensible than XML Web services because it allows developers to choose the protocol and format for message transport, or to build their own protocols and formatters. Using remoting, developers can intervene nearly at any stage within the communication cycle.

In this chapter we discuss remoting by covering some key concepts, including: application domains, remotable objects, channels, and serialization. We then discuss how to configure applications for remoting and show how to construct a host and client for the gasTIX AddressValidationService. Finally, we cover the concept of activation and lifetime control.

Application Domains

A .NET application is defined by one or more assemblies that run inside an Application Domain, or AppDomain. An assembly is essentially a collection of types represented as an executable (.exe) or a dynamic link library (.dll) file that share a common security and version boundary. It is a fundamental building block of all .NET applications.

Typically operating systems and runtime environments provide some sort of application isolation. AppDomains provide a way to isolate assemblies from others in the same operating system process as well as those loaded in different processes. The isolation of .NET assemblies allows for improved scalability, secure applications, and better fail-over capabilities.

By definition, all .NET application is type-safe. This allows assemblies to be grouped together along specific security policies, configuration settings, and runtime behavior. These characteristics define the boundary of an AppDomain.

NOTE

A *type* is a classification of similar categories or variables which share the same data and behavior. It can represent a class, interface, array, enum, or integral types such as integer, long, or decimal. The common type system provided by the .NET framework enables cross-language integration and a type-safe environment.

An AppDomain can be thought of as a “logical process.” Windows OS processes can contain more than one AppDomain with the same isolation level as if the multiple AppDomains are in separate processes. The AppDomains do not share information, such as global variables, static functions, etc. This isolation extends to type discovery. A type can discover the other types in its AppDomain and call them directly; however, it cannot discover types outside its AppDomain.

.NET remoting is the way in which AppDomains communicate with each other. By using remoting, an object in one AppDomain can access an object in another AppDomain. Let’s take a detailed look at how remote objects are called.

Remotable Versus Non-Remotable Objects

Since types are not shared across AppDomains, .NET remoting enables an object to be marshaled from one AppDomain to another AppDomain. In this way, an object within specific AppDomains can expose its functionality to other objects outside its own AppDomain.

.NET remoting draws a distinction between objects within an AppDomain. An object that can only be accessed by other objects within its AppDomain is said to be non-remotable. The functionality provided by the object is only available from within its AppDomain. An object that can be accessed from within its AppDomain and by other objects outside its AppDomain is said to be remotable. There are two different types of remotable objects: Marshal-By-Value and Marshal-By-Reference.

Marshal-By-Value

A remotable object whose instance data is copied from one AppDomain to another is considered a Marshal-By-Value (MBV) object. When an MBV object is requested from a remote AppDomain, .NET remoting creates a new instance of the remote object. The value or current state of the object is then copied back to the calling AppDomain where a new local instance is created. Any subsequent call to the object is handled by the local instance of the object. In order for an object to be copied, the .NET remoting must know how to serialize the object, i.e. write the current state of an object to a form that can be transported to another AppDomain. By adorning an object with the `Serializable` attribute as seen in Listing 13.1, the system will serialize the object state automatically. An object can also control its own serialization by implementing the `ISerializable` interface.

LISTING 13.1 Creating a Marshal-By-Value Object

```
 [Serializable]
public class GASException : ApplicationException
{
```

LISTING 13.1 Continued

```
    private GASErrors _errorList = null;
    public GASException(GASErrors errorList)
    {
        errorList = errorList;
    }
    /// <summary>
    /// Property ErrorList returns the error list from the Exception
    /// </summary>
    public GASErrors ErrorList
    {
        get
        {
            return _errorList;
        }
    }
}
```

CAUTION

Care should be taken when determining which objects are suitable to be marshaled-by-value. It is not good practice to declare large objects as marshal-by-value, or objects that require few round trips across a network which should be declared as marshal-by-reference.

NOTE

Once an object is marshaled-by-value, its state is never returned to the originating AppDomain. Any changes to the state of the object in the calling AppDomain are not communicated back to the source AppDomain. The object, and hence its state, can be returned to the originating AppDomain on a subsequent method call.

Marshal-By-Reference

The second type of remotable object is a Marshal-By-Reference (MBR) object. This type of object is not copied to the caller, but exists in a remote AppDomain. When a client requests a new instance of a MBR object, a proxy is created in the local AppDomain and a reference to that proxy is returned to the caller. When the client makes a call to the proxy, .NET remoting forwards the call to the actual object in the remote AppDomain.

An object is considered marshal-by-reference if it is derived from System.MarshalByRefObject or one of its children as shown in Listing 13.2. The `AddressValidation` object (Listing 13.2) is used by the gasTIX system to validate addresses. This object runs on a physically separate machine than the gasTIX site. Since it is desired to run this object on this separate machine, it must be an MBR. MBR objects are very useful when the state and functionality of the object should stay in the originating AppDomain, such as a database connection, file handle, or another dependent application running on the same machine.

LISTING 13.2 AddressValidation Marshal-By-Ref Class

```
using System;
public class AddressValidation : System.Web.Services.WebService
{
    public AddressValidation()
    {
        //CODEGEN: This call is required by the ASP.NET Web services Designer
        InitializeComponent();
    }

    /// <summary>
    /// Validate the passed-in address using default connection string.
    /// </summary>
    [WebMethod]
    public string ValidateAddress(string addressLine1, string addressLine2,
    string addressLine3, string city, string region, string postalCode, string
    country)
    {
        . . .
    }

    /// <summary>
    /// Lookup address in the database
    /// </summary>
    private void LookupAddress(string connectionString, string addressLine1,
    string addressLine2, string addressLine3, string city, string region,
    string postalCode, string country, Address addressData)
    {
        . . .
    }

}
```

Channels

A channel is used to send messages across remoting boundaries. Remoting boundaries occur between AppDomains, processes, or machines. A channel's primary responsibility is to convert messages to and from specific protocols. A channel listens on an endpoint for inbound messages to be processed or outbound messages to forward to another endpoint, or both. This design allows you to plug any channel, using a wide range of protocols, into the remoting framework.

When a client invokes a method on a remote object, the call information, such as parameters and other metadata, are transported to the remote object through a channel. After the remote object has completed the request, the results are returned to the caller in the same way (see Figure 13.1).

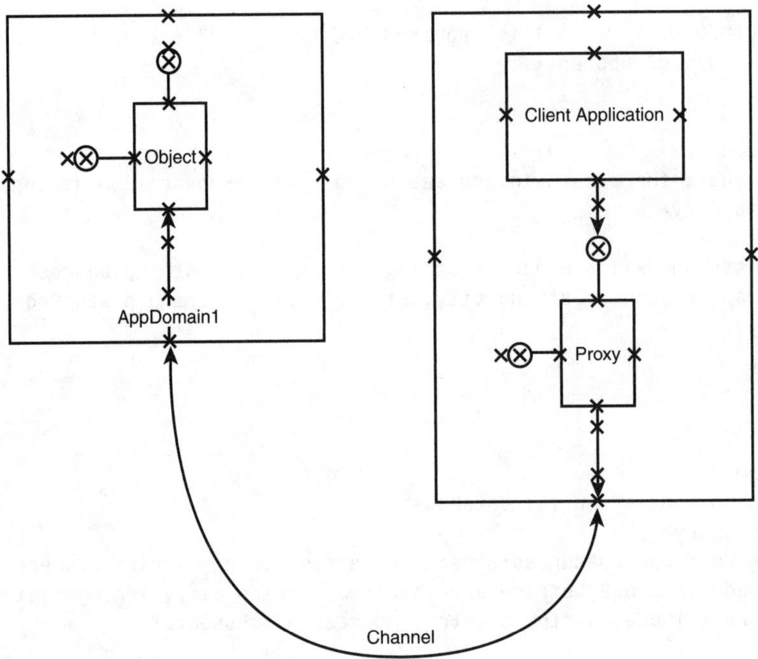

FIGURE 13.1
Communication using a channel across an AppDomain boundary.

All channel objects implement the `IChannel` interface. The `IChannel` interface provides a means to get information about a channel such as the name or priority. Channels designed to listen on an endpoint for a specific protocol implement the `IChannelReceiver` interface.

Channels designed to send messages to another endpoint implement the `IChannelSender` interface. Most channels included in the .NET framework implement both interfaces.

The server must register one or more channels before any remote objects can be used by a client. Channels are specific to an Application Domain and machine. For example, two AppDomains running on a single machine cannot register the same channel to listen on the same port. A client can select any channel provided by the server to communicate with a remote object. On the server, several remote objects can share a single channel. In order for a channel to handle multiple client requests concurrently, each connection is handled in its own thread.

The .NET framework includes two channels, the HttpChannel and the TcpChannel, to transmit messages using different protocols. The HTTPChannel class provides a way to communicate with a remote object using the SOAP protocol by default. Before a message is sent, it is formatted into XML and serialized for delivery. A binary format can also be used to serialize a message. In this case, the stream is transported using the HTTP protocol. The TcpChannel class provides the means to transmit a message using the TCP protocol. A binary formatter is used by default to serialize the message for transport. Message serialization and formatting are discussed in the following section.

Serializing Messages

As you have seen, messages that cross remoting boundaries are serialized before they are sent and de-serialized upon delivery. Serialization is the process of writing information into a transportable form.

.NET framework provides classes to serialize messages. The SoapFormatter class is used to serialize and deserialize messages in the SOAP format. The BinaryFormatter class is used to complete the same task in a binary format.

As described in the section "Marshal-By-Value" earlier in this chapter, an object adorned with the `Serializable` attribute is automatically serialized by the framework when requested by either the SoapFormatter or BinaryFormatter. An object can control its own serialization by implementing the `ISerializable` interface. At the time of serialization, the formatter calls the `GetObjectData` method which provides the data required to represent the remote object.

NOTE

You can think of the serialization classes as plug-ins for a channel. It is possible for an HttpChannel to use the BinaryFormatter class and a TcpChannel to use the SoapFormatter class.

Remoting Configuration Options

In the DCOM world, configuration for COM components occurred in the registry. The registry controlled where components were created by default, using a key that specified the name of the server on which to create a type. Unlike DCOM, which required that only the endpoint be specified, remoting requires that the protocol, formatter and endpoint be specified in order to remote a request to a type in another application domain. The .NET framework provides for two mechanisms to specify the remoting configuration on both the host and the client application: programmatic configuration and configuration files.

Programmatic configuration involves coding into your remoting host or client the appropriate configuration information. Listing 13.3 shows code that is used to programmatically configure a remoting host.

LISTING 13.3 Programmatic Remoting Configuration Code

```
HttpChannel hChannel = new HttpChannel(8095);
TcpChannel tChannel = new TcpChannel(8096);
ChannelServices.RegisterChannel(hChannel);
ChannelServices.RegisterChannel(tChannel);

RemotingConfiguration.RegisterWellKnownServiceType(
typeof(gasTIX.AddressValidation.AddressValidation), "AddressValidation",
WellKnownObjectMode.SingleCall);
```

The listing shows that the remoting host will accept remoting calls on both the TCP channel 8096 and HTTP channel 8095. The code registers those channels and registers the remoted typed with the endpoint `"AddressValidation"`.

Programmatic configuration may not be the most flexible way to configure your application. Changes in the remoting configuration, for example, using a different channel or using a separate formatter, would require recompilation and redeployment of both the remoting client and the remoting host. A better way to specify remoting configuration would be to load the configuration information from a file.

The use of Remoting Configuration files for both the remoting client and a remoting host allow for flexibility when it is uncertain which formatter and channel will be used for remoting. If the remoting channel needs to be changed, remoting configuration files allow for a configuration file to be deployed. No recompilation and redeployment of an application is necessary. In order to load the remoting configuration file, the following code must be placed in both the remoting client and remoting host:

```
RemotingConfiguration.Configure(filename);
```

Microsoft strongly recommends (but does not require) that configuration files be named app.exe.config in order to prevent naming collisions. This recommendation applies in all cases except when the remoting host or remoting client are run inside IIS's process space. In this case, remoting configuration information must be placed in the web.config file. Listing 13.4 is the equivalent remoting configuration to Listing 13.3 specified in a configuration file rather than in code.

LISTING 13.4 Remoting Configuration File

```
<configuration>
<system.runtime.remoting>
<application>
<service>
<wellknown mode="SingleCall" type="gasTIX.AddressValidation.AddressValidation",
AddressValidation" objectUri="AddressValidation" />
</service>
<channels>
<channel type="System.Runtime.Remoting.Channels.HTTP.HttpChannel,
System.Runtime.Remoting" port="8095" />
<channel type="System.Runtime.Remoting.Channels.TCP.TcpChannel,
System.Runtime.Remoting" port="8096" />
</channels>
</application>
</system.runtime.remoting>
</configuration>
```

The remoting configuration file requires the name of the assembly from which to load the type. The generic syntax to register a type in a remoting configuration file is:

```
Type="Namespace.Type","AssemblyName" objectUri="EndpointName"
```

If we need to change the HTTP channel number, simply change this file and redeploy the configuration file. There is no recompilation necessary. The use of remoting configuration files allows for a more transparent appearance for remoting than programmatic configuration; however, remember that both provide equivalent functionality.

Hosting a Remote Object

Like any .NET object, remote objects must be hosted within a process. The remoting framework provides three options for hosting your remote objects. These are:

- Any managed .exe or managed service
- Internet Information Server (IIS)
- .NET component services framework

It is important to point out that regardless of the mechanism used host a remote object, the remote object itself never knows what is hosting it, or how it is accessed via remoting, nor whether it is accessed via TCP or HTTP. Hosting a remote object inside each of the above processes requires a slightly different implementation.

Before we discuss the code required to host a remote object, we should first create a remote object that can be hosted. Listing 13.2 showed our marshal-by-ref AddressValidation class from the gasTIX application and that class is appropriate for the following discussions.

Hosting in a Managed .EXE or Managed Service

Building a managed .exe or managed Windows service to host a remote object is very straightforward. As stated before, gasTIX, remote calls to the `AddressValidation` object. This object is hosted in either a managed .exe or Windows service. The remoting configuration file shown in Listing 13.5 is the same in both the managed (custom) .exe and the Windows service. If the host process is a Windows service, the code to load the remoting configuration file would appear in the `OnStart` method. In a managed .exe, the code would be called somewhere during the .exe's startup code (possibly main).

LISTING 13.5 Remoting Configuration for AddressValidation Host

```
<configuration>
    <system.runtime.remoting>
        <application>
            <service>
                <wellknown mode="SingleCall" type=
                "gasTIX.AddressValidation.AddressValidation,
                gasTIX.AddressValidation"
                objectUri="AddressValidationService.soap" />
            </service>
            <channels>
                <channel type="System.Runtime.Remoting.Channels.TCP.TcpChannel,
                System.Runtime.Remoting" port="8086" />
            </channels>
        </application>
    </system.runtime.remoting>
</configuration>
```

The remoting host listens for requests on the TCP channel 8086, using the default binary formatter. The `"AddressValidationService.soap"` endpoint is registered and is mapped to the appropriate type in the gasTIX.AddressValidation assembly.

NOTE

The TCP channel using a binary formatter is nearly four times faster than an HTTP channel using the SOAP formatter. Given the performance increases of a TcpChannel, it should be used whenever the application requirements allow for either type of channel.

Listing 13.6 is the equivalent programmatic configuration to the remoting configuration file that would appear in the remote host.

LISTING 13.6 Programmatic Configuration for AddressValidation Managed EXE Host

```
TcpChannel tChannel = new TcpChannel(8086);
CannelServices.RegisterChannel(tChannel);

RemotingConfiguration.RegisterWellKnownServiceType(
typeof(gasTIX.AddressValidation.AddressValidation),
"AddressValidationService.soap", WellKnownObjectMode.SingleCall);
```

A custom .exe host allows for remoted components to be used over TCP and HTTP protocols simultaneously if desired. The custom .exe host also allows for the selection of a formatter (Binary, SOAP or other). For more information about selecting and using a formatter, see Chapter 6, "Implementing .NET Business Services."

Internet Information Server (IIS)

Now that we have seen how to host our object in a custom .exe, let's focus our attention on how to host this same object in IIS. The simplest way to host our object in IIS is to add the code from Listing 13.7 to the web.config file in the virtual directory in which we want our endpoint to reside, and then copy the .dll into the appropriate bin directory.

LISTING 13.7 Hosting `AddressValidation` in IIS Using Web.config

```
 <system.runtime.remoting>
  <application>
   <service>
    <wellknown mode="SingleCall"
type="gasTIX.AddressValidation.AddressValidation, gasTIX.AddressValidation"
objectUri="AddressValidationService.soap" />
   </service>
  </application>
 </system.runtime.remoting>
```

We also could have added the code from Listing 13.8 to the global.asax file to achieve the same results.

LISTING 13.8 Programmatic Configuration to Host AddressValidation in IIS

```
void Application_Start()
{
HttpChannel channel = new HttpChannel();
ChannelServices.RegisterChannel(channel);
RemotingConfiguration.RegisterWellKnownServiceType(typeof(
gasTIX.AddressValidation.AddressValidation),
"AddressValidationService.soap", WellKnownObjectMode.SingleCall);
}
```

When remote objects are hosted in IIS, IIS requires messages to be sent through an HttpChannel configured on whatever port the web site listens to. Therefore, there is no reason to specify a particular channel number. A client cannot send a message to a remote component hosted in IIS using a TcpChannel.

.NET Component Services Framework

Remoting objects can also be hosted in COM+. Remoting objects hosted by the .NET component services framework can take advantage of the services offered by COM+ including object pooling and transactions. Communication with these components occurs via COMInterop. In Visual Studio .NET, we set a reference to the component running in COM+, this creates a runtime callable wrapper that the .NET runtime uses to invoke method calls on the component.

Consuming a Remote Object

A client must be configured to know the endpoint, protocol and formatter to use in order to consume a remote object. As with the server, the client can be configured using code or a configuration file. In the case of gasTIX, the Business.Rule.OrderRules is the consumer of the remote Address validation service. The `AddressValidation` object is actually accessible as either a web service or through remoting. An object that is accessible through either remoting or a web service allows for flexibility in the future. The configuration file gasTIX uses to connect with can be seen in Listing 13.9. For more information on building and consuming XML Web services, see Chapters 6, and 11, "Purchasing A Ticket."

LISTING 13.9 Remoting Configuration file for `AddressValidationService` Client

```
<system.runtime.remoting>
    <application>
        <client url="tcp://localhost:8086">
```

LISTING 13.9 Continued

```
            <wellknown type= "gasTIX.AddressValidation.AddressValidation,
            gasTIX.AddressValidation"
            url="tcp://localhost:8086/AddressValidationService.soap" />
        </client>
        <channels>
            <channel type= "System.Runtime.Remoting.Channels.TCP.TcpChannel,
            System.Runtime.Remoting" />
        </channels>
    </application>
</system.runtime.remoting>
```

As stated in the "Remoting Configuration Options" section, Microsoft strongly suggests that the remoting configuration information go in a file called app.exe.config. Since the remoting client in the case of gasTIX runs in IIS's process space, the configuration information belongs in the web.config file.

The code required in the client to load this remoting configuration file is shown in Listing 13.10.

LISTING 13.10 Code for the Client Using a Remoting Configuration File

```
RemotingConfiguration.Configure(
AppDomain.CurrentDomain.SetupInformation.ConfigurationFile);
gasTIX.AddressValidation.AddressValidation addrValidation= new
gasTIX.AddressValidation.AddressValidation();

if (RemotingServices.IsTransparentProxy(addrValidation))
Console.WriteLine("TransparentProxy");
else
Console.WriteLine("Not a Transparent proxy");
```

If we had chosen to use programmatic configuration, the code required in the client would look like the code in Listing 13.11. One item to note is that although the client knows the channel, endpoint, and formatter to use, the client is not aware and does not require knowledge of what the host process is for the remote object.

LISTING 13.11 Remoting Configuration Code in the Client

```
ChannelServices.RegisterChannel(new HttpChannel());
AddressValidation.AddressValidation addrVal;
addrVal = (gasTIX.AddressValidation.AddressValidation)
Activator.GetObject(typeof(gasTIX.AddressValidation.AddressValidation),
```

LISTING 13.11 Continued

```
"http://localhost:8086/AddressValidationService.soap");
if (RemotingServices.IsTransparentProxy(addrVal))
{
Console.WriteLine("TransparentProxy");
}
else
Console.WriteLine("Not a Transparent proxy");
```

It is important to note the difference in the code between Listings 13.10 and 13.11. Listing 13.11 shows the use of `Activator.GetObject`, whereas Listing 13.10 uses the new operator to create the `AddressValidation` object. The appropriate question is: What is going on here? According to Microsoft, in order to use the new keyword, you must provide all the following about the remotable object before trying to create an instance:

- The type of activation required (Client or Server)
- Metadata describing the type
- Channel registered to handle requests for the type
- The URI (the path that comes after the protocol, the machine name, and any port information) that uniquely identifies a well-known object of that type.

We determine if the `addrVal` variable is a remote object by calling the `RemotingServices` `IsTransparentProxy` function. A *transparent proxy* is an object that forwards requests to the actual object through the remoting infrastructure. A transparent proxy has the interface and signature of the actual object.

It is important to know in our case if the object that we are dealing with is a proxy or the actual object. If our object requires access to database resources, creating an actual copy of the object in the client process rather than the server would cause the object to not function.

During deployment, we place a copy of the gasTIX.AddressValidation assembly on the local machine with the remoting client. When code requires a call to new, Microsoft purposely overloads the new operator. The runtime attempts to create a copy of the object using the remoting configuration information specified. If the runtime is unable to create the component remotely, the new operator will create an instance of the object in the local process space. If this has occurred, IsTransparentProxy will return `false` and the appropriate action can be taken.

Activation and Lifetime Control

When a caller requests a marshal-by-reference object, the remoting runtime must know when and how to create the object as well as how long the object is available to the caller. When designing and building marshal-by-reference components, it is important to understand two key concepts: activation and lifetime. These are discussed in the following sections.

Server Activation

An object whose lifetime is controlled by the server is considered server-activated. The object is only created when the caller invokes a method on the object, not when the caller creates the object. When the caller creates the object, only the proxy is constructed.

NOTE

An effect of this design is that only the default constructor is called when a server-activated object is initialized. Since the .NET remoting framework handles object creation, you cannot pass parameters during the construction of a server-activated object.

An object can be activated in two different modes on the server: Singleton and SingleCall. An object that has only one instance at any time is defined as a *Singleton*. A single object is created on the server. All client requests are forwarded to this instance. A `Singleton` object has a default lifetime or it can define its own lifetime. Depending on the lifetime of the object, a client will not always receive a reference to the same Singleton object. When the server creates one instance of the object per client request, the object is considered a `SingleCall` object. The lifetime of the instance is only the length of the client request. Each method invocation is serviced by a different object instance. The following code shows creating a server activated `SingleCall` object.

```
RemotingConfiguration.RegisterWellKnownServiceType(
typeof(MyRemotelyActivatedClass), "MyRemotelyActivatedClass",
WellKnownObjectMode.SingleCall);
```

This code would be placed inside the server in which MyRemotelyActivatedClass would be hosted. In order to create a Singleton, replace `WellKnownObjectMode.SingleCall` with `WellKnownObjectMode.Singleton`.

NOTE

`SingleCall` objects cannot hold state between multiple client requests since they exist only for the duration of a client request. In contract, `Singleton` objects can hold state since they stay alive between client requests.

Client Activation

Client-activated objects are those objects whose lifetime is controlled by the calling AppDomain. When the client creates a client-activated object, a round-trip is performed to create the new instance on the server, and the client proxy is returned. Once the remote object is created, it will only serve requests from the client reference until its lease expires.

To create a client-activated object, place the following code in the client that will consume the remote object:

```
RemoteObjectClass MyRemoteClass =
(RemoteObjectClass)Activator.CreateInstance(typeof(RemoteObjectClass),
"tcp://computername:8080/RemoteObjectApplicationName");
```

> **NOTE**
>
> Client-activated objects can hold state if the client instructs the remote object to stay alive.

Object Lifetimes

The lifetime of a client-activated or server-activated singleton object is controlled by its lifetime lease. When the client creates a remote object, it specifies how long the server should keep the object available, the lease time. The remote object contacts the client when the lease time has expired, and asks if it should stay available and for how long. If no client is available, an additional wait time can be specified before the remote object is recycled by the server application. This is in contrast to the DCOM method of object lifetime that used reference counts and the constant pinging between server and client to determine the availability of a remote object. Also, the development of remote objects is made easier than with DCOM since the object does not have to implement its own reference counting.

From Here

As we have seen, building remote components in .NET is very straightforward. We have seen that remote components can be hosted in IIS or in a custom exe or windows service. The client is unaware of exactly what process is hosting this service; the only thing the client must know is the port and formatter to use. A big advantage of choosing Remoting rather than Web services is that when using Web Service, we must use HttpChannel and the SOAP formatter. Using remoting, we can choose the protocol (HTTP, TCP, or Custom) and independently choose the formatter (SOAP, Binary, or Custom).

Testing and Deploying .NET Sites

In this last section we explore the necessity of debugging and tuning the performance of a .NET e-Business application prior to release. An entire chapter is dedicated to the issues surrounding deploying a .NET application. This section rounds out a complete discussion of the software development life cycle for a .NET e-Business application.

IN THIS PART

- **Chapter 14: Debugging a .NET Application 413**
- **Chapter 15: Performance Tuning in .NET 435**
- **Chapter 16: Deploying the Application 469**

Debugging a .NET Application

by John Pickett

CHAPTER

14

IN THIS CHAPTER

- .NET Debugging—The Basics 414
- Debugging an ASP.NET Web Application 423
- Exception Handling 427
- From Here 433

An essential element to delivering Enterprise Class applications with .NET is the ability to quickly and easily eliminate bugs. Once you have written your application and resolved any build errors, it is almost certain you will need to find and correct the logical errors that exist in your application.

In order to successfully resolve these issues, you must be able to inspect the state of your program at runtime. An effective debugger should allow you to break your application at any point during execution. Once stopped, you should be able to view and change variables or determine how the application reached its current state.

Visual Studio .NET provides an integrated debugger capable of providing the detailed information necessary to resolving these logical errors. A major enhancement to the Visual Studio debugger is cross-language debugging of application code written in Visual Basic .NET, C#, JScript, SQL, and managed extensions for C++. The ability to debug applications on the local machine or a remote machine is also a feature of the Visual Studio debugger.

This chapter describes in detail the Visual Studio .NET debugger. You will learn how to debug .NET applications in particular the gasTIX business components and the gasTIX web application. Also, several new features that aid in the debugging process are discussed. The conclusion of the chapter focuses on how the common language runtime manages exceptions. We will also discuss the fundamentals and best practices of exception handling.

.NET Debugging—The Basics

Application source code goes through two distinct steps before a user can run it. First, the source code is compiled to Microsoft Intermediate Language (MSIL) code using a .NET compiler. Then, at runtime, the MSIL code is compiled to native code. When you debug a .NET application, this process works in reverse. The debugger first maps the native code to the MSIL code. The MSIL code is then mapped back to the source code using the programmer's database (PDB) file. In order to debug an application, these two mappings must be available to the .NET runtime environment.

To accomplish the mapping between the source code and MSIL use the /debug:pdbonly compiler switch to create the PDB file. When building ASP.NET applications specify the `compilation debug="true"` in the computer or applications web.config file. The second mapping between the MSIL code and native code is accomplished by setting the `JITTracking` attribute in your assembly. By specifying the /debug compiler switch the PDB file is created and the `JITTracking` attribute are enabled. When using this compiler switch, a debugger can be attached to an application loaded outside of the debugger.

Once the required mappings exist, there are several means by which to debug your applications. You can use the integrated debugger with Visual Studio .NET or if you prefer, DbgClr, a GUI-based debugger. There is also a command line debugger, CorDBG, that is included in the .NET Framework SDK.

Debugging gasTIX

In general, Visual Studio .NET provides two approaches to debug applications. The first involves running the application within the debugger. The second requires you to attach the debugger to the running application. Both techniques require you to first compile the application.

TIP

Visual C++ allowed developers to attach the debugger to a running application; this is a new and useful feature available for applications written in VB .NET.

The follow steps summarize the general approach to debugging an application from within the Visual Studio debugger.

1. Open the Visual Studio solution.
2. Select the project file in the Solution Explorer.
3. From the **Project** menu, select **Properties**.
4. On the **Project Property** Pages, select **Configuration Properties**.
5. Select the **Build** option.
6. For a VB .NET project, select the **Define DEBUG constant** option under **Conditional compilation constants** as shown in Figure 14.1.
7. For a C# .NET project, ensure that that **DEBUG** is defined in the **Conditional Compilation Constants** under **Code Generation** as shown in Figure 14.2.
8. Compile the application.
9. Open the source code files you would like to debug.
10. Set break points by moving the cursor to the line of code you would like to break on and press **F9** or choose **New Breakpoint** from the **Debug** menu as shown in Figure 14.3.
11. Start the debugger by selecting **Start** from the **Debug** menu or press **F5**.

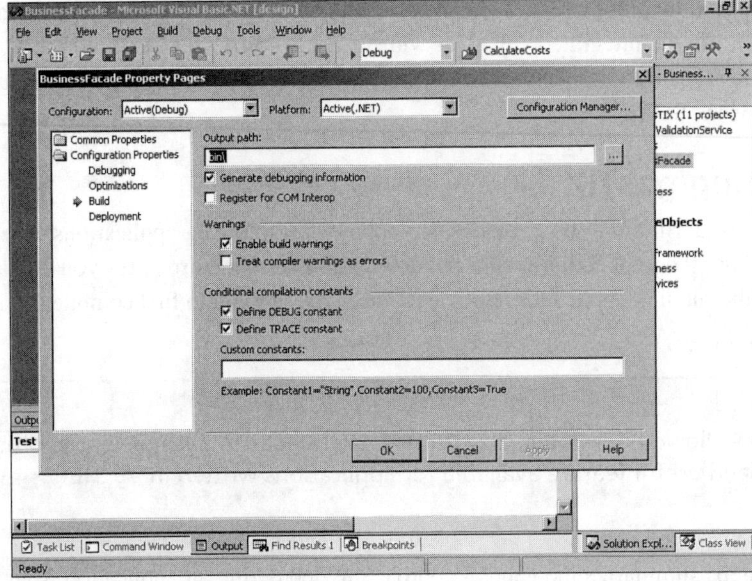

FIGURE 14.1
Define DEBUG constant for VB .NET project.

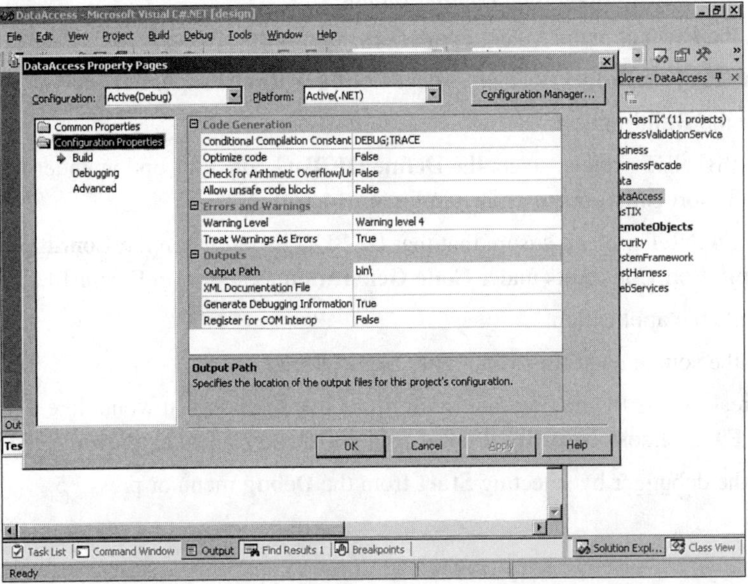

FIGURE 14.2
Define DEBUG constant for C# .NET project.

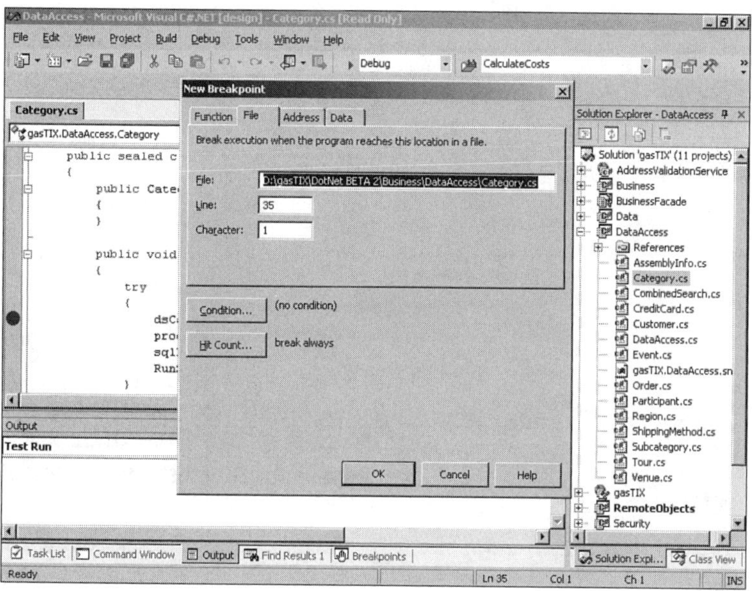

FIGURE 14.3
Setting a new breakpoint.

> **NOTE**
>
> Visual Studio saves breakpoint locations in the user settings of the project. They are available when the solution is reopened. Many times it is useful to save breakpoint locations when a solution is closed, especially if debugging an issue will continue at a later time.
>
> Breakpoints tell the debugger to pause, or break, the execution of an application. Once in break mode, you can inspect the current state of the application.

Figure 14.4 shows the gasTIX Business Services TestHarness application in the debugger after following the steps listed above.

Once an application is in break mode, several windows allow you to inspect the state of the program being debugged. In many cases it may be necessary to change the value of a variable. The Visual Studio debugger provides the Autos and Locals windows to view and modify the value of variables in the current context. The Call Stack window is also available. Other windows: Memory, Registers, Threads, and Modules enable you to get a detailed picture of the running application. Also, the Command window is available during a debugging session that is similar to the command window in previous versions of Visual Studio.

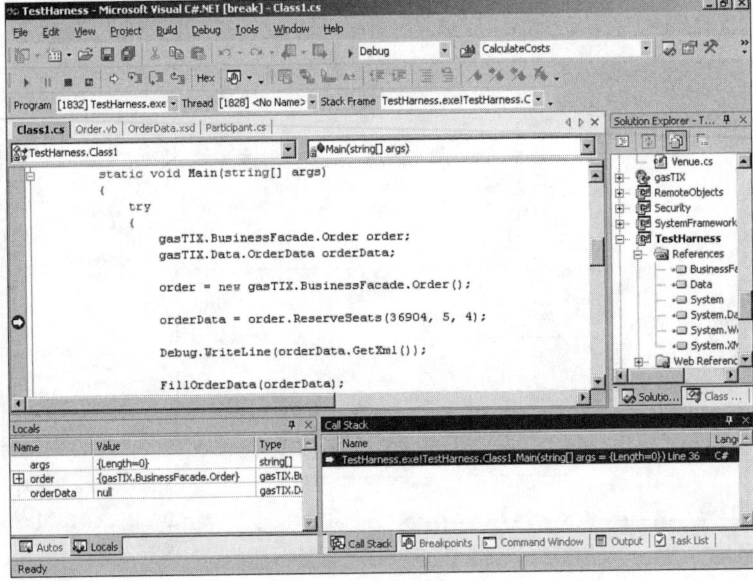

FIGURE 14.4
Debugging gasTIX.

Attaching to gasTIX Web

Many times it may not be possible to start an application in the debugger; for example, if you were attempting to debug an ISAPI DLL hosted by IIS or the application is running on a remote machine. Visual Studio provides a way to debug applications that are running outside the debugger. This second way to debug .NET applications is to attach the Visual Studio debugger to a running application.

The follows steps are used to attach the debugger to the gasTIX web application.

1. Open the gasTIX web solution.
2. Set break points.
3. From the **Debug** menu, select **Processes**.
4. Check Show system processes.
5. Select **aspnet_wp.exe** in the **Available Processes** list box as shown in Figure 14.5.
6. Click the **Attach button**.
7. In the **Attach to Process** dialog box, make sure the **Common Language Runtime** and **Native** options are selected in the **Choose the program types that you want to debug** list box as shown in Figure 14.6.

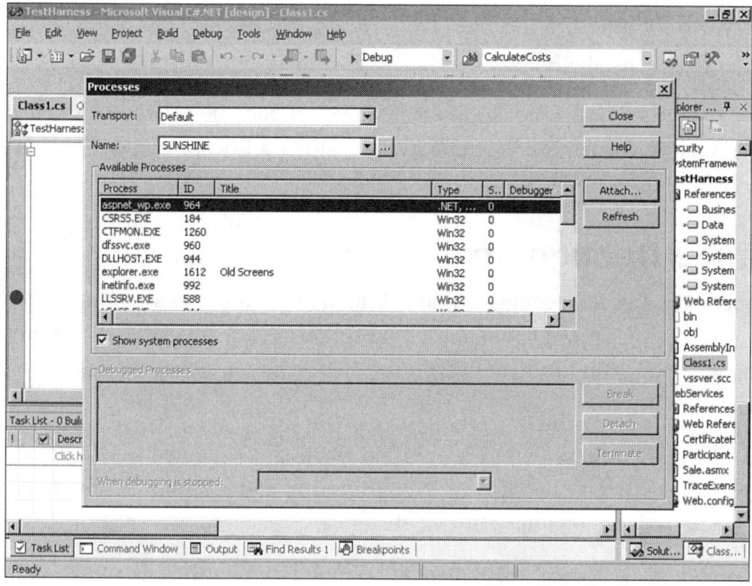

FIGURE 14.5

Processes dialog box.

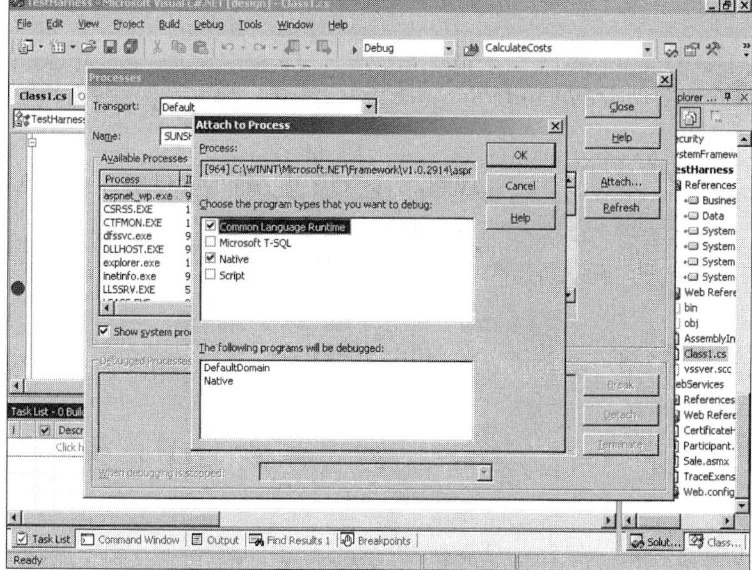

FIGURE 14.6

Attach to Process dialog box.

8. Click the **OK** button.
9. Close the **Processes** dialog box.

Once attached to a process, the breakpoints you have set become active. All the features for debugging from within Visual Studio, such as the Auto and Locals windows, are available to help you resolve issues with the application.

Just-In-Time Debugging

Starting an application in the debugger or attaching the debugger to a running application works well for resolving known application issues; however, many times it may not be feasible to always run an application inside the debugger. How can you debug an unknown exception when it occurs?

Just-In-Time debugging allows you to be notified when an unhandled exception occurs. The .NET runtime will break the execution of the application and present the option to begin a debugging session to determine the cause of the error.

When an unhandled exception is encountered, a dialog box like the one shown in Figure 14.7 is displayed. You now have the option to debug your application. You can debug with any running debugger or start a new instance of the debugger.

NOTE

If you choose to debug with a running instance or a new instance of Visual Studio, you will be asked to attach to the process that caused the exception.

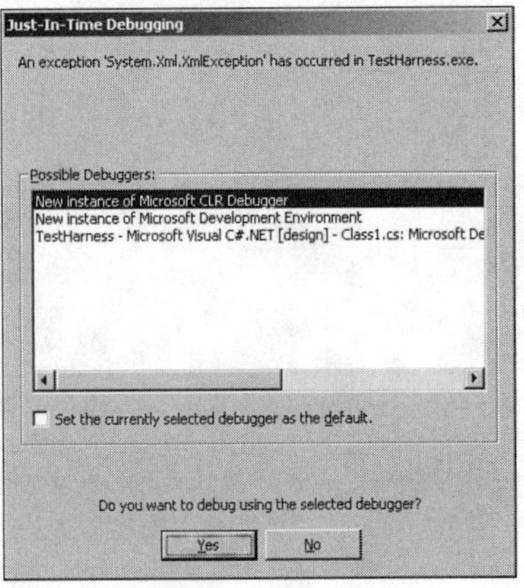

FIGURE 14.7
Just-In-Time Debugging dialog box.

Trace and Debug Classes

Stepping through each line of code in your application may not be the most efficient way to debug the application. There could be times when given a certain condition the application should go to break mode. Also, you might find it useful to log certain events that occur during normal program execution. The .NET framework provides two classes, `Trace` and `Debug`, in the `System.Diagnostics` namespace, to accomplish each of these tasks as well as other features to help you debug your application.

The `Trace` class provides a way to trace the execution of your code. The `Debug` class makes debugging your application easier. These two classes provide essentially the same functionality. The `Debug` class is available for any application that defines the Debug compiler option. The `Trace` class is available for any application that defines the Trace compiler option.

NOTE

The Trace compiler option can be set using Visual Studio in the same manner as the Debug compiler options from the **Project Settings|Configuration Properties|Build** option.

A `TraceListener` records the output for both classes. The `TraceListener` is an abstract class from which all listeners are derived. The follow listeners are also available in the `System.Diagnostics` namespace.

- The `DefaultTraceListener` provides the default listener that directs the output to the Windows system debugger using the `OutputDebugString` Windows API.
- The `EventLogTraceListener` provides a simple listener for directing tracing and debugging information to the Windows event log.
- The `TextWriterTraceListener` directs information to a `TextWriter` or to a `Stream`, such as the console or file.

The code in Listing 14.1 is used to trace the execution of the `gasTIX.BusinessFacade.Order` component `ReserveSeats` function. The function is called when the user has requested seats for an event, but before they enter the shipping and billing information. The output is directed to the `DefaultTraceListener` by default. Before each line of code, a message is written to the debug window.

LISTING 14.1 Function to ReserveSeats

```
Public Function ReserveSeats(ByVal eventId as Integer, ByVal sectionId as
Integer, ByVal numberSeats as Integer) as OrderData
    Dim returnValue as gasTIX.DataAccess.OrderData
    Dim orderRules as gasTIX.Business.Rules.OrderRules
    Dim orderDB as gasTIX.DataAccess.Order

    Trace.WriteLine("In ReserveSeats")

    Trace.WriteLine("Creating OrderRules")
    orderRules = new gasTIX.Business.Rules.OrderRules()

    Trace.WriteLine("Calling ValidateReserveSeats")
    orderRules.ValidateReserveSeats(eventId, sectionId, numberSeats)

    Trace.WriteLine("Creating DataAccess.Order")
    orderDB = new gasTIX.DataAccess.Order

    Trace.WriteLine("Calling ReserveSeats")
    orderDB.ReserveSeats(eventId, sectionId, numberSeats, returnValue)

    Trace.WriteLine("Done calling ReserveSeats")

    Trace.WriteLine( returnValue.GetXML() )

    return returnValue
End Function
```

The code in Listing 14.2 is an example of directing the debugging and tracing information to the Windows event log. First, a new `EventLog`, `newLog`, is created using the Windows Application log with gasTIX as the source. Next, a new `EventLogTraceListener` is initialized with `newLog`. The new listener is then added to the `Trace.Listeners` collection.

LISTING 14.2 Directing Debugging Output to the Windows Event Log

```
EventLog newLog = new EventLog("Application", ".", "gasTIX");
EventLogTraceListener newListener = new EventLogTraceListener(newLog);
Trace.Listeners.Add(newListener);
Trace.WriteLine("new event occurred");
```

Both classes, `Trace` and `Debug`, provide an `Assert` method that checks a condition and displays a message box is the condition evaluates to false. For example, when calculating the total cost of a purchase, we might want to ensure the shipping charges are not zero. The following code will display a dialog box like the one shown in Figure 14.8 if the value of the variable `shippingCharge` evaluates to zero.

```
decimal shippingCharge;
Trace.Assert( shippingCharge != 0, "shippingCharge is zero" );
```

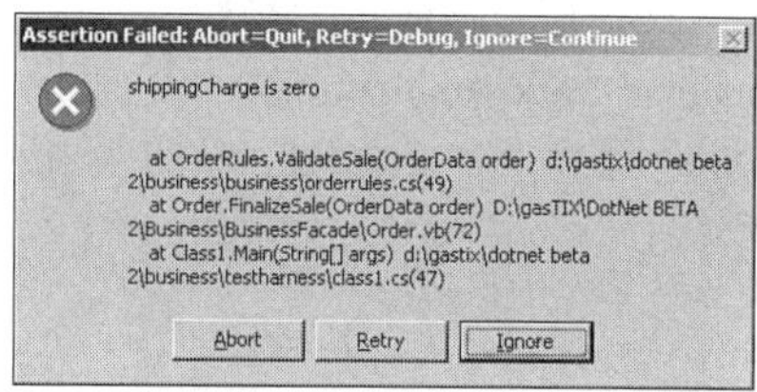

FIGURE 14.8
Assert dialog Box.

Debugging an ASP.NET Web Application

Debugging ASP.NET applications is accomplished in much the same way as any other .NET application. The features included with the Visual Studio integrated debugger are also available for debugging ASP.NET. The methods and features available for debugging ASP.NET applications are the same as any other .NET application. To enable debugging of an ASP.NET application, make sure the web.config file contains the following statements.

```
<configuration>
    <system.web>
        <compilation debug="true" />
    </system.web>
</configuration>
```

A debugging session can be started from within the Visual Studio .NET by following these steps.

1. Open the ASP.NET web Application.
2. Right click on an aspx file and select **Set as Start Page** to identify the first page requested.
3. From the **Debug** menu, select **Start**.

Instead, you can run the application outside the debugger and attach to the aspnet_wp.exe process as described in the previous section, "Attaching to gasTIX Web."

ASP.NET Tracing

An important new feature of the ASP.NET framework is tracing. Trace information, performance numbers, application and session state, server variables, query string collection, and trace messages are all available for inspection. Interpreting this information can aid you in understanding how the .NET framework processes a page.

Tracing information can be enabled at the application level or the page level. The following statements were added to the gasTIX web.config file to enable application level tracing.

```
<configuration>
      <system.web>
            <trace enabled="true" requestLimit="10" pageOutput="true"
      traceMode="SortByTime" />
   </system.web>
</configuration>
```

The trace information can be viewed by navigating to the trace viewer application, which is the trace.axd file located in the application root directory. In the case of gasTIX this is `http://localhost/gastix/trace.axd`. Each page request is listed in the trace viewer application as shown in Figure 14.9.

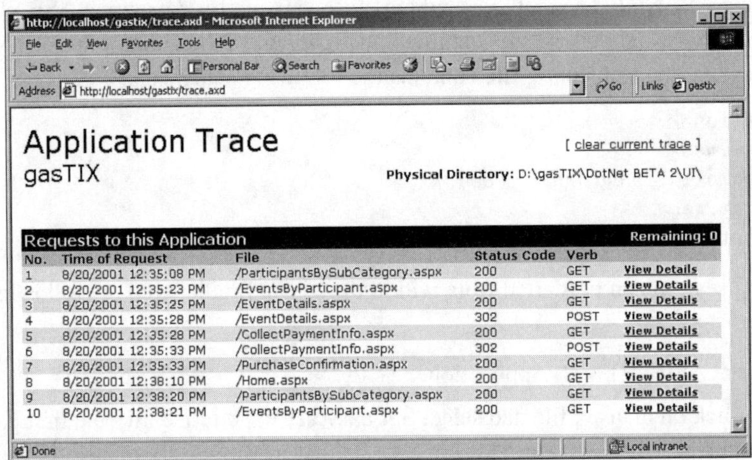

FIGURE 14.9
gasTIX Application Trace.

To enable page level tracing, set the trace attribute of the `@Page` directive:

```
<% Page Trace="true" %>
```

NOTE

When tracing is enabled at the application level, it is available for every page; however, to view the information on the page you must set the `pageOutput` attribute in the applications web.config file.

A built-in object, `Trace`, allows you to write custom messages into the trace information. The `TraceContext` class is used to store information about a request. Access to the `TraceContext` is available through the `Page.Trace` property.

```
Page.Trace.Write( "LoadEvents", "No events were found." );
```

Two methods, `Write` and `Warn`, are available on the `TraceContext` class. The difference being the Warn messages are displayed in red when you view the trace information.

Debugging and Testing a Web Service

Testing and debugging Web services created with Visual Studio .NET is similar to any other application. Visual Studio aids in the process by creating a test page for your web service. From the Debug menu, when you select Start, Visual Studio launches a new instance of Internet Explorer and the test page is dynamically generated. The gasTIX Participant Web Service test page is shown in Figure 14.10.

Using this test page, you can execute the functions available from the Participant web service. If we select `ReserveSeats`, we are presented with a new page that allows us to input the `EventId`, `SectionId`, and `NumberOfSeats` as shown in Figure 14.11. The sample SOAP request and response for the web service method are also displayed. When we invoke the method, a new page is presented with the response from the web service. In this case, an XML document is returned that represents the new gasTIX order.

While developing the gasTIX web services, the development team found it useful to log the incoming soap request as well as the outgoing soap response during the testing process. A custom attribute, `TraceExtension`, was developed derived from the `SoapExtensionAttribute` class. When applied to a web service method, as shown below, the `SoapMessage` is written to the specified file immediately before the server deserializes the request from the caller and immediately after the response is serialized but before it is returned to the caller.

```
[WebMethod]
[TraceExtensionAttribute(Filename=@"c:\gastix_soap.log")]
public string ReserveSeats(int eventID, int sectionID, int numberOfSeats)
```

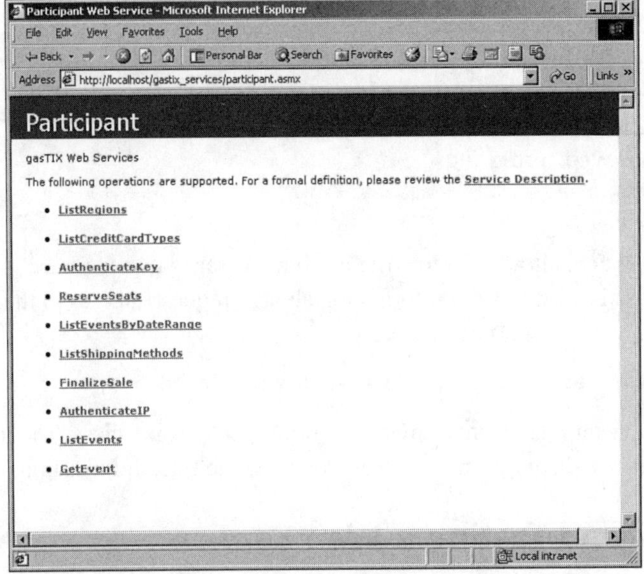

FIGURE 14.10
gasTIX Participant Web Service.

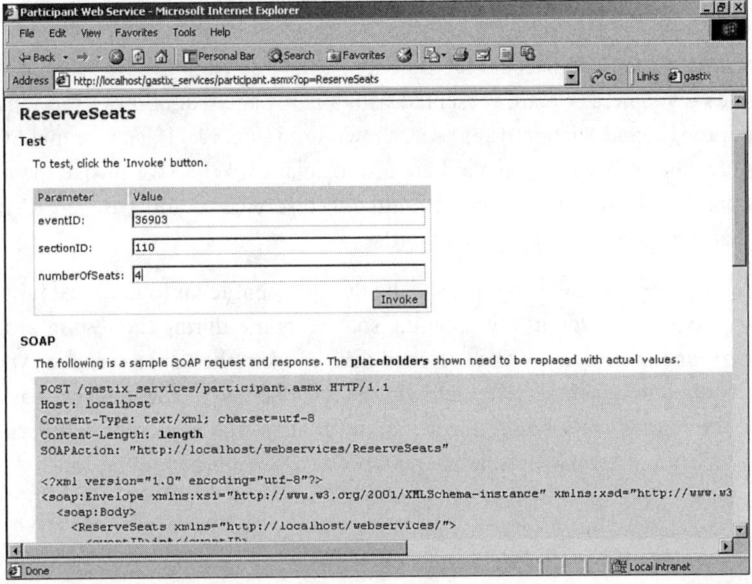

FIGURE 14.11
gasTIX Participant ReserveSeats.

Exception Handling

Even the most demanding quality assurance processes cannot guarantee a bug-free application. Programs must be able to handle unexpected errors that occur during execution. The common language runtime provides an environment for notifying an application when errors arise.

An exception is an error condition or unexpected behavior encountered by an application. In the .NET framework, an exception is an object that inherits from the `System.Exception` class. Both an application and the common language runtime environment can generate an exception. The exception is passed up the stack until it is handled by the application or the program terminates.

NOTE

All .NET framework methods indicate failure by throwing exceptions.

An exception can be thrown across process and even machine boundaries.

There are many advantages to using structured exception handling. The structured exception handling included in the common language runtime is an improvement over the previous unstructured exception handling, `on error goto`. Unstructured exception handling can degrade overall performance and result in an application that is hard to debug and maintain. Exceptions must be addressed; runtime errors cannot be ignored. Return values do not have to be checked. Exception handling code can easily be added to increase system reliability. Also, the runtime's exception handling is extremely efficient, even more so than Windows-based C++ error handling.

The `Exception` Object

The `Exception` class is the base class from which exceptions inherit. All exception objects are instances of the `System.Exception` class. The class contains public instance properties for getting details about the underlying error, each of which is described below.

- Use the `Source` property to get information about the application or object that threw the exception.
- The `InnerException` contains a reference to an inner exception. If an exception is caught, a new exception can be created to give the caller more meaningful information. The original exception can be saved in the `InnerException` property allowing the caller to inspect the causes of the initial error.
- The `Message` property contains a detailed description of the exception.

- The `HelpLink` property is used to get or set the help file associated with the exception.
- Use the `TargetSite` property to retrieve the method that threw the exception.
- The `StackTrace` contains a stack trace that determines where an error occurred. If debugging information is available, the stack trace includes the source file name and the program line number. This information is captured immediately before an exception is thrown.

TIP

Use the `Environment.StackTrace` static property to inspect the stack trace without throwing an exception. This might prove beneficial during testing to log the execution of a long running business process that involves multiple objects or might complete one or more database updates.

In general, two categories of exceptions derive from `System.Exception`. These are

- The pre-defined common language runtime exceptions derived from `SystemException`.
- User-defined application exceptions derived from `ApplicationException`.

NOTE

Most classes that inherit from `System.Exception` do not implement additional functionality. Exceptions are caught based on their type rather than some change to the state of the exception class, and hence don't need additional members or methods.

When the runtime encounters an error, a `SystemException` is thrown. The .NET framework contains a hierarchy of exceptions all derived from `SystemException`. For example, the `DivideByZeroException` is thrown when an attempt is made to divide a number by zero. The `DivideByZeroException` hierarchy is shown in Figure 14.12.

A program, rather than the runtime, throws an `ApplicationException`. When designing an application that creates new exceptions, derive those exceptions from the `ApplicationException` class.

Many applications find it useful to attempt several operations at once, testing each, and then recording those that fail. For example, gasTIX requires the validation of both the shipping and billing addresses. In order to provide a better user experience, gasTIX validates both addresses in the `OrderRules` class regardless if one fails, or any other business rule for that matter. The user is able to correct all data entry errors at once rather than rely on the "fix one error, resubmit the request" approach.

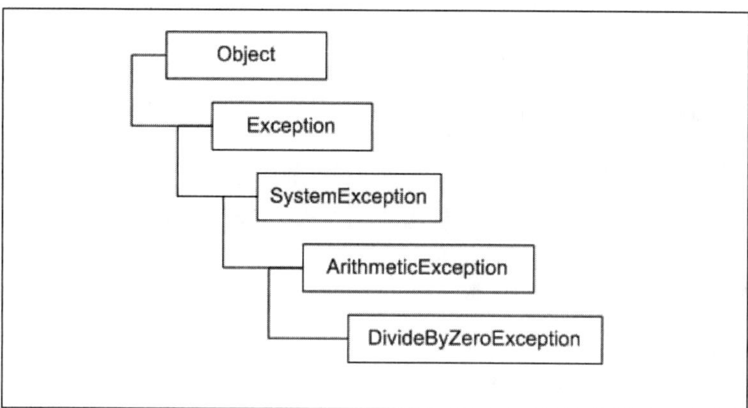

FIGURE 14.12
`DivideByZeroException` *hierarchy.*

To fulfill this requirement, gasTIX derives its own exception class `GASException` from `ApplicationException`. The `GASException` constructor requires an instance of the `GASErrors` class, a type-safe collection of `Exception` objects that implements the IEnumerable interface.

NOTE

The `GASException` object uses the IEnumerable interface to iterate over the type-safe collection exposed by `GASErrors`.

The `GASException` class overrides the instance properties of its base class to concatenate the information about each exception held in the `GASErrors` object. The code in listing 14.3 illustrates the `GASException` class.

LISTING 14.3 `GASException` class.

```
public class GASException : ApplicationException
{
    private GASErrors _errorList = null;
    public GASException(GASErrors errorList) : base()
    {
        errorList = errorList;
    }
```

LISTING 14.3 Continued

```
    public override string ToString()
    {
        string temp = null;
        foreach(Exception e in _errorList)
        {
            temp += e.ToString() + "\n\r";
        }
        return (temp);
    }
    public override string Message
    {
        get
        {
            string temp = null;
            foreach(Exception e in _errorList)
            {
                temp += e.Message + "\n\r";
            }
            return (temp);
        }
    }
    public override string Source
    {
        get
        {
            string temp = null;
            foreach(Exception e in _errorList)
            {
                temp += e.Source + "\n\r";
            }
            return (temp);
        }
    }
};
```

Fundamentals

Exception handling is supported by the common language runtime (CLR) with the use of objects and protected blocks of code. The runtime creates an object that represents an exception when it occurs. Code that may cause an exception is placed in a try block. Code that handles an exception is placed in a catch block. Every runtime language supports exception handling in a similar manner.

The code Listing 14.4 shows the use of exception handling. First, the try statement is used to begin a section of protected code. In this case, we are validating the XML buffer passed to a web services method, `FinalizeSale`, against the gasTIX order schema. The `OrderData.Read` method performs the validation and returns a new instance of an `OrderData` object. If successful, we complete the ticket purchase.

LISTING 14.4 Function to complete ticket purchase.

```
[WebMethod] public string FinalizeSale(string orderData)
{
    string retVal;
    gasTIX.Data.OrderData orderData;
    BusinessFaçade.Order order;

    try
    {
        gasTIX.Data.OrderData orderData;
        orderData = gasTIX.Data.OrderData.Read(orderData);

        order = new BusinessFacade.Order();

        retVal = order.FinalizeSale(od);
    }
    catch(XmlException xmlError)
    {
        System.Console.WriteLine(error.ToString());
        throw new ApplicationException(
        "Error validating input", xmlError);
    }
    catch(Exception error)
    {
        System.Console.WriteLine(error.ToString());
        throw;
    }
    finally
    {
    if( orderData != null )
        orderData.Dispose();
        if( order != null )
            order.Dispose();
    }
    return retVal;
}
```

NOTE

If an exception is generated during a SOAP request to a web service, the CLR converts the exception into a `SoapException`. The exception is return to the caller as a SOAP fault. If the caller is another .NET application, upon return the SOAP fault is "promoted" back to a `SoapException`.

When an exception is thrown during validation or purchase, an exception is passed back up the stack and each catch block is given an opportunity to handle the exception. The proper catch block is determined by comparing the type of exception object thrown to that of the name of the exception specified in the catch block. If there is no specific catch block for the exception, then the exception is caught by a general catch block.

TIP

The order of the catch blocks is important. You should place catch blocks targeted to specific exceptions before the general catch block, otherwise the compiler will issue an error.

The throw statement is used to initiate a new exception as well as to re-throw an existing exception. Many times it is useful to cleanup after an exception occurs, such as closing a file, releasing database connections. The `finally` statement is used to create a block of code which is always executed regardless if an exception is thrown.

Best Practices

Using exception handling can make an application more stable and less prone to fatal errors. It can also be very useful in debugging applications by allowing you to write specific application state in the event of an error to a log file or the Windows event viewer. The follow is a list of best practices for using exception handling:

- Know when to use exception handling. Exception handling should not be used to replace normal program flow. If an error rarely occurs it is a good candidate for exception handling. If an error may occur half the time, then use a return value or check a field on an object.
- Derive all user-defined exception classes from `ApplicationException`.
- If you develop your own exception class, always end the new class with `Exception`.

- When making use of user-defined exceptions, programs that handle these exceptions must have access to the metadata for the exception class. This is especially true for programs that execute remotely and generate user-defined exceptions.
- Be aware of when the stack trace begins. It is the point at which the exception is thrown not when the exception is created.
- Use meaningful exception messages to describe what error has occurred.
- Cleanup any application state after an exception is generated. The code that generated the error must be able to be called again once either the user or another program resolves the error.

From Here

The Visual Studio .NET integrated debugger combines the all the tools necessary to debug .NET applications into one common application. The new debugger is language independent. For example, you can step from C# code into VB .NET code into a SQL stored procedure lessening the difficulty of debugging complex applications or large development efforts. New robust tracing features included with ASP.NET allow you to understanding exactly how the web server responses to a client request.

One of the best new features of the CLR is structured exception handling. By using exception handling, applications become more stable and less prone to crashes, thereby improving the overall user experience.

For more information on building the gasTIX application, see Chapter 10, "gasTIX Event Searching," and Chapter 11, "Purchasing a Ticket." Chapter 15, "Performance Tuning in .NET," offers suggestions for improving the speed of your application, while Chapter 16, "Deploying the Application," demonstrates how the gasTIX application was deployed.

Performance Tuning in .NET

by Matthew Baute

CHAPTER

15

IN THIS CHAPTER

- **Performance Tuning Concepts 436**
- **.NET Performance Mechanisms 439**
- **.NET Performance Tuning Tools 450**
- **From Here 467**

Microsoft offers the .NET Framework as a robust platform on which to build and deploy technical solutions that solve the e-Business challenges businesses face today. However, the technical power and flexibility behind .NET is derived from its complex set of interlocking pieces, including the Common Language Runtime (CLR), ASP.NET, and SQL Server 2000.

A thorough understanding of the various pieces and how to best tune each is required by the individual assigned with the responsibility of either making an existing system achieve desired performance levels, or with planning a scalable and high-performance design of a new system. These pieces must be individually and collectively well-tuned for high performance. Additionally, a solid understanding of the tuning tools at the disposal of developers and testers must also be gained in order to uncover potential bottlenecks before a system is deployed.

This chapter examines fundamental tuning concepts, gives direction for tuning specific components of the .NET Framework to achieve optimal application performance, and explores the tools available for the .NET platform that are helpful for enhancing system performance.

Performance Tuning Concepts

Why should we tune? How should we tune? When should we tune? This section answers these three basic questions and presents the fundamental concepts behind tuning an application to achieve robust performance.

Why Performance Tune?

Beyond the obvious goal of making applications and systems run fast, there are a few more tangible reasons for undertaking a tuning effort and for justifying the resources that are needed.

First, applications are implemented to meet specific business goals. New systems are developed for a variety of reasons: to make a business process more efficient, to replace an outdated system, to take advantage of a new medium such as Web services, or to gain a competitive advantage by offering customers an enhanced or unique service. If the new application meets all requirements and fulfills all use cases but performs sub-par, it will not bring efficiency to the business process. Instead, it will feel as outdated as the system being replaced, and will not offer the desired competitive advantage. For this reason, we should pay close attention to performance in order to meet our business goals.

Second, in this increasingly technological age, we have come to expect applications to perform faster and faster. With the speed of affordable, widely available processors now reaching 2.0 GHz and the cost of RAM and disk continuing to drop, everyday computer users expect screens to update and refresh quickly. Web users will only wait a few seconds for each page to load, or else they're off to a competitor's site. In order to meet the general expectations of today's users, applications must be tuned so that database queries return results in a reasonable time, middle-tier components execute business logic quickly, and web pages process and send out HTML within a few seconds. Paying attention to meeting end-users' expectations and needs has always been a key strategy of Microsoft. We can take a page from the book of the most successful software company in history by listening to and learning from what users of our applications are saying.

Third, performance testing of existing systems is preparation for future growth. It was not uncommon for many Internet dot-com start-ups to experience double, triple, or even exponential growth rates within short time periods during the Internet boom of the late 1990s. Different industry sectors continue to exhibit strong growth patterns. In order to ensure a quality user experience is delivered during rates of high growth, performance testing helps answer the what if questions before such situations actually arise. It helps provide assurance that performance will be adequate as a system scales larger and larger. Testing gives the company a chance to make sure the proper hardware resources are in place in advance of the next big advertising campaign.

Additionally, saving the performance tuning results of an application at a particular point in time provides us with a baseline against which we may measure future releases. This can help us determine whether the features in a new release cause the application to slow down, and lets us know to focus on tuning these new features.

For these reasons, performance tuning should be a recurring task on our project plans.

How to Performance Tune

Measurable, concrete goals must be provided early in the design process, or else tuning will be without end. How do we know if we've reached our goal unless we have a specific mark for which to aim? Abstract business goals must be translated into concrete benchmarks such as number of pages served per second, number of transactions completed per minute, and so on. When performance goals are met, tuning has been completed until the business starts planning a new growth cycle.

After measurable goals have been set, tuning can begin. A load is put on the system using a tool such as Application Center Test (ACT—discussed in more detail later). Reports generated by the ACT tool along with Performance Monitor counters are analyzed to determine where bottlenecks exist. Is there a problem with specific ASPX pages? Is there enough RAM on the SQL Server box?

A solution to alleviate the current bottleneck is proposed, implemented, and the system is stressed again. Did the solution help? If so, take note and continue by stressing again, finding the next bottleneck, and testing potential solutions. This process is iterative, repeated over and over until performance goals are met.

TIP

The cost-effectiveness of each potential solution should be kept in mind. By nature, we as developers prefer rewriting ASPX pages or middle-tier C# components rather than simply adding more RAM to a server. However, if additional RAM solves the problem, this is a more cost-effective solution and should be chosen.

When To Performance Tune?

Performance testing and tuning at all stages in the software development life cycle, from early design to post-deployment, is critical to delivering and maintaining a high-performance system. This section discusses how to integrate performance tuning into all phases of the life cycle.

Tune from the Start!

A common misconception among developers and project managers alike is that performance testing should take place once development has reached the alpha or beta stage. Beginning our tuning efforts at such a late stage in the life cycle can have dire effects. Considering the performance requirements of an application should begin from the start of the software development life cycle.

The technical architect responsible for the overall design of the system should be considering performance requirements when designing the data model, the object model, and when choosing the implementation technologies. How normalized should the database be? To what level of abstraction should the object model be designed? Such questions must be carefully weighed by the architect early in the design phase. Trying to correct these early decisions once a product is in beta release can be an arduous and expensive task.

TIP

It is important to solicit feedback from colleagues about the choices being made in the design phase. See if the design makes sense to others who have been down a similar road before. Most importantly, request feedback from an experienced DBA on the data model—it is hard to overemphasize how important a well-designed data schema is to the success of a highly performing application.

Tune throughout Development

Performance should be kept in mind by programmers implementing a system during each day of the development phase. Algorithms must be implemented efficiently for the application to perform well. Poor choices or shallow comprehension can cause the overall performance of an application to suffer. If developers are trained to be mindful of how the code they are implementing has a direct effect on system performance, the burden of tuning further down the road will be lessened.

TIP

A helpful practice during development is to convene regular code reviews. In these meetings, small teams of developers examine code samples, discuss implementation approaches, and trade best practices. People new to a technology or language will benefit from this exercise by listening to more seasoned staff who have experienced the pain of real-world lessons. Poorly implemented code can be identified and fixed early in the life cycle, making it less likely expensive rework will be needed later.

Tune at Pre-Release

It makes sense to stress-test an application prior to release. Put a significant load on the system and see what happens. Does it meet the specific performance goals for the release? If not, tune the hardware and software configuration until it performs to specification. The goal is to eliminate problems before any users touch the system.

Tune Post-Release

Once an application has been deployed to the user community (see Chapter 16, "Deploying the Application"), analysis should be performed on log files to determine real-world usage patterns. Perhaps users really like a certain section of the web site we did not anticipate. In this case, it is beneficial to stress-test and tune that section to make sure it is performing well.

Is the overall application performing adequately now that it is live? If not, we may need to tune in emergency mode, monitoring production servers and making changes quickly to ensure users are getting the quality experience we have intended.

Capturing application usage patterns and performance metrics can be automated by simply turning on logging in Internet Information Server, and by setting a few performance counters in Windows. Reports can then be run on these logs offline to determine if exception conditions are being encountered that necessitate tuning.

.NET Performance Mechanisms

The .NET Framework provides several mechanisms application developers can use to gain performance boosts. Among these are caching technology in ASP.NET, application profiling, asynchronous processing support, and install-time code generation. By implementing some of these strategies, an application can perform significantly faster. We should consider these techniques when designing a new .NET e-Business application.

ASP.NET Caching Technologies

Caching web pages is an important concept to keep in mind when designing a high-performance dynamic web site. *Caching* is the concept of rendering a page a single time, and then storing the rendered output in memory for fast access thereafter. Caching can offer significant performance gains when implemented appropriately. Pages that are more static in nature, such as the main gasTIX home page, or a product catalog that does not change often, are good candidates for caching.

Output Caching

Output Caching in ASP.NET generates an ASPX page dynamically the first time, making the middle-tier call and the database hit required to fill out the data controls on the page. The page is then stored in memory so subsequent requests are served without traversing the various tiers again.

ASP.NET output caching is configurable on a page-by-page basis, so we should consider turning it on for the more static pages on our sites. The following directive, placed at the top of an ASPX page, will place this page in the output cache for five minutes (300 seconds):

```
<%@OutputCache Duration="300" VaryByParam="None" %>
```

Caching parameters for an ASPX page can also be set in the code-behind page using the `Response.Cache` properties. However, it is simpler to use the `@OutputCache` page directive and let ASP.NET handle the details.

The `VaryByParam` argument of the `@OutputCache` directive can be used to cache multiple versions of the same page. Dynamic pages often return different results based on the parameters passed in the `QueryString` or in a form post. Use the `VaryByParam` option to tell ASP.NET which parameters passed into the page will cause another version of the page to be cached. For example, in the gasTIX application, the main home page lists subcategories the user can pick. When a subcategory is chosen, such as Celtic under the Music category, the following URL is requested:

```
localhost/gastix/ParticipantsBySubCategory.aspx?SubCategory_ID=11&SubCategory_
Name=Celtic
```

Note the `SubCategory_ID` and `SubCategory_Name` parameters passed in the `QueryString`. We can choose to create a cached version of the `ParticipantsBySubCategory.aspx` page for each `SubCategory_ID` passed in by adding the following directive to the top of the page:

```
<%@OutputCache Duration="300" VaryByParam="SubCategory_ID" %>
```

If we need to cache an ASPX page for multiple parameters, we can semi-colon delimit the parameter list in the `VaryByParam` option.

We can also choose to cache Web Form User Controls independently from the ASPX page on which they are placed, effectively making it possible to cache only specific portions of a page.

Refer to Chapter 10, "GasTIX Event Searching," for an example of ASP.NET output caching in the gasTIX sample application.

Application Cache

Two other options are available in ASP.NET to cache data that is expensive to generate. Information can be stored in the `Application` object (`System.Web` namespace, HttpApplicationState class), or in the `Cache` object (`System.Web.Caching` namespace, Cache class). Both methods enable storing data across multiple web page requests, and both are scoped according to the application. Web pages in one application domain on the same web server cannot access the data in another application's cache.

The `Application` object is similar to its predecessor in ASP, and it is in fact backwards compatible with that version. This is helpful when we decide to migrate our ASP applications to ASP.NET—we are not required to worry about changing the guts of our application state mechanism.

The Cache class takes key/value pairs, and supports special functionality to optimize its use. It will clean itself up when system resources run low (similar to .NET CLR garbage collection), removing items that have not been used in some time. This built-in technique is called *scavenging*. We can set the expiration time of a specific item in the cache, and can also set a priority level that determines if other items are scavenged first.

The Cache class also enables a developer to specify a dependency on a file or on another cached item when creating a new cache entry. When the dependent item changes, the cached item with the specified dependency is removed from the cache, keeping data in synch. We could, for example, cache a list of the events in a tour on gasTIX setting a dependency on an XML file containing the tour cities. When we update the XML file to add new cities to a tour, the cached item will expire because the XML file on which it is dependent has been modified. The next user request for the tour list will cause ASP.NET to re-generate the item and place it in the cache.

.NET Application Profiling

Profiling an application in .NET is the concept of monitoring different aspects of its behavior while it is running, preferably under load. The various aspects we can monitor can be categorized into two groups: system-provided and application-provided.

System-provided counters are built-in to the Windows operating system, and allow us to monitor processor, memory, and disk usage, SQL Server locks and connections, ASP.NET page requests, and much more.

.NET Performance Counters

The .NET Framework provides us with a large number and variety of new performance counters that can help us track down problems with our .NET applications. These counters and their descriptions are shown in Table 15.1.

TABLE 15.1 .NET Performance Counters

Performance Object	*Description (per .NET Framework SDK)*
`.NET CLR Exceptions`	Exceptions are violations of semantic constraints of an implementation language, the runtime, or an application.
`.NET CLR Interop`	Interoperability deals with how the runtime interacts with all external entities, including COM, external libraries, and the operating system.
`.NET CLR Jit`	Just-in-time (JIT) compilation is used to compile IL methods to native machine language immediately before execution of the methods.
`.NET CLR Loading`	Loading is the process used to locate a binary form of a class and constructing from that binary form an object that represents the class.
`.NET CLR LocksAndThreads`	A lock, or mutex, is data associated with each object in the runtime that a program can use to coordinate multithreaded access to the object. A thread is an independent unit of execution with its own working memory that operates on values and objects that reside in a shared main memory.
`.NET CLR Memory`	Memory is the set of storage locations that a program uses to store its variables.
`.NET CLR Remoting`	Remoting is the mechanism used to make method calls between object instances across a boundary. Boundaries include calling between contexts, application domains, processes, and machines.
`.NET CLR Security`	Security is the set of mechanisms used to provide controlled access to resources.

TABLE 15.1 Continued

Performance Object	*Description (per .NET Framework SDK)*
`ASP.NET`	ASP.NET global performance counters are exposed which either aggregate information for all ASP.NET applications on a Web server computer or apply generally to the ASP.NET subsystem.
`ASP.NET Applications`	ASP.NET application performance counters can be used to monitor the performance of a single instance of an ASP.NET application. A unique instance appears for these counters, named __Total__, which aggregates counters for all applications on a Web server (similar to the global counters). The __Total__ instance is always available—the counters will display zero when no applications are present on the server.

Although the system-provided performance counters give us a wealth of information with which to profile our .NET applications, we might want to implement a few custom counters to help determine bottlenecks, or to provide administrators with general operational feedback. They can provide us with special insight into the workings of our custom application that is not possible with the Windows 2000 system-provided counters.

Application-provided performance counters are built into our code. We define categories and counters and choose when to increment or decrement our counter values. When we set our code in motion, we can watch our custom counters in action based on the application events that occur.

Application-provided counters are implemented using the classes located in the `System.Diagnostics` namespace. To implement a custom counter, implement code similar to that found in Listing 15.1.

LISTING 15.1 Creating a Custom Application Performance Counter in .NET is Done through the `System.Diagnostics` Namespace

```
using System;
using System.Diagnostics;

namespace gasTIXConsole
{
    class Class1
    {
```

LISTING 15.1 Continued

```
        static void Main(string[] args)
        {
            // first check to see if the category is already there
            if (!PerformanceCounterCategory.Exists("gasTIX") ||
!PerformanceCounterCategory.CounterExists("TicketsSold", "gasTIX"))
            {
                PerformanceCounterCategory.Create("gasTIX",

"The gasTIX performance counters report on a large variety of gasTIX metrics.",
"TicketsSold",

"This counter reports the number of overall tickets sold on the gasTIX site.");
            }

            PerformanceCounter pcTicketsSold = new PerformanceCounter("gasTIX",
"TicketsSold", false);

            // this loop would of course be replaced with a real ticket sale
            //event
            for (int i=1; i <= 90000; i++)
            {
                pcTicketsSold.Increment();
            }
        }
    }
}
```

Once the custom performance category and counters have been implemented, we can start monitoring using the Performance Monitor tool (described in more detail in the next section), shown in Figure 15.1.

Performance Monitor

The main tool used to track both system- and application-provided performance counters is the Windows Performance Monitor utility. To run this utility, enter perfmon in the Start/Run dialog box, or select Performance from the Administrative Tools program group.

The Performance Monitor lets us add the counters relevant to the situation we are monitoring. By choosing a few counters while our application is running (or while it is being stress-tested by a tool such as the Application Center Test tool, discussed later), we can watch the counters to see if they provide insights into why our application might not be performing as we desire. Picking a few sample counters with this tool is shown in Figure 15.2.

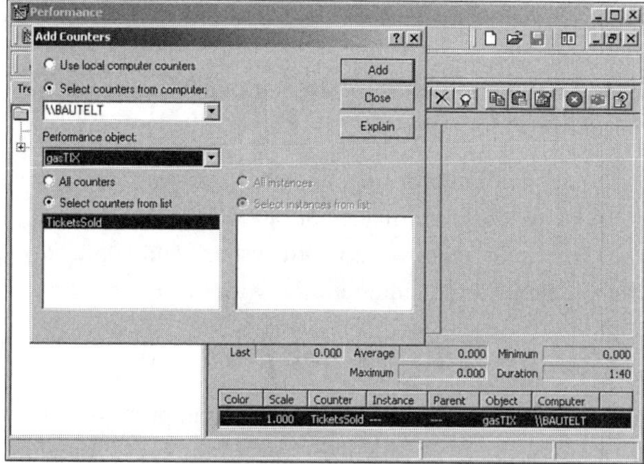

FIGURE 15.1

A custom counter is displayed in Performance Monitor.

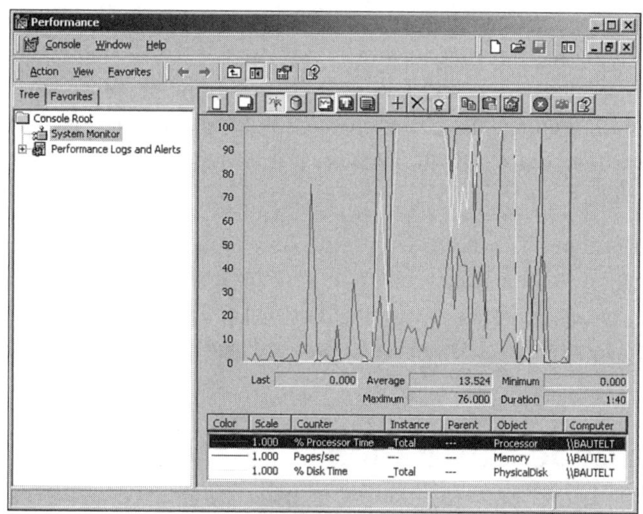

FIGURE 15.2

The Performance Monitor allows us to track system and application performance metrics.

We can also record a Performance Monitor session so we can play it back later. This is helpful for recording performance on production servers. The results can be brought down to a local server and re-run to keep the production server from being significantly impacted.

After we have made a modification to an ASPX file or we have added more RAM to a server, we should use the same counters and run the same tests to see if we have helped remove the bottleneck. Performance Monitor allows us to save a group of counters so we can quickly recall an entire counter group.

A thorough grounding in application profiling, creating, updating, and measuring performance counters, is a key to enhancing the performance of our .NET e-Business applications. The Performance Monitor is our main window into both system- and application-provided performance counters, so we should become quite familiar with this tool.

Asynchronous Processing in .NET

Many times an application can offload work to a background process so the user can go on to other tasks. The user can return later to view the status of the background process, or he can be notified through a mechanism such as e-mail. Consider implementing asynchronous processing where appropriate to improve overall application performance.

Business workflow is often a good candidate for asynchronous processing. Using gasTIX as a practical example, when a user completes a purchase, an entire series of business events needs to take place—notifying the fulfillment partner, exporting to the accounting system, notifying the artist, etc. The user does not want to wait for the web browser screen to refresh while all these events take place. Perhaps the communication link between the gasTIX systems and the fulfillment partner is temporarily down. The user just wants to know the order was placed and go on doing other things.

Such business events could be handled asynchronously in the background after saving the transaction information to the database and returning control to the user. Any errors encountered in the asynchronous process can be logged or sent via notification to an administrator. The user will perceive a more robust and high-performance system with such an asynchronous design.

Install-Time Code Generation

Microsoft provides a utility called Ngen.exe that allows an administrator to pre-compile (pre-JIT) IL application code into native machine language code after installation. This technique is called "install-time code generation."

The advantage of pre-compiling assemblies is the time it takes to invoke a segment of code at run-time is reduced. This is because the compilation to native machine language has already taken place at install-time. We take the performance hit during the Ngen run, rather than at application run-time.

The Ngen utility, shown in Figure 15.3, is called for all the assemblies (DLLs) we want to precompile. The results are placed in a reserved area called the native image cache.

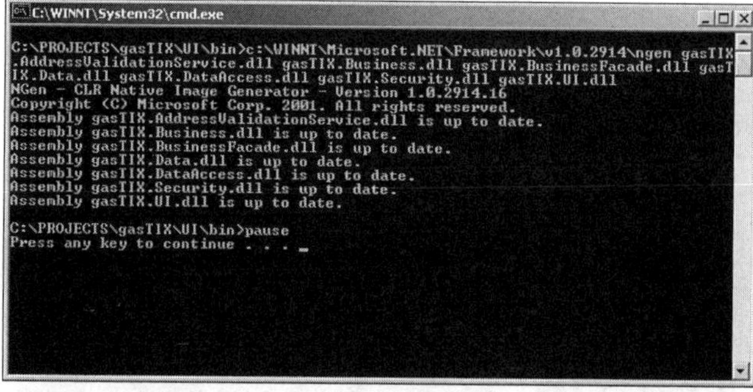

FIGURE 15.3

Running Ngen.exe on each gasTIX assembly.

To confirm our assemblies have been pre-compiled and have been placed in the native image cache, we can run the `Ngen` command again with the `/show` parameter.

For ease of use, it is appropriate to create a batch file with the Ngen command specifying all the assemblies to pre-compile. This will allow the administrator to simply double-click the batch file to run the install-time code generation process.

Another way to determine whether the assemblies are pre-JIT compiled or will be JIT compiled on demand at runtime is to view the C:\WINNT\Assembly folder in Windows Explorer, as shown in Figure 15.4.

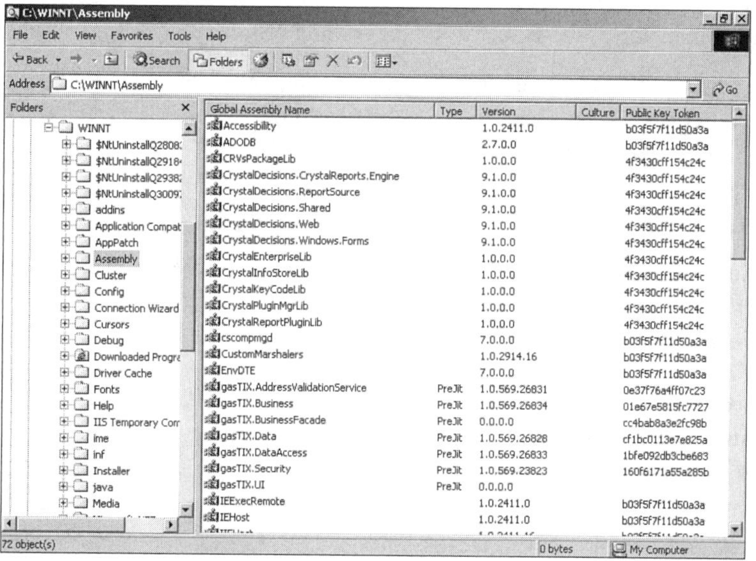

FIGURE 15.4

Windows Explorer lists the native image cache in the GAC.

When viewing this folder in Windows Explorer, a shell extension is invoked that categorizes the assembly types as either PreJit or normal (blank). The true directory structure on disk is a bit different, however. Using a command prompt to browse to the C:\WINNT\Assembly folder, we can see there are really a few different subfolders at this location.

```
C:\WINNT\System32\cmd.exe
Microsoft Windows 2000 [Version 5.00.2195]
(C) Copyright 1985-2000 Microsoft Corp.

C:\>cd winnt

C:\WINNT>cd ass*

C:\WINNT\Assembly>dir
 Volume in drive C has no label.
 Volume Serial Number is 00E4-08C7

 Directory of C:\WINNT\Assembly

06/30/2001  02:10p      <DIR>          downloaded
07/18/2001  04:30p      <DIR>          GAC
06/30/2001  02:10p      <DIR>          global
07/24/2001  09:03a      <DIR>          NativeImages1_v1.0.2914
07/23/2001  02:53p      <DIR>          temp
07/18/2001  04:30p      <DIR>          tmp
               0 File(s)              0 bytes
               6 Dir(s)   4,479,881,216 bytes free

C:\WINNT\Assembly>_
```

FIGURE 15.5
The native image cache is stored in a different subdirectory from the GAC.

The assemblies we compiled using the Ngen tool have been placed into the NativeImages1_v1.0.2914 folder, while the Global Assembly Cache shared assemblies are located in the GAC folder. Although in Windows Explorer it appears the native image cache is a part of the GAC, this is not in fact the case. They do share some similarities, however, such as persistence on disk when a machine reboots. This is different from JIT-compiled code, which is stored in memory and is lost when the owning process dies.

We should consider using the Ngen utility to pre-compile .NET code that takes a long time to start. This can help the users of our applications, especially the ones who first hit a page or function, get a performance boost.

Other .NET Performance Considerations

When working with specific pieces of the .NET Framework, we need to keep in mind a few techniques that will ensure a high performance system. This section covers the most important .NET tools and techniques that fall into this category.

ViewState

ASP.NET introduces a new feature that maintains the state of server controls on a web form between page postbacks called `ViewState`. Although this feature comes in quite handy and saves us from writing lots of extra code, it should be used wisely. The `ViewState` feature can increase the size of an ASPX page substantially, especially when used with repeating data controls like DataGrid and DataList.

Turn off ViewState on a control-by-control basis using the MaintainState parameter. It should be set to false when we do not need ASP.NET to remember control state between server trips. The default setting for ViewState is true. Turn off ViewState for an entire ASPX page by using the EnableViewState parameter in the @Page directive:

```
<%@Page Language="VB" EnableViewState="False" %>
```

Session State

Internet Information Server (IIS) session state should also be disabled when not needed. This can be done on a page-by-page basis with the following page directive:

```
<@Page EnableSessionState="false" %>
```

Session state generates a cookie sent over the HTTP header. This generation requires extra CPU cycles to perform, and if we are not using session variables on a page, we should disable it to get a performance boost.

Some ASPX pages may only need to read from Session variables. If this is the case, we can make the session state read-only with the following page-level directive:

```
<@Page EnableSessionState="ReadOnly" %>
```

In-process session state is the fastest option when state persistence is required in an application. However, it is also the least fault-tolerant, because it runs in the same process space as IIS. If IIS crashes, the session state will be lost. ASP.NET offers an out-of-process Session Windows service, which can be located on a completely separate machine. Additionally, state can be stored in SQL Server. Although these alternatives are more fault-tolerant, they are slower. We need to evaluate the speed requirements of our applications when deciding which state option to implement.

StringBuilder

Use the new StringBuilder class of the System.Text namespace for efficient string concatenation. Concatenations have been the bane of Visual Basic 6.0 programmers because of the inefficient way in which memory was used to perform the operation. StringBuilder offers a remedy to this situation, providing fast and efficient memory usage during operation.

Visual Basic .NET programmers no longer have to worry about performance degradations when concatenating with StringBuilder. The code in Listing 15.2 demonstrates a simple use of the StringBuilder class:

LISTING 15.2 The New StringBuilder Class Offers Performance Benefits Over Simple String Concatenation

```
using System;
using System.Text;

namespace gasTIXConsole
{
    class Class1
    {
        static void Main(string[] args)
        {
            StringBuilder tmpTickets = new StringBuilder();
            String tmpMyString = " this is number: ";
            for (int i=1; i <= 100; i++) {
                tmpTickets.Append(tmpMyString);
                tmpTickets.Append(i.ToString());
            }
            Console.Write(tmpTickets);
        }
    }
}
```

Secure Sockets Layer (SSL)

The Secure Sockets Layer (SSL) protocol, or HTTPS, should only be used when necessary. On gasTIX, the appropriate pages for SSL implementation are the order and order confirmation pages, on which credit card information is passed between the user's browser and the gasTIX web server over the Internet. It may be easier programmatically to turn on SSL for an entire web site, but using SSL where not really needed will frustrate users because of the performance hit taken for each page request.

Newer SSL accelerator technology can offload the CPU cycles it takes to encrypt and decrypt the HTTPS stream. One of these new products, BIP-IP from F5 Networks provides such functionality, speeding up the process by letting the CPU on the Web server focus on page generation, rather than on encryption. Intel's new Itanium chip supports on-chip SSL processing, also speeding throughput.

.NET Performance Tuning Tools

Microsoft offers several tools that can help us identify performance bottlenecks in our .NET e-Business applications. These tools are deeply integrated with the other components of the .NET platform. They offer us a wide variety of ways to tune all the logical tiers in the .NET architecture: presentation, business, and data.

Tuning the .NET Presentation Tier with Application Center Test (ACT)

The main tool used to test and tune the presentation tier in a .NET application is Application Center Test (ACT). This tool, shown in Figure 15.6, is based on Microsoft's previous stress-testing tool, the Web Application Stress (WAS) tool.

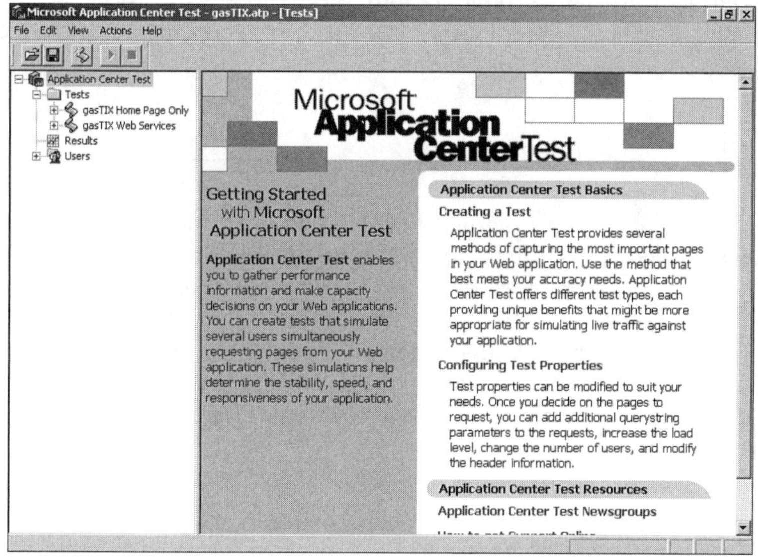

FIGURE 15.6

The main Application Center Test window.

The idea behind a load-testing tool is to place a heavy load on the system by executing many requests for ASPX pages per second. As this load is placed on the application, we can monitor performance counters to determine whether the application meets performance requirements.

Stress testing should be performed on a regular basis. We should not wait to put a load on an application just before we are ready to release to production. Putting a load on the application early in the development process will help us catch problems that may be too costly to fix later in the life cycle.

Simulate real-world scenarios as much as possible. We can use the ACT tool to record test scripts that simulate users' clicks on our web site. After we determine our application's peak load time, and we can use the ACT tool to simulate this heavy load. Focus on being able to meet the HTTP requests that will occur during such heavy usage periods. If we can meet the heaviest demand, the off-peak periods should be no problem.

TIP

The test environment should match the production environment as closely as possible. Although this may not be financially feasible, it is important to get as close as possible. If we have a multi-CPU box as our production SQL Server, we should also have a multi-CPU box for our testing SQL Server. We will encounter different problems with different hardware configurations. It is of little use to solve problems in the test environment that are different from the problems encountered in production.

TIP

Isolate the test environment from other network activity, placing the test box on its own network segment, if possible. This will provide more accurate test results. If there are limited resources, try testing overnight using development workstations as clients. Copying the ACT test scripts to multiple machines is a cost-effective way to gather more accurate results. Also, remember to populate SQL Server tables with realistic data volumes. If we are testing against only a few rows of data while the production database holds millions of rows, tests results will not be accurate, and in fact are likely to be badly skewed.

Multiple ACT tests are saved within a project file (.atp extension), similar to the way in which multiple files are saved in a Visual Studio.NET project. This allows us to group all of our tests into a single view. To create a new ACT test, select New Test… from the Actions menu. The New Test Wizard will be displayed.

The easiest way to create a simple test is to record our own user clicks in a browser window. This is done by selecting the Record a new test option on the Test Source screen of the wizard.

After clicking Next on this screen, the Browser Record screen is displayed. Clicking the Start recording button opens a new instance of Internet Explorer. In this browser window we can point to our application and traverse the desired application path. The ACT recorder captures all of the HTTP GET and POST messages passed between the browser and the web server, as shown in Figure 15.7.

When finished recording, click the Stop recording button to end the session. Click the Next button and enter a name for this test, and the test is created.

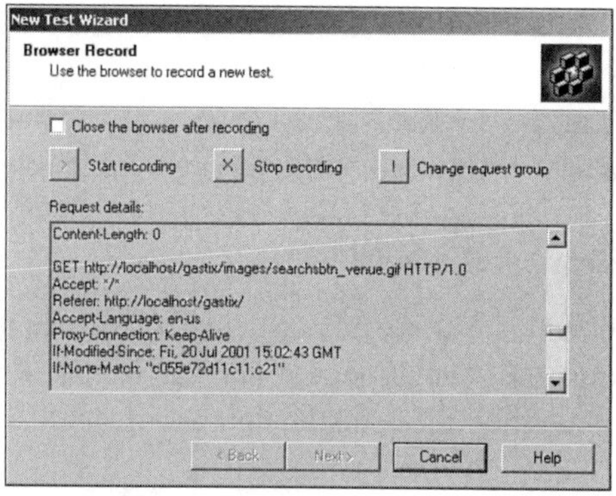

FIGURE 15.7
The ACT Recorder captures all HTTP GET and POST commands.

There are two types of tests in ACT: *static* and *dynamic*. Static tests, which can be created by recording a browser session, do not consider the responses received from the Web server. Static tests are useful for simple testing, and for testing sites without a lot of dynamic forms and input. Dynamic tests, constructed with VBScript, can dynamically send a custom request based on the response received from the Web server. While dynamic tests are much more flexible than static tests, programming knowledge is required. Note, however, that recording a browser session can also generate a dynamic test, if we so choose. The code for this test can then be modified in the script editor window, as displayed in Figure 15.8.

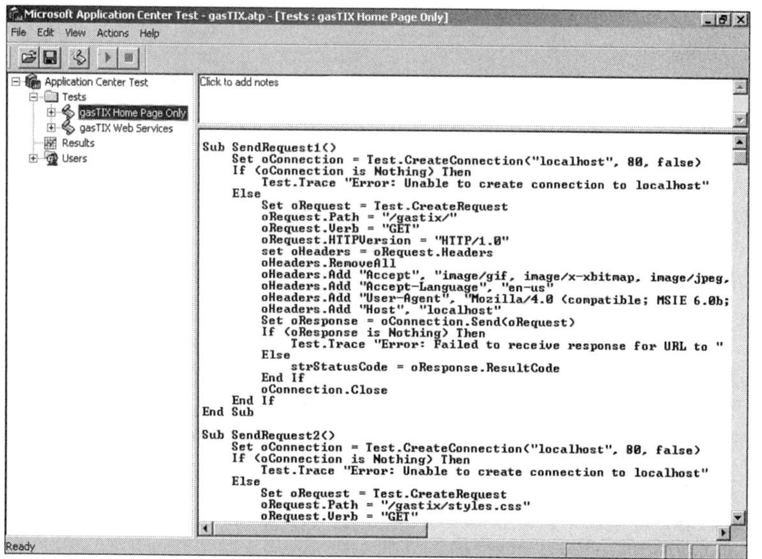

FIGURE 15.8
The Script Editor window enables us to configure dynamic scripts.

Dynamic tests provide us with a way to parse the Web server response for a specific parameter (such as an `EventID` in the gasTIX application), and then run subsequent HTTP GET commands with that parameter. ACT's predecessor, the WAS tool, did not support dynamically receiving and passing parameters. Although VBScript programming is required to take advantage of this functionality, it is a powerful enhancement that can help generate more realistic test scripts and provide more accurate test results.

An ACT test can be configured in a variety of ways. To set the parameters for a test, right-click the test name and select Properties. The General properties tab, shown in Figure 15.9, provides us with a way to set the test duration time and the number of simultaneous browser connections to open.

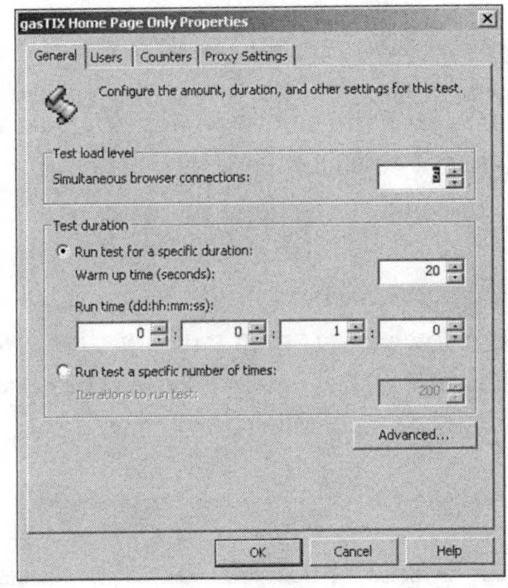

FIGURE 15.9

The ACT test configuration screen provides a wide array of testing options.

It is recommended that a warm-up time be entered so first-time ASPX page requests can be JIT-compiled. The first time any ASPX page is called, it must be JIT-compiled from IL to native machine language. This takes longer than subsequent requests, which are served from memory.

Once the properties have been set, it is time to run a test with the ACT tool. Select the test name and click the green Start Test button, or select Start Test from the Actions menu. The test will commence, and a screen similar to that shown in Figure 15.10 will be displayed.

By clicking the Show Details button, we can view a dynamically generated chart of ASPX requests per second, along with a few other metrics. When the test concludes, we can click the Close button to return to the main ACT console.

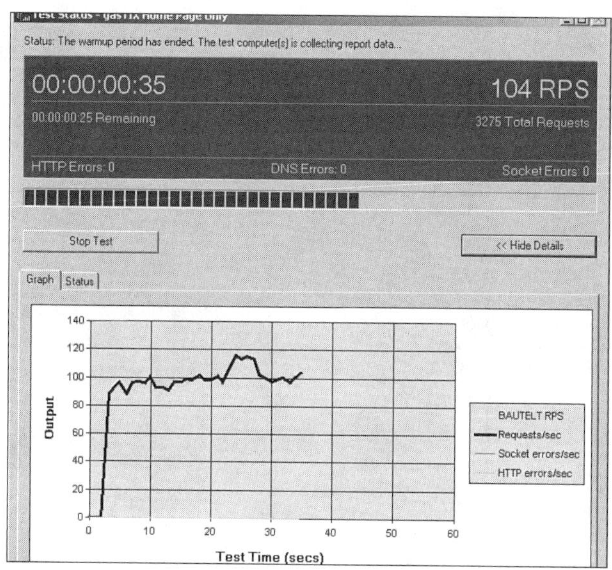

FIGURE 15.10
Running an ACT test.

To view detailed results of our ACT test, we expand the test and select the Results entry in the tree view. All the test results that have been gathered so far are displayed in the top right pane. A sample test results screen in shown in Figure 15.11. Selecting a specific test results entry displays the details for us.

The key metric in this window is Requests Per Second. If this number does not meet our stated performance goals, we need to identify potential bottleneck, try a solution, and test again.

The Visual Studio .NET environment and the ACT tool also provide us with the ability to stress-test our custom Web services. Visual Studio .NET generates an HTML page for us whenever an ASMX Web Service page is called through a browser. By passing the method name and parameter list in the URL, we can execute a method on a web service. This HTTP-GET request can be placed in an ACT test script, letting us load-test our Web service.

An easy way to get to the HTTP-GET request for a specific Web service is to navigate to the ASMX file. This page lists all the supported methods for the Web service. We can then select the `Web Service` method for which we want to generate a request. This provides us with a page where we enter sample parameters for the method, as shown in Figure 15.12.

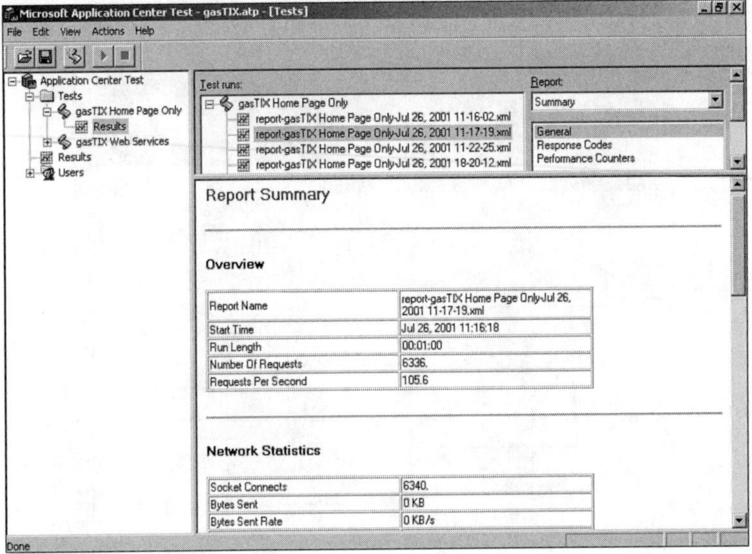

FIGURE 15.11

The ACT test results window lets us inspect different aspects of each test run.

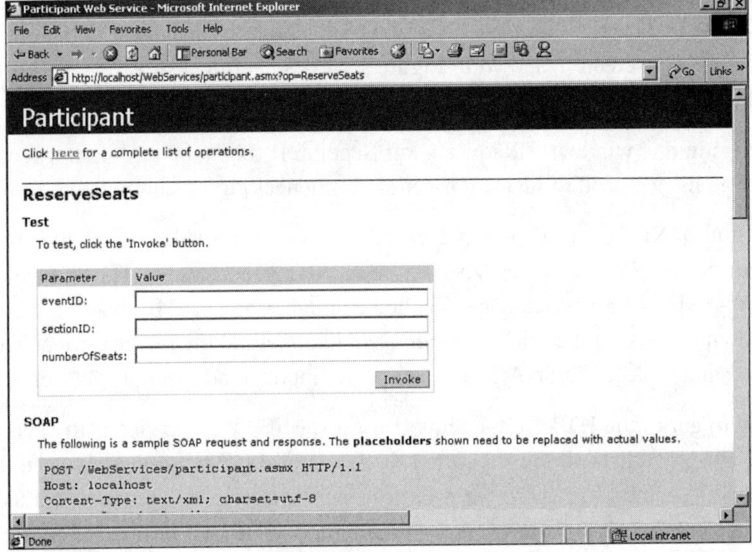

FIGURE 15.12

An HTML stub is created for each Web service method.

By entering the parameters and clicking the Invoke button, a new browser window is opened with the correctly formed URL in the QueryString window. We can cut and paste the contents of the browser's location window into an ACT test script, as in Figure 15.13.

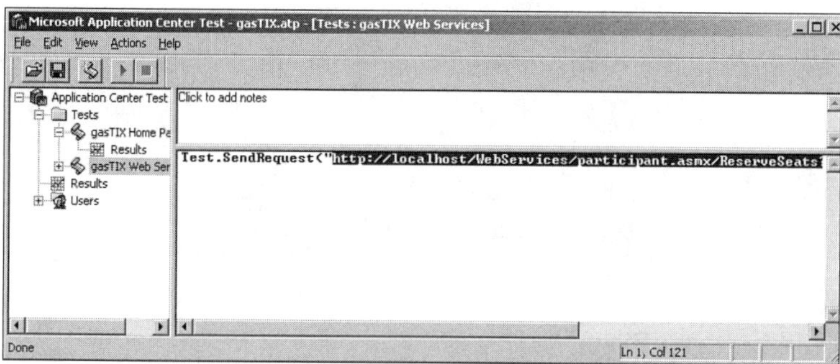

FIGURE 15.13
Pasting in the Web service method URL in an ACT test script.

This is an easy way to determine whether the methods we have exposed as .NET Web services will hold up under heavy loads.

Tuning the .NET Business Tier with Visual Studio Analyzer

One of the main tools used to tune the middle tier in .NET applications is Visual Studio Analyzer (VSA). VSA is designed to provide a picture of the lower-level operation of a Windows .NET application. Unlike debugging and tuning within a single language such as Visual Basic .NET, VSA shows us interactions between components, machines, and processes.

VSA captures data through events, and unwanted data can be filtered out. Graphical displays allow a technical architect to track down problems and bottlenecks. VSA operates within the familiar Visual Studio .NET IDE, and is made available with the Enterprise Edition of VS .NET.

When Visual Studio Analyzer is started, the Project Wizard dialog is displayed, shown in Figure 15.14. The first screen allows us to pick, in addition to our local machine, any other machines on the network our application might interact with that we want to monitor.

The next two screens in the wizard allow us to select which components we want to monitor, and which filters we want to activate. A wealth of data can be captured using these components, and if too many are selected, the data capture can be a bit overwhelming. It is a good idea to start with just a few events, then build up if more are needed.

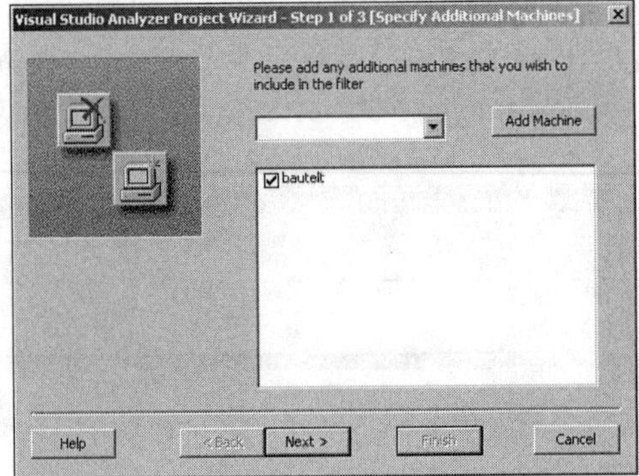

FIGURE 15.14
The Visual Studio Analyzer Project Wizard.

Once the VSA Project Wizard has been completed, we are placed in the Visual Studio .NET IDE. A new VSA Analyzer solution is created, and we can explore its different components in the VS .NET Solution Explorer window, shown in Figure 15.15.

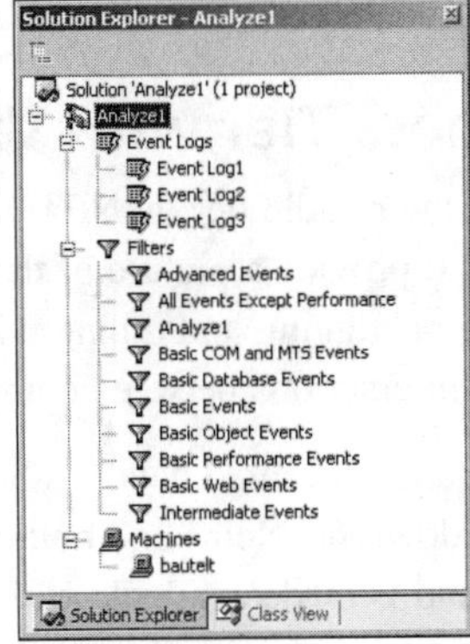

FIGURE 15.15
The Solution Explorer in VSA shows all the components of a VSA solution.

To begin a recording session, select Start Recording from the Analyzer menu. Each recording session generates a new Event Log in the Solution Explorer window.

TIP

It is a good idea to run our ACT test scripts while recording in VSA, as the user is doing in Figure 15.16. This will provide us with a lower-level view of all the events fired when our .NET application is placed under load.

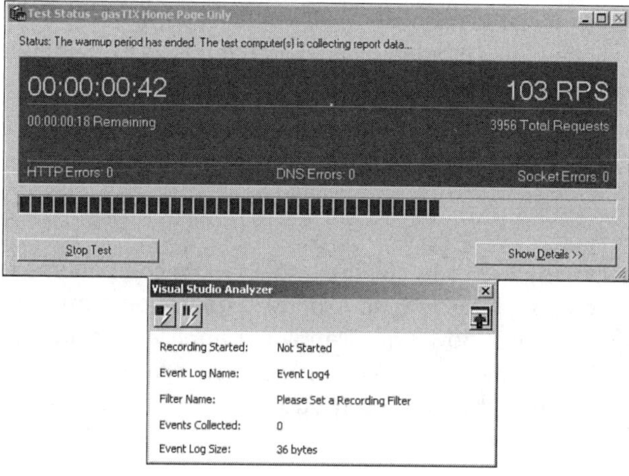

FIGURE 15.16

Recording a VSA test run while stressing the system with ACT.

When we feel like we have captured enough data, we can click the Stop Recording button on the recording details window. Now it is time to analyze the data we have just captured. Double-clicking the Event Log in the Solution Explorer will open up the event details view, shown in Figure 15.17.

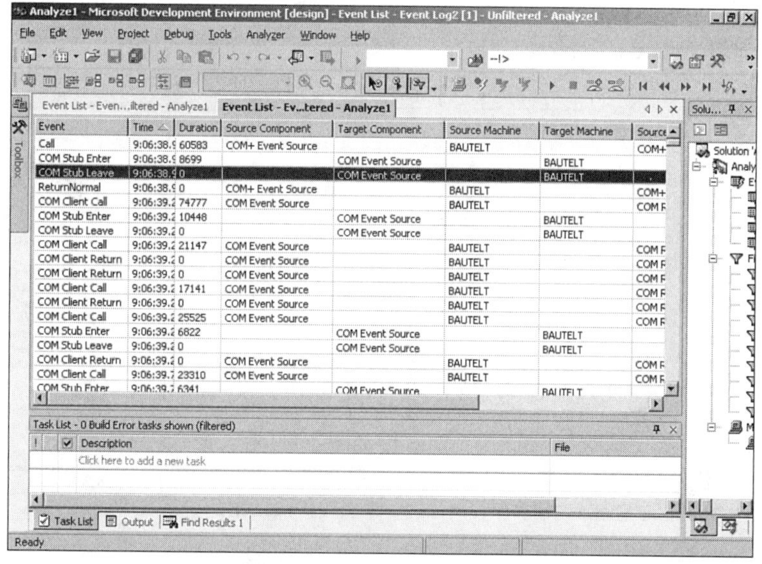

FIGURE 15.17

The VSA Event details view shows us all the events captured during a recording session.

We can use this screen to determine which events are taking a long time to execute. An easy way to do this is by clicking the Duration column header to sort by event duration time. Knowing which events are taking a long time provides us with a starting point for figuring out why our application is not performing as well as we would like.

CAUTION

.NET Interoperability enables us to call into legacy COM components from .NET managed code, and vice versa. Interop is an expensive operation, however, and VSA is a good tool to investigate just how significantly our applications are being impacted. Interop transitions should be minimized, perhaps by converting the unmanaged code to .NET. Refer to Chapter 9, "COM+ Integration," for a gasTIX interoperability example.

VSA provides several other helpful views, including the Machine Diagram (helpful for a distributed application with multiple servers), the Process Diagram, and the Component Diagram.

Click the New Process Diagram button to automatically generate a view of all the processes captured by the recorder. A sample VSA process diagram is shown in Figure 15.18.

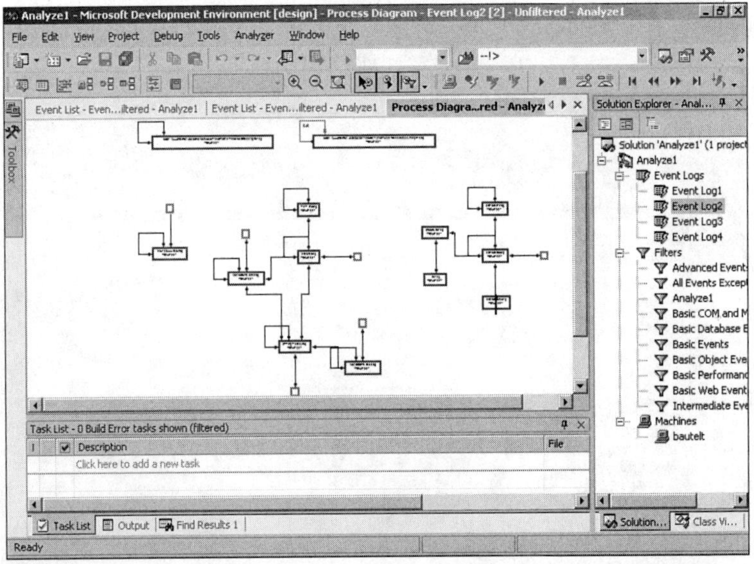

FIGURE 15.18

The Process Diagram displays how events move through application processes.

This view gives us a graphical look at interrelated .NET processes and when control is passed between the processes. Click the Replay Events button to see a slow-motion view of the process execution path. The currently executing inter-process communication will be highlighted in red.

Click the New Component Diagram button to automatically generate a view of all the components captured by the recorder. A sample VSA component diagram is shown in Figure 15.19.

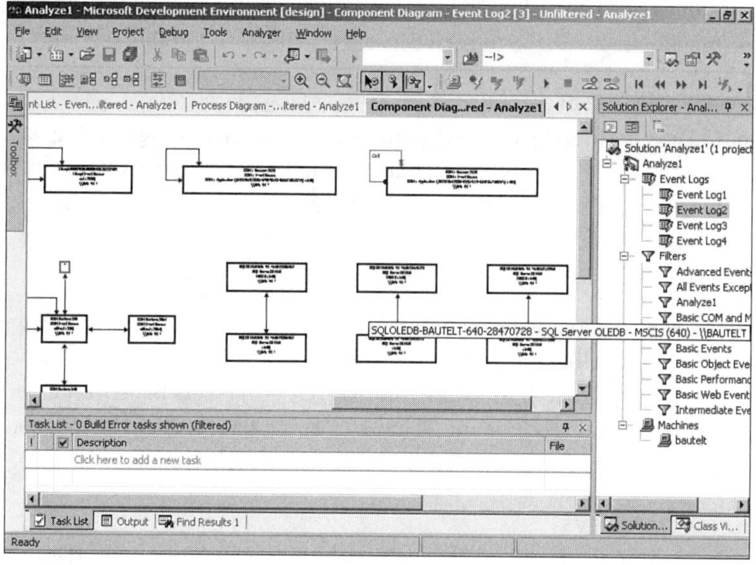

FIGURE 15.19

The Component Diagram displays how events move between the various components that make up an application.

This view gives us a graphical look at interrelated .NET components and when control is passed between the components. Again, the Replay Events button can be clicked to see a slow-motion view of the component execution path.

Visual Studio Analyzer provides the business tier developer with a wealth of information that shows how a .NET application is really executing under the covers. VSA is a great tool for identifying performance bottlenecks, and should be a key resource in the tuning toolkit of middle-tier programmers.

Tuning the .NET Data Tier

Data services in the .NET Framework are largely built around ADO.NET and Microsoft's enterprise-level relational database management system, SQL Server 2000. When planning, implementing, and tuning an application database in SQL Server, schema design and database operations should be given special consideration.

Refer to Chapter 7, "Implementing .NET Data Services," for a detailed data discussion of the implementation of the gasTIX data tier. This section will present general data tier tuning guidelines.

Schema Design

Many different things go into designing an efficient database schema. A few of the more important design guidelines related to performance are discussed in this section.

Normalization/Performance Tradeoff

It is important to keep performance considerations in mind when designing the database schema. As a general rule, avoid highly generalized models. Flexibility often comes at the expense of performance. If performance is a key design goal, we need to get specific with our tables and fields. A proper balance between deep tables with fewer columns and wide tables with fewer rows should be reached, based on how data will be queried.

An OLTP system generally requires a more normalized schema, while an OLAP application tends to be denormalized. However, an appropriate level of normalization and denormalization in each scenario must be reached. An overly normalized OLTP schema will not perform well. Designing the right level in each scenario is more of an art than a science. We should share our proposed designs with more experienced DBAs and solicit their feedback.

Primary and Foreign Keys

Keep primary keys short and avoid GUIDs unless absolutely necessary. GUIDs are appropriate in highly distributed applications where new row entries will be made at remote sites that will be replicated into a central data store. Employing GUIDs as primary keys prevents one remote site from overwriting another's data. However, GUIDs come with a performance penalty since they are 128-bit integers. A CHAR or INT column as a primary key will perform better in SELECT statements if a GUID is not really necessary.

When implementing foreign keys, refer to as few tables as possible. If updating or deleting rows in referenced tables, make sure the referencing columns are indexed. If no index exists, the referencing table will be locked and a full table scan will be performed, an operation that is usually quite costly.

Database Operations

Once a database schema has been implemented, ongoing maintenance and tuning of the database is crucial to keeping the application performing well. This section covers the most important database operation issues that should be investigated in any .NET eBusiness application.

Indexes

Indexes speed up SELECT queries, but slow down `INSERT`, `UPDATE`, and `DELETE` statements, so choose them wisely. The more selective an index is, the better. *Composite indexes*, those that include multiple columns, will only be used by queries if the leading column in the index is used in the query join or filter, so make sure to order the columns in indexes properly. It may be necessary to create additional indexes for a table with the same columns in a different order.

Stored procedures are pre-compiled and pre-optimized by the SQL Server 2000 engine, providing fast execution. Use them for performing database operations instead of inline SQL in middle-tier ADO.NET commands.

Generally speaking, dynamic SQL should be avoided within stored procedures. This includes any statement within a stored procedure that is concatenated together. Instead, perform conditional checks within the stored procedure, placing the statement to be executed within each check. More advanced options can sometimes mitigate the negative effects of dynamic SQL, but an advanced DBA is usually required to implement these options effectively.

Transact SQL (T/SQL)

Avoid SQL functions on columns in a `WHERE` clause or in a `JOIN`. Using a function in these contexts will prevent an index from being used that would normally provide fast access. The NOT IN keyword should also be avoided.

Sometimes a SQL cursor can be replaced with a complex SQL statement using a `GROUP BY` or `HAVING` clause. Less experienced Transact SQL programmers can especially be tempted to use a cursor because of how familiar it feels to a simple FOR loop in other programming languages such as Visual Basic .NET. However, cursors can quickly limit performance and scalability and should only be used when the work they perform cannot be done another way.

Locking Issues

Locks are placed on rows in the database each time a query is performed to make sure they are not updated in the middle of the query. Without such locking, skewed results would be returned, with the first half of the result set representing one state of the data, and the second half another state because an update was performed by another user mid-query.

Because locks are so integral to database integrity, they are necessary for operation and cannot altogether be avoided. However, too much locking in a system can cause contention for resources. Performance can be hampered because queries may spend a good deal of time waiting on locks to be released, rather than returning result sets.

SQL Server provides several ways to monitor the state of locking in a database. The sysprocesses table in the Master database can help track down processes that are blocked. SQL also exposes the Locks object to the Performance Monitor, providing several counters that can help identify high contention levels in the DB. If we think excessive locking may be causing contention in our application, these counters can help us locate the root cause and test solutions.

SQL Profiler / SQL Query Analyzer

The SQL Profiler tool can be used to determine which T/SQL statements are taking a long time to run. Profiler is a powerful tool, capturing a multitude of events and filtering out unwanted data. It should primarily be run on a test system during load testing. However, depending on the loads experienced in production, we might choose to run Profiler on a limited basis on production SQL Server boxes to obtain more accurate performance metrics.

Profiler, displayed in Figure 15.20, captures SQL statement execution by time slices, showing detailed timing metrics for each command.

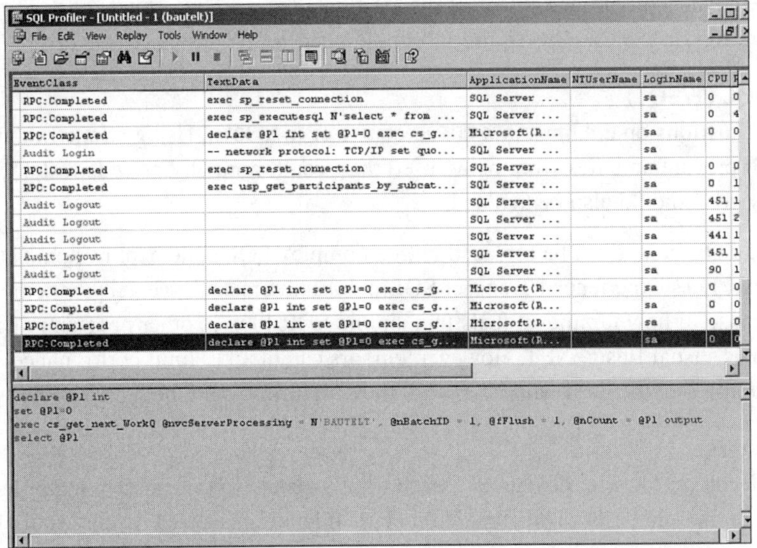

FIGURE 15.20

SQL Profiler captures all database operation at a low level.

Once we've captured an adequate amount of data in the Profiler window, we can stop the recording and copy and paste the data into Excel for further analysis. Excel gives us an easy way to sort the data by CPU time or by Duration in descending order, so that the longest-running queries are displayed at the top. We can run down the list and choose to tune the queries we think should be faster.

TIP

In order to filter out unwanted data, SQL Profiler allows us to capture just the commands or users we want. This gives us the ability to focus on just the execution statements we're interested in.

Profiler also features the Index Tuning Wizard. This tool can sometimes help optimize indexes on tables, based on commands captured in the execution window. The Index Tuning Wizard is shown in Figure 15.21.

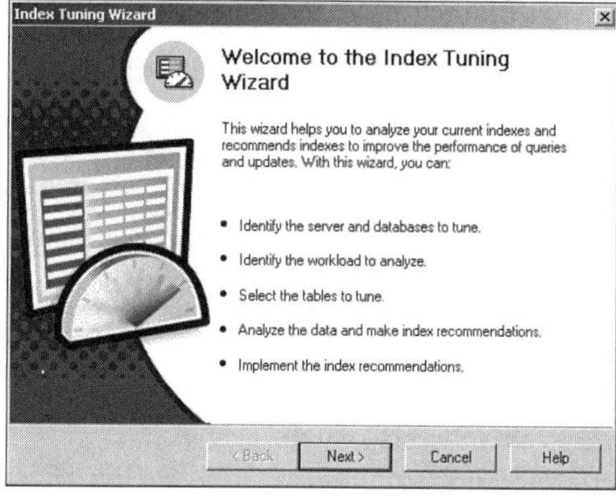

FIGURE 15.21
SQL Profiler's Index Tuning Wizard can suggest indexes we may have missed.

By specifying a trace file generated in SQL Profiler (.trc extension) and selecting which tables to analyze, the Index Tuning Wizard can analyze which indexes may help speed up performance. When analysis is complete, recommendations are listed (shown in Figure 15.22) and can be automatically executed or scheduled as a SQL Server job.

Although it may not always be selective enough to meet our needs, the Index Tuning Wizard can provide us with a good starting point and may catch some indexes we have overlooked. More information on the Index Tuning Wizard can be found in Chapter 7, "Implementing .NET Data Services."

Once we have identified the problem SQL statements using Profiler, SQL Query Analyzer's graphical Show Execution Plan feature, shown in Figure 15.23, can provide us with details on how queries are being executed:

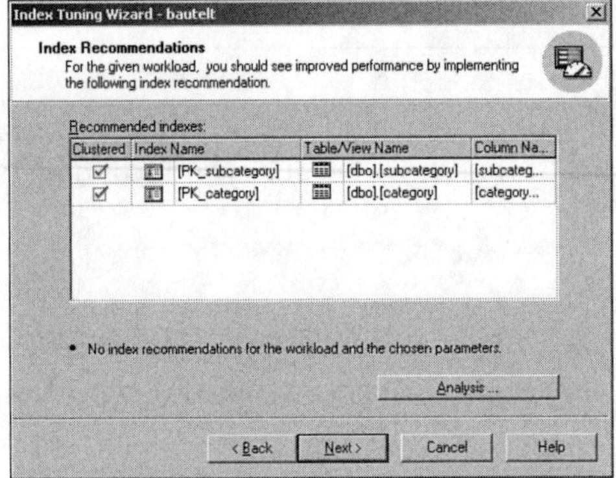

FIGURE 15.22
We can execute the suggested indexes made by the Index Tuning Wizard immediately.

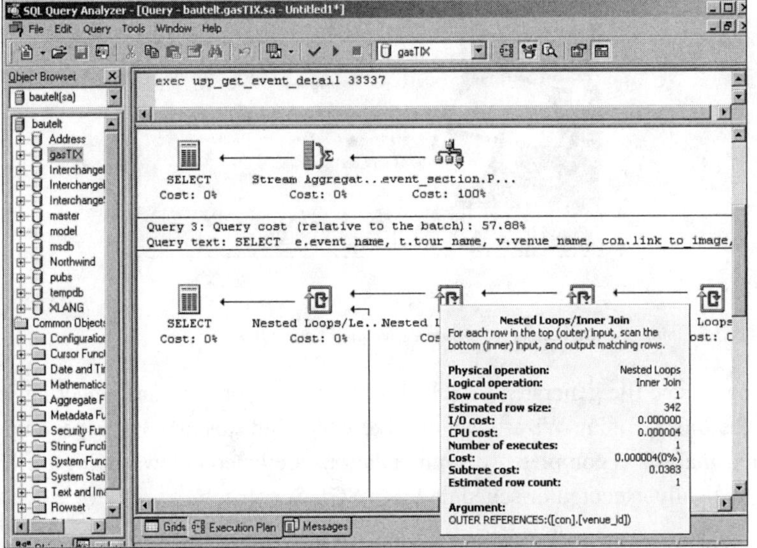

FIGURE 15.23
SQL Query Analyzer's Show Execution Plan feature gives us a graphical view of how our queries are run.

Hovering over a step in the execution plan gives details such as a description of the logical operation performed and the argument of the SQL command that generated the step.

As we develop a feel for why the problem T/SQL statements are not performing as desired, we can rewrite the queries until performance is improved. Alternatively, we can tune the indexes on the tables being joined in the queries. As a last resort, optimizer hints such as locking hints, join hints, query hints, and table hints can be tried if we still are not getting the performance we need.

From Here

Paying close attention to efficient coding practices in each of the logical tiers of the .NET architecture is an important part of writing a well-tuned application. Several different mechanisms such as ASP.NET caching help us to get more efficiency, and thus better performance, from our applications.

Microsoft also provides several performance utilities, including Application Center Test, Visual Studio Analyzer, and SQL Profiler. These tools are designed to help identify and resolve performance bottlenecks that may develop throughout the various logical and physical tiers.

Although performance testing may take persistence and determination, it is well worth the effort to track down and resolve problems with a poorly running system. It is quite satisfying to help meet the business goals of a company and deliver a quality user experience through tuning. Plus, simply put, it is a great feeling to see a system we have worked hard on tuning running like lightning!

To learn how to deploy a .NET application once it has been tuned for performance, refer to Chapter 16, "Deploying the Application.".

Deploying the Application

by Robert Amar

CHAPTER

16

IN THIS CHAPTER

- Putting the Application Together 470
- Infrastructure Considerations 473
- Executing Deployments with Visual Studio .NET 477
- Deploying a .NET Application to the World 484
- Creating Web Clusters with Application Center 2000 513
- From Here 518

Moving a distributed enterprise application from a development environment to its final destination has always been a very involved task. In the Windows DNA environment, the setup of each tier of the traditional *n*-tier application is essentially a separate event. The procedures to deploy the elements of each application layer and to construct their interaction mechanisms are mostly manual, and are thus error-prone.

The .NET Framework has been designed in part to reduce these common difficulties, and if successful, it stands to change the face of distributed application deployment. Many of the exciting new features of .NET assemblies, such as metadata and versioning (discussed in detail in Chapter 4, "Tools of the Trade"), form the cornerstone of such a revolution. However, it is the addition of Microsoft's Windows Installer as the vehicle for packaging files and managing deployment versions that completes the package. Through a combination of .NET language features and robust installer technology, the deployment of full-featured, enterprise-class distributed applications is greatly simplified.

We will begin our survey of deployment by examining the bare-bones requirements for a simple .NET Web server. We will then proceed to a more detailed description of the deployment of the gasTIX sample application discussed throughout this book to a set of production servers.

Putting the Application Together

Currently, in the world of the Component Object Model (COM, or COM+ in Windows 2000) and Visual Studio 6, deploying the individual tiers of an ordinary *n*-tier enterprise application requires a lot of tedious, manual effort in each tier. Setting up interactions between the various application layers can also get quite involved, requiring several extra steps such as setting up Data Source Names (DSNs) on client computers, tuning settings and permissions for Distributed COM (DCOM), and replicating COM+ applications.

This scenario is all too common among enterprise development projects using Microsoft technologies. For example, a user interface developer might use Visual InterDev to deploy classic ASP and Dynamic HTML pages for the presentation tier to a Web server. Similarly, a business object developer may use Visual Basic 6.0's Package and Deployment Wizard for ActiveX component deployment. COM+ applications (and legacy MTS packages), while reliable and modular, must be set up manually and then exported as installer packages or application proxies.

The .NET Framework dramatically improves this situation. Because .NET assemblies can run independent of the Windows Registry thanks to metadata and versioning, a much simpler installation mechanism is possible. A single Windows Installer package can contain all the files required for a particular application machine.

Windows Installer packages rely on an internal database that carefully records all changes made to a computer during the course of an installation. Because of this, uninstall and repair operations are cleaner and more reliable than ever. In addition, these installers can *themselves* be versioned, with old versions of the installed program automatically updated regardless of whether the new version consists of older or newer versions of the application assemblies.

Let us now examine what needs to be deployed within each layer of a .NET application.

The Presentation Tier

The pieces that make up an ASP.NET presentation tier from a deployment standpoint are:

- Configuration and XML Web service discovery files such as web.config, .vsdisco, and global.asax.
- Web page content such as files with extensions .html, .aspx, .asmx, .js, and .css.
- The code-behind file for each ASP.NET page with an extension indicating the source language, such as .aspx.cs or .aspx.vb.
- The assembly (.dll) created as a result of compiling the code-behind files and any other resources.
- Additional non-code resources such as images and sounds.

We might tend to feel uncomfortable with the proliferation of server-side source code types. However, we can rest assured that ASP.NET takes great pains to ensure that our server-side code is safe, as shown in Figure 16.1.

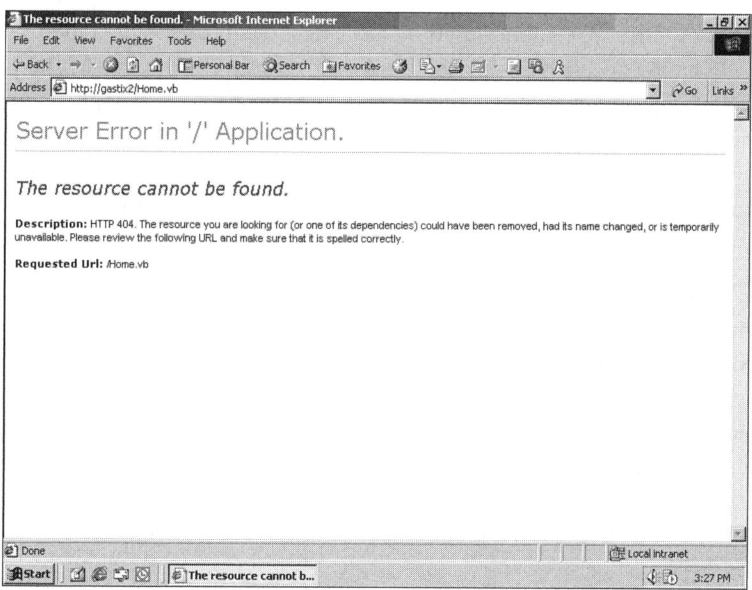

FIGURE 16.1
ASP.NET protects code-behind files.

This protection occurs because all .NET-specific source file extensions—including .cs, .vb, .csproj, and .vbproj—are mapped to the ASP.NET script handler by IIS, and are thus processed and protected by the handler. Only during remote debugging can these files be accessed over IIS.

CAUTION

DLLs are not script-mapped to the ASP.NET handler, so ASP.NET itself does not protect DLLs (or any other unmapped script extensions, for that matter). If we don't want our presentation or business DLLs downloaded and dissected with ILDasm, we need to be sure to protect the files manually by setting their read permissions appropriately in IIS. Fortunately, the Visual Studio .NET deployment process, as we will see, handles this for us.

The large number of presentation components may look daunting. The good news, as we will soon see, is that Visual Studio .NET provides us with deployment capabilities that help manage all of these different resources with a great deal of ease.

The Business Tier

The business and data access objects, as we might expect, need only be exposed by their respective assembly files. Assemblies used by more than one program on a machine must reside in the Global Application Cache. Private assemblies, on the other hand, may reside wherever deemed appropriate at development time, even inside of Web application folders. In the development of gasTIX and its related sites, we have only created private assemblies. When we walk through the deployment of the gasTIX application, we will see that the private assemblies for business objects are placed inside the Web application folders, together with the assemblies for the compiled presentation-tier pages. This is done because the presentation-tier DLLs depend on the middle-tier DLLs.

The fact that our business objects' DLLs coexist with Web pages in an application's virtual directory allows us, for most deployment procedures, to treat them as if they were simple content files, such as ASP.NET pages or image files, in the Web application. This lets us easily propagate and synchronize our business objects across multiple locations, such as related projects or computers in a Web farm. Middle-tier synchronization can be more difficult in COM+ because of the locking of DLLs in use; the fact that .NET assemblies can be replaced on-the-fly without shutting down a runtime process such as IIS or a COM+ application is a great help.

We will see a particularly compelling advantage to this approach when we introduce Web clusters into the picture (see "Creating Web Clusters with Application Center 2000" later in this chapter).

The Data Tier

Concerning deployment, the database-tier of an .NET enterprise application will not feel much different than in Windows DNA. Programmers working on Web pages and components that access databases may find data-bound Web controls, graphical designers and the strong typing of the new ADO.NET DataSet programming model useful new tools in development. (ADO.NET is discussed in detail in Chapter 6, "Implementing .NET Business Services.")

ADO.NET supports ODBC connectivity, and .NET Web applications are thus still flexible in terms of the variety of data sources accessible. However, Microsoft's .NET enterprise-class database product should always be highly considered. SQL Server 2000, besides being a rigorously tested upgrade to previous editions, adds support for XML-based queries and HTTP access to the database. This support is a major step towards realizing a SQL Server database as a generalized form of web service with which other XML Web services and BizTalk servers can communicate using XML. This interoperability using XML as the messaging format is a hallmark of SQL Server as a .NET Enterprise Server and a key part of the .NET initiative. The major features of SQL Server 2000, Microsoft's latest, Web-aware incarnation of its enterprise database service, as well as changes from SQL Server 7.0, are discussed more fully in Chapter 7, "Implementing .NET Data Services."

Infrastructure Considerations

Any computer that can support the .NET Framework components is a possible target server for a .NET deployment. In the future, this may include a variety of non-Microsoft platforms, but, for now, the supported platforms include all flavors of Windows from Windows 98 going forward. Now that we have examined what to deploy, we turn our attention towards good practices in designing and selecting actual deployment targets.

Technical Requirements for Deployment

Simply put, a .NET Web server should have the .NET redistributable components running on it. These components, which include the elements of the .NET Common Language Runtime (CLR) as well as the ASP.NET script handler for IIS, are free for download as a single package from the Microsoft .NET site, `www.microsoft.com/net`.

TIP

Installing the full .NET Software Development Kit (SDK) is not necessary for machines that will simply host .NET applications. The SDK contains compilers and development tools that simply take up space and encourage unwanted development on production boxes. In order to keep deployment machines as clean as possible, consider installing just the .NET redistributable components instead of the full SDK.

Application-Imposed Requirements

The application we are set to deploy, along with the XML Web services that it accesses, may place some constraints on our deployment setup. For example, any application that accesses a SQL Server 2000 database or implements the Microsoft Passport Single Sign-In (SSI) service must be running a Windows enterprise server operating system (such as NT 4.0 Server or Windows 2000 Server) to host the necessary software.

Even given the flexibility of the .NET Framework in terms of the platforms supported, we will want to make the investment in enterprise-class server software for our distributed enterprise applications. This will also allow us to take advantage of technologies which can increase the availability and scalability of your Web applications, such as Windows 2000 Network Load Balancing (NLB), which distributes TCP/IP Web requests to machines in a cluster. A whole host of advanced capabilities such as NLB exist to open the door for future growth, which is something we discuss next.

Performance Considerations

A critical part of any infrastructure plan includes a discussion of performance, scalability, and availability. At a local level, .NET assemblies take a performance hit during the conversion from Intermediate Language (IL) to native code, and also during type resolutions from metadata in shared assemblies. However, assuming that assemblies are converted into native code via the pre-JIT compiler as needed, .NET is not significantly hampered in terms of its performance by the use of IL. In fact, ASP.NET enjoys a scalability and performance advantage over classic ASP because all pages are now compiled, as opposed to interpreted server-side script. For more information on pre-JIT compilation using the NGen utility, see Chapter 15, "Performance Tuning in .NET."

Keep in mind that .NET was not developed simply as a performance enhancement over existing applications. Certainly, some attention was paid to scalability, especially for Web pages. Still, .NET is really about interoperability and publishing services over the Internet for a truly distributed, global user experience. In fact, Microsoft recommends the use of "smart devices" and XML Web services to distribute computing load across a network, and in doing so increasing overall performance.

Scaling Up Versus Scaling Out

To get high performance out of a website, deployment administrators usually focus attention at the hardware level. There are two different approaches to this. *Scaling up* is the term applied to boosting the computing power of a single server by increasing its internal resources, such as CPU (both CPU speed and number of processors), memory, and peripheral speed (for example, IDE versus SCSI). *Scaling out* is the term applied to boosting the computing power of an application by clustering servers together, all running the same software.

Scaling up is a technique generally used to increase performance without significantly impacting maintainability, and is generally used for increasing data-tier performance, in which data coherency is much more easily achieved using a non-clustering solution. Of course, scaling up can be both expensive and risky. Some machines are simply not designed for scaling up, and unless such machines can be redeployed in other capacities, they are wasted. A single scaled-up machine, while more powerful than a group of lower-end machines because all of its resources are internal, represents a single point of failure—lose this machine and the site is off the air until the machine is fixed or replaced. Additionally, the price of a machine that can support more processors, disk space, and memory will usually be significantly higher than separate, lower-end machines.

Scaling out is a method that is gaining more and more attention and favor with time. Scaling out can be economically friendly because several lower-end, workstation-class machines are used together to create a more powerful unit. However, maintenance is spread over several machines, and software may be more expensive because of the use of multiple machines and the possible need for multiple licenses. While network latency, message passing and management traffic can cause a performance decrease relative to the same amount of scaling up, scaling out has a significant advantage—high availability. Machines balance the load between each other. If one machine fails, the other machines can pick up the slack.

For Windows platforms, there are two major approaches to scaling out. First, there are traditional hardware-based load balancers such as Cisco's NetDirector and F5 Networks' BIG-IP family. Second, there is Windows NLB, which provides a software-based configuration, but has fewer options for traffic control than the typical hardware-based solution. NLB comes with Windows 2000 Advanced Server and Datacenter Server, as well as with Application Center 2000, a new product from Microsoft that provides easy graphical monitoring and configuration of Web clusters using NLB. We will discuss Application Center 2000 later in this chapter as a tool for creating a cluster of Web servers for our gasTIX application.

Deployment Platform for gasTIX Sites

To illustrate some of the previous discussion, we will select a scalable deployment platform for our gasTIX site. We have chosen to separate the Web sites onto different machines, which means there are really two sites—gasTIX and gasBAGS. Both of these sites are available over the Internet:

- gasTIX is at `www.gastix.com`.
- gasBAGS is at `www.gasbags.com`.

Figure 16.2 shows a diagram of the proposed site.

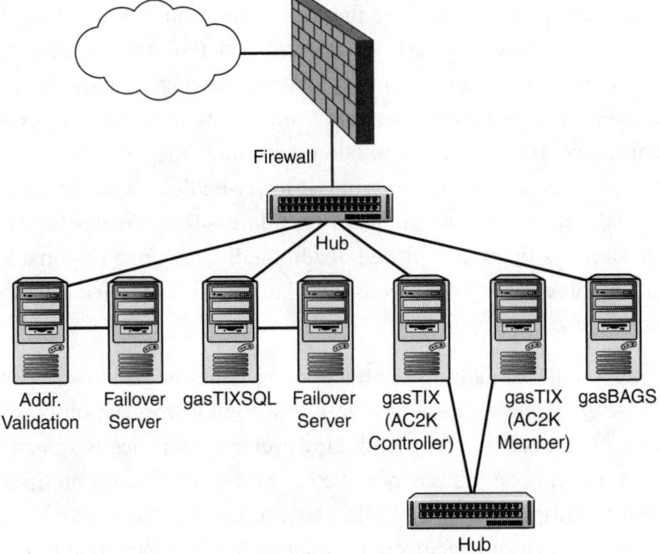

FIGURE 16.2
The infrastructure setup for the gasTIX sites.

Each of the Web servers is an Intel Pentium III 550-MHz machine with 128 MB of RAM. The data tier uses simple SQL Server failover and a standalone RAID for data protection. The database servers (both the main server and the failover server) are Pentium III 700-MHz machines with 256 MB of RAM. All machines are running Windows 2000 Advanced Server. While these machines won't withstand a large flood of traffic, they will perform adequately for a few hundred users at a time, which is the expected target traffic. Also, notice that two machines have been reserved for gasTIX.com. These two machines will be joined together in an Application Center 2000 cluster later in this chapter (see "Creating Web Clusters with Application Center 2000").

Executing Deployments with Visual Studio .NET

Visual Studio .NET, much like previous versions of Visual Studio, integrates within itself a full-featured facility for creating installer projects to deploy .NET applications. However, the packaging and deployment features of Visual Studio .NET represent a significant step towards setting up an *n*-tier application as a single application rather than *n* separate applications which must then be made to work together.

Visual Studio .NET Deployment Projects

The heart of all deployments in Visual Studio .NET is the Deployment Project. Deployment projects can be built and kept within the same solutions whose component parts they deploy, or they can be standalone projects. Just like DLLs and content files are outputs of a normal project, the output of a deployment project is one of four items:

- A .cab file containing the files from the project.
- A *merge module*, which represents a module for a shared component or assembly. This module can be incorporated into other Windows Installer packages.
- A *Web Setup* project, which is a Windows Installer setup package that installs its content directly into an IIS virtual directory on the target machine.
- A conventional Windows Installer setup package for a Windows application.

As our focus will be almost entirely on the last two options (Web Setup and conventional installer), let us quickly discuss the first two. The .cab file option, which produces a Microsoft cabinet format archive of the included files, is useful in compressing files to be used in other distributions or install packages, or as an internal distribution format. Merge modules are useful for creating standard install programs for shared assemblies and can be inserted into Windows Installers for applications that depend on them, insulating users of the shared assembly from any peculiar installation difficulties or procedures.

The following sections describe the other two deployment methods in detail, which both produce Windows Installer packages.

Dissecting the Web Setup Project

The Web Setup installer option, as mentioned before, creates a Windows Installer to install files into an IIS virtual directory. This is the simplest way to get a Web application deployed, but it also has some significant limitations. When we first decide to create a setup project, we are greeted with the screen shown in Figure 16.3.

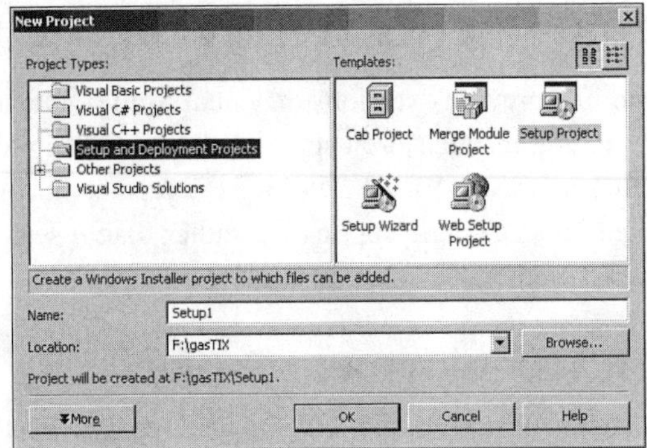

FIGURE 16.3
Different choices for Visual Studio .NET setup projects.

Since we want to deploy a web project in this instance, we will select Web Setup Project and proceed to the screen, shown in Figure 16.4.

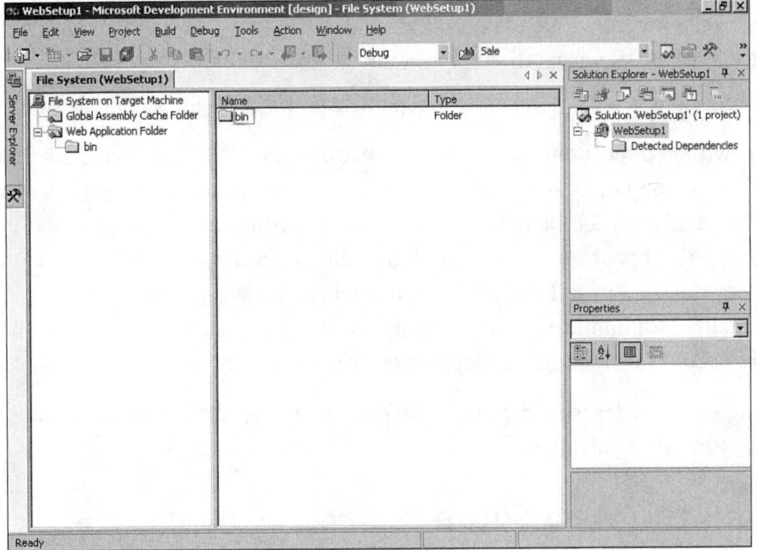

FIGURE 16.4
The structure of the file system for a Visual Studio .NET Web Setup project.

Notice that two destinations are allowed in this project by default: the Global Assembly Cache Folder and the Web Application Folder. These map to the target machine's GAC and the IIS virtual directory into which the application will be installed, respectively. For example, we can specify that a shared assembly is to go into the target machine's GAC by adding it to the Global Assembly Cache Folder. Alternately, we can place a file in the Web site virtual directory that will be created at install time by placing it in the Web Application Folder in the setup project.

At first, it seems like we might be in for a lot of work, adding each individual file from our Web Application project to the Web Application Folder and hoping we didn't miss anything. However, Visual Studio .NET steps in again and assists us by providing us with the ability to add *project outputs* to each of the file system entries. Project outputs are natural groupings of individual projects' component parts and compilation products. The major project outputs we will concern ourselves with for a Web Setup project include the following:

- **Primary output—**the DLL that results from compiling all of the Web pages' code-behind classes and any other resources.
- **Content files—**the project files with actual Web content or configuration information, such as .asax, .aspx and .resx files.
- **Source files—**the code-behind classes for each Web page in the project.

A Sample Web Setup: gasBAGS

Let's illustrate how to use the Web Setup features by configuring a deployment project for the gasBAGS website we developed earlier in this book. First, we will add the project outputs to the Setup project's File System view. Second, we will add images (extra resources) to the File System view. Finally, we will build and deploy the project.

To add the project outputs, we right-click the Web Application Folder, choose Add, and select Project Output… to bring up the Add Project Output Group dialog box, shown in Figure 16.5.

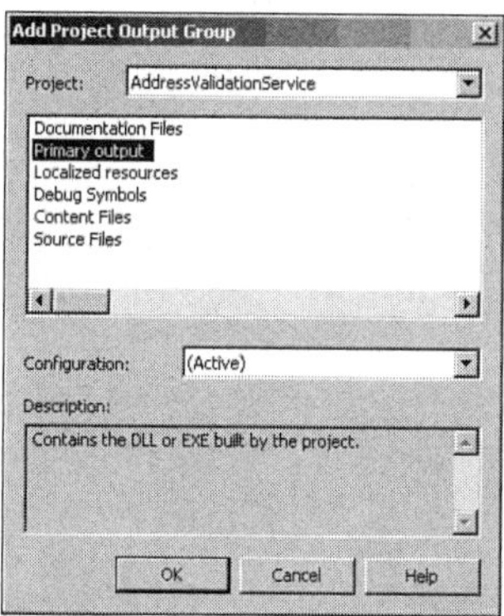

FIGURE 16.5

The Add Project Output Group dialog box allows us to add a project's file groups and compilation products to a deployment project.

If we compare the three project outputs to the list of what needs to be deployed from the presentation tier, we see that we've covered everything except non-code resources, such as images. In order to add the images on the pages, we will have to manually add folders and files to the Web Application folder.

All of the images in gasBAGS reside in an `/images` subdirectory underneath the Web application root, so we will mimic this structure by adding an `/images` Web folder to the Web Application folder. We can right-click on the folder, choose Add, and then choose Web Folder and specify images as the new folder name. Once we have done this, we can add files to it by right-clicking the new folder, selecting Add, and then choosing File….

TIP

We can use the Windows standard SHIFT and CTRL keys while choosing files in the Add files dialog to make multiple selections.

Once we have added all the images and subdirectories, we are ready to build this deployment project and deploy gasBAGS. The File System entries should look like the completed view in Figure 16.6.

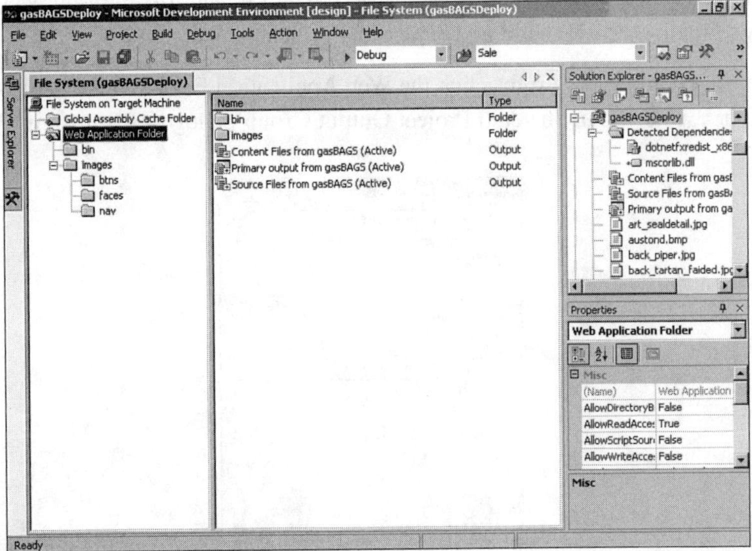

FIGURE 16.6

The completed file system for the gasBAGS deployment project.

CAUTION

At the time of this writing, there are subtle problems with building deployment projects containing image files from Web Application projects. We need to be sure that the property pages for each image file have None as the Build Action, rather than Compile. If image files are inadvertently compiled, it could cause a deployment project to fail with an unrecoverable (and unexplained) build error. If we are still receiving errors on build, we should try excluding images them from the Web Application project and rebuilding the project.

During a Visual Studio .NET setup project build, each project that is not up to date is automatically rebuilt, assemblies are constructed, and all specified files are added to the installation package. Upon installation, the correct files are automatically deployed to the server with default, sensible settings (e.g. content files can be read by Web users, while DLL files cannot), all without our manual intervention. While we still must manually transport the Windows Installer archive, the archive automatically takes care of setting up the IIS virtual directory in which it will reside using parameters configured at the time the deployment project was built. We will examine some of these parameters later in this chapter.

CAUTION

While these new deployment capabilities are truly powerful, there are a number of items that could easily trip up the unsuspecting user.

First, ASP.NET expects to find the DLL containing the compiled code-behind classes in the /bin subdirectory of the Web application's IIS virtual directory. However, by default, the primary output from a Visual Studio .NET Web Application project is automatically written to the /bin subdirectory of wherever it is placed in the File System view of the Web Setup project. **Do not** place the primary output in the /bin subdirectory of the Web Application Folder, or else we will write the primary output to the wrong place in the virtual directory (it will end up in /bin/bin).

Second, don't forget to include the "source files" project output for a Web project. This project output contains the source for the code-behind classes for the Web pages, and ASP.NET will not get too far if we leave them out.

Finally, we need to be sure that the project outputs we are adding to the project really belong to the project we intended. If we have several projects in the solution, the first project will be selected by default in the Add Project Output Group dialog box. Among all the details to contend with, this one is very easy to miss.

Once we are done with the file system setup, we build the deployment project just like we would build any other project in a Visual Studio .NET solution. The output of the project is a Windows Installer file (extension .msi) that ends up in either the /Debug or /Release subdirectory of the directory in which the deployment project resides, depending on whether the Web Setup project was in Debug or Release configuration.

TIP

We can use Debug and Release versions to store different configurations of the deployment, perhaps one for internal testing and one for final release.

NOTE

As project outputs are added, dependencies on common .NET DLLs or other DLLs in our project are automatically detected by Visual Studio .NET. When the project is built, the dependent projects are automatically compiled and their assemblies built and included in the setup project.

And, in case you are wondering, we can specify that common .NET runtime elements be copied to the Web server. By default, the .NET platform is automatically installed on the target server if needed. If we examine the dependencies in the deployment project, we can see the redistributable package, in the form of a merge module (extension .msm), added in with the rest of the files for deployment. This accounts for most of the rather large sizes of the Web Setup Windows Installers (usually around 15 MB for most moderate-sized Web sites, with about 1 to 2 MB of pure content and source files). If we wish, we can remove this component from the deployment project, but our users will need to install the .NET Framework separately.

To test the installer we just built, we can locate the .msi file and copy it to a target Web server. When we run the installer, it should look something like the installer in Figure 16.7.

As a quick check to be sure that we have things working correctly, make sure you can see and interact with the gasBAGS site after the installer is done. The site should be able to run with any other steps when the installation has completed since we have distributed the gasBAGS.dll assembly, and the .NET redistributable components.

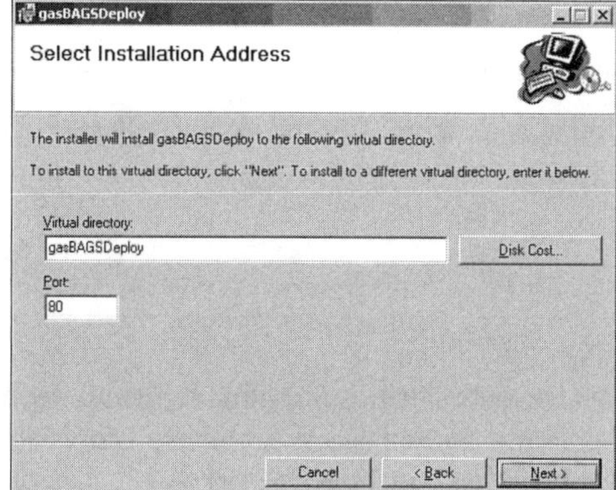

FIGURE 16.7
Our new gasBAGSDeploy installer at work.

TIP

During the execution of the installer, we may notice that the name of the virtual directory is something different than what you wanted. To change this, set the `VirtualDirectory` property of the Web Application Folder in the File System view. If we want a more elegant title than the name we assigned to the deployment project in the first place (for example, for an installer to be released to the world), then set the `ProductName` property of the Web Setup project itself.

"XCopy Deployment" Is Still Possible

To perform the deployment of a simple .NET Web application, it is not necessary to use the Windows Installer packages created by the deployment projects in Visual Studio .NET. Simply copying over all of the content and source files for the Website to a .NET Web server-capable computer will allow the application to run. This is known as XCopy deployment (named after the DOS XCopy command), and is literally as easy as issuing a command at a DOS prompt or dragging files in Windows Explorer. Although we don't derive the versioning and maintenance benefits of Windows Installers and the XCopy procedure is error-prone, it nevertheless makes it possible to simply copy files to the Web server and have the application work.

A Closer Look at the Setup Project

A number of items are customizable in a Web Setup project. These include things such as the permissions for the newly created IIS virtual directory on the target machine, the default document, and the IIS application protection setting. By changing these properties, which correspond to IIS metabase properties, we can be sure that the Web directory we set up doesn't need to be changed manually after the installer runs, which defeats the purpose of an installer.

All of these items can be found as properties of the Web Application Folder in the File System view. They are instantly accessible through the properties window in the Visual Studio .NET IDE.

TIP

The project's default permissions settings are almost always acceptable for a production deployment. For example, source access, directory browsing, and write access are disabled, and the site only allows execution of scripts.

Another aspect of all deployment projects is the support for Windows Installer versioning. There are several properties of each deployment project, found on the property page for the deployment project in the properties window of Visual Studio .NET, that control this versioning:

- The `Version` property identifies the number of the version of the application that this installer bears.
- The `UpgradeCode` is a GUID that uniquely identifies the product through its changing versions and deployment packages. Existing applications with the same upgrade code as an installer being executed on the same machine can be updated or removed automatically if the version numbers dictate it.
- The `DetectNewerInstalledVersion` property determines whether or not this installer should detect and warn the user of a newer installed version of the application.
- The `RemovePreviousVersions` property determines whether or not this installer should remove any versions found of this application that are different from previous versions.

Deploying a .NET Application to the World

Packaging and deploying software on a large-scale basis onto servers over which we have no control is a very different scenario from the local-deployment scenario described above. In the scenario already explored, we have deployed a .NET e-Business application onto Web servers on the other side of our firewall. We will now take a look at how we might package the gasTIX sample application for mass download by users. In fact, the package and deployment issues considered in this section were constructed to make the gasTIX application available for download from the Web to complement this book. Therefore, in this section we have "eaten our own dog food," so to speak.

NOTE

To download the sample gasTIX application, browse to the gasTIX Web site at `www.gasTIX.net`. The download includes the entire codebase for the gasTIX and gasBAGS applications, including databases, images, and presentation and middle-tier code.

We begin constructing our deployment by using the Visual Studio Deployment project, described earlier in this chapter. Instead of choosing a Web Setup Project, however, we base our install on a Windows Installer Setup Project. The reason for this is that we want our installation program to prompt the user for the target directory to install the source files to. The Web Setup Project prompts only for the name of the virtual directory to create, and does not give the user the option to change the installation directory. To offer more flexibility and to comply with standard software installation practices, we base our installation on the Windows Setup Project so that our users have more control.

After creating a Windows Setup Project, we add another Visual Basic .NET project called gasTIXInstall. This project will contain a main class called Install.vb, along with several utility classes, including DatabaseInstaller.vb, Exceptions.vb, and IISAdmin.vb. It is in the Install.vb file that we perform custom actions during gasTIX install, rollback, and uninstall, including changing database connection strings, creating virtual directories, registering COM+ components, and more. This class will be discussed in detail later in this chapter.

File System

In the File System view of the deployment project, the main Application Folder created by default will become our virtual directory (gasTIX). We add application subfolders underneath this main folder, including AddressValidation, Business, Database, and Web, based on the final folder hierarchy we want to provide to our users.

NOTE

We can choose to setup deployment folders in a different manner than the way they have been developed. In the gasTIX development environment, the Web folder is not called Web, and it could be located at a different folder level. We have the capability to be quite flexible when deciding upon an installation configuration, and we should make the folder hierarchy as intuitive as possible, both in development and in deployment.

We place the main gasTIX.sln Visual Studio .NET solution file in the Application Folder root. Providing a solution file allows users to open and compile the entire gasTIX solution with all its projects in one fell swoop. The solution file provides users with the ability to view all the code that makes up the application they have just downloaded, and lets them compile it after making changes.

Within each project subfolder (such as BusinessFacade, DataAccess, and so on), we place the .cs, .vb, .resx, .csproj, .vcproj, and any other files we want to deploy. Note that we do NOT deploy any .user or .suo files. These files are specific to each user working on the solution, and they will be created automatically by the Visual Studio .NET IDE when a new user opens the gasTIX solution. Deploying these files will cause problems for other users because VS.NET will attempt to read them if they exist, and settings on a developer's workstation have no relevance for a user that has downloaded the application.

Underneath the Web subfolder, we have created a `\bin` directory. We have placed all of the gasTIX assemblies in this folder so that if users choose to open their browsers and hit the gasTIX home page immediately after downloading and installing the sample application, the site will work properly. If the user chooses to open the gasTIX.sln solution file first and view the code, compile it, and then view the home page, these assemblies will be overwritten by the recompilation.

In the Setup subfolder, we need to add the primary output of the gasTIXInstall Visual Basic .NET project that we have added to this deployment solution. This is done by selecting Add\Project Output… on this subfolder, and selecting the Primary output for the gasTIXInstall project, as shown in Figure 16.8.

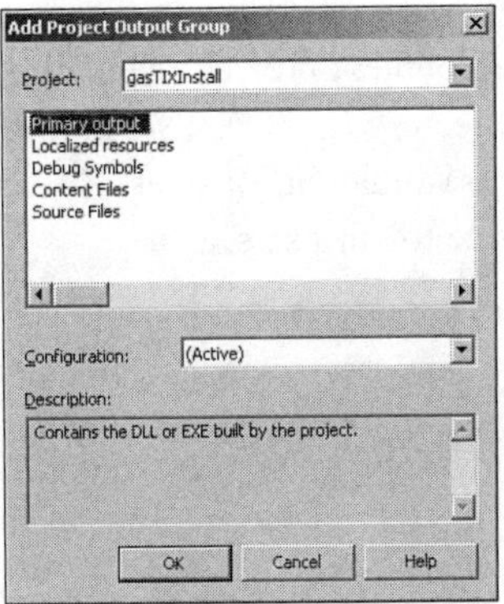

FIGURE 16.8
Adding the primary output for the gasTIXInstall project to our Visual Studio .NET deployment File System.

Registry

Note that we have not included any registry entries for the gasTIX setup application. We are able to do this by saving the relevant arguments entered by the user at installation time to an XML file called gasTIXInstall.InstallState, located in the Setup folder. This is standard practice for .NET installations, as dependence on the Windows Registry for custom applications is being phased out.

The InstallState file is an XML text file containing all of the information we need in order to uninstall the application later, including the database user ID and password (encrypted) information. Listing 16.1 shows a sample InstallState file for gasTIX.

LISTING 16.1 The gasTIXInstall.InstallState file contains all the information the uninstall program needs to remove the application at a later time.

```
<SOAP-ENV:Envelope xmlns:xsi="http://www.w3.org/2001/XMLSchema-instance"
xmlns:xsd="http://www.w3.org/2001/XMLSchema" xmlns:SOAP-
ENC="http://schemas.xmlsoap.org/soap/encoding/" xmlns:SOAP-
ENV="http://schemas.xmlsoap.org/soap/envelope/" SOAP-
ENV:encodingStyle="http://schemas.xmlsoap.org/soap/encoding/"
xmlns:a1="http://schemas.microsoft.com/clr/ns/System.Collections">
<SOAP-ENV:Body>
<a1:Hashtable id="ref-1">
<LoadFactor>0.72</LoadFactor>
<Version>2</Version>
<Comparer xsi:null="1"/>
<HashCodeProvider xsi:null="1"/>
<HashSize>11</HashSize>
<Keys href="#ref-2"/>
<Values href="#ref-3"/>
</a1:Hashtable>
<SOAP-ENC:Array id="ref-2" SOAP-ENC:arrayType="xsd:ur-type[2]">
<item id="ref-4" xsi:type="SOAP-
ENC:string">_reserved_lastInstallerAttempted</item>
<item id="ref-5" xsi:type="SOAP-ENC:string">_reserved_nestedSavedStates</item>
</SOAP-ENC:Array>
<SOAP-ENC:Array id="ref-3" SOAP-ENC:arrayType="xsd:ur-type[2]">
<item xsi:type="xsd:int">0</item>
<item href="#ref-6"/>
</SOAP-ENC:Array>
<SOAP-ENC:Array id="ref-6" SOAP-ENC:arrayType="a1:IDictionary[1]">
<item href="#ref-7"/>
</SOAP-ENC:Array>
<a1:Hashtable id="ref-7">
<LoadFactor>0.72</LoadFactor>
<Version>13</Version>
```

LISTING 16.1 Continued


```
<Comparer xsi:null="1"/>
<HashCodeProvider xsi:null="1"/>
<HashSize>23</HashSize>
<Keys href="#ref-8"/>
<Values href="#ref-9"/>
</a1:Hashtable>
<SOAP-ENC:Array id="ref-8" SOAP-ENC:arrayType="xsd:ur-type[12]">
<item id="ref-10" xsi:type="SOAP-ENC:string">gasTIXDatabase</item>
<item id="ref-11" xsi:type="SOAP-ENC:string">AddressRemote</item>
<item id="ref-12" xsi:type="SOAP-ENC:string">AddressDatabase</item>
<item id="ref-13" xsi:type="SOAP-ENC:string">PreCompile</item>
<item id="ref-14" xsi:type="SOAP-ENC:string">gasTIXServer</item>
<item id="ref-15" xsi:type="SOAP-ENC:string">AddressServer</item>
<item id="ref-16" xsi:type="SOAP-ENC:string">gasTIXUser</item>
<item id="ref-17" xsi:type="SOAP-ENC:string">gasTIXPassword</item>
<item href="#ref-4"/>
<item id="ref-18" xsi:type="SOAP-ENC:string">AddressPassword</item>
<item href="#ref-5"/>
<item id="ref-19" xsi:type="SOAP-ENC:string">AddressUser</item>
</SOAP-ENC:Array>
<SOAP-ENC:Array id="ref-9" SOAP-ENC:arrayType="xsd:ur-type[12]">
<item id="ref-20" xsi:type="SOAP-ENC:string">gasTIX</item>
<item id="ref-21" xsi:type="SOAP-ENC:string">2</item>
<item id="ref-22" xsi:type="SOAP-ENC:string">Address</item>
<item id="ref-23" xsi:type="SOAP-ENC:string">1</item>
<item id="ref-24" xsi:type="SOAP-ENC:string">gastixsql</item>
<item id="ref-25" xsi:type="SOAP-ENC:string">gastixsql</item>
<item id="ref-26" xsi:type="SOAP-ENC:string">sa</item>
<item id="ref-27" xsi:type="SOAP-ENC:string">ÊÆÊÎÆÆ</item>
<item xsi:type="xsd:int">-1</item>
<item id="ref-28" xsi:type="SOAP-ENC:string">ÊÆÊÎÆÆ</item>
<item href="#ref-29"/>
<item id="ref-30" xsi:type="SOAP-ENC:string">sa</item>
</SOAP-ENC:Array>
<SOAP-ENC:Array id="ref-29" SOAP-ENC:arrayType="a1:IDictionary[0]">
</SOAP-ENC:Array>
</SOAP-ENV:Body>
</SOAP-ENV:Envelope>
```


User Interface

Several screens are added to the User Interface view so that we can gather required information from the user at installation. In addition to a Splash screen on which shameless graphics are shown, we have added the Textboxes (A) and Textboxes (B) screens for gathering gasTIX and AddressValidation database installation options. The RadioButtons (2 buttons) screen is also added for prompting the user to choose to install the AddressValidation remoting host either as an out-of-process EXE or a Windows Service. Also added is the Checkboxes (A) screen, allowing users to select the pre-JIT option, which will run Ngen.exe on all the assemblies so that they are loaded into the .NET Native Image Cache. (For more information on using the NGen utility, see Chapter 15.)

The main drawback to the Visual Studio .NET Deployment User Interface screen is the lack of a graphical design surface. This feature will likely appear in a subsequent version, but for now, we can only design a screen by setting properties for pre-provided controls by using the properties window. Unfortunately, there is no way to add a custom button such as a "Test Data Source Connection" to a screen.

When we name a control on a custom User Interface screen, this name becomes available for use throughout the VS.NET deployment project. This allows us to retrieve the value of the named control so that it can be used during installation. For example, on the Textboxes (A) screen (which captures gasTIX database configuration choices), the properties shown in Table 16.1 are used to design this screen.

TABLE 16.1 .NET User Interface Properties Allow Us to Configure a Custom Installation Screen

Property Name	*Design-Time Value*
`BannerBitmap`	GASullivanLogo proTIX.jpg
`BannerText`	gasTIX database
`BodyText`	This dialog allows you to specify the name and location of the gasTIX database to be created on the database server.
`Edit1Label`	&Database Name:
`Edit1Property`	GASTIXDBNAME
`Edit1Value`	gasTIX
`Edit1Visible`	True
`Edit2Label`	&Machine Name:
`Edit2Property`	GASTIXMACHINENAME
`Edit2Value`	localhost
`Edit2Visible`	True
`Edit3Label`	&User ID:
`Edit3Property`	GASTIXUSERID

TABLE 16.1 Continued

Property Name	*Design-Time Value*
`Edit3Value`	sa
`Edit3Visible`	True
`Edit4Label`	&Password:
`Edit4Property`	GASTIXPASSWORD
`Edit4Value`	
`Edit4Visible`	True

`Edit1Property` is named GASTIXDBNAME, which will be available for use throughout the setup program, as will be shown in the listings later in this chapter. When the final user interface window is displayed to the user at install time, it will appear similar to Figure 16.9.

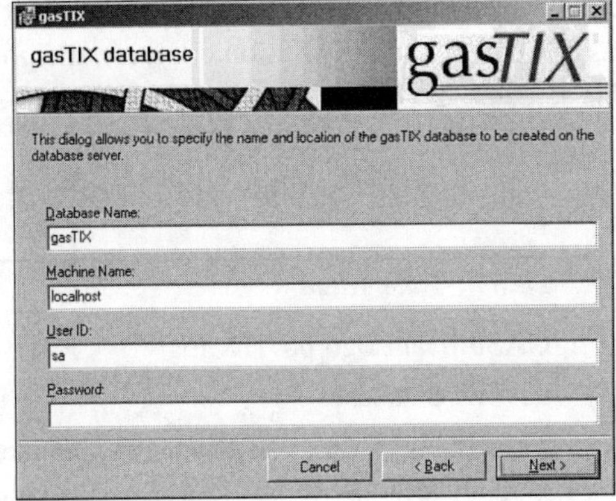

FIGURE 16.9
A custom user interface window is built to gather gasTIX database configuration properties.

Even though the first version of this User Interface screen is rudimentary, it does allow us to create screens that gather required information in order to complete a professional .NET installation.

Custom Actions

Custom actions in a Visual Studio .NET deployment project allow us to call custom code or scripts, and are the key to making a deployment project highly extensible. A custom action has been added to the gasTIX deployment project for the Install, Rollback, and Uninstall events. We have selected the custom action for each of these events to be the primary output of the

Install.vb class, which is described in detail in the following sections. Whenever one of the custom actions is fired, the related method in our Install.vb class will be called and our custom code will be run. User-entered parameters are passed in through the `stateSaver` variable, which is a collection of type System.Collections.IDictionary.

CAUTION

The primary output of another project (such as the gasTIXInstall Visual Basic .NET project used in the gasTIX deployment project) can only be added as a custom action if it has first been included in the File System view.

In the Install.vb class of the gasTIXInstall project, we have overridden the built-in `Install`, `Rollback`, and `Uninstall` methods provided with the System.Configuration.Install.Installer class, from which we have set this class to inherit, as shown in Listing 16.2. This ensures that Windows Installer custom actions call our code at the appropriate time.

LISTING 16.2 The Install.vb Class Inherits from System.Configuration.Install.Installer, which Provides the Built-in Install, Commit, Rollback, and Uninstall Classes

```
Imports System
Imports System.Data.SqlClient
Imports System.IO
Imports Microsoft.Win32
Imports gasTIXInstall.Exceptions
Imports System.Text
Imports System.Xml
Imports System.ServiceProcess
Imports System.EnterpriseServices

<System.ComponentModel.RunInstaller(True)> Public Class Install
    Inherits System.Configuration.Install.Installer
```

The main `Install` method is called when the installer reaches the custom action step (after installing source code files and folders, performing any conditional checks, and making any registry entries).

The `Install` method, detailed in Listing 16.3, is where we setup the gasTIX and AddressValidation databases with the options entered by the user, change connection strings in COM+ object constructor strings and an XML file, create a virtual directory, install the AddressValidation remoting host as either a Windows Service or a standalone out-of-process EXE, and pre-JIT the gasTIX assemblies, if desired by the user. As you can see, we are able to perform a tremendous amount of custom installation work by inheriting and extending the `Install` method.

LISTING 16.3 The `Install` Method is Where the Bulk of Custom Installation Actions are Performed

```
Public Overrides Sub Install(ByVal stateSaver As
System.Collections.IDictionary)

    Try

        MyBase.Install(stateSaver)

        Initialize(stateSaver)

        ' STEP 1: Install the databases
        Log("Installing databases.")
        Dim dbInstall As DatabaseInstaller

        Log("Installing gasTIX database.")
        dbInstall = New DatabaseInstaller(_gasTIXServer, _gasTIXDatabase,
_gasTIXUser, _gasTIXPassword)
        dbInstall.InstallDatabase(_TargetDir & GASTIX_DATABASE_DIR &
"create_gastix_database.sql")

        Log("Loading gasTIX data.")
        dbInstall.DataLoad(_TargetDir & GASTIX_DATABASE_DIR,
"gastix.data_load.xml")

        ' create sporting events
        Dim sportingEvents() As SqlParameter = {New
SqlParameter("@duplicate_schedule_count", ➥SqlDbType.Int), _
New SqlParameter("@category_id", SqlDbType.Int)}
        sportingEvents(0).Value = 5
        sportingEvents(1).Value = 2
        Log("Loading sports events.")
        dbInstall.ExecuteStoredProc("usp_create_sports_events", sportingEvents)

        'create non-sporting events
        Dim nonsportingEvents() As SqlParameter = {New
SqlParameter("@events_per_participant", ➥SqlDbType.Int)}
        nonsportingEvents(0).Value = 5
        Log("Loading non-sports events.")
```

LISTING 16.3 Continued

```
        dbInstall.ExecuteStoredProc("usp_create_non_sports_events",
nonsportingEvents)

        ' Create all venue sections, rows, & seats
        Dim venueSeating() As SqlParameter = {New
SqlParameter("@number_sections_per_venue", ➥SqlDbType.Int), _
                                               New
SqlParameter("@number_rows_per_section", ➥SqlDbType.Int)}
        venueSeating(0).Value = 3
        venueSeating(1).Value = 3
        Log("Creating venue seating.")
        dbInstall.ExecuteStoredProc("usp_create_venue_seating", venueSeating)

        ' Associate venue sections, rows, & seats to event configurations
        Log("Creating venue configuration.")
        dbInstall.ExecuteStoredProc("usp_create_venue_config", Nothing)

        ' Create event section prices & seat locking records
        Log("Creating event section data.")
        dbInstall.ExecuteStoredProc("usp_create_event_section_data", Nothing)

        ' Reset event dates
        Dim newDate() As SqlParameter = {New SqlParameter("@new_start_date",
SqlDbType.DateTime)}
        newDate(0).Value = Now()
        Log("Setting event dates.")
        dbInstall.ExecuteStoredProc("usp_reset_all_event_dates", newDate)
        dbInstall = Nothing

        Log("Installing address database.")
        dbInstall = New DatabaseInstaller(_AddressServer, _AddressDatabase,
_AddressUser, _AddressPassword)
        dbInstall.InstallDatabase(_TargetDir & GASTIX_DATABASE_DIR &
"create_address_database.sql")

        Log("Loading address data.")
        dbInstall.DataLoad(_TargetDir & GASTIX_DATABASE_DIR,
"address.data_load.xml")

        dbInstall = Nothing

        ' STEP 2: Register the gasTIX.Business and gasTIX.DataAccess objects in
        'COM+
```

LISTING 16.3 Continued

```
        Log("Registering gasTIX assemblies with COM+")
        Dim regHelper = New RegistrationHelper()

        Log("Registering gasTIX.Business assembly with COM+.")
        regHelper.InstallAssembly(_TargetDir & GASTIX_WEB_BIN_DIR &
"gasTIX.Business.dll", _Nothing, Nothing,
_InstallationFlags.FindOrCreateTargetApplication)

        Log("Registering gasTIX.DataAccess assembly with COM+.")
        regHelper.InstallAssembly(_TargetDir & GASTIX_WEB_BIN_DIR &
"gasTIX.DataAccess.dll", _Nothing, Nothing,
_InstallationFlags.FindOrCreateTargetApplication)

        regHelper = Nothing

        ' STEP 3: change the object constructor strings for all
        'gasTIX.DataAccess components
        ModifyDataAccessConstructorString()

        ' STEP 4: Change the Address Validation connection string
        ModifyAddressValidationConnectionString()

        ' STEP 5: Register the remoting host
        '          (either as a Windows Service or as an out-of-process EXE)
        If _AddressRemote = REMOTING_WINDOWS_SERVICE_OPTION Then

            Log("Installing Address Validation remoting host as a Windows
Service.")
            InstallUtil.ExecuteProcess(Chr(34) & _DotNetDir & "installutil.exe
" & Chr(34), Chr(34) & _TargetDir & ADDRESS_VALIDATIONSVC_BIN &
"AddressValidationSvc.exe " & Chr(34))

            Log("Starting Address Validation remoting host Windows Service.")
            Dim addressService As New ServiceProcess.ServiceController("Address
Validation")
            addressService.Start()
            addressService = Nothing

        Else

            Log("Starting Address Validation remoting host as an out-of-process
EXE.")
```

LISTING 16.3 Continued

```
            Dim cmdProcess As Process
            cmdProcess = Process.Start(Chr(34) & _TargetDir &_
ADDRESS_VALIDATIONSVC_BIN & "AddressValidationSvc.exe " & Chr(34))
            cmdProcess = Nothing

        End If

        ' STEP 6: Ngen the gasTIX assemblies if the user chose this option
        HandlePreJIT(True)

        ' STEP 7: Create a virtual directory in IIS for gasTIX
        '         based on the installation location chosen
        Log("Setting up IIS.")
        Log("Stopping IIsAdmin service.")
        InstallUtil.ExecuteProcess("iisreset", "/stop")

        Dim vDir As New gasTIXInstall.IISAdmin("localhost")
        Log("Creating gasTIX virtual directory.")
        vDir.CreateVirtualDir(GASTIX_PRODUCT_NAME, _TargetDir & GASTIX_WEB_DIR)
        vDir = Nothing

        Log("Starting IIsAdmin service.")
        InstallUtil.ExecuteProcess("iisreset", "/start")

    Catch e As Exception

        Log("Error encountered: " & _LastLogMsg & vbCrLf & e.Message)
        Throw New ApplicationException(_LastLogMsg)

    Finally

        Uninitialize(stateSaver)

    End Try
End Sub
```

Note especially Step 5 in the previous listing. At install time, we offer the user the option to configure the AddressValidation remoting host as either a Windows Service, or a standalone out-of-process EXE. Based on the user's choice, we perform different tasks. This step contains code to run and configure a process as a Service, and code to simply run the EXE out-of-process.

The databases gasTIX and AddressValidation are run via the SQL Server command-line utility bcp.exe called in Step 1 in the previous listing. The development team first tried doing a simple `RESTORE` and `BACKUP` in the InstallClass, but SQL Server hard-codes the name of the database as it appears in Enterprise Manager in the backup itself. This prevents the user from renaming the database at install time, which we should certainly allow them to do. This prompted us to resort to bcp, as shown in Listing 16.4.

LISTING 16.4 The DatabaseInstaller.vb Class is Where the gasTIX Databases are Actually Installed, Based on the User-Entered Options

```
Imports System.Text
Imports System.Data.SqlClient
Imports System.ServiceProcess
Imports System.IO
Imports System.Xml

Public Class DatabaseInstaller

    Private Const connectionString As String = "server={0};database={1};user
id={2};password={3}"

    Private Const createDatabaseCmd As String = "create database {0}"
    Private Const deleteDatabaseCmd As String = "if exists (SELECT name FROM
master.dbo.sysdatabases WHERE name = N'{0}') drop database {0}"
    Private Const truncLogCmd As String = "sp_dboption '{0}', 'trunc. log',
'true'"
    Private Const autoShrinkCmd As String = "sp_dboption '{0}', 'autoshrink',
'true'"
    Private Const bulkCopyCmd As String = "sp_dboption '{0}', 'bulkcopy',
'true'"
    Private Const killCnnCmd As String = "kill {0}"
    Private Const schemaCmdArgs As String = "-S {0} -d {1} -U {2} -P {3} -i
{4}"

    Private Const bcpCmd As String = """{0}..{1}"" in ""{2}"" -S""{3}"" -
U""{4}"" -P""{5}"" -c -k -E"

    Private _Server As String
    Private _Database As String
    Private _User As String
    Private _Password As String

    Public Sub New(ByVal server As String, ByVal database As String, _
                   ByVal user As String, ByVal password As String)
```

LISTING 16.4 Continued

```
        MyBase.New()

        _Server = server
        _Database = database
        _User = user
        _Password = password

    End Sub

    Public Sub InstallDatabase(ByVal schema As String)

        CreateDatabase()

        Dim streamReader As New StreamReader(schema)
        CreateSchema(streamReader.ReadToEnd())

    End Sub

    Public Sub UninstallDatabase()

        DeleteDatabase()

    End Sub

    Public Sub ExecuteStoredProc(ByVal procName As String, ByRef procParameters
As Array)
        ExecuteStoredProc(String.Format(connectionString, _Server, _Database,
_User, _Password), procName, CommandType.StoredProcedure, procParameters)
    End Sub

    Public Sub KillConnections()
        Dim ds As DataSet
        ds = ExecuteStoredProcReturnDS(String.Format(connectionString, _Server,
"master", _User, _Password), _"sp_who", _CommandType.StoredProcedure, _Nothing)
        Dim dr As DataRow
        For Each dr In ds.Tables(0).Rows
            If dr.Item("dbname").ToString().Equals(_Database) Then
                ExecuteStoredProc(String.Format(connectionString, _Server,
"master", _User, _Password), _String.Format(killCnnCmd,
dr.Item("spid").ToString()), CommandType.Text, _Nothing)
```

LISTING 16.4 Continued

```
            End If
        Next
    End Sub

    Public Sub DataLoad(ByVal sourceDirectory As String, ByVal sourceFile As
String)

        Dim sourceDoc As New XmlDocument()

        sourceDoc.Load(sourceDirectory & sourceFile)

        Dim nodeList As XmlNodeList = sourceDoc.SelectNodes("/data_load/table")
        Dim node As XmlNode

        For Each node In nodeList
            InstallUtil.ExecuteProcess("bcp.exe ", _
                                       String.Format(bcpCmd, _
                                       _Database,
node.Attributes("name").Value, sourceDirectory & node.Attributes("file").Value,
_Server, _User, _Password))
        Next

        sourceDoc = Nothing
    End Sub

    Private Sub CreateDatabase()

        ExecuteStoredProc(String.Format(connectionString, _Server, "master",
_User, _Password), _
                          String.Format(createDatabaseCmd, _Database), _
                          CommandType.Text, _
                          Nothing)
        ExecuteStoredProc(String.Format(connectionString, _Server, "master",
_User, _Password), _
                          String.Format(truncLogCmd, _Database), _
                          CommandType.Text, _
                          Nothing)
        ExecuteStoredProc(String.Format(connectionString, _Server, "master",
_User, _Password), _
                          String.Format(autoShrinkCmd, _Database), _
                          CommandType.Text, _
                          Nothing)
```

LISTING 16.4 Continued

```
        ExecuteStoredProc(String.Format(connectionString, _Server, "master",
_User, _Password), _
                             String.Format(bulkCopyCmd, _Database), _
                             CommandType.Text, _
                             Nothing)

    End Sub

    Private Sub DeleteDatabase()
        ExecuteStoredProc(String.Format(connectionString, _Server, "master",
_User, _Password), _
                             String.Format(deleteDatabaseCmd, _Database), _
                             CommandType.Text, _
                             Nothing)
    End Sub

    Private Sub CreateSchema(ByRef schema As String)
        Dim cnn As New SqlConnection(String.Format(connectionString, _Server,
_Database, _User, _Password))
        Dim cmd As SqlCommand
        Dim result As Integer

        cnn.Open()

        Dim lines() As String
        Dim sep(0) As Char
        sep(0) = vbNewLine
        lines = Schema.Split(sep)

        Dim buffer As New StringBuilder()
        Dim l As String
        For Each l In lines
            Dim line As String = l.Trim()
            If line.ToLower().Equals("go") Then
                cmd = New SqlCommand(buffer.ToString(), cnn)
                cmd.CommandType = CommandType.Text
                cmd.CommandTimeout = 1200
                Try
                    result = cmd.ExecuteNonQuery()
                Catch e As Exception
                    Console.WriteLine(e.ToString())
```

LISTING 16.4 Continued

```
            End Try
            cmd.Dispose()
            buffer = New StringBuilder()
        ElseIf Not line.StartsWith("--") Then
            buffer.Append(line)
            buffer.Append(vbNewLine)
        End If
    Next
    cnn.Close()
    cnn.Dispose()
End Sub

Private Sub ExecuteStoredProc(ByVal connectionString As String, _
                              ByVal procName As String, _
                              ByVal commandType As CommandType, _
                              ByRef procParameters As Array)
    Dim cnn As New SqlConnection(connectionString)
    Dim cmd As New SqlCommand(procName, cnn)
    Dim param As SqlParameter

    cmd.CommandType = commandType
    cmd.CommandTimeout = 1200

    If Not procParameters Is Nothing Then
        For Each param In procParameters
            cmd.Parameters.Add(param)
        Next
    End If

    cnn.Open()
    cmd.ExecuteNonQuery()
    cnn.Close()

    cmd = Nothing
    cnn = Nothing
End Sub

Private Overloads Function ExecuteStoredProcReturnDS(ByVal connectionString
As String, _
                                     ByVal procName As String, _
                                     ByVal commandType As CommandType, _
                                     ByRef procParameters As Array) As
DataSet
    Dim cnn As New SqlConnection(connectionString)
    Dim cmd As New SqlDataAdapter(procName, cnn)
```

LISTING 16.4 Continued

```
        Dim param As SqlParameter
        Dim dsOut As New DataSet()

        cmd.SelectCommand.CommandType = commandType

        If Not procParameters Is Nothing Then
            For Each param In procParameters
                cmd.SelectCommand.Parameters.Add(param)
            Next
        End If

        cnn.Open()
        cmd.Fill(dsOut)
        cnn.Close()

        cmd = Nothing
        cnn = Nothing

        Return dsOut
    End Function
End Class
```

The DatabaseInstaller class expects text files of the data in ASCII tab-delimited format, auto-generated by the SQL Server bcp utility. A batch file has been written for both the gasTIX and AddressValidation databases which runs the bcp command for each table in the database, as shown in Listing 16.5. This batch file exports all the relevant data in a format that is appropriate for the `DataLoad()` method in the DatabaseInstaller class.

LISTING 16.5 The bcp_Export_gastix.bat Batch File Generates Text Files with the Data from the gasTIX Database, which Can then be Used in the DatabaseInstaller Class to Recreate the Database

```
bcp "gastix..category" out "category.txt" -c -q -v -Usa -P -S%1
bcp "gastix..tax_rate" out "tax_rate.txt" -c -q -v -Usa -P -S%1
bcp "gastix..subcategory" out "subcategory.txt" -c -q -v -Usa -P -S%1
bcp "gastix..shipping_method" out "shipping_method.txt" -c -q -v -Usa -P -S%1
bcp "gastix..region_map" out "region_map.txt" -c -q -v -Usa -P -S%1
bcp "gastix..map" out "map.txt" -c -q -v -Usa -P -S%1
bcp "gastix..country" out "country.txt" -c -q -v -Usa -P -S%1
bcp "gastix..credit_card_type" out "credit_card_type.txt" -c -q -v -Usa -P -S%1
bcp "gastix..venue" out "venue.txt" -c -q -v -Usa -P -S%1
```

LISTING 16.5 Continued

```
bcp "gastix..region" out "region.txt" -c -q -v -Usa -P -S%1
bcp "gastix..participant" out "participant.txt" -c -q -v -Usa -P -S%1
bcp "gastix..tour" out "tour.txt" -c -q -v -Usa -P -S%1
bcp "gastix..configuration" out "configuration.txt" -c -q -v -Usa -P -S%1
bcp "gastix..sponsor" out "sponsor.txt" -c -q -v -Usa -P -S%1
```

We have created an XML file, the name of which is passed into the `DataLoad()` method, that contains a list of all the text files (one per table) that are to be created in the new, empty database on the target server. An example of this XML file is shown in Listing 16.6. The `DataLoad()` method parses through this XML file, and for each `<table />` node, the bcp utility is called to load in the data in the table from the respective text file.

LISTING 16.6 The gastix.data_load.xml File Tells the DataLoad Method which Text Files to bcp Into the Database

```
<data_load>
    <table name="category" file="category.txt" />
    <table name="subcategory" file="subcategory.txt" />
    <table name="map" file="map.txt" />
    <table name="country" file="country.txt" />
    <table name="region" file="region.txt" />
    <table name="credit_card_type" file="credit_card_type.txt" />
    <table name="shipping_method" file="shipping_method.txt" />
    <table name="region_map" file="region_map.txt" />
    <table name="tax_rate" file="tax_rate.txt" />
    <table name="venue" file="venue.txt" />
    <table name="configuration" file="configuration.txt" />
    <table name="sponsor" file="sponsor.txt" />
    <table name="tour" file="tour.txt" />
    <table name="participant" file="participant.txt" />
</data_load>
```

In order to provide a basic level of security, we hash the database passwords entered by the user at install time. To do this, we use a simple algorithm shown in Listing 16.7, detailed on MSDN. We make a slight modification by adding `70` to the `Xor` statement so that we receive only text characters and no control characters.

LISTING 16.7 The Simple Encrypt Method Provides a Hash of the Database Passwords So They Will Not Appear in Clear Text

```
Public Shared Function Encrypt(ByVal secret, ByVal password) As String
    ' This simple string hash encryption routine was found
    ' on MSDN.  It has been modified to add 70 to the Xor
    ' so that only text characters result.

    ' secret = the string you wish to encrypt or decrypt.
    ' password = the password with which to encrypt the string.
    Dim encryptData = secret & ENCRYPT_PADDING
    Dim R As String
    Dim L As Integer = Len(password)
    Dim X As Integer
    Dim myChar As Integer
    For X = 1 To Len(encryptData)
        myChar = Asc(Mid(password, (X Mod L) - L * ((X Mod L) = 0), 1))
        R = R & Chr(Asc(Mid(encryptData, X, 1)) Xor myChar + 70)
    Next
    Return R
End Function
```

The gasTIX application is configured so that the database connection strings are located in the object constructor strings of the middle-tier gasTIX.DataAccess components. In order for the application to find the gasTIX database successfully, we need to change these constructor strings at installation based on the options entered by the user. The `ModifyDataAccessConstructorString` method performs this work for us, wrapping the legacy COMAdmin component to provide the functionality needed to manipulate COM+ Applications, components, and properties. By simply adding a reference to the COMAdmin.dll (normally located in `C:\WINNT\system32\Com`), .NET allows us to interoperate with this legacy DLL. For more information on COM+ Interoperability, see Chapter 9, "COM+ Integration." Listing 16.8 demonstrates the method that performs this work.

LISTING 16.8 A Method is Included in the gasTIX Install Program to Access and Modify COM+ Constructor Strings for Database Connectivity

```
Private Sub ModifyDataAccessConstructorString()

    Log("Modifying COM+ constructor strings for gasTIX.DataAccess components.")

    Dim Catalog As New COMAdmin.COMAdminCatalog()
    Dim Applications As COMAdmin.COMAdminCatalogCollection
```

LISTING 16.8 Continued

```
    Applications = Catalog.GetCollection("Applications")
    Applications.Populate()

    Dim oApplication As COMAdmin.COMAdminCatalogObject
    Dim gasTIXDataAccess As COMAdmin.COMAdminCatalogObject

    For Each oApplication In Applications
        If oApplication.Name = "gasTIX.DataAccess" Then
            gasTIXDataAccess = oApplication
        End If
    Next

    If gasTIXDataAccess Is Nothing Then
        Throw New ApplicationException("Failed to find gasTX.DataAccess in COM+
catalog.")
    End If

    Dim oComponent As COMAdmin.COMAdminCatalogObject
    Dim Components As COMAdmin.COMAdminCatalogCollection

    Components = Applications.GetCollection("Components", gasTIXDataAccess.Key)
    Components.Populate()

    Dim strgasTIXObjConst = String.Format(CONNECTION_STRING, _gasTIXServer,
_gasTIXDatabase, _gasTIXUser, _gasTIXPassword)
    For Each oComponent In Components
        oComponent.Value("ConstructorString") = strgasTIXObjConst
    Next

    Components.SaveChanges()
End Sub
```

Because the AddressValidation remoting host is not a COM+ application, its database connection string is stored in a different location. We have chosen to place the connection string in a .config file, found in the `\AddressValidation\AddressValidationSvc\AddressValidationSvc.exe.config` file. This is an XML file, so the relevant method in Listing 16.9 enables us to find and modify the appropriate XML node in this file.

LISTING 16.9 Another Method is Included in the gasTIX Install Program to Access and Modify the AddressValidation Database Connection String in an XML Configuration Text File

```
Private Sub ModifyAddressValidationConnectionString()
    Log("Modifying connection string for the AddressValidation database.")

    Dim strAVS As String = _TargetDir & ADDRESS_VALIDATIONSVC_BIN

    Dim xmlFile As New XmlDocument()
    xmlFile.Load(strAVS & "AddressValidationSvc.exe.config")
    Dim myNodeList As XmlNodeList =
xmlFile.SelectNodes("configuration/appSettings/add")
    Dim myNode As XmlNode
    For Each myNode In myNodeList
        If myNode.Attributes("key").Value = "dsn" Then
            myNode.Attributes("value").Value = String.Format(CONNECTION_STRING,
_AddressServer, _AddressDatabase, _AddressUser, _AddressPassword)
            xmlFile.Save(strAVS & "AddressValidationSvc.exe.config")
            Exit For
        End If
    Next
    xmlFile = Nothing
End Sub
```

The method to pre-JIT the gasTIX assemblies is named `HandlePreJIT`, and is shown in Listing 16.10. The multiple use of `Chr(34)` in this method and throughout the InstallClass.vb class exists so that a doublequote (" ") wraps each command-line argument. This is needed in case the user is installing to a file location with a space, such as the default `C:\Program Files\G.A. Sullivan\`. Without a `""` `Chr(34)`, the command-line `NGen` utility will not be able to read the arguments with embedded spaces, and will produce unexpected results.

LISTING 16.10 The HandlePreJIT Method Will Invoke the NGen Utility to Pre-JIT the gasTIX Assemblies If the User Has Selected this Option

```
Private Sub HandlePreJIT(ByVal executeInstall As Boolean)

    If _PreCompile = PRECOMPILE_OPTION Then

        Log("Running Ngen utility on gasTIX assemblies.")

        Dim args As New StringBuilder()
```

LISTING 16.10 Continued

```
        If executeInstall Then
            args.Append(Chr(34) & _TargetDir)
            args.Append(ADDRESS_VALIDATIONSVC_BIN & "AddressValidation.dll" &
Chr(34) & " ")
            args.Append(Chr(34) & _TargetDir)
            args.Append(ADDRESS_VALIDATIONSVC_BIN & "AddressValidationSvc.exe "
& Chr(34) & " ")
            args.Append(Chr(34) & _TargetDir)
            args.Append(GASTIX_WEB_BIN_DIR & "gasTIX.Business.dll" & Chr(34) &
" ")
            args.Append(Chr(34) & _TargetDir)
            args.Append(GASTIX_WEB_BIN_DIR & "gasTIX.BusinessFacade.dll" &
Chr(34) & " ")
            args.Append(Chr(34) & _TargetDir)
            args.Append(GASTIX_WEB_BIN_DIR & "gasTIX.Data.dll" & Chr(34) & " ")
            args.Append(Chr(34) & _TargetDir)
            args.Append(GASTIX_WEB_BIN_DIR & "gasTIX.DataAccess.dll" & Chr(34)
& " ")
            args.Append(Chr(34) & _TargetDir)
            args.Append(GASTIX_WEB_BIN_DIR & "gasTIX.Security.dll" & Chr(34) &
" ")
            args.Append(Chr(34) & _TargetDir)
            args.Append(GASTIX_WEB_BIN_DIR & "gasTIX.UI.dll" & Chr(34) & " ")
            args.Append(Chr(34) & _TargetDir)
            args.Append(GASTIX_WEB_BIN_DIR & "gasTIX.SystemFramework.dll" &
Chr(34) & " ")
        Else
            args.Append("/delete ")
            args.Append("AddressValidation ")
            args.Append("AddressValidationSvc ")
            args.Append("gasTIX.Business ")
            args.Append("gasTIX.BusinessFacade ")
            args.Append("gasTIX.Data ")
            args.Append("gasTIX.DataAccess ")
            args.Append("gasTIX.Security ")
            args.Append("gasTIX.UI ")
            args.Append("gasTIX.SystemFramework ")
        End If

        InstallUtil.ExecuteProcess(Chr(34) & _DotNetDir & "ngen.exe " &
Chr(34), args.ToString())
    End If
End Sub
```

TIP

Any Visual Studio .NET deployment package should be tested on many different platforms, and each permutation of each installation option should be tried. We should test our installs to remote machines and to folders with spaces in the folder name. Purposefully try to crash the installation program. After install, remove pieces of the application to see if the uninstall program can still proceed. The overall goal is to make the install and uninstall processes as smooth as possible for our users. There is no overstating the beauty of a clean, well-delivered installation program, especially when you are on the receiving end.

Several additional helper methods related to IIS virtual directory administration, called by the main `Install` method, are contained in the IISAdmin.vb class, shown in its entirety in Listing 16.11.

LISTING 16.11 The IISAdmin.vb Class Contains Several Helper Methods Related to Virtual Directory Administration, Called by the Install and UninstallBase Methods

```
Imports System
Imports System.DirectoryServices
Imports gasTIXInstall.Exceptions

Public Class IISAdmin
    Private _server As String

    Public Sub New(ByVal server As String)
        _server = server
    End Sub

    Public Sub CreateVirtualDir(ByVal directoryName As String, ByVal path As
String)

        Dim newSite As DirectoryEntry
        Dim webroot As DirectoryEntry

        Try

            If Not DirectoryEntry.Exists("IIS://" & _server & "/W3SVC/1") Then
                Throw New DefaultWebSiteNotFoundException("Failed to find
default web site.")
            End If
```

LISTING 16.11 Continued

```
            If DirectoryEntry.Exists("IIS://" & _server & "/W3SVC/1/Root/" &
directoryName) Then
                Throw New VirtualDirectoryExistsException("Virtual directory "
& directoryName & " already exists.")
            End If

            webroot = New DirectoryEntry("IIS://" & _server & "/W3SVC/1/Root")

            newSite = webroot.Children().Add(directoryName, "IIsWebVirtualDir")
            newSite.CommitChanges()

            newSite.Properties("AccessExecute")(0) = True
            newSite.Properties("AccessWrite")(0) = True
            newSite.Properties("AccessScript")(0) = True
            newSite.Properties("AccessRead")(0) = True
            newSite.Properties("AccessSource")(0) = True
            newSite.Properties("Path")(0) = path
            newSite.CommitChanges()

            Dim args(0) As Object
            args(0) = 2
            newSite.Invoke("AppCreate2", args)
            newSite.Properties("AppFriendlyName")(0) = directoryName
            newSite.CommitChanges()

        Catch ex As Exception
            Throw ex
        End Try
    End Sub

    Public Sub DeleteVirtualDir(ByVal directoryName As String)

        Try
            If Not DirectoryEntry.Exists("IIS://" & _server & "/W3SVC/1") Then
                Throw New DefaultWebSiteNotFoundException("Failed to find
default web site.")
            End If

            If Not (DirectoryEntry.Exists("IIS://" & _server & "/W3SVC/1/Root/"
& directoryName)) Then
                Throw New VirtualDirectoryNotFoundException("Virtual directory
" & directoryName & " does not exists.")
            End If
```

LISTING 16.11 Continued

```
            Dim webItem As DirectoryEntry = New DirectoryEntry("IIS://" &
_server & "/W3SVC/1/Root/" & directoryName)
            Dim webParent As DirectoryEntry = New DirectoryEntry("IIS://" &
_server & "/W3SVC/1/Root")

            webItem.Invoke("AppDelete", Nothing)

            webParent.Children.Remove(webItem)

        Catch ex As Exception
            Throw ex
        End Try
    End Sub
End Class
```

The `Uninstall` and `Rollback` methods need to do the same basic work. Rollback will continue if it encounters any error condition in case it tries to perform an uninstall function that was not yet reached during the aborted install process. (We instruct the installer to continue during Rollback by using `Try...Catch` blocks without throwing errors, but instead only displaying message boxes). Because `Uninstall` and `Rollback` do the same work, we have abstracted the implementation out to a separate method which both of these methods call, simply passing in a parameter to notify the method of identity (either `Rollback` or `Uninstall`) of the caller. This abstraction is shown in Listing 16.12.

LISTING 16.12 The `Rollback` and `Uninstall` Methods Need to Perform the Same Work, So They Call the Same Sub-Method

```
Public Overrides Sub Rollback(ByVal savedState As
System.Collections.IDictionary)

    MyBase.Rollback(savedState)
    UninstallBase(savedState)

End Sub


Public Overrides Sub Uninstall(ByVal savedState As
System.Collections.IDictionary)

    MyBase.Uninstall(savedState)
    UninstallBase(savedState)

End Sub
```

The `UninstallBase` method itself is where custom uninstallation actions, such as removing the databases, removing the virtual directory, and removing assemblies from the Native Image Cache are performed. This method is shown in its entirety in Listing 16.13.

LISTING 16.13 The UninstallBase Method Performs the Custom Uninstallation Actions Required for Completely Removing the gasTIX Application

```
Private Sub UninstallBase(ByVal savedState As System.Collections.IDictionary)
    Try

        Initialize(savedState)

        ' STEP 1: Remove the gasTIX virtual directory in IIS
        Dim vDir As gasTIXInstall.IISAdmin
        Try
            Log("Deleting gasTIX virtual directory.")
            vDir = New gasTIXInstall.IISAdmin("localhost")
            vDir.DeleteVirtualDir(GASTIX_PRODUCT_NAME)
        Catch e As Exception
            Log("Error encountered: " & _LastLogMsg & vbCrLf & e.Message)
        Finally
            vDir = Nothing
        End Try

        ' STEP 2: From here we need to stop IIS
        Log("Stopping IIsAdmin service.")
        InstallUtil.ExecuteProcess("iisreset", "/stop")

        ' STEP 3: Uninstall the databases

        Log("Removing databases.")
        Dim dbInstall As DatabaseInstaller

        Try
            Log("Removing gasTIX database.")
            dbInstall = New DatabaseInstaller(_gasTIXServer, _gasTIXDatabase,
_gasTIXUser, _gasTIXPassword)
            Log("Terminating gasTIX database connections.")
            dbInstall.KillConnections()
            Log("Deleting gasTIX database.")
            dbInstall.UninstallDatabase()
        Catch e As Exception
            Log("Error encountered: " & _LastLogMsg & vbCrLf & e.Message)
        Finally
```

LISTING 16.13 Continued

```
            dbInstall = Nothing
        End Try

        Try
            Log("Removing Address database.")
            dbInstall = New DatabaseInstaller(_AddressServer, _AddressDatabase,
_AddressUser, _AddressPassword)
            Log("Terminating Address database connections.")
            dbInstall.KillConnections()
            Log("Deleting Address database.")
            dbInstall.UninstallDatabase()
        Catch e As Exception
            Log("Error encountered: " & _LastLogMsg & vbCrLf & e.Message)
        Finally
            dbInstall = Nothing
        End Try

        ' Step 4: Remove all the gasTIX objects from the native image cache
        HandlePreJIT(False)

        ' STEP 5: Unregister the gasIX.Business and gasTIX.DataAccess objects
        'in COM+
        Log("Unregistering gasTIX assemblies with COM+.")
        Dim regHelper As RegistrationHelper = New RegistrationHelper()

        Log("Unregistering gasTIX.Business assembly with COM+.")
        regHelper.UninstallAssembly(_TargetDir & GASTIX_WEB_BIN_DIR &
"gasTIX.Business.dll", Nothing, Nothing)

        Log("Unregistering gasTIX.DataAccess assembly with COM+.")
        regHelper.UninstallAssembly(_TargetDir & GASTIX_WEB_BIN_DIR &
"gasTIX.DataAccess.dll", Nothing, Nothing)

        regHelper = Nothing

        Log("Deleting COM+ TypLibs.")
        Try
            File.Delete(_TargetDir & GASTIX_WEB_BIN_DIR &
"gasTIX.Business.tlb")
        Catch e As Exception
            Log("Error encountered: " & _LastLogMsg & vbCrLf & e.Message)
        End Try
        Try
            File.Delete(_TargetDir & GASTIX_WEB_BIN_DIR &
```

LISTING 16.13 Continued

```
"gasTIX.DataAccess.tlb")
        Catch e As Exception
            Log("Error encountered: " & _LastLogMsg & vbCrLf & e.Message)
        End Try

        ' STEP 6: Uninstall the Address Validation remoting host
        '         (either a Windows Service or an out-of-process EXE)
        If _AddressRemote = REMOTING_WINDOWS_SERVICE_OPTION Then

            Log("Stopping Address Validation remoting host Windows Server.")
            Dim addressService As New ServiceProcess.ServiceController("Address
Validation")
            If Not addressService Is Nothing Then
                addressService.Stop()
                addressService = Nothing
            Else
                Log("Error encountered: " & _LastLogMsg & vbCrLf & "Address
Validation Windows service not found.")
            End If

            Log("Uninstalling Address Validation remoting host as a Windows
Service.")
            InstallUtil.ExecuteProcess(Chr(34) & _DotNetDir & "installutil.exe
" & Chr(34), "/u " & Chr(34) & _TargetDir & ADDRESS_VALIDATIONSVC_BIN &
"AddressValidationSvc.exe " & Chr(34))

        End If

    Catch e As Exception

        Log("Error encountered: " & _LastLogMsg & vbCrLf & e.Message)
        Throw New ApplicationException(_LastLogMsg)

    Finally

        ' STEP 7: Lets restart IIS
        InstallUtil.ExecuteProcess("iisreset", "/start")

        Uninitialize(savedState)

    End Try
End Sub
```

As you can see, we have created a highly extensible Windows Installer program by overriding the built-in `Install`, `Rollback`, and `Uninstall` methods of

System.Configuration.Install.Installer (we have not used the Commit method). Custom actions call our methods at the appropriate time during installation, ensuring that the custom tasks specific to our application are performed, setting up the application as the user has specified in our user interface screens. We have built-in error handling in `Try…Catch` blocks to ensure a smooth process that degrades gracefully when an error condition is encountered.

Visual Studio .NET has made great strides in providing a powerful environment in which to create Windows Installer packages for our .NET eBusiness applications.

Creating Web Clusters with Application Center 2000

As an illustration of creating scalable and available Web sites, we're going to deploy the application using Visual Studio .NET in tandem with a new product for enterprise Web cluster management on the Windows server platform, Microsoft Application Center 2000 (AC2K).

About Application Center 2000

Application Center is another one of the .NET Enterprise Servers, and as such is positioned as the technology of choice for creating load-balanced, highly available clusters for Internet and intranet enterprise applications (see Figure 16.10).

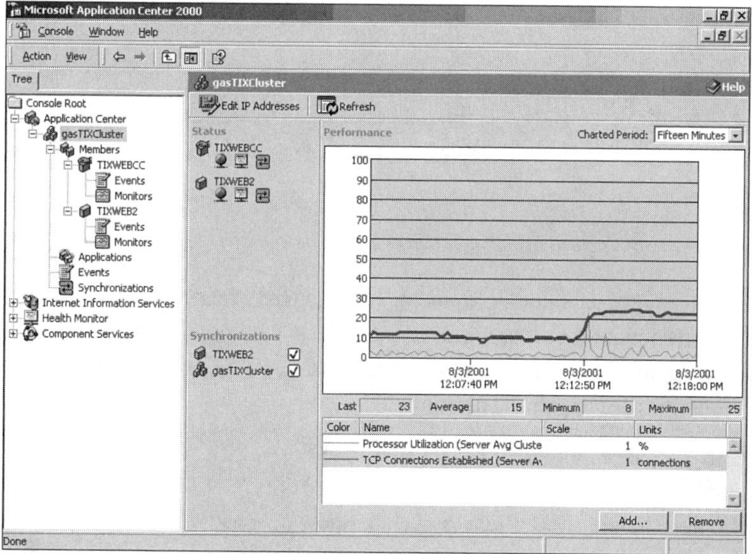

FIGURE 16.10
Application Center 2000 in action.

AC2K manages content on the machines that make up a Web cluster. A machine is designated as the *controller* for the cluster, and is considered to have the master copy of all relevant Web content for the site. Changes to the cluster controller content can be automatically propagated to other members of the cluster.

AC2K provides several powerful performance monitoring capabilities, in the form of *health monitors*. These monitors can gather performance data such as website performance statistics, or they can gather system health data such as memory utilization and the status of forwarded requests. Some of the different kinds of health monitors available are depicted in Figure 16.11.

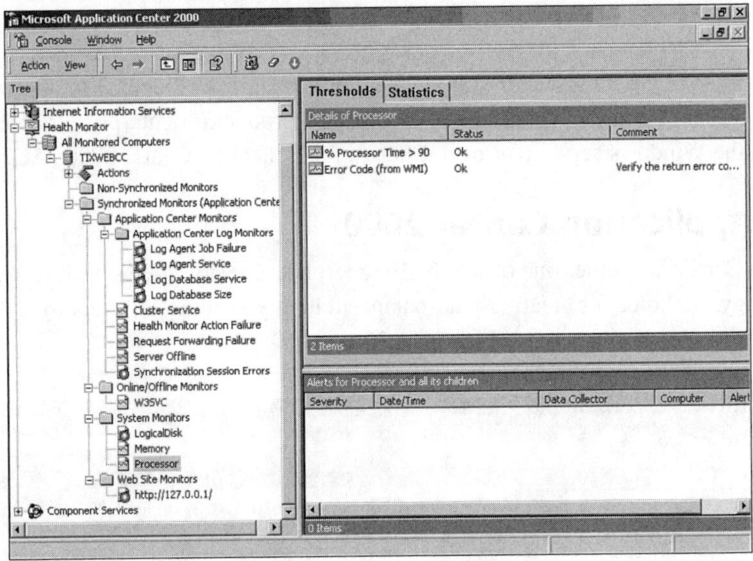

FIGURE 16.11

Many health monitors are available in Application Center 2000 to monitor and measure performance of a Web cluster.

AC2K also manages incremental deployment. If a change is made to an application that requires IIS to shut down on all the machines, AC2K will automatically handle the draining of connections, the application update, and the restarting of IIS on each machine in the cluster without intervention from an administrator.

Although AC2K has been dubbed a .NET Enterprise Server, it still has plenty of support mechanisms for COM+. Specialized clusters can be created for COM+ applications using Component Load Balancing, and there is even support for clusters which route COM+ requests to COM+ application clusters. Replacement of COM+ components requires shutting down and restarting COM+ applications, so content does not propagate automatically through these clusters; the changes must be initiated manually. Since COM+ is not part of the .NET Framework, we will not discuss these clusters further, limiting ourselves to a discussion of Web clusters under AC2K.

Preparing a Web Cluster for Use with .NET and AC2K

CAUTION

As of the time of this writing, Application Center 2000 installs poorly on Windows 2000 machines already running Service Pack 2 or later. In fact, it may not even work at all if installed on such machines. There is no real solution other than to think ahead and install Application Center 2000 before applying SP2. Keep this in mind if you plan to install Application Center 2000 and Visual Studio .NET on the same machine—Visual Studio .NET requires Service Pack 2.

It is safe to install Service Pack 2 after installing Application Center 2000, as long as the machine is not part of a cluster.

NOTE

If we plan to use Windows Network Load Balancing as our load distribution mechanism, each computer in the cluster must have two network cards. One network card from each computer will hook to a private "heartbeat" network that circulates Application Center-specific management traffic; the other network card is the external interface. Under Windows Network Load Balancing, the machine that will be the cluster controller needs to have a static IP address for its external network card. Network Load Balancing will identify the cluster according to this IP address.

TIP

Cluster members need only be running Windows 2000 Server, as AC2K will automatically add Windows Network Load Balancing on any machines on which it is installed. Network Load Balancing comes automatically as part of Windows 2000 Advanced Server.

To add members to a cluster, we must first create the cluster. This can be done by opening Application Center and choosing to connect to a server. We will see a prompt that asks us whether to create a new cluster or join an existing cluster. Use the first option to create a cluster and make the computer to which we are connecting the controller for that cluster; use the second option, as shown in Figure 16.12, to join machines to the cluster we just created. We will be asked to verify some information about the network card(s) and network configuration in the machine to be joined.

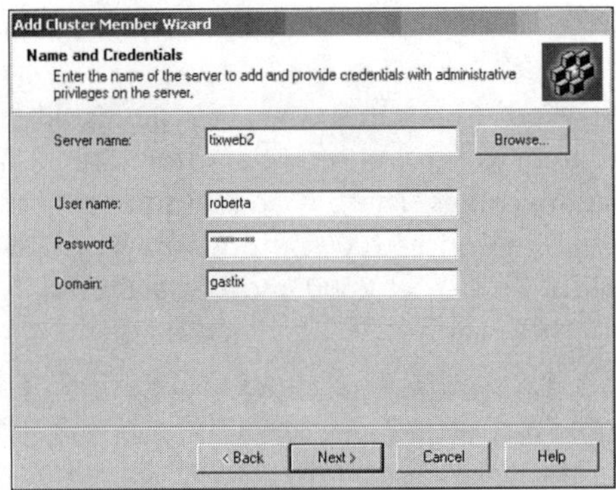

FIGURE 16.12
Adding a member to a cluster.

TIP

Be patient when preparing a Web cluster. It takes time to add computers to clusters. A lot of work goes on "under the hood" to support adding a new member to a cluster, including changing Network Load Balancing settings and other network properties, as well as beginning synchronization of content to new cluster members.

Going forward, we will work with the AC2K Web cluster depicted in Figure 16.13, which consists of two machines. TIXWEBCC is the cluster controller, while TIXWEB2 is the other cluster member.

Deploying .NET Applications on Application Center 2000 Clusters

AC2K automatically propagates changes made to Web applications on the cluster controller to the other members of the cluster. In the traditional Windows DNA setting, any discussion of AC2K would by necessity involve most of the features and attributes of Application Center 2000 applications, which are simply collections of IIS virtual directories and associated local resources that are to be replicated across different machines. This is because the trappings of

COM+ can involve a lot of registry settings and quite a few external resources such as DSNs. To make matters worse, COM+ packages do not automatically replicate, as we briefly discussed earlier, and we would have to perform a manual synchronization in order to propagate COM+ application changes.

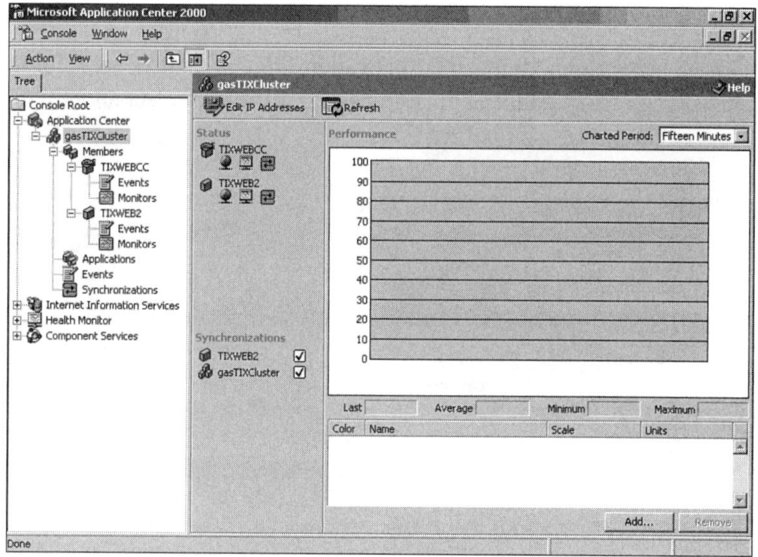

FIGURE 16.13

The gasTIX cluster in Application Center.

The .NET Framework changes all of this. Because there is no locking of shared DLLs in use, no processes need to shut down in order to install changes to .NET assemblies. In addition, since we are treating all assemblies as private, we store our business and data objects directly in the Web application folders as simple content. Application Center 2000 will automatically propagate changes in our application.

CAUTION

At this time, it is risky to replicate DLLs stored in the global assembly cache (GAC). Shared assemblies are stored in a very specific directory structure inside the `WINNT\Assembly\` folder. While copying the GAC directory tree between machines as a File System Path resource in the corresponding Application Center 2000 application is possible, the Microsoft-recommended way is to use a Windows Installer to manipulate the GAC. Installer projects specifically designed for the GAC (such as those created by Visual Studio .NET) have special features, such as assembly reference counting, which make working with the GAC safe.

AC2K applications are still very useful for propagating any registry keys utilized by the application, or any DSNs needed by each machine that exist on the cluster controller. In our case, we have compiled the proper database connection strings into our application files, so we will not need to use the local resource propagation features of AC2K. If we were using these features, items such as registry keys and DSNs would be bundled with an Application Center application as local resources, and would also be propagated to other cluster members.

In order to add resources, simply view the Applications item in the tree view for the Web cluster, select the resource type to add, and click the Add… button to select an item to add. This process is shown in Figure 16.14.

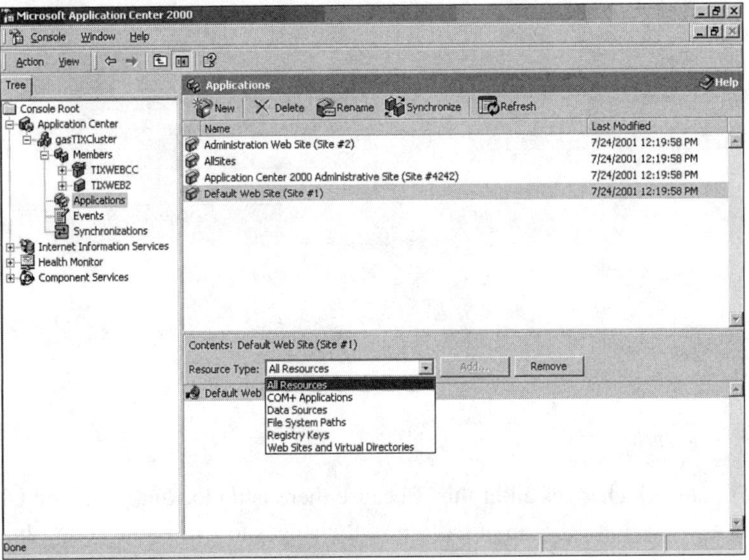

FIGURE 16.14
Adding resources to an AC2K application.

We are now ready to deploy content to the cluster controller. In our case, it is as simple as running the installer we created for gasTIX on the cluster controller. Once the application is installed on the controller, if automatic synchronization is enabled, the application will be replicated to the other cluster members at the next synchronization interval.

From Here

In this chapter, we have gotten a taste of the powerful options available to us for .NET distributed application deployment. While XCopy Deployment is a viable option (which some people swear by), the ability to create version-checked, easily maintained installation packages is worth the extra effort. With practice, deployment projects can become as straightforward as simple deployment via copying files, but with many more benefits.

As this is a book on .NET e-Business architecture, we have focused primarily on Web deployments and considerations relating to Website scalability and availability. As we have seen, .NET has a rich set of features for traditional Windows client deployment as well. These features behave in a similar manner to those for Web deployments, and should be familiar to users of installer programs like InstallShield and the Package and Deployment Wizard in Visual Basic 6.0.

As .NET is a new technology, we will no doubt continue to see improvements to the platform that will provide further robustness and ease in deploying next-generation distributed enterprise applications. We hope that this chapter, and indeed this entire book, has provided you with a set of practical, usable skills that will help you master the new, ever-changing world of .NET e-Business. From all of us to all of you, happy programming! Return often to `www.gasTIX.net` for product updates and further learning topics!

Design Documents

by Matthew Baute

APPENDIX

IN THIS APPENDIX

- **gasTIX Requirements 522**
- **gasTIX Use Cases 526**
- **gasTIX Site Map 529**
- **gasTIX Object Models 531**
- **gasTIX Data Model 541**

The purpose of this section is to provide additional design documentation material to aid in the understanding of the gasTIX sample .NET application. See Chapter 2, "gasTIX: A Sample .NET eBusiness," for a detailed explanation of the sample application.

gasTIX Requirements

The high-level requirements for the gasTIX application are described in this section. It focuses on user, financial, back office, and administrative requirements of the system. Functionality is also divided into the requirements that are implemented in this version of gasTIX, and those that have been deferred to a future version.

Implemented Functionality

This section describes the functional requirements that are implemented in the current version of the gasTIX .NET sample application. The requirements are grouped by major functional area: User, Financial, Back Office, and Administration.

I. User Functional Requirements

1. The system will provide a set of venues for users to pick from, and will track seating for those venues.
2. The system will display demographic information for each venue, such as address, phone numbers, directions, parking information, and so on. This will allow users to make informed choices when purchasing tickets.
3. The system will contain a graphical seating chart for venues (when a graphics file is made available by the venue) which will help users make buying decisions.
4. The system will sell tickets for a number of events and will allow users to query for available seating still remaining at those events.
5. The system will allow users to search for specific events for an artist or team, events within a certain category (sports, music, with subcategories), events at a specific venue, and events in a specific state.
6. The system will allow users to specify the number of tickets desired for an event, with a maximum of eight tickets per purchase.
7. The system will allow users to locate seats in a specific venue section, or query for the best seats still available for an event.
8. The system will allow users to purchase tickets using a credit card through the Internet.
9. The system will e-mail a purchase confirmation to users.

10. By tracking a number of events for a specific artist or team, the system will support a tour schedule for artists/teams.
11. The system will offer the user a variety of ticket shipping methods (next day, three business days, standard postal mail, etc.).
12. The system will support an address validation feature that will query a database of valid addresses during address entry, and prompt users if an address cannot be verified.
13. The system will support the display of banner advertisements.

II. Financial Functional Requirements

1. The system will provide transactional support for purchasing, ensuring that either all steps in the process are completed, or none are completed.
2. The system will ensure the security of sensitive financial data such as credit card information during the purchase process.

III. Back Office Functional Requirements

1. The system will be designed to support a large number of users.
2. The system will provide an XML Web service that will allow other web sites to query for pricing, availability, and event information.
3. The system will provide an XML Web service that will allow other web sites to make ticket purchases.
4. The system will integrate with a Transaction Processing Authority (TPA) business partner. This partner will handle all ticket printing and shipping fulfillment. Communications between the gasTIX system and the TPA system will occur in an asynchronous, loosely coupled manner.

Future Functionality

This section describes the functional requirements that are deferred to a future version of the gasTIX .NET sample application. While these requirements have not been implemented at this time, careful consideration was given to their future implementation during design.

I. User Functional Requirements (Future)

1. The system will support online help for commonly accessed features.
2. The system will provide users with a feature to track the status of orders.
3. The user account area will track "purchase points" which can be applied to future orders.

4. The system will provide users with the capability to sign up for email notifications of specific promotions and events.
5. The system will provide a "forgotten password" functionality to registered users, allowing them to receive their password via e-mail.
6. The system will support online user registration of demographic information and optionally, credit card information. Registration will also allow the user to enter artist/team/event preferences, and a customized home page will then display specific events based on these preferences. Registration will be accomplished through integration with Microsoft Passport .NET, enabling the site to begin offering HailStorm services.
7. The system will provide users with a password-protected login screen to enter the personal user account area where they can modify preferences. Login will be accomplished through integration with Microsoft Passport .NET.
8. If a user has logged in to a personal account and is making a purchase, billing information is read from the user's personal account and is displayed. The user may optionally change the billing information for the purchase. Billing information will be retrieved via Microsoft Passport .NET Express Purchase.
9. The system will allow users to print purchased tickets online (bar code scanners will be required at venues to read these tickets).
10. The system will offer an extended product line (posters, T-shirts, and other merchandise) related to events featured on the site.
11. The system will support internationalization features (language and monetary conversions, date formatting, and so on), offering service to users in overseas markets.

II. Financial Functional Requirements (Future)

The system will integrate with an external accounting system's general ledger.

III. Back Office Functional Requirements (Future)

1. The system will support mobile device connectivity. Wireless devices such as digital telephones, Personal Digital Assistants (PDAs), and other WAP-compliant devices will access the site over the web. These users will be presented with pages tailored for the small screen.
2. The system will support XML-based exchange with venues for seating information for different venue layouts.
3. The system will query shipping web sites (FedEx, UPS, and so on) to determine shipping pricing for tickets.

IV. Administration Functional Requirements (Future)

1. The system will provide a login screen for administrators of the ticketing application. This login will be accomplished through integration with Microsoft Passport .NET.
2. The administration area will allow adding, editing, or deleting a venue. The venue maintenance area will allow the administrator to enter seating detail for different venue configurations. This area will also allow the administrator to enter the filename of the graphical seating chart for each configuration.
3. The administrator will not be allowed to delete a venue with events with tickets sold. Only venues with no tickets sold (or a venue where all tickets for all events have been refunded) can be deleted.
4. The administration area will allow an administrator to add, edit, or delete an artist/team. The artist/team will contain a name, web site, picture, and category. The artist/team can be designated as a featured performer. With this designation enabled, an artist/team will be featured on the gasTIX home page under the appropriate category.
5. The administrator will not be allowed to delete an artist/team with tickets sold. Only artists/teams with no tickets sold (or artists/teams where all tickets for all events have been refunded) can be deleted.
6. The administration area will allow an admin to add, edit, or delete an event, joining an artist/team with a venue for a specific date/time. Data such as special instructions (for example, no cameras or recorders), ticket limit, date/time tickets go on sale, and so on can be entered for an event.
7. The administrator will not be allowed to delete an event with tickets sold. Only events with no tickets sold (or an event where all tickets have been refunded) can be deleted.
8. The administrator will be able to process a refund for all tickets for an event in case of rain out, cancellation, low sales, etc.
9. The system will allow an administrator to mark specific seats for an event as sold prior to the event going on sale (promotional giveaways, etc.).
10. The system will provide standard transactional reports listing sales and other relevant data.
11. The system will allow executives to produce ad-hoc OLAP reports to determine purchasing trends and patterns.

gasTIX Use Cases

The gasTIX design team used the Unified Modeling Language (UML) during the design phase. One of the most important artifacts generated during UML modeling is the use case diagram. This diagram shows the entire system scope, and is supported by use case documents that describe the system scope in more detail.

The following use cases were constructed at a high level, and contain only simple extension conditions. In a real-world client engagement, much more detail would be provided.

The actor for each use case (actor in the UML sense of the word, not a gasTIX performer) is the customer browsing the application, searching for events and purchasing tickets.

Use Case 1—Select Event by Category

Extends: None (A use case that extends another use case builds upon the functionality of the use case it extends).

Assumption: The actor can cancel this use case at any time.

Purpose: Select an event based on the category of an artist or team.

The actor picks a category and a list of artist or team names having events fitting the category is displayed. The actor then picks a specific artist or team name, and a list of events for that artist or team with summary information is displayed. The actor next selects a specific event and the system displays detailed information for that event.

Use Case 2—Select Event by Venue

Extends: None

Assumption: The actor can cancel this use case at any time.

Purpose: Select an event based on the venue in which an event is being held.

Outputs: Detailed information for a specific event.

The actor decides whether to search for the venue by name or by state and proceeds according to one of the following two paths.

a. Venue Search

The actor inputs the name of a venue and issues the search for a venue command. The system determines that the number of characters input is greater than or equal to one character in length. If not, the user is prompted to enter a venue name and must restart the process.

Upon successful venue name entry, the system searches for the venue input by the user. A list of venues is displayed to the actor if matches are found. A "no venues found" message is displayed to the actor if no matches are found.

The actor picks a venue from the list of matches and a list of events at that venue with summary information is displayed. The actor then selects a specific event and the system displays detailed information for that event.

b. Select Venue by State

A list of states and a graphical U.S. state map is displayed to the actor, who then picks a state. A list of cities with a covered venue is displayed. If no covered venue cities are found for the selected state, a "no venues found" message is displayed.

The actor next selects a city, and a list of venues is displayed. The actor picks a venue and a list of events at that venue with summary information is displayed. The actor then selects a specific event and the system displays detailed information for that event.

Use Case 3—Select Event by State

Extends: None

Assumption: The actor can cancel this use case at any time.

Purpose: To select an event based on the state in which the event is taking place.

Outputs: Detailed information for a specific event.

A list of states and a graphical U.S. state map is displayed to the actor. The actor selects a state, and a list of artist or team names with upcoming events in the state is displayed, ordered by category. The actor selects an artist or team name and the system displays a list of events with limited event summary information for the selected name. The actor then selects a specific event and the system displays detailed information for that event.

Use Case 4—Select Event by Artist/Team Name

Extends: None

Assumption: The actor can cancel this use case at any time.

Purpose: Select an event based on the name of the artist/team.

Outputs: Detailed information for a specific event.

The actor inputs the name of an artist or team name and issues the search for artist/team name command. The system determines that the number of characters input is greater than or equal to one character in length. If not, the user is prompted to enter an artist or team name and must restart the process.

Upon successful artist/team name entry, the system searches for the name input by the user. A list of names is displayed to the actor if matches are found. A "no artists/teams found" message is displayed to the actor if no matches are found.

The actor picks an artist/team name from the list, and a list of events for that name with summary information is displayed. The actor then selects a specific event and the system displays detailed information for that event.

Use Case 5—Pricing/Availability Check

Extends: Select Event by Category, Select Event by Venue, Select Event by State, Select Event by Artist/Team Name

Assumptions: The actor can cancel this use case at any time. A specific event has been selected in order to run this use case.

Purpose: Determine which seats are still available for a specific event and the pricing for those seats.

Outputs: A list of available seats and prices for a specific event.

The actor enters the number of seats desired for the event (up to eight), and optionally the price range willing to pay. The system issues the check pricing/availability search function, and a list of available seating options meeting the criteria is displayed. Detailed pricing information, along with service charges and any applicable taxes, is displayed to the user.

Use Case 6—View Seating Chart

Extends: Select Event by Category, Select Event by Venue, Select Event by State, Select Event by Artist/Team Name

Assumption: The actor can cancel this use case at any time. A venue must be selected in order to proceed with this use case.

Purpose: To provide the actor with a graphical view of the seating chart for a specific venue.

Outputs: A graphical display for the selected venue.

The actor picks the view seating chart option for a specific venue. If a seating chart is available for the venue, it is displayed to the user. If no chart is available, a "no seating chart available" message is displayed. The actor is able to view the different seating configurations for the venue, if available.

Use Case 7—Purchase Tickets

Extends: Pricing/Availability Check

Assumptions: The actor cannot cancel this use case once the final purchase has been submitted. A specific event has been selected, and a pricing/availability check has been run for this event.

Purpose: Enable the actor to purchase a specific number of tickets for a specific price for a specific event.

Outputs: A confirmation of purchase for the selected event, pricing, and seating.

The actor enters the shipping option, billing address, and credit card information. If a shipping option is not picked, if required billing address fields are not completed, or if credit card information is not completed, the system displays an error message to the user and provides an opportunity to fill in the required fields.

Once the system determines all information is entered correctly, the system calls the purchase ticket function. The credit card information is processed. The system removes the seats purchased from the available list for the event. The system displays a "purchase completed" message to the user. If any errors are encountered during the purchasing process, the purchase is rolled back. Any error messages are displayed to the user, who is given the opportunity to resubmit the purchase if appropriate.

gasTIX Site Map

The following site map provides a graphical view of the general web page navigation path of the gasTIX application.

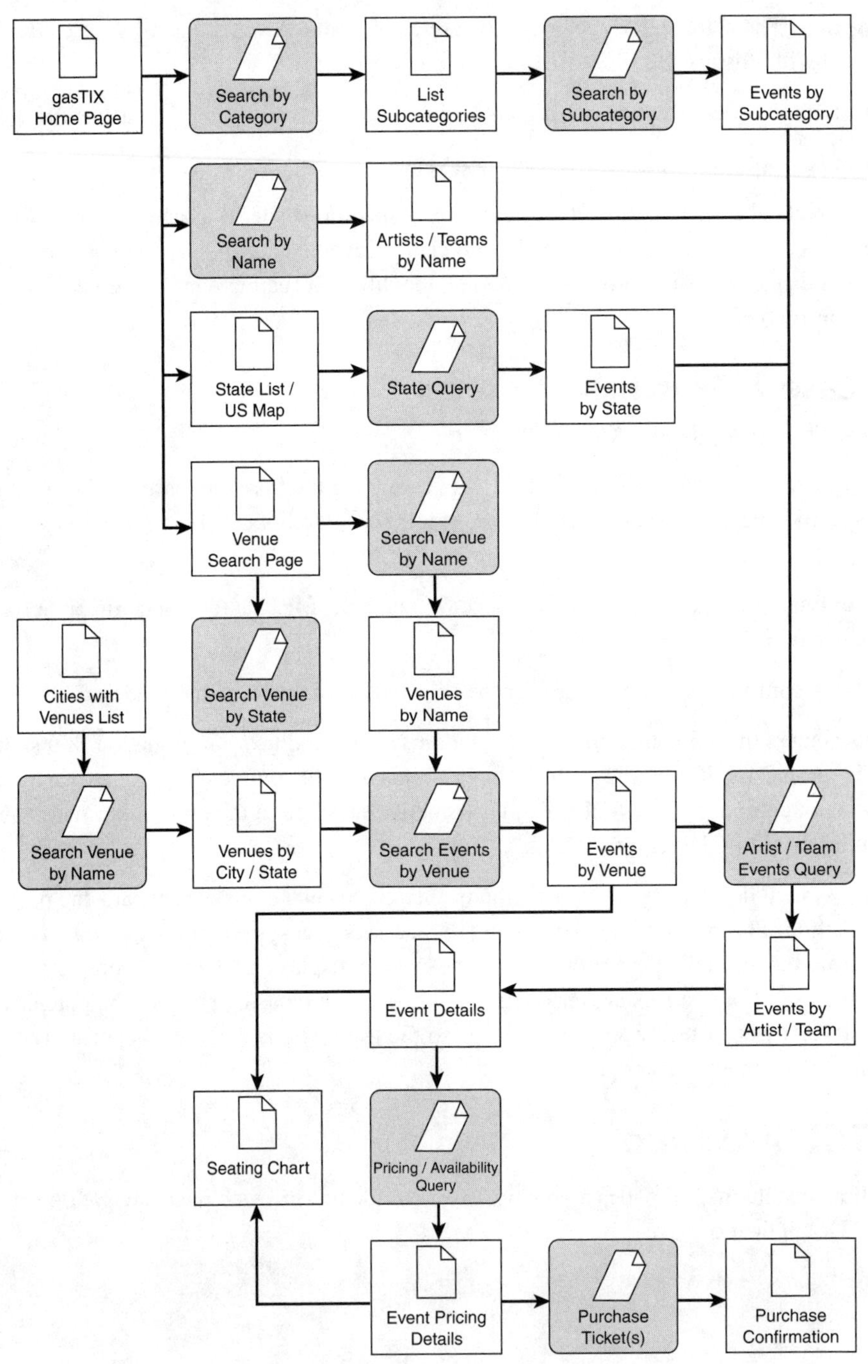

FIGURE A.1
gasTIX Application Web Page Navigation Path.

gasTIX Object Models

The following object models present a graphical view of the gasTIX middle-tier components. These diagrams were generated in Visual Studio .NET using the Visio UML Reverse Engineer feature, found on the Project menu. VS .NET automatically generates a Visio UML file when this feature is selected on a project. This can be done on the solution level as well as at the individual project and class level.

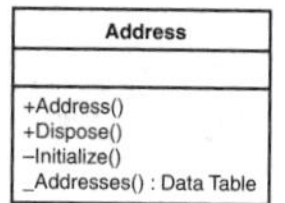

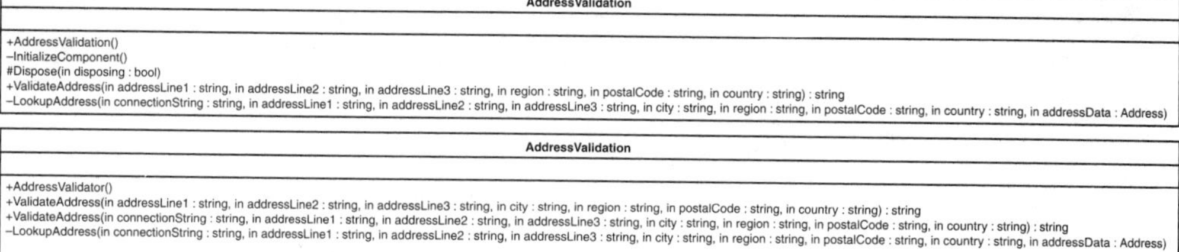

FIGURE A.2
Address Validation.

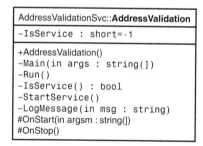

AddressValidationSvc::**AddressValidation**
-IsService : short=-1
+AddressValidation() -Main(in args : string[]) -Run() -IsService() : bool -StartService() -LogMessage(in msg : string) #OnStart(in argsm : string[]) #OnStop()

AddressValidationSvc::**AddressValidationInstaller**
+AddressValidationInstaller()

FIGURE A.3
Address Validation Service.

Business::**CreditCardProcessor**
+CreditCardProcessor() +ChargeCard(in ccName : string, in ccType : int, in ccNumber : string, ccExpireDate : datetime, in purchaseAmount : float) : string

Business::**UpdateOrder**
+UpdateOrder() +Add(in order : OrderData) +UpdateSaleStatus(in saleID : int, in status : string)

Rules::**OrderRules**
+OrderRules() +ValidateSale(in order : OrderData) +ValidateReserveSeats(in evenId : int, in sectionId : int, numberSeats : int) –GenerateConfirmation() : string –CalculateCosts(in saleItem : SaleDetail, in numberSeats : int, in priceTicket : decimal, in shippingCharge : decimal, in taxRate : decimal) –ValidateAddress(in saleItem : SaleDetail, in shipToRegion : string, in billToRegion : string, in shipToCountry : string, in billToCountry : string)

FIGURE A.4
Business.

BusinessFacade::**Category**
+ListCategories() : ListCategoriesData +ListSubCategories(in categoryId : Integer) : ListSubCategoriesData

BusinessFacade::**Category**
+New() +ListMultiple(in searchName : String) : CombinedSearchResultsData

BusinessFacade::**CreditCard**
+ListCreditCardTypes() : ListCreditCardTypesData

BusinessFacade::**Customer**
+ListCategories(in customerid : Integer) : ListCategoriesData +Add(in emailAddress : String) : Integer

BusinessFacade::**Event**
+GetEvent(in eventId : Integer) : EventData +GetEvent(in eventId : Integer, in wantSections : Boolean) : EventData +ListEvents(in startDate : Date, in endDate : Date) : ListEventsData

BusinessFacade::**Order**
+ReserveSeats(in eventId : integer, in sectionId : Integer, in numberSeats : Integer) : OrderData +ValidateCosts(in order : OrderData) : OrderData +FinalizeSale(in order : orderData) : OrderData +UpdateSaleStatus(in saleID : Integer, in status : String)

FIGURE A.5
Business Facade.

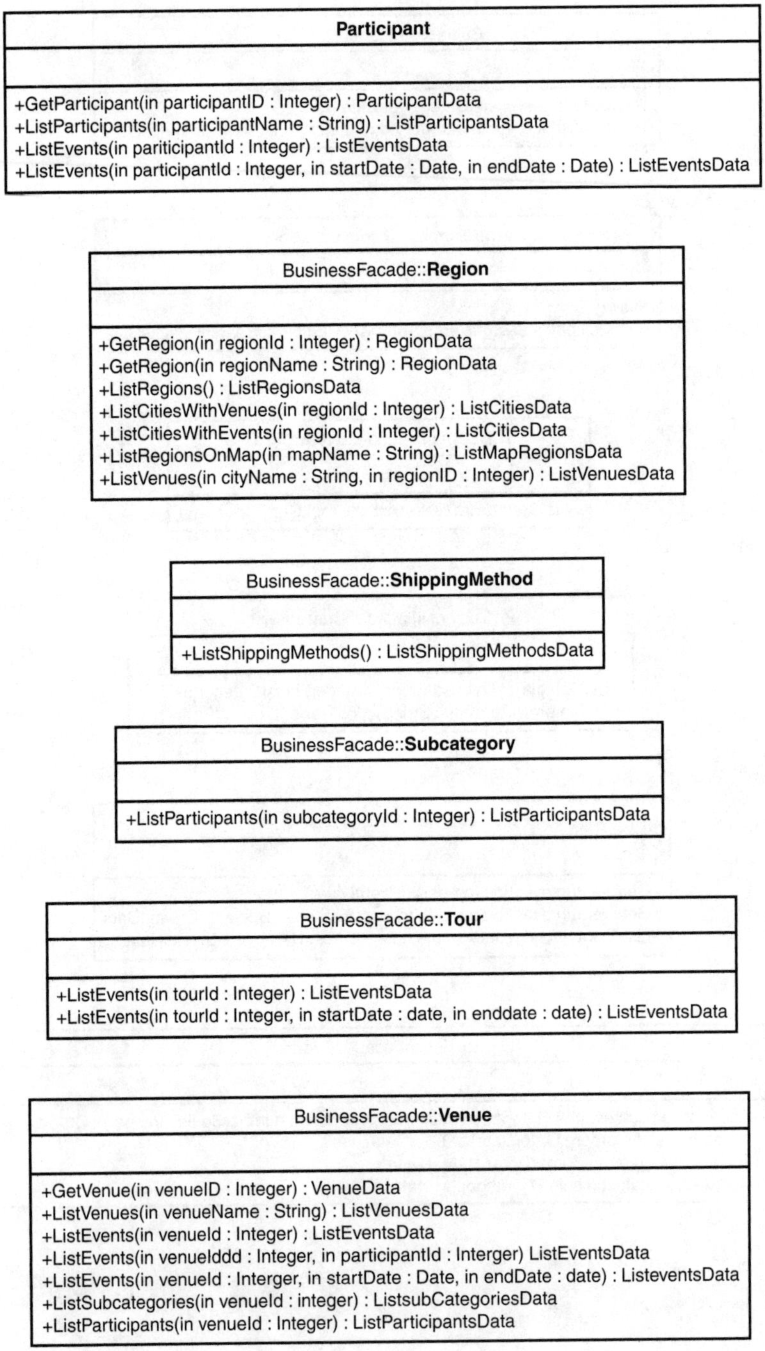

Participant
+GetParticipant(in participantID : Integer) : ParticipantData +ListParticipants(in participantName : String) : ListParticipantsData +ListEvents(in pariticipantId : Integer) : ListEventsData +ListEvents(in participantId : Integer, in startDate : Date, in endDate : Date) : ListEventsData

BusinessFacade::**Region**
+GetRegion(in regionId : Integer) : RegionData +GetRegion(in regionName : String) : RegionData +ListRegions() : ListRegionsData +ListCitiesWithVenues(in regionId : Integer) : ListCitiesData +ListCitiesWithEvents(in regionId : Integer) : ListCitiesData +ListRegionsOnMap(in mapName : String) : ListMapRegionsData +ListVenues(in cityName : String, in regionID : Integer) : ListVenuesData

BusinessFacade::**ShippingMethod**
+ListShippingMethods() : ListShippingMethodsData

BusinessFacade::**Subcategory**
+ListParticipants(in subcategoryId : Integer) : ListParticipantsData

BusinessFacade::**Tour**
+ListEvents(in tourId : Integer) : ListEventsData +ListEvents(in tourId : Integer, in startDate : date, in enddate : date) : ListEventsData

BusinessFacade::**Venue**
+GetVenue(in venueID : Integer) : VenueData +ListVenues(in venueName : String) : ListVenuesData +ListEvents(in venueId : Integer) : ListEventsData +ListEvents(in venueIdddd : Integer, in participantId : Interger) ListEventsData +ListEvents(in venueId : Interger, in startDate : Date, in endDate : date) : ListeventsData +ListSubcategories(in venueId : integer) : ListsubCategoriesData +ListParticipants(in venueId : Integer) : ListParticipantsData

FIGURE A.6

Business Facade, continued.

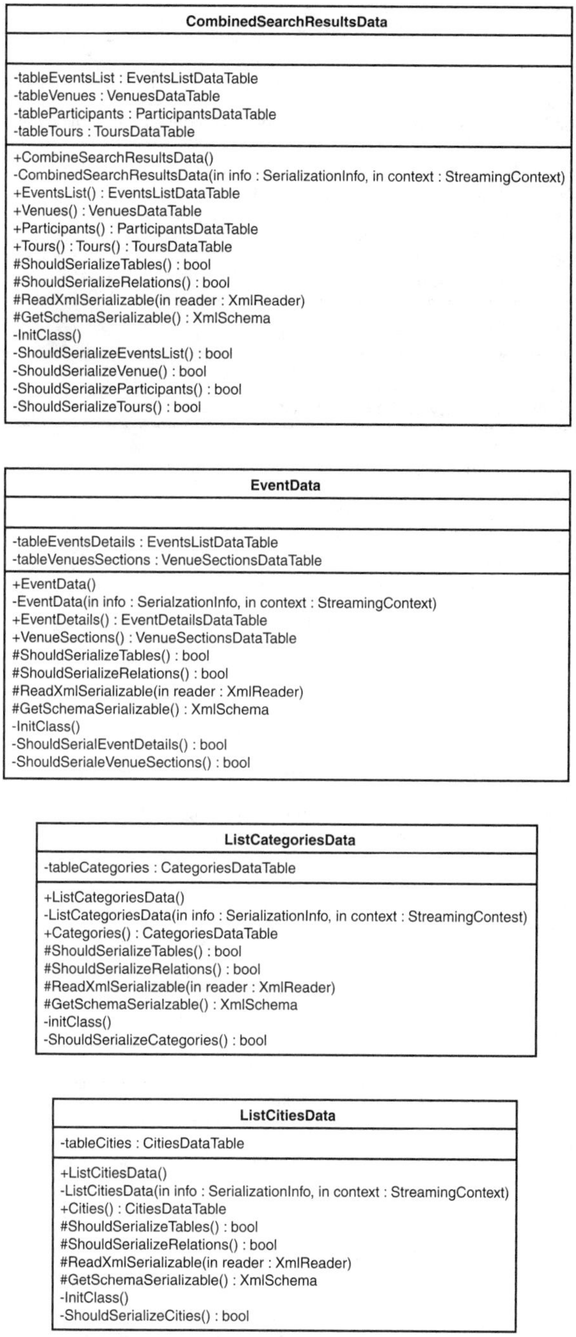

```
CombinedSearchResultsData
-----------------------------------------------------------
-tableEventsList : EventsListDataTable
-tableVenues : VenuesDataTable
-tableParticipants : ParticipantsDataTable
-tableTours : ToursDataTable
-----------------------------------------------------------
+CombineSearchResultsData()
-CombinedSearchResultsData(in info : SerializationInfo, in context : StreamingContext)
+EventsList() : EventsListDataTable
+Venues() : VenuesDataTable
+Participants() : ParticipantsDataTable
+Tours() : Tours() : ToursDataTable
#ShouldSerializeTables() : bool
#ShouldSerializeRelations() : bool
#ReadXmlSerializable(in reader : XmlReader)
#GetSchemaSerializable() : XmlSchema
-InitClass()
-ShouldSerializeEventsList() : bool
-ShouldSerializeVenue() : bool
-ShouldSerializeParticipants() : bool
-ShouldSerializeTours() : bool
```

```
EventData
-----------------------------------------------------------
-tableEventsDetails : EventsListDataTable
-tableVenuesSections : VenueSectionsDataTable
-----------------------------------------------------------
+EventData()
-EventData(in info : SerialzationInfo, in context : StreamingContext)
+EventDetails() : EventDetailsDataTable
+VenueSections() : VenueSectionsDataTable
#ShouldSerializeTables() : bool
#ShouldSerializeRelations() : bool
#ReadXmlSerializable(in reader : XmlReader)
#GetSchemaSerializable() : XmlSchema
-InitClass()
-ShouldSerialEventDetails() : bool
-ShouldSerialeVenueSections() : bool
```

```
ListCategoriesData
-----------------------------------------------------------
-tableCategories : CategoriesDataTable
-----------------------------------------------------------
+ListCategoriesData()
-ListCategoriesData(in info : SerializationInfo, in context : StreamingContest)
+Categories() : CategoriesDataTable
#ShouldSerializeTables() : bool
#ShouldSerializeRelations() : bool
#ReadXmlSerializable(in reader : XmlReader)
#GetSchemaSerialzable() : XmlSchema
-initClass()
-ShouldSerializeCategories() : bool
```

```
ListCitiesData
-----------------------------------------------------------
-tableCities : CitiesDataTable
-----------------------------------------------------------
+ListCitiesData()
-ListCitiesData(in info : SerializationInfo, in context : StreamingContext)
+Cities() : CitiesDataTable
#ShouldSerializeTables() : bool
#ShouldSerializeRelations() : bool
#ReadXmlSerializable(in reader : XmlReader)
#GetSchemaSerializable() : XmlSchema
-InitClass()
-ShouldSerializeCities() : bool
```

FIGURE A.7
Data.

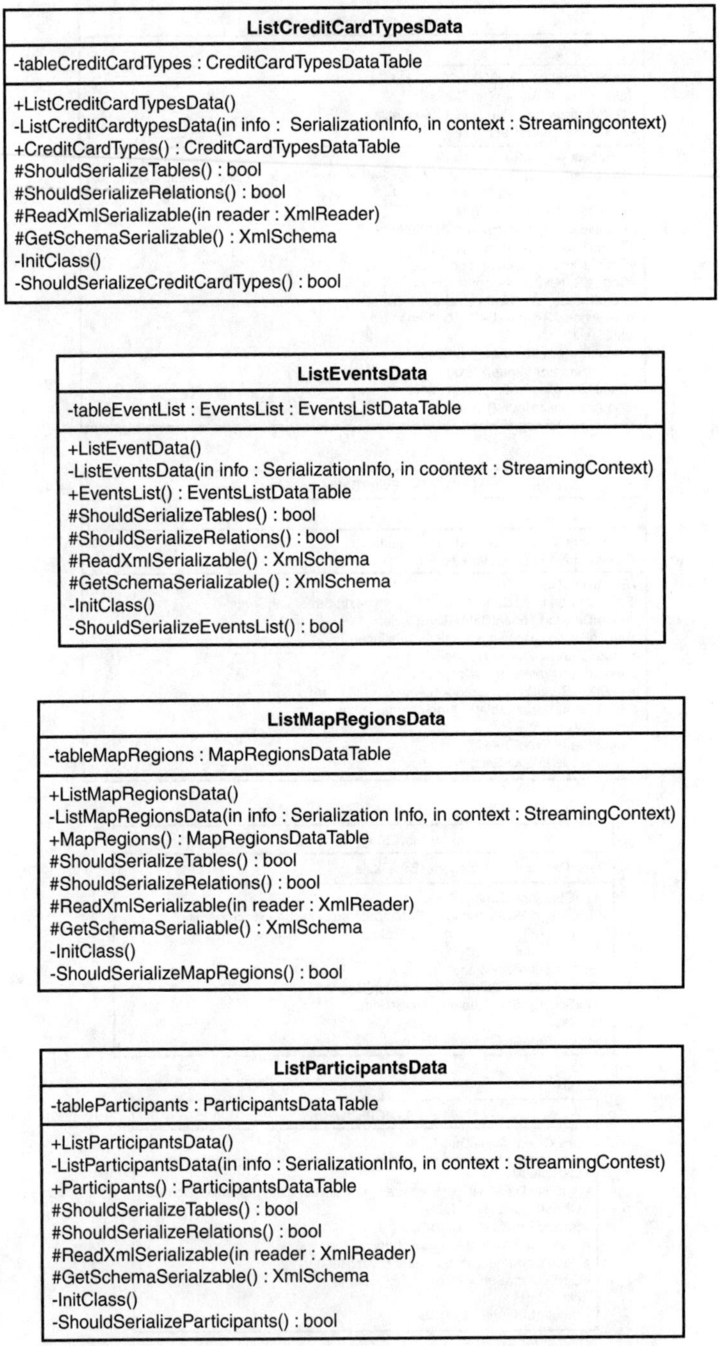

```
ListCreditCardTypesData
-------------------------------------------------
-tableCreditCardTypes : CreditCardTypesDataTable
-------------------------------------------------
+ListCreditCardTypesData()
-ListCreditCardtypesData(in info :  SerializationInfo, in context : Streamingcontext)
+CreditCardTypes() : CreditCardTypesDataTable
#ShouldSerializeTables() : bool
#ShouldSerializeRelations() : bool
#ReadXmlSerializable(in reader : XmlReader)
#GetSchemaSerializable() : XmlSchema
-InitClass()
-ShouldSerializeCreditCardTypes() : bool
```

```
ListEventsData
-------------------------------------------------
-tableEventList : EventsList : EventsListDataTable
-------------------------------------------------
+ListEventData()
-ListEventsData(in info : SerializationInfo, in coontext : StreamingContext)
+EventsList() : EventsListDataTable
#ShouldSerializeTables() : bool
#ShouldSerializeRelations() : bool
#ReadXmlSerializable() : XmlSchema
#GetSchemaSerializable() : XmlSchema
-InitClass()
-ShouldSerializeEventsList() : bool
```

```
ListMapRegionsData
-------------------------------------------------
-tableMapRegions : MapRegionsDataTable
-------------------------------------------------
+ListMapRegionsData()
-ListMapRegionsData(in info : Serialization Info, in context : StreamingContext)
+MapRegions() : MapRegionsDataTable
#ShouldSerializeTables() : bool
#ShouldSerializeRelations() : bool
#ReadXmlSerializable(in reader : XmlReader)
#GetSchemaSerialiable() : XmlSchema
-InitClass()
-ShouldSerializeMapRegions() : bool
```

```
ListParticipantsData
-------------------------------------------------
-tableParticipants : ParticipantsDataTable
-------------------------------------------------
+ListParticipantsData()
-ListParticipantsData(in info : SerializationInfo, in context : StreamingContest)
+Participants() : ParticipantsDataTable
#ShouldSerializeTables() : bool
#ShouldSerializeRelations() : bool
#ReadXmlSerializable(in reader : XmlReader)
#GetSchemaSerialzable() : XmlSchema
-InitClass()
-ShouldSerializeParticipants() : bool
```

FIGURE A.8

Data, continued.

ListCreditCardTypesData
-tableRegions : RegionsDataTable
+ListRegionsData() -ListRegions(in info : SerializationInfo, in context : Streamingcontext) +Regions() : RegionsTable #ShouldSerializeTables() : bool #ShouldSerializeRelations() : bool #ReadXmlSerializable(in reader : XmlReader) #GetSchemaSerializable() : XmlSchema -InitClass() -ShouldSerializeRegions() : bool

ListShippingMethodsData
-tableShippingMethods : ShippingMethodsDataTable
+ListShippingMethodsData() -ListShippingMethodsData(in info : SerializationInfo, in context : StreamingContext) +ShippingMethods() : ShippingMethodsDataTable #ShouldSerializeTables() : bool #ShouldSerializeRelations() : bool #ShouldSerializeRelations(in reader : XmlReader) #GetSchemaSerializable() : XmlSchema -InitClass() -ShouldSerializeShippingMethods() : bool

ListSubCategoriesData
-tableSubCategories : SubCategoriesTable
+ListSubCategoriesData() -ListSubCategoriesData(in info : Serialization Info, in context : StreamingContext) +SubCategories() : SubCategoriesDataTable #ShouldSerializeTables() : bool #ShouldSerializeRelations() : bool #ReadXmlSerializable(in reader : XmlReader) #GetSchemaSerialiable() : XmlSchema -initClass() -ShouldSerialize#ShouldSerializeRelations() : bool

ListVenuesData
-tableVenues : VenuesDataTable
+ListVenuesData() -ListVenueData(in info : SerializationInfo, in context : StreamingContest) +Venue() : ParticipantsDataTable #ShouldSerializeTables() : bool #ShouldSerializeRelations() : bool #ReadXmlSerializable(in reader : XmlReader) #GetSchemaSerialzable() : XmlSchema -initClass() -ShouldSerializeParticipants() : bool

FIGURE A.9
Data, continued.

OrderData
-tableSaleDetails : SaleDetailsDataTable -tableSeatDetails : SeatDetailsDataTable
+OrderData() -OrderData(in info : SerializationInfo, in context : StreamingContext) +SaleDetails() : SaleDetailsDataTable +SeatDetails() : SeatDetailsDataTable #ShouldSerializeTables() : bool #ShouldSerializeRelations() : bool #ReadXMlSerializable(in reader : XmlReader) #GetSchemaSerializable) : XmlSchema -initClass() -ShouldSerializeSaleDetails() : bool -ShouldSerialSeatDetails() : bool

ParticipantData
-tableParticipantDetails : ParticipantDetailsDataTable
+ParticipantData() -ParticipantData()(in info : SerializationInfo, in context : StreamingContext) +ParticipantDetails() : ParticipantDetails DataTable #ShouldSerializeTables() : bool #ShouldSerializeRelations() : bool #ReadXmlSerializable(in reader : XmlReader) #GetSchemaSerializable() : XmlSchema -InitClass() -ShouldSerializeParticipantDetails() : bool

RegionData
-tableRegionDetails : RegionDetailsDataTable
+RegionData() -RegionData(in info : Serialization Info, in context : StreamingContext) +RegionDetails() : RegionDataTable #ShouldSerializeTables() : bool #ShouldSerializeRelations() : bool #ReadXmlSerializable(in reader : XmlReader) #GetSchemaSerialiable() : XmlSchema -initClass() -ShouldSerialize#ShouldSerializeRelations() : bool

VenueData
-tableVenueDetails : VenueDetailsDataTable
+VenueData -VenueData(in info : SerializationInfo, in context : StreamingContest) +VenueDetails() : VenueDetailsDataTable #ShouldSerializeTables() : bool #ShouldSerializeRelations() : bool #ReadXmlSerializable(in reader : XmlReader) #GetSchemaSerialzable() : XmlSchema -initClass() -ShouldSerializeParticipants() : bool

FIGURE A.10

Data, continued.

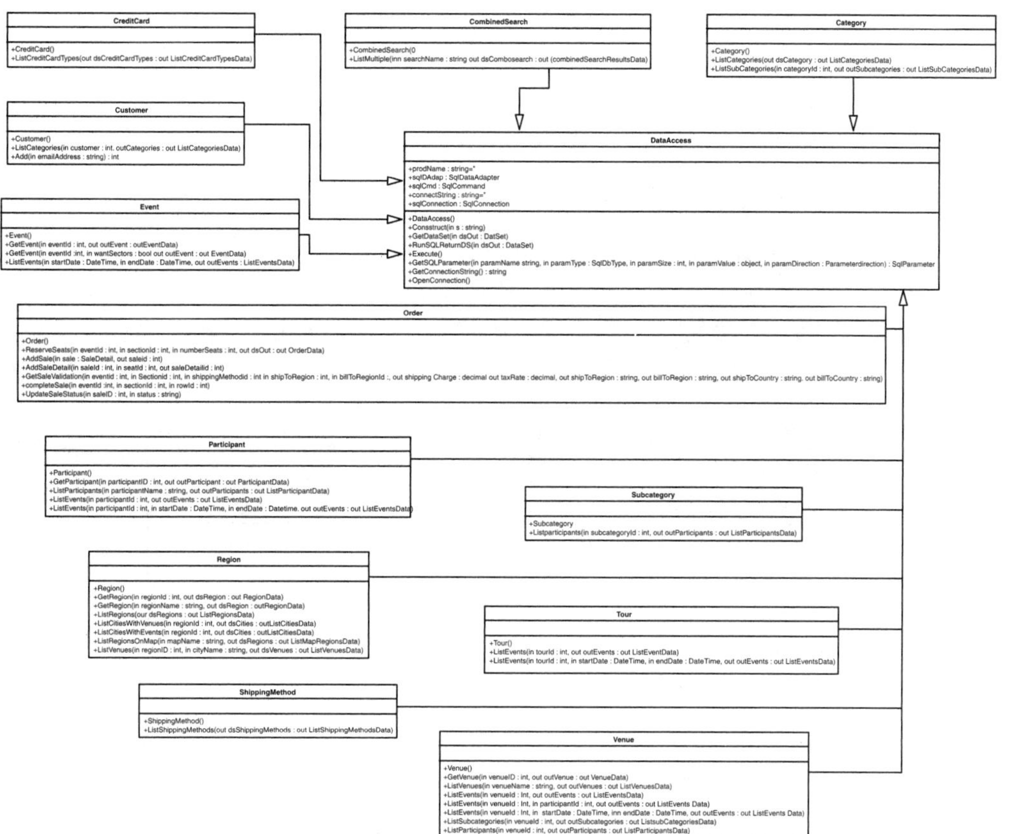

FIGURE A.11

Data Access.

```
Install
-----------------------------------------------------------------
-components : Container
-_Log : TextWriter
-_LastLogMsg : String
-_TargetDir : String
-_gasTIXDatabase : String
-_gasTIXServer : String
-_gasTIXUser : String
-_gasTIXPassword : String
-_AddressDatabase : String
-_AddressServer : String
-_AddressUser : String
-_AddressPassword : String
-_AddressRemote : String
-_PreCompile : String
-_DotNetDir : String
-PRECOMPILE_OPTION : String = "1"
-REMOTING_WINDOWS_SERVICE_OPTION : String="1"
-DOTNET_REG_KEY : String = "Software\Microsoft\.NETFramework"
-DOTNET_INSTALL_ROOT_KEY : String = "InstallRoot"
-DOTNET_VERSION_KEY : String = "Version"
-ENCRYPT_KEY : String = "gasTIXSampleApp"
-GASTIX_WEB_DIR : String = "Web\"
-GASTIX_WEB_BIN_DIR : String = "Web\bin\"
-GASTIX_SETUP_DIR : String = "Setup\"
-GASTIX_PRODUCT_NAME : String = "gasTIX"
-ADDRESS_VALIDATIONSVC_BIN : String = "AddressValidation\AddressValidationSvc\bin\"
-GASTIX_DATABASE_DIR : String = "Database\"
-CONNECTION_STRING : String = "server = {0}:database={1}:uid={2}:pwd={3}:"
-----------------------------------------------------------------
+New()
-InitializeComponent()
+Install(in stateSaver : IDictionary)
+Rollback(in savedState : IDictionary)
+Uninstall(in savedState : IDictionary)
-UninstallBase(in savedState : IDictionary)
-Intialize(in savedState : IDictionary)
-Uninitialize(in state : IDictionary)
-ModifyDataAccessConstructorString()
-HandlePreJIT(in executeInstall : Boolean)
-Log(in msg : String)
```

```
InstallUtil
-----------------------------------------------------------------
-ENCRYPT_PADDNG : String = "ForJacob_10171999"
-----------------------------------------------------------------
+ExecuteProcess(in fileName : String, processArgs : String)
+Encrypt(in secret : Object, in password : Object) : String
+Decrypt(in secret : Object, in password : Object) : String
+BuildLogFileName(in action : String, in targetDir ; String, in subDirectory : String, in productName : String) : String
+OpenLogFile(in action : String, in fileName : String, inout outFile : TextWriter)
+CloseLogFile(in action : String, inout outFile : TextWriter)
```

FIGURE A.12

gasTIX Setup.

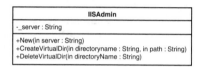

```
DatabaseInstaller
-connectionString : String = "server={0}:database=[1}:user?id={2};passsword=3"
-createDatabaseCmd : String = "create?database?{0}"
-deleteDatabaseCmd : String = "if?exists?(SELECT?name?Name?FROM?master.dbo.sysdatabases?WHERE?name?=?N'{0}')?drop?database?[0}"
-truncLogCmd : String = "sp_dboption?'{0}'.?'trunc.?log".?"true"
-autoShrinkCmd : String = "sp dboption?'{0}'.?autoshrink".?"true"'
-bulkCopyCmd : String = "sp dboption?'{0}'.?'autoshrink'.?"true'"
-killCnnCmd : String = "kill?{0}"
-schemaCmdArgs : String = "-S?{0}?-d?{1}?-U?{2}?-P?{3}?-?{4}"
-bcpCmd : String = """{0}…{1}""?in?""{2}""?-S""{3}""?-U""{4}""?-P""{5}""?-c?-k?-E"
-_Server : String
-_Database : String
-_User : String
-_Password : String
+New(inserver : String, in database : String, in user : String, in password : String)
+InstallDatabase(in schema : String)
+UninstallDatabase()
+ExecuteStoredProc(in procName : String, inout procParameters : Array)
+KillConnections()
+DataLoad(in sourceDirectory : String, in sourceFile : String)
-CreateDatabase()
-DeleteDatabase()
-CreateSchema(inout schema : String)
-ExecuteStoredProc(in connectionString : String, in procName : String, in commandType : CommandType, inout procParameters : Array)
-ExecuteStoredProcReturnDS(in conncectionString : String, in procName : String, in commandType : CommandType, inout procParameters : Array) : DataSet
```

```
IISAdmin
-_server : String
+New(in server : String)
+CreateVirtualDir(in directoryname : String, in path : String)
+DeleteVirtualDir(in directoryName : String)
```

FIGURE A.13

gasTIX Setup, continued.

gasTIX Data Model

The following figures depict the gasTIX data model, generated with the Erwin ER Studio design tool.

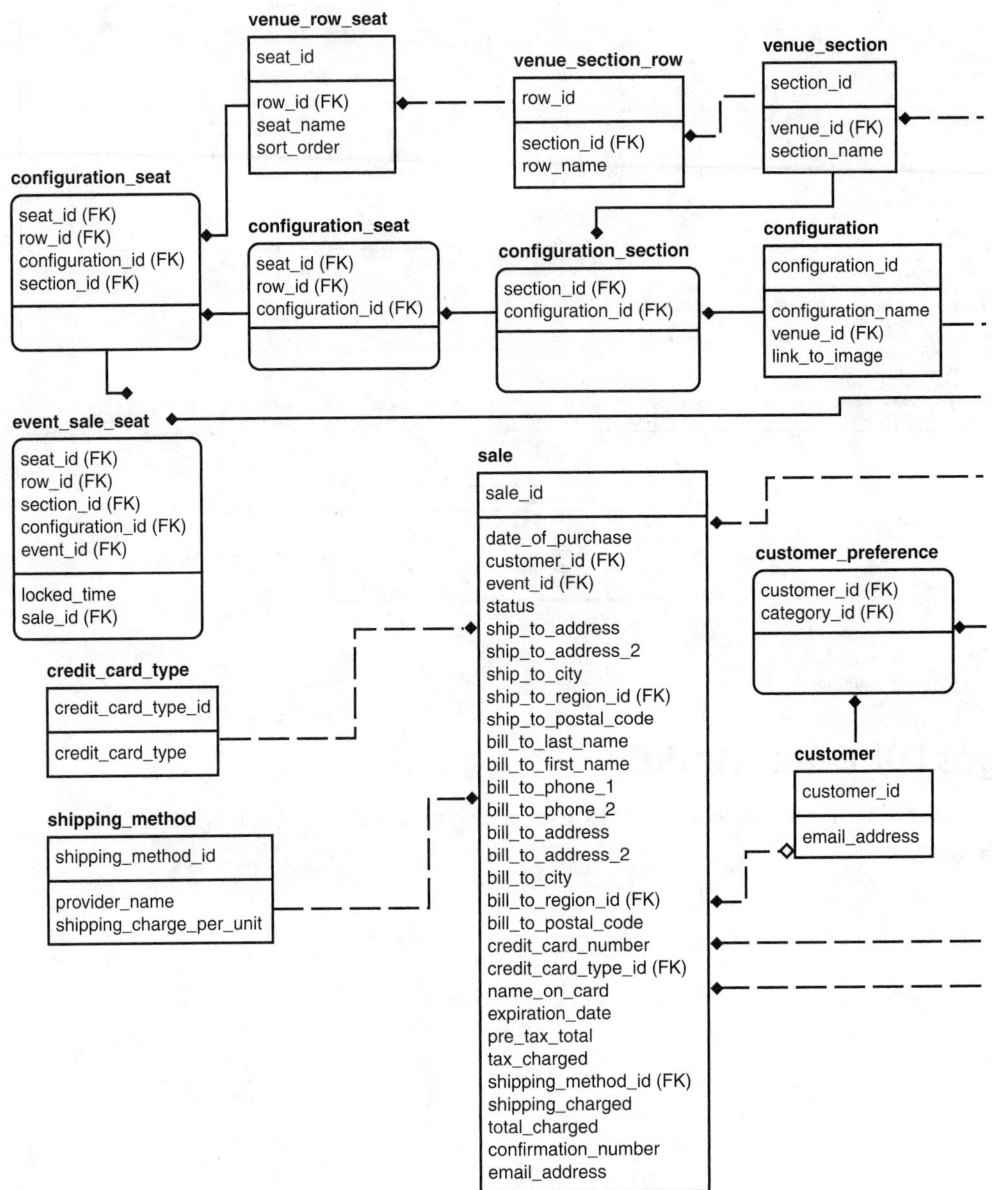

FIGURE A.14

gasTIX Data Model Generated with Erwin ER Studio.

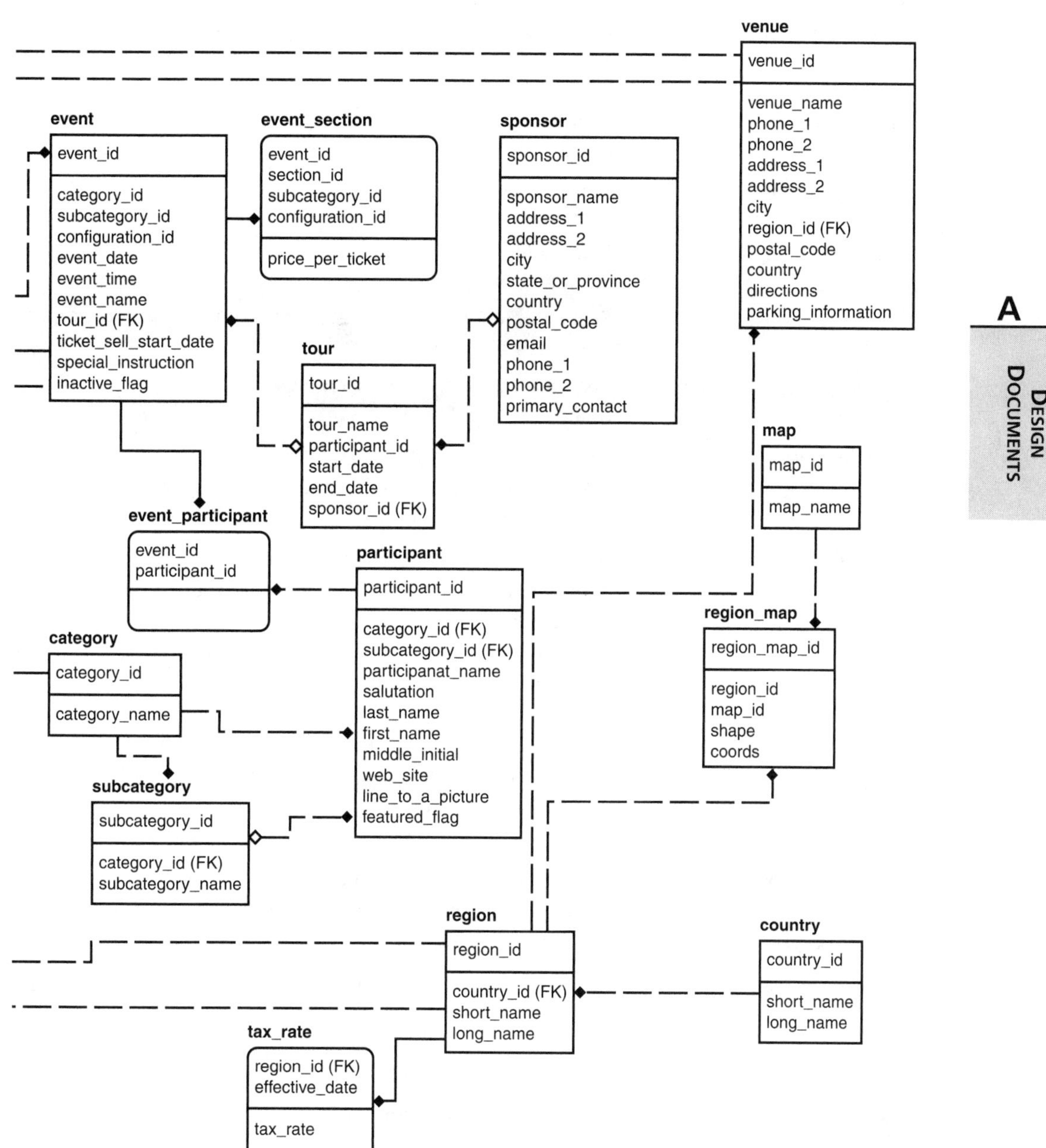

FIGURE A.15
gasTIX Data Model Generated with Erwin ER Studio.

TABLE AP.1 The gasTIX Tables Support the Required Application Functionality

Table Name	*Description*
Category	A grouping of participants by type. Examples include Music and Sports.
Configuration	A specific arrangement of sections, rows, and seats within a venue.
Configuration_Row	Rows within a section that are available within a given configuration.
Configuration_Seat	Seats within a row that are available within a given configuration.
Configuration_Section	Sections within a venue that are used within a given configuration.
Credit_Card_Type	Type of credit card used in transaction.
Country	Country in which a region is located. Used for customer shipping and billing addresses as well as venue locations.
Customer	Individual purchasing tickets.
Customer_Preference	Favorite event categories for a given user. Examples include Music, Sports, etc.
Event	A specific occasion at a venue for which for which tickets are available. Examples include a football game or a concert. An event can have more than one participant and is assigned to a specific configuration for the venue at which the event occurs. Events occur at a specific date and time. Tickets cannot go on sale before a specific date.
Event_Participant	A participant that is schedule to appear at a given event.
Event_Section	Assignment of a configuration section to an event. Used to set ticket prices which are the same for an entire section.
Event_Sale_Seat	Available seats for a given event.
Map	Represents an image from which the user can graphical choose a region.
Participant	An individual or group for which tickets can be sold for associated events.
Region	Represents a state or province.
Region_Map	Map coordinates of a particular region.
Sale	The purchase of one or more seats by a customer. Includes the information about the customer.

TABLE AP.1 Continued

Table Name	*Description*
Shipping_Method	The method by which tickets will be shipped to customer. (UPS, FedEx, etc.)
Sponsor	A group that subsidizes a particular tour.
Subcategory	A grouping of participants within a given category. Examples with the category of Music might include Country, Rock, etc.
Tax_Rate	The percentage of tax applied to the sale by region and effective date.
Tour	A series of common events.
Venue	A location at which one or more events can be hosted.
Venue_Row_Seat	A location for an individual to sit within a row.
Venue_Section	A group of related rows available within a venue. This table (and related tables Venue_Section_Row and Venue_Row_Seat) collectively list all available seating options within a venue.
Venue_Section_Row	A group of adjacent seats within a section.

INDEX

A

absolute positioning, Web controls, 145
accounting, gasTIX, 56
ACT (Application Center Test), 437
performance tuning presentation tier, 451-452, 454-457
Visual Studio .NET, 455
Actions menu commands, New Test, 452
activation
MBR client, 410
MBR server, 409
activation MBR serverlifetimes, 410
Active Server Pages. *See* ASP; ASP.NET
ActiveX Data Objects. ADO, 34, 42
actors, 58
Add Project Group dialog box, 479
Add Reference command (Project menu), 278
Add References dialog box, 274-275, 296, 307
Address Windowing Extensions (AWE), 36
address validation service, gasTIX, 505, 531
address validator, 375
address verification, gasTIX, 56
administration, gasTIX, 55
ADO (ActiveX Data Objects), 34, 42
ADO.NET
classes, 169
DataReader, 169-170
Dataset, 170-172
typed datasets, 172-177
XML views of data, 172
component development, 169
DataReader class, 169-170
Dataset class, 170-172
typed datasets, 172-177
XML views of data, 172

OLEDB, 169
SQLClient, 169
XML Support, 34
AFTER triggers, 211-213
AIC (Application Integration Component), 362
aliases, 100
ALTER DATABASE command, 199
ALTER PROC statement, 208
ALTER VIEW statement, 201
AlternatingItemTemplate, 303-304
Analysis Services, 180
ANSI (American National Standards Institute), 194
APIs
AWE (Address Windowing Extensions), 36
Class library, 32-33
AppDomains, 396-397
assemblies, 396-397
channels, 400
communication, 400
HttpChannel, 401
IChannel interface, 400
TcpChannel, 401, 405
non-remotable objects, 397
remotable objects, 397
consuming, 406-408
hosting, 403-406
MBR, 398-399, 409-410
MBV, 397-398
application caching, 441
Application Center 2000
adding members to clusters, 515-517
creating Web clusters, 513-515
deploying applications in clusters, 516-518
installation, 515
load balancing, 359
Application Center Server 2000, 37-39
Application Center Test, 437
Application Integration Component. *See* AIC
Application object, 441
application profiling, counters, 441-443
creating, 443-444
Performance Monitor, 444-446
application-based requirements, 474
Application-Memory Tuning (4GT), 32, 36
application-provided counters, 442-443
creating, 443-444
Performance Monitor, 444-446
ApplicationException class, 428
applications, 471
Business tier, 472-473
creating, 360-361
Data tier, 473
definition, 360
Presentation tier, 471-472
scale, 20
Web sites as, 17-19
Applications model (MSF), 70
architecture
COM+ integration, 256-257
gasTIX, 52-53
availability, 159
Back Office, 56
conceptual, 53-56
design goals, 156-157
future considerations, 56
interoperability, 157-158
performance, 158-159
purchasing mechanisms, 54-55
scalability, 159-160
security, 160-161
ticket engine, 55
ticketing interface, 55
tools, 92-93, 108
classes, 93, 95-97
CLR (Common Language Runtime), 97-99
CTS (Common Type System), 99-101
device independence, 104, 106
metadata, 101-104
performance, 107-108
scalability, 107-108
security, 106-107
server integration, 104, 106
arguments, VaryByParam, 440
artists by subcategory page, gasTIX, 66
Artists/Teams by Name page, gasTIX, 66
AS (Analysis Services), 180
ascx files, 311
ASP (Active Server Pages), 17, 104, 124
versus ASP.NET, 125-128
ASP.NET 30-32
@ Assebly directive, 129
Business tier, 472-473
code-behind files, 471-472, 481
@ Control directive, 129
Data tier, 473
debugging, 423-425
DLLs, 472
@ Import directive, 129
@ OutputCache directive, 129
Page object, 128-130

presentation services, 288
gasTIX_Search project, 294-319
goals, 288-290
user controls, 310-319
Web controls, 290-293, 297-310
Presentation tier, 471-472
@ Register directive, 129
versus ASP, 125-128
Web controls, 130-131, 290
compared to DTCs, 131
Control class, 290-291
cross-browser development, 133
CSS (Cascading Style Sheet), 132
event-driven programming, 133-134
event-handling, 138-140
handheld devices, 132
Page object, 143-144
round-tripping, 140-143
TemplateControl class, 291-293
third-party, 133
Visual Studio .NET, 134-137
ASPCompat attribute, Page object, 128
aspx files, 297
aspx pages (decimal point), 127
assemblies, 30, 257-258
AppDomains, 396-397
@ Assembly, 129
BusinessFacade, 307, 324
Global Application Cache, 472
Global Cache Assembly Folder, 478
multiple versions, 29
private, 29, 104
signing, 247-248
testing, 281-283
AssemblyInfo.vb, 295
Assert dialog box, 423
asynchronous processing, 446
Attach to Process dialog box, 418
attribute-based programming, 101-102
attributes
AutoEventWireup, 306
CodeBehind, 297
CUSTOMERRORS tag, 322
JITTracking, 414
MarshalAs, 269
Page object, 128-129
TraceExtension, 425
authentication, 106-107, 234-236. *See also* security
built-in methods, 236
certificates, 240-243
client certificates, 167
cookies, 237-240
digest, 235-236
Kerberos Version 5, 31
Microsoft Passport, 235-236
principals, 235
protocols, 31
authorization, 234-235
principals, 235
role-based security, 243-246
AutoEventWireup attribute, 306
AutoPostBack property, 146
AWE (Address Windows Extensions), 36

B

Back Office, gasTIX, 56, 523
bcp_Export_gastix.bat batch file (gasTIXInstall project), 501-502
BIA (Business Internet Analytics), 44
BIGINT data type, 184-185
Billing Details section (CollectPaymentInfo page), 334
BizTalk Server, 38, 364, 371, 383
communications, 353
data transformation, 355
delivery receipts, 378-380
enhanced receipts, 381-383
framework limitations, 381
framework reliability, 380-381
queues, 379
transport acknowledgement, 378
formatting orders, 365, 370
functoids, 367-370
Framework, 45
Host Integration Server 2000 integration, 41
initiative, 45
Mapper, 365-366
Messaging Binding Wizard, 374-375, 390
Messaging Manager, 359
notification of new orders (fulfillment), 354
message format, 355
message transport, 355-359
orchestration, 46
organization, 45
order status, 381-388
correlation, 388-389, 391-393
implementation, 393
updates, 393-394
processing orders, 370
activating orchestration from messaging, 371
business process, 372-374
creating component ports, 376-377

creating components, 375-376
mapping data, 377-378
receiving messages in schedule, 373-375
TPA orchestration, 372
receiving orders, 371
sending orders, 359
creating applications, 360-361
creating channels, 363-365
creating organizations, 360-361
creating ports, 361-363
messaging, 360
Steering Committee, 29
submitting messages to, 358
trading partners, 355
W3C (World Wide Web Consortium), 45
Web site, 28, 380
XLANG schedules, 360, 362, 371
activating orchestration of, 371
creating component ports, 376-377
creating components, 375-376
delivery receipts, 378-383
mapping data, 377-378
order status, 381-389, 391-394
processing orders, 370
queues, 379
receiving messages, 373-375
receiving orders, 371
TPAs, 372
transport acknowledgement, 378
transports, 360

black box, legacy systems, 252
blittable data types, 267
box offices, gasTIX, 55
breakpoints, debugging applications, 417
BTS (BizTalk Server), 352
communications, 353
data transformation, 355
delivery receipts, 378-380
enhanced receipts, 381-383
framework limitations, 381
framework reliability, 380-381
queues, 379
transport acknowledgement, 378
formatting orders, 365-370
Framework, 28-29
initiative, 28
Mapper, 365-366
Messaging Binding Wizard, 374-375, 390
Messaging Manager, 359
notification of new orders (fulfillment), 354
message format, 355
message transport, 355-359
orchestration, 29
order status, 381-388
correlation, 388-389, 391-393
implementation, 393
updates, 393-394
processing orders, 370
activating orchestration from messaging, 371
business process, 372-374

creating component ports, 376-377
creating components, 375-376
mapping data, 377-378
receiving messages in schedule, 373-375
TPA orchestration, 372
receiving orders, 371
sending orders, 359
creating applications, 360-361
creating channels, 363-365
creating organizations, 360-361
creating ports, 361-363
messaging, 360
Steering Committee, 29
submitting messages to, 358
trading partners, 355
Web site, 28, 380
XLANG schedules, 360, 362, 371
activating orchestration of, 371
creating component ports, 376-377
creating components, 375-376
delivery receipts, 378-383
mapping data, 377-378
order status, 381-389, 391-394
processing orders, 370
queues, 379
receiving messages, 373-375
receiving orders, 371
TPAs, 372
transport acknowledgement, 378
transports, 360

bugs. *See* debugging
BUILTIN keyword, 245
Business Internet Analytics (BIA), 44
Business namespace, 102
business services, 156, 161-163, 532
BizTalk Server 2000. *See* BTS
Business area, 162-163
component development, 167-168
ADO.NET, 169—177
remoting versus DCOM, 168
data access objects, 163-164
Data area, 163
exposing as Web services, 165, 167
façade, 161-162, 533-534
goals, 51
high-level design, 161-162
objects, 324-326
performance tuning business tier, 457-461
processes (fulfillment), creating, 372-374
system framework, 164-165
Business tier, 472-473
BusinessFacade assembly, 307, 324
Button control, 297-300

C

C# aliases, 100
C++ Managed Extensions, 111
cab file option, 477
Cache class, 441
caching technologies, 440
application, 441
ouput caching, 440-441
Call Stack, 268
CAST function, 200
Categories user control, 315
CCW (COM-Callable Wrapper), 260-261
CEILING function, 200
certificates, authentication, 240-243
channels, 400
communication, 400
creating, 363-365
definition, 360
HttpChannel, 401
IChannel interface, 400
TcpChannel, 401, 405
CHAR data type, 184
cities with venue list page, gasTIX, 67
class library, 32-33
classes, 93, 95-96. *See also* objects
ADO.NET, 169
DataReader, 169-170
Dataset, 170-172
typed datasets, 172-173, 175-177
XML views of data, 172
ApplicationException, 428
Cache, 441
Control, 290-291, 294
DatabaseInstaller.vb (gasTIXInstall project), 496, 501
DataSet, 309
Debug, 421-423
DefaultTraceListener, 421
EventLogTraceListener, 421
Exception, 427-430
gasTellTime, 275
gasTime, 278
gasTIX, 96-97
gasTIX.DataAccess, 164
HTMLControl, 293
IISAdmin.vb, 507, 509
Install.vb (gasTIXInstall project), 491
libraries, 277-279
OrderRules, 163, 428
Page, 292-293
Participant, 162
Repeater, 293
RepeaterItem, 293
SoapExtensionAttribute, 425
StringBuilder, 449-450
System.Exception, 427
TellTime, 278
TemplateControl, 291-293
TextWriterTraceListener, 421
Trace, 421-423
TraceContext, 425
TraceListener, 421
UpdateOrder, 102
UserControl, 293
Venue, 162
WebControl, 293
clauses
GROUP BY, 198
SELECT, 199
client-side event handling, 133
clients, 16-17
activation, MBR, 410
certificates, Web services, 167
COM+ migration, 253-255
CLB (Component Load Balancing), 38
CLR (Common Language Runtime), 28, 98, 234, 473
assemblies. *See* assemblies
calling DLLs, 258-259
cross-platform functionality, 29
design goals, 28
development environment, 28
Garbage Collection, 98-99
IL (Intermediate Language), 97

languages supported, 30
managed code, 29
MSIL, 29
partial ports, 261
CCW, 262-263
performance, 263-265
quick approach, 262-263
RCW, 261-262
performance counters, 442-443
security, 31, 160, 234
code access, 28
evidence-based, 234
role-based, 28, 234, 243-246

CLS (Common Language Specification), 99

clusters
adding members, 515-517
creating, 513-515
deploying applications in, 516-518
indexes, versus non-clustered, 189-193
NLB, 515

code
access security, 28
assemblies, 257-258
comments, 130
cross-platform functionality, 29
debugging, 414-415
ASP.NET applications, 423-425
attaching debugger to applications, 418-420
breakpoints, 417
Debug class, 421-423
exception handling, 427-433
gasTIX, 417
just-in-time, 420
MSIL, 414-415
Trace class, 421-423
Visual C++, 415
Web services, 425
declaration blocks, 129
include directives, 130
install-time code generation, 446-448
listings. *See* listings
managed code, 29
managed versus unmanaged, 257-258
MSIL, 29
object tags, 130
performance reviews, 439
render blocks, 129
separation, 296-297
separation from UI, 153-154

code-access security, 246-247
permissions, 248-249
signing assemblies, 247-248

code-behind files
ASP.NET, 481
protection of, 471-472

CodeBehind attribute, 297

CollectPaymentInfo page, 332-333
Billing Details section, 334
Payment Details section, 334-335
Shipping Details section, 333-334

columns
nullable, 184
partitioning, 204

COM (Component Object Model), 470

COM Transaction Integrator (COMTI), 41

COM+. *See also* Enterprise Services
calling operating systems, 258-259
CLR, 261-265
components
creating, 375-376
creating ports, 376-377
unmanaged code, 257
components. *See* components (COM+)
direct calls, 355-358
hosting remote objects, 406
integration architecture, 256-257
legacy systems, 252-255
managed code versus unmanaged code, 257-258
RCW (Runtime-Callable Wrapper), 259-261
security, compared to .NET, 244-245
unmanaged code versus managed, 257-258

COM-Callable Wrapper, 260-261

CombinedSearch object, ListMultiple method, 306

CombinedSearch.aspx, 305-306, 308

CombinedSearch_Init event, 305

CombinedSearch_Load event, 305

command line compilers, 120-121

commands
Actions menu, New Test, 452
ALTER DATABASE, 199
DEALLOCATE, 199
Debug menu
New Breakpoint, 415
Processes, 418
Start, 415
EXEC, 208
New menu
Project, 135
Virtual Directory, 227
OPEN, 199
procedure_name, 208
Project menu
Add Reference, 278
Properties, 415
RegAsm, 282
TlbImp, 273

comments, 130

Commerce Server 2000, 39
Common Language Runtime. ***See* CLR**
Common Type System. ***See* CTS**
Common Language Specification. ***See* CLS**
communications
channels, 400
inter-application, 76
BizTalk Server 2000, 85-87
challenges, 76-77
SOAP, 82-84
Web services, 82-84
XML, 77-79
XSD, 79-82
TPAs, 353-354
compilers, 414
Component Load Balancing (CLB), 38
Component Object Model. ***See* COM**
components (COM+), 252, 254
ADO.NET, 169
DataReader class, 169-170
Dataset class, 170-172
typed datasets, 172-173, 175-177
XML views of data, 172
creating, 375-377
myClient.dll, 253
myServer.dll, 253
remoting versus DCOM, 168
TPASender, 375
unmanaged code, 257
Visual Basic 6, 254
COMTI (COM Transaction Integrator), 41
conceptual architecture, gasTIX, 53
Back Office, 56
future considerations, 56
purchasing mechanisms, 54-55
ticket engine, 55
ticketing interface, 55
configuration
Global.asax file, 323-324
remoting, 402-403
Web.config file, 322
constraints, PRIMARY KEY, 191
consumption, 406-408
content files, 479
ContentType attribute, Page object, 128
Content Management Server 2001, 39
Control class, 290-291, 294
controls
code declaration blocks, 129
code render blocks, 129
custom, 129
data, 149
DataList, 297
DropDownList server, 328-330
binding to XML Web services, 343-345
loading from XML strings, 333-334
HTML, 129
RangeValidator, 330
RequiredField, 330
server-side, 131
user. *See* user controls
validation, 150
Web (ASP.NET), 130-131, 290
absolute positioning, 145
advanced features, 145-147, 149-150
compared to DTCs, 131
Control class, 290-291
creating demonstrations of, 139
cross-browser development, 133
CSS (Cascading Style Sheet), 132
data binding, 147-148
event handling, 138-143
event-driven programming, 133-134
handheld devices, 132
Page object, 143-144
round-tripping, 140-143
System.Web.UI, 145
TemplateControl class, 291-293
third-party, 133
validation, 150
Visual Studio .NET, 134-137
Web. *See* Web controls
cookies, authentication, 237-240
CorDBG, 415
correlation, order status (fulfillment), 388-393
cost
legacy systems, 252
performance tuning, 438
counters (performance)
application-provided, 442-444
Performance Monitor, 444-446
system-provided, 442-444
CREATE PROCEDURE statement, 206
CREATE VIEW statement, 201-202
credit card processors, gasTIX, 56
cross-language debugging, 113-114

CSC.exe, 121, 348
CTS (Common Type System), 99-101
CType function, 332
CURSOR data type, 184-186
cursors, Transact-SQL, 198-200
custom actions, gasTIXInstall project, 490-491
- accessing/modifying AddressValidation string in XML configuration, 505
- accessing/modifying strings for database connectivity, 503-504
- bcp_Export_gastix.bat batch file, 501-502
- DatabaseInstaller.vb class, 496, 501
- gastix.data_load.xml file, 502
- HandlePreJIT method, 505-506
- IISAdmin.vb class, 507-509
- Install method, 492, 495
- Install.vb class, 491
- Rollback and Uninstall methods, 509-510
- simple encrypt method, 503
- UninstallBase method, 510-513

custom attributes, 102
custom controls, 129
CUSTOMERRORS tag (Web.config file), 322
customers, gasTIX, 48, 54

D

data, gasTIX, 535-539
Data Access object, 163-164
Data area (gasTIX business services), 163
data binding, Web controls, 147-148
Data Center Server, 32
data controls, 149
data modeling, 181
- gasTIX, 521, 541
- logical models, 181
- normalization, 182
- physical modeling, 183
  - *data types, 183-184*
  - *RI (Referential Integrity), 186-189*
  - *SQL Server 2000 data types, 184-186*
- relational versus dimensional, 181-183

Data Modification Language. *See* DML
data providers
- OLEDB, 169
- SQLClient, 169

data services, 18, 180-181
- physical modeling, 183-189
- relational versus dimensional, 181-183

Data Source Names. *See* DSNs
Data tier, 473
- performance
  - *foreign keys, 462*
  - *indexes, 463*
  - *locks, 463-464*
  - *normalization, 462*
  - *pimary keys, 462*
  - *schema design, 462*
  - *SQL Profiler, 464-466*
  - *SQL Query ANalyzer, 464-466*
  - *Transact SQL, 463*

Data Transformation Services. *See* DTS
data types
- blittable, 267
- ismorphic, 267
- physical modeling, 183-184
  - *RI (Referential Integrity), 186-189*
  - *SQL Server 2000, 184-186*
- TABLE, 194
- Visual Basic .NET, 266-268

data warehousing, SQL Server 2000, 180
Database Lookup functoid, 369
Database Management Systems. *See* DBMS
DatabaseInstaller.vb class (gasTIXInstall project), 496, 501
databases. *See also* SQL Server 2000
- abstract connectivity, Visual Basic, 164
- federated, 203
- indexes
  - *clustered versus non-clustered, 189-193*
  - *Index Tuning Wizard, 193*
  - *key lengths, 193*
  - *number, 189*
  - *performance, 189*
- normalization, 182
- scale, 20

DataBing() method, Control class, 291
DataCenter Server 2000, 35-36
datagrid control, 301
datalist control, 300, 314-317
DataList controls, 297
DataReader class (ADO.NET), 169-170
DataSet class, ReadXML method, 309

Dataset class (ADO.NET), 170-172
datasets, typed, 172-173, 175-177
DataTable object, 330
DBMS (Database Management Systems), 180
DCOM (Distributed COM), 168, 470
DDL statements, 207
DEALLOCATE command, 199
Debug class, 421-423
Debug menu commands
- New Breakpoint, 415
- Processes, 418
- Start, 415

Debug versions, 482
debugging, 414-415
- ASP.NET applications, 423-425
- breakpoints, 417
- CorDBG, 415
- cross-language, 113-114
- Debug class, 421-423
- exception handling, 427, 430, 432
  - *best practices, 432-433*
  - *Exception class, 427-430*
- gasTIX, 417-418, 420
- just-in-time, 420
- MSIL, 414-415
- Trace class, 421-423
- Visual C++, 415
- Web services, 425

decision support systems. *See* DSS
declarative security, 245
DECLARE statement, 194-195, 199
DefaultTraceListener class, 421
deferred name resolution, 206
DELETE statement, 187, 191
delivery receipts (fulfillment), 378-380
- BTS queues, 379
- enhanced receipts, 381-383
- framework limitations, 381
- framework reliability, 380-381
- transport acknowledgement, 378

deployment
- gasTIX, 484-485
  - *tests, 507*
  - *Windows Setup project, 485-513*
- in AC2K clusters, 517
- in Application center 2000 clusters, 516, 518
- infrastructure (.NET Web servers), 473
  - *application-based requirements, 474*
  - *gasTIX sites, 476*
  - *performance considerations, 474-475*
  - *scaling out, 475*
  - *scaling up, 475*
  - *technical requirements, 473-474*
  - *VisualStudio .NET, 477*
- Visual Studio .NET, 477
  - *Web Setup project, 477-484*
  - *XCopy deployment, 483*

Description attribute, Page object, 129
design, 70
- business services, 161-162
- code separatation, 296-297
- gasTIX
  - *architectural goals, 156-157*
  - *availability, 159*
  - *criteria, 51-52*
  - *interoperability, 157-158*
  - *performance, 158-159*
  - *scalability, 159-160*
  - *security, 160-161*
- MSF, 70
- OLTP, 182
- schema, 462
  - *foreign keys, 462*
  - *indexes, 463*
  - *locks, 463-464*
  - *normalization, 462*
  - *primary keys, 462*
  - *SQL Profiler, 464-466*
  - *SQL Query Analyzer, 464-466*
  - *Transact-SQL, 463*

Design view, Web forms, 298
Design-Time Control. *See* DTCs
DetectNewerInstalledVersion property (Windows Installer versioning), 484
deterministic functions, 200
developers, 111
Developing phase (MSF), 72
development
- component, 167-168
  - *ADO.NET, 169-173, 175-177*
  - *remoting versus DCOM, 168*
- MSF, 70
  - *Developing phase (Process model), 72*
  - *Envisoning phase (Process model), 72*

models, 70-72
Planning phase (Process model), 72
Stabilizing phase (Process model), 72
performance tuning, 438-439
devices, independence, 104, 106
dialog boxes
Add Project Output Group, 479
Add Reference, 274-275, 307
Add References, 296
Assert, 423
Attach to Process, 418
Juts-in-Time, 420
Messaging Port Properties, 371
New Project, 135, 274, 295
New Virtual Directory, 228
digest authentication, 31, 235-236
digital certificates. *See* certificates
dimensional modeling, versus relational, 181-183
direct COM+ calls, 355-358
DISCO (Discovery of Web services), 26-27, 84
Distributed COM, 168, 470
Distributed Transaction Coordinator (DTC), 204
DLLs (dynamic link library), 270, 396
ASP.NET, 472
calling, 258-259
from class libraries, 277-279
from executables, 279-283
from Web services, 271-277
creating, 270
registration, 271
TellTime function, 270-271
Web Setup projects, 482
DML (Data Modification Language), 202
statements, 202
triggers, 210
AFTER triggers, 211-213
INSTEAD OF triggers, 213
nested, 210
RECURSIVE TRIGGERS option, 210-211
documents, 360
DOM (Document Object Model), 32
downloads, gasTix, 485
DROP TABLE statement, 186
DROP VIEW statement, 202
DropDownList server control, 328-330, 343-345
DropDownlist server control, 333-334
DSNs (Data Source Names), 470
DSS (decision support system), 181-182
DTC (Distributed Transaction Coordinator), 204
DTCs (Design-Time Control), 131
DTS (Data Transformation Services), 180
Dynamic Help, 114
dynamic SQL, stored procedures, 463
dynamic link library. *See* DLLs

E

EMA (Enterprise Memory Architecture), 36
email, gasTIX, 56
EnableSessionState attribute, Page object, 129
EnableViewState parameter, 449
encapsulation, 150
Encoding option, 362
encrypt method (gasTIXInstall project), 503
Encryption option, 362
enterprise class attributes, 14-15
Enterprise Memory Architecture, 36
enterprise servers, 30, 37
Application Center Server 2000, 37-38
BizTalk Server 2000, 38, 41
Commerce Server 2000, 39
Content Management Server 2001, 39
Exchange Server 2000, 40
Host Integration Server 2000, 40-41
ISA Server, 42
Mobile Information Server, 42-43
Share Point Portal Server 2000, 43
SQL Server 2000, 43-44
enterprise services, 32. *See also* COM+
Application Center Server2000, 37-38
Biztalk Server 2000, 38, 41
Commerce Server 2000, 39
Content Management Server 2001, 39
Exchange Server 2000, 40
Host Integration Server 2000, 40-41
ISA Server, 42

Mobile Information Server 2001, 42-43
Share Point Portal Server 2001, 43
SQL Server 2000, 43-44
enterprise services, 32. *See also* COM+
envelopes, definition, 360
Envelopes option, 362
Envisioning phase (MSF), 72
Error Return functoid, 369
ErrorPage attribute, Page object, 129
errors, InvalidCastException, 332
Event Details page, 328-330
creating orders, 330-331
Data Entry section, 328
Event Summary section, 328
event details page, gasTIX, 68
Event Details page, saving orders, 331-332
event handlers
JavaScript, 133
ListBox1_SelectedIndexChanged, 138
round-tripping, 140-143
Web controls, 138-140, 305-306
ViewState field, 140-143
Web forms, 138
WebForm_Init, 138-139
WebForm_Load form, 138
event pricing details page, gasTIX, 68
EventData object, 329
EventLogTraceListener class, 421
events
CombinedSearch_Init, 305
CombinedSearch_Load, 305
handlers. *See* event handlers
Page_Load, 144
programming, 133-134
searching services (gasTIX), 55, 288
building with ASP.NET, 288, 290-293
gasTIX_Search project, 294-319
goals, 288-290
events by artist/team page, gasTIX, 68
events by venue page, gasTIX, 67
evidence-based security, 234
Exception class, 427-430
exception handling, 427, 430, 432
best practices, 432-433
Exception class, 427-430
Exchange Server 2000, 40-41
exe files, 396, 404-405
EXEC command, 208
EXEC statement, 196
executables
calling DLLs, 279
creating, 279-281
testing assemblies, 281-283
EXECUTE statement, 196
explicit type variables, 100
Extensible Markup Language. *See* XML

F

façade, business, 161-162
fault tolerance, 38
federated databases, 203
fields, gasTIX, 366
File System view, 485-486
files
.ascx, 311
.aspx, 297
bcp_Export_gastix.bat batch (gasTIXInstall project), 501-502
.cab, 477
code-behind, 471-472, 481
CombinedSeach.aspx, 305-306
CombinedSearch.aspx, 308
content, 479
.dll, 396
.exe, 404-405
gastix.data_load.xml (gasTIXInstall project), 502
gasTIX_Search project, 295-296
InstallState, 487
interoperability systems, 157
source, 479
vb, 297
Windows Installer, 482
finally statement, 432
financial functionality, gasTIX, 523
First Normal Form, OLTP, 182
FLOOR function, 200
folders
Global Assembly Cache, 478
Web Application, 478, 480, 483
FooterTemplates, 302
foreign keys, data tier performance, 462
formatting orders (fulfillment), 365,, 367-370
forms, Web, 130
event handlers, 138
views, 298
Fortezza, 31
fulfillment, 55-56, 352-353
business requirements, 352
communications overview, 353-354
delivery receipts, 378-380
BTS queues, 379
enhanced receipts, 381-383
framework limitations, 381

framework reliability, 380-381
transport acknowledgement, 378
formatting orders, 365-370
notification of new orders, 354
message format, 355
message transport, 355-359
order status, 381-388
correlation, 388-389, 391-393
implementation, 393
updates, 393-394
processing orders, 370
activating orchestration from messaging, 371
business process, 372-374
creating component ports, 376-377
creating components, 375-376
mapping data, 377-378
receiving messages in schedule, 373-375
TPA orchestration, 372
receiving orders, 371
sending orders, 359
creating applications, 360-361
creating channels, 363-365
creating organizations, 360-361
creating ports, 361-363
messaging, 360

functions
CAST, 200
CEILING, 200
CType, 332
FLOOR, 200
ISNULL, 200
LEN, 200
MessageBox, 258
Now, 270
ReserveSeats, 421-422
SQL Server 2000, 213-216
SUBSTRING, 200
TellTime, 270-271
Transact-SQL, 200-201
ValidateAddress, 375

functoids, 367-370

G

G.A. Sullivan, Web site, 485
GAC (global assembly case), 517
Garbage Collection, 98-99
gasBags
Global.asax, 323-324
Web.config file, 322
Web Setup project, 479-482
output, 481-482
Web Application Folder properties, 483
Windows Installer versioning, 484
XCopy deployment, 483
GASException object, 429-430
gasTellTime class, 275
gasTime class, 278
gasTIX project Web site, 48, 151
architecture, 52-53
availability, 159
Back Office, 56
conceptual, 53-56
design goals, 156-157
future considerations, 56
interoperability, 157-158
performance, 158-159
purchasing mechanisms, 54-55
scalability, 159-160
security, 160-161
ticket engine, 55
ticketing interface, 55
business goals, 51
business services, 156, 161
Business area, 162-163
business façade, 161-162
data access objects, 163-164
Data area, 163
exposing as Web services, 165, 167
high-level design, 161-162
system framework, 164-165
code behind page, 153-154
COM+ integration, 256-257
company background, 48, 54
credit card processor, 56
customers, 48, 54
data model, 521, 541
data services, 181-189
debugging, 417-418, 420
deployment, 484-485
tests, 507
Windows Setup project, 485-513
design, 51-52
download, 485
email, 56
event searching services, 288
gasTIX_Search project, 294-319
presentation services, 288-293
fields, 366
fulfillment, 352-353
business requirements, 352
communications overview, 353-354
delivery receipts, 378-383
formatting orders, 365, 367-370
notification of new orders, 354-359
order status, 381-394

processing orders, 370-378
receiving orders, 371
sending orders, 359-365
home page, 65-66
hosting remote objects, 404-405
infrastructure, 73
infrastructure deployment, 476
Microsoft passport wallet, 56
MSF, 70-72
namespaces, 96-97
object models, 531
address validation, 531
business, 532-534
data, 535-539
gasTIXSetup, 540-541
Page object attributes, 128-129
Passport support, 58
presentation services, 124
building with ASP.NET, 288-293
gasTIX_Search project, 294-319
goals, 288-290
problem statement, 49
project trade-off matrix, 50-51
purchasing tickets, 322
business objects, 324-325
gasBAGS UI, 342-345
Global.asax file configuration, 323-324
interface, 326-342
Web.CONFIG file configuration, 322
XML Web services, 325-326
requirements, 522
Back Office, 523
financial functionality, 523
future functionality, 523-525
site map, 65, 529
artists by subcategory, 66
artists/teams by name, 66
cities with venues list, 67
event details, 68
event pricing details, 68
events by artist/team, 68
events by venue, 67
home page, 65-66
purchase confirmation, 69
seating chart, 68
shipment status, 69-70
state list, 66
subcategories by category, 66
ticket purchase, 69
update profile, 69
US map, 66
venue search page, 67
venues by city/state, 67
venues name, 67
solution concept, 49-51
tables, 544-545
tracing, 424-425
use cases, 56-57, 526
actors, 58
display main page, 58
financial transactions, 64
personal account setup, 63-64
personal options, 64
pricing/availability, 61, 528
purchasing tickets, 61-62, 529
requesting ticket delivery, 63
select event by artist/team name, 60, 528
select event by category, 60, 526
select event by state, 59, 527
select event by venue, 59-60, 526-527
shipment status, 64
updating shipment status, 63
viewing seating chart, 61, 528-529
user controls, 151-153
vision statement, 49
Web services, 84
business components as, 165, 167
testing, 425
gasTIX.Data namespace, 163
gasTIX.DataAccess class, 164
gastix.data_load.xml file (gasTIXInstall project), 502
gasTIX.System.Framework namespace, 164
gasTIXInstall project, 485
custom actions, 490-491
accessing/modifying AddressValidation string in XML configuration, 505
accessing/modifying strings for database connectivity, 503-504
bcp_Export_gastix.bat batch file, 501-502
DatabaseInstaller.vb class, 496, 501
gastix.data_load.xml file, 502
HandlePreJIT method, 505-506
IISAdmin.vb class, 507, 509
Install method, 492, 495
Install.vb class, 491

Rollback and Uninstall methods, 509-510
simple encrypt method, 503
UninstallBase method, 510, 512-513
File System view, 485-486
Registry, 487-488
user interface, 488-490
gasTIXSetup, 540-541
gasTIX_Search project, 294
code separation, 296-297
creating, 294-296
files, 295-296
user controls, 310-311
creating, 311-314
DataList, 314-317
nested, 314, 317-319
Web controls, 297
binding data, 306-310
Button, 297-300
event handling, 305-306
Repeater, 300-305
TextBox, 297-300
GenericPrincipal object, 241
GetObjectData method, 401
Global Application Cache, 472
Global Assembly Cache Folder, 478
global assembly case, 517
Global Positioning System (GPS), 23
global variables, Transact-SQL, 196
Global.asax, 295, 323-324
GPS, 23
GROUP BY clause, 198

H

HailStorm Web services, 106
handheld devices, Web controls, 132
HandlePreJIT method, 505-506
HeaderTemplates, 302-303
HelpLink property, 428
home organizations, 360
home pages, gasTIX, 65-66
horizontal partitioning, 203
Host Integration Server 2000, 40-41
hosting remote objects, 403-404
COM+, 406
IIS, 405-406
managed exe, 404-405
managed services, 404-405
HTML (Hypertext Markup Language), 11, 78
controls, 129
view, Web forms, 298
and XML, 78-79
HTMLControl class, 293
HTTP (HyperText Transfer Protocol), 11, 158-159
HttpChannel, 401
Hypertext Markup Language. *See* HTML

I

IChannel interface, 400
IDEs, Visual Studio .NET Web controls, 136
Iinterchange object, 358
IIS (Internet Information Server), 30-32, 405, 449
hosting remote objects, 405-406
session state, 449
SQL Server 2000 integration, 227-230
IISAdmin.vb class, 507, 509
IL (Intermediate Language), 97
ILDasm, 119
IMAGE data type, 186
include directives, 130
IncomingPrintOrder port, 371, 373
Index Tuning Wizard, 193
indexes
data tier performance, 463
performance, 189
clustered versus non-clustered, 189-193
Index Tuning Wizard, 193
key lengths, 193
number, 189
views, 204-205
infrastructure
application-based requirements, 474
gasTIX, 73, 476, 484-513
performance considerations, 474-475
scaling out, 475
scaling up, 475
technical requirements, 473-474
Visual Studio .NET, 477-484
inline table-valued functions, 214
InnerException property, 427
INSERT statement, 191, 202

Install method (gasTIXInstall project), 492, 495
install-time code generation, 446-448
Install.vb class (gasTIXInstall project), 491
InstallState file, 487
INSTEAD OF triggers, 202, 213
IntelliSense, 116, 276
inter-application communications, 76
- BizTalk Server 2000, 85
  - *business document exchange, 85-86*
  - *Messaging, 87*
  - *Orchestration, 86*
- challenges, 76-77
- SOAP, 82
  - *Call Message code listing, 82-83*
  - *Response Message code listing, 83*
  - *Web sites, 84*
- Web services, 82-83
  - *DISCO, 84*
  - *UDDI, 84*
  - *Web sites, 84*
  - *WSDL, 84*
- XML, 77-78
  - *and HTML, 78-79*
  - *XSD, 79-82*

inter-process communication (IPC), 33
interfaces
- gasTIXInstall project, 488-490
- IChannel, 400
- Iserializable, 401
- ticket purchases on gasTIX, 326-327
  - *CollectPaymentInfo page, 332-335*
  - *Event Details page, 328-332*
  - *gasBAGS, 342-345*
  - *Microsoft Passport Express Purchase, 335-337*
  - *OrderData object, 335-337*
  - *organization, 327-328*
  - *PurchaseConfirmation page, 337-339*
  - *PurchaseReceipt page, 339-341*
  - *ViewSeatingChart page, 341-342*

Intermediate Language. *See* IL
internationalization, gasTIX, 56
Internet
- enterprise class attributes, 14-15
- .NET and, 10-11
- partners, 48, 55
- standards, 11
  - *SOAP, 12-14*
  - *XML, 12*
- third generation applications, 93

Internet Information Server. *See* IIS
Internet Security and Acceleration Server 2000, 42
interoperability, gasTIX, 157-158
Interoperability Services, 257
InteropServices, 259
InvalidCastException error, 332
IPC (inter-process communication), 33
Ipipeline, 41
ISA Server, 42
Iserializable interface, 401
ISNULL function, 200
isomorphic data types, 267
ItemTemplates, 149, 297, 302-303

J

Java Upgrade Migration Plan (JUMP), 111
JavaScript, client-side event handling, 133
JIT (Just-In-Time) compiler, 97
JITTracking attribute, 414
JUMP (Java Upgrade Migration Plan), 111
Just-In-Time compiler. *See* JIT
Just-In-Time debugging, 420
Jut-in-Time dialog box, 420

K

Kerberos Version 5, 31
keys, indexes, 193
keywords
- BUILTIN, 245
- OPENQUERY, 204
- OPENROWSET, 204
- VARYING, 197
- WITH SCHEMABINDING, 205

Kids Passport service, 25
kiosks, gasTIX, 48, 54

L

language tools, 108, 112
- choosing, 110-111
- Visual Basic. *See* Visual Basic
- Visual C#. *See* Visual C#
- Visual C++. *See* Visual C++

legacy systems, COM+, 252-255

LEN function, 200

lifecycle tools, 118

lifetimes, MBR clients/servers, 410

linked servers, 204

ListBox1_SelectedIndexChanged event handler, 138

listings
- accessing/modifying AddressValidation string in XML configuration, 505
- accessing/modifying strings for database connectivity, 503-504
- AddressValidation Marshal-by-Ref Class, 399
- authenticating users and clearing cookies, 238, 240
- authentication credentials, 239
- bcp_Export_gastix.bat batch file (gasTIXInstall project), 501-502
- binding DropDownList to XML Web services, 343-345
- client-side JavaScript, 141
- code-behind page, 153-154
- completing purchases, 338
- creating a Marshal-By-Value object, 397-398
- creating annotated schemas, 175-177
- creating inline table-valued functions, 214
- creating multistatement table-valued functions, 215-216
- creating performance counters, 443-444
- creating stored procedures, 208-210
- creating triggers, 211-212
- creating views, 201-202, 205
- CURSOR data type, 185-186
- data binding and DropDownList server control, 329-330
- DatabaseInstaller.vb class (gasTIXInstall project), 496, 501
- displaying receipts, 340-341
- EXEC statement, 196
- GASException class, 429-430
- gastix.data_load.xml file (gasTIXInstall project), 502
- gasTIXInstall.InstallState file, 487-488
- HandlePreJIT method, 505-506
- hosting AddressValidation in IIS, 405-406
- HTML order page, 345
- IISAdmin.vb class, 507, 509
- impersonated users and certificates, 242
- Install method (gasTIXInstall project), 492, 495
- Install.vb class (gasTIXInstall project), 491
- ItemTemplate, 149
- loading DropDownList server control from XML strings, 333-334
- OPENXML function, 225-227
- ORDER BY clause, 220, 222, 224
- querying databases in EXPLICIT mode, 219-220
- remoting configuration code, 402-403
- remoting configuration files for AddressValidationService client, 406-408
- remoting configuration for Address Validation Managed EXE host, 405
- remoting configuration for AddressValidation host, 404
- ReserveSeats function, 422
- reserving seats and creating orders, 330
- retrieving data into datasets, 171-172
- returning column names as separate elements, 218
- returning XML from SQL Server 2000 AUTO and RAW modes, 217
- Rollback and Uninstall methods, 509-510
- scalar local variables, 196
- SELECT statement with functions, 200-201
- simple encrypt method providing hashes of database passwords (gasTIXInstall project), 503
- single-mode XML tree for multitable joins, 217-218
- SOAP Call Message, 82-83

SOAP Response Message, 83
SQLDataReader, 170
submitting messages to BizTalk, 358
TABLE data type, 186
ticket purchases, 431
UninstallBase method, 510, 512-513
updating OrderData object, 335-337
ViewState field, 142
Web.config file using forms-based security, 237
Web.config file using integrated security, 236
Web.config using certificates, 241-243
XML description of household pets, 77-78
XSD Schema household pets, 80-82

@listings
stored procedures accepting input parameters, 197
stored procedures using output parameters, 198
using output parameters from stored procedures, 198

ListMultiple method, CombinedSearch object, 306

load balancing, 20-21, 359
NLB (Network Load Balancing), 21
WLBS (Windows Load Balancing Service), 20

local variables, Transact-SQL, 194-196

locks (database), performance, 463-464

logical data models, 181

login, gasTIX, 55

M

Machine Diagram, 460

mainState property (Web controls), 142

MaintainState attribute, Page object, 129

MaintainState parameter, 449

managed code, 29

Managed Extensions (C++), 111

managed services, hosting remote objects, 404-405

manifests (assemblies), 29

Mapper (BTS), 365-366

maps, site, gasTIX, 529

Marshal-By-Reference object. *See* MBR

Marshal-By-Value object. *See* MBV

MarshalAs attribute, 269

mathematical functoids, 369

MBR, 398-399
client activation, 410
server activation, 409-410

MBV (Marshal-By-Value object), 397-398

MDX (Multi-Dimensional Services), 180

members, adding to clusters, 515-517

memory, Garbage Collection, 98-99

merge modules, 477

Message property, 427

MessageBox function, 258

Message-Oriented Middleware (MOM), 41

messages, fulfillment
format, 355
transport, 355-359

Messaging (BizTalk Server 2000), 87
Messaging Binding Wizard, 374-375, 390
Messaging Manager, 359
Messaging Port Properties dialog box, 371

metadata, 101-104

methods
Control class, 291
GetObjectData, 401
HandlePreJIT method, 505-506
Install, 492, 495
ListMultiple, 306
MessageBox, 258
OrderData.Read, 431
overloading, 103
ReadXML, 172
ReadXML (DataSet class), 309
Rollback, 509-510
SendFail, 376
SendSuccess, 376
SendTicket, 375
SubmitSynch, 356
TellTime, 273, 275
Uninstall, 509-510
UninstallBase, 510, 512-513
Warn, 425
Write, 425
WriteXML, 172
WriteXMLSchema, 172

Microsoft
Intermediate Language (MSIL), 29, 257, 414-415
Management Console (MMC), 32
Message Queue. *See* MSMQ
.NET site, 473

Passport Express Purchase, 56, 235-236
Single Sign-In (SSI), 474
ticket purchasing interface, 335-337
Solution Framework. *See* MSF
SNA Server, 40-41
Transaction Server (MTS), 18, 32, 52
Wallet, 337
Web Distributed Authoring Version (WebDAV), 43

migration, COM+ legacy systems, 252-255

MMC (Microsoft Management Console), 32

Mobile Information Server 2001, 42-43

MOM (Message-Oriented Middleware), 41

momentum, legacy systems, 252

MQ Series, 41

MSF (Microsoft Solution Framework) models, 70
Applications, 70
Process, 70-72
Team, 70

MSIL (Microsoft Intermediate Language), 29, 257, 414-415

MSMQ (Microsoft Message Queue), 33-34, 355
message transports, 359
MQSeries integration, 41

MTS (Microsoft Transaction Server), 18, 32, 52

Multi-Dimensional eXpressions. *See* MDX

multi-tier programming, 17-19
load balancing, 20-21
scale, 20
state information, 21-22

multistatement table-valued functions, 214-216

myApp.exe, 253

myClient.dll, 253

myServer.dll, 253

N

name searches, gasTIX, 66

namespaces, 93-96
Business, 102
gasTIX, 96-97, 163
gasTIX.System.Framework, 164
System, 32
System.Data, 33
System.Data.SqlClient, 34
System.Data.Odbc, 169
System.Diagnostics, 443-444
System.Runtime.Interop.Services, 257
System.Text, 449
System.Web.UI, 32, 291
System.Web.UI.Control, 293

National Resource for Global Standards. *See* NSSN

nested triggers, 210

nested user controls, 314, 317-319 , 322

.NET, 10

.NET Framework, 15, 93, 95-96
class library, 32-33
clients, 16-17
Common Language Runtime. *See* CLR
CTS (Common Type System), 99-101
defined, 10
device independence, 104, 106
gasTIX, 96-97
metadata, 101-104
performance, 107-108
remoting. *See* remoting
scalability, 107-108
security, 106-107
compared to COM+, 244-245
server integration, 104, 106
servers, 16-17

Network Load Balancing. *See* NLB

network operating system. *See* NOS

New Breakpoint command (Debug menu), 415

New menu commands
Project command, 135
Virtual Directory, 227

New Project dialog box, 135, 274, 295

New Test command (Actions menu), 452

New Test Wizard, 452

New Virtual Directory dialog box, 228

Ngen.exe, 446-448

NLB (Network Load Balancing), 21, 38, 474
Application Center Server 2000, 38
Web clusters, 515
Windows 2000 Advanced Server, 515

non-clustered indexes, versus clustered, 189-193

non-deterministic functions, 200

normalization, 182, 462

NOS (network operating system), 32

notification of new orders (fulfillment), 354
message format, 355
message transport, 355-359

Now function, 270

NSSN (National Resource for Global Standards), 194

NT LAN Manager. *See* NTLM
NTEXT data type, 186
NTLM (NT LAN Manager), 36
nullable columns, 184

O

objects. *See also* classes
Application, 441
business, 324-326
CombinedSearch, 306
Data Access, 163-164
Data Table, 330
EventData, 329
Exception, 427-430
GASExceptinon, 429-430
GenericPrincipal, 241
IInterchange, 358
models, 531
address validation, 531
address validation service, 531
business, 532
business facade, 533-534
data, 535-538
data access, 539
gasTIXSetup, 540-541
non-remotable, 397
OrderData, 330-332
OrderData object, 335-337
Page (ASP.NET), 128-130
attributes, 128-129
life cycle, 143-144
remotable, 397
consuming, 406-408
hosting, 403-406
MBR, 398-399, 409-410
MBV, 397-398
SingleCall, 409
Singletons, 409
tags, 130
transparent proxies, 408
WindowsPrincipal, 235, 245-246
OLAP (online analytical processing), 181-183
OLEDB, 169
Exchange Server 2000, 40
Host Integration Server 2000, 41
OLTP (online transaction processing), 32, 181-183
OPEN command, 199
OPENQUERY keyword, 204
OPENROWSET keyword, 204
OPENXML function, 225-227
operating systems, calling (COM+ integration), 258-259
Orchestration BizTalk Server 2000, 46, 86
OrderData object, 330-332, 335-337
OrderData.Read method, 431
OrderRules class, 163, 428
orders
creating, 330-331
saving, 331-332
status (fulfillment), 381-388
correlation, 388-389, 391-393
implementation, 393
updates, 393-394
organizations
creating, 360-361
definition, 360
output
caching, 440-441
Visual Studio .NET Web applications, 481
overloading (methods), 103

P

P/Invoke, 258
PAE (Physical Address Extension), 36
Page class, 292-293
Page object (ASP.NET), 128-130
attributes, 128-129
life cycle, 143-144
Page_load event, 144
parameters
EnableViewState, 449
MaintainState, 449
SubCategory_ID, 440
SubCategory_Name, 440
Transact-SQL, 196-198
partial ports, 261
CCW, 262-263
performance, 263-265
quick approach, 262-263
RCW, 261-262
Participant class, 162
partitioned views, 203-204
partitioning
column, 204
horizontal, 203
vertical, 202
partners, gasTIX, 48, 55
Passport, 106-107, 235-236
gasTIX support, 58
Passport service, 24-25
Kids Passport, 25
Passport Express Purchase, 25, 335-337
Passport Single Sign-in, 25
Passport Single Sign-in service, 25, 106
passport wallet, gasTIX, 56
Payment Details section (CollectPaymentInfo page), 334-335
payments, processing, 55
performance, 107-108
code, 439
DSS, 182

gasTIX, 158-159
indexes, 189
clustered versus non-clustered, 189-193
Index Tuning Wizard, 193
key lengths, 193
number, 189
infrastructure deployment, 474-475
OLTP, 182
partial ports, 263-265
Transact-SQL stored procedures, 207-210
tuning, 436
application profiling, 441-446
asynchronous processing, 446
business tier, 457-461
caching technologies, 440-441
cost effectiveness, 438
data tier, 462-466
during development, 438-439
goals, 436-437
install-time code generation, 446-448
post-releases, 439
pre-releases, 439
presentation tier, 451-452, 454-457
session state, 449
SSL (Secure Sockets Layer), 450
StringBuilder class, 449-450
ViewState, 448-449
when to tune, 438
Performance Monitor, 444-446
permissions, code-access security, 248-249
personalization, gasTIX, 55-56
phone sales, gasTIX, 48
Physical Address Extension (PAE), 36
physical modeling, 183
data types, 183-184
RI (Referential Integrity), 186-189
SQL Server 2000 data types, 184-186
Planning phase (MSF), 72
Platform Invoke. *See* P/Invoke
ports
components, creating, 376-377
creating, 361-363
definition, 360
IncomingPrintOrder, 371, 373
partial
CCW, 262-263
performance, 263-265
quick approach, 262-263
RCW, 261-262
post-releases, performance tuning, 439
pre-releases, performance tuning, 439
presentation services, 17, 124
performance tuning presentation tier, 451-452, 454-457
Presentation tier, 471-472
presentations services
building with ASP.NET, 288
user controls, 310-319
Web controls, 290-293, 297-310
gasTIX_Search project, 294
code separation, 296-297
creating, 294-296
user controls, 310-319
Web controls, 297-310
goals, 288-290
PRIMARY KEY constraints, 191
primary keys, data tier performance, 462
primary outpur, 479
principals, 235
private assemblies, 29, 104
problem statements, gasTIX, 49
procedures, stored. *See* stored procedures
procedure_name command, 208
Process model (MSF), 70-72
Processes command (Debug menu), 418
Process Control (DataCenter Server 2000), 36
processing orders (fulfillment), 370
activating orchestration from messaging, 371
business process, 372-374
creating component ports, 376-377
creating components, 375-376
mapping data, 377-378
receiving messages in schedules, 373-375
TPA orchestration, 372
productivity tools, 112, 121
command line compilers, 120-121
Visual Studio, 112
cross-language debugging, 113-114
Enterprise features, 119
ILDasm, 119

lifecycle tools, 118
single IDE, 112-113
usability, 114-116
Web services support, 116-117
ProductName property (Web Application Folder), 483
profiling counters, 442-443
creating, 443-444
Performance Monitor, 444-446
programming models, 15
attribute-based, 101-102
clients, 16-17
event-driven, 133-134
load balancing, 20-21
NLB (Network Load Balancing), 21
WLBS (Windows Load Balancing Service), 20
scale, 20
servers, 16-17
state information, 21-22
three-tier architecture, 17-18
Project command (New menu), 135
Project menu commands
Add Reference, 278
Properties, 415
Project Wizard, 458
projects
creating in Visual Studio .NET, 135
management, 70
Web Setup, 477-482
output, 481-482
Web Application Folder properties, 483
Windows Installer versioning, 484
XCopy deployment, 483
Windows Setup, gasTIXInstall, 485-513
properties
AutoPostBack, 146
gasTIXInstall project, 489-490
HelpLink, 428
InnerException, 427
mainState (Web controls), 142
Message, 427
Page class, 292-293
ProductName (Web Application Folder), 483
Response.Cache, 440
Source, 427
StackTrace, 428
TargetSite, 428
VirtualDirectory (Web Application Folder), 483
Web Application Folder, 483
Properties command (Project menu), 415
protocols
authentication, 31
Simple Object Access Protocol. *See* SOAP
SOAP, SDK, 25-26
purchase confirmation page, gasTIX, 69
PurchaseConfirmation page, ticket purchasing interface, 337-339
PurchaseReceipt page, ticket purchasing interface, 339-341
purchasing mechanisms, gasTIX, 54-55
purchasing tickets (gasTIX), 322
business objects, 324-325
gasBAGS UI, 342-345
Global.asax file configuration, 323-324
interface, 326-327
CollectPaymentInfo page, 332-335
Event Details page, 328-332
Microsoft Passport Express Purchase, 335-337
OrderData object, 335-337
organization, 327-328
PurchaseConfirmation page, 337-339
PurchaseReceipt page, 339-341
ViewSeatingChart page, 341-342
Web.CONFIG file configuration, 322
XML Web services, 325-326

R

RangeValidator control, 330
RCW (Runtime-Callable Wrapper), 259-261
creating, 272
partial ports, 261-262
ReadXML method, 172
DataSet class, 309
receipts. *See* delivery receipts
receive functions, 355-356
receiving orders (fulfillment), 371
Record Count functoid, 368
RECUSRSIVE TRIGGERS option, 210-211
Referential Integrity. *See* RI
REGASM (.NET Assembly Registration Utilty), 261, 282
registration, DLLs, 271
Registry, gasTIXInstall project, 487-488

relational modeling, versus dimensional modeling, 181-183
Release versions, 482
reliability, BTS delivery receipts, 380-381
remoting, 396
channels, 400
communication, 400
HttpChannel, 401
IChannel interface, 400
TcpChannel, 401, 405
configuration options, 402-403
non-remotable objects, 397
remotable objects, 397
consuming, 406-408
hosting, 403-406
MBR, 398-399, 409-410
MVB, 397-398
versus DCOM, 168
RemovePreviousVersions property (Windows Installer versioning), 484
Repeater class, 293
Repeater control, 300-301
binding data, 306-310
templates, 301-305
RepeaterItem class, 293
RequiredField control, 330
requirements, gasTIX, 522
Back Office, 523
financial functionality, 523
fulfillment, 352
functionality, 522-523
future functionality, 523-525
ReserveSeats function, 421-422
Response.Cache properties, 440
retail box offices, gasTIX, 48
retry queues (BTS), 379
RI (Referential Integrity), 186-189
role-based security, 28, 234
authorization, 243-246
Rollback method, 509-510
round-tripping, 140-143
routing
AppDomains. *See* AppDomains
serialization, 401
Runtime-Callable Wrapper (RCW), 259

S

SANs (system area networks), 32
scalability, 107-108, 159-160
scalar local variables, 196
scaling out, 475
scaling up, 475
scheduled queues (BTS), 379
schedules (XLANG), 360-364, 371, 383
creating component ports, 376-377
creating components, 375-376
delivery receipts, 378-380
BTS queues, 379
enhanced receipts, 381-383
framework limitations, 381
framework reliability, 380-381
transport acknowledgement, 378
mapping data, 377-378
order status, 381-383
correlation, 388-389, 391-393
implementation, 393
transactions, 383-388
updates, 393-394
processing orders, 370-371
receiving messages, 373-375
receiving orders, 371
TPAs, 372
transports, 360
schema design (data tier), 462
foreign keys, 462
indexing, 463
locks, 463-464
normalization, 462
primary keys, 462
SQL Profiler, 464-466
SQL Query Analyzer, 464-466
Transact-SQL, 463
Script Editor, 453
SDKs (Software Development Kit), 25-26, 474
seating charts, gasTIX, 55, 68
Second Normal Form (OLTP), 182
Secure Sockets Layer. *See* SSL
security, 106-107, 234
authentication, 31, 234-236
built-in methods, 236
certificates, 240-243
cookies, 237-240
digest, 235-236
Microsoft Passport, 235-236
principals, 235
authorization, 234-235
principals, 235
role-based, 243-246
CLR, 31, 234
evidence-based, 234
role-based, 234, 243-246
code-access, 28, 246-247
permissions, 248-249
signing assemblies, 247-248

COM+, compared to .NET, 244-245
declarative, 245
gasTIX, 55, 160-161
ISA Server, 42
.NET, compared to COM+, 244-245
Passport, 106-107
role-based, 28
SSL, 31
TSL, 31
SELECT clause, DECLARE statement, 199
SELECT statement, 191, 195
functions, 200-201
GROUP BY clause, 198
SendFail method, 376
sending orders (fulfillment), 359
applications, 360-361
channels, 363-365
organizations, 360-361
ports, 361-363
messaging, 360
SendSuccess method, 376
SendTicket method, 375
SeparatorTemplate, 303
serialization, routing, 401
Server Explorer, 115-116, 173
Server-Gated Cryptography (SGC), 31
server-side controls, writing HTML, 131
servers, 16-17, 35
activation, MBR, 409-410
Application Center Server 2000, 39
BizTalk Server 2000, 29, 39-40, 85
business document exchange, 85-86
Messaging, 87
Orchestration, 86
BizTalk. *See* BTS
Commerce Server 2000, 41-42
COM+ migration, 253-255
DataCenter Server 2000, 35-36
enterprise. *See* enterprise servers
Exchange Server 2000, 40-41
Host Integration Server 2000, 42-43
IIS, 30
integration, 104, 106
Internet Information. *See* IIS
ISA Server, 44
linked, 204
Mobile Information Server 2001, 45
MTS, 32
Share Point Portal, 42
SQL Server 2000, 37-38
Windows 2000 Advanced Server, 36-37
Windows 2000 Server, 36
Windows XP, 35-36
XML support, 35
Service Window option, 362
services
business. *See* business services
data, 18
managed, hosting remote objects, 404-405
presentation. *See* presentation services
Web, 22-24
Discovery of Web services. See DISCO
Kids Passport, 25
Passport, 24-25
SOAP, 25-26
Web. *See* Web services
session state, 449
SET statement, 195
SET XACT ABORT option, 204
SGC (Server-Gated Cryptography), 31
Share Point Portal Server, 43
shipment status page, gasTIX, 69-70
Shipping Details section (CollectPaymentInfo page), 333-334
Signature option, 362
signing assemblies, 247-249
Simple Object Access Protocol. *See* SOAP
single IDE, 112-113
Single Sign-In. *See* SSI
SingleCall objects, 409
Singletons, 409
site administration, gasTIX, 55
site maps, gasTIX, 65, 529
artists, 66
cities with venues list, 67
event details,67-68
home page, 65-66
purchase confirmation, 69
seating chart, 68
shipment status, 69-70
state list, 66
subcategories by category, 66
ticket purchase, 69
update profile, 69
US map, 66
venues, 67
SOAP (Simple Object Access Protocol), 12-14, 25, 82, 116-117, 158-159
Call Message code listing, 82-83
exception handling, 432
HTTP, 326
Response Message code listing, 83
SDK, 25-26
specifications, 325-326

Web services, 104
Web sites, 84
XML Web services, 325-326
SoapExtensionAttribute class, 425
Software Development Kit. *See* SDKs
solution concepts, gasTIX, 49-51
Solution Explorer (VSA), 458
source code, MSIL, 29
source files, 479
Source property, 427
specifications, SOAP, 325-326
sp_helptext stored procedure, 207
SQL (Structured Query Language), 20
SQL Server 2000, 43-44, 180-181. *See also* databases
Client, 169
data types, 184-186
data warehousing, 180
functions, user-defined, 213-216
IIS integration, 227-230
Profiler, 464-466
Query Analyzer, 464-466
scale, 20
total cost of ownership, 180
Transact-SQL, 194
cursors, 198-200
functions, 200-201
parameters, 196-198
stored procedures, 206-210
variables, 194-196
views, 201-205
XML extensions, 216-220, 222, 224-227
triggers. *See* triggers
XML, 216
IIS integration, 227-230
Transact-SQL extensions, 216-227
SQL Server Windows CE, 38
SQL VARIANT data type, 185-186
SSI (Single-In), 474
SSI (Passport Single Sign-In), 106
SSL (Secure Sockets Layer), 31, 450
Stabilizing phase (MSF), 72
StackTrace property, 428
Start command (Debug menu), 415
state, multi-tier programming, 21-22
state maps, gasTIX, 66
statements. *See also* functions
ALTER PROC, 208
ALTER VIEW, 201
CREATE PROCEDURE, 206
CREATE VIEW, 201-202
DDL, 207
DECLARE, 194-195, 199
DELETE, 187, 191
DML, 202
DROP TABLE, 186
DROP VIEW, 202
EXEC, 196
EXECUTE, 196
finally, 432
INSERT, 191, 202
SELECT, 191, 195
functions, 200-201
GROUP BY clause, 198
SET, 195
throw, 432
UPDATE, 187, 191
stored procedures
dynamic SQL, 463
performance, 463
Transact-SQL, 206
creating, 206-207
performance, 207-210
sp_helptext, 207
stress testing, 451, 455
String Concatenation functoid, 368-369
StringBuilder class, 449-450
Styles.css, 295
subcategories by category page, gasTIX, 66
SubCategory_ID parameter, 440
SubCategory_Name parameter, 440
SubmitSynch method, 356
SUBSTRING function, 200
suspended queues (BTS), 379
SYSCOMMENTS table, 207
system area networks. *See* SANs
system-provided counters, 442-443
creating, 443-444
Performance Monitor, 444-446
System namespace, 32
System.Configuration namespace, 94
System.Data namespace, 33, 94
System.Data.Odbc namespace, 169
System.Data.SqlClient namespace, 34
System.Diagnostics namespace, 94, 443-444
System.DirectoryServices namespace, 94
System.EnterpriseServices namespace, 94

System.Exception class, 427
System.IO namespace, 94
System.Messaging namespace, 94
System.Net namespace, 94
System.Runtime namespace, 94
System.Runtime.InteropServices namespace, 257
System.Security namespace, 95
System.Text namespace, 449
System.Textn namespace, 95
System.Threading namespace, 95
System.Web namespace, 95
System.Web.UI, 145
System.Web.UI namespace, 32, 291
System.Web.UI.Control namespace, 293
System.XML namespace, 95

T

table-valued functions, SQL Server 2000
- inline, 214
- multistatement, 214-216

tables (database)
- gasTIX, 544-545
- indexes
  - *clustered versus non-clustered, 189-193*
  - *Index Tuning Wizard, 193*
  - *key lengths, 193*
  - *number, 189*
  - *performance, 189*
- SYSCOMMENTS, 207

TargetSite property, 428
Task List, 116
TCO, SQL Server 2000, 180
TCP, 159
TcpChannel, 401, 405
TDL (Template Description Language), 119
Team model (MSF), 70
technical requirements, Web servers, 473-474
telephone sales, gasTIX, 48
TellTime class, 278
TellTime function, 270-275
Template Description Language (TDL), 119
TemplateControl class, 291-293
templates
- ItemTemplate, 149
- Repeater control, 301-305

TemplateTop user control, 152
testing
- assemblies, 281-283
- Visual Studio .NET deployments, 507
- Web services, 425

TexBox control, 297-300
TEXT data type, 186
TextWriterTraceListener class, 421
third generation applications, 93
Third Normal Form, OLTP, 182
third-party administrators. ***See*** **TPAs**
third-party Web controls, 133
throw statement, exception handling, 432
ticket engine, gasTIX, 55
ticket purchases (gasTIX), 322
- business objects, 324-325
- gasBAGS UI, 342-345
- Global.asax file configuration, 323-324
- interface, 326-327
  - *CollectPaymentInfo page, 332-335*
  - *Event Details page, 328-332*
  - *Microsoft Passport Express Purchase, 335-337*
  - *OrderData object, 335-337*
  - *organization, 327-328*
  - *PurchaseConfirmation page, 337-339*
  - *PurchaseReceipt page, 339-341*
  - *ViewSeatingChart page, 341-342*
- Web.config file configuration, 322
- XML Web services, 325-326

ticketing interface, gasTIX, 55
TIMESTAMP data type, 186
TINYINT data type, 184
TlbExp (Type Library Exporter Utility), 260-261, 279
TlbImp (Type Library Importer Utility), 260-261, 272-273
TLS (Transport Layer Security), 31
total cost of ownership. ***See*** **TCO**
TPAs (third-party administrators), 352
- communications overview, 353-354
- creating business process, 372-374

creating channels, 363-365
creating components, 375-377
creating ports, 361-363
delivery receipts, 378-380
BTS queues, 379
enhanced receipts, 381-383
framework limitations, 381
framework reliability, 380-381
transport acknowledgement, 378
formatting orders, 365, 370
mapping data, 377-378
orchestration, 372
order status, 381-388
correlation, 388-389, 391-393
implementation, 393
updates, 393-394
processing orders, 370-371
receiving messages in schedules, 373-375
receiving orders, 371
sending orders, 359-360
creating applications, 360-361
creating organizations, 360-361

TPASender component, 375
Trace attribute, Page object, 129
Trace class, 421-423
TraceContext class, 425
TraceExtension attribute, 425
TraceListener class, 421
tracing (ASP.NET debugging), 424-425
trade-off matrix, gasTIX, 50-51
trading partners, 355
Transact-SQL, 194
cursors, 198-200
functions, SELECT statement, 200-201
parameters, 196-198
performance, 463
stored procedures, 206
creating, 206-207
performance, 207-210
variables, 194
global, 196
local, 194-196
views, 201-202
advantages, 202-203
creating, 201-202
disadvantages, 203
indexed, 204-205
partitioned, 203-204
XML extensions, 216-220, 222, 224-227

transactional systems, 180
transparent proxies, 408
Transport Layer Security (TLS), 31
Transport option, 362
triggers, 210
AFTER triggers, 211-213
INSTEAD OF, 202
INSTEAD OF triggers, 213
nested, 210
RECURSIVE TRIGGERS option, 210-211

tuning. *See* performance, tuning
Type Library Exporter Utility. *See* TlbExp
Type Library Importer Utility. *See* TlbImxp
typed datasets, ADO.NET component development, 172-177

U

UBR (UDDI Business Registry), 24
UDDI (Universal Description Discovery Integration), 24, 84
Uninstall method, 509-510
UninstallBase method, 510, 512-513
update profile page, gasTIX, 69
UPDATE statement, 187, 191
UpdateOrder class, 102
updates, status order (fulfillment), 393-394
UpgradeCode property (Windows Installer versioning), 484
US map, gasTIX, 66
use cases, gasTIX, 56-57, 526
actors, 58
display main page, 58
financial transactions, 64
personal account setup, 63-64
personal options, 64
pricing/availability, 61, 528
purchasing tickets, 61-62, 529
requesting ticket delivery, 63
select event by artist/team name, 60, 528
select event by category, 60, 526
select event by state, 59, 527
select event by venue, 59-60, 526-527
shipment status, 64
updating shipment status, 63
viewing seating chart, 61, 528-529

user controls, 150-151, 310-311
Categories, 315
creating, 311-314
DataList, 314-317
gasTIX Web site, 151-153
nested, 314, 317-319
TemplateTop, 152
user interfaces, gasTIXInstall project, 488-490
user-defined functions, SQL Server 2000, 213-214
inline table-valued, 214
multistatement table-valued, 214-216
table-valued, 214
UserControl class, 293
users
gasTIX, 48, 54
principals, 235

V

ValidateAddress function, 375
validation controls, 150
Value Extractor function, 369
VARBINARY data type, 184
VARCHAR data type, 184
variables
explicit types, 100
Transact-SQL, 194
global, 196
local, 194-196
Variant, 100
VARIANT data type, 186
Variant variables, 100
VaryByParam argument, 440
VARYING keyword, 197
vb files, 297
VB .NET aliases, 100
VBC.exe, 121
venue box offices, gasTIX, 48
Venue class, 162
@venue_id parameter, 197
venue search page, gasTIX, 67
venues by city/state page, gasTIX, 67
venues by name page, gasTIX, 67
Version property (Windows Installer versioning), 484
versioning, 102-103, 484
vertical partitioning, 202
views
Transact-SQL, 201-202
advantages, 202-203
disadvantages, 203
indexed, 204-205
partitioned, 203-204
Web forms, 298
ViewSeatingChart page, ticket purchasing interface, 341-342
ViewState field, 140-143, 448-449
Virtual Directory command (New menu), 227
VirtualDirectory property (Web Application Folder), 483
vision statements, gasTIX, 49
Visual Basic, 109, 112
abstract database connectivity, 164
COM+ components, 254
DLLs. *See* DLLs
versus Visual C#, 110-111
Visual Basic .NET, 127
Ctype function, 332
data types, 266-268
Visual C#, 108-109, 112
versus Visual Basic 6.0, 110-111
Visual C++, debugging, 415
Visual J++, 111
Visual SourceSafe (VSS), 118
Visual Studio 6, 112, 470
cross-language debugging, 113-114
Enterprise features, 119
ILDasm, 119
lifecycle tools, 118
single IDE, 112-113
usability, 114-116
Web services support, 116-117
Visual Studio Analyzer. *See* VSA
Visual Studio .NET, 477
ACT, 455
code, managed versus unmanaged, 257-258
debugging, 414-415
ASP.NET applications, 423-425
attaching debugger to applications, 418, 420
breakpoints, 417
Debug class, 421-423
exception handling, 427-430, 432-433
gasTIX, 417
just-in-time, 420
MSIL, 414-415
Trace class, 421-423
Web services, 425
deployment tests, 507
Web controls, 134-137

Web Setup project, 477-479
gasBags, 479-482
output, 481-482
Web Application Folder properties, 483
Windows Installer versioning, 484
XCopy deployment, 483
XML Web services, 345-349
VSA (Visual Studio Analyzer), 118, 457
Event details view, 459
performance tuning business tier, 457-461
Solution Explorer, 458
VSS (Visual SourceSafe), 118

W

Wallet (Microsoft), 337
wallets, gasTIX, 56
Warn method, 425
WAS (Web Application Stress), 451, 454
WDSL (Web Service Description Language), 84
Web Application Folder, 478, 480
ProductName property, 483
properties, 483
VirtualDirectory property, 483
Web Application Stress. *See* WAS
Web applications, 423-425
Web clusters
adding members, 515-517
creating, 513-515
deploying applications in, 516-518
NLB, 515
Web controls, 130-131, 290, 297
absolute positioning, 145
advanced features, 145-150
Button, 297-300
compared to DTCs, 131
Control class, 290-291
creating demonstrations of, 139
cross-browser development, 133
CSS (Cascading Style Sheet), 132
data binding, 147-148
datagrid, 301
datalist, 300
event handling, 138-140, 305-306
round-tripping, 140-143
ViewState field, 140-143
event-driven programming, 133-134
handheld devices, 132
Page object, 143-144
Repeater, 300-301
binding data, 306-310
templates, 301-305
System.Web.UI, 145
TemplateControl class, 291-293
TextBox, 297-300
third-party, 133
validation, 150
Visual Studio .NET, 134-137
Web Distributed Authoring and Versioning. (WebDAV), 43
Web forms, 130
event handlers, 138
views, 298
Web pages (gasTIX). *See* site maps, gasTIX
Web references, 117
Web servers
application-based requirements, 474
gasTIX, 55
performance considerations, 474-475
scaling, 475
technical requirements, 473-474
Web Service Description Language. *See* WDSL
Web services, 22-24, 82-84
business components as, 165, 167
calling DLLs, 271-273
client certificates, 167
creating, 274-277
debugging, 425
DISCO, 84
Discovery of Web services, 26-27, 84
gasTIX, 55
HailStorm, 106
Passport, 24-25
SOAP, 25-26, 104, 116-117
stress testing, 455
testing, 425
UDDI, 84
WSDL, 84
XML
binding DropDownList server control to, 343-345
business objects, 325-326
Visual Studio .NET, 345-349
Web Setup project, 477-479
gasBags, 479-482
Visual Studio .NET
output, 481-482
Web Application Folder properties, 483

Windows Installer versioning, 484
XCopy deployment, 483
Web sites
ANSI, 194
as applications, 17-19
BizTalk, 28, 380
G.A. Sullivan, 485
gasTIX. *See* gasTIX
Microsoft .NET, 473
NSSN, 194
physical architecture, 19
SOAP, 84
Web services, 84
XML Developer Center, 79
XML-Zone, 79
Web Storage System, (Exchange Server 2000), 40
Web.config file, 295, 322
WebControl class, 293
WebDAV (Web Distributed Authoring and Versioning), 43
WebForm_Init event handler, 138-139
WebForm_Load event handler, 138
windows
Dynamic Help, 114
Task List, 116
Windows 2000, 31-32
Windows 2000 Advanced Server, 36-37, 515
Windows 2000 Data Center Server, 35-36
Windows 2000 Server, 36
Windows Installer, 470, 477
msi file, 482
versioning, 484
Windows Load Balancing Service. (WLBS), 20
Windows Setup project, gasTIXInstall, 485
custom actions, 490-513
File System view, 485-486
Registry, 487-488
tests, 507
user interface, 488-490
Windows XP, 35-36
WindowsPrincipal object, 235, 245-246
Winsock Direct, 36
Wireless Markup Language. *See* WML
wireless services, 48
wireless users, 55
wizards
Index Tuning Wizard, 193
Messaging Binding (BizTalk), 390
New Test, 452
Project, 458
WLBS (Windows Load Balancing Service), 20
WML (Wireless Markup Language), 105
work queues (BTS), 379
World Wide Web Consortium (W3C), 45
Write method, 425
WriteXML method, 172
WriteXMLSchema method, 172
WSSL.exe, 348

X

XCopy deployment, 483
XLANG schedules, 360, 362, 364, 371, 383
creating component ports, 376-377
creating components, 375-376
delivery receipts, 378-380
BTS queues, 379
enhanced receipts, 381-383
framework limitations, 381
framework reliability, 380-381
transport acknowledgement, 378
mapping data, 377-378
order status, 381-383
correlation, 388-393
implementation, 393
transactions, 383-388
updates, 393-394
processing orders, 370-371
receiving messages, 373-375
receiving orders, 371
TPAs, 372
transports, 360
XML (Extensible Markup Language), 12, 77-78
ADO.NET component development, 34, 172
and HTML, 78-79
BizTalk Server 2000, 85
business document exchange, 85-86
Messaging, 87
Orchestration, 86
data sharing, 92-93
DISCO, 84
SQL Server 2000, 216
IIS integration, 227-230
Transact-SQL extensions, 216- 222, 224-227
system integration, 92-93
UDDI, 84
WDSL, 84

Web services
binding DropDownList server control to, 343-345
Visual Studio .NET, 345-349
well formed, 78
Windows XP, 35
XSD, 79-82
XSL, 32
XML Developer Center, 79
XML Schema Definition. *See* XSD
XML Stylesheet Language. *See* XSL
XML Web services, 24, 325-326. *See also* Web services
XML-Zone Web site, 79
XSD (XML Schema Definition), 79-82
XSL (XML Stylesheet Language), 32